Test Booklet No. 3947201

Test Booklet Code CH1

MEDACE

NEET (UG)

SELF ASSESSMENT KIT

Some Basic Concepts of Chemistry

Topics Covered

- Nature of matter, Significant Figures and Laws of Chemical Combinations
- Atomic and Molecular Masses, Percentage Composition, Empirical and Molecular Formula
- Mole Concepts, Stoichiometry and Concentration Terms

Important Instructions

- This Booklet Contains – 3 Topic Tests and One Test on Complete Chapter.
- Each question carries 4 marks.
- For each correct response the candidate will get 4 marks and for every incorrect response 1 mark will be additionally deducted from the total score.
- Use **Blue/Black** point pen only for filling the OMR.
- Rough work is to be done in the space provided for this purpose in the test booklet only.

Name of the Candidate (In Capitals) ____________________

____

Candidate's Signature ____________________

Invigilator's Signature ____________________

Facsimile signature stamp of center superintendent ____________________

Do not open this Booklet until you start attempting the Test

Topical Follow Thru

Test 1

Syllabus

- Matter and its Nature
- Concept of Atom, Molecule, Element and Compound
- Dalton's Atomic Theory
- Laws of Chemical Combinations

For deeper insight **Scan the QR Code**

Important Instructions

- The test is of 30 minutes duration and contains 15 multiple choice questions (Four options with a single correct answer).
- Choose the correct option and fill the OMR given on the last page of test accordingly.
- At some instances, you may find more than 1 option may be correct. In such circumstances, you have to judge the most appropriate answer as per the conditions given in the question.

1. Which of the following statement is incorrect?

(a) Matter has mass and occupies space.
(b) Mixture contains two or more substances present in it (in any ratio).
(c) Mixtures are always a combination of the same compounds that are in different states.
(d) Heterogeneous mixture can be separated by physical method such as filtration.

2. Given below are two statements.

Statement I Glucose is an example of pure substances.

Statement II Pure substance cannot be separated by simple physical method.

In the light of the above statements, choose the correct answer from the options given below.

(a) Both Statement I and Statement II are incorrect.
(b) Statement I is correct but Statement II is incorrect.
(c) Statement I is incorrect but Statement II is correct.
(d) Both Statement I and Statement II are correct.

3. Match List-I with List-II.

List-I (Physical quantity)	List-II (Derived unit)
A. Frequency	I. $kg\ m^2\ s^{-2}$
B. Energy	II. s^{-1}
C. Electrical resistance	III. A
D. Electric current	IV. VA^{-1}

Choose the correct answer from the options given below.

(a) A-III, B-I, C-II, D-IV
(b) A-II, B-I, C-IV, D-III
(c) A-II, B-III, C-I, D-IV
(d) A-III, B-II, C-IV, D-I

4. Arrange the following in increasing order of submultiples of prefix

yotta, mega, kilo and hecto

Choose the correct answer from the options given below.

(a) hecto < kilo < mega < yotta
(b) kilo < mega < hecto < yotta
(c) kilo < hecto < yotta < mega
(d) hecto < kilo < yotta < mega

5. Select the correct statements.

I. In the following numbers, 0.0020, 0.00200, 0.002000 and 0.002, the only number in which all zeros are not significant is 0.002.
II. 1 bar = 0.987 atm = 10^5 Pa and 133.322 Pa = 1 mm of Hg.
III. All measured quantities are reported in such a way that only the last digit is uncertain usually by ± 1.
IV. 1 lb = 453.6 g and 1 quart = 0.9463 kg of water.
V. Significant figure in 0.300 is 1 whereas in 0.003 significant figure is 3.

Choose the correct answer from the options given below.

(a) I, II and V
(b) II, III and IV
(c) I, II, III, IV and V
(d) I, II, III and IV

6. Given below are two statements, one is labelled as Assertion (A) and the other is labelled as Reason (R).

Assertion (A) Significant figure for 0.300 is 3 whereas for 400 it is 1.

Reason (R) Zeroes at the end of right of a number are significant provided, they are not on the right side of the decimal point.

In the light of the above statements, choose the correct answer from the options given below.

(a) Both (A) and (R) are true and (R) is the correct explanation of (A).
(b) Both (A) and (R) are true but (R) is not the correct explanation of (A).
(c) (A) is true but (R) is false.
(d) (A) is false but (R) is true.

7. Which of the following statement is incorrect about Dalton's atomic theory?

(a) Atoms of the same element are similar to one another in all respects and equal in weights.
(b) Atoms of different elements have different masses and different properties.
(c) Matter is made up of tiny indivisible particles called atom.
(d) The relative number and kinds of atoms in a given compound is variable.

8. The mass of precious stones is expressed in terms of "Carat''. What will be the total mass of a ring in grams and kilograms, which contains 0.500 Carat diamond and 7.00 grams gold?
(Given, 1 carat = 3.168 grains, 1 gram = 15.4 grains)

(a) 8.20 g, 0.0065 kg
(b) 0.10 g, 0.0071 kg
(c) 0.20 g, 0.0031 kg
(d) 0.10 g, 0.0056 kg

9. In the reaction,

$$2H_2(g) + O_2(g) \longrightarrow 2H_2O(g)$$

The ratio of volume of hydrogen, oxygen and water is 2 : 1 : 2. This statement illustrates the law of

(a) constant proportion
(b) Gay-Lussac
(c) multiple proportion
(d) reciprocal proportion

10. Given below are two statements.

Statement I Under identical condition, 1 L of O_2 gas and 1 L of O_3 gas contains the same number of oxygen atoms.

Statement II 1 L of O_2 and 1 L of O_3 contains the same number of moles under identical conditions.

In the light of the above statements, choose the correct answer from the options given below.

(a) Both Statement I and Statement II are incorrect.
(b) Statement I is correct but Statement II is incorrect.
(c) Statement I is incorrect but Statement II is correct.
(d) Both Statement I and Statement II are correct.

11. 4.90 g of $KClO_3$ when heated produced 1.92 g of oxygen and the residue (KCl) left behind weighs 2.96 g. Which of the following law illustrated by above statement?

(a) Law of conservation of mass.
(b) Law of definite proportion.
(c) Law of multiple proportion.
(d) Law of reciprocal proportion.

12. From the given values, how many values have significant number as 2 in the following?

$$6.62 \times 10^{-34}, 0.72, 8.35, 0.0075, \frac{22}{7}$$

(a) 1 (b) 2
(c) 3 (d) 4

13. H_2S contains 94.11% sulphur, SO_2 contains 50% oxygen and H_2O contains 11.11% hydrogen. Thus it follows

(a) law of conservation of mass
(b) law of reciprocal proportion
(c) law of multiple proportion
(d) law of definite proportion

14. Which of the following statements are incorrect?

I. Law of constant proportion is true for all type of compound.

II. Molar volume of gas at standard condition is 22.4 L.

III. Vapour density of a gas is twice of its molecular mass.

IV. According to law of definite proportion, a chemical compound is always found to be made up of the same elements combined together in the same fixed proportion by mass.

V. Ethane and benzene illustrates the law of multiple proportions.

Choose the correct answer from the options given below.

(a) I, II and V (b) I, II and III
(c) II, III and IV (d) I, III and IV

15. Carbon combine with hydrogen to form three compounds *A, B* and *C*. The percentage of hydrogen in *A, B* and *C* is 25, 14.3 and 7.7 respectively. Which law of chemical combination is illustrated by the given data?

(a) Law of multiple proportion
(b) Law of reciprocal proportion
(c) Law of Gay-Lussac
(d) Law of conservation of mass

Response Index

01	a	b	c	d	10	a	b	c	d	19	a	b	c	d
02	a	b	c	d	11	a	b	c	d	20	a	b	c	d
03	a	b	c	d	12	a	b	c	d	21	a	b	c	d
04	a	b	c	d	13	a	b	c	d	22	a	b	c	d
05	a	b	c	d	14	a	b	c	d	23	a	b	c	d
06	a	b	c	d	15	a	b	c	d	24	a	b	c	d
07	a	b	c	d	16	a	b	c	d	25	a	b	c	d
08	a	b	c	d	17	a	b	c	d					
09	a	b	c	d	18	a	b	c	d					

Performance Scanner

> 90% Excellent !	You have mastered these topics. The concepts of these topics are at your fingertips. Move on to the next test and maintain this momentum.
76-90% Very Good !	You have a good command over these topics. Revise these topics again after a few days and enhance your performance.
60-75% Good !	You have a wide scope to learn for these topics. Revise these topics again.
<60 Not Satisfactory!	You have a long way ahead of you to master these topics. Revise it thoroughly.

Test 2

Syllabus
- Atomic and Molecular Masses
- Percentage Composition
- Empirical and Molecular Formula

For deeper insight Scan the QR Code 

Important Instructions
- The test is of 30 minutes duration and contains 15 multiple choice questions (Four options with a single correct answer).
- Choose the correct option and fill the OMR given on the last page of test accordingly.
- At some instances, you may find more than 1 option may be correct. In such circumstances, you have to judge the most appropriate answer as per the conditions given in the question.

1. Chlorine has two isotopes of atomic mass units 34.97 g/mol and 36.97 g/mol. The relative abundance of these two isotopes are 0.755 and 0.245 respectively. Average atomic mass of chlorine (in g) is

(a) 35.01 (b) 35.00
(c) 35.30 (d) 35.46

2. Naturally occurring boron consist of two isotopes *A* and *B* where atomic weights are 10.01 g/mol and 11.01 g/mol respectively. The atomic weight of natural boron is 10.81. The percentage of each isotope is

	A	*B*		*A*	*B*
(a)	10%	90%	(b)	85%	15%
(c)	20%	80%	(d)	80%	20%

3. Given below are two statements, one is labelled as Assertion (A) and the other is labelled as Reason (R).

Assertion (A) The empirical mass of ethene is one fourth of its molecular mass.

Reason (R) The empirical formula represent the simplest whole number ratio of various atoms present in a compound.

In the light of the above statements, choose the correct answer from the options given below.

(a) Both (A) and (R) are true and (R) is the correct explanation of (A).
(b) Both (A) and (R) are true but (R) is not the correct explanation of (A).
(c) (A) is true but (R) is false.
(d) (A) is false but (R) is true.

4. Select the incorrect statement.

(a) Single C^{12} atom has a mass exactly 12 amu and a mole of these atom has a mass of exactly 12 grams.
(b) The standard unit for expressing the mass of atoms is amu.
(c) Average atomic mass of an element depends mainly on the heavier isotopes.
(d) Atomic mass of oxygen is 16 u.

5. Given below are two statements, one is labelled as Assertion (A) and the other is labelled as Reason (R).

Assertion (A) Atomic mass of sodium is 23 u.

Reason (R) An atom of sodium is 23 times heavier than an atom of C-12 isotope.

In the light of the above statements, choose the correct answer from the options given below.

(a) Both (A) and (R) are true and (R) is the correct explanation of (A).
(b) Both (A) and (R) are true but (R) is not the correct explanation of (A).
(c) (A) is true but (R) is false.
(d) (A) is false but (R) is true.

6. Which of the following has maximum percentage of nitrogen by mass?

(a) LSD, $C_{20}H_{25}N_3O$
(b) Phencylidine, $C_{17}H_{25}N$
(c) Heroin, $C_{21}H_{23}NO_5$
(d) Morphine, $C_{17}H_{19}NO_3$

7. Match List-I with List-II.

List-I (Compound)		List-II (Equivalent mass of the compound)	
A.	HBr	I.	56.10
B.	NaCl	II.	80.91
C.	NH_3	III.	58.5
D.	KOH	IV.	17

Choose the correct answer from the options given below.

(a) A-I, B-IV, C-III, D-II
(b) A-II, B-III, C-IV, D-I
(c) A-I, B-III, C-II, D-IV
(d) A-II, B-IV, C-I, D-III

8. Consider the statements given below.

Statement I The empirical formula of a compound is the chemical formula which express the simplest whole number ratio of the atom of the various element present in one molecule of the compound.

Statement II Empirical formula of a compound represents only the atomic ratio of various element present in the molecule.

In the light of the above statements, choose the most appropriate answer from the options given below.

(a) Both Statement I and Statement II are incorrect.
(b) Statement I is correct but Statement II is incorrect.
(c) Statement I is incorrect but Statement II is correct.
(d) Both Statement I and Statement II are correct.

9. Which of the following statements are correct?

I. Equivalent weight of $Ca_3(PO_4)_2$ is $\frac{\text{mol. wt.}}{6}$

II. Equivalent weight of $Na_3PO_4 \cdot 12H_2O$ is $\frac{\text{mol.wt.}}{3}$

III. Equivalent weight of K_2SO_4 is $\frac{\text{mol. wt.}}{2}$

IV. The equivalent weight of potash alum $K_2SO_4 \cdot Al_2(SO_4)_3 \cdot 24H_2O$ is $\frac{\text{mol. wt.}}{8}$

V. Equivalent weight of $KMnO_4$ in acidic medium is $\frac{\text{mol. wt.}}{5}$

Choose the correct answer from the options given below.

(a) I and II
(b) I, II and III
(c) II, II and IV
(d) I, II, III, IV and V

10. A 0.2075 g sample of an oxide of cobalt on analysis was found to contain 0.1475 g cobalt empirical formula of oxide is

(a) CoO
(b) Co_2O_3
(c) CoO_3
(d) Co_2O

11. Consider the following compounds.

$$H_2O, Al_2(SO_4)_3, BaSO_4, AlCl_3, H_3PO_4$$

Total number of species that have valency factor three is ....

(a) 1 (b) 2 (c) 3 (d) 5

12. If an organic compound contains C, H and N atoms in 9:1:3.5 by weight, then what will be the molecular formula of the compound? (Molecular mass of the compound = 108 g/mol)

(a) $C_7H_{10}N$
(b) $C_5H_6N_3$
(c) $C_6H_8N_2$
(d) $C_4H_8N_2$

13. Consider the following reaction sequence.

$$CaCl_2(aq) + CO_2(g) + H_2O \longrightarrow CaCO_3(s) + 2HCl(aq)$$

$$CaCO_3(s) \xrightarrow{\Delta} CaO(s) + CO_2(g)$$

If the percentage yield of I[st] step is 70% and that of 2nd step is 65%. What is expected overall percentage yield for producing CaO from $CaCl_2$?

(a) 45.5% (b) 60% (c) 55.5% (d) 65%

14. Match List-I with List-II.

List-I (Species with reference of potash alum)		List-II (% Composition)
A.	K_2SO_4	I. 40.50%
B.	$Al_2(SO_4)_3$	II. 45.56%
C.	H_2O	III. 36.07%
D.	SO_4^{2-}	IV. 18.35%

Choose the correct answer from the options given below.

(a) A-IV, B-III, C-II, D-I
(b) A-I, B-II, C-III, D-IV
(c) A-II, B-I, C-IV, D-III
(d) A-II, B-IV, C-III, D-I

15. Generally, Kevlar is used in making bullet proof vests. Suppose, it contains 70.6% of C, 4.2% of H, 11.8% of N and 13.4% of oxygen. Then, the empirical formula of Kevlar is

(a) C_7H_5NO (b) C_7H_9NO
(c) $C_7H_5N_2O$ (d) $C_7H_5NO_2$

Response Index

01	a	b	c	d	10	a	b	c	d	19	a	b	c	d
02	a	b	c	d	11	a	b	c	d	20	a	b	c	d
03	a	b	c	d	12	a	b	c	d	21	a	b	c	d
04	a	b	c	d	13	a	b	c	d	22	a	b	c	d
05	a	b	c	d	14	a	b	c	d	23	a	b	c	d
06	a	b	c	d	15	a	b	c	d	24	a	b	c	d
07	a	b	c	d	16	a	b	c	d	25	a	b	c	d
08	a	b	c	d	17	a	b	c	d					
09	a	b	c	d	18	a	b	c	d					

Performance Scanner

> 90% Excellent !	You have mastered these topics. The concepts of these topics are at your fingertips. Move on to the next test and maintain this momentum.
76-90% Very Good !	You have a good command over these topics. Revise these topics again after a few days and enhance your performance.
60-75% Good !	You have a wide scope to learn for these topics. Revise these topics again.
<60 Not Satisfactory!	You have a long way ahead of you to master these topics. Revise it thoroughly.

Test 3

Syllabus
- Mole Concept
- Molar Mass
- Chemical Equation and Stoichiometry

For deeper insight **Scan the QR Code**

Important Instructions

- The test is of 30 minutes duration and contains 15 multiple choice questions (Four options with a single correct answer).
- Choose the correct option and fill the OMR given on the last page of test accordingly.
- At some instances, you may find more than 1 option may be correct. In such circumstances, you have to judge the most appropriate answer as per the conditions given in the question.

1. 40 g of a magnesium carbonate sample decomposes on heating to give carbon dioxide and 16 g magnesium oxide. What will be the percentage purity of magnesium carbonate in the sample?

(a) 42% (b) 32%
(c) 63% (d) 84%

2. The molarity (M) and molality (m) of 16% aqueous methanol (CH_3OH) solution by volume. (Density of the solution = 0.9 g/mL) are respectively.

(a) 2.232 M, 1.875 m (b) 1.023 M, 2.032 m
(c) 1.875 M, 3.323 m (d) 1.875 M, 2.232 m

3. Which of the following statements is/are correct about the given conclusion?

A mixture containing 64 g of H_2 and 64 g of O_2 is ignited so that water is formed as follows

$$2H_2 + O_2 \longrightarrow 2H_2O$$

I. H_2 is the limiting reagent.
II. O_2 is the limiting reagent.
III. The reaction mixture contains 72 g of H_2O and 56 g of unreacted H_2.
IV. The reaction mixture contains 56 g of H_2O and 72 g of unreacted H_2.
V. The reaction mixture contains 72 g of H_2O and 28 g of unreacted H_2.

Choose the most appropriate answer from the options given below.

(a) I, II and V
(b) II and III
(c) III, IV, II and V
(d) I, II, III and IV

4. Match List-I with List-II.

	List-I (Mass of reactant)		List-II (Mass of product)
A.	$\underset{1.0\,g}{2H_2} + \underset{1.0\,g}{O_2} \longrightarrow \underset{?}{2H_2O}$	I.	0.56 g
B.	$\underset{1.0\,g}{N_2} + \underset{1.0\,g}{3H_2} \longrightarrow \underset{?}{2NH_3}$	II.	1.333 g
C.	$\underset{1.0\,g}{CaCO_3} \xrightarrow{\Delta} CaO + \underset{?}{CO_2}$	III.	1.125 g
D.	$\underset{1.0\,g}{C} + \underset{1.0\,g}{2H_2} \longrightarrow \underset{?}{CH_4}$	IV.	1.214 g

Choose the correct answer from the options given below.

(a) A-III, B-IV, C-I, D-II
(b) A-IV, B-III, C-II, D-I
(c) A-I, B-III, C-II, D-IV
(d) A-I, B-IV, C-III, D-II

5. The mass of 0.50 molal solution of sodium acetate in water would use to obtain 0.150 mol sodium acetate (82 g mol^{-1}) is

(a) 312.3 g (b) 31.2 g
(c) 42.3 g (d) 412.3 g

6. Which of the following quantities are independent of temperature?

I. Molarity II. Normality
III. Mole fraction IV. Molality
V. Formality

Choose the most appropriate answer from the options given below.

(a) I, III and V (b) I, II and V
(c) III and IV (d) III and II

7. Arrange the following in order of increasing masses.

I. 1 molecule of oxygen
II. 1 atom of nitrogen
III. 1 mole of water
IV. 1×10^{-10} g of iron

Choose the correct answer from the options given below.

(a) II < I < III < IV
(b) I < II < IV < III
(c) II < I < IV < III
(d) I < II < III < IV

8. 50% (*w*/*V*) NaCl has specific gravity 1.12 g/mL. The concentration of NaCl in ppm is

(a) 11.86×10^6 (b) 4.45×10^6
(c) 445×10^5 (d) 4.45×10^5

9. Given below are two statements, one is labelled as Assertion (A) and the other is labelled as Reason (R).

Assertion (A) Both 106 g Na_2CO_3 and 12 g carbon have same number of carbon atoms.

Reason (R) Both contains 1 g atom of carbon which contains 6.023×10^{23} carbon atoms.

In the light of the above statements, choose the correct answer from the options given below.

(a) Both (A) and (R) are true and (R) is the correct explanation of (A).
(b) Both (A) and (R) are true but (R) is not the correct explanation of (A).
(c) (A) is true but (R) is false.
(d) (A) is false but (R) is true.

10. Calculate the amount of $KClO_3$ needed to supply sufficient oxygen for burning 112 L of CO gas at NTP.

(a) 248 g
(b) 306 g
(c) 104 g
(d) 204 g

11. During the complete combustion of 200 cm^3 of acetylene, the volume of oxygen (at STP) required and volume of CO_2 formed respectively are

(a) 500 cm^3 and 400 cm^3
(b) 400 cm^3 and 500 cm^3
(c) 200 cm^3 and 300 cm^3
(d) 300 cm^3 and 200 cm^3

12. Consider the following compounds with mass.
8 g O_2, 7 g CO, 14 g N_2, 11 g CO_2, 16 g SO_2
Total number of species having same number of moles is ....

(a) 1
(b) 2
(c) 3
(d) 4

13. 2.0 g of magnesium is burnt with 0.65 g of O_2 in a closed vessel. Which reactant is left in excess and how much?

(a) Mg, 1.025 g
(b) Mg, 0.975 g
(c) O_2, 0.975 g
(d) O_2, 1.33 g

14. The number of molecules present in 250 mL of 0.02 N H_2SO_4 is

(a) 15.05×10^{20}
(b) 15.05×10^{23}
(c) 15.05×10^{18}
(d) 15.05×10^{18}

15. Which of the following statements are not correct?

I. Sum of mole fraction of all components of mixture is always less than 1.

II. Molality is temperature independent.

III. In molality, amount of solvent is measured in terms of volume.

IV. Formality is the concentration term used particularly for covalent compounds.

V. Molality (m) and molarity (M) are related by the following relation.

$$m = \frac{1000\,m}{100d - Mm'}$$

Choose the most appropriate answer from the options given below.

(a) I, III and IV (b) I, II and IV

(c) II, III and IV (d) III, IV and V

Response Index

01	ⓐ ⓑ ⓒ ⓓ	10	ⓐ ⓑ ⓒ ⓓ	19	ⓐ ⓑ ⓒ ⓓ
02	ⓐ ⓑ ⓒ ⓓ	11	ⓐ ⓑ ⓒ ⓓ	20	ⓐ ⓑ ⓒ ⓓ
03	ⓐ ⓑ ⓒ ⓓ	12	ⓐ ⓑ ⓒ ⓓ	21	ⓐ ⓑ ⓒ ⓓ
04	ⓐ ⓑ ⓒ ⓓ	13	ⓐ ⓑ ⓒ ⓓ	22	ⓐ ⓑ ⓒ ⓓ
05	ⓐ ⓑ ⓒ ⓓ	14	ⓐ ⓑ ⓒ ⓓ	23	ⓐ ⓑ ⓒ ⓓ
06	ⓐ ⓑ ⓒ ⓓ	15	ⓐ ⓑ ⓒ ⓓ	24	ⓐ ⓑ ⓒ ⓓ
07	ⓐ ⓑ ⓒ ⓓ	16	ⓐ ⓑ ⓒ ⓓ	25	ⓐ ⓑ ⓒ ⓓ
08	ⓐ ⓑ ⓒ ⓓ	17	ⓐ ⓑ ⓒ ⓓ		
09	ⓐ ⓑ ⓒ ⓓ	18	ⓐ ⓑ ⓒ ⓓ		

Performance Scanner

> 90% Excellent !	You have mastered these topics. The concepts of these topics are at your fingertips. Move on to the chapter test and maintain this momentum.
76-90% Very Good !	You have a good command over these topics. Revise these topics again after a few days and enhance your performance.
60-75% Good !	You have a wide scope to learn for these topics. Revise these topics again.
<60 Not Satisfactory!	You have a long way ahead of you to master these topics. Revise it thoroughly.

Chapter Break Thru

Syllabus			
Syllabus	• Matter and its Nature • Dalton's Atomic Theory • Concept of Atom, Molecule, Element and Compound • Laws of Chemical Combinations	• Atomic and Molecular Masses • Percentage Composition • Empirical and Molecular Formula	• Mole Concepts and Molar Mass • Chemical Equations and Stoichiometry

Important Instructions

- The test is of 1 hour duration and contains 50 multiple choice questions (Four options with a single correct answer).
- Choose the correct option and fill the OMR given on the last page of test accordingly.
- At some instances, you may find more than 1 option may be correct. In such circumstances, you have to judge the most appropriate answer as per the conditions given in the question.

1. Select the incorrect statement regarding conversion of one unit to another.

(a) In S.I. unit 360 miles per hour is equal to 160 m/s.

(b) In S.I. unit 100 million miles is equal to 1.6×10^{11} m.

(c) In S.I. unit 0.54 Å is equal to 5.4×10^{-11} m.

(d) In S.I. unit 10 pounds is equal to 3.54 kg.

2. Which of the following statements are incorrect?

I. Unit of physical quantity represented by volume is dm^3.

II. The SI unit of measurement of volume of liquid is litre.

III. The unit of work done is represented by kg/m.

IV. Air sometimes is considered as heterogeneous mixture due to the presence of dust particles.

V. Matter consists of very small indivisible particle called as atoms.

Select the correct answer from the options given below.

(a) I and II (b) II and III

(c) II, IV and V (d) II and IV only

3. Consider the following species.

I. Air II. Brass III. Dry ice

IV. Aerated drink V. Diesel

The total number of species that are mixture is ....

(a) 1 (b) 2

(c) 3 (d) 4

4. Which of the following have same number of significant figures ?

I. 6.023×10^{23} II. 7.70×10^{-20}

III. 7.50 IV. 0.75

V. 0.92

Choose the correct answer from the options given below.

(a) I and II only

(b) I, II and IV

(c) II and III only

(d) II, III and V

5. Which of the following pair of compounds do not illustrate the law of multiple proportion?

(a) SO_2 and SO_3

(b) NO_2 and N_2O

(c) MgO and $Mg(OH)_2$

(d) NO and N_2O_5

6. There are two common oxides of sulphur, one of which contains 50 % oxygen by weight, the other almost contain exactly 60 %. The weight of sulphur which combine with 1g O_2 are in the ratio of

(a) 2 : 1 (b) 1 : 1

(c) 2 : 3 (d) 3 : 2

7. The simplest formula of a compound containing 50 % of element X (atomic weight 10) and 50 % of element Y (atomic weight 20) is

(a) XY (b) X_2Y
(c) XY_2 (d) X_2Y_3

8. 0.1653 g of aluminium react completely with 0.652 g chlorine to form chloride of aluminium. If molecular mass of the compound is 267 amu. Calculate the molecular formula of the compound.

(a) Al_2Cl_3 (b) $AlCl_3$
(c) Al_2Cl_6 (d) Al_2Cl_5

9. What is percentage composition of each element in zinc phosphate?

	Zn (%)	P (%)	O (%)
(a)	33.15	16.05	50.80
(b)	16.05	33.15	50.80
(c)	33.15	50.80	16.05
(d)	50.80	16.05	33.15

10. $BrO_3^- + 5Br^- \longrightarrow Br_2 + 3H_2O$

If 50 mL of 0.1 M BrO_3^- is mixed with 30 mL of 0.5 M Br^- solution that contains excess of H^+ ion, the moles of Br_2 formed is

(a) 6.0×10^{-4}
(b) 1.2×10^{-4}
(c) 9.0×10^{-3}
(d) 1.8×10^{-3}

11. Consider the following statements.

Statement I In a gaseous reaction, the ratio of volume of reactant and gaseous product is in agreement with their molar ratio.

Statement II Volume of gas is inversely proportional to its moles at particular temperature and pressure.

In the light of the above statements, choose the correct answer from the options given below.

(a) Both Statement I and Statement II are incorrect.
(b) Statement I is correct but Statement II is incorrect.
(c) Statement I is incorrect but Statement II is correct.
(d) Both Statement I and Statement II are correct.

12. If 10.0 g of $CaCO_3$ is reacted with 10.0 g of HCl, what mass of CO_2 will be produced and which reactant is limiting reagent?

(a) $CaCO_3$, 44 g CO_2
(b) $CaCO_3$, 4.4 g CO_2
(c) CO_2, 44 g CO_2
(d) CO_2, 4.4 g CO_2

13. Which of the following statement is incorrect?

(a) Molecular mass of a substance expressed in grams is called gram molecular mass.
(b) The atomic mass of an element expressed in grams called gram atomic mass.
(c) One atomic mass unit is equal to $\frac{1}{12}$th of the mass of an atom of oxygen-16 isotope.
(d) The atomic mass of an element is the average relative mass of its atoms as compared with an atom of carbon-12 taken as 12.

14. Which of the following illustrate the law of conservation of mass?

I. 90 g of $KClO_3$ when heated produced 1.92 g of oxygen and the residue (KCl) left behind weight 2.96 g.
II. 17.0 g mass of silver nitrate will react with 5.85 g of sodium chloride to produce 14.35 g of silver chloride and 8.5 g of silver nitrate.
III. When 4.2 g of $NaHCO_3$ is added to a solution of acetic acid weighing 10.0 g it is observed that 2.2 g of CO_2 is released into the atmosphere.
IV. Atoms in a chemical reactions are neither created nor destroyed .
V. Law of conservation of mass was put forth by Antoine Lavoisier.

Select the correct answer from the options given below.

(a) Only I and V (b) I, II and IV
(c) Only II and III (d) I, II, III, IV and V

15. Which of the following has largest number of atoms ?

(a) 0.5 g atom of Cu
(b) 0.635 g of Cu
(c) 0.25 moles of Cu atom
(d) 1 g of Cu

16. Total number of electrons present in 3.2 g oxygen gas is

(a) 9.205×10^{22} electrons
(b) 9.635×10^{23} electrons
(c) 8.635×10^{22} electrons
(d) 8.625×10^{23} electrons

17. How many moles of electrons weigh one kilograms ?

(a) 6.023×10^{23} (b) $\frac{1}{9.108}\times10^{31}$
(c) $\frac{6.023}{9.108}\times10^{54}$ (d) $\frac{1}{9.108\times6.023}\times10^{8}$

18. Given below are two statements, one is labelled as Assertion (A) and the other is labelled as Reason (R).

Assertion (A) Pure water obtained from different sources such as rivers, well, spring sea etc always contain hydrogen and oxygen in the ratio of 1 : 8 by mass.

Reason (R) Total mass of reactant and product during chemical or physical changes is always the same.

In the light of the above statements, choose the most appropriate answer from the options given below.

(a) Both (A) and (R) are true and (R) is the correct explanation of (A).
(b) Both (A) and (R) are true but (R) is not the correct explanation of (A).
(c) (A) is true but (R) is false.
(d) (A) is false but (R) is true.

19. The mass of N_2F_4 produced by the reaction of 2.0 g of NH_3 and 8.0 g of F_2 is 3.56 g. What is the percentage yield?

$$2NH_3 + 5F_2 \longrightarrow N_2F_4 + 6HF$$

(a) 79.04 % (b) 71.23 %
(c) 84.61 % (d) 81.30 %

20. 7.4 gram of a metal hydroxide on heating gives 5.6 g of metal oxide. Equivalent weight of metal is

(a) 20 (b) 40
(c) 60 (d) 10

21. Moles and gram equivalent in 196 g of H_3PO_4 are

(a) 1 and 2
(b) 2 and 2
(c) 2 and 4
(d) 2 and 6

22. In the final answer of the expression,

$$\frac{(29.2-20.2)(1.79\times10^5)}{137}$$

The number of significant figure is

(a) 2 (b) 3
(c) 4 (d) 1

23. Given below are two statements.

Statement I A single ^{12}C atom has a mass exactly 12 amu and a mole of these atom has a mass of exactly 12 g.

Statement II A mole of atoms of any element has a mass in grams equal to its atomic mass.

In the light of above statements, choose the most appropriate answer from the options given below.

(a) Both Statement I and Statement II are incorrect
(b) Statement I is correct but Statement II is incorrect.
(c) Statement I is incorrect but Statement II is correct.
(d) Both Statement I and Statement II are correct.

24. Hydrogen peroxide in aqueous solution decomposes on warming to give oxygen according to the equation.

$$2H_2O_2(aq) \longrightarrow 2H_2O(l) + O_2(g)$$

Under condition where 1 mole of gas occupies 24 dm^3, 100 cm^3 of "X" M solution of H_2O_2 produce 3 dm^3 of O_2. Thus "X" is

(a) 2.5 (b) 0.5
(c) 0.25 (d) 1

25. An aqueous solution of urea is 3.0 molal. The mole fraction of urea is

(a) 0.33 (b) 0.25
(c) 0.66 (d) 0.05

26. Select the correct statements about the Dalton's atomic theory.

I. Matter consists of very small indivisible particles named as atom.

II. Atoms of different elements have different masses and also have different chemical properties.

III. Fractions of atom do not take part in a chemical reaction.

IV. Atoms in a chemical reactions are neither created nor destroyed but they get reorganised.

V. All atoms of a given element may or may not have identical properties.

Choose the most appropriate answer from the options given below.

(a) I, II and V (b) I, II, III and IV

(c) I, II, III, IVand V (d) I, III and IV

27. A sample of H_2SO_4 (density 1.8 g/mL) is 90 % by weight. What is the volume of the acid that has to be used to make 1 L of 0.2 M H_2SO_4 ?

(a) 16 mL (b) 18 mL

(c) 12 mL (d) 10 mL

28. Elements *X* and *Y* combine to form two compounds XY_2 and X_3Y_2 when 0.1 mole of former weigh 10 g, while 0.05 mole of the latter weigh 9 g. What are the atomic weights of *X* and *Y* ?

(a) 40, 30 (b) 60, 40

(c) 20, 30 (d) 30, 20

29. Given below are two statements, one is labelled as Assertion (A) and the other is labelled as Reason (R).

Assertion (A) 10 g of N_2, CO pair has equal number of molecule with 10 g of N_2O and CO_2 pair.

Reason (R) Equal number of molecules are present as number of moles are same.

In the light of the above statements, choose the correct answer from the options given below.

(a) Both (A) and (R) are true and (R) is the correct explanation of (A).

(b) Both (A) and (R) are true but (R) is not the correct explanation of (A).

(c) (A) is true but (R) is false.

(d) (A) is false but (R) is true.

30. The elemental analysis of an organic compound given composition of carbon as 38.71%, hydrogen as 9.67% and oxygen as 51.62%. The empirical formula of the compound would be

(a) CH_2O (b) CH_4O

(c) CHO (d) CH_3O

31. 500 mL of NH_3 contain 6.00×10^{23} molecule at STP. How many molecules are present in 100 mL of CO_2 at STP?

(a) 6×10^{23} (b) 1.5×10^{21}

(c) 1.2×10^{23} (d) 8.4×10^{20}

32. 10 g of hydrogen and 64 g of O_2 were filled in a steel vessel and exploaded. Amount of water produced in this reaction will be

(a) 3 mole (b) 4 mole

(c) 1 mole (d) 2 mole

33. 100 g of ethylene polymerises to polyethene according to the equation,

$$nCH_2{=}CH_2 \longrightarrow \text{+}CH_2{-}CH_2\text{+}_n$$

The mass of polyethene produced will be

(a) 100 ng (b) 100/n g

(c) 100 n/2 g (d) 100 g

34. Which of the following combinations illustrate law of reciprocal proportions?

(a) NaCl, NaBr, NaI

(b) CO_2, CH_4, H_2O

(c) N_2O_3, N_2O_4, N_2O_5

(d) PH_3, P_2O_3, P_2O_5

35. Consider the following reactions and select the incorrect statement regarding reactions.

I. $P_4 + 5O_2 \longrightarrow P_4O_{10}$

II. $P_4 + 3O_2 \longrightarrow P_4O_6$

1.24 g of P_4 react with 8.0 g of O_2

(A) P_4 is the limiting quantity.

(B) O_2 is the limiting quantity.

(C) Mass of P_4O_{10} obtained 2.2 g.

(D) Mass of P_4O_6 obtained is 2.84 g.

Choose the correct answer from the options given below.

(a) A and B (b) B only

(c) A and D (d) B, C and D

36. Which of the following is correct regarding composition of 10 g $CaCO_3$ it contains?

(a) 10 mole of $CaCO_3$ (b) 0.1 g atom of Ca
(c) 6×10^{23} atoms of Ca (d) 6.1 equivalent of Ca

37. If two oxides of same metal were found to contain 32% and 51.2% of oxygen respectively. If the formula of first oxide is represented by M_2O_3, then the formula of second oxide is

(a) MO_2 (b) MO_3
(c) M_2O (d) M_2O_2

38. What is the valency of an element of which the equivalent weight is 12 and specific heat is 0.25?

(a) 1 (b) 2
(c) 3 (d) 4

39. 36.5 % HCl has density equal to 1.20 g/ml. The molarity (*M*) and molality (*m*) respectively are

	(*M*)	(*m*)
(a)	15.7	15.7
(b)	12	12
(c)	15.7	12
(d)	12	15.7

40. A gas mixture of 3.0 litre of propane and butane on complete combustion at 25 °C produced 10 litre of CO_2. Find the volume of gas.

	Propane	Butane
(a)	2 L	1 L
(b)	0.5 L	1 L
(c)	1 L	2.5 L
(d)	1.5 L	2 L

41. How many years would it take to spend Avogadro's number of rupees at the rate of 10 lakh rupees per second?

(a) 1.02×10^3 years (b) 2.02×10^{10} years
(c) 1.9×10^{10} years (d) 2.9×10^8 years

42. Given below are two statements.

Statement I Calomel is a chemical compound, whereas brass is a mixture.

Statement II Calomel always contains 5.6 times as much mercury as chlorine by weight. Brass can be made with widely different ratio of Cu and Zn.

In the light of the above statements, choose the most appropriate answer from the options given below.

(a) Both Statement I and Statement II are incorrect.
(b) Statement I is correct but Statement II is incorrect.
(c) Statement I is incorrect but Statement II is correct.
(d) Both Statement I and Statement II are correct.

43. The empirical formula of an oxide of iron which has 69.9 % iron and 30.1 % oxygen by mass is (atomic mass of Fe = 56, O = 16)

(a) FeO (b) Fe_2O_3
(c) Fe_3O_4 (d) FeO_3

44. The same amount of metal combines with 0.200 g oxygen and 3.17 g of halogen. Hence, equivalent mass of halogen is

(a) 127 g eq^{-1} (b) 80 g eq^{-1}
(c) 35.5 g eq^{-1} (d) 9 g eq^{-1}

45. Match List-I with List-II

List-I (Reaction)	List-II (Equivalent weight)
A. $MnO_4^- \longrightarrow Mn^{2+}$	I. $\frac{M}{5}$
B. $H_3PO_2 \longrightarrow H_2PO_2^- + H^{\oplus}$	II. $\frac{M}{2}$
C. $2H_2O_2 \longrightarrow 2H_2O + O_2$	III. $\frac{M}{6}$
D. $N_2 + 3H_2 \longrightarrow 2NH_3$	IV. M

Choose the correct answer from the options given below.

(a) A-I, B-IV, C-II, D-III
(b) A-II, B-III, C-IV, D-I
(c) A-III, B-II, C-IV, D-I
(d) A-IV, B-III, C-II, D-I

46. A gaseous hydrocarbon *X* was burnt in excess of oxygen. A 0.112 dm^3 sample of *X*, at STP gave 0.88 g of CO_2. How many C- atoms are there in one molecule of *X*?

(a) 1 (b) 2 (c) 3 (d) 4

47. A solution contains 410.3 g H_2SO_4 per litre of the sodium at 20 °C. If the density is 1.243 g/mL, then what will be its molarity and molality?

	M	m
(a)	4.186	5.027
(b)	5.027	4.186
(c)	3.025	1.286
(d)	1.286	3.025

48. The common salt obtained from sea water contains 95 % NaCl by mass. The appropriate number of molecules in 10 g salt is

(a) 10^{21} (b) 10^{22}
(c) 10^{23} (d) 10^{24}

49. Given below are two statements, one is labelled as Assertion (A) and Reason (R).

Assertion (A) The mass of the product formed in a reaction depends upon the limiting reagent.

Reason (R) Limiting reagent react completely in the reaction.

In the light of the above statements, choose the correct answer from the options given below.

(a) Both (A) and (R) are true and (R) is the correct explanation of (A).
(b) Both (A) and (R) are true but (R) is not the correct explanation of (A).
(c) (A) is true but (R) is false.
(d) (A) is false but (R) is true.

50. Molecular weight of NH_3 and N_2 are x_1 and x_2 respectively in the given reaction. Their equivalent weights are y_1 and y_2 respectively.

$$N_2 + 3H_2 \longrightarrow 2NH_3$$

Then $y_1 - y_2$ is

(a) $\frac{(2x_1 - x_2)}{6}$ (b) $(3x_1 - x_2)$
(c) $(x_1 - 3x_2)$ (d) $(x_1 - x_2)$

Response Index

01	ⓐ	ⓑ	ⓒ	ⓓ	14	ⓐ	ⓑ	ⓒ	ⓓ	27	ⓐ	ⓑ	ⓒ	ⓓ	40	ⓐ	ⓑ	ⓒ	ⓓ
02	ⓐ	ⓑ	ⓒ	ⓓ	15	ⓐ	ⓑ	ⓒ	ⓓ	28	ⓐ	ⓑ	ⓒ	ⓓ	41	ⓐ	ⓑ	ⓒ	ⓓ
03	ⓐ	ⓑ	ⓒ	ⓓ	16	ⓐ	ⓑ	ⓒ	ⓓ	29	ⓐ	ⓑ	ⓒ	ⓓ	42	ⓐ	ⓑ	ⓒ	ⓓ
04	ⓐ	ⓑ	ⓒ	ⓓ	17	ⓐ	ⓑ	ⓒ	ⓓ	30	ⓐ	ⓑ	ⓒ	ⓓ	43	ⓐ	ⓑ	ⓒ	ⓓ
05	ⓐ	ⓑ	ⓒ	ⓓ	18	ⓐ	ⓑ	ⓒ	ⓓ	31	ⓐ	ⓑ	ⓒ	ⓓ	44	ⓐ	ⓑ	ⓒ	ⓓ
06	ⓐ	ⓑ	ⓒ	ⓓ	19	ⓐ	ⓑ	ⓒ	ⓓ	32	ⓐ	ⓑ	ⓒ	ⓓ	45	ⓐ	ⓑ	ⓒ	ⓓ
07	ⓐ	ⓑ	ⓒ	ⓓ	20	ⓐ	ⓑ	ⓒ	ⓓ	33	ⓐ	ⓑ	ⓒ	ⓓ	46	ⓐ	ⓑ	ⓒ	ⓓ
08	ⓐ	ⓑ	ⓒ	ⓓ	21	ⓐ	ⓑ	ⓒ	ⓓ	34	ⓐ	ⓑ	ⓒ	ⓓ	47	ⓐ	ⓑ	ⓒ	ⓓ
09	ⓐ	ⓑ	ⓒ	ⓓ	22	ⓐ	ⓑ	ⓒ	ⓓ	35	ⓐ	ⓑ	ⓒ	ⓓ	48	ⓐ	ⓑ	ⓒ	ⓓ
10	ⓐ	ⓑ	ⓒ	ⓓ	23	ⓐ	ⓑ	ⓒ	ⓓ	36	ⓐ	ⓑ	ⓒ	ⓓ	49	ⓐ	ⓑ	ⓒ	ⓓ
11	ⓐ	ⓑ	ⓒ	ⓓ	24	ⓐ	ⓑ	ⓒ	ⓓ	37	ⓐ	ⓑ	ⓒ	ⓓ	50	ⓐ	ⓑ	ⓒ	ⓓ
12	ⓐ	ⓑ	ⓒ	ⓓ	25	ⓐ	ⓑ	ⓒ	ⓓ	38	ⓐ	ⓑ	ⓒ	ⓓ					
13	ⓐ	ⓑ	ⓒ	ⓓ	26	ⓐ	ⓑ	ⓒ	ⓓ	39	ⓐ	ⓑ	ⓒ	ⓓ					

Performance Scanner

> 90% Excellent !	You have mastered this chapter. The concepts of this chapter are at your fingertips. Move on to the next chapter and maintain this momentum.
76-90% Very Good !	You have a good command over this chapter. Revise the chapter again after a few days and enhance your performance.
60-75% Good !	You have a wide scope to learn for this chapter. Revise this chapter again.
<60 Not Satisfactory!	You have a long way ahead of you to master this chapter. Revise it thoroughly.

Scan for Online Chapter Test

Scan for Online Unit Test

Test Booklet No. **3947202**

Test Booklet Code **CH2**

MEDACE

NEET (UG)

SELF ASSESSMENT KIT

Structure of Atom

Topics Covered

Preliminary Model and Dual Nature of Light

Bohr's Model and Hydrogen Spectrum

Dual Nature of Matter and Quantum Mechanical Model

Important Instructions

- This Booklet Contains – 3 Topic Tests and One Test on Complete Chapter.
- Each question carries 4 marks.
- For each correct response the candidate will get 4 marks and for every incorrect response 1 mark will be additionally deducted from the total score.
- Use **Blue/Black** point pen only for filling the OMR.
- Rough work is to be done in the space provided for this purpose in the test booklet only.

Name of the Candidate (In Capitals) ______

______

Candidate's Signature ______

Invigilator's Signature ______

Facsimile signature stamp of center superintendent______

Do not open this Booklet until you start attempting the Test

Topical Follow Thru

Test 1

Syllabus
- Preliminary Models, Nature of Electromagnetic Radiation, Photoelectric Effect

For deeper insight **Scan the QR Code**

Important Instructions
- The test is of 30 minutes duration and contains 15 multiple choice questions (Four options with a single correct answer).
- Choose the correct option and fill the OMR given on the last page of test accordingly.
- At some instances, you may find more than 1 option may be correct. In such circumstances, you have to judge the most appropriate answer as per the conditions given in the question.

1. Select the incorrect statement regarding cathode rays.
(a) They themselves are not visible but their behaviour can be observed with the help of flourescent material.
(b) The charge to mass ratio (*e/m*) of the particles constituting cathode rays depend upon the nature of the gas present in discharge tube.
(c) The charge and mass of the particles does not depend upon the material of the cathode.
(d) They consist of negatively charged particles.

2. The number of protons, electrons and neutrons in sulphide ion are respectively.
(a) 16, 16, 16 (b) 16, 18, 16
(c) 16, 18, 18 (d) 18, 16, 16

3. Given below are two statements.
Statement I R.A Millikan advised a method known as oil drop experiment to determine the charge and mass of electrons.
Statement II Rutherford found that α-rays consist of high energy particles carrying two units of positive charge and four units of atomic mass.
In the light of the above statements, choose the correct answer from the options given below.
(a) Both Statement I and Statement II are incorrect.
(b) Statement I is correct but Statement II is incorrect.
(c) Statement I is incorrect but Statement II is correct.
(d) Both Statement I and Statement II are correct.

4. An electromagnetic wave has an electric field and magnetic field component, which of the following statement is incorrect regarding it?
(a) They have same frequency.
(b) They travel with same speed.
(c) They are coplanar.
(d) They have same wavelength and amplitude.

5. Which of the following statement(s) is/are correct?
I. In Rutherford's gold foil experiment, the path of the α-particles is hyperbolic and in the scattering of α-particles, nuclear force are involved.
II. Canal rays carries positively charged particles.
III. Energy of electromagnetic radiation are proportional to wave number, frequency and number of photons.
IV. Energy equivalent of 10.0 cm^{-1} is 2×10^{-22} J/photon or 0.12 kJ/mol.
V. The value of (*e/m*) for cathode ray is constant and value is 1.7588×10^{8} C/g.

Choose the correct answer from the options given below.
(a) I, II, III only
(b) II, III, IV, V only
(c) I, II, III, IV only
(d) I, II, III, IV, V

6. The number of photons of light having wave number $\overline{\nu}$ in 10J of energy is
(a) $\frac{h}{10c\overline{\nu}}$ (b) $\frac{10}{h\overline{\nu}c}$ (c) $\frac{hc}{10\overline{\nu}}$ (d) $10h\overline{\nu}c$

7. Among the following, the total number of radiations having lower wavelength than the visible light is
Cosmic rays, γ-rays, infrared, microwave, radiowave.

(a) 1 (b) 2 (c) 3 (d) 4

8. Which of the following statement is/are incorrect?

I. Anode rays are deflected by electric field towards negative charged plate.
II. Charge to mass ratio of the particles of canal rays depends on nature of the gas from which these originate.
III. When Rutherford bombarded a thin foil of Be with fast moving α-particles he observed that electrically neutral particles having a mass slightly greater than protons were emitted.
IV. Proton is a fundamental particles of atom carrying one unit positive charge and having mass nearly equal to the mass of an atom of helium.
V. *e/m* ratio is minimum when H_2 gas is used in the discharge tube during anode rays.

Choose the correct answer from the options given below.

(a) I and II (b) II and III
(c) IV and V (d) III and V

9. Match Column I with Column II.

	Column I (Property)		Column II (Pair of species)
A.	Isobar	I.	$_8O^{2-}$, $_9F^-$
B.	Isotone	II.	$^{14}_{6}C$, $^{13}_{6}C$
C.	Isotope	III.	$^{14}_{6}C$, $^{16}_{8}O$
D.	Isoelectronic	IV.	$^{14}_{6}C$, $^{14}_{7}N$

Choose the correct answer from the options given below.

(a) A-I, B-II, C-III, D-IV
(b) A-II, B-I, C-III, D-IV
(c) A-III, B-I, C-II, D-IV
(d) A-IV, B-III, C-II, D-I

10. Which of the following statement is correct about electromagnetic radiation?

I. IR radiation have larger wavelength than cosmic rays.
II. The frequency of microwave is less than that of UV rays.
III. X-rays have larger wave number than microwaves.
IV. The velocity of X-ray is more than that of microwave in a given medium.
V. The frequency of microwave is greater than that of radiowaves.

Choose the correct answer from the options given below.

(a) I and II (b) I, III and IV
(c) I, II, III and IV (d) I, II, III and V

11. The work function of a metal is 4.2 eV. If radiations 2000Å fall on the metal, then the kinetic energy of the fastest photoelectron is

(a) 1.6×10^{-19} J
(b) 16×10^{10} J
(c) 3.2×10^{-19} J
(d) 6.4×10^{-10} J

12. Which of the following statement is incorrect regarding atomic models?

(a) According to plum pudding model or watermelon model the mass of an atom is uniformly distributed over the atom.
(b) It helped to compare the behaviour of elements in terms of both physical and chemical properties.
(c) It plays no role in understanding the origin and nature of the characteristic of EM radiation observed or emitted by atoms.
(d) It helps to explain the formation of different kind of molecules.

13. What will be the ratio of frequencies of violet light ($\lambda_1 = 4.1 \times 10^{-5}$ cm) to that of red light ($\lambda_2 = 6.56 \times 10^{-5}$ cm) ?

(a) 1.2 :1 (b) 1 : 1
(c) 1.6 : 1 (d) 1.4 : 1

14. Which graph shows how the energy *E* of the photon of light is related to its wavelength (λ) ?

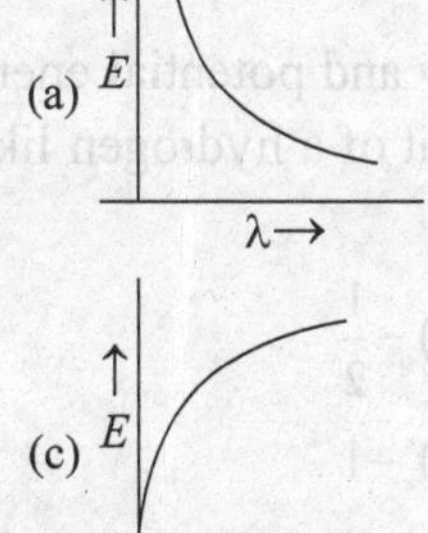

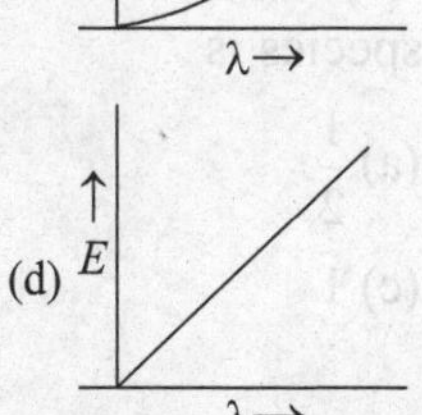

15. How long would it take a radiowave of frequency $6\times10^{-3}\ s^{-1}$ to travel from mars to earth, a distance of 8×10^{7} km?

(a) 4 min 26 s
(b) 2 min 20 s
(c) 1 min 10 s
(d) 4 min 5 s

Response Index

01	ⓐ	ⓑ	ⓒ	ⓓ	10	ⓐ	ⓑ	ⓒ	ⓓ	19	ⓐ	ⓑ	ⓒ	ⓓ
02	ⓐ	ⓑ	ⓒ	ⓓ	11	ⓐ	ⓑ	ⓒ	ⓓ	20	ⓐ	ⓑ	ⓒ	ⓓ
03	ⓐ	ⓑ	ⓒ	ⓓ	12	ⓐ	ⓑ	ⓒ	ⓓ	21	ⓐ	ⓑ	ⓒ	ⓓ
04	ⓐ	ⓑ	ⓒ	ⓓ	13	ⓐ	ⓑ	ⓒ	ⓓ	22	ⓐ	ⓑ	ⓒ	ⓓ
05	ⓐ	ⓑ	ⓒ	ⓓ	14	ⓐ	ⓑ	ⓒ	ⓓ	23	ⓐ	ⓑ	ⓒ	ⓓ
06	ⓐ	ⓑ	ⓒ	ⓓ	15	ⓐ	ⓑ	ⓒ	ⓓ	24	ⓐ	ⓑ	ⓒ	ⓓ
07	ⓐ	ⓑ	ⓒ	ⓓ	16	ⓐ	ⓑ	ⓒ	ⓓ	25	ⓐ	ⓑ	ⓒ	ⓓ
08	ⓐ	ⓑ	ⓒ	ⓓ	17	ⓐ	ⓑ	ⓒ	ⓓ					
09	ⓐ	ⓑ	ⓒ	ⓓ	18	ⓐ	ⓑ	ⓒ	ⓓ					

Performance Scanner

> 90% Excellent !	You have mastered these topics. The concepts of these topics are at your fingertips. Move on to the next test and maintain this momentum.
76-90% Very Good !	You have a good command over these topics. Revise these topics again after a few days and enhance your performance.
60-75% Good !	You have a wide scope to learn for these topics. Revise these topics again.
<60 Not Satisfactory!	You have a long way ahead of you to master these topics. Revise it thoroughly.

Test 2

Syllabus

- Spectrum of the Hydrogen Atom
- Bohr's Model of Hydrogen Atom and its Postulates, Relation for the Energy of Electron and Radii of Different Orbits, Limitations of Bohr's Model.

For deeper insight **Scan the QR Code**

Important Instructions

- The test is of 30 minutes duration and contains 15 multiple choice questions. (Four options with a single correct answer).
- Choose the correct option and fill the OMR given on the last page of test accordingly.
- At some instances, you may find more than 1 option may be correct. In such circumstances, you have to judge the most appropriate answer as per the conditions given in the question.

1. The wavelength of H_α line of Balmer series is X Å. What is the X of H_β line of Balmer series?

(a) $X\dfrac{108}{80}$ Å (b) $X\dfrac{80}{108}$ Å
(c) $\dfrac{1}{X}\dfrac{80}{108}$ Å (d) $\dfrac{1}{X}\dfrac{108}{80}$ Å

2. The ratio of kinetic energy and potential energy of an electron in Bohr orbit of a hydrogen like species is

(a) $\dfrac{1}{2}$ (b) $-\dfrac{1}{2}$
(c) 1 (d) -1

3. Given below are two statements, one is labelled as Assertion (A) and the other is labelled as Reason (R).

Assertion (A) Bohr's model could explain the stability of an atom.

Reason (R) Bohr's model explain spectrum of hydrogen, carbon and nitrogen.

In the light of the above statements, choose the correct answer from the options given below.

(a) Both (A) and (R) are true and (R) is the correct explanation of (A).
(b) Both (A) and (R) are true but (R) is not the correct explanation of (A).
(c) (A) is true but (R) is false.
(d) (A) is false but (R) is true.

4. The wave number of the first line of Balmer series of hydrogen is 15200 cm^{-1}. The wave number of the first Balmer line of Li^{2+} ion is

(a) 15200 cm^{-1} (b) 60800 cm^{-1}
(c) 76000 cm^{-1} (d) 136800 cm^{-1}

5. If the radius of the 1st orbit of hydrogen is 5.29×10^{-11} m, then the radius of the 2nd orbit of hydrogen is

(a) 10.58×10^{-11} m (b) 2.645×10^{-11} m
(c) 21.16×10^{-11} m (d) 27.98×10^{-11} m

6. Match List-I with List-II.

List-I (Spectrum series)		List-II (Region)	
A.	Lyman series	I	Visible region
B.	Paschen series	II	Ultraviolet region
C.	Balmer series	III	Far infrared region
D.	Humphrey series	IV	Infrared region

Choose the correct answer from the options given below.

(a) A-IV, B-III, C-II, D-I
(b) A-II, B-IV, C-I, D-III
(c) A-IV, B-I, C-III, D-II
(d) A-I, B-II, C-III, D-IV

7. For a hydrogen atom, the total energy of the electron in the nth orbit is given by $E_n = \frac{-ke^2}{2r_n}$.

Which of the following statement is correct about the total energy E_n and the radius r_n of the orbit?

(a) E_n increases as r_n increases.
(b) E_n is independent of r_n.
(c) E_n decreases as r_n increases.
(d) E_n and r_n are directly proportional to each other.

8. The energy of an electron in the first Bohr orbit for hydrogen is −13.6 eV. Which one of the following is a possible excited state for electrons in Bohr orbit of hydrogen atom?

(a) – 3.4 eV (b) – 6.8 eV
(c) – 1.7 eV (d) 13.6 eV

9. Consider the statements given below.

Statement I In Lyman series of H-spectrum, the maximum wavelength of lines is 121.56 nm.

Statement II Wavelength is maximum if there is transition from the very next level.

In the light of the above statements, choose the correct answer from the options given below.

(a) Both Statement I and Statement II are incorrect.
(b) Statement I is correct but Statement II is incorrect.
(c) Statement I is incorrect but Statement II is correct.
(d) Both Statement I and Statement II are correct.

10. The energy of second Bohr orbit of the hydrogen atom is 328 kJ/mol. Then, the energy of third Bohr orbit is

(a) – 164 kJ/mol
(b) – 237 kJ/mol
(c) – 82 kJ/mol
(d) – 145.8 kJ/mol

11. What will be the lowest energy of the spectral line emitted by the hydrogen atom in the Lyman series (symbols have their usual meaning) ?

(a) $\frac{3hcR_H}{4}$ (b) $\frac{2hcR_H}{12}$
(c) $\frac{7hcR_H}{12}$ (d) $\frac{5hcR_H}{36}$

12. Consider the statements given below.

I. The solar spectrum.
II. The spectrum of hydrogen molecule.
III. Spectrum of an atom or ion containing one electron only.
IV. The spectrum of hydrogen atom only.
V. The spectrum of helium atom.

The total number of statement that can be explained by Bohr's model of atom is ......

(a) 2 (b) 5
(c) 1 (d) 4

13. The wavelength of the radiation emitted, when in a hydrogen atom, the electron falls from infinity to the stationary state will be

(a) 196 nm (b) 498 nm
(c) 47 nm (d) 91 nm

14. The frequency of radiation emitted when the electron falls from $n = 3$ to $n = 1$ in a hydrogen atom, will be, (Given that ionisation energy of $H = 2.18 \times 10^{-18}$ J/atom and $h = 6.625 \times 10^{-34}$ Js).

(a) $4.96 \times 10^{8} s^{-1}$ (b) $2.93 \times 10^{15} s^{-1}$
(c) $2.94 \times 10^{16} s^{-1}$ (d) $4.96 \times 10^{7} s^{-1}$

15. In hydrogen atom, energy of first excited state is -6.8 eV. Then the kinetic energy of same orbit of hydrogen atom is

(a) -6.8 (b) $+6.8$
(c) -3.4 (d) $+3.4$

Response Index

01	a b c d	10	a b c d	19	a b c d
02	a b c d	11	a b c d	20	a b c d
03	a b c d	12	a b c d	21	a b c d
04	a b c d	13	a b c d	22	a b c d
05	a b c d	14	a b c d	23	a b c d
06	a b c d	15	a b c d	24	a b c d
07	a b c d	16	a b c d	25	a b c d
08	a b c d	17	a b c d		
09	a b c d	18	a b c d		

Performance Scanner

> 90% Excellent !	You have mastered these topics. The concepts of these topics are at your fingertips. Move on to the next test and maintain this momentum.
76-90% Very Good !	You have a good command over these topics. Revise these topics again after a few days and enhance your performance.
60-75% Good !	You have a wide scope to learn for these topics. Revise these topics again.
<60 Not Satisfactory!	You have a long way ahead of you to master these topics. Revise it thoroughly.

Test 3

Syllabus Dual Nature of Matter : de-Broglie's Relationship and Heisenberg Uncertainty Principle, Quantum Mechanical Model of the Atom, Its Important Features. Quantum Numbers and their Significance, Rules for Filling Electrons in Orbitals, Aufbau Principle, Pauli's Exclusion Principle and Hund's rule, Electronic Configuration of Elements.

For deeper insight **Scan the QR Code**

Important Instructions

- The test is of 30 minutes duration and contains 25 multiple choice questions (Four options with a single correct answer).
- Choose the correct option and fill the OMR given on the last page of test accordingly.
- At some instances, you may find more than 1 option may be correct. In such circumstances, you have to judge the most appropriate answer as per the conditions given in the question.

1. Which of the following statement about quantum numbers is incorrect?

(a) If the value of $l = 0$, the electron distribution is spherical.
(b) The shape of the orbital is given by subsidiary quantum number.
(c) The Zeeman's effect is explained by magnetic quantum number.
(d) The spin quantum number gives the orientation of electron cloud.

2. Which of the following statement is/are correct?

I. There is no probability of finding a p-electron right at the nucleus.
II. The orbital d_{z^2} has two lobes of electron density directed along the z-axis and a ring of electron density centred in the XY-plane.
III. The orientation of p- and d-orbitals minimize electron repulsion in many electron atoms.

IV. An orbital can accommodate a maximum of two electrons with parallel spins.

V. The energy of various subshell in the same shell are in the order $s > p > d > f$.

Choose the correct answer from the options given below.

(a) I, II and III
(b) II, III and IV
(c) III, IV and V
(d) I, III and V

3. Match List-I with List-II.

	List-I		List-II
A.	Angular momentum	I.	$\sqrt{n(n+2)}$
B.	Orbital angular momentum	II.	$\frac{nh}{2\pi}$
C.	Spin angular momentum	III.	$\sqrt{s(s+1)}\,\hbar$
D.	Magnetic momenta	IV.	$\sqrt{l(l+1)}\,\hbar$

Choose the correct answer from the options given below.

(a) A-I, B-II, C-III, D-IV
(b) A-II, B-IV, C-III, D-I
(c) A-III, B-IV, C-II, D-I
(d) A-I, B-III, C-II, D-IV

4. If E_1, E_2 and E_3 represent respectively the kinetic energy of electron, an alpha particle and a proton each having same de-Broglie wavelength, then

(a) $E_1 > E_3 > E_2$
(b) $E_2 > E_3 > E_1$
(c) $E_1 < E_3 < E_2$
(d) $E_1 = E_2 = E_3$

5. Among the following orbitals, described by three quantum number as given, then how many of them will have same energy in the absence of magnetic and electric fields?

I. $n=1, l=0. m=0$
II. $n=2, l=0, m=0$
III. $n=2, l=1, m=1$
IV. $n=3, l=2, m=+2$
V. $n=3, l=2, m=0$

Choose the correct answer from the options given below.

(a) II, I and II
(b) II, III and IV
(c) III and IV
(d) II, III, IV and V

6. Principal, azimuthal and magnetic quantum numbers are respectively, related to

(a) size, orientation and shape
(b) size, shape and orientation
(c) shape, size and orientation
(d) orientation, shape and size

7. Given below are two statements.

Statement I Heisenberg's uncertainty principle is applicable to microscopic as well as macroscopic particles.

Statement II Heisenberg's uncertainty principle is due to the limitation of the measuring instrument to measure accurately the position and velocity of microscopic particles.

In the light of the above statements, choose the correct answer from the options given below.

(a) Both Statement I and Statement II are incorrect.
(b) Statement I is correct but Statement II is incorrect.
(c) Statement I is incorrect but Statement II is correct.
(d) Both Statement I and Statement II are correct.

8. Given below are two statements, one is labelled as Assertion (A) and the other is labelled as Reason (R).

Assertion (A) The de-Broglie equation is significant for any microscopic or sub microscopic particles.

Reason (R) The de-Broglie wavelength is inversely proportional to the mass of the object if velocity is constant.

In the light of the above statements, choose the correct answer from the options given below.

(a) Both (A) and (R) are true and (R) is the correct explanation of (A).
(b) Both (A) and (R) are true but (R) is not the correct explanation of (A).
(c) (A) is true but (R) is false.
(d) (A) is false but (R) is true.

9. The mass of particle is 10^{-10} g and its radius 2×10^{-4} cm. If its velocity is 10^{-6} cm/s with 0.0001% uncertainty in measurement. The uncertainty in its position is

(a) 5.2×10^{-9} m
(b) 5.2×10^{-6} m
(c) 5.2×10^{-7} m
(d) 5.2×10^{-8} m

10. All the energy levels are called excited state when the value of the principal quantum number is

(a) $n=1$ (b) $n>1$
(c) $n<1$ (d) $n>-1$

11. What is the atomic number of an element if the quantum number of the highest energy electron of the element in the ground state are $n=4, l=1, m=-1, s=+\frac{1}{2}$?

(a) 31 (b) 35
(c) 30 (d) 32

12. Given below are two statements.

Statement I $2s$ and $2p$-orbitals having the same energy called degenerates orbitals.

Statement II In hydrogen atom, there is only one electron corresponds to most stable condition called ground state.

In the light of the above statements, choose the correct answer from the options given below.

(a) Both Statement I and Statement II are incorrect.
(b) Statement I is correct but Statement II is incorrect.
(c) Statement I is incorrect but Statement II is correct.
(d) Both Statement I and Statement II are correct.

13. Consider the following elements.

N, Cr, Se, Kr, B

The total number of elements that have two unpaired electrons.

(a) 1 (b) 2
(c) 3 (d) 4

14. Given below are two statements, one is labelled as Assertion (A) and the other is labelled as Reason (R).

Assertion (A) Electronic configuration of Cr^{+3} is same as that of Sc $(Z=21)$.

Reason (R) Orbitals of atoms as well as ions are filled in order of increasing energy according to Aufbau principle.

In the light of the above statements, choose the correct answer from the options given below.

(a) Both (A) and (R) are true and (R) is the correct explanation of (A).
(b) Both (A) and (R) are true but (R) is not the correct explanation of (A).
(c) (A) is true but (R) is false.
(d) (A) is false but (R) is true.

15. Select the correct notation for the subshell denoted by the following quantum numbers.

	Quantum number	Notation
(a)	$n=5,\ l=2$	$5p$
(b)	$n=6,\ l=3$	$6f$
(c)	$n=4,\ l=0$	$4p$
(d)	$n=5,\ l=4$	$5f$

16. Which of the following is not according to the Hund's rule ?

(a) [↑↑][ ][ ] (b) [↑↑][↑][ ]
(c) [↑↓][↑][↑] (d) Both (a) and (b)

17. If the value of $n+l=7$, what would be the increasing order of energy of the possible subshells?

(a) $4f<5d<6p<7s$ (b) $7s<6p<5d<4f$
(c) $7s>6p>6d<4f$ (d) $4f<5d<6p>7s$

18. Which of the following would be correct according to Hund's rule?

(a) ${}_6C = 1s^2 2s^2$ [↑↓][ ][ ]
(b) ${}_8O = 1s^2 2s^2$ [↑↓][↑↓][ ]
(c) ${}_7N = 1s^2 2s^2$ [↑↓][↑][ ]
(d) ${}_9F = 1s^2 2s^2$ [↑↓][↑↓][↑]

19. Match List-I with List-II.

	List-I (Configuration)		List-II (Angular and spherical node)
A.	$3p$	I.	0, 2
B.	$3d$	II.	0, 1
C.	$2s$	III.	2, 0
D.	$3s$	IV.	1, 1

Choose the correct answer from the options given below.

(a) A-I, B-II, C-III, D-IV

(b) A-I, B-III, C-II, D-IV

(c) A-IV, B-I, C-II, D-III

(d) A-IV, B-III, C-II, D-I

20. Which of the following statement is incorrect?

(a) A node is a point in space where the wave function (ψ) has zero amplitude.

(b) The number of peaks in radial distribution is $n-1$.

(c) Radial probability density,

$$\pi_{n,\,l}(r)=4\pi r^2 R^2_{n,\,l}(r).$$

(d) ψ^2 represents the atomic orbital.

21. The variation of radial probability density $R^2(r)$ as a function of distance r of the electron from the nucleus for $2p$ orbital. Which of the following graph correctly represents $R^2(r)$ *vs* r ?

(a)

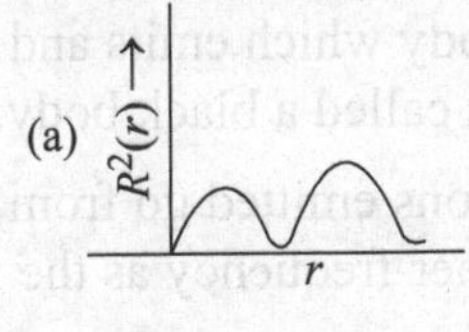

(b)

(c)

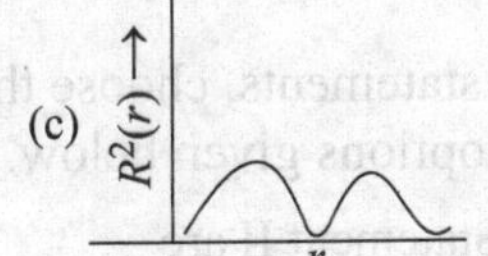

(d)

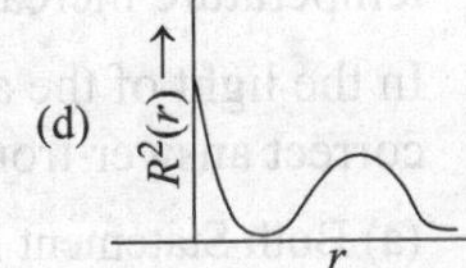

22. Which of the following statement is false?

(a) The electron density in the XY plane in $3d_{xy}$ orbital is zero.

(b) The electron densities in the XY and XZ plane in $3d_{yz}$ orbitals are zero.

(c) The electron density in the XY plane in $3d_{z^2}$ orbital is zero.

(d) Pauli exclusion principle does not followed by Boson's which have integral spin.

23. Which two orbitals are located along the axis and not between the axis?

(a) d_{xy}, d_{z^2} (b) d_{xy}, p_z (c) d_{yx}, p_x (d) $p_z, d_{x^2-y^2}$

24. The radii of maximum probability for $3s$, $3p$ and $3d$ electrons are in the order

(a) $(r_{\max})_{3s} > (r_{\max})_{3p} > (r_{\max})_{3d}$

(b) $(r_{\max})_{3d} > (r_{\max})_{3s} > (r_{\max})_{3p}$

(c) $(r_{\max})_{3d} > (r_{\max})_{3p} > (r_{\max})_{3s}$

(d) $(r_{\max})_{3p} > (r_{\max})_{3d} > (r_{\max})_{3s}$

25. Which of the following orbital has two spherical nodes?

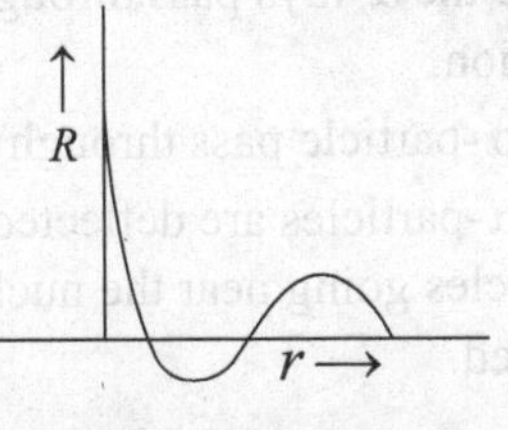

(a) $1s$ (b) $2s$ (c) $3s$ (d) $2p$

■ **Response Index**

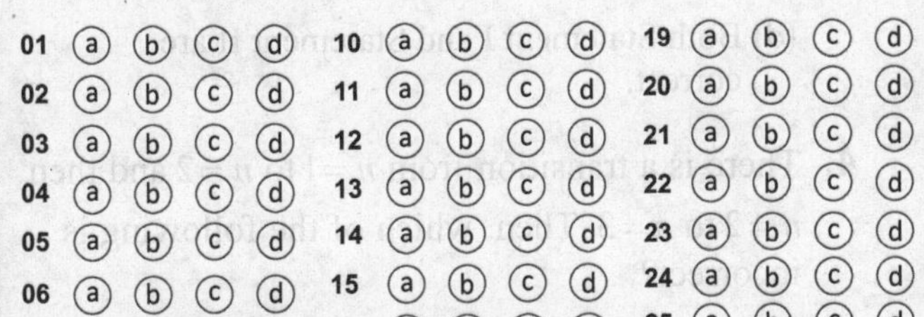

■ **Performance Scanner**

> 90% Excellent !	You have mastered these topics. The concepts of these topics are at your fingertips. Move on to the chapter test and maintain this momentum.
76-90% Very Good !	You have a good command over these topics. Revise these topics again after a few days and enhance your performance.
60-75% Good !	You have a wide scope to learn for these topics. Revise these topics again.
<60 Not Satisfactory!	You have a long way ahead of you to master these topics. Revise it thoroughly.

Chapter Break Thru

Syllabus	Preliminary Models, Nature of Electromagnetic Radiation, Photoelectric Effect	Spectrum of the Hydrogen Atom Bohr Model of Hydrogen Atom and its Postulates, Relation for the Energy of Electron and Radii of Different Orbits, Limitations of Bohr's Model.	Dual Nature of Matter : de-Broglie's Relationship and Heisenberg Uncertainty Principle, Quantum Mechanical Model of the Atom, Its Important Features. Quantum Numbers and their Significance, Rules for Filling Electrons in Orbitals, Aufbau Principle, Pauli's Exclusion Principle and Hund's rule, Electronic Configuration of Elements.

Important Instructions

- The test is of 1 hour duration and contains 50 multiple choice questions (Four options with a single correct answer).
- Choose the correct option and fill the OMR given on the last page of test accordingly.
- At some instances, you may find more than 1 option may be correct. In such circumstances, you have to judge the most appropriate answer as per the conditions given in the question.

1. In Rutherford's scattering experiment, which of the following observation does not occur?

(a) Most of the α-rays pass through without deflection.

(b) A few α-particle pass through the nucleus.

(c) A few α-particles are deflected back.

(d) α-particles going near the nucleus are slightly deflected.

2. Match List-I with List-II.

List-I (Outermost configuration)		List-II (Atomic number)	
A.	$3s^1$	I.	26
B.	$2p^3$	II.	17
C.	$3p^5$	III.	11
D.	$3d^6$	IV.	7

Choose the correct answer from the options given below.

(a) A-I, B-IV, C-II, D-III

(b) A-IV, B-III, C-II, D-I

(c) A-III, B-IV, C-II, D-I

(d) A-III, B-IV, C-I, D-II

3. Given below are two statements.

Statement I The ideal body which emits and absorbs all frequencies is called a black body.

Statement II The radiations emitted go from a lower frequency to a higher frequency as the temperature increases.

In the light of the above statements, choose the correct answer from the options given below.

(a) Both Statement I and Statement II are incorrect.

(b) Statement I is correct but Statement II is incorrect.

(c) Statement I is incorrect but Statement II is correct.

(d) Both Statement I and Statement II are correct.

4. There is a transition from $n=1$ to $n=2$ and then $n=2$ to $n=3$. Then, which of the following is incorrect?

(a) $\Delta E = \Delta E_1 + \Delta E_2$

(b) $\lambda = \lambda_1 + \lambda_2$

(c) $\nu = \nu_1 + \nu_2$

(d) $\dfrac{1}{\lambda} = \dfrac{1}{\lambda_1} + \dfrac{1}{\lambda_2}$

5. Given below are two statements, one is labelled as Assertion (A) and other is labelled as Reason (R).

Assertion (A) The magnitude of an electron's spin angular momentum cannot be changed.

Reason (R) Spin angular momentum is an intrinsic property of a particle.

In the light of the above statements, choose the correct answer from the options given below.

(a) Both (A) and (R) are true and (R) is the correct explanation of (A).
(b) Both (A) and (R) are true but (R) is not the correct explanation of (A).
(c) (A) is true but (R) is false.
(d) (A) is false but (R) is true.

6. Given below are two statements.

Statement I $2p$-orbitals do not have any spherical node.

Statement II The number of nodes in p-orbitals is given by $(n-2)$ where n is the principal quantum number.

In the light of the above statements, choose the correct answer from the options given below.

(a) Both Statement I and Statement II are incorrect.
(b) Statement I is correct but Statement II is incorrect.
(c) Statement I is incorrect but Statement II is correct.
(d) Both Statement I and Statement II are correct.

7. Among the following pairs of orbitals, which have electronic density along the axis?

(a) d_{xy}, d_{xz}
(b) $d_{x^2-y^2}, d_{z^2}$
(c) d_{xy}, d_{yz}
(d) d_{xy}, d_{z^2}

8. Which of the following set of quantum numbers is/are not permitted?

I. $n=3, l=2, m=-2, s=+\frac{1}{2}$

II. $n=3, l=2, m=-1, s=0$

III. $n=2, l=2, m=+1, s=\frac{1}{2}$

IV. $n=2, l=0, m=+1, s=-\frac{1}{2}$

V. $n=3, l=3, m=+3, s=+\frac{1}{2}$

Choose the correct answer from the options given below.

(a) I, II and III
(b) II, III and IV
(c) II, III, IV and V
(d) I, II, III and IV

9. Arrange the following orbitals in increasing order of energy

$$5p, 5d, 4f, 6s$$

Choose the correct answer from the options given below.

(a) $5p < 5d < 4f < 6s$
(b) $6s < 4f < 5d < 5p$
(c) $5p < 6s < 4f < 5d$
(d) $4f < 5p < 5d < 6s$

10. Match List-I with List-II.

	List-I (Quantum number)		List-II (Information provided)
A.	Principal quantum number	I.	Shape of orbital
B.	Spin quantum number	II.	Size of orbital
C.	Magnetic quantum number	III.	Orientation of orbital
D.	Azimuthal quantum number	IV.	Orientation of spin of an electron

Choose the correct answer from the options given below.

(a) A-I, B-III, C-II, D-IV
(b) A-III, B-IV, C-I, D-II
(c) A-III, B-IV, C-II, D-I
(d) A-II, B-IV, C-III, D-I

11. Consider the following orbitals.

I. $3d_{xy}$ II. $3d_{z^2}$ III. $4d_{xy}$ IV. $4d_{z^2}$ V. $3d_{yz}$ VI. $4d_{yz}$ VII. $5d_{xy}$

The total number of degenerate orbitals is

(a) 4 (b) 5 (c) 6 (d) 3

12. Given below are two statements.

Statement I The number of electrons ejected is proportional to the intensity or brightness of light.

Statement II The kinetic energy of the ejected electron is proportional to the wavelength of the electromagnetic radiation.

In the light of the above statements, choose the correct answer from the options given below.

(a) Both Statement I and Statement II are incorrect.
(b) Statement I is correct but Statement II is incorrect.
(c) Statement I is incorrect but Statement II is correct.
(d) Both Statement I and Statement II are correct.

13. Given below are two statements.

Statement I The effect of the Heisenberg uncertainty principle is significant for the motion of microscopic objects as well as macroscopic objects.

Statement II The important implication of the Heisenberg uncertainty principle is that it rules out the existence of definite paths or trajectories of electrons and other similar particles.

In the light of the above statements, choose the correct answer from the options given below.

(a) Both Statement I and Statement II are incorrect.
(b) Statement I is correct but Statement II is incorrect.
(c) Statement I is incorrect but Statement II is correct.
(d) Both Statement I and Statement II are correct.

14. Which of the following matter waves has the shortest wavelength?

(a) Electron (b) Alpha particle
(c) Neutron (d) Proton

15. Match List-I with List-II.

List-I (Frequency ≈ in Hz)		List-II (Different regions of the spectrum)
A.	10^{10}	I. Infrared region
B.	10^{13}	II. Radio frequency region
C.	10^{16}	III. Microwave region
D.	10^{6}	IV. Ultraviolet region

Choose the correct answer from the options given below.

(a) A-I, B-III, C-II, D-IV
(b) A-III, B-I, C-IV, D-II
(c) A-III, B-IV, C-II, D-I
(d) A-II, B-IV, C-III, D-I

16. Arrange these radiations in the increasing order of their energies,

$\lambda(A)=300$ nm, $\lambda(B)=300\ \mu$m, $\lambda(C)=3$ nm, $\lambda(D)=30$ Å

Choose the correct answer from the options given below.

(a) $(A)<(B)<(C)=(D)$
(b) $(B)<(A)<(C)=(D)$
(c) $(C)<(D)=(A)<(B)$
(d) $(D)<(C)<(B)<(A)$

17. The angular momentum of electron present in d-orbital is equal to

I. $\frac{h}{2\pi}\sqrt{6}$ II. $\hbar\sqrt{6}$ III. $h\sqrt{2}$

IV. $\frac{h}{2\pi}\sqrt{2}$ V. $\frac{2\pi}{h}\sqrt{6}$

Choose the correct answer from the options given below.

(a) I and III (b) I and II
(c) I, III and IV (d) I, II, III and V

18. The number of radial nodes in 4p subshell will be

(a) 1 (b) 2
(c) 0 (d) 3

19. Which of the following pairs represents isobars?

(a) $^{3}_{2}$He and $^{4}_{2}$He (b) $^{40}_{19}$K and $^{25}_{12}$Mg
(c) $^{40}_{19}$K and $^{40}_{20}$Ca (d) $^{40}_{19}$K and $^{39}_{19}$K

20. Select the correct statement.

(a) Atomic orbital is the circular path of the electron.
(b) Atomic orbital is an elliptical shaped orbit.
(c) Atomic orbital is three-dimensional field around nucleus.
(d) Atomic orbital is the region in which there is a maximum probability of finding an electron.

21. According to Aufbau principle, the condition for a new electron to enters the orbitals is

(a) $(n+1)$ should be minimum
(b) $(n+1)$ should be maximum
(c) $(n-1)$ should be minimum
(d) $(n-1)$ should be maximum

22. The ionisation energy of He^+ is 19.6×10^{-18} J/atom. The energy of first stationary state of Li^{2+}- ion will be

(a) 84.2×10^{-18} J/atom

(b) 44.1×10^{-18} J/atom

(c) 63.2×10^{-18} J/atom

(d) 21.2×10^{-18} J/atom

23. Which of the following statement is incorrect regarding α-particle scattering effect?

(a) α-particles mostly move through the gold foil having zero deflection.

(b) A small fraction are deflected.

(c) One in twenty thousand turns 180°.

(d) The thickness of the gold foil is about 100 μm.

24. The ratio of the atomic radius of the 5th orbit in chlorine atom and 3rd orbit in helium atom is

(a) 125:52

(b) 50:153

(c) 153:100

(d) 100:125

25. Given below are two statements.

Statement I Bohr could not explain the ability of atoms to form molecules by chemical bonds.

Statement II The splitting of spectral lines in the magnetic field that is Stark effect.

In the light of the above statements, choose the correct answer from the options given below.

(a) Both Statement I and Statement II are incorrect.

(b) Statement I is correct but Statement II is incorrect.

(c) Statement I is incorrect but Statement II is correct.

(d) Both Statement I and Statement II are correct.

26. Mass of a photon is given by 3.31×10^{-34} kg. The wavelength of a photon is

(a) 0.37 Å

(b) 0.67 nm

(c) 67 Å

(d) 1.73 Å

27. The magnetic quantum number of the orbital $2p_z$ is

(a) 1 (b) ±1

(c) −1 (d) 0

28. Which of the following set of quantum numbers is not valid?

(a) $n=5, l=2, m=0, s=\frac{1}{2}$

(b) $n=1, l=2, m=0, s=\frac{1}{2}$

(c) $n=5, l=3, m=2, s=\frac{1}{2}$

(d) $n=5, l=2, m=0, s=-\frac{1}{2}$

29. What will be the mass of photon with wavelength 3.6 Å ?

(a) 2.135×10^{-19} kg (b) 1.135×10^{-19} kg

(c) 2.135×10^{-29} kg (d) 6.135×10^{-33} kg

30. In a H-atom, if an electron jumps from n^{th} level to the first level. Then, correct facts about H-atom is/are

I. Number of spectral lines $= \frac{n(n-1)}{2}$

II. If $n = 4$, number of spectral lines = 6

III. Number of spectral lines $= \frac{n(n+1)}{2}$

IV. If $n = 6$, number of spectral lines = 12

V. If $n = 5$, number of spectral lines = 10

Choose the correct answer from the options given below.

(a) I, II and V

(b) I, II and III

(c) II and IV

(d) II, III and IV

31. What will be the wave number of violet colour in electromagnetic spectrum ?

(a) 25×10^3 min^{-1}

(b) 25×10^3 m^{-1}

(c) 25×10^3 cm^{-1}

(d) 25×10^3 nm^{-1}

32. An object has a mass of 6 kg and velocity of 10 m/s. The speed is measured with 5% accuracy, then the value of Δx in m is

(a) 0.12676×10^{-34} (b) 0.1566×10^{-34}
(c) 0.176×10^{-34} (d) 0.276×10^{-34}

33. How many electrons can exist with the principal quantum number's value as 4?

(a) 16 (b) 4
(c) 32 (d) 12

34. Given below are two statements, one is labelled as Assertion (A) and the other is labelled as Reason (R).

Assertion (A) Angular momentum of an electron is quantised.

Reason (R) The energy of an electron revolving in a particular orbit is fixed and doesn't change over time.

In the light of the above statements, choose the correct answer from the options given below.

(a) Both (A) and (R) are true and (R) is the correct explanation of (A).
(b) Both (A) and (R) are true but (R) is not the correct explanation of (A).
(c) (A) is true but (R) is false.
(d) (A) is false but (R) is true.

35. Select the statement which is not a part of Bohr's theory.

(a) Energy of the electrons in the orbit is quantised.
(b) The electron in the orbit nearest the nucleus has the lowest energy.
(c) Electrons revolve in different orbits around the nucleus.
(d) The position and velocity of the electrons in the orbit cannot be determined simultaneously.

36. What should be the ratio of the velocities of CH_4 and O_2 molecules so that they are associated with de-Broglie waves of equal wavelength?

(a) $v_{CH_4}=1.5\,v_{O_2}$ (b) $v_{CH_4}=3\,v_{O_2}$
(c) $v_{CH_4}=2v_{O_2}$ (d) $v_{CH_4}=v_{O_2}$

37. If the threshold wavelength (λ_0) for ejection of an electron from metal is 330 nm, then work function for the photoelectric emission is

(a) 1.2×10^{-18} J (b) 1.2×10^{-20} J
(c) 6×10^{-19} J (d) 6×10^{-12} J

38. Which of the following statements are incorrect?

I. According to Pauli's exclusion principle, no two electrons in an atom can have the same value of quantum numbers n, l and m.
II. The total energy of an electron in an orbit is half of its potential energy.
III. The velocity of an electron in an orbit increases with increase in its quantum number n.
IV. The energy of an electron in an orbit decreases with increase of its principal quantum number n.
V. Hund's rule deals with the filling of electrons into the orbitals belonging to the same subshell.

Choose the correct answer from the options given below.

(a) I, III and V (b) I, III and IV
(c) I, II and III (d) I, II, III and IV

39. If radius of third Bohr orbit of Li^{2+} ion is 154.2 pm, then what is the radius of second Bohr orbit of Be^{3+} ion?

(a) 51.4 pm (b) 32.70 pm
(c) 46.32 pm (d) 98.13 pm

40. Select the correct notation for the subshell denoted by the following quantum numbers.

	Quantum number	Notation
(a)	$n=5, l=2$	$5p$
(b)	$n=6, l=3$	$6f$
(c)	$n=4, l=0$	$4p$
(d)	$n=5, l=4$	$5f$

41. Calculate the uncertainty in the position of an electron (mass 9.1×10^{-28} g) moving with a velocity of 3×10^4 cm/sec, if the uncertainty in velocity is 0.001%?

(a) 1.93 cm (b) 7.68 cm
(c) 0.175 cm (d) 3.84 cm

42. In hydrogen atom, the de-Broglie wavelength of an electron in the fourth Bohr orbit is
[Given that, Bohr radius, $a_0 = 54.3$]
(a) 240.6 πpm
(b) 210.4 πpm
(c) 250.2 πpm
(d) 434.4 πpm

43. Given below are two statements.

Statement I In Bohr's model, the velocity of electrons increases with a decrease in the positive charge of the nucleus as electrons are not held tightly.

Statement II Velocity decreases with an increase in principal quantum number.
In the light of the above statements, choose the correct answer from the options given below.
(a) Both Statement I and Statement II are incorrect.
(b) Statement I is correct but Statement II is incorrect.
(c) Statement I is incorrect but Statement II is correct.
(d) Both Statement I and Statement II are correct.

44. Select the correct statements about limitation of Bohr's model.
I. Bohr's model could not explain the spectra of atoms containing more than one electron.
II. Splitting of spectral line in magnetic field (Zeeman effect) explain by Bohr's model.
III. Splitting of spectral line in electric field (Stark effect) could not be explained by Bohr's model.
IV. Geometry and shapes of the molecule could not be explained by Bohr's model.
V. It could not explain the ability of atoms to form molecules by chemical bonds.

Choose the correct answer from the options given below.
(a) I, II and V
(b) I, III, IV and V
(c) I, II and III
(d) I, II, III and IV

45. Hydrogen atoms in the ground state are excited by monochromatic radiation of wavelength λ Å. The resulting spectrum consists of maximum 15 different lines. What is the wavelength λ?
($R_H = 109737\ cm^{-1}$)
(a) 937.3 Å (b) 1025 Å
(c) 1236 Å (d) 1573 Å

46. The number of radial nodes of 3s and 2p orbitals are respectively
(a) 2, 0 (b) 0, 2 (c) 1, 2 (d) 2, 1

47. Which of the following statement is incorrect?
(a) Energies of stationary states in hydrogen like atoms is inversely proportional to the square of the principal quantum number.
(b) The radius of the first orbit of He^+ is half that of the first orbit of hydrogen atom.
(c) Angular quantum number signifies the shape of orbital.
(d) Total number of nodes for 3s-orbital is three.

48. Arrange the following type of radiations in increasing order of frequency.
(i) Radiation from microwave oven
(ii) Amber light from traffic signal
(iii) Radiation from FM radio
(iv) Cosmic rays from outer space and
(v) X-rays

The correct order is
(a) (i) < (iii) < (ii) < (iv) < v)
(b) (iii) < (i) < (v) < (ii) < (iv)
(c) (iii) < (i) < (ii) < (v) < (iv)
(d) (iii) < (v) < (i) < (ii) < (iv)

49. Given below are two statements, one is labelled as Assertion (A) and the other is labelled as Reason (R).

Assertion (A) Black body is an ideal body that emits and absorbs radiations of all frequencies.

Reason (R) The frequency of radiation emitted by a body goes from a higher frequency to lower frequency with an increase in temperature.

In the light of the above statements, choose the correct answer from the options given below.

(a) Both (A) and (R) are true and (R) is the correct explanation of (A).

(b) Both (A) and (R) are true but (R) is not the correct explanation of (A).

(c) (A) is true but (R) is false.

(d) (A) is false but (R) is true.

50. Which options is not correct regarding the order of frequency of electromagnetic radiation?

(a) Radiowaves < Microwaves < X-rays

(b) X-rays < UV rays < Microwaves

(c) Gamma rays > Infrared > Radiowaves

(d) Microwaves < Infrared rays < UV rays

Response Index

01 ⓐ ⓑ ⓒ ⓓ	14 ⓐ ⓑ ⓒ ⓓ	27 ⓐ ⓑ ⓒ ⓓ	40 ⓐ ⓑ ⓒ ⓓ
02 ⓐ ⓑ ⓒ ⓓ	15 ⓐ ⓑ ⓒ ⓓ	28 ⓐ ⓑ ⓒ ⓓ	41 ⓐ ⓑ ⓒ ⓓ
03 ⓐ ⓑ ⓒ ⓓ	16 ⓐ ⓑ ⓒ ⓓ	29 ⓐ ⓑ ⓒ ⓓ	42 ⓐ ⓑ ⓒ ⓓ
04 ⓐ ⓑ ⓒ ⓓ	17 ⓐ ⓑ ⓒ ⓓ	30 ⓐ ⓑ ⓒ ⓓ	43 ⓐ ⓑ ⓒ ⓓ
05 ⓐ ⓑ ⓒ ⓓ	18 ⓐ ⓑ ⓒ ⓓ	31 ⓐ ⓑ ⓒ ⓓ	44 ⓐ ⓑ ⓒ ⓓ
06 ⓐ ⓑ ⓒ ⓓ	19 ⓐ ⓑ ⓒ ⓓ	32 ⓐ ⓑ ⓒ ⓓ	45 ⓐ ⓑ ⓒ ⓓ
07 ⓐ ⓑ ⓒ ⓓ	20 ⓐ ⓑ ⓒ ⓓ	33 ⓐ ⓑ ⓒ ⓓ	46 ⓐ ⓑ ⓒ ⓓ
08 ⓐ ⓑ ⓒ ⓓ	21 ⓐ ⓑ ⓒ ⓓ	34 ⓐ ⓑ ⓒ ⓓ	47 ⓐ ⓑ ⓒ ⓓ
09 ⓐ ⓑ ⓒ ⓓ	22 ⓐ ⓑ ⓒ ⓓ	35 ⓐ ⓑ ⓒ ⓓ	48 ⓐ ⓑ ⓒ ⓓ
10 ⓐ ⓑ ⓒ ⓓ	23 ⓐ ⓑ ⓒ ⓓ	36 ⓐ ⓑ ⓒ ⓓ	49 ⓐ ⓑ ⓒ ⓓ
11 ⓐ ⓑ ⓒ ⓓ	24 ⓐ ⓑ ⓒ ⓓ	37 ⓐ ⓑ ⓒ ⓓ	50 ⓐ ⓑ ⓒ ⓓ
12 ⓐ ⓑ ⓒ ⓓ	25 ⓐ ⓑ ⓒ ⓓ	38 ⓐ ⓑ ⓒ ⓓ	
13 ⓐ ⓑ ⓒ ⓓ	26 ⓐ ⓑ ⓒ ⓓ	39 ⓐ ⓑ ⓒ ⓓ	

Performance Scanner

> 90% Excellent !	You have mastered this chapter. The concepts of this chapter are at your fingertips. Move on to the next chapter and maintain this momentum.
76-90% Very Good !	You have a good command over this chapter. Revise the chapter again after a few days and enhance your performance.
60-75% Good !	You have a wide scope to learn for this chapter. Revise this chapter again.
<60 Not Satisfactory!	You have a long way ahead of you to master this chapter. Revise it thoroughly.

Scan for Online **Chapter Test**

Scan for Online **Unit Test**

Test Booklet No. **3947203**

Test Booklet Code **CH3**

MEDACE
NEET (UG)
SELF ASSESSMENT KIT

Classification of Elements and Periodicity in Properties

Topics Covered

- Modern Periodic Table
- Periodic Properties and their Trends-1, (Atomic radius, Ionisation Enthalpy, Electron Gain Enthalpy, Electronegativity, Metallic Character)
- Periodic Properties and their Trends-2 (Lattice Enthalpy, Hydration Enthalpy, Oxidation State and Chemical Properties)

Important Instructions

- This Booklet Contains – 3 Topic Tests and One Test on Complete Chapter.
- Each question carries 4 marks.
- For each correct response the candidate will get 4 marks and for every incorrect response 1 mark will be additionally deducted from the total score.
- Use **Blue/Black** point pen only for filling the OMR.
- Rough work is to be done in the space provided for this purpose in the test booklet only.

Name of the Candidate (In Capitals)

____

____

Candidate's Signature __________

Invigilator's Signature __________

Facsimile signature stamp of center superintendent__________

Do not open this Booklet until you start attempting the Test

Topical Follow Thru

Test 1

Syllabus

- Modern Periodic Law and Present Form of the Periodic Table
- *s*, *p*, *d* and *f*-Block Elements

For deeper insight **Scan the QR Code**

Important Instructions

- The test is of 30 minutes duration and contains 15 multiple choice questions (Four options with a single correct answer).
- Choose the correct option and fill the OMR given on the last page of test accordingly.
- At some instances, you may find more than 1 option may be correct. In such circumstances, you have to judge the most appropriate answer as per conditions given in the question.

1. Select the incorrect statement regarding the element having atomic number 119.

(a) Outermost electronic configuration will be $8s^1$.

(b) It will lie in group IA along with alkali metals.

(c) The formula of its oxide will be *M*O.

(d) Its ionisation enthalpy will be low.

2. Match List-I with List-II.

List-I (Properties)	List-II (Element)
A. An element that is present in group 13 and in 5th period.	I. Cs
B. A highly reactive metal in the 6th period.	II. I
C. An element that is present in group 17 and in 5th period.	III. Xe
D. An element with atomic number greater than 50 but similar to the element with atomic number 18.	IV. In

Choose the correct answer from the options given below.

(a) A-I, B-III, C-II, D-IV

(b) A-IV, B-I, C-II, D-III

(c) A-III, B-I, C-II, D-IV

(d) A-III, B-II, C-I, D-IV

3. Given below are two statements.

Statement I Elements of groups IB and IIB are transition elements.

Statement II Elements of VB group can be a metalloid.

In the light of the above statements, choose the correct answer from the options given below.

(a) Both Statement I and Statement II are incorrect.

(b) Statement I is correct but Statement II is incorrect.

(c) Statement I is incorrect but Statement II is correct.

(d) Both Statement I and Statement II are correct.

4. In which group, element with atomic number 114 will be placed

(a) 10 (b) 7

(c) 14 (d) 11

5. Given below are two statements, one is labelled as Assertion (A) and the other is labelled as Reason (R).

Assertion (A) Elements in the same group have similar chemical properties and physical properties.

Reason (R) Elements of same group are isoelectronic.

In the light of the above statements, choose the correct answer from the options given below.

(a) Both (A) and (R) are true and (R) is the correct explanation of (A).
(b) Both (A) and (R) are true but (R) is not the correct explanation of (A).
(c) (A) is true but (R) is false.
(d) (A) is false but (R) is true.

6. Lanthanoids are the elements in which electrons are progressively filled in
(a) 6*p*-orbital (b) 5*d*-orbital
(c) 3*f*-orbital (d) 4*f*-orbital

7. Match List-I with List-II.

List-I (Element)		List-II (Atomic number)
A. Unq	I.	103
B. Uns	II.	104
C. Unt	III.	112
D. Uub	IV.	107

Choose the correct answer from the options given below.
(a) A-II, B-IV, C-I, D-III
(b) A-IV, B-III, C-II, D-I
(c) A-II, B-IV, C-III, D-I
(d) A-III, B-I, C-IV, D-II

8. The element with the electronic configuration as [Ar] $3d^{10}4s^2 4p^4$ represents a
(a) metal
(b) non-metal
(c) metalloid
(d) transition element

9. Given below are two statements.
Statement I Lu is an element with atomic number 71 and belongs to lanthanoid series.
Statement II The last electron of Lu goes into 5*d*-orbital.
In the light of the above statements, choose the correct answer from the options given below.
(a) Both Statement I and Statement II are incorrect.
(b) Statement I is correct but Statement II is incorrect.
(c) Statement I is incorrect but Statement II is correct.
(d) Both Statement I and Statement II are correct.

10. Elements *A*, *B*, *C*, *D* and *E* have the following electronic configurations. Which among these belongs to the same group in the periodic table?
A. $1s^2 2s^2 2p^1$ B. $1s^2 2s^2 2p^6 3s^2 3p^1$
C. $1s^2 2s^2 2p^6 3s^2 3p^2$ D. $1s^2 2s^2 2p^6 3s^2 3p^5$
E. $1s^2 2s^2 2p^6 3s^2 3p^6 4s^2$
Choose the most appropriate answer from the options given below.
(a) A and B
(b) B and C
(c) B, C and D
(d) C and E

11. Select the incorrect statement from the following.
(a) Ce, Pr and Nd are *f*-block elements.
(b) Cu, Pd and Ni are *d*-block elements.
(c) Si, Ge and As are metalloids.
(d) Cu ([Ar] $3d^{10}4s^1$) and K ([Ar] $4s^1$) have been placed in same group.

12. The element with five electrons in the outer subshell belongs to which family?
(a) Chalcogens
(b) Halogens
(c) Noble gases
(d) Alkaline earth metals

13. Given below are two statements, one is labelled as Assertion (A) and the other is labelled as Reason (R).
Assertion (A) All transition elements are *d*-block elements but all *d*-block elements are not transition elements.
Reason (R) Completely filled electronic configuration is responsible for the given contradiction.
In the light of the above statements, choose the correct answer from the options given below.
(a) Both (A) and (R) are true and (R) is the correct explanation of (A).
(b) Both (A) and (R) are true but (R) is not the correct explanation of (A).
(c) (A) is true but (R) is false.
(d) (A) is false but (R) is true.

14. The period number in modern periodic table corresponds to the highest
(a) principal quantum number
(b) spin quantum number
(c) magnetic quantum number
(d) azimuthal quantum number

15. Given below are two statements.

Statement I The fourth period of modern periodic table ends with the element called krypton.

Statement II 3*d*-transition series starts from zinc and ends with argon.

In the light of the above statements, choose the correct answer from the options given below.
(a) Both Statement I and Statement II are incorrect.
(b) Statement I is correct but Statement II is incorrect.
(c) Statement I is incorrect but Statement II is correct.
(d) Both Statement I and Statement II are correct.

Response Index

01	a	b	c	d	10	a	b	c	d	19	a	b	c	d
02	a	b	c	d	11	a	b	c	d	20	a	b	c	d
03	a	b	c	d	12	a	b	c	d	21	a	b	c	d
04	a	b	c	d	13	a	b	c	d	22	a	b	c	d
05	a	b	c	d	14	a	b	c	d	23	a	b	c	d
06	a	b	c	d	15	a	b	c	d	24	a	b	c	d
07	a	b	c	d	16	a	b	c	d	25	a	b	c	d
08	a	b	c	d	17	a	b	c	d					
09	a	b	c	d	18	a	b	c	d					

Performance Scanner

> 90% Excellent !	You have mastered these topics. The concepts of these topics are at your fingertips. Move on to the next test and maintain this momentum.
76-90% Very Good !	You have a good command over these topics. Revise these topics again after a few days and enhance your performance.
60-75% Good !	You have a wide scope to learn for these topics. Revise these topics again.
<60 Not Satisfactory!	You have a long way ahead of you to master these topics. Revise it thoroughly.

Test 2

Syllabus

Periodic Properties and their Trends-1 (Atomic Radius, Ionisation Enthalpy, Electron Gain Enthalpy, Electronegativity, Metallic Character)

For deeper insight **Scan the QR Code**

Important Instructions

- The test is of 30 minutes duration and contains 15 multiple choice questions (Four options with a single correct answer).
- Choose the correct option and fill the OMR given on the last page of test accordingly.
- At some instances, you may find more than 1 option may be correct. In such circumstances, you have to judge the most appropriate answer as per conditions given in the question.

1. Arrange the following atoms in order of increasing radius.

A. Na^+ B. Cl^- C. O^{2-} D. Ne

Choose the correct answer from the options given below.

(a) B < C < D < A (b) A < D < C < B

(c) D < C < B < A (d) D < A < C < B

2. The atom/ions that has the highest number of unpaired electrons is

(a) Na^+ (b) B

(c) N (d) O^{2-}

3. Given below are two statements.

Statement I The values of van der Waals' radii are larger than those of covalent radii because the van der Waals' forces are much weaker than the forces operating between atoms in covalently bonded molecules.

Statement II The metallic radii are smaller than the van der Waals' radii, since the bonding forces in the metallic crystal lattice are much stronger than the van der Waals' forces.

In the light of the above statements, choose the correct answer from the options given below.

(a) Both Statement I and Statement II are incorrect.

(b) Statement I is correct and Statement II is incorrect.

(c) Statement I is incorrect and Statement II is correct.

(d) Both Statement I and Statement II are correct.

4. Among halogens, the correct order of amount of energy released in electron gain enthalpy is

(a) F > Cl > Br > I

(b) F < Cl < Br < I

(c) F < Cl > Br > I

(d) F < Cl < Br > I

5. Which of the atoms having following electronic configurations will have the highest first ionisation energy?

(a) [Ne] $3s^2 3p^2$

(b) [Ne] $3s^2 3p^3$

(c) [He] $2s^2 2p^3$

(d) [Ne] $3s^2 3p^4$

6. Given below are two statements.

Statement I First ionisation enthalpy of the corresponding elements of 3*d* and 4*d*-series are almost similar.

Statement II First ionisation enthalpy of 5*d*-series elements are smaller than that of 3*d* and 4*d*-series elements.

In the light of the above statements, choose the correct answer from the options given below.

(a) Both Statement I and Statement II are incorrect.

(b) Statement I is correct and Statement II is incorrect.

(c) Statement I is incorrect and Statement II is correct.

(d) Both Statement I and Statement II are correct.

7. Select the incorrect statement from the following.

(a) Greater the energy released in the process of taking up an extra electron, greater is the electron affinity.

(b) Halogens have low electron affinities.

(c) The electron affinity of an element is equal to the enthalpy change that accompanies the ionisation process of its ion.

(d) Electron affinity of nitrogen is less favourable than that of carbon.

8. Arrange the following elements in the order of increasing electronegativity.

C, N, O, F

Choose the correct answer from the options given below.

(a) N < C < O < F (b) C < N < O < F
(c) C < F < O < N (d) N < O < F < C

9. Arrange the elements in the increasing order of metallic character. Their electronic configuration is as follows

I. [Ar] $3d^{10}4s^2$ II. [Ar] $4s^2$
III. [Ar] $3d^{10}4s^2 4p^5$ IV. [Ar] $3d^{10}4s^2 4p^6 5s^1$

Choose the correct answer from the options given below.

(a) III < I < II < IV (b) I < IV < III < II
(c) III < II < I < IV (d) II < I < III < IV

10. Following is the successive ionisation enthalpies (in kJ/mol) of an element.

I. 577.5 II. 1810 III. 2750
IV. 11580 V. 14280

Choose the correct answer from the options given below.

(a) Na (b) Mg (c) P (d) Al

11. Given below are two statements, one is labelled as Assertion (A) and the other is labelled as Reason (R).

Assertion (A) Noble gases have positive electron gain enthalpy

Reason (R) Noble gases have no tendency to take extra electron.

In the light of the above statements, choose the correct answer from the options given below.

(a) Both (A) and (R) are true and (R) is the correct explanation of (A).

(b) Both (A) and (R) are true but (R) is not the correct explanation of (A).

(c) (A) is true but (R) is false.

(d) (A) is false but (R) is true.

12. Match List-I with List-II.

	List-I (Property of element)		List-II (Relevant element)
A.	Element having maximum electron affinity.	I.	Cs
B.	Most electronegative element.	II.	He
C.	Element having maximum ionisation enthalpy.	III.	F
D.	Element having highest metallic character.	IV.	Cl

Choose the correct answer from the options given below.

(a) A-IV, B-III, C-II, D-I
(b) A-III, B-IV, C-I, D-II
(c) A-II, B-I, C-IV, D-III
(d) A-IV, B-II, C-III, D-I

13. Arrange the following elements in the order of increasing non-metallic character,

N, P, S, O

Choose the correct answer from the options given below.

(a) N < P < S < O (b) P < N < S < O
(c) P < S < N < O (d) P < N < O < S

14. Which of the following represents the most electropositive element?

(a) [Ar] $3d^{10}4s^2$

(b) [He] $2s^1$

(c) [Xe] $6s^2$

(d) [Xe] $6s^1$

15. Arrange the following in increasing order of reducing property.

F^-, Br^-, Cl^-, I^-

Choose the correct answer from the options given below.

(a) $F^- < Cl^- < Br^- < I^-$

(b) $I^- < Br^- < Cl^- < F^-$

(c) $F^- < Cl^- < I^- < Br^-$

(d) $Cl^- < F^- < Br^- < I^-$

■ Response Index

01	(a) (b) (c) (d)	10	(a) (b) (c) (d)	19	(a) (b) (c) (d)
02	(a) (b) (c) (d)	11	(a) (b) (c) (d)	20	(a) (b) (c) (d)
03	(a) (b) (c) (d)	12	(a) (b) (c) (d)	21	(a) (b) (c) (d)
04	(a) (b) (c) (d)	13	(a) (b) (c) (d)	22	(a) (b) (c) (d)
05	(a) (b) (c) (d)	14	(a) (b) (c) (d)	23	(a) (b) (c) (d)
06	(a) (b) (c) (d)	15	(a) (b) (c) (d)	24	(a) (b) (c) (d)
07	(a) (b) (c) (d)	16	(a) (b) (c) (d)	25	(a) (b) (c) (d)
08	(a) (b) (c) (d)	17	(a) (b) (c) (d)		
09	(a) (b) (c) (d)	18	(a) (b) (c) (d)		

■ Performance Scanner

> 90% Excellent !	You have mastered these topics. The concepts of these topics are at your fingertips. Move on to the next test and maintain this momentum.
76-90% Very Good !	You have a good command over these topics. Revise these topics again after a few days and enhance your performance.
60-75% Good !	You have a wide scope to learn for these topics. Revise these topics again.
<60 Not Satisfactory!	You have a long way ahead of you to master these topics. Revise it thoroughly.

Test 3

Syllabus Periodic Properties and their Trends-2 (Lattice Enthalpy, Hydration Enthalpy, Oxidation State and Chemical Properties)

For deeper insight **Scan the QR Code** 

Important Instructions

- The test is of 30 minutes duration and contains 15 multiple choice questions (Four options with a single correct answer).
- Choose the correct option and fill the OMR given on the last page of test accordingly
- At some instances, you may find more than 1 option may be correct. In such circumstances, you have to judge the most appropriate answer as per conditions given in the question.

1. Which of the following is the best oxidising agent?

(a) Pb^{4+} (b) Ge^{4+} (c) Sn^{2+} (d) Sn^{4+}

2. Select the incorrect order of lattice energy among the following set.

(a) $Li_3N > Li_2O$ (b) $NaCl > LiF$

(c) $AlF_3 > MgF_2$ (d) $NaF < MgF_2$

3. Select the correct statement.

(a) Chemical reactivity decreases in the alkali metals but increases in the halogen with increase in atomic number.

(b) Chemical reactivity increases with increase in atomic number down the group in both the alkali metals and halogens.

(c) Chemical reactivity increases in alkali metals but it decreases in halogens with increase in atomic number down the group.

(d) In both alkali metals and halogens, the chemical reactivity decreases with increase in atomic number down the group.

4. X, Y and Z are the elements of a third point. The oxide of X is ionic, that of Y is amphoteric and that of Z is a giant molecule. The correct order of these element with respect to their atomic number is

(a) $X < Y < Z$ (b) $Z < Y < X$

(c) $X < Z < Y$ (d) $Y < X < Z$

5. Given below are two statements, one is labelled as Assertion (A) and the other is labelled as Reason (R).

Assertion (A) LiCl is hydrated but NaCl is always anhydrous.

Reason (R) Li^+ is smaller in size than Na^+.

In the light of the above statements, choose the correct answer from the options given below.

(a) Both (A) and (R) are true and (R) is the correct explanation of (A).

(b) Both (A) and (R) are true but (R) is not the correct explanation of (A).

(c) (A) is true but (R) is false.

(d) (A) is false but (R) is true.

6. Among the following compounds, which has a higher hydration energy than the lattice energy?

(a) $MgSO_4$ (b) $CaSO_4$ (c) $BaSO_4$ (d) $SrSO_4$

7. Which of the following processes involve absorption of energy?

(a) $S(g) + e^- \longrightarrow S^-(g)$

(b) $Cl(g) + e^- \longrightarrow Cl^-(g)$

(c) $O^-(g) + e^- \longrightarrow O^{2-}(g)$

(d) $O(g) + e^- \longrightarrow O^-(g)$

8. Consider the following compounds.

(i) Cl_2O_7 (ii) Na_2O (iii) Al_2O_3 (iv) N_2O

(v) SO_2 (vi) ZnO (vii) PbO

The number of compounds which are amphoteric in nature is ....

(a) 2 (b) 3 (c) 4 (d) 5

9. The valence electrons in the element A are 3 and that in element B are 6. The compound formed from A and B is

(a) A_2B (b) AB_2 (c) A_6B_3 (d) A_2B_3

10. Given below are two statements, one is labelled as Assertion (A) and the other is labelled as Reason (R).

Assertion (A) P_4O_{10} is a stronger acid than P_4O_6.

Reason (R) Higher the oxidation state of element, stronger is the acid.
In the light of the above statements, choose the correct answer from the options given below.
(a) Both (A) and (R) are true and (R) is the correct explanation of (A).
(b) Both (A) and (R) are true but (R) is not the correct explanation of (A).
(c) (A) is true but (R) is false.
(d) (A) is false but (R) is true.

11. Given below are two statements.
Statement I With increase in ionic charge, the value of lattice energy increases.
Statement II Smaller the ions, higher the lattice energy.
In the light of the above statements, choose the correct answer from the options given below.
(a) Both Statement I and Statement II are incorrect.
(b) Statement I is correct but Statement II is incorrect.
(c) Statement I is incorrect but Statement II is correct.
(d) Both Statement I and Statement II are correct.

12. Match List-I with List-II.

	List-I (Element)		List-II (Atomic radius, pm)
A.	Be	I.	66
B.	C	II.	77
C.	O	III.	88
D.	B	IV.	111

Choose the correct answer from the options given below.
(a) A-IV, B-II, C-III, D-I
(b) A-III, B-I, C-II, D-IV
(c) A-II, B-IV, C-I, D-III
(d) A-IV, B-II, C-I, D-III

13. Which of the following compounds does not act as a reducing agent?
(a) SO_2
(b) SeO_2
(c) TeO_2
(d) SeO_2 and TeO_2

14. For the properties mentioned, choose the correct trend for the different species given.
(a) Strength as Lewis acid – $BCl_3 > AlCl_3 > GaCl_3$
(b) Inert pair effect – $Al > Ga > In$
(c) Oxidising property – $Al^{3+} > In^{3+} > Tl^{3+}$
(d) First ionisation enthalpy – $B > Al > Tl$

15. Elements X, Y and Z belong to the same period in the long form of the periodic table. The nature of the oxides of X, Y and Z is amphoteric, basic and acidic respectively. Then what will be the correct order of the atomic numbers of these elements ?
(a) $Z > Y > X$
(b) $Z > X > Y$
(c) $X > Y > Z$
(d) $Y > X > Z$

Response Index

01	a	b	c	d	10	a	b	c	d	19	a	b	c	d
02	a	b	c	d	11	a	b	c	d	20	a	b	c	d
03	a	b	c	d	12	a	b	c	d	21	a	b	c	d
04	a	b	c	d	13	a	b	c	d	22	a	b	c	d
05	a	b	c	d	14	a	b	c	d	23	a	b	c	d
06	a	b	c	d	15	a	b	c	d	24	a	b	c	d
07	a	b	c	d	16	a	b	c	d	25	a	b	c	d
08	a	b	c	d	17	a	b	c	d					
09	a	b	c	d	18	a	b	c	d					

Performance Scanner

> 90% Excellent !	You have mastered these topics. The concepts of these topics are at your fingertips. Move on to the chapter test and maintain this momentum.
76-90% Very Good !	You have a good command over these topics. Revise these topics again after a few days and enhance your performance.
60-75% Good !	You have a wide scope to learn for these topics. Revise these topics again.
<60 Not Satisfactory!	You have a long way ahead of you to master these topics. Revise it thoroughly.

Chapter Break Thru

Syllabus	Modern Periodic Law and Present form of Periodic Table, *s, p, d* and *f*-Block Elements	Periodic Properties and their Trends-1 (Atomic Radius, Ionisation Enthalpy, Electron Gain Enthalpy, Electronegativity, Metallic Character)	Periodic Properties and their Trends-2 (Lattice Enthalpy, Hydration Enthalpy, Oxidation State and Chemical Properties)

Important Instructions

- The test is of 1 hour duration and contains 50 multiple choice questions (Four options with a single correct answer).
- Choose the correct option and fill the OMR given on the last page of test accordingly.
- At some instances, you may find more than 1 option may be correct. In such circumstances, you have to judge the most appropriate answer as per the conditions given in the question.

1. Which of the following species has lowest ionisation enthalpy?

(a) O_2^- (b) O
(c) O_2 (d) O_2^+

2. The electronic configuration of atom having maximum difference in first and second ionisation enthalpies is

(a) $1s^2 2s^2 2p^6 3s^1$ (b) $1s^2 2s^2 2p^6 3s^2$
(c) $1s^2 2s^2 2p^1$ (d) $1s^2 2s^2 2p^3$

3. The correct order of decreasing first ionisation potential is

(a) Rb > K > Cl > Ca
(b) Ca > K > Rb > Cs
(c) Ca > Cs > K > Rb
(d) Ca > Rb > Cs > K

4. Correct sequence of increasing order of density is

(a) Li < K < Na < Rb
(b) Li < Na < K < Rb
(c) Rb < K < Na < Li
(d) K < Li < Na < Rb

5. Which of the following statements is correct about Lothar-Meyer's plot between atomic volume and atomic weight?

A. The most strongly electropositive alkali metals occupy peaks on the curve.
B. The strongly electronegative halogen atoms occupy ascending positions on the curve.
C. The less strongly electropositive alkaline earth metals occupy descending positions on the curve.
D. Lothar-Meyer proposed that the physical properties of the elements are a periodic function of their atomic numbers.
E. The most strongly electropositive alkali metals occupy the bottom position of the graph.

Choose the most appropriate answer from the options given below.

(a) A, B and D (b) A, C and D
(c) B, C and E (d) A, B and C

6. Match List-I with List-II.

	List-I		List-II
A.	Radioactive element	I.	Ba
B.	Alkaline earth metal	II.	Fr
C.	Metalloid	III.	Po
D	Chalcogen	IV.	As

Choose the correct answer from the options given below.

(a) A-II, B-I, C-IV, D-III
(b) A-III, B-II, C-I, D-IV
(c) A-I, B-III, C-II, D-IV
(d) A-III, B-IV, C-II, D-I

7. The correct family, group and electronic configuration of the element Z (atomic number $=118$) respectively are

(a) oxygen family, $[Rn]\,5f^{14}6d^{10}7s^2 7p^4$
(b) halogen family, $[Rn]\,5f^{14}6d^{10}7s^2 7p^5$
(c) carbon family, $[Rn]\,5f^{14}6d^{10}7s^2 7p^2$
(d) noble gas family, $[Rn]5f^{14}6d^{10}7s^2 7p^6$

8. Which of the following statements is/are correct about modified Mendeleev's periodic table?

A. Group VIII has been divided into two sub-groups *A* and *B*.
B. The group of an element in the periodic table represents its valency.
C. The elements of group IB are called coinage metals.
D. It consists of eight groups and seven periods.
E. Some proper place was alloted to lanthanoids and actinoids.

Choose the most appropriate answer from the options given below.

(a) A, B and C (b) B, C and D
(c) B, C and E (d) A, C and E

9. The correct order of second ionisation potential of C, N, O, F is

(a) C > N > O > F (b) O > N > F > C
(c) O > F > N > C (d) C > O > N > F

10. Among the given statements, which one is incorrect?

(a) Caesium is the most electropositive element.
(b) Cl has highest negative electron gain enthalpy.
(c) Electron gain enthalpy of N and noble gases are positive.
(d) In any period, the atomic radius of noble gas is lowest.

11. Match List-I with List-II.

	List-I (Atomic number)		List-II (Block)
A.	44	I.	*s*-block
B.	83	II.	*d*-block
C.	62	III.	*p*-block
D.	55	IV.	*f*-block

Choose the correct answer from the options given below.

(a) A-II, B-III, C-IV, D-I
(b) A-I, B-II, C-III, D-IV
(c) A-II, B-IV, C-III, D-I
(d) A-II, B-I, C-III, D-IV

12. Given below are two statements, one is labelled as Assertion (A) and other is labelled as Reason (R).

Assertion (A) Na_2SO_4 is soluble while $BaSO_4$ is insoluble.

Reason (R) Lattice energy of $BaSO_4$ exceeds its hydration energy.

In the light of above statements, choose the correct answer from the options given below.

(a) Both (A) and (R) are true and (R) is the correct explanation of (A).
(b) Both (A) and (R) are true but (R) is not the correct explanation of (A).
(c) (A) is true but (R) is false.
(d) (A) is false but (R) is true.

13. Which of the following order of metallic character is correct?

(a) P < Si < Be < Na < Mg
(b) P < Si < Mg < Be < Na
(c) P < Si < Be < Mg < Na
(d) P > Si > Be > Mg > Na

14. The electronic configuration of the element with highest electron affinity is

(a) $3s^2 3p^5$ (b) $2s^2 2p^3$
(c) $2s^2 2p^5$ (d) $2s^2 2p^2$

15. Given below are two statements, one is labelled as Assertion (A) and other is labelled as Reason (R).

Assertion (A) F atom has less negative electron gain enthalpy than Cl atom.

Reason (R) Additional electrons are repelled more efficiency by $3p$ electron in Cl than by $2p$ electron in F atom.

In the light of above statements, choose the correct answer from the options given below.

(a) Both (A) and (R) are true and (R) is the correct explanation of (A).
(b) Both (A) and (R) are true but (R) is not the correct explanation of (A).
(c) (A) is true but (R) is false.
(d) (A) is false but (R) is true.

16. Given below are two statements.

Statement I For the same element, as the *s*-character of hybrid orbitals decreases, the electronegativity also decreases.

Statement II More the participation of *s*-block in the state of hybridisation, more is the attraction towards bonded pair of electrons.

In the light of above statements, choose the correct answer from the options given below.

(a) Both Statement I and Statement II are incorrect.
(b) Statement I is correct but Statement II is incorrect.
(c) Statement I is incorrect but Statement II is correct.
(d) Both Statement I and Statement II are correct.

17. Which of the following order is incorrect?

(a) $IE_1(Al) < IE_1(Mg)$
(b) $IE_1(Na) < IE_1(Mg)$
(c) $IE_2(Mg) > IE_2(Na)$
(d) $IE_3(Mg) > IE_3(Al)$

18. Given below are two statements.

Statement I Chlorine has higher electron gain enthalpy than fluorine.

Statement II Chlorine is a poor oxidising agent than fluorine.

In the light of above statements, choose the correct answer from the options given below.

(a) Both Statement I and Statement II are incorrect.
(b) Statement I is correct but Statement II is incorrect.
(c) Statement I is incorrect but Statement II is correct.
(d) Both Statement I and Statement II are correct.

19. The screening effect of *d*-electrons is

(a) equals of that of *p*-electrons
(b) more than that of *p*-electrons
(c) same as *f*-electron
(d) less than that of *p*-electron

20. The correct order of energy of 2*s*-orbitals in H, Li, Na and K is

(a) H > Li > Na > K (b) H > Na > Li > K
(c) Li > H > Na > K (d) Li > K > Na > H

21. The atomic radii of Li, F, Na and Si follow the order

(a) Si < Li < Na < F (b) F < Si < Li < Na
(c) Si < F < Li < Na (d) Si < F < Na < Li

22. Among Mg, Mg^{2+}, Al and Al^{3+} which have the largest and smallest size respectively.

(a) Al^{3+}, Mg (b) Mg^{2+}, Al
(c) Al, Mg^{2+} (d) Mg, Al^{3+}

23. Given below are two statements, one is labelled as Assertion (A) and the other is labelled as Reason (R).

Assertion (A) Atomic number of the element copernicium is 112.

Reason (R) IUPAC name of this element is ininbium in which in and bi are used for 1 and 2 respectively in latin words.

In the light of the above statements, choose the correct answer from the options given below.

(a) Both (A) and (R) are true and (R) is the correct explanation of (A).
(b) Both (A) and (R) are true but (R) is not the correct explanation of (A).
(c) (A) is true but (R) is false.
(d) (A) is false but (R) is true.

24. The decreasing order of basic character of given oxides is

(a) $Na_2O > Al_2O_3 > CuO$
(b) $MgO > Al_2O_3 > Na_2O$
(c) $Al_2O_3 > MgO > Na_2O$
(d) $CuO > Na_2O > MgO$

25. The correct increasing order of acidic nature is

(a) $Li_2O < BeO < CuO < B_2O_3$
(b) $BeO < CuO < B_2O_3 < Li_2O$
(c) $Li_2O < CuO < BeO < B_2O_3$
(d) $B_2O_3 < CuO < BeO < Li_2O$

26. Match List-I with List-II.

	List-I	List-II
A.	ZnO	I. Acidic oxide
B.	K_2O	II. Neutral oxide
C.	N_2O	III. Basic
D.	P_4O_{10}	IV. Amphoteric oxide

Choose the correct answer from the options given below.
(a) A-IV, B-III, C-II, D-I
(b) A-III, B-II, C-I, D-IV
(c) A-IV, B-II, C-I, D-III
(d) A-III, B-IV, C-I, D-II

27. Which of the following is the correct increasing order of electron affinity?
(a) Al < O < N < Cl (b) O < N < Cl < Al
(c) N < Al < O < Cl (d) Cl < O < N < Al

28. O^{2-} ion is isoelectronic with which of the following group of ions?
(a) Zn^{2+}, N^{3-}, F^{+} (b) Mg, Mg^{+}, Al^{3+}
(c) K, Na, Ca (d) Mg^{2+}, Na^{+}, Al^{3+}

29. The atomic numbers of other elements, which lies in the same group as the tenth element in the periodic table are
(a) 2, 18, 36, 54 (b) 2, 8, 18, 36
(c) 8, 16, 36, 86 (d) 18, 36, 54, 96

30. Given below are two statements, one is labelled as Assertion (A) and the other is labelled as Reason (R).

Assertion (A) Na^{+} and Al^{3+} are isoelectronic but the magnitude of ionic radius of Al^{3+} is less than that of Na^{+}.

Reason (R) The magnitude of effective nuclear charge of the outer shell electrons in Al^{3+} is greater than that in Na^{+}.

In the light of the above statements, choose the correct answer from the options given below.
(a) Both (A) and (R) are true and (R) is the correct explanation of (A).
(b) Both (A) and (R) are true but (R) is not the correct explanation of (A).
(c) (A) is true but (R) is false.
(d) (A) is false but (R) is true.

31. The group of elements in which the differentiating electron enter in the antipenultimate shell of atom are called
(a) *f*-block element
(b) *s*-block element
(c) *p*-block element
(d) *d*-block element

32. The plot/graph of atomic number against square root of frequency of X-ray emitted led to the suggestion of which rule?
(a) Periodic law
(b) Modern periodic law
(c) Hund's rule
(d) Avogadro's law

33. In general, outer electronic configuration of group 6 element is
(a) $(n-1)\,d^5\,4s^1$ (b) $(n-1)\,d^{1-5}\,4s^2$
(c) $ns^2\,(n-1)\,p^3$ (d) ns^1

34. How does the electron gain enthalpies vary across a period and down a group?
(a) More negative across a period, less negative down a group.
(b) More negative across a period, less positive down a group.
(c) More positive across a period, more negative down a group.
(d) More positive across a period, less negative down a group.

35. Which one of the following constitutes a group of isoelectronic species?
(a) N_2, O_2^-, NO^+, CO (b) $NO^+, C_2^{2-}, CN^-, N_2$
(c) C_2^{2-}, O_2^-, CO, NO (d) $CN^-, N_2, O_2^{2-}, C_2^{2-}$

36. Which of the following sequence correctly represents the decreasing acidic nature of oxides ?
(a) $CO_2 > BeO > Li_2O > B_2O_3$
(b) $CO_2 > B_2O_3 > BeO > Li_2O$
(c) $Li_2O > BeO > B_2O_3 > CO_2$
(d) $Li_2O > B_2O_3 > BeO > CO_2$

37. Choose the incorrect statement from the following
(a) The process of adding an electron to the atom can be either exothermic or endothermic.
(b) Group 17 elements have very low negative electron gain enthalpy.
(c) Noble gases have large positive electron gain enthalpy.
(d) Electron gain enthalpy have large negative values towards the upper right of the periodic table preceeding the noble gases.

38. Which of the following statements is/are incorrect?

I. The last member of the 7th period of the periodic table will have atomic number 118.
II. All the transition elements are metal and paramagnetic.
III. The maximum number of elements are present in the 5th period of the periodic table.
IV. Every period of periodic table starts with a member of alkali group.
V. The size of Zr and Hf are almost similar due to lanthanoid contraction.

Choose the correct answer from the options given below.

(a) I, II and IV
(b) I, III and V
(c) II, III and IV
(d) III and IV

39. Match List-I with List-II.

List-I	List-II
A. Transition elements	I. Thorium
B. Noble gases	II. Cerium
C. Lanthanoids	III. Krypton
D. Actinoids	IV. Manganese

Choose the correct answer from the options given below.

(a) A-II, B-III, C-IV, D-I
(b) A-IV, B-III, C-II, D-I
(c) A-I, B-III, C-II, D-IV
(d) A-III, B-IV, C-II, D-I

40. Which of the following is/are correctly matched with their respective properties?

I. Li < Na < K < Rb → Metallic radii
II. I < Br < F < Cl → Electron gain enthalpy
III. B < C < N < O → Ionisation enthalpy
IV. $Al^{3+} > Mg^{2+} > Na^{+} > F^{-}$ → Ionic radii
V. $Ca^{2+} < K^{+} < Cl^{-} < S^{2-}$ → Ionic radii

Choose the correct answer from the options given below.

(a) I, II, III and V (b) I, II, IV and V
(c) II, III and IV (d) I, II and V

41. Given below are two statements, one is labelled as Assertion (A) and the other is labelled as Reason (R).

Assertion (A) Metallic character order is K > Mg > Al > B.

Reason (R) Along the period metallic character increases and down the group decreases.

In the light of the above statements, choose the most appropriate answer from the options given below.

(a) Both (A) and (R) are true and (R) is the correct explanation of (A).
(b) Both (A) and (R) are true but (R) is not the correct explanation of (A).
(c) (A) is true but (R) is false.
(d) (A) is false but (R) is true.

42. Among the following element arrange in decreasing order of electronegativity.

F, Cl, O,S, C, P

Choose the correct answer from the options given below.

(a) F > O > Cl > S > C > P
(b) Cl > O > F > C > S > P
(c) S > Cl > O > F > P > C
(d) O > F > Cl > S > C > P

43. Which among the following species has the highest value of ionisation potential?

(a) Li^{+} (b) Mg^{+} (c) Al^{2+} (d) Na

44. $BaSO_4$ is water soluble although it is an ionic compound because

(a) it has high hydration energy
(b) its hydration energy is more than lattice energy
(c) its lattice energy is more than hydration energy
(d) it has low hydration energy

45. Given below are two statements, one is labelled as Assertion (A) and other is labelled as Reason (R).

Assertion (A) The negative ion is always larger than its neutral atom.

Reason (R) As the number of electrons increases, the nuclear charge per electron is reduced.

In the light of the above statements, choose the mosta ppropriate answer from the options given below.

(a) Both (A) and (R) are true and (R) is the correct explanation of (A).
(b) Both (A) and (R) are true but (R) is not the correct explanation of (A).
(c) (A) is true but (R) is false.
(d) (A) is false but (R) is true.

46. Ununennium is the systematic name for element having atomic number
(a) 113
(b) 115
(c) 117
(d) 119

47. Which of the following statement is not correct for periodic classification of elements?
(a) The properties of elements are the periodic function of their atomic number.
(b) Non-metallic elements are less in number than metallic elements.
(c) The first ionisation energies of elements along a period do not vary in a regular manner with an increase in atomic number.
(d) For transition elements, the ionisation energies increase gradually with increase in atomic number.

48. Which of the following species are isoelectronic?

$$NO_3^-, CO_3^{2-}, ClO_3^-, SO_2$$

(a) $NO_3^-, CO_3^{2-}, ClO_3^-$ (b) NO_3^-, CO_3^{2-}, SO_2
(c) CO_3^{2-}, ClO_3^-, SO_2 (d) NO_3^- and ClO_3^-

49. Which of the following process requires the largest amount of energy?
(a) $Al(g) \longrightarrow Al^{\oplus} + e^-$
(b) $Al^{2+}(g) \longrightarrow Al^{3+} + e^-$
(c) $Al^{\oplus}(g) \longrightarrow Al^{2+} + e^-$
(d) All require same amount of energy.

50. An element A of short period having configuration ns^2np^1. The nature of its oxide is
(a) basic (b) neutral
(c) acidic (d) amphoteric

Response Index

01	ⓐ ⓑ ⓒ ⓓ	14	ⓐ ⓑ ⓒ ⓓ	27	ⓐ ⓑ ⓒ ⓓ	40	ⓐ ⓑ ⓒ ⓓ
02	ⓐ ⓑ ⓒ ⓓ	15	ⓐ ⓑ ⓒ ⓓ	28	ⓐ ⓑ ⓒ ⓓ	41	ⓐ ⓑ ⓒ ⓓ
03	ⓐ ⓑ ⓒ ⓓ	16	ⓐ ⓑ ⓒ ⓓ	29	ⓐ ⓑ ⓒ ⓓ	42	ⓐ ⓑ ⓒ ⓓ
04	ⓐ ⓑ ⓒ ⓓ	17	ⓐ ⓑ ⓒ ⓓ	30	ⓐ ⓑ ⓒ ⓓ	43	ⓐ ⓑ ⓒ ⓓ
05	ⓐ ⓑ ⓒ ⓓ	18	ⓐ ⓑ ⓒ ⓓ	31	ⓐ ⓑ ⓒ ⓓ	44	ⓐ ⓑ ⓒ ⓓ
06	ⓐ ⓑ ⓒ ⓓ	19	ⓐ ⓑ ⓒ ⓓ	32	ⓐ ⓑ ⓒ ⓓ	45	ⓐ ⓑ ⓒ ⓓ
07	ⓐ ⓑ ⓒ ⓓ	20	ⓐ ⓑ ⓒ ⓓ	33	ⓐ ⓑ ⓒ ⓓ	46	ⓐ ⓑ ⓒ ⓓ
08	ⓐ ⓑ ⓒ ⓓ	21	ⓐ ⓑ ⓒ ⓓ	34	ⓐ ⓑ ⓒ ⓓ	47	ⓐ ⓑ ⓒ ⓓ
09	ⓐ ⓑ ⓒ ⓓ	22	ⓐ ⓑ ⓒ ⓓ	35	ⓐ ⓑ ⓒ ⓓ	48	ⓐ ⓑ ⓒ ⓓ
10	ⓐ ⓑ ⓒ ⓓ	23	ⓐ ⓑ ⓒ ⓓ	36	ⓐ ⓑ ⓒ ⓓ	49	ⓐ ⓑ ⓒ ⓓ
11	ⓐ ⓑ ⓒ ⓓ	24	ⓐ ⓑ ⓒ ⓓ	37	ⓐ ⓑ ⓒ ⓓ	50	ⓐ ⓑ ⓒ ⓓ
12	ⓐ ⓑ ⓒ ⓓ	25	ⓐ ⓑ ⓒ ⓓ	38	ⓐ ⓑ ⓒ ⓓ		
13	ⓐ ⓑ ⓒ ⓓ	26	ⓐ ⓑ ⓒ ⓓ	39	ⓐ ⓑ ⓒ ⓓ		

Performance Scanner

> 90% Excellent !	You have mastered this chapter. The concepts of this chapter are at your fingertips. Move on to the next chapter and maintain this momentum.
76-90% Very Good !	You have a good command over this chapter. Revise the chapter again after a few days and enhance your performance.
60-75% Good !	You have a wide scope to learn for this chapter. Revise this chapter again.
<60 Not Satisfactory!	You have a long way ahead of you to master this chapter. Revise it thoroughly.

Scan *for Online*
Chapter Test

Scan *for Online*
Unit Test

Space for Rough Work

Test Booklet No. **3947204**

Test Booklet Code **CH4**

MEDACE
NEET (UG)
SELF ASSESSMENT KIT

Chemical Bonding and Molecular Structure

Topics Covered

Ionic and Covalent Bonding, Fajans' Rule, Dipole Moment, Bond Parameters

VSEPR, Hybridisation and VBT

MOT, Metallic and Hydrogen Bonding

Important Instructions

- This Booklet Contains – 3 Topic Tests and One Test on Complete Chapter.
- Each question carries 4 marks.
- For each correct response the candidate will get 4 marks and for every incorrect response 1 mark will be additionally deducted from the total score.
- Use **Blue/Black** point pen only for filling the OMR.
- Rough work is to be done in the space provided for this purpose in the test booklet only.

Name of the Candidate (In Capitals) ________________

____

Candidate's Signature ________

Invigilator's Signature ________

Facsimile signature stamp of center superintendent________

Do not open this Booklet until you start attempting the Test

Topical Follow Thru

Test 1

Syllabus
- Kossel Lewis Approach to Chemical Bond Formation
- Concept of Ionic Bonds : Formation of Ionic Bonds and Factors Affecting the Formation of Ionic Bonds, Lattice Enthalpy
- Covalent Bonding, Concept of Electronegativity, Fajans' Rule, Dipole Moment

For deeper insight **Scan the QR Code**

Important Instructions
- The test is of 30 minutes duration and contains 25 multiple choice questions (Four options with a single correct answer).
- Choose the correct option and fill the OMR given on the last page of test accordingly.
- At some instances, you may find more than 1 option may be correct. In such circumstances, you have to judge the most appropriate answer as per the conditions given in the question.

1. In HNO_2 molecule, the type of bond present in O—H and N—O are
(a) both polar covalent bond
(b) non-polar covalent and polar covalent bond respectively
(c) polar covalent and non-polar covalent bond respectively
(d) both non-polar covalent bond

2. Compound with maximum ionic character is formed from
(a) Na and Cl (b) Cs and F
(c) Cs and I (d) Na and F

3. Which combination is best explained by the co-ordinate covalent bond?
(a) $H^+ + H_2O$ (b) $Cl + Cl$
(c) $Mg + \frac{1}{2}O_2$ (d) $H_2 + I_2$

4. The correct increasing order of dipole moment is
(a) $CH_4 < NF_3 < NH_3 < H_2O$
(b) $NF_3 < CH_4 < NH_3 < H_2O$
(c) $NH_3 < NF_3 < CH_4 < H_2O$
(d) $H_2O < NH_3 < NF_3 < CH_4$

5. Least dipole moment will be observed in
(a) SO_2 (b) SO_3^{2-}
(c) SO_3 (d) SO_2Cl_2

6. Given below are two statements, one is labelled as Assertion (A) and other is labelled as Reason (R).
Assertion (A) Generally, ionic bonds are stronger than covalent bonds.
Reason (R) Ionic bonds break only when bombarded with electrons.
In the light of the above statements, choose the most appropriate answer from the options given below.
(a) Both (A) and (R) are true and (R) is the correct explanation of (A).
(b) Both (A) and (R) are true but (R) is not the correct explanation of (A).
(c) (A) is true but (R) is false.
(d) (A) is false but (R) is true.

7. Which of the following is the correct decreasing order of polarisability of ion?
(a) $Cl^- > Br^- > I^- > F^-$
(b) $F^- > I^- > Br^- > Cl^-$
(c) $I^- > Br^- > Cl^- > F^-$
(d) $F^- > Cl^- > Br^- > I^-$

8. The correct order in which the O—O bond length increases is
(a) $H_2O_2 < O_2 < O_3$
(b) $O_3 < H_2O_2 < O_2$
(c) $O_2 < H_2O_2 < O_3$
(d) $O_2 < O_3 < H_2O_2$

9. Which of the following statement is correct for bond angle?

(a) It is the angle between the orbitals containing bonding electron pairs around the central atom in a molecule.

(b) It is the angle between the orbitals containing non-bonding electrons pairs around the central atom in a molecule.

(c) It is the angle between the orbitals containing bonding electrons and lone pair electrons around the central atom in a molecule.

(d) It can be between the orbitals containing bonding electrons and lone pair electrons around the central atom or it can be between two lone pair of electrons around the central atom.

10. Which of the following statements is incorrect regarding lattice energy?

(a) Greater is the charge on the ions, more is the lattice energy.

(b) It is inversely proportional to the size of an ion.

(c) Lattice energy for KCl is greater than $CaCl_2$.

(d) More is the lattice energy, stronger is the ionic bond.

11. Consider pair of compounds given below.

I. BF_3 and CO_2 follow octet rule.

II. CO_2 and CH_4 follow octet rule.

III. NH_3 and H_2O follow octet rule.

IV. NH_3 and BF_3 follow octet rule.

V. CO_2 and SF_4 follow octet rule.

Total number of correct statement regarding the octet rule is

(a) 2 (b) 3 (c) 4 (d) 5

12. Consider the following compounds,

$$KCl, PH_3, B_2H_6, H_2SO_4$$

The compound that contain no covalent bond is

(a) KCl

(b) KCl, B_2H_6

(c) KCl, H_2SO_4

(d) B_2H_6, KCl, PH_3

13. The compound which contains both ionic and covalent bond is

(a) CH_4 (b) H_2

(c) KCN (d) KCl

14. Which of the following statement is wrong regarding ionic compounds?

(a) These are generally in solid state at room temperature.

(b) The force of attraction between ions is non-directional.

(c) Ionic compounds are soluble in all solvents.

(d) They conduct electricity in molten and solution state.

15. The number of molecules among the following which do not satisfy octet rule is

$$BeCl_2, AlCl_3, H_2O_2, H_2SO_4, HNO_3, SO_3, PCl_5$$

(a) 7 (b) 2 (c) 4 (d) 5

16. Which of the following has largest bond angle?

(a) H_2O (b) F_2O

(c) Cl_2O (d) H_2S

17. The number of species among the following which have zero dipole moment is

$$SO_2, CO_2, BF_3, CH_4, NF_3$$

(a) 5 (b) 4 (c) 3 (d) 2

18. Which of the following molecule has highest dipole moment?

(a) BF_3 (b) NH_3 (c) NF_3 (d) B_2H_6

19. The correct order of the bond angles is

(a) $NH_3 > H_2O > PH_3 > H_2S$

(b) $NH_3 > PH_3 > H_2O > H_2S$

(c) $NH_3 > H_2S > PH_3 > H_2O$

(d) $PH_3 > H_2S > NH_3 > H_2O$

20. Which of the following pair of molecule contain odd electron molecule and an expanded octet molecule?

(a) BF_3 and SF_6 (b) NO and H_2SO_4

(c) BCl_3 and NO (d) NH_3 and H_2O

21. NH_3 and BF_3 combine readily due to the formation of

(a) a covalent bond

(b) a hydrogen bond

(c) a co-ordinate bond

(d) an ionic bond

22. CaO and NaCl have the same crystal structure and approximately the same ionic radii. If u is the lattice energy of NaCl, the approximate lattice energy of CaO is

(a) $\frac{u}{2}$ (b) u

(c) $2u$ (d) $4u$

23. Out of following which one has maximum ionic character?

(a) NaCl

(b) KCl

(c) $CaCl_2$

(d) $MgCl_2$

24. Which of the following molecule is polar in nature?

(a) PF_3 (b) XeF_4 (c) CO_3^{2-} (d) I_3^-

25. The charge/size ratio of a cation determines its polarising power. Which one of the following sequence represent the increasing order of the polarising power of the cationic species, K^+, Ca^{+2}, Mg^{+2}, Be^{+2}?

(a) $Ca^{+2} < Mg^{+2} < Be^+ < K^+$

(b) $Mg^{2+} < Be^{2+} < K^+ < Ca^{2+}$

(c) $Be^{+2} < K^+ < Ca^{2+} < Mg^{+2}$

(d) $K^+ < Ca^{2+} < Mg^{+2} < Be^{+2}$

Response Index

Q					Q					Q				
01	a	b	c	d	10	a	b	c	d	19	a	b	c	d
02	a	b	c	d	11	a	b	c	d	20	a	b	c	d
03	a	b	c	d	12	a	b	c	d	21	a	b	c	d
04	a	b	c	d	13	a	b	c	d	22	a	b	c	d
05	a	b	c	d	14	a	b	c	d	23	a	b	c	d
06	a	b	c	d	15	a	b	c	d	24	a	b	c	d
07	a	b	c	d	16	a	b	c	d	25	a	b	c	d
08	a	b	c	d	17	a	b	c	d					
09	a	b	c	d	18	a	b	c	d					

Performance Scanner

> 90% Excellent !	You have mastered these topics. The concepts of these topics are at your fingertips. Move on to the next test and maintain this momentum.
76-90% Very Good !	You have a good command over these topics. Revise these topics again after a few days and enhance your performance.
60-75% Good !	You have a wide scope to learn for these topics. Revise these topics again.
<60 Not Satisfactory!	You have a long way ahead of you to master these topics. Revise it thoroughly.

Test 2

Syllabus
- The Concept of Hybridisation, Involving *s,p,d*-orbitals
- VSEPR Theory and Shapes of Molecules
- Valence Bond Theory-Its Important Features

For deeper insight **Scan the QR Code**

Important Instructions
- The test is of 30 minutes duration and contains 15 multiple choice questions (Four options with a single correct answer).
- Choose the correct option and fill the OMR given on the last page of test accordingly.
- At some instances, you may find more than 1 option may be correct. In such circumstances, you have to judge the most appropriate answer as per the conditions given in the question.

1. Which statement is not true according to VBT?
(a) A sigma bond has no free rotation about the internuclear axis.
(b) *p*-orbitals always have sidewise overlapping.
(c) *s*-orbitals never form π-bonds.
(d) There is only one sigma bond between two atoms.

2. Which of the following molecule is incorrectly matched with the hybridisation type?
(a) $PF_5 \longrightarrow sp^3d$
(b) $BrF_5 \longrightarrow sp^3d^2$
(c) $SF_6 \longrightarrow sp^3d^2$
(d) $[Co(NH_3)_6]^{3+} \longrightarrow sp^3d^2$

3. Which one of the following compound will have a tetrahedral shape?
(a) SO_2 (b) SO_3
(c) SO_4^{2-} (d) SO_3^{2-}

4. Which plot best represents the potential energy (PE) of two hydrogen atoms as they approach one another to form hydrogen molecule?

(a) 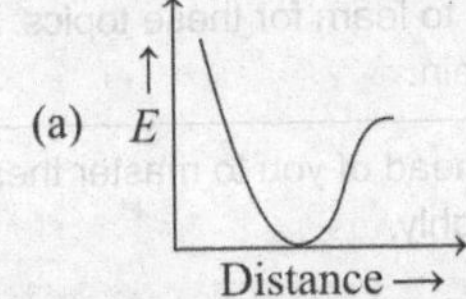

(b) 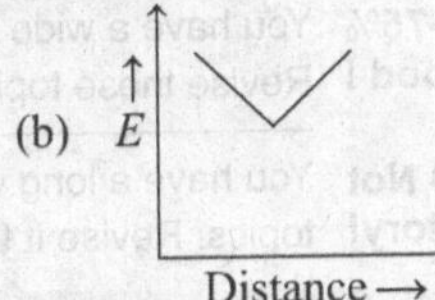

(c) 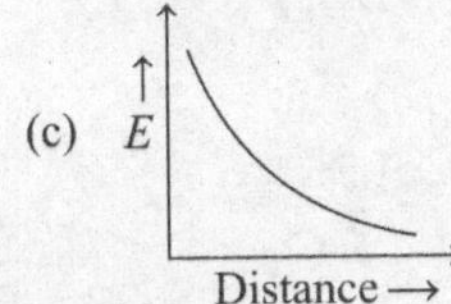

(d) 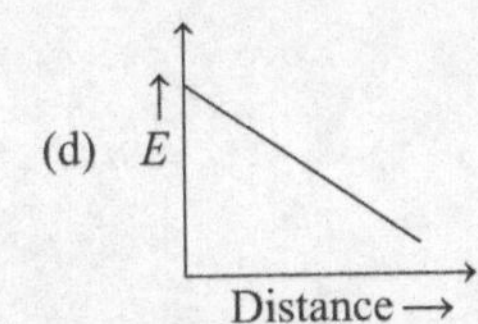

5. The maximum number of 180° angle is possible between *X*—*M*—*X* bond for compounds with sp^3d^2 and sp^3d hybridisation respectively are
(a) 3, 3 (b) 3, 1
(c) 1, 3 (d) 3, 0

6. In a regular octahedral molecule of SF_6, the number of F—S—F bonds at 180° is
(a) four (b) three
(c) two (d) five

7. Which of the following have undistorted octahedral structures?
A. SF_6 B. PF_6^- C. SiF_6^{2-} D. BrF_5
Choose the most appropriate answer from options given below.
(a) B, C and D
(b) A, C and D
(c) A, B and C
(d) A, B and D

8. In which of the following molecules, the central atom does not have sp^3-hybridisation?
(a) CH_4 (b) SF_4
(c) BF_4^- (d) NH_4^+

9. Select incorrect statement regarding σ and π-bonds.
(a) σ-bond lies on the internuclear axis of bonded atoms.
(b) π-electron cloud lies in the molecular plane of the bonded atoms.

(c) $(3p\pi - 3d\pi)$ π-bonds is weaker than $(2p\pi - 3d\pi)$ π-bond.

(d) σ-bonds affect the geometry of the molecule whereas π-bonds are present in same plane of participating orbitals.

10. The pair of species with planar structure is

(a) NH_3 and I_3^-

(b) H_3O^+ and XeF_4

(c) I_3^- and XeF_4

(d) XeF_4 and NH_3

11. Consider the following statements.

Statement I Both H_2O and $SnCl_2$ are bent molecules.

Statement II Both H_2O and $SnCl_2$ have sp^3 hybridisation of the central atom.

In the light of the above statements, choose the most appropriate answer from the options given below.

(a) Both Statement I and Statement II are incorrect.

(b) Statement I is correct but Statement II is incorrect.

(c) Statement I is incorrect but Statement II is correct.

(d) Both Statement I and Statement II are correct.

12 SF_2, SF_4 and SF_6 have the hybridisation of sulphur atom respectively as

(a) sp^2, sp^3, sp^3d^2

(b) sp^3, sp^3, sp^3d^2

(c) sp^3, sp^3d, sp^3d^2

(d) sp^3, spd^2, d^2sp^3

13 Shape and hybridisation of IF_5 respectively are

(a) trigonal bipyramidal, sp^3d

(b) see-saw, sp^3d

(c) square pyramidal, sp^3d^2

(d) pentagonal pyramidal, sp^3d^3

14. The number of species among the following that has linear shape is

H_2S, XeF_2, NO_2^-, I_3^-, ICl_2^-

(a) 4 (b) 5 (c) 3 (d) 2

15. Among the following species, identify the isostructural pairs.

NF_3, NO_3^-, BF_3, H_3O^+, HN_3

(a) [NF_3, NO_3^-] and [BF_3, H_3O^+]

(b) [NF_3, HN_3] and [NO_3^-, BF_3]

(c) [NF_3, H_3O^+] and [NO_3^-, BF_3]

(d) [NF_3, H_3O^+] and [HN_3, BF_3]

Response Index

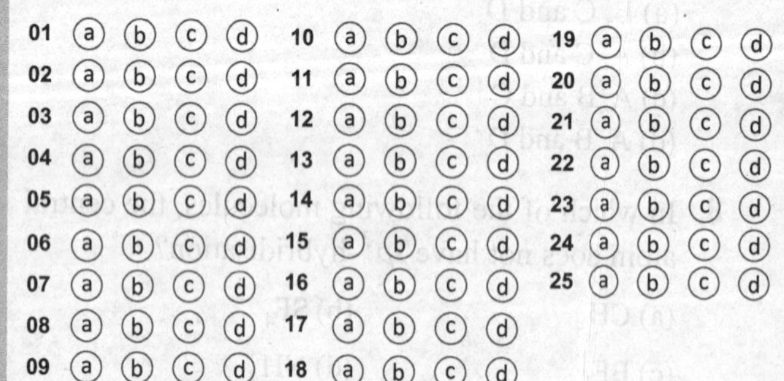

Performance Scanner

> 90% Excellent ! You have mastered these topics. The concepts of these topics are at your fingertips. Move on to the next test and maintain this momentum.

76-90% Very Good ! You have a good command over these topics. Revise these topics again after a few days and enhance your performance.

60-75% Good ! You have a wide scope to learn for these topics. Revise these topics again.

<60 Not Satisfactory! You have a long way ahead of you to master these topics. Revise it thoroughly.

Test 3

Syllabus

MOT : Its Important Features, LCAOs, Types of Molecular Orbitals (Bonding and Antibonding) Sigma and pi-Bonds, Molecular Orbital Electronic Configuration of Homonuclear Diatomic Molecules, Concept of Bond Order, Bond Length and Bond Energy, Elementary Idea of Metallic Bonding, Hydrogen Bonding and Its Applications

For deeper insight **Scan the QR Code**

Important Instructions

- The test is of 30 minutes duration and contains 25 multiple choice questions (Four options with a single correct answer).
- Choose the correct option and fill the OMR given on the last page of test accordingly.
- At some instances, you may find more than 1 option may be correct. In such circumstances, you have to judge the most appropriate answer as per the conditions given in the question.

1. Which of the following will have a higher boiling point than *meta*-nitrophenol?

(a) *Ortho*-nitrophenol
(b) *Para*-nitrophenol
(c) Benzene
(d) Nitrobenzene

2. Why is metallic bonding different from ionic or covalent bonding?

(a) It is difficult to determine the number of valence electrons involved in a metallic bond.
(b) Metallic bonding is the only type of bonding that involves metal atoms.
(c) The valence electrons in a metallic bond are delocalised while those of ionic or covalent bonds are localised.
(d) Metallic bonds are rare while ionic and covalent bonds are more common in nature.

3. Methanol and ethanol are miscible with water due to their

(a) covalent character
(b) hydrogen bonding character
(c) oxygen bonding character
(d) non-polar nature

4. The number of lobes and nodal planes present in π^*3d_{xy} respectively will be

(a) 4 and 3
(b) 6 and 2
(c) 5 and 3
(d) 8 and 2

5. Choose the correct statement.

(a) Bonding molecular orbitals (BMOs) always have higher energy than antibonding molecular orbitals (ABMO) as well as atomic orbitals, from which they are formed.
(b) Bonding molecular orbitals have higher electron density between the two nuclei.
(c) Higher is the electron density in a BMO lower will be the bond order and smaller will be the bond length.
(d) The bonding molecular orbitals has less stability than anti-bonding molecular orbitals.

6. In the molecule of N_2, which of the following set of orbitals represents HOMO and LUMO?

(a) $\pi 2p_x$ and $\sigma 2p_z$
(b) $\sigma 2p_z$ and $\pi^* 2p_x$
(c) $\pi^* 2p_x$ and $\sigma 2p_z$
(d) $\pi^* 2p_y$ and $\sigma 2p_x$

7. When O_2 changes to O_2^- the electron goes to which of the following orbitals?

(a) π-orbitals (b) σ-orbitals
(c) π^*-orbitals (d) σ^*-orbitals

8. Which of the following is correctly based on molecular orbital theory for peroxide ion?

(a) Its bond order is three and it is paramagnetic.
(b) Its bond order is three and it is diamagnetic.
(c) Its bond order is one and it is diamagnetic.
(d) Its bond order is one and it is paramagnetic.

9. Using MO theory, predict which of the following species has the largest bond length?

(a) F_2 (b) NO (c) C_2 (d) CN^-

10. In which of the following metallic bond is present?
(a) Cupric chloride
(b) Stannous chloride
(c) Mercurous chloride
(d) Mercuric chloride

11. Assuming that Hund's rule is violated, the bond order and magnetic nature of the diatomic molecule B_2 is
(a) 1 and diamagnetic
(b) 0 and diamagnetic
(c) 1 and paramagnetic
(d) 0 and paramagnetic

12. Among the following species,
$N_2, N_2^+, N_2, N_2^{-2}, O_2, O_2^+, O_2, O_2^{-2}$
The number of species showing diamagnetism is
(a) 5 (b) 4 (c) 2 (d) 3

13. Given below are two statements,
Statement I O_2 and N_2^{-2} have the same bond order.
Statement II O_2 and N_2^{-2} have same number of electron and same molecular orbital configuration.
In the light of the above statements, choose the most appropriate answer from the options given below.
(a) Both Statement I and Statement II are incorrect.
(b) Statement I is correct but Statement II is incorrect.
(c) Statement I is incorrect but Statement II is correct.
(d) Both Statement I and Statement II are correct.

14. Which of the species CN^-, O_2^-, NO^+ and CN^+ have the same bond order?
(a) CN^- and O_2^- (b) NO^+ and CN^+
(c) O_2^- and NO^+ (d) NO^+ and CN^-

15. Choose the correct match from the following.
(a) O_2^{2-} — Bond order 1.0, Diamagnetic
(b) O_2^+ — Bond order 2.5, Diamagnetic
(c) N_2^+ — Bond order 1.5, Paramagnetic
(d) N_2^- — Bond order 1.5, Diamagnetic

16. For the species, NO, NO^+, NO^{+2} and NO^-, the correct order of bond lengths is
(a) $NO^+ < NO \approx NO^{+2} < NO^-$
(b) $NO^{+2} < NO^+ < NO^- < NO$
(c) $NO < NO^- < NO^+ < NO_2^+$
(d) $NO < NO^- \simeq NO^+ < NO_2^+$

17. The hydrogen bond is strongest in
(a) O—H ..... S
(b) S—H ..... O
(c) F—H ..... F
(d) F—H ..... O

18. The maximum possible number of hydrogen bonds, a water molecules can form is
(a) 2 (b) 4
(c) 3 (d) 1

19. Which one of the following does not exhibit paramagnetism?
(a) NO (b) NO_2
(c) ClO_2 (d) ClF_2^-

20. In which of the following pairs of molecules/ions, both the species are not likely to exist?
(a) H_2^{+2}, He_2
(b) H_2^-, He_2^{+2}
(c) H_2^+, He_2
(d) H_2^-, He_2^{-2}

21. The number of paramagnetic species among the following is
$B_2, Li_2, C_2, C_2^-, O_2^{-2}, O_2^+$ and He_2^+
(a) 6 (b) 5
(c) 3 (d) 4

22. In an antibonding molecular orbital, electron density is minimum
(a) around one atom of the molecules
(b) between the two nuclei of the molecules
(c) at the region away from the nuclei of the molecules
(d) at no place

23. N_2 and O_2 are converted into monoanions, N_2^- and O_2^- respectively. Which of the following statement is wrong?

(a) In N_2^-, N—N bond weakens.
(b) In O_2^-, O—O bond order increase.
(c) In O_2^-, O—O bond order decrease.
(d) N_2^- become paramagnetic.

24. In which of the following pair, both the molecular orbital are either gerade or ungerade?

(a) $\pi 2p_x, \pi^* 2p_x$ (b) $\sigma 2s, \sigma^* 2s$
(c) $\sigma 2s, \pi^* 2p_x$ (d) $\sigma^* 2s, \pi^* 2p_x$

25. The distribution of electrons in the O_2 molecule is as follow

$\sigma 1s^2\, \sigma^* 1s^2\, \sigma 2s^2\, \sigma^* 2s^2\, \sigma 2p_z^2 \ldots$

(a) $\pi 2p_x^2\ \pi 2p_y^2\ \pi^* 2p_x^2\ \pi^* 2p_y^0$
(b) $\pi 2p_x^2\ \pi 2p_y^2\ \pi^* 2p_x^1\ \pi^* 2p_y^1$
(c) $\pi 2p_x^2\ \pi 2p_y^2\ \pi^* 2p_x^2\ \pi^* 2p_y^1$
(d) $\pi 2p_x^2\ \pi 2p_y^2\ \pi^* 2p_x^1\ \pi^* 2p_y^0$

Response Index

01	(a) (b) (c) (d)	10	(a) (b) (c) (d)	19	(a) (b) (c) (d)
02	(a) (b) (c) (d)	11	(a) (b) (c) (d)	20	(a) (b) (c) (d)
03	(a) (b) (c) (d)	12	(a) (b) (c) (d)	21	(a) (b) (c) (d)
04	(a) (b) (c) (d)	13	(a) (b) (c) (d)	22	(a) (b) (c) (d)
05	(a) (b) (c) (d)	14	(a) (b) (c) (d)	23	(a) (b) (c) (d)
06	(a) (b) (c) (d)	15	(a) (b) (c) (d)	24	(a) (b) (c) (d)
07	(a) (b) (c) (d)	16	(a) (b) (c) (d)	25	(a) (b) (c) (d)
08	(a) (b) (c) (d)	17	(a) (b) (c) (d)		
09	(a) (b) (c) (d)	18	(a) (b) (c) (d)		

Performance Scanner

> 90% Excellent !	You have mastered these topics. The concepts of these topics are at your fingertips. Move on to the chapter test and maintain this momentum.
76-90% Very Good !	You have a good command over these topics. Revise these topics again after a few days and enhance your performance.
60-75% Good !	You have a wide scope to learn for these topics. Revise these topics again.
<60 Not Satisfactory!	You have a long way ahead of you to master these topics. Revise it thoroughly.

Chapter Break Thru

Syllabus	Kossel Lewis Approach to Chemical Bond Formation, Concept of Ionic Bond : Formation of Ionic Bonds, and Factors Affecting the Formation of Ionic Bonds, Lattice Enthalpy, Concept of Electronegativity Fajans' Rule, Dipole moment	The Concept of Hybridisation, Involving *s,p,d*-orbitals, VSEPR Theory and Shapes of Molecules, Valence Bond Theory-Its Important Features	MOT, its Important Features, LCAOs, Types of Molecular Orbitals (Bonding and Antibonding) Sigma and pi-Bonds, Molecular Orbital Electronic Configuration of Homonuclear Diatomic Molecules, Concept of Bond Order, Bond Length and Bond Energy, Elementary Idea of Metallic Bonding, Hydrogen Bonding and Its Applications

Important Instructions

- The test is of 1 hour duration and contains 50 multiple choice questions (Four options with a single correct answer).
- Choose the correct option and fill the OMR given on the last page of test accordingly.
- At some instances, you may find more than 1 option may be correct. In such circumstances, you have to judge the most appropriate answer as per the conditions given in the question.

1. Select the correct statement(s) about Kössel-Lewis approach and covalency.

A. According to Lewis, atoms achieve the stable octet state when they are linked by chemical bonds.

B. In Cl_2, H_2 and F_2 molecules, the bond is formed by sharing a pair of electrons between the atoms.

C. The elements having vacant *d*-orbitals in their valence shell such as P, S, Cl, Br and I show variable covalency by increasing the number of unpaired electrons under the excited conditions.

D. The negative and positive ions are stabilised by magnetic forces.

E. In calcium, the covalency is two while chlorine has a covalency of one.

Choose the most appropriate answer from the options given below.

(a) A, B and E (b) B, C and D

(c) A and C (d) A, B and C

2. Among the compounds KCl, PH_3, O_2, B_2H_6, H_2SO_4 the compounds which contain covalent bond(s) are

(a) KCl, B_2H_6, PH_3

(b) B_2H_6, PH_3, H_2SO_4, O_2

(c) B_2H_6, PH_3

(d) KCl, H_2SO_4

3. Match the List-I with List-II.

	List-I		List-II
A.	CH_4	I.	Square pyramidal
B.	$XeOF_4$	II.	Tetrahedral
C.	H_2O	III.	Trigonal pyramidal
D.	NH_3	IV.	V-shape

Choose the correct answer from the options given below.

(a) A-II, B-I, C-IV, D-III

(b) A-I, B-II, C-III, D-IV

(c) A-II, B-III, C-I, D-IV

(d) A-I, B-II, C-III, D-IV

4. H_2O has a net dipole moment, while BeF_2 has zero dipole moment because

(a) H_2O molecule is linear while BeF_2 is bent

(b) BeF_2 molecule is linear, while H_2O is bent

(c) fluorine is more electronegative than oxygen.

(d) Be is more electronegative than oxygen.

5. The correct decreasing order of dipole moment value of

(A) CH_3Br, (B) CH_2Br_2, (C) $CHBr_3$, (D) CBr_4.

(a) D > C > B > A

(b) A > B > C > D

(c) B > A > C > D

(d) C > B > A > D

6. Which of the following overlapping shows zero overlapping?

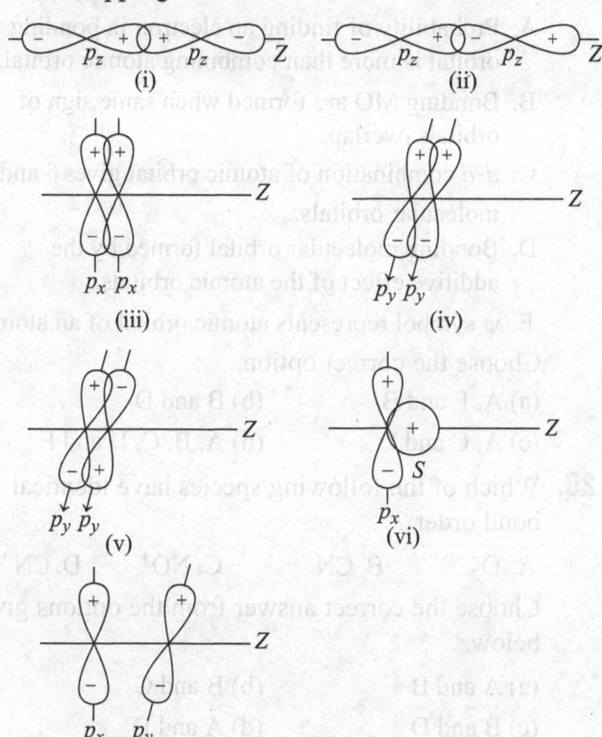

Choose the correct orbitals and mark the options accordingly.

(a) (vi) and (vii) (b) (i), (ii) and (iii)
(c) (iv) and (v) (d) (ii) and (v)

7. The types of bonds present in $CuSO_4 \cdot 5H_2O$ are only

(a) electrovalent and covalent
(b) electrovalent and coordinate covalent bond
(c) electrovalent, covalent, coordinate covalent and hydrogen bonds
(d) covalent and coordinate covalent

8. Which one of the following is more soluble in non-polar solvent?

(a) LiCl (b) NaCl
(c) KCl (d) $BaCl_2$

9. CuCl is more covalent than NaCl because of the

I. smaller size of Cu^+ ion.
II. larger size of Na^+ ion.
III. greater polarising power of 18 e^- shells than 8 e^- shell.
IV. electronegativity difference between Cu and Cl is less as compared to Na and Cl.
V. electronegativity difference between Cu and Cl is more as compared to Na and Cl.

Choose the correct option.

(a) I and II (b) III and IV
(c) I and III (d) I and IV

10. Calculate the percentage of ionic character, when the dipole moment of HBr is 2.6×10^{-30} Cm and interatomic spacing is 1.14 Å.

(a) 12.52% (b) 9.56%
(c) 14.25% (d) 15.65%

11. Which of the following statements are correct about bond angle ($B—A—B$) for AB_x type molecule?

A. Bond angle $\propto$ E.N. of central atom A.
B. Bond angle $\propto 1/$ E.N. of the central atom A.
C. Bond angle $\propto$ size of central atom.
D. Bond angle $\propto \dfrac{1}{\text{Size of central atom}}$
E. Bond angle does not depend on electronegativity of central atom.

Choose the correct option.

(a) A, B and C (b) B and D
(c) A and D (d) B and C

12. Given below are two statements, one is labelled as Assertion (A) and the other is labelled as Reason (R).

Assertion (A) The geometries of NH_3 and H_2O are distorted tetrahedral, bond angle in water is less than that of ammonia.

Reason (R) The repulsions on the bond pairs in H_2O molecule are greater than that in NH_3.

In the light of the above statements, choose the most appropriate answer from the options given below.

(a) Both (A) and (R) are true and (R) is the correct explanation of (A).
(b) Both (A) and (R) are true but (R) is not the correct explanation of (A).
(c) (A) is true but (R) is false.
(d) (A) is false but (R) is true.

13. Which of the following statement regarding valence bond theory (VBT) is not true ?

(a) A molecule is considered to be collection of atoms and then interaction between different atoms is considered.

(b) For a molecule to be stable, the electrostatic attraction must predominate over the repulsion.

(c) The potential energy of diatomic molecule is less than the sum of potential energy of free atoms.

(d) Overlapping of two distinct atomic orbital, each having an unpaired electron do not formed a covalent bond.

14. The shapes of PCl_4^+, PCl_4^- and $AsCl_5$ are respectively

(a) square planar, tetrahedral and *see-saw*

(b) tetrahedral, *see-saw*, trigonal bipyramidal

(c) tetrahedral, square planar, pentagonal bipyramidal

(d) trigonal bipyramidal, tetrahedral, square pyramidal

15. In which of the following pair of species, both have the similar geometry?

(a) CO_2, SO_2 (b) NH_3, BH_3

(c) CO_3^{2-}, SO_4^{2-} (d) SO_4^{2-}, ClO_4^-

16. A σ-bonded molecule MX_3, is T-shaped. The number of non-bonded pair of electrons are

(a) 2 (b) 4 (c) 0 (d) 1

17. AsF_5 molecule is sp^3d-hybridised and is trigonal bipyramidal (TBP) geometry. Which of the following *d*-orbital is involved in sp^3d-hybridisation?

(a) $d_{x^2-y^2}$ (b) d_{z^2}

(c) d_{xy} (d) d_{zx}

18. Consider the following compounds.

I. XeF_4 II. XeO_3 III. XeF_2 IV. H_2SO_4

The decreasing order of number of lone pair of electrons associated with the central atom in the above compounds is

(a) I > II > III > IV

(b) II > III > I > IV

(c) II > I > III > IV

(d) III > I > II > IV

19. Which of the following statements about molecular orbital (M.O.) is/are correct?

A. Probability of finding an electron in bonding orbital is more than combining atomic orbital.

B. Bonding MO are formed when same sign of orbitals overlap.

C. *d-d* combination of atomic orbital gives δ and δ* molecular orbitals.

D. Bonding molecular orbital formed by the additive effect of the atomic orbitals.

E. ψ symbol represents atomic orbital of an atom.

Choose the correct option.

(a) A, E and B (b) B and D

(c) A, C and D (d) A, B, C, D and E

20. Which of the following species have identical bond order ?

A. O_2^- B. CN^- C. NO^+ D. CN^+

Choose the correct answer from the options given below.

(a) A and B (b) B and C

(c) B and D (d) A and D

21. The decreasing order of bond order as well as bond dissociation energy of (A) O_2, (B) O_2^+ (C) O_2^- and (D) O_2^{2-} is

(a) A > B > C > D (b) B > A > C > D

(c) C > D > B > A (d) A > C > D > B

22. Which of the following is incorrectly matched with the properties mention in the bracket?

(a) $O_2^+ < O_2 < O_2^- < O_2^{2-}$ (Order of bond length)

(b) $CO^+ > CO$ (Bond strength)

(c) $CN^+ < CN < CN^-$ (Bond order)

(d) $N_2 > N_2^+ > N_2^{2-}$ (Bond energy)

23. Select the correct statements regarding MOT.

I. The electrons in a molecules are present in the various atomic orbitals as the electrons of atoms are present in the various atomic orbitals.

II. The atomic orbitals of comparable energies and proper symmetry combine to form molecular orbitals.

III. By combining two atomic orbitals two bonding molecular orbital are formed.

IV. The electron probability distribution around a group of nuclei in a molecule is given by a molecular orbital.

V. The bonding molecular orbital has lower energy and greater stability than the corresponding antibonding molecular orbitals.

Choose the correct answer from the options given below.

(a) II, IV and V
(b) II, III and V
(c) I, III and V
(d) I, II, III, IV and V

24. Given below are two statements.

Statement I CO and NO have same bond order.

Statement II NO_2^- and BF_3 have same hybridisation.

In the light of the above statements, choose the correct answer from the options given below.

(a) Both Statement I and Statement II are incorrect.
(b) Statement I is correct but Statement II is incorrect.
(c) Statement I is incorrect but Statement II is correct.
(d) Both Statement I and Statement II are correct.

25. Consider the following compounds.

I. Hydrogen peroxide
II. Hydrogen cyanide
III. Cellulose
IV. Concentrated acetic acid
V. Salicylic acid

Select the compounds that shows the presence of intra-molecular H-bonding.

(a) I and IV (b) II and V
(c) II and III (d) III and V

26. Given below are two statements.

Statement I LiCl is predominently covalent compound.

Statement II Electronegativity difference between Li and Cl is too small.

In the light of the above statements, choose the correct answer from the options given below.

(a) Both Statement I and Statement II are incorrect.
(b) Statement I is correct but Statement II is incorrect.
(c) Statement I is incorrect but Statement II is correct.
(d) Both Statement I and Statement II are correct.

27. The possible number of resonance structures for NO_3^- is

(a) 2 (b) 3 (c) 4 (d) 5

28. Which of the following compounds, will have a zero dipole moment?

(a) *trans*-1,2 - dichloroethylene
(b) *cis*-1,2-dichloroethylene
(c) 1, 1-dichloroethylene
(d) *trans*-1,2-dichloropent-2-ene

29. In which of the following pairs do the species have identical shapes?

(a) XeO_3 and I_3^-
(b) $SnCl_4$ and XeF_4
(c) SO_2 and SO_3
(d) $SnCl_2$ and O_3

30 Which of the following metal carbides are ionic in nature?

I. CaC_2 II. Al_4C_3 III. SiC IV. Be_2C

Choose the correct answer from the options given below.

(a) I and II (b) II and IV
(c) I, II and IV (d) Only III

31. Which of the MOs has more than one nodal plane?

(a) $\pi 2p_y$ (b) $\sigma 2s$
(c) $\sigma^* 2p_x$ (d) $\pi^* 2p_y$

32. The incorrect order of the boiling point is

(a) $H_2O > CH_3OH$
(b) $H_3PO_4 > Me_3PO_4$
(c) $NH_3 > HN_3$
(d) $CH_3N_3 > HN_3$

33. How many of the following species are planar?

PCl_3, NH_2^-, BrF_3, XeO_2F_2, XeF_4, SiO_2, CO_2, SF_4

Choose the correct option given below.

(a) 4 (b) 5 (c) 3 (d) 6

34. Given below are two statements, one is labelled as Assertion (A) and the other is labelled as Reason (R).

Assertion (A) Peroxide is diamagnetic in nature.

Reason (R) According to MOT it has no unpaired electrons.

In the light of the above statements, choose the most appropriate answer from the options given below.

(a) Both (A) and (R) are true and (R) is the correct explanation of (A).

(b) Both (A) and (R) are true but (R) is not the correct explanation of (A).

(c) (A) is true but (R) is false.

(d) (A) is false but (R) is true.

35. Coordination number of hydrogen in a hydrogen bond is

(a) 8 (b) 4
(c) 2 (d) 1

36. Which of the following order is incorrect with respect to the mentioned property?

(a) Ionic character = $MCl < MCl_2 < MCl_3$

(b) Polarisability = $F^- < Cl^- < Br^- < I^-$

(c) Polarising power = $Na^+ < Ca^{2+} < Mg^{2+} < Al^{3+}$

(d) Covalent character = LiF < LiCl < LiBr < LiI.

37. The hybridisation state of the central atom in $HgCl_2$ is

(a) sp (b) sp^2
(c) sp^3 (d) sp^3d^2

38. In sp^3d^3 hybridisation,

(a) the axial bond are longer and weaker than the equatorial.

(b) the d-orbitals participating are d_{xy}, d_{yz} and d_{zx}.

(c) the d-orbitals participating are $d_{x^2-y^2}$, d_{xy} and d_{z^2}.

(d) it is a combination of two sets of hybridisation, i.e. sp^2d^2 (sp_x, p_y, d_{xy}) while d_{zx} and pd includes (p_z, d_{z^2}).

39. Lattice energy of an ionic compound depend upon

(a) charge on the ion only

(b) size of the ion only

(c) packing of the ion only

(d) charge as well as size of the ion

40. In C_2H_6 (ethane), the C—C sigma (σ) bond is formed by .... overlap.

(a) p—p (b) sp—s
(c) s—s (d) sp^3—sp^3

41. Given below are two statements.

Statement I VBT cannot explain the colour exhibited by transition metal complexes.

Statement II VBT cannot distinguish ligands as weak and strong field ligands.

In the light of the above statements, choose the correct answer from the options given below.

(a) Both Statement I and Statement II are incorrect.

(b) Statement I is correct but Statement II is incorrect.

(c) Statement I is incorrect but Statement II is correct.

(d) Both Statement I and Statement II are correct.

42. Which of the following has highest bond energy?

(a) F_2 (b) Cl_2
(c) N_2 (d) O_2

43. The percentage ionic character of a bond having 1.257 Å length and 1.032 D dipole moment is ($q = 4.8 \times 10^{-10}$ esu)

(a) 10% (b) 15%
(c) 16.86% (d) 18.88%

44. Given below are two statements, one is labelled as Assertion (A) and other is labelled as Reason (R).

Assertion (A) Sigma (σ) is a strong bond while (π) is a weak bond.

Reason (R) Atoms rotate freely about (π) bond.

In the light of the above statements, choose the most appropriate answer from the options given below.

(a) Both (A) and (R) are true and (R) is the correct explanation of (A).

(b) Both (A) and (R) are true but (R) is not the correct explanation of (A).

(c) (A) is true but (R) is false.

(d) (A) is false but (R) is true.

45. According to MO theory, which of the following ranks the nitrogen species in terms of increasing bond order?

(a) $N_2^{2-} < N_2^- < N_2$ (b) $N_2 < N_2^{2-} < N_2^-$

(c) $N_2^- < N_2^{2-} < N_2$ (d) $N_2^- < N_2 < N_2^{2-}$

46. Which of the following statement is incorrect?

(a) The dipole moment of NH_3 is non-zero.

(b) The dipole moment of NF_3 is less than NH_3.

(c) The dipole moment of NF_3 is more than NH_3.

(d) The dipole moment of NF_3 is equal to NH_3.

47. Choose the incorrect statement from the following.

(a) Bonding orbital has greater stability then corresponding antibonding molecular orbital.

(b) Atomic orbital is monocentric while a molecular orbital is polycentric

(c) Molecular orbitals are filled according to Pauli's exclusion principle, Aufbau's principle and Hund's rule.

(d) The number of molecular orbital formed and number of combining orbitals are different in number.

48. Amongst LiCl, RbCl, $BeCl_2$ and $MgCl_2$ the compounds with the greatest and the least ionic character respectively are

(a) LiCl and $MgCl_2$

(b) RbCl and $BeCl_2$

(c) LiCl and $BeCl_2$

(d) $BeCl_2$ and $RbCl_2$

49. Which of the following is a correct set with respect to molecule, hybridisation and shape?

(a) $BeCl_2$, sp^2, linear

(b) $BeCl_2$, sp^2, triangular

(c) BCl_3, sp^2, trigonal planar

(d) BCl_3, sp^3, tetrahedral

50. In BrF_3 molecule, the lone pairs occupy equatorial position to minimize

(a) lone pair-bond pair repulsion only

(b) bond pair-bond pair repulsion only

(c) lone pair-lone pair repulsion and lone pair-bond pair repulsion

(d) lone pair-bond pair repulsion and bond pair-bond pair repulsion

Response Index

01 ⓐ ⓑ ⓒ ⓓ	14 ⓐ ⓑ ⓒ ⓓ	27 ⓐ ⓑ ⓒ ⓓ	40 ⓐ ⓑ ⓒ ⓓ
02 ⓐ ⓑ ⓒ ⓓ	15 ⓐ ⓑ ⓒ ⓓ	28 ⓐ ⓑ ⓒ ⓓ	41 ⓐ ⓑ ⓒ ⓓ
03 ⓐ ⓑ ⓒ ⓓ	16 ⓐ ⓑ ⓒ ⓓ	29 ⓐ ⓑ ⓒ ⓓ	42 ⓐ ⓑ ⓒ ⓓ
04 ⓐ ⓑ ⓒ ⓓ	17 ⓐ ⓑ ⓒ ⓓ	30 ⓐ ⓑ ⓒ ⓓ	43 ⓐ ⓑ ⓒ ⓓ
05 ⓐ ⓑ ⓒ ⓓ	18 ⓐ ⓑ ⓒ ⓓ	31 ⓐ ⓑ ⓒ ⓓ	44 ⓐ ⓑ ⓒ ⓓ
06 ⓐ ⓑ ⓒ ⓓ	19 ⓐ ⓑ ⓒ ⓓ	32 ⓐ ⓑ ⓒ ⓓ	45 ⓐ ⓑ ⓒ ⓓ
07 ⓐ ⓑ ⓒ ⓓ	20 ⓐ ⓑ ⓒ ⓓ	33 ⓐ ⓑ ⓒ ⓓ	46 ⓐ ⓑ ⓒ ⓓ
08 ⓐ ⓑ ⓒ ⓓ	21 ⓐ ⓑ ⓒ ⓓ	34 ⓐ ⓑ ⓒ ⓓ	47 ⓐ ⓑ ⓒ ⓓ
09 ⓐ ⓑ ⓒ ⓓ	22 ⓐ ⓑ ⓒ ⓓ	35 ⓐ ⓑ ⓒ ⓓ	48 ⓐ ⓑ ⓒ ⓓ
10 ⓐ ⓑ ⓒ ⓓ	23 ⓐ ⓑ ⓒ ⓓ	36 ⓐ ⓑ ⓒ ⓓ	49 ⓐ ⓑ ⓒ ⓓ
11 ⓐ ⓑ ⓒ ⓓ	24 ⓐ ⓑ ⓒ ⓓ	37 ⓐ ⓑ ⓒ ⓓ	50 ⓐ ⓑ ⓒ ⓓ
12 ⓐ ⓑ ⓒ ⓓ	25 ⓐ ⓑ ⓒ ⓓ	38 ⓐ ⓑ ⓒ ⓓ	
13 ⓐ ⓑ ⓒ ⓓ	26 ⓐ ⓑ ⓒ ⓓ	39 ⓐ ⓑ ⓒ ⓓ	

Performance Scanner

> 90% Excellent !	You have mastered this chapter. The concepts of this chapter are at your fingertips. Move on to the next chapter and maintain this momentum.
76-90% Very Good !	You have a good command over this chapter. Revise the chapter again after a few days and enhance your performance.
60-75% Good !	You have a wide scope to learn for this chapter. Revise this chapter again.
<60 Not Satisfactory!	You have a long way ahead of you to master this chapter. Revise it thoroughly.

Scan for Online **Chapter Test**

Scan for Online **Unit Test**

Space for Rough Work

Test Booklet No. **3947205**

Test Booklet Code **CH5**

MEDACE
NEET (UG)
SELF ASSESSMENT KIT

Thermodynamics

Topics Covered

Fundamentals and First Law of Thermodynamics

Second Law of Thermodynamics, Entropy, Free Energy Change and Spontaneity

Reactions Related to Enthalpies and Hess Law

Important Instructions

- This Booklet Contains – 3 Topic Tests and One Test on Complete Chapter.
- Each question carries 4 marks.
- For each correct response the candidate will get 4 marks and for every incorrect response 1 mark will be additionally deducted from the total score.
- Use **Blue/Black** point pen only for filling the OMR.
- Rough work is to be done in the space provided for this purpose in the test booklet only.

Name of the Candidate (In Capitals) ______________________

____

Candidate's Signature ______________

Invigilator's Signature ______________

Facsimile signature stamp of center superintendent______________

Do not open this Booklet until you start attempting the Test

Topical Follow Thru

Test 1

Syllabus

- Fundamentals of Thermodynamics : System and Surroundings, Extensive and Intensive Properties, State Functions, Types of Processes
- First Law of Thermodynamics : Concept of Work, Heat, Internal Energy, Enthalpy

For deeper insight **Scan the QR Code**

Important Instructions

- The test is of 30 minutes duration and contains 25 multiple choice questions (Four options with a single correct answer).
- Choose the correct option and fill the OMR given on the last page of test accordingly.
- At some instances you may find more than 1 option may be correct. In such circumstances, you have to judge the most appropriate answer as per conditions given in the question.

1. A tightly closed dessicator in action is an example of

(a) closed system
(b) open system
(c) isolated system
(d) insulated system

2. 8g of O_2 gas at STP is expanded so that volume is doubled. Thus, work done is

(a) 22.4 L atm (b) –5.6 L atm
(c) 5.6 L atm (d) –11.2 L atm

3. According to the first law of thermodynamics, the internal energy of which system remains constant?

(a) Open system
(b) Isolated system
(c) Closed system
(d) Dynamic system

4. An ideal gas is compressed to half of its initial volume by means of several processes. Which of the following process results in the maximum work done on the gas?

(a) Isothermal
(b) Adiabatic
(c) Isobaric
(d) Isochoric

5. In a cyclic process, heat transfers are +14.7 kJ, –25.2 kJ, –3.56 kJ and +31.5 kJ. What is the net work done in the net cyclic process?

(a) +10.56 kJ (b) –10.56 kJ
(c) –17.44 kJ (d) +17.44 kJ

6. Consider the following properties.

I. Enthalpy II. Entropy
III. Concentration IV. Density
V. Volume

Total number of extensive property is......... .

(a) 2 (b) 3 (c) 4 (d) 5

7. What will be the work done when 1 mole water at 373 K vaporises against at atmospheric pressure of 1.0 atmosphere? Assume ideal gas behaviour

(a) –6200 J (b) –306 J
(c) –3100 J (d) –1550 J

8. During isothermal expansion of one mole of an ideal gas from 10 atm to 1 atm at 27°C, the work done is (Gas constant $= 2\,\text{cal deg}^{-1}\,\text{mol}^{-1}$).

(a) –895.8 cal
(b) –1172.6 cal
(c) –124.4 cal
(d) 1499.6 cal

9. Changes in a system from an initial state to the final state were made by a different manner that ΔH remains same but q changes because
(a) ΔH is a path function but q is a state function
(b) ΔH is a state function but q is a path function
(c) both ΔH and q are state function
(d) both ΔH and q are path function

10. A gas expands against a constant external pressure of 2.00 atm, increasing its volume by 3.40 L. Simultaneously, the system absorbs 400 J of heat from its surroundings. What is ΔU in Joules, for this gas?
(a) –689 (b) –289
(c) +400 (d) +289

11. Consider the following properties.
I. Pressure II. Volume III. Temperature
IV. Heat V. Work
The number of properties which are not a state function is
(a) 4 (b) 2
(c) 3 (d) 1

12. A gas absorbs 250 J of heat and expands from external pressure of 0.5 atm. The value of q, W and ΔU will be respectively
(a) 250 J, 455 J, 710 J
(b) 250 J, –454.5 J, –204.5 J
(c) –250 J, –455 J, –205 J
(d) –250 J, 454.5 J, 204.5 J

13. Under which of the following conditions is the relation $\Delta H = \Delta U + p\Delta V$ valid for a closed system?
(a) Constant pressure
(b) Constant temperature
(c) Constant temperature and pressure
(d) Constant temperature, pressure and composition

14. In the expansion of a system, work of 500 cal takes place and 80 cal heat is given out then the value of internal energy change of the system will be
(a) – 420 cal (b) 420 cal
(c) 80 cal (d) – 500 cal

15. If ΔH is the enthalpy change and ΔU is the change in internal energy accompanying a gaseous reaction then
(a) ΔH is always less than ΔU
(b) ΔH is always greater than ΔU
(c) ΔH is less than ΔU if the number of moles of gaseous product is greater than the number of moles of gaseous reactants
(d) ΔH is less than ΔU if the number of moles of gaseous product is less than the number of moles of gaseous reactants

16. Match List-I with List-II.

List-I (Process)	List-II (Property)
A. Adiabatic process	I. $q = 0$
B. Isothermal process	II. $\Delta V = 0$
C. Isobaric process	III. $\Delta T = 0$
D. Isochoric process	IV. $\Delta p = 0$

Choose the correct answer from the options given below.
(a) A-II, B-I, C-IV, D-III
(b) A-IV, B-II, C-III, D-I
(c) A-I, B-III, C-IV, D-II
(d) A-III, B-IV, C-II, D-I

17. Given below are two statements, one is labelled as Assertion (A) and the other is labelled as Reason (R).
Assertion (A) The presence of reactants in a closed vessel made of conducting material is an example of a closed system.
Reason (R) In a closed system, there is no exchange of matter but exchange of energy is possible between the system and the surroundings.
In the light of the above statements, choose the correct answer from the options given below.
(a) Both (A) and (R) are true and (R) is the correct explanation of (A).
(b) Both (A) and (R) are true but (R) is not the correct explanation of (A).
(c) (A) is true and (R) is false.
(d) (A) is false and (R) is true.

18. A gas expands against a variable pressure given by $p = \frac{20}{V}$ (p in atm and V in L). During expansion from volume of 1 L to 10 L, the gas undergoes a change in internal energy of 500 J. How much heat is absorbed by the gas during expansion? [Given, 1 L atm = 101.3 J]

(a) 4665.8 J
(b) 5166.8 J
(c) 5265 J
(d) 6265 J

19. Match List-I with List-II.

List-I	List-II
A. A process carried out infinitesimally slowly	I. Adiabatic
B. A process in which heat transfer does not take place	II. $\Delta G = 0$
C. A process is in equilibrium	III. $\Delta U = 0, \Delta H = 0$
D. Cyclic process	IV. Reversible

Choose the correct answer from the options given below.

(a) A-IV, B-I, C-II, D-III
(b) A-I, B-II, C-III, D-IV
(c) A-II, B-III, C-IV, D-I
(d) A-IV, B-II, C-I, D-III

20. The total work done for 2 moles of a gas undergoing changes shown in the following p-V graph is

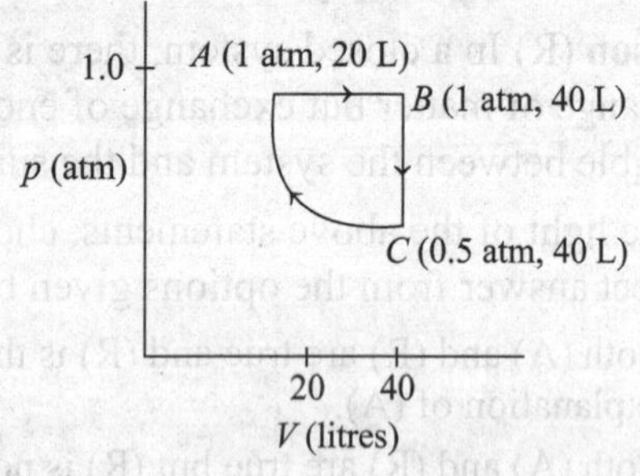

(a) –523.66 J
(b) –621.58 J
(c) –600.1 J
(d) –595.21 J

21. The value of ΔU for a certain change is –1455 J. During the change, the system absorbs 812 J of heat. How much work, expressed (in Joules), was involved?

(a) – 2267
(b) – 1325
(c) – 3021
(d) – 2856

22. An ideal gas expands from an initial volume V into vacuum under isothermal conditions. For this process,

(a) $\Delta U \neq 0, W = 0$ and $q \neq 0$
(b) $\Delta U \neq 0, W \neq 0$ and $q \neq 0$
(c) $\Delta U \neq 0, W \neq 0$ and $q = 0$
(d) $\Delta U = 0, W = 0,$ and $q = 0$

23. Which of the following equations does not correctly represent the first law of thermodynamics?

(a) Expansion of a gas into vacuum, $\Delta U = q$
(b) Adiabatic process, $\Delta U = -W$
(c) Cyclic process, $q = -W$
(d) Isothermal process, $q = -W$

24. Which of the following is not a path function?

(i) q
(ii) W
(iii) q_V
(iv) $q + W$
(v) T

Choose the most appropriate answer from the options given below.

(a) (i), (ii), (iii) and (iv)
(b) (iii), (iv) and (v)
(c) (i), (ii) and (v)
(d) (i), (ii) and (iii)

25. Given below are two statements.

Statement I If the value of the property of a system is equal to the sum of the values for the parts of the system, then such a property is called intensive property.

Statement II Volume, energy and mass are the examples of extensive properties.

In the light of the above statements, choose the correct answer from the options given below.

(a) Both Statement I and Statement II are incorrect.

(b) Statement I is correct but Statement II is incorrect.

(c) Statement I is incorrect but Statement II is correct.

(d) Both Statement I and Statement II are correct.

Response Index

01	a	b	c	d	10	a	b	c	d	19	a	b	c	d
02	a	b	c	d	11	a	b	c	d	20	a	b	c	d
03	a	b	c	d	12	a	b	c	d	21	a	b	c	d
04	a	b	c	d	13	a	b	c	d	22	a	b	c	d
05	a	b	c	d	14	a	b	c	d	23	a	b	c	d
06	a	b	c	d	15	a	b	c	d	24	a	b	c	d
07	a	b	c	d	16	a	b	c	d	25	a	b	c	d
08	a	b	c	d	17	a	b	c	d					
09	a	b	c	d	18	a	b	c	d					

Performance Scanner

> 90% Excellent !	You have mastered these topics. The concepts of these topics are at your fingertips. Move on to the next test and maintain this momentum.
76-90% Very Good !	You have a good command over these topics. Revise these topics again after a few days and enhance your performance.
60-75% Good !	You have a wide scope to learn for these topics. Revise these topics again.
<60 Not Satisfactory!	You have a long way ahead of you to master these topics. Revise it thoroughly.

Test 2

Syllabus
- Hess's Law of Constant Heat Summation
- Enthalpies of Bond Dissociation, Combustion, Formation, Atomisation, Sublimation, Phase Transition, Hydration, Ionisation and Solution, Heat Capacity.

For deeper insight **Scan the QR Code**

Important Instructions

- The test is of 30 minutes duration and contains 25 multiple choice questions (Four options with a single correct answer).
- Choose the correct option and fill the OMR given on the last page of test accordingly.
- At some instances you may find more than 1 option may be correct. In such circumstances, you have to judge the most appropriate answer as per conditions given in the question.

1. During the process of conversion of ice into the water, the specific heat capacity is given by

(a) zero
(b) positive
(c) infinity
(d) negative

2. For which of the following, Hess's law is not applicable?

(a) Determination of lattice energy.
(b) Determination of resonance energy.
(c) Determination of enthalpy of transformation of one allotropic form to another.
(d) Determination of entropy.

3. What will be the bond enthalpy of the O—H bond using the following thermochemical equation?

$H_2O(g) \longrightarrow H(g) + OH(g); \Delta_{bond} H^\circ = 502$ kJ

$OH(g) \longrightarrow H(g) + O(g); \Delta_{bond} H^\circ = 427$ kJ

(a) 502 kJ
(b) 464.5 kJ
(c) 427 kJ
(d) 929 kJ

4. Standard enthalpies of combustion for $H_2(g)$, $CO(g)$, $CH_4(g)$ and $C_6H_{12}O_6(s)$ are –285, –283, –890 and –2802 kJ/mol, respectively. Which of the following has minimum calorific value?

(a) $C_6H_{12}O_6(s)$ (b) $CH_4(s)$
(c) $CO(g)$ (d) $H_2(g)$

5. Which of the following equation does not correspond to the standard enthalpy of atomisation?

(a) $H_2(g) \longrightarrow 2H(g)$
(b) $CH_4(g) \longrightarrow C(g) + 4H(g)$
(c) $Na(s) \longrightarrow Na(g)$
(d) $Br_2(l) \longrightarrow 2Br(s)$

6. Hess's law of constant heat summation is applied to calculate

(a) the enthalpy of combustion
(b) the enthalpy of neutralisation
(c) the entropy of a substance
(d) the enthalpy changes for the reaction which are not known experimentally

7. Lattice enthalpy is the enthalpy change for completely separating one mole of a solid ionic compound into its constituent ions which is present in

(a) solid phase (b) gas phase
(c) liquid phase (d) solution phase

8. How many steps are involved in the Born-Haber cycle for $NaCl(s)$?

(a) Four (b) Five
(c) Six (d) Seven

9. When 0.5 g of sulphur is burnt to SO_2, 4.6 kJ of heat is liberated. What is the enthalpy of formation of sulphur dioxide ?

(a) +1472 kJ (b) –1472 kJ
(c) –294.4 kJ (d) +294.4 kJ

10. Which of the following has maximum standard enthalpy of combustion per gram?

(a) C_3H_8 (b) C_4H_{10}

(c) C_2H_4 (d) C_2H_2

11. Enthalpy of fusion of a liquid is 1.435 kcal mol^{-1} and molar entropy change is 5.26 cal mol^{-1} K^{-1}. Hence, melting point in liquid is

(a) 100°C

(b) 0°C

(c) 373 K

(d) –273°C

12. The enthalpy of vaporisation of a liquid is 30 kJ mol^{-1} and entropy of vaporisation is 75 JK^{-1} mol^{-1}. The boiling point of the liquid at one atmosphere is

(a) 250 K (b) 400 K

(c) 450 K (d) 600 K

13. Given below are two statements, one is labelled as Assertion (A) and the other is labelled as Reason (R).

Assertion (A) Combustion of all organic compounds is an exothermic reaction.

Reason (R) The enthalpies of all elements in their standard state are zero.

In the light of the above statements, choose the correct answer from the options given below.

(a) Both (A) and (R) are true and (R) is the correct explanation of (A).

(b) Both (A) and (R) are true but (R) is not the correct explanation of (A).

(c) (A) is true and (R) is false.

(d) (A) is false and (R) is true.

14. Which of the following reaction defines ΔH_f°?

(a) $C_{(Diamond)} + O_2(g) \longrightarrow CO_2(g)$

(b) $\frac{1}{2}H_2(g) + \frac{1}{2}F_2(g) \longrightarrow HF(g)$

(c) $N_2(g) + 3H_2(g) \rightleftharpoons 2NH_3(g)$

(d) $CO(g) + \frac{1}{2}O_2(g) \longrightarrow CO_2(g)$

15. The enthalpy of hydration and enthalpy of solution of $CuSO_4(s)$ are –18.69 kcal and –15.89 kcal respectively. The enthalpy of solution of the hydrated salt, $CuSO_4 \cdot 5H_2O(s)$ is

(a) –2.80 kcal

(b) +2.80 kcal

(c) –15.89 kcal

(d) –34.58 kcal

16. The enthalpy change ΔH for the neutralisation of 1 M HCl by caustic potash in dilute solution at 298 K is

(a) 68 kJ (b) 65 kJ

(c) 57.3 kJ (d) 50 kJ

17. The heat of combustion of yellow P and red P are –9.91 kJ mol^{-1} and –8.78 kJ mol^{-1} respectively. The heat of transition of yellow P $\rightarrow$ red P is

(a) –18.69 kJ (b) +1.13 kJ

(c) +18.69 kJ (d) –1.13 kJ

18. The ΔH_f° for $CO_2(g)$, $CO(g)$ and $H_2O(g)$ are –393.5, –110.5 and –241.8 kJ mol^{-1} respectively. The standard enthalpy change (in kJ) for the reaction

$CO_2(g) + H_2(g) \longrightarrow CO(g) + H_2O(g)$ is

(a) 524.1 (b) 41.2

(c) –262.5 (d) –41.2

19. Value of heat of formations for SiO_2 and MgO are –48.4 and –34.7 kJ respectively. The heat of the reaction.

$$2Mg + SiO_2 \longrightarrow 2MgO + Si \text{ is}$$

(a) 21.16 kJ (b) –21.00 kJ

(c) –13.62 kJ (d) 13.6 kJ

20. Which of the following equation represents a reaction that provides the enthalpy of formation of CH_3Cl?

(a) $C(s) + HCl(g) + H_2(g) \longrightarrow CH_3Cl(g)$

(b) $C(s) + 3H(g) + Cl(g) \longrightarrow CH_3Cl(g)$

(c) $C(s) + \frac{3}{2}H_2(g) + \frac{1}{2}Cl_2(g) \longrightarrow CH_3Cl(g)$

(d) $CH_4(g) + Cl_2(g) \longrightarrow CH_3Cl(g) + HCl(g)$

21. Enthalpy of hydrogenation of benzene is q_1 and for cyclohexene it is q_2, then resonance energy of benzene is

(a) $3q_1 - q_2$ (b) $3q_2 - q_1$

(c) $3q_1 + q_2$ (d) $q_1 - 3q_2$

22. The enthalpy of combustion of a substance

(a) is always positive

(b) is always negative

(c) can be either zero or greater than zero

(d) is unpredictable till the calculations are done

23. For the allotropic change represented by the equation,

C (graphite) $\longrightarrow$ C (diamond), the enthalpy change $\Delta H = 1.9$ kJ. If 6 g of diamond and 6 g of graphite are separately burnt to yield CO_2, the heat liberated in first case is

(a) less than in the second case by 1.9 kJ

(b) more than in the second case by 11.4 kJ

(c) more than in the second case by 0.95 kJ

(d) less than in the second case by 11.4 kJ

24. When ethyne is passed through a red hot tube, then formation of benzene takes place.

$$\Delta_f H^{\ominus}\ (C_2H_2)(g) = 230\ \text{kJ mol}^{-1}$$

$$\Delta_f H^{\ominus}\ (C_6H_6)(g) = 85\ \text{kJ mol}^{-1}$$

Calculate the standard heat of trimerisation of ethyne to benzene.

$$3C_2H_2(g) \longrightarrow C_6H_6(g)$$

(a) 205 kJ mol^{-1}

(b) 605 kJ mol^{-1}

(c) –605 kJ mol^{-1}

(d) –205 kJ mol^{-1}

25. The bond energies of C—C, C=C, H—H and C—H linkages are 350, 600, 400 and 410 kJ per mole respectively. The heat of hydrogenation of ethylene is

(a) –170 kJ mol^{-1}

(b) –260 kJ mol^{-1}

(c) –400 kJ mol^{-1}

(d) –450 kJ mol^{-1}

Response Index

01	a	b	c	d	10	a	b	c	d	19	a	b	c	d
02	a	b	c	d	11	a	b	c	d	20	a	b	c	d
03	a	b	c	d	12	a	b	c	d	21	a	b	c	d
04	a	b	c	d	13	a	b	c	d	22	a	b	c	d
05	a	b	c	d	14	a	b	c	d	23	a	b	c	d
06	a	b	c	d	15	a	b	c	d	24	a	b	c	d
07	a	b	c	d	16	a	b	c	d	25	a	b	c	d
08	a	b	c	d	17	a	b	c	d					
09	a	b	c	d	18	a	b	c	d					

Performance Scanner

> 90% Excellent !	You have mastered these topics. The concepts of these topics are at your fingertips. Move on to the next test and maintain this momentum.
76-90% Very Good !	You have a good command over these topics. Revise these topics again after a few days and enhance your performance.
60-75% Good !	You have a wide scope to learn for these topics. Revise these topics again.
<60 Not Satisfactory!	You have a long way ahead of you to master these topics. Revise it thoroughly.

Test 3

Syllabus Second Law of Thermodynamics : Spontaneity of Processes, ΔS of Universe and ΔG of the System as Criteria for Spontaneity, $\Delta G°$ and Equilibrium Constant

For deeper insight **Scan the QR Code**

Important Instructions

- The test is of 30 minutes duration and contains 15 multiple choice questions. (Four options with a single correct answer).
- Choose the correct option and fill the OMR given on the last page of test accordingly.
- At some instances you may find more than 1 option may be correct. In such circumstances, you have to judge the most appropriate answer as per conditions given in the question.

1. Which of the following process is associated with a decrease in entropy?

(a) $H_2(g) \longrightarrow 2H(g)$

(b) $2NaHCO_3(s) \longrightarrow Na_2CO_3(s) + CO_2(g) + H_2O(g)$

(c) Temperature of a crystalline solid is raised from 0 K to 115 K.

(d) A liquid crystallises into a solid.

2. Considering entropy (S) as a thermodynamic parameter, the criteria for the spontaneity of any process is

(a) only $\Delta S_{\text{surrounding}} > 0$

(b) $\Delta S_{\text{system}} + \Delta S_{\text{surrounding}} > 0$

(c) $\Delta S_{\text{system}} + \Delta S_{\text{surrounding}} < 0$

(d) only $\Delta S_{\text{system}} > 0$

3. The free energy change for the following reactions are given below.

$$C_2H_2(g) + \frac{5}{2}O_2(g) \longrightarrow 2CO_2(g) + H_2O(l); \quad \Delta G° = -1234 \text{ kJ}$$

$$C(s) + O_2(g) \longrightarrow CO_2(g); \Delta G° = -394 \text{ kJ}$$

$$H_2(g) + \frac{1}{2}O_2(g) \longrightarrow H_2O(l); \Delta G° = -237 \text{ kJ}$$

The standard free energy change for the reaction is

$$H_2(g) + 2C(s) \longrightarrow C_2H_2(g)$$

(a) – 209 kJ

(b) – 2259 kJ

(c) 2259 kJ

(d) 209 kJ

4. For a chemical reaction, ΔG will always be negative if

(a) ΔH and $T\Delta S$ both are positive

(b) ΔH and $T\Delta S$ both are negative

(c) ΔH is negative and $T\Delta S$ is positive

(d) ΔH is positive and $T\Delta S$ is negative

5. Which of the following is incorrect about entropy (S)?

(a) It is a thermodynamic property.

(b) It is a direct measure of the randomness or disorder of a system.

(c) It is an intensive property.

(d) It is a state function.

6. In a reversible process, the total change in entropy is

(a) > 0 (b) < 0

(c) ≥ 0 (d) $= 0$

7. For the reaction, $X_2Y_4(l) \longrightarrow 2XY_2(g)$ at 300K the values of ΔU and ΔS are 2 kcal and d 40 cal K^{-1} respectively. The value of $\Delta G°$ for the reaction is

(a) – 3400 kcal (b) 3400 kcal

(c) – 8800 cal (d) 8800 cal

8. 2 moles of an ideal gas at 27°C temperature is expanded reversibly from 2L to 20 L. The entropy change (in cal K^{-1} mol^{-1}) will be ($R = 2$ cal $mol^{-1}K^{-1}$).

(a) 92.1 (b) 0

(c) 4 (d) 9.2

9. A process is non-spontaneous at every temperature if

(i) $\Delta H > 0, \Delta S = 0$ (ii) $\Delta H < 0, \Delta S > 0$
(iii) $\Delta H > 0, \Delta S < 0$ (iv) $\Delta H = 0, \Delta S < 0$
(v) $\Delta H = 0$ and $\Delta S = 0$

Choose the most appropriate answer from the options given below.

(a) (i), (ii), (iii) and (v)
(b) (ii), (iii), (iv) and (v)
(c) (i), (ii), (iii) and (iv)
(d) (i), (iii) and (iv)

10. In a reaction, if the value of Gibbs free energy is greater than zero what does it infer?

(a) K is less than 1
(b) K is greater than 1
(c) K is equal to 1
(d) Cannot deduce K from Gibbs free energy

11. The second law of thermodynamics states that in a cyclic process

(a) work cannot be converted into heat
(b) heat cannot be converted into work
(c) work cannot be completely converted into heat
(d) heat cannot be completely converted into work

12. The entropy change involved in the isothermal reversible expansion of 5 moles of an ideal gas from a volume of 10 dm^3 to 100 dm^3 at 300 K is approximately.

(a) 95.7 JK^{-1} (b) 19 JK^{-1}
(c) 9.5 JK^{-1} (d) 41.5 JK^{-1}

13. The standard Gibb's free energy change, $\Delta G°$ is related to equilibrium constant, K as

(a) $K = -RT \ln \Delta G°$
(b) $K = \left[\frac{e}{RT}\right]^{\Delta G°}$
(c) $K = \frac{\Delta G}{RT}$
(d) $K = e^{-\Delta G°/RT}$

14. For the reaction, $A(g) + B(g) \longrightarrow C(g)$, at 25°C

$\Delta U = -5$ cal and $\Delta S = -10$ cal K^{-1}

(a) $\Delta G = +2379$ cal
(b) $\Delta G = -2379$ cal
(c) $\Delta G = +237.9$ cal
(d) $\Delta G = -237.9$ cal

15. Given below are two statements, one is labelled as Assertion (A) and the other is labelled as Reason (R).

Assertion (A) In the process, $H_2(g) \rightarrow 2H(g)$ entropy increases.

Reason (R) Breaking of bonds is an endothermic process.

In the light of the above statements, choose the correct answer from the options given below.

(a) Both (A) and (R) are true and (R) is the correct explanation of (A).
(b) Both (A) and (R) are true but (R) is not the correct explanation of (A).
(c) (A) is true and (R) is false.
(d) (A) is false and (R) is true.

Response Index

01	a b c d		10	a b c d		19	a b c d
02	a b c d		11	a b c d		20	a b c d
03	a b c d		12	a b c d		21	a b c d
04	a b c d		13	a b c d		22	a b c d
05	a b c d		14	a b c d		23	a b c d
06	a b c d		15	a b c d		24	a b c d
07	a b c d		16	a b c d		25	a b c d
08	a b c d		17	a b c d			
09	a b c d		18	a b c d			

Performance Scanner

> 90% Excellent !	You have mastered these topics. The concepts of these topics are at your fingertips. Move on to the chapter test and maintain this momentum.
76-90% Very Good !	You have a good command over these topics. Revise these topics again after a few days and enhance your performance.
60-75% Good !	You have a wide scope to learn for these topics. Revise these topics again.
<60 Not Satisfactory!	You have a long way ahead of you to master these topics. Revise it thoroughly.

Chapter Break Thru

Syllabus	• Fundamentals of Thermodynamics : System and Surroundings, Extensive and Intensive Properties, State Functions, Types of Processes • First Law of Thermodynamics : Concept of Work, Heat, Internal Energy, Enthalpy	• Hess's Law of Constant Heat Summation • Enthalpies of Bond Dissociation, Combustion, Formation, Atomisation, Sublimation, Phase Transition, Hydration, Ionisation and Solution, Heat Capacity.	Second Law of Thermodynamics : Spontaneity of Processes, ΔS of Universe, ΔG the System as Criteria for Spontaneity, $\Delta G°$ and Equilibrium Constant

Important Instructions

- The test is of 1 hour duration and contains 50 multiple choice questions (Four options with a single correct answer).
- Choose the correct option and fill the OMR given on the last page of test accordingly.
- At some instances, you may find more than 1 option may be correct. In such circumstances, you have to judge the most appropriate answer as per the conditions given in the question.

1. The standard entropies of $CO_2(g)$, $C(s)$ and $O_2(g)$ are 213.5, 5.690 and 205 JK^{-1} respectively. The standard entropy of formation of $CO_2(g)$ is

(a) 4.86 JK^{-1} (b) 1.96 JK^{-1}
(c) 2.81 JK^{-1} (d) 3.86 JK^{-1}

2. Which of the following reactions has/have positive entropy change?

I. $2NH_3(g) \longrightarrow N_2(g) + 3H_2(g)$
II. $2NH_4Cl(s) \longrightarrow NH_3(g) + HCl(g)$
III. $Ag^+(aq) + Cl^-(aq) \longrightarrow AgCl(s)$
IV. $2N_2(g) + O_2(g) \longrightarrow 2N_2O(g)$
V. $PCl_3(g) + Cl_2(g) \longrightarrow PCl_5(g)$

Choose the most appropriate answer from the options given below.

(a) II, III and IV
(b) I and II
(c) I, III and V
(d) I, II and III

3. A gas occupies 2 L at STP. It is provided 300 J heat. So, that its volume become 2.5 L at 1 atm. Calculate the change in its internal energy.

(a) 101.2 J (b) 249.35 J
(c) 92.57 J (d) 450 J

4. A mole of an ideal gas for which $C_V = \frac{3}{2}R$ is heated reversibly at a constant pressure of 1 atm from 25°C to 100°C. The change in enthalpy of the process will be [Given : $R = 2$ cal/K mol]

(a) 3.725 cal mol^{-1}
(b) 25.7 cal mol^{-1}
(c) 250 cal mol^{-1}
(d) 375 cal mol^{-1}

5. The enthalpy change for a reaction does not depend upon the

(a) physical states of reactants and products
(b) use of different reactants for same product
(c) nature of intermediate reaction steps
(d) difference in initial and final temperature of involved substances

6. Which of the following options given below are correctly matched ?

	ΔH	ΔS	Nature of reaction
(a)	–	+	Spontaneous at all temperature
(b)	–	–	Spontaneous at all temperature
(c)	+	+	Spontaneous only at very low temperature
(d)	+	–	Spontaneous at all temperature

7. C_p and C_V are specific heats at constant pressure and constant volume respectively. It is observed that $C_p - C_V = a$ for hydrogen gas

$C_p - C_V = b$ for nitrogen gas

The correct relation between a and b is

(a) $a = 28\ b$ (b) $a = \frac{1}{14} b$

(c) $a = b$ (d) $a = 14\ b$

8. 1 mol of NH_3 ($\gamma = 1.33$) gas at 27°C is expanded under adiabatic condition to make volume 8 times. Final temperature and work done are respectively. [Given, for $NH_3 (C_V = 3R)$]

(a) 150 K, 900 cal

(b) 150 K, 400 cal

(c) 250 K, 1000 cal

(d) 200 K, 800 cal

9. Work done for one mole of an ideal gas is heated at constant pressure from 0°C to 100°C will be

(a) –198.4 J (b) 831.4 J

(c) 607.7 J (d) –831.4 J

10. Given below are two statements.

Statement I A compound is formed from its elements only if free energy of formation of the compound is positive.

Statement II Many photochemical reactions have positive value for the free energy change.

In the light of the above statements, choose the most appropriate answer from the options given below.

(a) Both Statement I and Statement II are incorrect.

(b) Statement I is correct but Statement II is incorrect.

(c) Statement I is incorrect but Statement II is correct.

(d) Both Statement I and Statement II are correct.

11. Given below are two statements.

Statement I No process is possible whose sole result is the absorption of heat from a reservoir and complete conversion of the heat into work.

Statement II No process is possible whose sole result is the transfer of heat from a colder object to a hotter object.

In the light of the above statements choose the correct answer from the options given below.

(a) Both Statement I and Statement II are incorrect

(b) Statement I is correct but Statement II is incorrect

(c) Statement I is incorrect but Statement II is correct.

(d) Both Statement I and Statement II are correct.

12. Consider the reaction at 300 K,

$$C_6H_6(l) + \frac{15}{2}O_2(g) \longrightarrow 6CO_2(g) + 3H_2O(l); \quad \Delta H = -3271\,\text{kJ}$$

What is the value of ΔU for the combustion of 1.5 mole of benzene at 27°C?

(a) –3267.25 kJ (b) –4900.88 kJ

(c) –4906.5 kJ (d) –3274.25 kJ

13. The favourable conditions for a spontaneous reaction are

(a) $T\Delta S > \Delta H$, $\Delta H = +$ ve, $\Delta S = +$ ve

(b) $T\Delta S > \Delta H$, $\Delta H = +$ ve, $\Delta S = -$ ve

(c) $T\Delta S = \Delta H$, $\Delta H = -$ ve, $\Delta S = -$ ve

(d) $T\Delta S = \Delta H$, $\Delta H = +$ ve, $\Delta S = +$ ve

14. The heat energy required to ionise the following molecules is given as follows,

$$N_2(g) \xrightarrow{\Delta H_1} N_2^{\oplus}(g), O_2(g) \xrightarrow{\Delta H_2} O_2^{\oplus}(g)$$

$$Li_2(g) \xrightarrow{\Delta H_3} Li_2^{\oplus}(g), C_2(g) \xrightarrow{\Delta H_4} C_2^{\oplus}(g)$$

Arrange the heat terms in decreasing order of energy.

(a) $\Delta H_1 > \Delta H_3 > \Delta H_2 > \Delta H_4$

(b) $\Delta H_2 > \Delta H_3 > \Delta H_1 > \Delta H_4$

(c) $\Delta H_3 > \Delta H_4 > \Delta H_1 > \Delta H_2$

(d) $\Delta H_3 > \Delta H_1 > \Delta H_4 > \Delta H_2$

15. The species which by definition has zero standard molar enthalpy of formation at 298 K is

(a) $Br_2(g)$ (b) $Cl_2(g)$

(c) $H_2O(g)$ (d) $CH_4(g)$

16. Calculate the entropy change when 2 moles of an ideal gas expand isothermally and reversing from an initial volume of 2 dm^3 to 20 dm^3 at 300 K.

(a) 19.15 JK^{-1} (b) 38.294 JK^{-1}

(c) 95.73 JK^{-1} (d) 109.456 JK^{-1}

17. What will be the work done when 2 moles of hydrogen expand isothermally and reversibly at 27°C from 15 to 50 litres?

(a) −14.45 kcal (b) −1445 J

(c) −1445 cal (d) −14.45 kJ

18. Change in entropy is negative for

(a) Bromine $(l) \longrightarrow$ Bromine(g)

(b) $C(s) + H_2O(g) \longrightarrow CO(g) + H_2(g)$

(c) $N_2(g, 10\text{ atm}) \longrightarrow N_2(g, 1\text{ atm})$

(d) Fe (1 mol, 400 K) $\longrightarrow$ Fe (1 mol, 300 K)

19. The enthalpy of neutralisation of a strong acid by a strong base is $-57.32\text{ kJ mol}^{-1}$. The enthalpy of formation of water is $-285.84\text{ kJ mol}^{-1}$. The enthalpy of formation of hydroxylation is

(a) $+228.52\text{ kJ mol}^{-1}$

(b) $-114.26\text{ kJ mol}^{-1}$

(c) $-228.52\text{ kJ mol}^{-1}$

(d) $+114.2\text{ kJ mol}^{-1}$

20. Given below are two statements, one is labelled as Assertion (A) and the other is labelled as Reason (R).

Assertion (A) In adiabatic system, $\Delta U = W_{ad.}$

Reason (R) In adiabatic system, no transfer of heat takes place.

In the light of the above statements, choose the correct answer from the options given below.

(a) Both (A) and (R) are true and (R) is the correct explanation of (A).

(b) Both (A) and (R) are true but (R) is not the correct explanation of (A).

(c) (A) is true but (R) is false.

(d) (A) is false but (R) is true.

21. Consider the following properties.

I. Temperature II. Pressure III. Volume

IV. Energy V. Dipole moment

The number of intensive properties is ....

(a) 2 (b) 5

(c) 4 (d) 3

22. Given the reaction at 967°C and 1 atm,

$CaCO_3(s) \rightleftharpoons CaO(s) + CO_2(g)$; $\Delta H = 176\text{ kJ mol}^{-1}$

then ΔU equal

(a) 156.6 kJ (b) 165.69 kJ

(c) 16.6 kJ (d) 1.6569 kJ

23. The enthalpy and entropy change for a chemical reaction are -2.5×10^3 cal and 74 cal deg^{-1} respectively. The reaction at 298 K will be

(a) spontaneous

(b) reversible

(c) irreversible

(d) non-spontaneous

24. The work done by a system is 10 J, when 40 J heat is supplied to it. Calculate the increase in the internal energy of system.

(a) 30 J (b) 101.2 J

(c) 50 J (d) 10 J

25. Work done in the expansion of an ideal gas from 4 dm^3 to 6 dm^3 against a constant external pressure of 2.5 atm was used to heat up 1 mole of water at 20°C. The final temperature of water will be (Take specific heat of water as 4.2 $Jg^{-1}K^{-1}$).

(a) 23.4°C (b) 26.7°C

(c) 25.1°C (d) 28.2°C

26. For a reaction to be spontaneous at all temperature

(a) ΔH and ΔG should be negative

(b) ΔG for the reaction is zero

(c) ΔG and ΔH should be positive

(d) $\Delta H < \Delta G$

27. If the door of a refrigerator is kept open, the room in which the refrigerator is kept

(a) gets cooled

(b) gets heated

(c) neither gets cooled nor gets heated

(d) gets cooled or heated depending on the initial temperature of the room

28. For the reaction of one mole of zinc dust with one mole of sulphuric acid in a bomb calorimeter, ΔU and W correspond to

(a) $\Delta U < 0, W = 0$ (b) $\Delta U < 0, W < 0$

(c) $\Delta U > 0, W = 0$ (d) $\Delta U > 0, W > 0$

29. Given an ideal gas is expanded adiabatically and irreversibly from volume V_1 to V_2, then which one of the following is correct?

(a) ΔS (system) = 0 and ΔS (surrounding) is positive.

(b) ΔS (system) is positive and ΔS (surrounding) = 0.

(c) ΔS (system) = 0 and ΔS (surrounding) = 0.

(d) ΔS (system) is positive and ΔS (surrounding) is negative.

30. What will be the value of equilibrium constant for the following reaction at 298 K?

$2NH_3(g)+CO_2(g) \rightleftharpoons NH_2CONH_2(aq)+H_2O(l)$

Standard Gibb's energy change, $\Delta_r G^\ominus$ at the given temperature is -13.6 kJ mol^{-1}.

(a) 0.5×10^2

(b) 398×10^2

(c) 9.9×10^2

(d) 4×10^2

31. Calculate $\Delta G^\ominus$ for the following reaction.

$$CO(g)+\left(\frac{1}{2}\right)O_2(g) \longrightarrow CO_2(g);$$

$$\Delta H^\ominus = -282.84 \text{ kJ}$$

Given : $S^\ominus_{CO_2} = 213.8 \text{ JK}^{-1} \text{ mol}^{-1}$,

$S^\ominus_{CO(g)} = 197.9 \text{ JK}^{-1} \text{ mol}^{-1}$,

$S^\ominus_{O_2} = 205.0 \text{ JK}^{-1} \text{ mol}^{-1}$

(a) 97.02 kJ
(b) 257.033 kJ
(c) 394.56 kJ
(c) –257.033 kJ

32. Determine the entropy change for the reaction given below, $2H_2(g)+O_2(g) \longrightarrow 2H_2O(l)$ at 300 K. If standard entropies of $H_2(g), O_2(g)$ and $H_2O(l)$ are 126.6, 201.20 and 68.0 JK^{-1} mol^{-1} respectively.

(a) 318.4 JK^{-1}

(b) 95.73 JK^{-1}

(c) –318.4 JK^{-1}

(d) 8.314 JK^{-1}

33. When 1.0 mole of water at 413 K temperature vaporises against an atmospheric pressure, then work done against 1.0 atmospheric pressure is (assume ideal gas behaviour)

(a) – 3434.8 J

(b) – 2834.3 J

(c) – 3233.3 J

(d) – 3590.3 J

34. Given below are two statements.

Statement I Entropy of all elements is zero at 0 K.

Statement II Standard entropy of all elements is greater than zero.

In the light of the above statements, choose the most appropriate answer from the options given below.

(a) Both Statement I and Statement II are incorrect.

(b) Statement I is correct but Statement II is incorrect.

(c) Statement I is incorrect but Statement II is correct.

(d) Both Statement I and Statement II are correct.

35. The standard heat of formation listed for gaseous NH_3 is –13.00 kcal/mol at 298 K. Given that at 298 K, heat capacities at constant pressure of gases N_2, H_2 and NH_3 are respectively 7.0, 6.0 and 8.0 cal/mol, then $\Delta H^\ominus_{298\text{ K}}$ and $\Delta H^\ominus_{773\text{ K}}$ for the reaction are

$$\frac{1}{2}N_2(g)+\frac{3}{2}H_2(g) \longrightarrow NH_3(g)$$

(a) – 13.00 kcal/mol, – 10.137 kcal/mol

(b) – 13.137 kcal/mol, – 13.00 kcal/mol

(c) – 13.00 kcal/mol, – 13.137 kcal/mol

(d) – 13.00 kcal/mol, – 15.137 kcal/mol

36. 0.06 mole of KNO_3 is added to 100 cm^3 of water at 298 K. The enthalpy of $KNO_3(aq)$ solution is 35.8 kJ mol^{-1}. After the solute is dissolved, the temperature of the solution will be

(a) 293 K
(b) 298 K
(c) 301 K
(d) 303 K

37. 8.5 g of NH_3 is passed over heated CuO to reduce it to copper. The heat evolved will be given standard enthalpies of $NH_3(g)$, CuO(s) and $H_2O(l)$ are – 46.0, –155.0 and –285.0 kJ mol^{-1} respectively.

(a) 149 kJ
(b) 74.5 kJ
(c) 103 kJ
(d) 196 kJ

38. Given below are two statements, one is labelled as Assertion (A) and the other is labelled as Reason (R).

Assertion (A) The difference between ΔH and ΔU is not significant for system consisting of only solids and/or liquid.

Reason (R) Solid and liquid do not suffer any significant volume change upon heating.

In the light of the above statements, choose the correct answer from the options given below.
(a) Both (A) and (R) are true and (R) is the correct explanation of (A).
(b) Both (A) and (R) are true but (R) is not the correct explanation of (A).
(c) (A) is true and (R) is false.
(d) (A) is false and (R) is true.

39. Consider the statements given below.
I. Temperature is an intensive property.
II. Enthalpy and entropy are intensive properties.
III. Heat capacity and free energy are extensive properties.
IV. Volume is an extensive property.
V. Concentration is an extensive property.

Total number of correct statement is ....
(a) 2 (b) 3
(c) 1 (d) 4

40. Given the following data,
$\Delta H_f\ (C_2H_4) = 12.5$ kcal
Heat of atomisation of C = 171 kcal
Heat of atomisation of H = 52.1 kcal
Bond energy of C—H bond = 99.3 kcal
What is C=C bond energy?
(a) 140.7 kcal
(b) 36 kcal
(c) 40 kcal
(d) 76 kcal

41. $(\Delta H - \Delta U)$ for the formation of carbon monoxide (CO) from its elements at 298 K is
$(R = 8.314\ JK^{-1}\ mol^{-1})$
(a) $-1237.78\ J\ mol^{-1}$
(b) $1238.78\ J\ mol^{-1}$
(c) $-2477.57\ J\ mol^{-1}$
(d) $2477.57\ J\ mol^{-1}$

42. Two moles of an ideal gas is expanded isothermally and reversibly from 1 litre to 10 litre at 300 K. The enthalpy change (in kJ) for the process is
(a) 11.4 kJ (b) –11.4 kJ
(c) 0 kJ (d) 4.8 kJ

43. A hypothetical reaction, $A \rightarrow 2B$, proceeds through following sequence of steps
$$A \longrightarrow C; \Delta H = q_1$$
$$C \longrightarrow D; \Delta H = q_2$$
$$\frac{1}{2}D \longrightarrow B; \Delta H = q_3$$
The heat of reaction is
(a) $q_1 - q_2 + 2q_3$ (b) $q_1 + q_2 - 2q_3$
(c) $q_1 + q_2 + 2q_3$ (d) $q_1 + 2q_2 - 2q_3$

44. Which one of the following equation does not correctly represent the first law of thermodynamics for the given process?
(a) Isothermal process : $q = -W$
(b) Cyclic process : $q = -W$
(c) Isochoric process : $\Delta U = q$
(d) Adiabatic process : $\Delta U = -W$

45. The difference between the heats of reaction at constant pressure and a constant volume for the reaction.
$$2C_6H_6(l) + 15O_2(g) \longrightarrow 12CO_2(g) + 6H_2O(l)$$
at 25°C in kJ is
(a) –7.43 (b) +3.72 (c) –372 (d) + 743

46. The heat liberated when 1.89 g of benzoic acid is burnt in a bomb calorimeter at 25°C increase the temperature of 18.94 kg of water by 0.632°C. If the specific heat of water at 25°C is 0.998 cal/g-deg, the value of the heat of combustion of benzoic acid is
(a) 881.1 kcal (b) 771.12 kcal
(c) 981.1 kcal (d) 871.21 kcal

47. Among the following, which one is not a type of exergonic reaction?
(a) Combustion reaction
(b) Chemiluminescence
(c) Photosynthesis
(d) Formation of NaCl from sodium and chlorine

48. Calculate the entropy change when 1 mole of an ideal gas expands reversibly from an initial volume of 2 L to a final volume of 20 L at 25°C.
(a) $79.47\ J\ mol^{-1}\ K^{-1}$
(b) $101\ J\ mol^{-1}\ K^{-1}$
(c) $19.15\ J\ mol^{-1}\ K^{-1}$
(d) $101.2\ J\ mol^{-1}\ K^{-1}$

49. For an isothermal reversible expansion process, the value of q can be calculated by the expression

(a) $q = 2.303nRT \log \frac{V_2}{V_1}$

(b) $q = -2.303nRT \log \frac{V_2}{V_1}$

(c) $q = -nRT \log \frac{V_1}{V_2}$

(d) $q = -p_{\text{exp}} nRT \log \frac{V_1}{V_2}$

50. The enthalpy of neutralisation of oxalic acid by a strong base is -25.4 kcal mol^{-1}. The enthalpy of neutralisation of strong acid and strong base is -13.7 kcal equiv^{-1}. The enthalpy of dissociation of $H_2C_2O_4 \rightleftharpoons 2H^+ + C_2O_4^{-2}$ is

(a) 1.0 kcal mol^{-1}

(b) 2.0 kcal mol^{-1}

(c) 18.55 kcal mol^{-1}

(d) 11.7 kcal mol^{-1}

Response Index

01	ⓐ ⓑ ⓒ ⓓ	14	ⓐ ⓑ ⓒ ⓓ	27	ⓐ ⓑ ⓒ ⓓ	40	ⓐ ⓑ ⓒ ⓓ
02	ⓐ ⓑ ⓒ ⓓ	15	ⓐ ⓑ ⓒ ⓓ	28	ⓐ ⓑ ⓒ ⓓ	41	ⓐ ⓑ ⓒ ⓓ
03	ⓐ ⓑ ⓒ ⓓ	16	ⓐ ⓑ ⓒ ⓓ	29	ⓐ ⓑ ⓒ ⓓ	42	ⓐ ⓑ ⓒ ⓓ
04	ⓐ ⓑ ⓒ ⓓ	17	ⓐ ⓑ ⓒ ⓓ	30	ⓐ ⓑ ⓒ ⓓ	43	ⓐ ⓑ ⓒ ⓓ
05	ⓐ ⓑ ⓒ ⓓ	18	ⓐ ⓑ ⓒ ⓓ	31	ⓐ ⓑ ⓒ ⓓ	44	ⓐ ⓑ ⓒ ⓓ
06	ⓐ ⓑ ⓒ ⓓ	19	ⓐ ⓑ ⓒ ⓓ	32	ⓐ ⓑ ⓒ ⓓ	45	ⓐ ⓑ ⓒ ⓓ
07	ⓐ ⓑ ⓒ ⓓ	20	ⓐ ⓑ ⓒ ⓓ	33	ⓐ ⓑ ⓒ ⓓ	46	ⓐ ⓑ ⓒ ⓓ
08	ⓐ ⓑ ⓒ ⓓ	21	ⓐ ⓑ ⓒ ⓓ	34	ⓐ ⓑ ⓒ ⓓ	47	ⓐ ⓑ ⓒ ⓓ
09	ⓐ ⓑ ⓒ ⓓ	22	ⓐ ⓑ ⓒ ⓓ	35	ⓐ ⓑ ⓒ ⓓ	48	ⓐ ⓑ ⓒ ⓓ
10	ⓐ ⓑ ⓒ ⓓ	23	ⓐ ⓑ ⓒ ⓓ	36	ⓐ ⓑ ⓒ ⓓ	49	ⓐ ⓑ ⓒ ⓓ
11	ⓐ ⓑ ⓒ ⓓ	24	ⓐ ⓑ ⓒ ⓓ	37	ⓐ ⓑ ⓒ ⓓ	50	ⓐ ⓑ ⓒ ⓓ
12	ⓐ ⓑ ⓒ ⓓ	25	ⓐ ⓑ ⓒ ⓓ	38	ⓐ ⓑ ⓒ ⓓ		
13	ⓐ ⓑ ⓒ ⓓ	26	ⓐ ⓑ ⓒ ⓓ	39	ⓐ ⓑ ⓒ ⓓ		

Performance Scanner

> 90% Excellent !	You have mastered this chapter. The concepts of this chapter are at your fingertips. Move on to the next chapter and maintain this momentum.
76-90% Very Good !	You have a good command over this chapter. Revise the chapter again after a few days and enhance your performance.
60-75% Good !	You have a wide scope to learn for this chapter. Revise this chapter again.
<60 Not Satisfactory!	You have a long way ahead of you to master this chapter. Revise it thoroughly.

Scan for Online **Chapter Test**

Scan for Online **Unit Test**

Test Booklet No. **3947206**

Test Booklet Code **CH6**

MEDACE
NEET (UG)
SELF ASSESSMENT KIT

Chemical Equilibrium

Topics Covered

Chemical Equilibrium, Law of Mass Action and Equilibrium Constant

Factors Affecting Equilibrium and Le-Chatelier's Principles

Important Instructions

- This Booklet Contains – 2 Topic Tests and One Test on Complete Chapter.
- Each question carries 4 marks.
- For each correct response the candidate will get 4 marks and for every incorrect response 1 mark will be additionally deducted from the total score.
- Use **Blue/Black** point pen only for filling the OMR.
- Rough work is to be done in the space provided for this purpose in the test booklet only.

Name of the Candidate (In Capitals)

____

____

Candidate's Signature ____________

Invigilator's Signature ____________

Facsimile signature stamp of center superintendent____________

Do not open this Booklet until you start attempting the Test

Topical Follow Thru

Test 1

Syllabus

- Meaning of Equilibrium :The Concept of Dynamic Equilibrium
- Equilibrium Involving Physical Processes : Solid-Solid, Liquid-Gas and Solid-Gas Equilibrium, their Characteristics
- Law of Chemical Equilibrium
- Equilibrium Constant (K_p and K_C) and their Significance
- Significance of ΔG and $\Delta G°$ in Chemical Equilibrium

For deeper insight **Scan the QR Code**

Important Instructions

- The test is of 30 minutes duration and contains 25 multiple choice questions (Four options with a single correct answer).
- Choose the correct option and fill the OMR given on the last page of test accordingly.
- At some instances you may find more than 1 option may be correct. In such circumstances, you have to judge the most appropriate answer as per the conditions given in the question.

1. For which of the following equilibrium reaction, K_C and K_p are not equal?

(a) $2C(s) + O_2(g) \rightleftharpoons 2CO_2(g)$
(b) $2NO(g) \rightleftharpoons N_2(g) + O_2(g)$
(c) $SO_2(g) + NO_2(g) \rightleftharpoons SO_3(g) + NO(g)$
(d) $H_2(g) + Cl_2(g) \rightleftharpoons 2HCl(g)$

2. Consider the following gaseous equilibria with equilibrium constants K_1 and K_2 respectively,

$$SO_2(g) + \frac{1}{2}O_2(g) \rightleftharpoons SO_3(g)$$

$$2SO_3(g) \rightleftharpoons 2SO_2(g) + O_2(g)$$

The relation between equilibrium constants is

(a) $2K_1 = K_2^2$ (b) $K_1^2 = \frac{1}{K_2}$
(c) $K_2^2 = \frac{1}{K_1^{1/2}}$ (d) $K_2 = \frac{2}{K_1^3}$

3. Select the incorrect statement from the following.

A. For solid $\rightleftharpoons$ liquid equilibrium, there is only one temperature at 1 atm at which the two phases can coexist.

B. For liquid $\rightleftharpoons$ vapour equilibrium, the vapour pressure is constant at a given temperature.

C. For dissolution of solids in liquids, the solubility increases at a given temperature.

D. For dissolution of gases in liquids, the concentration of a gas in liquid is inversely proportional to the pressure of the gas over the liquid.

E. If there is no exchange of heat with the surroundings, the mass of the two phases remains constant.

Choose the correct answer from the options given below.

(a) A, B and E (b) Only C and D
(c) Only B and E (d) A, B, C and D

4. Match List-I with List-II.

List-I (Process)		List-II (Conclusion)
A.	Sugar $(s) \rightleftharpoons$ Sugar (solution)	I. Melting point is fixed at constant pressure.
B.	$H_2O(s) \rightleftharpoons H_2O(l)$	II. p_{H_2O} is constant at given temperature.
C.	$CO_2(g) \rightleftharpoons CO_2(aq)$	III. Concentration of solute in solution is constant at a given temperature.
D.	$H_2O(l) \rightleftharpoons H_2O(g)$	IV. [gas (aq)/gas (g)] is constant at a given temperature.

Choose the correct answer from the options given below.

(a) A-I, B-III, C-II, D-IV

(b) A-III, B-I, C-IV, D-II

(c) A-III, B-II, C-IV, D-I

(d) A-I, B-II, C-IV, D-III

5. If K_1 and K_2 are equilibrium constants for reactions (i) and (ii) respectively for,

$$N_2 + O_2 \rightleftharpoons 2NO \quad ...(i)$$

$$\frac{1}{2}N_2 + \frac{1}{2}O_2 \rightleftharpoons NO \quad ...(ii)$$

Then the relation between both K_1 and K_2 is

(a) $K_2 = K_1$ (b) $K_2 = \sqrt{K_1}$

(c) $K_1 = 2K_2$ (d) $K_1 = \frac{1}{2}K_2$

6. Consider the following reactions.

(i) $2NH_3 \longrightarrow N_2 + 3H_2$

(ii) $PCl_5 \longrightarrow PCl_3 + Cl_2$

(iii) $2KClO_3 \longrightarrow 2KCl + 3O_2$

(iv) $2SO_3 \longrightarrow 2SO_2 + O_2$

(v) $2Pb(NO_3)_2 \longrightarrow 2PbO + O_2 + 4NO_2$

Number of reactions that are irreversible is

(a) 2 (b) 3 (c) 4 (d) 5

7. Given below are two statements, one is labelled as Assertion (A) and the other is labelled as Reason (R).

Assertion (A) For the reaction,

$$N_2(g) + 3H_2(g) \rightleftharpoons 2NH_3(g)$$

Unit of $K_p = L^2\ mol^{-2}$

Reason (R) For the reaction,

$$N_2(g) + 3H_2(g) \rightleftharpoons 2NH_3(g)$$

Equilibrium constant, $K_p = \frac{(p_{NH_3})^2}{(p_{N_2}) \times (p_{H_2})^3}$

In the light of the above statements, choose the correct answer from the options given below.

(a) Both (A) and (R) are true and (R) is the correct explanation of (A).

(b) Both (A) and (R) are true but (R) is not the correct explanation of (A).

(c) (A) is true but (R) is false.

(d) (A) is false but (R) is true.

8. The equilibrium constant is found to decrease after 2100°C when hydrogen and oxygen were heated together in a closed vessel. Which is responsible for this?

(a) Backward reaction predominates over forward reaction.

(b) Forward reaction predominates over backward reaction.

(c) The rate of forward reaction is equal to the rate of backward reaction.

(d) It is a property of the system, hence no reason for lower value.

9. Consider the following statements.

A. Equilibrium is possible in all type of system at a given temperature.

B. Two opposing processes occur at the same rate and that is a dynamic but stable condition.

C. All measurable properties of the system remain constant.

D. When equilibrium is attained for a physical process, it is characterised by constant value of one of its parameters at a given temperature.

E. The magnitude of such quantities at any stage indicates the extent to which the physical process has proceeded after reaching equilibrium.

Choose the correct answer from the options given below.

(a) A, B, C and E

(b) B, C and D

(c) Only D and E

(d) Only B and C

10. The equilibrium constants for the following reactions are given as

$$H_3PO_4 \overset{K_1}{\rightleftharpoons} H^+ + H_2PO_4^-;\ K_1$$

$$H_2PO_4^- \overset{K_2}{\rightleftharpoons} H^+ + HPO_4^{2-};\ K_2$$

$$HPO_4^{2-} \overset{K_3}{\rightleftharpoons} H^+ + PO_4^{3-};\ K_3$$

Give the equilibrium constant for the reaction given below.

$$H_3PO_4 \rightleftharpoons 3H^+ + PO_4^{3-} \text{ will be}$$

(a) $\frac{K_1}{K_2K_3}$ (b) $K_1 \times K_2 \times K_3$

(c) $\frac{K_2}{K_1K_3}$ (d) $K_1 + K_2 + K_3$

11. Which of the following statement(s) is/are correct ?

A. Expression for equilibrium constant is applicable only when concentrations of the reactants and products have attained constant value at equilibrium state.

B. The value of equilibrium constant is dependent of initial concentrations of the reactants and products.

C. Equilibrium constant is temperature independent having one unique value for a particular reaction represented by a balanced equation at a given temperature.

D. The equilibrium constant for the reverse reaction is equal to the inverse of the equilibrium constant for the forward reaction.

E. The equilibrium constant K for a reaction is related to the equilibrium constant of the corresponding reaction, whose equation is obtained by multiplying or dividing the equation for the original reaction of a small integer.

Choose the correct answer from the options given below.

(a) A, D and E (b) Only B and E
(c) Only C and D (d) A, B and C

12. According to law of mass action, rate of a chemical reaction is proportional to

(a) concentration of products
(b) molar concentration of products
(c) concentration of reactants
(d) molar concentration of reactants

13. Which oxide of nitrogen in the given options is the most stable?

(a) $2NO_2(g) \rightleftharpoons N_2(g)+2O_2(g); K=6.7\times10^{16}$
(b) $2NO(g) \rightleftharpoons N_2(g)+O_2(g); K=2.5\times10^{28}$
(c) $2N_2O_5(g) \rightleftharpoons 2N_2(g)+5O_2(g); K=1.4\times10^{30}$
(d) $2N_2O(g) \rightleftharpoons 2N_2(g)+O_2(g); K=2.8\times10^{32}$

14. Which statement is not correct about the characteristics of equilibria?

(a) Equilibrium is possible only in a closed container.
(b) Both the opposing processes occurs at the same rate.
(c) All the measurable properties of the system keep changing in equilibrium.
(d) When equilibrium is attained for a physical process, it is characterised by constant value of one of its parameters at a given temperature.

15. Consider the following reactions,

(i) $2N_2O(g) \rightleftharpoons 2N_2(g)+O_2(g)$
(ii) $2NH_3(g) \rightleftharpoons N_2(g)+3H_2(g)$
(iii) $2Cu(NO_3)_2(s) \rightleftharpoons 2CuO(s)+4NO_2(g)+O_2(g)$
(iv) $Ca(OH)_2(s) \rightleftharpoons Ca^{2+}(aq)+2OH^-(aq)$
(v) $PCl_3(l)+Cl_2(g) \rightleftharpoons PCl_5(s)$

The number of homogeneous reaction from the above reactions are

(a) 2 (b) 3 (c) 4 (d) 5

16. Given below are two statements, one is labelled as Assertion (A) and the other is labelled as Reason (R).

Assertion (A) The equilibrium constant is fixed and a characteristic for any given chemical reaction at a specified temperature.

Reason (R) The composition of the final equilibrium mixture at a particular temperature depends upon the starting amount of reactants.

In the light of the above statements, choose the correct answer from the options given below.

(a) Both (A) and (R) are true and (R) is the correct explanation of (A).
(b) Both (A) and (R) are true but (R) is not the correct explanation of (A).
(c) (A) is true but (R) is false.
(d) (A) is false but (R) is true.

17. The value of equilibrium constant for α-D-glucose $\rightleftharpoons$ β-D-glucose is 1.8. The percentage of α-D-glucose at equilibrium is

(a) 35.7 (b) 55.6 (c) 44.4 (d) 64.3

18. Consider the following statements.

Statement I The concentration of pure liquid and pure solid is taken as 1.

Statement II Molar concentration is directly proportional to density of liquids and solids.

In the light of the above statements, choose the correct answer from the options given below.

(a) Both Statement I and Statement II are incorrect.
(b) Statement I is correct but Statement II is incorrect.
(c) Statement I is incorrect but Statement II is correct.
(d) Both Statement I and Statement II are correct.

19. If 1.0 mole of I_2 is introduced into 1.0 litre flask at 1000 K. At equilibrium, $[K_C = 10^{-6}]$ is true for the condition

(a) $[I_2(g)] > [I^-(g)]$ (b) $[I_2(g)] < [I^-(g)]$

(c) $[I_2(g)] = [I^-(g)]$ (d) $[I_2(g) = \frac{1}{2}[I^-(g)]$

20. The equilibrium reaction of a gas AB_2 can be represented as,

$$2AB_2(g) \rightleftharpoons 2AB(g) + B_2(g)$$

If the degree of dissociation is x and is small compared to 1, then the expression relating the degree of dissociation (x) with equilibrium constant K_p and total pressure p will be

(a) $(2K_p / p)^{1/3}$ (b) $\left(\frac{2K_p}{p}\right)^2$

(c) (K_p / p) (d) $(2K_p / p)^3$

21. Consider the following given reaction,

$$A_2(g) + B_2(g) \rightleftharpoons 2AB(g)$$

At equilibrium, the concentrations of given gases are

$$A_2 = 3.0 \times 10^{-3}\text{ M}, B_2 = 4.2 \times 10^{-3}\text{ M},$$
$$AB = 2.8 \times 10^{-3}\text{ M}$$

If the reaction takes place in a sealed vessel at 527°C then the value of K_C will be

(a) 1.62 (b) 3.59

(c) 0.62 (d) 4.62

22. If the value of an equilibrium constant for a particular reaction is 1.6×10^{12}, what is the condition of the system at equilibrium?

(a) Mainly reactants are involved.

(b) Major portion are products.

(c) Both reactants and products are same.

(d) All are reactants.

23. In the reaction, $A + 2B \rightleftharpoons 2C + D$, initial concentration of B was 1.5 times that of A. But the equilibrium concentration of A and B were found to be equal. Then the K_C for the reaction is

(a) 4 (b) 5 (c) 6 (d) 8

24. The equilibrium constant of a reaction is 20 units and the equilibrium constant of other reaction is 30 units when both the reactions are added up together then the equilibrium constant of the resultant reaction is given by

(a) 150 units (b) 50 units

(c) 600 units (d) 10 units

25. A definite amount of solid NH_4HS is placed in a flask already containing NH_3 gas at certain temperature and 0.50 atm pressure. NH_4HS decomposes to give NH_3 and H_2S and total equilibrium pressure in flask is 0.75 atm. The equilibrium constant for the reaction is

(a) 0.33 (b) 0.28

(c) 0.027 (d) 0.078

Response Index

01	a	b	c	d	10	a	b	c	d	19	a	b	c	d
02	a	b	c	d	11	a	b	c	d	20	a	b	c	d
03	a	b	c	d	12	a	b	c	d	21	a	b	c	d
04	a	b	c	d	13	a	b	c	d	22	a	b	c	d
05	a	b	c	d	14	a	b	c	d	23	a	b	c	d
06	a	b	c	d	15	a	b	c	d	24	a	b	c	d
07	a	b	c	d	16	a	b	c	d	25	a	b	c	d
08	a	b	c	d	17	a	b	c	d					
09	a	b	c	d	18	a	b	c	d					

Performance Scanner

> 90% Excellent !	You have mastered these topics. The concepts of these topics are at your fingertips. Move on to the next test and maintain this momentum.
76-90% Very Good !	You have a good command over these topics. Revise these topics again after a few days and enhance your performance.
60-75% Good !	You have a wide scope to learn for these topics. Revise these topics again.
<60 Not Satisfactory!	You have a long way ahead of you to master these topics. Revise it thoroughly.

Test 2

Syllabus

- The Significance of ΔG and ΔG° in Chemical Equilibrium
- Factors Affecting Equilibrium : Concentration, Pressure, Temperature, The Effect of Catalyst
- Le-Chatelier's Principle

For deeper insight **Scan the QR Code**

Important Instructions

- The test is of 30 minutes duration and contains 25 multiple choice questions (Four options with a single correct answer).
- Choose the correct option and fill the OMR given on the last page of test accordingly.
- At some instances you may find more than 1 option may be correct. In such circumstances, you have to judge the most appropriate answer as per conditions given in the question.

1. For a given reaction $A + B \rightleftharpoons C + D$, the equilibrium constant is 100 at 298 K. If the initial concentration of all the four species were 1 M each, then the equilibrium concentration of D and its value wrt intial concentration will (in mol L^{-1})

(a) 1.812, increase (b) 1.818, increase
(c) 0.881, decrease (d) 0.850, decrease

2. The standard Gibb's energy change at 200 K for the reaction, $2A \rightleftharpoons B + C$ is 2249.5 J. At a given time, the composition of the reaction mixture is $[A] = \frac{1}{2}$, $[B] = 2$ and $[C] = \frac{1}{2}$. The reaction proceeds in the $[R = 8314 \text{ J/K/mol}]$

(a) forward direction because $Q > K_C$
(b) backward direction because $Q > K_C$
(c) forward direction because $Q < K_C$
(d) backward direction because $Q < K_C$

3. A vessel at 500 K, contains CO_2 with a pressure of 1.0 atm. Some amount of the CO_2 is converted into CO on the addition of graphite. If the total pressure at equilibrium is 1.5 atm, the value of K_p is

(a) 1.5 atm (b) 2 atm
(c) 3 atm (d) 3.5 atm

4. The equilibrium constant for the reaction,

$$N_2(g) + O_2(g) \rightleftharpoons 2NO(g)$$

is 2×10^{-4} at 1000 K. In presence of a catalyst, the equilibrium is attained ten times faster. Therefore, the equilibrium constant, in presence of the catalyst, at 1000 K is

(a) 20×10^{-4} (b) 2×10^{-4}
(c) 5×10^{-3} (d) 2×10^{-2}

5. Given below are two statements.

Statement I The reaction is spontaneous and proceeds in the forward direction, if $\Delta G > 0$.

Statement II The reaction is non-spontaneous and the products of the forward reaction shall be converted to the reactants, if $\Delta G < 0$.

In the light of the above statements, choose the correct answer from the options given below.

(a) Both Statement I and Statement II are incorrect.
(b) Statement I is correct but Statement II is incorrect.
(c) Statement I is incorrect but Statement II is correct.
(d) Both Statement I and Statement II are correct.

6. In which one of the following equilibria will the point of equilibrium shift to left when the pressure of the system is increased?

(a) $H_2(g) + I_2(g) \rightleftharpoons 2HI(g)$
(b) $2NH_3(g) \rightleftharpoons N_2(g) + 3H_2(g)$
(c) $C(s) + O_2(g) \rightleftharpoons CO_2(g)$
(d) $2H_2(g) + O_2(g) \rightleftharpoons 2H_2O(g)$

7. Given below are two statements.

Statement I The endothermic reactions are favoured at lower temperature in comparison to exothermic reactions which are favoured at high temperature.

Statement II When a system in equilibrium is disturbed by changing the temperature, it will tend to adjust itself to neutralise the effect of change.

In the light of the above statements, choose the most appropriate answer from the options given below

(a) Both Statement I and Statement II are incorrect.
(b) Statement I is correct but Statement II is incorrect.
(c) Statement I is incorrect but Statement II is correct.
(d) Both Statement I and Statement II are correct.

8. Consider the following equilibrium equation,

$$H_2S \rightleftharpoons H^+ + HS^-$$

If dilute hydrochloric acid is added to an aqueous solution of hydrogen sulphide without any change in temperature, then

(a) the equilibrium constant will change.
(b) the concentration of HS^- will increase by 4 times.
(c) the concentration of undissociated hydrogen sulphide will decrease.
(d) the concentration of HS^- will decrease.

9. Which of the following statement is correct for a reversible chemical reaction where the forward process is exothermic?

(a) The backward reaction has higher activation energy than the forward reaction.
(b) Same activation energy is involved in forward and backward reaction.
(c) The activation energy of backward reaction is lower than that of forward reaction.
(d) Since energy is liberated in the process, no activation energy is required at all.

10. A reversible chemical reaction have two reactants, in equilibrium. If concentration of the reactants are doubled, then the equilibrium constant will

(a) also be doubled (b) become one-fourth
(c) be get halved (d) remain constant

11. Given below are two statements, one is labelled as Assertion (A) and the other is labelled as Reason (R).

Assertion (A) For the given reaction,

$$2NO(g) + O_2(g) \rightleftharpoons 2NO_2(g)$$

increase in pressure favours the formation of NO_2.

Reason (R) The reaction is exothermic.

In the light of the above statements, choose the correct answer from the options given below.

(a) Both (A) and (R) are true and (R) is the correct explanation of (A).
(b) Both (A) and (R) are true but (R) is not the correct explanation of (A).
(c) (A) is true but (R) is false.
(d) (A) is false but (R) is true.

12. For the reaction,

$$CH_4(g) + 2O_2(g) \rightleftharpoons CO_2(g) + 2H_2O(l),$$
$$\Delta_r H = -170.8 \text{ kJ mol}^{-1}$$

Which of the following statement is not true?

(a) The concentrations of $CO_2(g)$ and $H_2O(l)$ are not equal at equilibrium.
(b) The equilibrium constant for the reaction is given by $K_p = \frac{[CO_2]}{[CH_4][O_2]}$ as reaction is gaseous in nature.
(c) Addition of $CH_4(g)$ or $O_2(g)$ at equilibrium will move it to the forward direction.
(d) The reaction absorbs more heat.

13. For a reaction $2A + B \rightleftharpoons C + D$, the equilibrium concentrations for all the species is 0.1 M. For $T = 300$ K, the free energy change for the given reaction would be
(Consider all species to the gaseous)

(a) –5010.25 J/mol (b) –5744.14 J/mol
(c) +5744.14 J/mol (d) 0 J/mol

14. Which condition is favourable at equilibrium when $NaNO_3$ is heated in a closed vessel, oxygen is liberated and $NaNO_2$ is left behind?

(a) Insertion of $NaNO_2$ favours backward reaction.
(b) Insertion of $NaNO_2$ favours forward reaction.
(c) Enhancement in temperature favours forward reaction.
(d) Lowering in pressure favours reverse reaction.

15. Which information can be obtained from Le-Chatelier's principle?

(a) Shift in equilibrium position on changing p, T and concentration.
(b) Dissociation constant of a strong acid.
(c) Entropy change in a reaction.
(d) The value of equilibrium constant.

16. In the following reaction, predict the effect of increased pressure on equilibrium.

$$2SO_2(g) + O_2(g) \rightleftharpoons 2SO_3(g)$$

(a) Equilibrium gets shifted to the right.
(b) Equilibrium favours the reactant concentration.
(c) No effect on equilibrium.
(d) Reaction stops on increasing the pressure.

17. Given below are two statements, one is labelled as Assertion (A) and the other is labelled as Reason (R).

Assertion (A) The melting point of solid (except ice) increases with increase in pressure.

Reason (R) An increase in pressure favours the change where volume decreases.

In the light of the above statements, choose the correct answer from the options given below.

(a) Both (A) and (R) are true and (R) is the correct explanation of (A).

(b) Both (A) and (R) are true but (R) is not the correct explanation of (A).

(c) (A) is true but (R) is false.

(d) (A) is false but (R) is true.

18. Given below are two statements, one is labelled as Assertion (A) and the other is labelled as Reason (R).

Assertion (A) The red colour shown by $[Fe(SCN)]^{2+}(aq)$ in a reversible reaction between Fe^{3+} and SCN^-

$Fe^{3+}(aq) + SCN^-(aq) \rightleftharpoons Fe(SCN)^{2+}(aq)$

deepens if few more drops KCNS are added in equilibrium mixture.

Reason (R) Addition of of KCNS favours backward reaction.

In the light of the above statements, choose the correct answer from the options given below

(a) Both (A) and (R) are true and (R) is the correct explanation of (A).

(b) Both (A) and (R) are true but (R) is not the correct explanation of (A).

(c) (A) is true but (R) is false.

(d) (A) is false but (R) is true.

19. In the given exothermic reaction,

$CoCl_4^{2-}(aq) + 6H_2O(l) \rightleftharpoons [Co(H_2O)_6]^{2+} + 4Cl^-$

Which one of the following will decrease the equilibrium concentration of $CoCl_4^{2-}$?

(a) On increasing concentration of HCl.

(b) Increasing the concentration of $Co(NO_3)_2$.

(c) Increasing the amount of water.

(d) Enhancing the temperature.

20. The following reaction is performed at 25°C

$$2NO(g) + O_2(g) \rightleftharpoons 2NO_2(g)$$

The standard free energy of formation of NO(*g*) is 86.6 kJ/mol at 298 K. What is the standard free energy of formation of $NO_2(g)$ at 298 K? $(K_p = 1.6 \times 10^{12})$

(a) $0.5\,[-R \times 298 \ln(1.6 \times 10^{-12})]$

(b) $0.2\,[-R \times 298] + 0.5[86600]$

(c) $0.6\,[-R \times 298 \ln(86.6)]$

(d) $0.5\,[2 \times 86600 - R \times 298 \ln(1.6 \times 10^{12})]$

21. The equilibrium constants K_{p_1} and K_{p_2} for the reactions $X \rightleftharpoons 2Y$ and $Z \rightleftharpoons P + Q$, respectively are in the ratio of 1 : 8. If the degree of dissociation of *X* and *Z* be equal, then the ratio of total pressure at these equilibria is

(a) 1 : 9 (b) 1 : 32

(c) 1 : 1 (d) 1 : 3

22. The standard state Gibbs free energy change for the given isomerisation reaction

cis-2-butene $\rightleftharpoons$ *trans*-2-butene

is –11.5 kJ/mol at 300 K. If more amount of given *trans*-isomer is added to the reaction vessel, then

(a) equilibrium is shifted in the forward direction

(b) equilibrium remains unaffected

(c) more amount of *cis*-2-butene is formed

(d) more *trans*-2-butene is formed

23. The % yield of ammonia as a function of time in the reaction

$$N_2(g) + 3H_2(g) \rightleftharpoons 2NH_3(g), \Delta H < 0$$

at (p, T_1) is given below.

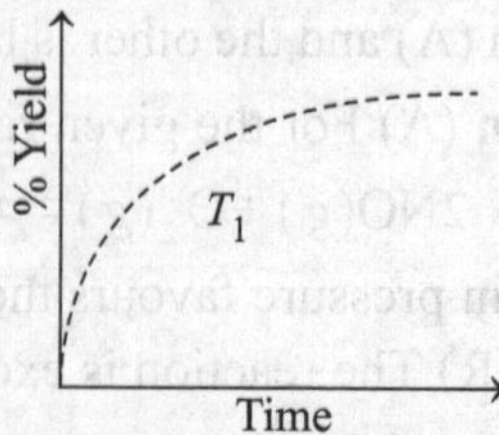

If this reaction is conducted at (p, T_2), with $T_2 > T_1$, the % yield of ammonia as a function of time is represented by

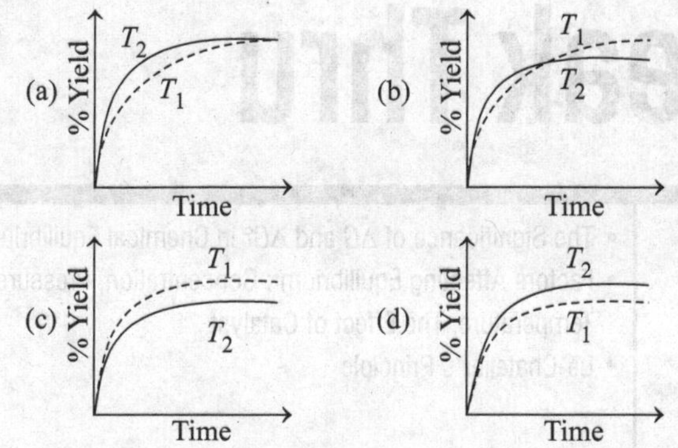

24. A 10 litre container at 300 K contains $CO_2(g)$ at pressure 0.2 atm and an excess of SrO (neglect the volume of solid SrO). The volume of the container is now decreased by moving the movable piston fitted in the container. The maximum volume of the container, when pressure of CO_2 attains its maximum value, will be

(Given that :

$SrCO_3(s) \rightleftharpoons SrO(s) + CO_2(g)$; $K_p = 0.800$ atm)

(a) 2.5 litre (b) 8 litre

(c) 5 litre (d) 20 litre

25. For the reaction, $N_2(g) + O_2(g) \rightleftharpoons 2NO(g)$, the production of NO will be favoured by

(a) high pressure

(b) low pressure

(c) presence of catalyst

(d) high concentration of N_2

Response Index

01	ⓐ	ⓑ	ⓒ	ⓓ	10	ⓐ	ⓑ	ⓒ	ⓓ	19	ⓐ	ⓑ	ⓒ	ⓓ
02	ⓐ	ⓑ	ⓒ	ⓓ	11	ⓐ	ⓑ	ⓒ	ⓓ	20	ⓐ	ⓑ	ⓒ	ⓓ
03	ⓐ	ⓑ	ⓒ	ⓓ	12	ⓐ	ⓑ	ⓒ	ⓓ	21	ⓐ	ⓑ	ⓒ	ⓓ
04	ⓐ	ⓑ	ⓒ	ⓓ	13	ⓐ	ⓑ	ⓒ	ⓓ	22	ⓐ	ⓑ	ⓒ	ⓓ
05	ⓐ	ⓑ	ⓒ	ⓓ	14	ⓐ	ⓑ	ⓒ	ⓓ	23	ⓐ	ⓑ	ⓒ	ⓓ
06	ⓐ	ⓑ	ⓒ	ⓓ	15	ⓐ	ⓑ	ⓒ	ⓓ	24	ⓐ	ⓑ	ⓒ	ⓓ
07	ⓐ	ⓑ	ⓒ	ⓓ	16	ⓐ	ⓑ	ⓒ	ⓓ	25	ⓐ	ⓑ	ⓒ	ⓓ
08	ⓐ	ⓑ	ⓒ	ⓓ	17	ⓐ	ⓑ	ⓒ	ⓓ					
09	ⓐ	ⓑ	ⓒ	ⓓ	18	ⓐ	ⓑ	ⓒ	ⓓ					

Performance Scanner

> 90% Excellent !	You have mastered these topics. The concepts of these topics are at your fingertips. Move on to the chapter test and maintain this momentum.
76-90% Very Good !	You have a good command over these topics. Revise these topics again after a few days and enhance your performance.
60-75% Good !	You have a wide scope to learn for these topics. Revise these topics again.
<60 Not Satisfactory!	You have a long way ahead of you to master these topics. Revise it thoroughly.

Chapter Break Thru

Syllabus

- Meaning of Equilibrium :The Concept of Dynamic Equilibrium
- Equilibrium Involving Physical Processes : Solid-Solid, Liquid-Gas and Solid-Gas Equilibrium, their Characteristics
- Law of Chemical Equilibrium
- Equilibrium Constant (K_p and K_C) and their Significance
- Significance of ΔG and $\Delta G°$ in Chemical Equilibrium
- The Significance of ΔG and $\Delta G°$ in Chemical Equilibrium
- Factors Affecting Equilibrium : Concentration, Pressure, Temperature, The Effect of Catalyst
- Le-Chatelier's Principle

Important Instructions

- The test is of 1 hour duration and contains 50 multiple choice questions (Four options with a single correct answer).
- Choose the correct option and fill the OMR given on the last page of test accordingly.
- At some instances, you may find more than 1 option may be correct. In such circumstances, you have to judge the most appropriate answer as per the conditions given in the question.

1. One mole of N_2O_4 gas at 300 K is kept in a closed container at 1 atm. It is heated to 600 K when 20% by mass of N_2O_4 decomposes to $NO_2(g)$. The resultant pressure in the container would be

(a) 2.4 atm (b) 24 atm
(c) 0.24 atm (d) 240 atm

2. The dissociation of PCl_5 take place as,

$$PCl_5(g) \rightleftharpoons PCl_3(g) + Cl_2(g)$$

If the degree of dissociation is α at equilibrium pressure p, the equilibrium constant for the reaction is

(a) $K_p = \dfrac{\alpha^2 p}{1-\alpha^2}$ (b) $K_p = \dfrac{\alpha p}{1-\alpha^2}$
(c) $\dfrac{\alpha^3 p^2}{1-\alpha^2}$ (d) $\dfrac{(\alpha p)^{1/2}}{1-\alpha^2}$

3. Given below are two statements.

Statement I Addition of inert gas at constant volume shifts the equilibrium toward lesser number of moles.

Statement II Addition of inert gas at constant pressure shifts the equilibrium toward larger number of moles.

In the light of above statements, choose the correct answer from the options given below

(a) Both Statement I and Statement II are incorrect.
(b) Statement I is correct but Statement II is incorrect.
(c) Statement I is incorrect but Statement II is correct.
(d) Both Statement I and Statement II are correct.

4. During thermal dissociation of a gas, the vapour density

(a) increases
(b) decreases
(c) remains constant
(d) change in both ways i.e. increases as well as decreases

5. If 340 g of a mixture of N_2 and H_2 in the correct ratio gave at 20% yield of NH_3, the mass produced would be

(a) 34 g (b) 60 g (c) 68 g (d) 124 g

6. Hydrolysis of sucrose gives,

Sucrose + $H_2O \rightleftharpoons$ Glucose + Fructose

Equilibrium constant K_C for the reaction is 2×10^{13} at 300 K. Gibbs energy change for this reaction at 300 K is

(a) -76×10^4 J/mol (b) -7.64×10^4 J/mol
(c) -7.64×10^3 J/mol (d) -76×10^3 J/mol

7. A cylinder provided with a piston has some PCl_5 which is in equilibrium with PCl_3 and Cl_2. The system is compressed with the help of piston. Which statement below is correct?
(a) Some more PCl_5 will decompose.
(b) The system remain unaffected.
(c) PCl_3 and Cl_2 will combine to form PCl_5.
(d) Explosion occurs.

8. Chemical equilibrium is a dynamic equilibrium because
(a) the rate of forward reaction is non zero.
(b) the rate of backward reaction is non zero.
(c) concentrations of reactants and products always keep changing.
(d) both forward and backward reactions occur simultaneously at the rate which is non zero.

9. Which of the following is a reversible reaction?
(a) $2Na(s) + H_2O(l) \longrightarrow 2NaOH(aq) + H_2(g)$
(b) $AgNO_3(aq) + HCl(aq) \longrightarrow AgCl(s) + HNO_3(aq)$
(c) $KNO_3(aq) + NaCl(aq) \longrightarrow KCl(aq) + NaNO_3(aq)$
(d) $Pb(NO_3)_2(aq) + 2NaI(aq) \longrightarrow PbI_2(s) + 2NaNO_3(aq)$

10. In the gaseous equilibrium, $A + 2B \rightleftharpoons C + \text{heat}$; the forward reaction is favoured
(a) low p, high T (b) low p, low T
(c) high p, low T (d) high p, high T

11. The equilibrium constant for the following reaction is 10.5 at 500 K. A system at equilibrium has $[CO] = 0.25$ M and $[H_2] = 0.12$ M. What is concentration of CH_3OH?
(a) 0.0378 (b) 0.0435
(c) 0.5461 (d) 0.0499

12. At 527°C, the reaction given below has $K_C = 4$

$$NH_3(g) \rightleftharpoons \frac{1}{2}N_2(g) + \frac{3}{2}H_2(g)$$

What is the value of K_p for the reaction?

$$N_2(g) + 3H_2(g) \rightleftharpoons 2NH_3(g)$$

(a) $16 \times (800\,R)^2$ (b) $\left(\frac{800R}{4}\right)^{-2}$
(c) $\left(\frac{1}{4 \times 800R}\right)^2$ (d) $64 \times \left(\frac{1}{800R}\right)^2$

13. Which of the following is not true for solid-liquid equilibrium?
(a) It can be established at any given temperature.
(b) The mass of solid does not change with time.
(c) The mass of liquid does not change with time.
(d) There is no exchange of heat between the system and its surroundings.

14. Which of the following reactions will not get affected on increasing the pressure?
(a) $2H_2(g) + CO(g) \rightleftharpoons CH_3OH(g)$
(b) $4NH_3(g) + 5O_2(g) \rightleftharpoons 4NO(g) + 6H_2O(g)$
(c) $CH_4(g) + 2S_2(g) \rightleftharpoons CS_2(g) + 2H_2S(g)$
(d) $PCl_5(g) \rightleftharpoons PCl_3(g) + Cl_2(g)$

15. When a catalyst is added to a reversible reaction,
(a) it increases the forward reaction's speed only
(b) it increases forward reaction speed more than backward reaction speed
(c) it increases the value of equilibrium constant
(d) equilibrium is not disturbed but attained quickly

16. In the synthesis of ammonia by Haber's process, the addition of inert gas favours
(a) forward reaction
(b) backward reaction
(c) no effect on equilibrium
(d) favours both forward and backward reaction

17. Given below are two statements, one is labelled as Assertion (A) and other is Reason (R).
Assertion (A) When $Q_C = K_C$, reaction is in equilibrium.
Reason (R) At equilibrium, $\Delta G = 0$.
In the light of above statements, choose the correct answer from the options given below
(a) Both (A) and (R) are true and (R) is the correct explanation of (A).
(b) Both (A) and (R) are true but (R) is not the correct explanation of (A).
(c) (A) is true but (R) is false.
(d) (A) is false but (R) is true.

18. The equilibrium constant for the synthesis of HI at 490°C is 50.0. The value of K of the dissociation of HI will be
(a) 50 (b) 2
(c) 20 (d) 0.02

19. With increase in temperature, equilibrium constant of a reaction

(a) always increases
(b) may increase or decrease depending on whether the reaction is endothermic or exothermic
(c) always decreases
(d) remains constant

20. For the given reaction, the unit of K_p will be

$$2NH_3(g) \rightleftharpoons N_2(g) + 3H_2(g)$$

(a) atm^3 (b) atm^{-2} (c) atm^{-4} (d) atm^2

21. The equilibrium constant of a reaction is 300. If the volume of the reaction flask is tripled, the equilibrium constant will be

(a) 300 (b) 200 (c) 600 (d) 1500

22. Given below are two statements, one is labelled as Assertion (A) and other as Reason (R).

Assertion (A) The value of K gives us a relative idea about the extent to which the reaction proceeds.

Reason (R) The value of K is independent of the stoichiometry of the reactant and the product at the point of equilibrium.

In the light of above statements, choose the correct answer from the options given below

(a) Both (A) and (R) are true and (R) is the correct explanation of (A).
(b) Both (A) and (R) are true but (R) is not the correct explanation of (A).
(c) (A) is true but (R) is false.
(d) (A) is false but (R) is true.

23. For the reaction,

$$SnO_2(s) + 2H_2(g) \rightleftharpoons 2H_2O(g) + Sn(l)$$

at 900 K, the equilibrium steam-hydrogen mixture was found to be 40% H_2 by volume. The K_p is

(a) 1.15 (b) 2.25 (c) 8.25 (d) 9

24. In the equilibrium, $N_2O_4(g) \rightleftharpoons 2NO_2(g)$ when 5 moles of each is taken and the temperature is kept at 298 K, the total pressure was found to be 20 bar [$\Delta G_f^\circ (N_2O_4) = 100$ kJ, $\Delta G_f^\circ (NO_2) = 50$ kJ]. The reaction will be

(a) forward (b) backward
(c) equilibrium (d) cannot predict

25. Given below are two statements, one is labelled as Assertion (A) and other as Reason (R).

Assertion (A) If reaction quotient (Q_C) is less than the equilibrium constant (K_C), the equilibrium tends to shift in the direction of product.

Reason (R) The expression for equilibrium constant is different than the expression for reaction quotient.

In the light of above statements, choose the correct answer from the options given below

(a) Both (A) and (R) are true and (R) is the correct explanation of (A).
(b) Both (A) and (R) are true but (R) is not the correct explanation of (A).
(c) (A) is true but (R) is false.
(d) (A) is false but (R) is true.

26. Given below are two statements, one is labelled as Assertion (A) and the other is labelled as Reason (R).

Assertion (A) K_p can be less than, greater than or equal to K_C.

Reason (R) $K_p = K_C(RT)^{\Delta n}$ Relation between K_p and K_C depends on the change in the number of moles of gaseous reactants and product (Δn).

In the light of the above statements, choose the correct answer from the options given below

(a) Both (A) and (R) are true and (R) is the correct explanation of (A).
(b) Both (A) and (R) are true but (R) is not the correct explanation of (A).
(c) (A) is true but (R) is false.
(d) (A) is false but (R) is true.

27. 5 mole of PCl_5 is heated in a closed 5 dm^3 vessel. At equilibrium, 40% of PCl_5 is dissociated into PCl_3 and Cl_2. Then what will be the equilibrium constant.

(a) 0.266 (b) 0.133
(c) 0.334 (d) 0.533

28. When 3 moles of A and 1 mole of B are mixed in 1 litre vessel the following reaction takes place,

$$A(g) + B(g) \rightleftharpoons 2C(g)$$

1.5 moles of C are formed. The equilibrium constant for the reaction is

(a) 4 (b) 0.4 (c) 0.004 (d) 40

29. Given below are two statements.

Statement I In Bosch process for manufacture of H_2 from water gas, pressure has no effect on equilibrium.

Statement II If the initial concentration of reactants in a reaction increase, then the value of equilibrium constant also increases.

In the light of above statements, choose the correct answer from the options given below

(a) Both Statement I and Statement II are incorrect.
(b) Statement I is correct but Statement II is incorrect.
(c) Statement I is incorrect but Statement II is correct.
(d) Both Statement I and Statement II are correct.

30. XY_2 dissociated as $XY_2(g) \rightleftharpoons XY(g) + Y(g)$, When the initial pressure of XY_2 is 600 mm Hg, the total equilibrium pressure is 800 mm Hg. Calculate K_p for the reaction, assuming that the volume of the system remains unchanged.

(a) 10 (b) 0.100
(c) 100 (d) 60

31. The equilibrium constant for the reaction,

$2G + J \rightleftharpoons D + 2T$ is 1.5×10^{-3}.

When 1 mole of *G*, 2 mole of *J* and 0.5 mole of *D* are put in a 1.0 L flask and allowed to reach equilibrium, then the equilibrium concentration of *T* is

(a) 0.087 M (b) 0.077 M
(c) 0.05 M (d) 0.5 M

32. $K_p = 63$ atm at 100 K for the given reaction,

$C(s) + CO_2(g) \longrightarrow 2CO(g)$

If at equilibrium, $p_{CO} = 10 p_{CO_2}$, then total pressure of gas at equilibrium is

(a) 5.91 atm (b) 69 atm
(c) 0.069 atm (d) 6.93 atm

33. For the reaction, $AB(g) \rightleftharpoons A(g) + B(g)$, *AB* is 33% dissociated at a total pressure of *p*. Therefore *p* is related to K_p by which relation?

(a) $p = 4K_p$ (b) $p = \frac{1}{K_p}$
(c) $p = 16K_p^2$ (d) $p = 8K_p$

34. Given below are two statements.

Statement I At high pressure, melting of ice is favoured.

Statement II Density of ice is less than of water.

In the light of above statements, choose the correct answer from the options given below

(a) Both Statement I and Statement II are incorrect.
(b) Statement I is correct but Statement II is incorrect.
(c) Statement I is incorrect but Statement II is correct.
(d) Both Statement I and Statement II are correct.

35. For the chemical reaction,

$3X(g) + Y(g) \rightleftharpoons X_3Y(g)$

the amount of X_3Y at equilibrium is affected by

(a) temperature and pressure
(b) temperature only
(c) pressure only
(d) temperature, pressure and catalyst

36. Given below is an exothermic reaction,

$CoCl_4^{2-}(aq) + 6H_2O(l) \rightleftharpoons [Co(H_2O)_6]^{2+} + 4Cl^-$

Which one of the following will decreases the equilibrium concentration of $CoCl_4^{2-}$?

(a) Addition of HCl.
(b) Addition of $Co(NO_3)_2$.
(c) The solution is diluted with water.
(d) The temperature is increased.

37. Match List-I with List-II

List-I (Reaction)	List-II (K_p/K_C)
A. $A_2(g) + 3B_2(g) \rightleftharpoons 2AB_3(g)$	I. $(RT)^{-2}$
B. $A_2(g) + B_2(g) \rightleftharpoons 2AB(g)$	II. $(RT)^0$
C. $A(s) + \frac{3}{2}B_2(g) \rightleftharpoons AB_3(g)$	III. $(RT)^{1/2}$
D. $AB_2(g) \rightleftharpoons A(g) + \frac{1}{2}B_2(g)$	IV. $(RT)^{-3/2}$

Choose the correct answer from the options given below.

(a) A-II, B-I, C-IV, D-III
(b) A-I, B-II, C-IV, D-III
(c) A-I, B-II, C-III, D-IV
(d) A-II, B-IV, C-I, D-III

38. Reactions that have standard free energy changes less than zero, always have equilibrium constant
(a) equal to zero
(b) greater than one
(c) equal to one
(d) less than one

39. Sodium sulphate dissolves in water with evolution of heat. Consider a saturated solution of sodium sulphate. If the temperature is raised, then according to Le-Chatelier principle
(a) more solid will dissolve
(b) some solid will precipitate out from the solution
(c) the solution will become supersaturated
(d) solution concentration remains unchanged

40. 1.7 g of $NH_3(g)$ is present in a 2 L flask. The active mass of $NH_3(g)$ is
(a) 0.1 M (b) 0.02 M
(c) 0.05 M (d) 0.5 M

41. Consider the following reaction,
$$2NO_2(g) \longrightarrow 2NO(g) + O_2(g)$$
In the figure given below, identify the curves X, Y and Z associated with the three species in the reaction.

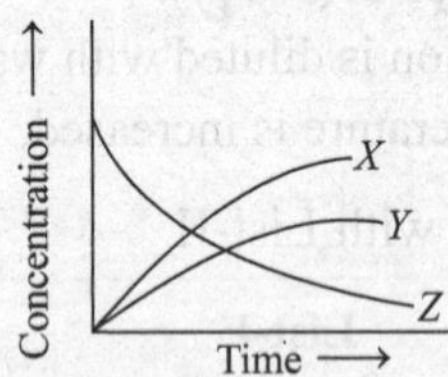

(a) $X = NO, Y = O_2, Z = NO_2$
(b) $X = O_2, Y = NO, Z = NO_2$
(c) $X = NO_2, Y = NO, Z = O_2$
(d) $X = O_2, Y = NO_2, Z = NO$

42. Consider the following reaction,
$$SO_2(g) + \frac{1}{2}O_2(g) \overset{K_1}{\rightleftharpoons} SO_3(g)$$
$$2SO_3(g) \overset{K_2}{\rightleftharpoons} 2SO_2(g) + O_2(g)$$
What is the relation between K_1 and K_2?
(a) $K_1 = \frac{1}{K_2}$ (b) $K_1 = \frac{1}{\sqrt{K_2}}$
(c) $K_1 = K_2$ (d) $K_1 = \frac{1}{K_2^2}$

43. Which of the following graph represents an exothermic reaction ?

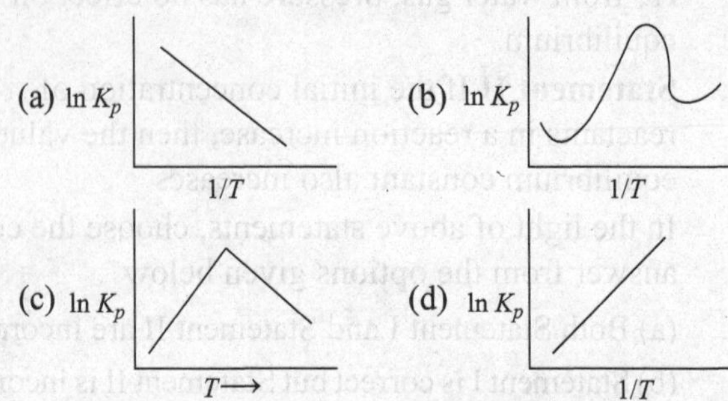

44. 1 mole of N_2 is mixed with 3 moles of H_2 in 1 litre container. If 50% of N_2 is converted into ammonia by the following reaction,
$$N_2(g) + 3H_2(g) \rightleftharpoons 2NH_3(g)$$
Then the total number of moles of gas at the equilibrium are
(a) 1.5 (b) 4.5
(c) 3.0 (d) 6.0

45. The vapour density of N_2O_4 at a certain temperature is 30. The percentage dissociation of N_2O_4 at this temperature is
(a) 25%
(b) 50.5%
(c) 53.3%
(d) 62%

46. Match List-I with List-II.

List-I (Relation)	List-II (Conclusion)
A. $Q = K$	I. Reaction is nearer to completion.
B. $Q < K$	II. Reaction is not at equilibrium.
C. $Q > K$	III. Reaction is fast in forward direction.
D. $K >> 1$	IV. Reaction is at equilibrium.

Choose the correct answer from the options given below.
(a) A-IV, B-III, C-II, D-I
(b) A-II, B-I, C-IV, D-III
(c) A-II, B-III, C-IV, D-I
(d) A-IV, B-I, C-III, D-II

47. Calculate the pressure of CO_2 gas at 700 K in the following heterogeneous equilibrium reaction,

$$CaCO_3(s) \rightleftharpoons CaO(s) + CO_2(g)$$

If $\Delta G°$ for this reaction is 83.14 kJ/mol.
[Given $R = 8.314$ J/K/mol]

(a) 6.30×10^{-8} atm (b) 6.30×10^{-7} atm
(c) 6.30×10^{-4} atm (d) 3.14×10^{-7} atm

48. Given below are two statements, one is labelled as Assertion (A) and the other is labelled as Reason (R).

Assertion (A) For any chemical reaction at a particular temperature the equilibrium constant is fixed and is a characteristic property.

Reason (R) Equilibrium constant is independent of temperature.

In the light of the above statements, choose the correct answer from the options given below.

(a) Both (A) and (R) are true and (R) is the correct explanation of (A).
(b) Both (A) and (R) are true but (R) is not the correct explanation of (A).
(c) (A) is true but (R) is false.
(d) (A) is false but (R) is true.

49. Which of the following statements are true for the given equilibrium reaction?

$$N_2(g) + O_2(g) \rightleftharpoons 2NO(g);\ \Delta H = 180\,\text{kJ mol}^{-1}$$

(i) The formation of NO is increased at higher temperature.
(ii) The volume change at constant pressure does not affect the equilibrium.
(iii) The pressure change at constant volume does not affect the equilibrium.
(iv) The formation of NO is decreased at higher temperature.
(v) No effect is observed on the addition of inert gas at constant pressure and volume.

Choose the correct option.

(a) (i), (iii) and (iv)
(b) (i), (ii), (iii) and (v)
(c) (i), (iv) and (v)
(d) (ii), (iii) and (v)

50. Which of the following is not correct about chemical equilibrium?

(a) At equilibrium the concentration of each of the reactants and the products becomes constant.
(b) At equilibrium, the rate of forward reaction becomes equal to the rate of backward reaction, and hence, the equilibrium is dynamic in nature.
(c) A chemical equilibrium can be established only if none of the products is allowed to escape out or separate out as a solid.
(d) Chemical equilibrium for the reversible reaction $N_2 + 3H_2 \rightleftharpoons 2NH_3$ can be attained from forward direction only.

Response Index

01 ⓐ ⓑ ⓒ ⓓ	14 ⓐ ⓑ ⓒ ⓓ	27 ⓐ ⓑ ⓒ ⓓ	40 ⓐ ⓑ ⓒ ⓓ
02 ⓐ ⓑ ⓒ ⓓ	15 ⓐ ⓑ ⓒ ⓓ	28 ⓐ ⓑ ⓒ ⓓ	41 ⓐ ⓑ ⓒ ⓓ
03 ⓐ ⓑ ⓒ ⓓ	16 ⓐ ⓑ ⓒ ⓓ	29 ⓐ ⓑ ⓒ ⓓ	42 ⓐ ⓑ ⓒ ⓓ
04 ⓐ ⓑ ⓒ ⓓ	17 ⓐ ⓑ ⓒ ⓓ	30 ⓐ ⓑ ⓒ ⓓ	43 ⓐ ⓑ ⓒ ⓓ
05 ⓐ ⓑ ⓒ ⓓ	18 ⓐ ⓑ ⓒ ⓓ	31 ⓐ ⓑ ⓒ ⓓ	44 ⓐ ⓑ ⓒ ⓓ
06 ⓐ ⓑ ⓒ ⓓ	19 ⓐ ⓑ ⓒ ⓓ	32 ⓐ ⓑ ⓒ ⓓ	45 ⓐ ⓑ ⓒ ⓓ
07 ⓐ ⓑ ⓒ ⓓ	20 ⓐ ⓑ ⓒ ⓓ	33 ⓐ ⓑ ⓒ ⓓ	46 ⓐ ⓑ ⓒ ⓓ
08 ⓐ ⓑ ⓒ ⓓ	21 ⓐ ⓑ ⓒ ⓓ	34 ⓐ ⓑ ⓒ ⓓ	47 ⓐ ⓑ ⓒ ⓓ
09 ⓐ ⓑ ⓒ ⓓ	22 ⓐ ⓑ ⓒ ⓓ	35 ⓐ ⓑ ⓒ ⓓ	48 ⓐ ⓑ ⓒ ⓓ
10 ⓐ ⓑ ⓒ ⓓ	23 ⓐ ⓑ ⓒ ⓓ	36 ⓐ ⓑ ⓒ ⓓ	49 ⓐ ⓑ ⓒ ⓓ
11 ⓐ ⓑ ⓒ ⓓ	24 ⓐ ⓑ ⓒ ⓓ	37 ⓐ ⓑ ⓒ ⓓ	50 ⓐ ⓑ ⓒ ⓓ
12 ⓐ ⓑ ⓒ ⓓ	25 ⓐ ⓑ ⓒ ⓓ	38 ⓐ ⓑ ⓒ ⓓ	
13 ⓐ ⓑ ⓒ ⓓ	26 ⓐ ⓑ ⓒ ⓓ	39 ⓐ ⓑ ⓒ ⓓ	

Performance Scanner

> 90% Excellent !	You have mastered this chapter. The concepts of this chapter are at your fingertips. Move on to the next chapter and maintain this momentum.
76-90% Very Good !	You have a good command over this topic. Revise the chapter again after a few days and enhance your performance.
60-75% Good !	You have a wide scope to learn for this chapter. Revise this chapter again.
<60 Not Satisfactory!	You have a long way ahead of you to master this chapter. Revise it thoroughly.

Scan for Online **Chapter Test**

Space for Rough Work

Test Booklet No. **3947207**

Test Booklet Code **CH7**

NEET Self Assessment Kit

Ionic Equilibrium

Topics Covered

- Acid-Base Concepts and Ostwald's Dilution Law
- Solubility Product and Common Ion Effect
- pH, Buffer and Salt Hydrolysis

Important Instructions

- This Booklet Contains – 3 Topic Tests and One Test on Complete Chapter.
- Each question carries 4 marks.
- For each correct response the candidate will get 4 marks and for every incorrect response 1 mark will be additionally deducted from the total score.
- Use **Blue/Black** point pen only for filling the OMR.
- Rough work is to be done in the space provided for this purpose in the test booklet only.

Name of the Candidate (In Capitals) ____________

Candidate's Signature ____________

Invigilator's Signature ____________

Facsimile signature stamp of center superintendent____________

Do not open this Booklet until you start attempting the Test

Topical Follow Thru

Test 1

Syllabus
- Various Concepts of Acids and Bases (Arrhenius, Bronsted-Lowry and Lewis)
- Weak and Strong Electrolytes
- Acid-Base
- Ionisation of Electrolytes
- Ionisation Constants
- Ionisation of Water

For deeper insight **Scan the QR Code**

Important Instructions
- The test is of 30 minutes duration and contains 15 multiple choice questions (Four options with a single correct answer).
- Choose the correct option and fill the OMR given on the last page of test accordingly.
- At some instances, you may find more than 1 option may be correct. In such circumstances, you have to judge the most appropriate answer as per conditions given in the question.

1. Arrange the following conjugate bases in the decreasing order of their basic strength.

$$OH^-, Cl^-, RO^-, CH_3COO^-$$

Choose the correct answer from the options given below.

(a) $OH^- > RO^- > Cl^- > CH_3COO^-$
(b) $Cl^- > CH_3COO^- > OH^- > RO^-$
(c) $RO^- > OH^- > CH_3COO^- > Cl^-$
(d) $CH_3COO^- > RO^- > OH^- > Cl^-$

2. According to Lewis-base concept, the correct trend of the acidic strength is

(a) $HClO_4 < HClO_3 < HClO_2$
(b) $HClO_4 > HClO_3 > HClO_2$
(c) $HClO_2 = HClO_3 = HClO_4$
(d) $HClO_2 > HClO_4 > HClO_3$

3. Choose the incorrect statement from the following.

(a) Boric acid acts as a base and water as an acid in the reaction.

$$B(OH)_3(aq) + H_2O(l) \rightleftharpoons B(OH)_4^- + H^+$$

(b) BF_3 and $AlCl_3$ do not have any hydrogen and hence behave as acid.

(c) Arrhenius theory cannot explain the basic nature of certain salts like PH_3, NH_3.

(d) Cl^- and NO_3^- are conjugate acids of HCl and HNO_3 respectively.

4. CH_3COOH is considered as a weak acid but it can behave as strong acid as compare to which of the following species?

(a) HNO_3 (b) H_3PO_4
(c) NH_3 (d) H_3O^+

5. Given below are two statements.

Statement I HNO_2 is an Arrhenius acid in

$$HNO_2(aq) \rightleftharpoons H^+(aq) + NO_2^-(aq)$$

Statement II HNO_2 acts as Bronsted-Lowry base in

$$HNO_2(l) + H_2O(aq) \rightleftharpoons H_3O^+(aq) + NO_2^-(aq)$$

In the light of above statements, choose the correct answer from the options given below.

(a) Both Statement I and Statement II are incorrect.
(b) Statement I is correct but Statement II is incorrect
(c) Statement I is incorrect but Statement II is correct.
(d) Both Statement I and Statement II are correct.

6. Consider the following reaction.

$$\underset{[A]}{[Al(H_2O)_6]^{3+}} + \underset{[B]}{HCO_3^-} \rightleftharpoons \underset{[C]}{[Al(H_2O)_5OH]^{2+}} + \underset{[D]}{H_2CO_3}$$

Choose the species which behave as Bronsted-Lowry acids from the options given below.

(a) A, B, D (b) B, C, D
(c) A, C, D (d) A, D

7. Given below are two statements, one is labelled as Assertion (A) and the other is labelled as Reason (R).

Assertion (A) $H_2PO_3^-$, HPO_3^{2-} and HCO_3^- are the amphiprotic species.

Reason (R) Amphiprotic species are those which act as proton acceptor as well as proton donor.

In the light of the above statements, choose the correct answer from the options given below.

(a) Both (A) and (R) are true and (R) is the correct explanation of (A).
(b) Both (A) and (R) are true but (R) is not the correct explanation of (A).
(c) (A) is true but (R) is false.
(d) (A) is false but (R) is true.

8. When 100 mL of 1 M HCl is mixed with 50 mL of 2M HCl, then the concentration of H_3O^+ ion is

(a) 0.013 M (b) 0.13 M
(c) 3.01 M (d) 1.33 M

9. Given below are certain reactions.

A. $HF(aq) + NH_3(aq) \rightleftharpoons NH_4^+(aq) + F^-(aq)$
B. $HSO_4^-(aq) + CN^-(aq) \rightleftharpoons HCN(aq) + SO_4^{2-}(aq)$
C. $H_2CO_3(aq) + HSO_4^-(aq) \rightleftharpoons H_2SO_4(aq) + HCO_3^-(aq)$
D. $HF(aq) + Cl^-(aq) \rightleftharpoons HCl(aq) + F^-(aq)$

The reactions proceeding to the forward direction are

(a) A and B
(b) B and D
(c) A, B and C
(d) C and D

10. The value of ionisation constant of weak bases at particular temperature are given below.

$A = 5.14 \times 10^{-4}$ $B = 1.13 \times 10^{-14}$
$C = 1.67 \times 10^{-9}$ $D = 1.67 \times 10^{-6}$

Choose the correct order of their basic strength from the options given below.

(a) $A > D > C > B$
(b) $D > B > C > A$
(c) $C > B > D > A$
(d) $B > C > D > A$

11. The concentration of solution of sulphuric acid is 0.2 M.

Given, $H_2SO_4 \longrightarrow H^+ + HSO_4^-$ (strong)

$HSO_4^- \rightleftharpoons H^+ + SO_4^{2-}, K_a = 1.3 \times 10^{-2}$

The concentration of H^+, HSO_4^- and SO_4^{2-} will be respectively.

(a) 1.1×10^{-2} M, 0.116 M and 0.187 M
(b) 0.2116 M, 0.0116 M and 0.188 M
(c) 1.81 M, 2.15 M and 0.301 M
(d) 0.213 M, 0.012 M and 0.13 M

12. The value of K_a for the acid HA is 1.0×10^{-6}.

For the reaction, $A^- + H_3O^+ \rightleftharpoons HA + H_2O$

The value of K is

(a) 1.0×10^{-3} (b) 1.0×10^{6}
(c) 1.0×10^{8} (d) 1.0×10^{-8}

13. Consider the following reaction.

$(CH_3)_3N + H_2O \rightleftharpoons (CH_3)_3NH^+ + OH^-$

The concentration of $(CH_3)_3N$ is 1.02 M and the value of K_b is 6.2×10^{-5}. What will be the concentration of $[(CH_3)_3NH^+]$?

(a) 7.02×10^{-5} M
(b) 12.06×10^{-10} M
(c) 7.95×10^{-3} M
(d) 1.12×10^{-4} M

14. Given below are two statements.

Statement I If autoprotolysis constant of a weak acid HA is 4×10^{-8}, then $[A^-]$ is 2×10^{-4} M.

Statement II Autoprotolysis constant of NH_3 is $[NH_4^+][NH_2^-]$.

In the light of the above statements, choose the correct answer from the options given below.

(a) Both Statement I and Statement II are incorrect.
(b) Statement I is correct but Statement II is incorrect.
(c) Statement I is incorrect but Statement II is correct.
(d) Both Statement I and Statement II are correct.

15. Consider the following equilibrium,

$$NH_4^+ + H_2O \rightleftharpoons NH_4OH + H^+$$

The equilibrium constant for this reaction is 5.55×10^{-10}.

Then, the value of equilibrium constant will be

(a) 1.08×10^{-6} (b) 1.8×10^{-5}
(c) 5.5×10^{-10} (d) 1.5×10^{-10}

Response Index

01	a	b	c	d	10	a	b	c	d	19	a	b	c	d
02	a	b	c	d	11	a	b	c	d	20	a	b	c	d
03	a	b	c	d	12	a	b	c	d	21	a	b	c	d
04	a	b	c	d	13	a	b	c	d	22	a	b	c	d
05	a	b	c	d	14	a	b	c	d	23	a	b	c	d
06	a	b	c	d	15	a	b	c	d	24	a	b	c	d
07	a	b	c	d	16	a	b	c	d	25	a	b	c	d
08	a	b	c	d	17	a	b	c	d					
09	a	b	c	d	18	a	b	c	d					

Performance Scanner

> 90% Excellent !	You have mastered these topics. The concepts of these topics are at your fingertips. Move on to the next test and maintain this momentum.
76-90% Very Good !	You have a good command over these topics. Revise these topics again after a few days and enhance your performance.
60-75% Good !	You have a wide scope to learn for these topics. Revise these topics again.
<60 Not Satisfactory!	You have a long way ahead of you to master these topics. Revise it thoroughly.

Test 2

Syllabus
- Solubility of Sparingly Soluble Salts and Solubility Products
- Common Ion Effect

For deeper insight **Scan the QR Code**

Important Instructions
- The test is of 30 minutes duration and contains 15 multiple choice questions (Four options with a single correct answer).
- Choose the correct option and fill the OMR given on the last page of test accordingly.
- At some instances, you may find more than 1 option may be correct. In such circumstances, you have to judge the most appropriate answer as per conditions given in the question.

1. If solubility of $BaSO_4$ in aqueous solution is 1×10^{-5} M, then the solubility in 0.1 M $BaCl_2$ is

(a) 1×10^{-2} M (b) 1×10^{-4} M
(c) 1×10^{-6} M (d) 1×10^{6} M

2. Given below are two statements, one is labelled as Assertion (A) and the other is labelled as Reason (R).

Assertion (A) Molar solubility of $Al(OH)_3$ is increased in the presence of both NaOH and HCl.

Reason (R) $Al(OH)_3$ is amphoteric, it can react with both of them.

In the light of the above statements, choose the correct answer from the options given below.

(a) Both (A) and (R) are true and (R) is the correct explanation of (A).
(b) Both (A) and (R) are true but (R) is not the correct explanation of (A).
(c) (A) is true but (R) is false.
(d) (A) is false but (R) is true.

3. If the solubility of $Ca(OH)_2$ is $\sqrt{3}$, then its solubility product will be

(a) $3\sqrt{3}$ (b) $12\sqrt{3}$
(c) $4\sqrt{3}$ (d) 3

4. Given below are two statements.

Statement I A solution is super saturated if $Q > K_{sp}$.

Statement II For PbI_2, the value of solubility product is $2S^3$.

In the light of above statements, choose the correct answer from the options given below.

(a) Both Statement I and Statement II are incorrect
(b) Statement I is correct but Statement II is incorrect.
(c) Statement I is incorrect but Statement II is correct.
(d) Both Statement I and Statement II are correct.

5. The minimum volume of water required to dissolve 1g of calcium sulphate at 298 K is (For calcium sulphate, $K_{sp} = 9\times10^{-6}$)

(a) 4.13 L
(b) 2.52 L
(c) 3×10^{-3} L
(d) 2.45 L

6. Match List-I with List-II.

	List-I (Solute)	List-II (K_{sp} related to solubility)
A.	Ag_2CrO_4	I. $K_{sp} = 108S^5$
B.	$Fe(OH)_3$	II. $K_{sp} = 4S^3$
C.	$BaCrO_4$	III. $K_{sp} = S^2$
D.	$Ca_3(PO_4)_2$	IV. $K_{sp} = 27S^4$

Choose the correct answer from the options given below.
(a) A-II, B-IV, C-III, D-I
(b) A-IV, B-II, C-III, D-I
(c) A-I, B-IV, C-II, D-III
(d) A-III, B-I, C-IV, D-II

7. K_{sp} of $Mg(OH)_2$ is 1.8×10^{-11} at 32°C. At pH $=12$, its molar solubility is
(a) 1.34×10^{-5} M (b) 1.6×10^{-11} M
(c) 1.8×10^{-7} M (d) 1.7×10^{-9} M

8. Choose the incorrect statement from the following.
(a) Silver chloride is more soluble in aqueous ammonia than water.
(b) Solubility of Ag_2CrO_4 is decreased in the presence of AgCl instead of $AgNO_3$.
(c) The common ion-effect is based on Le-Chatelier's principle.
(d) Completeness of precipitation is favoured by small value of K_{sp} and high concentration of common ion.

9. The maximum pH that can be established in $Ca(OH)_2(aq)$ is ....
$Ca(OH)_2 \rightleftharpoons Ca^{2+}(aq)+2OH^-(aq)$; $K_{sp}=5.5\times10^{-6}$
(a) 1.72 (b) 11.66
(c) 1.65 (d) 12.35

10. The solubility product of CuS, CdS and HgS are $10^{-31}, 10^{-44}$ and 10^{-54} respectively. The solubility of these sulphides are in the order
(a) CdS > HgS > CuS
(b) HgS > CdS > CuS
(c) CdS > CuS > HgS
(d) CuS > CdS > HgS

11. Given below are some sulphides with their K_{sp} values, which compound have solubility in range of 10^{-14} M to 10^{-20} M ?
I. CuS ($K_{sp}=8\times10^{-37}$)
II. MnS($K_{sp}=7\times10^{-16}$)
III. Bi_2S_3 ($K_{sp}=1\times10^{-70}$)
IV. Ag_2S($K_{sp}=6\times10^{-51}$)
V. FeS($K_{sp}=1\times10^{-16}$)

Choose the most appropriate answer from the options given below.
(a) Only I and II
(b) I, III and IV
(c) Only II
(d) Only III and IV

12. The solubility product constant of Ag_2CrO_4 and AgBr are 1.1×10^{-12} and 5×10^{-13} respectively. The ratio of solubility of Ag_2CrO_4 to AgBr is
(a) 92 : 1
(b) 1 : 5
(c) 7 : 2
(d) 0.92 : 10

13. 0.150 L of 0.10 M $Pb(NO_3)_2$ and 0.1 L of 0.20 M NaCl are mixed. The K_{sp} of $PbCl_2$ is 1.2×10^{-5}.
Choose the correct observation regarding the above statement.
(a) Precipitate of $PbCl_2$ will form.
(b) Precipitate of $PbCl_2$ will not form.
(c) Their resultant concentrations are not affected.
(d) The concentration of Pb^{2+} and Cl^- are equal.

14. Consider the following statements.
Statement I Cu(II) reacts with sulphide ions extremely quickly to give a solid.
Statement II The equilibrium constant of $Cu^{2+}(aq)+S^{2-}(aq) \rightleftharpoons CuS(s)$ is high, as the solubility product is low.
Choose the correct answer from the options given below.
(a) Both Statement I and Statement II are incorrect.
(b) Statement I is correct but Statement II is incorrect.
(c) Statement I is incorrect but Statement II is correct.
(d) Both Statement I and Statement II are correct.

15. Given below are two statements, one is labelled as Assertion (A) and the other is labelled as Reason (R).

Assertion (A) The solubility of AgCl is minimum in 0.01 M $CaCl_2$ than 0.001 M $AgNO_3$.

Reason (R) Due to common ion effect, solubility of AgCl is decreased.

In the light of the above statements, choose the correct answer from the options given below.

(a) Both (A) and (R) are true and (R) is the correct explanation of (A).

(b) Both (A) and (R) are true but (R) is not the correct explanation of (A).

(c) (A) is true but (R) is false.

(d) (A) is false but (R) is true.

Response Index

01	ⓐ ⓑ ⓒ ⓓ	10	ⓐ ⓑ ⓒ ⓓ	19	ⓐ ⓑ ⓒ ⓓ
02	ⓐ ⓑ ⓒ ⓓ	11	ⓐ ⓑ ⓒ ⓓ	20	ⓐ ⓑ ⓒ ⓓ
03	ⓐ ⓑ ⓒ ⓓ	12	ⓐ ⓑ ⓒ ⓓ	21	ⓐ ⓑ ⓒ ⓓ
04	ⓐ ⓑ ⓒ ⓓ	13	ⓐ ⓑ ⓒ ⓓ	22	ⓐ ⓑ ⓒ ⓓ
05	ⓐ ⓑ ⓒ ⓓ	14	ⓐ ⓑ ⓒ ⓓ	23	ⓐ ⓑ ⓒ ⓓ
06	ⓐ ⓑ ⓒ ⓓ	15	ⓐ ⓑ ⓒ ⓓ	24	ⓐ ⓑ ⓒ ⓓ
07	ⓐ ⓑ ⓒ ⓓ	16	ⓐ ⓑ ⓒ ⓓ	25	ⓐ ⓑ ⓒ ⓓ
08	ⓐ ⓑ ⓒ ⓓ	17	ⓐ ⓑ ⓒ ⓓ		
09	ⓐ ⓑ ⓒ ⓓ	18	ⓐ ⓑ ⓒ ⓓ		

Performance Scanner

> 90% Excellent !	You have mastered these topics. The concepts of these topics are at your fingertips. Move on to the next test and maintain this momentum.
76-90% Very Good !	You have a good command over these topics. Revise these topics again after a few days and enhance your performance.
60-75% Good !	You have a wide scope to learn for these topics. Revise these topics again.
<60 Not Satisfactory!	You have a long way ahead of you to master these topics. Revise it thoroughly.

Test 3

Syllabus
- pH Scale
- Hydrolysis of Salts
- pH of Solutions
- Buffer Solutions

For deeper insight **Scan the QR Code**

Important Instructions
- The test is of 30 minutes duration and contains 15 multiple choice questions (Four options with a single correct answer).
- Choose the correct option and fill the OMR given on the last page of test accordingly.
- At some instances, you may find more than 1 option may be correct. In such circumstances, you have to judge the most appropriate answer as per the conditions given in the question.

1. The pH of 0.05 M calcium acetate solution ($pK_a = 4.74$) is
(a) 8.87 (b) 7.54
(c) 6.05 (d) 7.13

2. If weak monobasic acid is 0.1% ionised at 0.1 M. Then its pH is
(a) 2 (b) 3
(c) 4 (d) 5

3. Given below are two statements.
Statement I Dilution of a buffer solution does not affect its pH.
Statement II $NH_4Cl + NH_4OH$ buffer is used for the precipitation of hydroxides of third group in qualitative analysis.
In the light of above statements, choose the correct answer from the options given below.
(a) Both Statement I and Statement II are incorrect.
(b) Statement I is correct but Statement II is incorrect.
(c) Statement I is incorrect but Statement II is correct.
(d) Both Statement I and Statement II are correct.

4. The solubility product of $Al(OH)_3$ is 2.7×10^{-11}. Select the incorrect answer regarding the given statement.
(a) The value of K_{sp} related to solubility is $27\, S^4$.
(b) Solubility of $Al(OH)_3$ is less than 0.002 mol L^{-1}.
(c) pH of the solution is less than 11.
(d) The value of solubility of $Al(OH)_3$ in gL^{-1} is 7.8×10^{-2}.

5. Arrange the following elements in increasing order of pH.
KNO_3, NH_4Cl, CH_3COONa, Na_2CO_3
Choose the correct answer from the options given below.
(a) $Na_2CO_3 < NH_4Cl < CH_3COONa < KNO_3$
(b) $KNO_3 < Na_2CO_3 < NH_4Cl < CH_3COONa$
(c) $NH_4Cl < KNO_3 < CH_3COONa < Na_2CO_3$
(d) $CH_3COONa < KNO_3 < NH_4Cl < Na_2CO_3$

6. What will be the pH of 0.01 M $(NH_4)_2SO_4$ and 0.02 M NH_4OH buffer (pK_a of $NH_4^+ = 9.26$)?
(a) 9.36 (b) 7.42
(c) 9.26 (d) 4.74

7. How many times a solution of pH = 3 has higher acidity than the solution of pH = 6 ?
(a) 1000 (b) 1200
(c) 10000 (d) 300

8. The value of K_a for acetic acid is 1.8×10^{-5} and K_b for ammonium hydroxide is 1.8×10^{-5}. The pH of ammonium acetate will be
(a) 7.0 (b) 4.8
(c) 9.2 (d) 6.0

9. Hydrolysis constants of two salts KA and KB of weak acid HA and HB are 10^{-9} and 10^{-6}. If the dissociation constant of the third acid HC is 10^{-3}. The order of acidic strength of the three acids will be
(a) $HA > HB > HC$ (b) $HB > HA > HC$
(c) $HC > HA > HB$ (d) $HA = HB = HC$

10. Given below are two statements, one is labelled as Assertion (A) and the other is labelled as Reason (R).

Assertion (A) Degree of hydrolysis of salts of weak acid and weak base is independent of the concentration of the solution.

Reason (R) pH of solution of salts of weak acid and weak base depends upon their relative strengths, i.e. their pK_a and pK_b values.

In the light of the above statements, choose the correct answer from the options given below.

(a) Both (A) and (R) are true and (R) is the correct explanation of (A).
(b) Both (A) and (R) are true but (R) is not the correct explanation of (A).
(c) (A) is true but (R) is false.
(d) (A) is false but (R) is true.

11. 100 mL of 0.1 M HCl is titrated against 0.1 M NaOH using phenolphthalein as an indicator. What will be the pH after the addition of 50 mL of NaOH?

(a) 7.4 (b) 1.48
(c) 5.0 (d) 6.82

12. A solution of 0.1 M acetic acid is titrated with a solution of 0.1 M sodium hydroxide solution. The pH at the equivalence point is (K_a for acetic acid $=2\times10^{-5}$)

(a) 7.813 (b) 8.712
(c) 8.424 (d) 8.695

13. Given below are two statements.

Statement I Greater the difference between pH of the solution and pK_a of the acid, lower is buffer capacity of the solution.

Statement II pH of an acidic buffer increases if the concentration of both salt and acid are doubled.

In the light of the above statements, choose the correct answer from the options given below.

(a) Both Statement I and Statement II are incorrec
(b) Statement I is correct but Statement II is incorrect.
(c) Statement I is incorrect but Statement II is correct.
(d) Both Statement I and Statement II are correct.

14. Arrange the following species in increasing order of $[H_3O^+]$.

$A: 0.01\ M\ H_2S$ $B: 0.01\ M\ H_2SO_4$
$C: 0.01\ M\ NaNO_2$ $D: 0.01\ M\ NaCl$

Choose the correct answer from the options given below.

(a) $A< B< C< D$ (b) $B< A< D< C$
(c) $C< D< A< B$ (d) $C< A< D< B$

15. What will be the pOH of a solution at 25°C that contains 1×10^{-5} M of H_3O^+ ion?

(a) 7 (b) 4
(c) 12 (d) 9

Response Index

01	(a) (b) (c) (d)	10	(a) (b) (c) (d)	19	(a) (b) (c) (d)
02	(a) (b) (c) (d)	11	(a) (b) (c) (d)	20	(a) (b) (c) (d)
03	(a) (b) (c) (d)	12	(a) (b) (c) (d)	21	(a) (b) (c) (d)
04	(a) (b) (c) (d)	13	(a) (b) (c) (d)	22	(a) (b) (c) (d)
05	(a) (b) (c) (d)	14	(a) (b) (c) (d)	23	(a) (b) (c) (d)
06	(a) (b) (c) (d)	15	(a) (b) (c) (d)	24	(a) (b) (c) (d)
07	(a) (b) (c) (d)	16	(a) (b) (c) (d)	25	(a) (b) (c) (d)
08	(a) (b) (c) (d)	17	(a) (b) (c) (d)		
09	(a) (b) (c) (d)	18	(a) (b) (c) (d)		

Performance Scanner

> 90% Excellent !	You have mastered these topics. The concepts of these topics are at your fingertips. Move on to the chapter test and maintain this momentum.
76-90% Very Good !	You have a good command over these topics. Revise these topics again after a few days and enhance your performance.
60-75% Good !	You have a wide scope to learn for these topics. Revise these topics again.
<60 Not Satisfactory!	You have a long way ahead of you to master these topics. Revise it thoroughly.

Chapter Break Thru

Syllabus			
Syllabus	• Various Concepts of Acids and Bases (Arrhenius, Bronsted-Lowry and Lewis) • Weak and Strong Electrolytes • Acid-Base • Ionisation of Electrolytes • Ionisation Constants • Ionisation of Water	• Solubility of Sparingly Soluble Salts and Solubility Products • Common Ion Effects	• pH scale • Hydrolysis of Salts • Buffer Solutions • pH of Solutions

Important Instructions

- The test is of 1 hour duration and contains 50 multiple choice questions (Four options with a single correct answer).
- Choose the correct option and fill the OMR given on the last page of test accordingly.
- At some instances, you may find more than 1 option may be correct. In such circumstances, you have to judge the most appropriate answer as per the conditions given in the question.

1. Which of the following Bronsted acids has the weakest conjugate base?

(a) H_2O (b) HCN
(c) HCOOH (d) HF

2. Which of the following can act both as a Bronsted acid as well as a Bronsted base?

(a) H_2SO_4 (b) HCO_3^-
(c) O^{2-} (d) NH_4^+

3. Which of the following statements are correct about Ostwald's dilution law?

(i) A decrease in concentration of salts shows an increase in its degree of dissociation (α).
(ii) As $C \rightarrow 0$, the degree of dissociation (α) approaches unity.
(iii) A plot of α^2 *versus* $\frac{1}{C}$ gives a straight line with a slope equal to dissociation constant of weak electrolyte when $\alpha < 0.05$.
(iv) A plot of α^2 *versus* C gives a straight line with a slope equal to dissociation constant of weak electrolyte.
(v) A decrease in concentration of salts shows a decrease in its degree of dissociation (α).

Choose the correct answer from the options given below.

(a) (ii) and (v)
(b) (i), (ii) and (iii)
(c) (ii), (iii) and (iv)
(d) (i), (ii), (iii) and (iv)

4. Given below are two statements, one is labelled as Assertion (A) and the other is labelled as Reason (R).

Assertion (A) pK_a of a weak acid becomes equal to the pH of the solution at the midpoint of its titration.

Reason (R) The molar concentrations of the proton donor and proton acceptor becomes equal at midpoint.

In the light of above statements, choose the correct answer from the options given below.

(a) Both (A) and (R) are true and (R) is the correct explanation of (A).
(b) Both (A) and (R) are true but (R) is not the correct explanation of (A).
(c) (A) is true but (R) is false.
(d) (A) is false but (R) is true.

5. If the equilibrium constant of the reaction of weak acid HA with strong base is 10^9, then pH in 0.1 M NaA is

(a) 5 (b) 9
(c) 7 (d) 8

6. Match List-I with List-II.

List-I (Salt/Acid/Base)	List-II (Formula for pH)
A. Sodium nitrate	I. $pH=\frac{1}{2}[pK_w - pK_b - \log C]$
B. Anilinium chloride	II. $pH=\frac{1}{2}[pK_w + pK_a - pK_b]$
C. Ammonium cyanide	III. $pH=\frac{1}{2}[pK_w + pK_a + \log C]$
D. Hydrogen cyanide	IV. $pH=\frac{1}{2}[pK_a - \log C]$

Choose the correct answer from the options given below.

(a) A-III, B-I, C-II, D-IV
(b) A-III, B-IV, C-I, D-II
(c) A-I, B-II, C-IV, D-III
(d) A-IV, B-I, C-II, D-III

7. What amount of sodium formate should be added to one litre of an aqueous solution containing 0.04 mole of formic acid ($K_a = 1.0\times10^{-4}$ at 25°C) to obtain a buffer solution of $pH = 5.0$?

(a) 0.5 M (b) 0.04 M
(c) 0.4 M (d) 0.02 M

8. Among the following, the strongest conjugate base is

(a) NO_3^- (b) Cl^-
(c) SO_4^{2-} (d) CH_3COO^-

9. Which of the following buffer solution has the pH value greater than 7?

(a) $CH_3COOH + CH_3COONa$
(b) $HCOOH + HCOOK$
(c) CH_3COONa
(d) $NH_4OH + NH_4Cl$

10. The ionisation constant of acetic acid is 1.74×10^{-5}. The degree of dissociation of acetic acid in its 0.05 M solution will be

(a) 1.86×10^{-2} (b) 1.8×10^{-2}
(c) 0.186×10^{2} (d) 1.86×10^{-2}

11. For 100 times increase in concentration of H^+ ions

(a) pH decreases by 10
(b) pH increases by 10
(c) pH decreases by 2
(d) pH increases by 2

12. A saturated solution of Ag_2SO_4, has solubility 2.5×10^{-2} M. The value of its solubility product is

(a) 625×10^{-6} (b) 6.25×10^{-8}
(c) 62.5×10^{-6} (d) 62.5×10^{-8}

13. The concentration of $[H^+]$ and concentration of $[OH^-]$ of a 0.1 aqueous solution of 2% ionised weak acid is (Ionic product of water $= 1\times10^{-14}$)

(a) 2×10^{-3} M and 5×10^{-12} M
(b) 1×10^{3} M and 3×10^{-11} M
(c) 0.02×10^{-3} M and 5×10^{-11} M
(d) 3×10^{-2} M and 4×10^{-13} M

14. The value of K_{sp} for $HgCl_2$ is 4×10^{-15}. The concentration of Cl^- ion in its aqueous solution at saturated point is

(a) 4×10^{-5} M (b) 2×10^{-5} M
(c) 2×10^{-6} M (d) 4×10^{-6} M

15. What concentration of $HCOO^-$ is present in a solution of 0.01 M HCOOH ($K_a = 1.8\times10^{-4}$) and 0.01 M HCl?

(a) 1.8×10^{-3} (b) 1.8×10^{-2}
(c) 1.8×10^{-4} (d) 1.8×10^{-5}

16. If H^+ ion concentration of a solution is increased by 10 times, its pH will

(a) increase by one
(b) decrease by one
(c) increase by 10 times
(d) decrease by 10 times

17. The K_α value of formic acid and acetic acid are respectively given as 3.54×10^{-4} and 3.50×10^{-5}. The ratio of acid strength at 0.1 N acid is

(a) 31.78 (b) 3.180
(c) 317.8 (d) 0.3180

18. Which one is not an acid salt?

(a) NaH_2PO_4 (b) NaH_2PO_2
(c) NH_4Cl (d) $(NH_4)_2SO_4$

19. The pH of 0.1 M solution of the following compounds in the decreasing order is

(a) HCl > NaCN > NH_4Cl > NaCl
(b) NaCN > NaCl > NH_4Cl > HCl
(c) HCl > NaCl > NH_4Cl > NaCN
(d) NH_4Cl > NaCN > NaCl > HCl

20. Which has the highest pH among the given compounds?

(a) CH_3COOK (b) Na_2CO_3
(c) NH_4Cl (d) $NaNO_3$

21. 100 mL of a buffer solution contains 0.1 M each of weak acid H*A* and salt Na*A*. How many grams of NaOH should be added to the buffer so that its pH becomes 6? (K_a for H*A* $=10^{-5}$)

(a) 0.327 g (b) 0.458 g
(c) 4.19 g (d) 3.27 g

22. What is $[H^+]$ of a solution that have 0.1 M HCN and 0.2 M NaCN? (K_α for HCN $=6.2\times10^{-10}$)

(a) 31×10^{-10} (b) 3.09×10^{-10}
(c) 0.310×10^{-10} (d) $6.2\times10^{+10}$

23. Calculate the pH of aqueous solution of 1.0 M ammonium formate assuming complete dissociation. pK_a for formic acid $=3.8$ and pK_b of ammonia $=4.8$.

(a) 8.5 (b) 6.5
(c) 5.5 (d) 4.5

24. Ammonium cyanide is a salt of NH_4OH ($K_b=1.8\times10^{-5}$) and HCN ($K_\alpha=4\times10^{-10}$). The hydrolysis constant of 0.1 M NH_4CN at 25°C is

(a) 14 (b) 1.4×10^{-6}
(c) 1.4 (d) 1.4×10^{-2}

25. If the equilibrium constant of the reaction of weak acid H*A* with strong base is 10^9, then pH in 0.1 M Na*A* is,

(a) 9 (b) 6
(c) 4 (d) 12

26. The pH of 0.05 M ammonia solution is 10.97. Find the ionisation constant of the conjugate acid of ammonia.
[Given : K_b for ammonia $=1.77\times10^{-5}$].

(a) 567×10^{-10} (b) 574×10^{-10}
(c) 56.4×10^{-10} (d) 5.64×10^{-10}

27. The pH at which an acid indicator will change colour when the indicator concentration is 1×10^{-3} M and $K_\alpha=1\times10^{-5}$ is

(a) 3 (b) 2
(c) 5 (d) 1

28. Choose the correct statement regarding constant acidity and alkalinity of buffer solutions.

(a) They have fixed value of pH.
(b) They give unionised acid or base on reaction with added acid or alkali.
(c) They have large excess of H^+ or OH^- ions.
(d) Acids and alkalies in these solutions are shielded from attack by other ions.

29. Given below are two statements.
Statement I HCO_3^- ion acts as a strong acid as well as a strong base.
Statement II CO_3^{2-} ions acts only as weak base.
In the light of the above statements, choose the most appropriate answer from the options given below.

(a) Both Statement I and Statement II are incorrect.
(b) Statement I is correct but Statement II is incorrect.
(c) Statement I is incorrect but Statement II is correct.
(d) Both Statement I and Statement II are correct.

30. Which of the following is arranged in the order of increasing ionisation constants of H_3PO_4?

(a) $K_3<K_1<K_2$ (b) $K_1<K_2<K_3$
(c) $K_2<K_1<K_3$ (d) $K_3<K_2<K_1$

31. The pH of a solution of given mixture (0.1 mole CH_3COOH + 0.2 mole CH_3COONa) in 100 mL of mixture is ($K_a = 2\times10^{-5}$)

(a) 4.6 (b) 5 (c) 6.6 (d) 7.6

32. Given below are two statements.

Statement I pH of HCl is less than that of acetic acid of same concentration.

Statement II In equimolar solutions, the number of titratable proton present in HCl is less than that present in acetic acid.

In the light of above statements, choose the correct answer from the options given below.

(a) Both Statement I and Statement II are incorrect.
(b) Statement I is correct but Statement II is incorrect.
(c) Statement I is incorrect but Statement II is correct.
(d) Both Statement I and Statement II are correct.

33. Given below are two statements, one is labelled as Assertion (A) and the other is labelled as Reason (R).

Assertion (A) Phenolphthalein is not used as indicator if the base is NH_4OH or Na_2CO_3.
Reason (R) NH_4OH is a weak base and phenolphthalein is also a weak base.

In the light of above statements, choose the correct answer from the options given below.

(a) Both (A) and (R) are true and (R) is the correct explanation of (A).
(b) Both (A) and (R) are true but (R) is not the correct explanation of (A).
(c) (A) is true but (R) is false.
(d) (A) is false but (R) is true.

34. A solution of 0.1 m NaZ has pH = 8.90, then the K_a of HZ is

(a) 6.3×10^{-11} (b) 6.3×10^{-10}
(c) 1.6×10^{-5} (d) 1.6×10^{-4}

35. If the equilibrium constant of $BOH \rightleftharpoons B^+ + OH^-$ at 25°C is 2.5×10^{-6}, then the equilibrium constant for $BOH + H^+ \rightleftharpoons B^+ + H_2O$ at the same temperature is

(a) 40×10^{-9} (b) 4.0×10^5
(c) 2.5×10^8 (d) 25×10^{-6}

36. Equal volumes of 0.02 M $CaCl_2$ and 0.0004 M Na_2SO_4 are mixed. What will happen? (K_{sp} for $CaSO_4 = 2.4\times 10^{-5}$)

(a) $CaSO_4$ cannot precipitate.
(b) $CaSO_4$ precipitated.
(c) $CaSO_4$ decomposed.
(d) Not predicted.

37. Given below are two statements.

Statement I pH of 10^{-8} M HCl is not equal to 8.

Statement II HCl does not dissociate properly in very dilute solution.

In the light of above statements, choose the correct answer from the options given below.

(a) Both Statement I and Statement II are incorrec
(b) Statement I is correct but Statement II is incorrect.
(c) Statement I is incorrect but Statement II is correct.
(d) Both Statement I and Statement II are correct.

38. What is the percentage hydrolysis of NaCN $\frac{N}{80}$ solution when dissociation constant for HCN is 1.3×10^{-9} and $K_w = 1\times10^{-14}$?

(a) 2.48 % (b) 24.8 %
(c) 0.248 % (d) 0.248×10^{-3} %

39. A weak monobasic acid is half neutralised by a strong base. If pH of solution is 5.4. Its pK_a is

(a) 2.7 (b) 5.4
(c) 10.8 (d) 6.4

40. Degree of dissociation of 0.1 N CH_3COOH is ($K_{acid} = 1\times10^{-5}$)

(a) 10^{-4} (b) 10^{-6}
(c) 10^{-2} (d) 10^{+2}

41. Consider the following statements.

I. AgCl is more soluble in very concentrated NaCl solution than in pure water.

II. Mg^{2+} ion is essential for selective precipitation of $Fe(OH)_3$ by aqueous NH_3.

III. pH of some solution is given by

$$pH = \frac{pK_{a_1} + pK_{a_2}}{2}$$

IV. 0.5 mmol of NaCN and 1 mmol of HCl in 1 L solution is a buffer.

V. During dissociation of hydrogen iodide, degree of dissociation is influenced by the increase of temperature.

Choose the correct statements from options given below.

(a) II and V (b) III and IV
(c) I, III and V (d) I, II, III and IV

42. In the following reaction,

$$HC_2O_4^-(aq) + PO_4^{3-}(aq) \rightleftharpoons HPO_4^-(aq) + C_2O_4^{2-}(aq)$$

The two Bronsted bases are

(a) $HC_2O_4^-$ and PO_4^{3-} (b) HPO_4^{2-} and $C_2O_4^-$
(c) $HC_2O_4^-$ and HPO_4^{2-} (d) PO_4^{3-} and $C_2O_4^{2-}$

43. Identify the incorrect statement out of the following.

(a) Lewis concept cannot explain the acidic nature of H_2SO_4.
(b) Bronsted Lowry theory can explain the acidic nature of CO_2.
(c) HSO_4^- and $HClO_4^-$ can acts as a base.
(d) A molecule in which the central atom has vacant orbitals available acts as an acid.

44. If pK_b for fluoride ion at 25°C is 10.83, the ionisation constant of hydrofluoric acid in water at this temperature is

(a) 1.74×10^{-5} (b) 3.52×10^{-3}
(c) 6.76×10^{-4} (d) 5.38×10^{-2}

45. Given below are two statements.

Statement I The degree of dissociation or ionisation of any weak electrolytes is inversely proportional to the square root of concentration.

Statement II Ostwald's dilution law is applicable for strong electrolytes.

In the light of the above statements, choose the most appropriate answer from the options given below.

(a) Both Statement I and Statement II are incorrect.
(b) Statement I is correct but Statement II is incorrect.
(c) Statement I is incorrect but Statement II is correct.
(d) Both Statement I and Statement II are correct.

46. Amongst the following hydroxides, the one which has the lowest value of K_{sp} at ordinary temperature (about 25°C) is

(a) $Ba(OH)_2$ (b) $CaSO_4$
(c) $Al_2(SO_4)_3$ (d) Na_3PO_4

47. Which one of the following mixture does not act as a buffer solution?

(a) Boric acid and borax.
(b) Sodium phosphate and disodium hydrogen phosphate.
(c) Sodium propionate and propionic acid.
(d) Sodium acetate and sodium propionate.

48. Which of the following metal sulphide solutions will have the maximum concentration of cation?

(a) MnS ($K_{sp} = 6.0 \times 10^{-16}$)
(b) FeS ($K_{sp} = 1.1 \times 10^{-19}$)
(c) ZnS ($K_{sp} = 1.2 \times 10^{-21}$)
(d) CdS ($K_{sp} = 3.5 \times 10^{-29}$)

49. A buffer solution contains 0.1 mol each of CH_3COONa and CH_3COOH. On diluting the solution to double its volume, the pH of the solution

(a) will become half
(b) will remain unchanged
(c) will be doubled
(d) cannot be predicted

50. Given below are two statements, one is labelled as Assertion (A) and the other is labelled as Reason (R).

Assertion (A) Addition of HCl(aq) to HCOOH(aq) decreases the ionisation of HCOOH(aq).

Reason (R) Due to common ion effect of H^+, ionisation of HCOOH decreases.

In the light of the above statements, choose the correct answer from the options given below.

(a) Both (A) and (R) are true and (R) is the correct explanation of (A).
(b) Both (A) and (R) are true but (R) is not the correct explanation of (A).
(c) (A) is true but (R) is false.
(d) (A) is false but (R) is true.

■ **Response Index**

01 ⓐ ⓑ ⓒ ⓓ	14 ⓐ ⓑ ⓒ ⓓ	27 ⓐ ⓑ ⓒ ⓓ	40 ⓐ ⓑ ⓒ ⓓ
02 ⓐ ⓑ ⓒ ⓓ	15 ⓐ ⓑ ⓒ ⓓ	28 ⓐ ⓑ ⓒ ⓓ	41 ⓐ ⓑ ⓒ ⓓ
03 ⓐ ⓑ ⓒ ⓓ	16 ⓐ ⓑ ⓒ ⓓ	29 ⓐ ⓑ ⓒ ⓓ	42 ⓐ ⓑ ⓒ ⓓ
04 ⓐ ⓑ ⓒ ⓓ	17 ⓐ ⓑ ⓒ ⓓ	30 ⓐ ⓑ ⓒ ⓓ	43 ⓐ ⓑ ⓒ ⓓ
05 ⓐ ⓑ ⓒ ⓓ	18 ⓐ ⓑ ⓒ ⓓ	31 ⓐ ⓑ ⓒ ⓓ	44 ⓐ ⓑ ⓒ ⓓ
06 ⓐ ⓑ ⓒ ⓓ	19 ⓐ ⓑ ⓒ ⓓ	32 ⓐ ⓑ ⓒ ⓓ	45 ⓐ ⓑ ⓒ ⓓ
07 ⓐ ⓑ ⓒ ⓓ	20 ⓐ ⓑ ⓒ ⓓ	33 ⓐ ⓑ ⓒ ⓓ	46 ⓐ ⓑ ⓒ ⓓ
08 ⓐ ⓑ ⓒ ⓓ	21 ⓐ ⓑ ⓒ ⓓ	34 ⓐ ⓑ ⓒ ⓓ	47 ⓐ ⓑ ⓒ ⓓ
09 ⓐ ⓑ ⓒ ⓓ	22 ⓐ ⓑ ⓒ ⓓ	35 ⓐ ⓑ ⓒ ⓓ	48 ⓐ ⓑ ⓒ ⓓ
10 ⓐ ⓑ ⓒ ⓓ	23 ⓐ ⓑ ⓒ ⓓ	36 ⓐ ⓑ ⓒ ⓓ	49 ⓐ ⓑ ⓒ ⓓ
11 ⓐ ⓑ ⓒ ⓓ	24 ⓐ ⓑ ⓒ ⓓ	37 ⓐ ⓑ ⓒ ⓓ	50 ⓐ ⓑ ⓒ ⓓ
12 ⓐ ⓑ ⓒ ⓓ	25 ⓐ ⓑ ⓒ ⓓ	38 ⓐ ⓑ ⓒ ⓓ	
13 ⓐ ⓑ ⓒ ⓓ	26 ⓐ ⓑ ⓒ ⓓ	39 ⓐ ⓑ ⓒ ⓓ	

■ **Performance Scanner**

> 90% Excellent !	You have mastered this chapter. The concepts of this chapter are at your fingertips. Move on to the next chapter and maintain this momentum.
76-90% Very Good !	You have a good command over this chapter. Revise the chapter again after a few days and enhance your performance.
60-75% Good !	You have a wide scope to learn for this chapter. Revise this chapter again.
<60 Not Satisfactory!	You have a long way ahead of you to master this chapter. Revise it thoroughly.

Scan for Online **Chapter Test**

Scan for Online **Unit Test**

Space for Rough Work

Test Booklet No. **3947208**

Test Booklet Code **CH8**

MEDACE

NEET (UG)

SELF ASSESSMENT KIT

Redox Reactions

Topics Covered

Oxidation-Reduction and Oxidation Number

Types of Redox Reactions and Balancing of Redox Equations

Important Instructions

- This Booklet Contains – 2 Topic Tests and One Test on Complete Chapter.
- Each question carries 4 marks.
- For each correct response the candidate will get 4 marks and for every incorrect response 1 mark will be additionally deducted from the total score.
- Use **Blue/Black** point pen only for filling the OMR.
- Rough work is to be done in the space provided for this purpose in the test booklet only.

Name of the Candidate (In Capitals)

____

____

Candidate's Signature __________

Invigilator's Signature __________

Facsimile signature stamp of center superintendent__________

Do not open this Booklet until you start attempting the Test

Topical Follow Thru

Test 1

Syllabus
- Electronic Concepts of Oxidation and Reduction
- Oxidation Number
- Rules for Assigning Oxidation Number

For deeper insight **Scan the QR Code**

Important Instructions
- The test is of 30 minutes duration and contains 25 multiple choice questions (Four options with a single correct answer).
- Choose the correct option and fill the OMR given on the last page of test accordingly.
- At some instances, you may find more than 1 option may be correct. In such circumstances, you have to judge the most appropriate answer as per conditions given in the question.

1. Which of the following behaves as an oxidising as well as reducing agents?

(a) H_2SO_4 (b) SO_2
(c) H_2S (d) HNO_3

2. The brown ring complex compound is formulated as $[Fe(H_2O)_5(NO)]SO_4$. The oxidation state of iron is

(a) 1 (b) 2
(c) 3 (d) 0

3. The reaction in which N gets oxidised is

(a) $NH_4^+ \longrightarrow N_2$
(b) $NO_3^- \longrightarrow N_2$
(c) $NO_2 \longrightarrow NO_2^-$
(d) $NO_3^- \longrightarrow NH_4^+$

4. Match List-I with List-II.

List-I (Compound)		List-II (Oxidation number of nitrogen)	
A.	N_2O_5	I.	−2
B.	NaN_3	II.	+5
C.	NO	III.	−1/3
D.	N_2H_4	IV.	+2

Choose the correct answer from the options given below.

(a) A-II, B-III, C-IV, D-I
(b) A-I, B-II, C-III, D-IV
(c) A-IV, B-I, C-II, D-III
(d) A-III, B-I, C-IV, D-II

5. Which of the following has been arranged in order of increasing oxidation number of nitrogen?

(a) $NH_3 < N_2O_5 < NO < N_2$
(b) $NH_3 < N_2 < N_2O_5 < NO$
(c) $NH_4^+ < N_2H_4 < NH_2OH < N_2O$
(d) $NaN_3 < N_2O < NH_4^+ < NO_2$

6. The oxidation number of sulphur in S_8, S_2F_2, H_2S respectively, are

(a) 0, +1 and −2 (b) +2, +1 and −2
(c) 0, +1 and +2 (d) −2, +1 and +2

7. Oxidation number of potassium in K_2O, K_2O_2 and KO_2 respectively is

(a) +1, +1 and + 1
(b) + 2, + 1 and $+\frac{1}{2}$
(c) +1, +2 and + 4
(d) + 1, + 4 and +2

8. The oxidation number of P in $HP_2O_7^-$ ion is

(a) + 5 (b) + 6
(c) + 7 (d) + 3

9. The oxidation number of Mn is +7 in
(a) manganese dioxide
(b) manganese chloride
(c) manganese sulphate
(d) potassium permanganate

10. In which one of the following compounds the oxidation number of oxygen is positive?
(a) H_2O_2
(b) Na_2O_2
(c) OF_2
(d) H_2O

11. The oxidation number of C in sucrose is
(a) +4 (b) +3
(c) +2 (d) zero

12. Oxidation number of carbon in carbon suboxide (C_3O_2) is
(a) +2/3 (b) +4/3
(c) +4 (d) –4/3

13. The oxidation number of Cr in CrO_5 is
(a) +3 (b) +5
(c) +6 (d) 0

14. Which of the following acts as a reducing agent?
(a) HNO_3 (b) $KMnO_4$
(c) H_2SO_4 (d) $(COOH)_2$

15. Which of the following chemical reaction depicts the oxidising behaviour of H_2SO_4?
(a) $2HI + H_2SO_4 \longrightarrow I_2 + SO_2 + 2H_2O$
(b) $Ca(OH)_2 + H_2SO_4 \longrightarrow CaSO_4 + 2H_2O$
(c) $NaCl + H_2SO_4 \longrightarrow NaHSO_4 + HCl$
(d) $2PCl_5 + H_2SO_4 \longrightarrow 2POCl_3 + 2HCl + SO_2Cl_2$

16. Which of the following arrangements represents increasing oxidation number of the central atom ?
(a) $CrO_2^-, ClO_3^-, CrO_4^{2-}, MnO_4^-$
(b) $ClO_3^-, CrO_4^{2-}, MnO_4^-, CrO_2^-$
(c) $CrO_2^-, ClO_3^-, MnO_4^-, CrO_4^{2-}$
(d) $CrO_4^{2-}, MnO_4^-, CrO_2^-, ClO_3^-$

17. The oxidation number of oxygen atom in O_2^{2-} ion is
(a) – 1 (b) – 2
(c) – 3 (d) – 4

18. Oxidation number of Fe in Fe_3O_4 is
(a) $\frac{1}{2}$ (b) $\frac{2}{6}$
(c) $\frac{8}{3}$ (d) $\frac{3}{2}$

19. In which of the following compounds, an element exhibits two different oxidation states?
(a) NH_2OH (b) NH_4NO_3
(c) N_2H_4 (d) N_3H

20. Out of the following, select species with different oxidation states of the underlined atoms.
I. $Ca\underline{O}Cl_2$ II. $H_2\underline{S}_2O_8$
III. $Na_2\underline{S}_4O_6$ IV. $Cr\underline{O}_5$
V. $\underline{N}_2H_4O_3$
(a) All except I (b) All except II
(c) All except III (d) All except V

21. The oxidation number of an element in a compound is evaluated on the basis of certain rules. Which of the following is incorrect in this respect?
(a) The oxidation number of hydrogen is always +1.
(b) The algebraic sum of all the oxidation numbers in a compound is zero.
(c) An element in the free or the uncombined state bears oxidation number zero.
(d) In all its compounds, the oxidation number of fluorine is –1.

22. Select the correct statement about the following reaction.

$$NH_4^+ + NO_2^- \longrightarrow N_2 + 2H_2O$$

(a) Oxidation number of N has changed from – 2 to +2.
(b) Oxidation number of N in NH_4^+ changed from –3 to 0 and that in NO_2^- changed from + 3 to 0.
(c) Oxidation number of N in NH_4^+ changed from +1 to 0 and that in NO_2^- changed from –1 to 0.
(d) No change in oxidation number.

23. Which one has maximum oxidation number of the underlined atoms in the following compounds?

(a) $\underline{Mn}O_4^{2-}$

(b) $\underline{Cr}O_5$

(c) $\underline{Cr}O_2Cl_2$

(d) Equal in all the options

24. The oxidation number of Cr in $K_2Cr_2O_7$ is

(a) +2 (b) + 4 (c) + 6 (d) + 5

25. The oxidation state of M^{3+} after removing three electrons is

(a) −3 (b) + 3 (c) + 6 (d) − 6

Response Index

01	(a)	(b)	(c)	(d)	10	(a)	(b)	(c)	(d)	19	(a)	(b)	(c)	(d)
02	(a)	(b)	(c)	(d)	11	(a)	(b)	(c)	(d)	20	(a)	(b)	(c)	(d)
03	(a)	(b)	(c)	(d)	12	(a)	(b)	(c)	(d)	21	(a)	(b)	(c)	(d)
04	(a)	(b)	(c)	(d)	13	(a)	(b)	(c)	(d)	22	(a)	(b)	(c)	(d)
05	(a)	(b)	(c)	(d)	14	(a)	(b)	(c)	(d)	23	(a)	(b)	(c)	(d)
06	(a)	(b)	(c)	(d)	15	(a)	(b)	(c)	(d)	24	(a)	(b)	(c)	(d)
07	(a)	(b)	(c)	(d)	16	(a)	(b)	(c)	(d)	25	(a)	(b)	(c)	(d)
08	(a)	(b)	(c)	(d)	17	(a)	(b)	(c)	(d)					
09	(a)	(b)	(c)	(d)	18	(a)	(b)	(c)	(d)					

Performance Scanner

> 90% Excellent !	You have mastered these topics. The concepts of these topics are at your fingertips. Move on to the next test and maintain this momentum.
76-90% Very Good !	You have a good command over these topics. Revise these topics again after a few days and enhance your performance.
60-75% Good !	You have a wide scope to learn for these topics. Revise these topics again.
<60 Not Satisfactory!	You have a long way ahead of you to master these topics. Revise it thoroughly.

Test 2

Syllabus
- Redox Reactions
- Balancing of Redox Reactions

For deeper insight **Scan the QR Code**

Important Instructions
- The test is of 30 minutes duration and contains 15 multiple choice questions (Four options with a single correct answer).
- Choose the correct option and fill the OMR given on the last page of test accordingly.
- At some instances, you may find more than 1 option may be correct. In such circumstances, you have to judge the most appropriate answer as per conditions given in the question.

1. The decomposition of $KClO_3$ to KCl and O_2 on heating is an example of
(a) intermolecular redox reaction
(b) intramolecular redox reaction
(c) autoredox reaction
(d) displacement reaction

2. The number of electrons required to balance the following equation

$NO_3^- + 4H^+ + e^- \longrightarrow 2H_2O + NO$ is

(a) 5 (b) 4 (c) 3 (d) 2

3. $8Al + 3Fe_3O_4 \longrightarrow 4Al_2O_3 + 9Fe$

How many electrons were accepted by Fe ions in above reaction?
(a) 12 (b) 24
(c) 20 (d) 14

4. The total number of electrons involved in redox change is $3Fe + 4H_2O \longrightarrow Fe_3O_4 + 4H_2$.
(a) 9 (b) 6
(c) 3 (d) 8

5. For the redox reaction

$MnO_4^- + C_2O_4^{-2} + H^+ \longrightarrow Mn^{+2} + CO_2 + H_2O$,

the correct coefficient of the reactant, i.e. MnO_4^-, $C_2O_4^{-2}$, H^+ for the balanced reaction are respectively
(a) 2, 5, 16 (b) 16, 3, 12
(c) 15, 16, 12 (d) 2, 16, 5

6. Balanced form of this reaction

$N_2O_4 + BrO_3^- \longrightarrow NO_3^- + Br^-$ (in acidic medium) is

(a) $2N_2O_4 + BrO_3^- + 2H_2O \longrightarrow 4NO_3^- + 4H^+ + Br^-$

(b) $3N_2O_4 + BrO_3^- + 3H_2O \longrightarrow 4NO_3^- + 4H^+ + Br^-$

(c) $3N_2O_4 + BrO_3^- + 3H_2O \longrightarrow 6NO_3^- + 6H^+ + Br^-$

(d) $3N_2O_4 + BrO_3^- + 2H_2O \longrightarrow 4NO_3^- + 4H^+ + Br^-$

7. Consider the reaction given below.

$H_2O + Br_2 \longrightarrow HOBr + HBr$

(a) It accepts proton.
(b) It undergoes disproportionation.
(c) It undergoes oxidation.
(d) It undergoes reduction.

8. Consider the following reaction.

$5H_2O_2 + xClO_2 + 2OH^- \longrightarrow xCl^- + yO_2 + 6H_2O$

The reaction is balanced if
(a) $x = 5$, $y = 2$ (b) $x = 2$, $y = 5$
(c) $x = 4$, $y = 10$ (d) $x = 5$, $y = 5$

9. In the balanced chemical reactions

$IO_3^- + aI^- + bH^+ \longrightarrow cH_2O + dI_2$

a, *b*, *c* and *d* respectively corresponds to
(a) 5, 6, 3, 3
(b) 5, 3, 6, 3
(c) 3, 5, 3, 6
(d) 5, 6, 5, 5

10. Which of the following is a redox reaction?
(a) Reaction of H_2SO_4 with NaOH.
(b) In atmosphere, formation of O_3 from O_2 by lightening.
(c) Formation of oxides of nitrogen from nitrogen and oxygen by lightening.
(d) Evaporation of H_2O.

11. An example of a disproportionation reaction is
(a) $2KMnO_4 \longrightarrow K_2MnO_4 + MnO_2 + O_2$
(b) $2NaBr + Cl_2 \longrightarrow 2NaCl + Br_2$
(c) $2CuBr \longrightarrow CuBr_2 + Cu$
(d) $2MnO_4^- + 10I^- + 16H^+ \longrightarrow 2Mn^{+2} + 5I_2 + 8H_2O$

12. Which of the given reaction is not an example of disproportionation reaction?
(a) $2H_2O_2 \longrightarrow 2H_2O + O_2$
(b) $2NO_2 + H_2O \longrightarrow HNO_3 + HNO_2$
(c) $MnO_4 + 4H^+ + 3e^- \longrightarrow MnO_2 + 2H_2O$
(d) $3MnO_4^{-2} + 4H^+ \longrightarrow 2MnO_4^- + MnO_2 + 2H_2O$

13. In the displacement reaction

$$X + YZ \longrightarrow XZ + Y$$

Which one of the following statement is correct?
(a) X is oxidised while Y is reduced.
(b) X is reduced while Y is oxidised.
(c) X is oxidised while Z is reduced.
(d) All X, Y and Z remains unaffected.

14. Which of the following represents a disproportionation reaction?
(a) $Cl_2 + 2OH^- \longrightarrow ClO^- + Cl^- + H_2O$
(b) $Cu_2O + H^+ \longrightarrow Cu + Cu^{+2} + OH^-$
(c) $2HCuCl_2 \xrightarrow[\text{with } H_2O]{\text{Dilution}} Cu + Cu^{2+} + 4Cl^- + 2H^+$
(d) All of the above

15. In the reaction,

$$xBrO_3^- + yCr^{+3} + zH_2O \longrightarrow Br_2 + CrO_4^{-2} + H^+ + ne^-$$

The coefficient x, y, z are
(a) 6, 8, 22 (b) 6, 10, 22
(c) 6, 10, 11 (d) 6, 10, 20

Response Index

01	a	b	c	d	10	a	b	c	d	19	a	b	c	d
02	a	b	c	d	11	a	b	c	d	20	a	b	c	d
03	a	b	c	d	12	a	b	c	d	21	a	b	c	d
04	a	b	c	d	13	a	b	c	d	22	a	b	c	d
05	a	b	c	d	14	a	b	c	d	23	a	b	c	d
06	a	b	c	d	15	a	b	c	d	24	a	b	c	d
07	a	b	c	d	16	a	b	c	d	25	a	b	c	d
08	a	b	c	d	17	a	b	c	d					
09	a	b	c	d	18	a	b	c	d					

Performance Scanner

> 90% Excellent !	You have mastered these topics. The concepts of these topics are at your fingertips. Move on to the chapter test and maintain this momentum.
76-90% Very Good !	You have a good command over these topics. Revise these topics again after a few days and enhance your performance.
60-75% Good !	You have a wide scope to learn for these topics. Revise these topics again.
<60 Not Satisfactory!	You have a long way ahead of you to master these topics. Revise it thoroughly.

Chapter Break Thru

Syllabus

- Electronic Concepts of Oxidation and Reduction
- Oxidation Number
- Rules for Assigning Oxidation Number
- Redox Reactions
- Balancing of Redox Reactions

Important Instructions

- The test is of 1 hour duration and contains 50 multiple choice questions (Four options with a single correct answer).
- Choose the correct option and fill the OMR given on the last page of test accordingly.
- At some instances, you may find more than 1 option may be correct. In such circumstances, you have to judge the most appropriate answer as per the conditions given in the question.

1. On the basis of structure, the two sulphur atoms in $Na_2S_2O_3$ have

(a) +2 and +4 oxidation states

(b) –2 and +6 oxidation states

(c) +4 and +6 oxidation states

(d) same oxidation state +2

2. The oxidation number of C in HCN and HNC respectively are

(a) +2, +2 (b) +2, +4

(c) +4, +4 (d) –2, –2

3. In the conversion of $K_2Cr_2O_7$ to K_2CrO_4, the oxidation number of chromium

(a) remains same (b) increase

(c) decrease (d) double

4. The equivalent weight of Mohr's salt, $FeSO_4 \cdot (NH_4)_2SO_4 \cdot 6H_2O$ is equal to

(a) its molecular weight

(b) atomic weight

(c) half its molecular weight

(d) one-third its molecular weight

5. Coefficients *x*, *y* and *z* in the following balanced equation $xMnO_4^- + yH_2S + zH^+ \rightarrow S + Mn^{+2} + H_2O$ are respectively.

(a) 2, 3, 4 (b) 6, 8, 10

(c) 2, 5, 6 (d) 2, 6, 5

6. The ratio of coefficients of HNO_3, $Fe(NO_3)_2$ and NH_4NO_3 in the following redox equation $Fe + HNO_3 \longrightarrow Fe(NO_3)_2 + NH_4NO_3 + H_2O$ in the balanced form will be

(a) 10 : 1 : 4 (b) 10 : 4 : 1

(c) 4 : 10 : 1 (d) 4 : 1 : 10

7. Which of the following reaction is an example of a redox reaction?

(a) $XeF_6 + H_2O \longrightarrow XeOF_4 + 2HF$

(b) $XeF_6 + 2H_2O \longrightarrow XeO_2F_2 + 4HF$

(c) $XeF_4 + O_2F_2 \longrightarrow XeF_6 + O_2$

(d) $XeF_2 + PF_5 \longrightarrow [XeF]^+ PF_6^-$

8. Which of the following reaction shows the reducing property of SO_2?

(i) $Cl_2 + SO_2 \longrightarrow SO_2Cl_2$

(ii) $2H_2S + SO_2 \longrightarrow 3S + 2H_2O$

(iii) $2FeCl_3 + SO_2 + 2H_2O \longrightarrow 2FeCl_2 + H_2SO_4 + 2HCl$

(iv) $SO_2 + H_2O \longrightarrow H_2SO_3$

Choose the most appropriate answer from the options given below.

(a) (i) only

(b) (ii) and (iii)

(c) (ii) and (iv)

(d) (i), (ii) and (iv)

9. Consider the statement given below.

I. Oxidation number of carbon in glucose is zero.
II. Oxidation number of sulphur is +6 in H_2SO_4.
III. Oxidation number of Cr is +6 in CrO_5.
IV. Oxidation number of Mn is +3 in Mn_2O_3.
V. Oxidation number of Mn is +6 in MnO_4^-.

Total number of correct statements are ....

(a) 2 (b) 3 (c) 4 (d) 5

10. Hydrogen can have oxidation number(s) of

(a) –1 only (b) +1 only
(c) 0 only (d) –1, 0, +1

11. Consider the following reaction.

I. $3Mg(s)+N_2(g)\xrightarrow{\Delta}Mg_3N_2(s)$
II. $C(s)+O_2(g)\xrightarrow{\Delta}CO_2(g)$
III. $CH_4(g)+2O_2(g)\xrightarrow{\Delta}CO_2(g)+2H_2O(l)$
IV. $Li(s)+N_2(g)\xrightarrow{\Delta}Li_3N(s)$
V. $H_2O(l)\xrightarrow{\Delta}2H_2(g)+O_2(g)$

The number of combination reaction among the given reactions is ....

(a) 2 (b) 3 (c) 4 (d) 5

12. Which of the following statement is not correct about the given reaction?

$$K_4[Fe(CN)_6]\xrightarrow{\text{Oxidation}}Fe^{+3}+CO_2+NO_3^-$$

(a) Fe is oxidised from Fe^{+2} to Fe^{+3}.
(b) Carbon is oxidised from C^{+2} to C^{+4}.
(c) N is oxidised from N^{-3} to N^{+5}.
(d) Carbon is not oxidised.

13. Select the incorrect statement.

(a) Oxidation number of S in $(NH_4)_2S_2O_8$ is +6.
(b) Oxidation number of Os in OsO_4 is +8.
(c) Oxidation number of S in H_2SO_5 is +8.
(d) Oxidation number of O in KO_2 is $-\frac{1}{2}$.

14. The oxidation state of the most electronegative element in the products of the reaction between BaO_2 and H_2SO_4 are

(a) 0 and –1 (b) –1 and –2
(c) –2 and 0 (d) –2 and +1

15. Match List-I with List-II.

List-I (Reactions)	List-II (Type of reactions)
A. $2H_2O_2\xrightarrow{\Delta}2H_2O+O_2$	I. Disproportionation and redox reaction
B. $2NaH\xrightarrow{\Delta}2Na+H_2$	II. Decomposition reaction
C. $V_2O_5+5Ca\xrightarrow{\Delta}2V+5CaO$	III. Decomposition and redox reaction
D. $CaCO_3\xrightarrow{\Delta}CaO+CO_2$	IV. Redox and metal displacement reaction

Choose the correct answer from the options given below.

(a) A-I, B-III, C-IV, D-II
(b) A-III, B-II, C-I, D-IV
(c) A-II, B-III, C-IV, D-I
(d) A-IV, B-I, C-II, D-III

16. Which of the following is the correct match?

(a) $2H_2O\xrightarrow{\Delta}2H_2+O_2$ (Non-metal displacement reaction)
(b) $CuSO_4+Zn\longrightarrow Cu+ZnSO_4$ (Decomposition reaction)
(c) $Cl_2+6OH^-\longrightarrow 5Cl^-+ClO_3^-+3H_2O$ (Disproportionation reaction)
(d) $Zn+2HCl\longrightarrow ZnCl_2+H_2$ (Metal displacement reaction)

17. The species given below that does not show disproportionation reaction is

(a) BrO^-
(b) BrO_2^-
(c) BrO_3^-
(d) BrO_4^-

18. Which one of the following is an example of disproportionation reaction?

(a) $3MnO_4^{-2}+4H^+\longrightarrow 2MnO_4^-+MnO_2+2H_2O$
(b) $MnO_4^-+4H^++4e^-\longrightarrow MnO_2+2H_2O$
(c) $10I^-+2MnO_4^-+16H^+\longrightarrow 2Mn^{2+}+8H_2O+5I_2$
(d) $8MnO_4^-+3S_2O_3^{-2}+H_2O\longrightarrow 8MnO_2+6SO_4^{-2}+2OH^-$

19. In the following decomposition reaction

$$2H_2O \xrightarrow{\Delta} 2H_2 + O_2$$

(a) Hydrogen is oxidised.
(b) Oxygen is reduced.
(c) Hydrogen is reduced.
(d) Oxygen remains unaffected.

20. Match List-I with List-II.

List-I	List-II
I. $Ni(CO)_4$	(p) +6 oxidation state
II. H_2SO_4	(q) Zero oxidation state
III. Cl_2O_7	(r) +5 oxidation state
IV. HNO_3	(s) +7 oxidation state

Choose the correct answer from the options given below.
(a) I-(q), II-(p), III-(s), IV-(r)
(b) I-(p), II-(q), III-(r), IV-(s)
(c) I-(r), II-(s), III-(p), IV-(q)
(d) I-(s), II-(r), III-(q), IV-(p)

21. What is the value of oxidation number of nitrogen atoms in $N_A H_4 N_B O_3$?
(a) Both N_A and N_B has +1 oxidation state.
(b) N_A has –3 and N_B has +5.
(c) N_A has –4 and N_B has +6.
(d) Cannot be calculated.

22. The oxidation state of phosphorus is +3 in
(a) pyrophosphoric acid
(b) metaphosphoric acid
(c) orthophosphoric acid
(d) phosphorus acid

23. Consider the reactions given below.

I. $CuSO_4(aq) + Zn(s) \xrightarrow{\Delta} Cu(s) + ZnSO_4(aq)$
II. $Cr_2O_3(s) + 2Al(s) \longrightarrow 2Cr(s) + Al_2O_3(s)$
III. $V_2O_5(s) + 2Ca(s) \xrightarrow{\Delta} 5CaO(s) + 2V(s)$
IV. $TiBr_4(l) + 2Mg(s) \xrightarrow{\Delta} 2MgBr_2(s) + Ti(s)$
V. $2NaH \xrightarrow{\Delta} 2Na(s) + H_2(g)$

The number of reactions that are metal displacement reactions is ………

(a) 4 (b) 3 (c) 2 (d) 5

24. Amongst the following, identify the species with an atom in +6 oxidation state.
(a) MnO_4^- (b) $[Cr(CN)_6]^{-3}$
(c) $[NiF_6]^{-2}$ (d) CrO_2Cl_2

25. The correct decreasing order of the oxidation state of nitrogen is
(a) HNO_3, NO, NH_4Cl, N_2
(b) HNO_3, NO, N_2, NH_4Cl
(c) HNO_3, NH_4Cl, NO, N_2
(d) NO, HNO_3, NH_4Cl, N_2

26. Match List-I with List-II.

List-I	List-II
A. Hydrolysis	I. $2AuCl_3 + 3HCHO + 3H_2O \longrightarrow 2Au(sol) + 3HCOOH + 6HCl$
B. Reduction	II. $As_2O_3 + 3H_2S \longrightarrow As_2S_3(sol) + 3H_2O$
C. Oxidation	III. $SO_2 + 2H_2S \longrightarrow 3S(sol)$
D. Double decomposition	IV. $FeCl_3 + 3H_2O \longrightarrow Fe(OH)_3(sol) + 3HCl$

Choose the most appropriate answer from the options given below.
(a) A-I, B-III, C-II, D-IV
(b) A-IV, B-I, C-III, D-II
(c) A-I, B-II, C-IV, D-III
(d) A-IV, B-II, C-III, D-I

27. Given below are two statements, one is labelled as Assertion (A) and the other labelled as Reason (R).

Assertion (A) H_2S is passed through an acidified solution of copper sulphate and a black precipitate of cupric sulphide is formed.

Reason (R) The precipitation reaction is possible due to oxidation of Cu^{2+}.

In the light of the above statements, choose the correct answer from the optins given below.
(a) Both (A) and (R) are true and (R) is the correct explanation of (A).
(b) Both (A) and (R) are true but (R) is not the correct explanation of (A).
(c) (A) is true but (R) is false.
(d) (A) is false but (R) is true.

28. The oxidation state of sulphur in the anions SO_3^{-2}, $S_2O_4^{-2}$ and $S_2O_6^{-2}$ follow the order

(a) $S_2O_4^{-2} < SO_3^{-2} < S_2O_6^{-2}$

(b) $SO_3^{-2} < S_2O_4^{-2} < S_2O_6^{-2}$

(c) $S_2O_4^{-2} < S_2O_6^{-2} < SO_3^{-2}$

(d) $S_2O_6^{-2} < S_2O_4^{-2} < SO_3^{-2}$

29. Which of the following is not a redox reaction?

(a) $2Na + Cl_2 \longrightarrow 2NaCl$

(b) $C + O_2 \longrightarrow CO_2$

(c) $AgNO_3 + NaCl \longrightarrow AgCl + NaNO_3$

(d) $Zn + H_2SO_4 \longrightarrow ZnSO_4 + H_2$

30. Given below are two statements.

Statement I $KMnO_4$ acts as an oxidant only.

Statement II Mn in $KMnO_4$ is in its highest oxidation state.

In the light of the above statements, choose the most appropriate answer from the options given below.

(a) Both Statement I and Statement II are incorrect.

(b) Statement I is correct but Statement II is incorrect.

(c) Statement I is incorrect but Statement II is correct.

(d) Both Statement I and Statement II are correct.

Response Index

01 ⓐ ⓑ ⓒ ⓓ	14 ⓐ ⓑ ⓒ ⓓ	27 ⓐ ⓑ ⓒ ⓓ	40 ⓐ ⓑ ⓒ ⓓ
02 ⓐ ⓑ ⓒ ⓓ	15 ⓐ ⓑ ⓒ ⓓ	28 ⓐ ⓑ ⓒ ⓓ	41 ⓐ ⓑ ⓒ ⓓ
03 ⓐ ⓑ ⓒ ⓓ	16 ⓐ ⓑ ⓒ ⓓ	29 ⓐ ⓑ ⓒ ⓓ	42 ⓐ ⓑ ⓒ ⓓ
04 ⓐ ⓑ ⓒ ⓓ	17 ⓐ ⓑ ⓒ ⓓ	30 ⓐ ⓑ ⓒ ⓓ	43 ⓐ ⓑ ⓒ ⓓ
05 ⓐ ⓑ ⓒ ⓓ	18 ⓐ ⓑ ⓒ ⓓ	31 ⓐ ⓑ ⓒ ⓓ	44 ⓐ ⓑ ⓒ ⓓ
06 ⓐ ⓑ ⓒ ⓓ	19 ⓐ ⓑ ⓒ ⓓ	32 ⓐ ⓑ ⓒ ⓓ	45 ⓐ ⓑ ⓒ ⓓ
07 ⓐ ⓑ ⓒ ⓓ	20 ⓐ ⓑ ⓒ ⓓ	33 ⓐ ⓑ ⓒ ⓓ	46 ⓐ ⓑ ⓒ ⓓ
08 ⓐ ⓑ ⓒ ⓓ	21 ⓐ ⓑ ⓒ ⓓ	34 ⓐ ⓑ ⓒ ⓓ	47 ⓐ ⓑ ⓒ ⓓ
09 ⓐ ⓑ ⓒ ⓓ	22 ⓐ ⓑ ⓒ ⓓ	35 ⓐ ⓑ ⓒ ⓓ	48 ⓐ ⓑ ⓒ ⓓ
10 ⓐ ⓑ ⓒ ⓓ	23 ⓐ ⓑ ⓒ ⓓ	36 ⓐ ⓑ ⓒ ⓓ	49 ⓐ ⓑ ⓒ ⓓ
11 ⓐ ⓑ ⓒ ⓓ	24 ⓐ ⓑ ⓒ ⓓ	37 ⓐ ⓑ ⓒ ⓓ	50 ⓐ ⓑ ⓒ ⓓ
12 ⓐ ⓑ ⓒ ⓓ	25 ⓐ ⓑ ⓒ ⓓ	38 ⓐ ⓑ ⓒ ⓓ	
13 ⓐ ⓑ ⓒ ⓓ	26 ⓐ ⓑ ⓒ ⓓ	39 ⓐ ⓑ ⓒ ⓓ	

Performance Scanner

> 90% Excellent !	You have mastered this chapter. The concepts of this chapter are at your fingertips. Move on to the next chapter and maintain this momentum.
76-90% Very Good !	You have a good command over this chapter. Revise the chapter again after a few days and enhance your performance.
60-75% Good !	You have a wide scope to learn for this chapter. Revise this chapter again.
<60 Not Satisfactory!	You have a long way ahead of you to master this chapter. Revise it thoroughly.

Scan for Online Chapter Test

Space for Rough Work

Space for Rough Work

Space for Rough Work

Space for Rough Work

Space for Rough Work

Space for Rough Work

Test Booklet No. **3947209**

Test Booklet Code **CH9**

MEDACE

NEET (UG)

SELF ASSESSMENT KIT

p-Block Elements-I

Topics Covered

Group 13 Elements

Group 14 Elements

Important Instructions

- This Booklet Contains – 2 Topic Tests and One Test on Complete Chapter.
- Each question carries 4 marks.
- For each correct response the candidate will get 4 marks and for every incorrect response 1 mark will be additionally deducted from the total score.
- Use **Blue/Black** point pen only for filling the OMR.
- Rough work is to be done in the space provided for this purpose in the test booklet only.

Name of the Candidate (In Capitals) ______________________

Candidate's Signature ______________

Invigilator's Signature ______________

Facsimile signature stamp of center superintendent ______________

Do not open this Booklet until you start attempting the Test

Topical Follow Thru

Test 1

Syllabus
- Electronic Configuration, General Trends in Physical and Chemical Properties of Elements
- Unique Behaviour of Boron

For deeper insight **Scan the QR Code**

Important Instructions
- The test is of 30 minutes duration and contains 25 multiple choice questions (Four options with a single correct answer).
- Choose the correct option and fill the OMR given on the last page of test accordingly.
- At some instances you may find more than 1 option may be correct. In such circumstances, you have to judge the most appropriate answer as per conditions given in the question.

1. Arrange the following elements in increasing order of their first ionisation energy.

Boron, Gallium, Aluminium

Choose the correct answer from the options given below:

(a) Boron < Aluminium < Gallium
(b) Gallium < Aluminium < Boron
(c) Aluminium < Gallium < Boron
(d) Boron < Gallium < Aluminium

2. What is the covalency and oxidation state of boron in the tetrafluoroborate ion $[BF_4]^-$?

(a) Covalency: 4, Oxidation state: + 3
(b) Covalency: 3, Oxidation state: + 5
(c) Covalency: 3, Oxidation state: + 4
(d) Covalency: 4, Oxidation state: + 4

3. Given below are two statements.

Statement I Boron exhibits exceptional hardness, suggesting a high lattice energy.

Statement II Boron possesses the highest melting and boiling point among its group members.

In the light of the above statements, choose the correct answer from the options given below.

(a) Both Statement I and Statement II are incorrect.
(b) Statement I is correct but Statement II is incorrect.
(c) Statement I is incorrect but Statement II is correct.
(d) Both Statement I and Statement II are correct.

4. Identify the element that would exist in a liquid state when immersed in pure boiling water.

(a) Gallium (b) Lithium
(c) Cesium (d) Aluminium

5. Arrange the boron trihalides in ascending order of Lewis acid character:

(a) $BBr_3 < BI_3 < BCl_3 < BF_3$
(b) $BF_3 < BCl_3 < BBr_3 < BI_3$
(c) $BI_3 < BBr_3 < BCl_3 < BF_3$
(d) $BI_3 < BBr_3 > BF_3 < BCl_3$

6. When aluminium chloride dissolves in an acidic aqueous solution, it forms a complex ion with water molecules. What is the hybridisation of the aluminium atom in this complex ion?

(a) sp^3 (b) dsp^2
(c) sp^3d^2 (d) d^2sp^3

7. Which of the following elements from group 13 is unable to form a stable MF_6^{3-} ion?

(a) Gallium (b) Aluminium
(c) Indium (d) Boron

8. Boric acid (H_3BO_3) exhibits acidic properties due to its ability to

(a) release a proton (H^+) directly
(b) accept a hydroxide ion (OH^-) from water and releasing a proton
(c) combine with a proton from water
(d) contain a replaceable H^+ ion

9. Aluminium fluoride (AlF_3) is only soluble in hydrofluoric acid (HF) in the presence of potassium fluoride (KF). This is because of the formation of which complex ion?

(a) $K_3[AlF_6]$ (b) $K[AlF_4]$
(c) AlH_3 (d) $K_3[AlF_3H_3]$

10. Arrange the following group 13 elements in order of increasing stability of their +1 oxidation state.

Al, Ga, Tl, In

Choose the correct answer from the options given below.

(a) Al < Ga < In < Tl (b) Tl < In < Ga < Al
(c) Ga < In < Al < Tl (d) In < Tl< Ga < Al

11. Which of the following substances has a layered structure similar to graphite?

(a) Boron nitride (b) Boron
(c) Boron carbide (d) Diborane

12. The electron-deficient species among the following is

(a) Si_2H_6 (b) B_2H_6
(c) PH_5 (d) C_2H_6

13. Select the correct statement from the following.

A. Boron is a non-metal, while the rest of the elements in the group 13 are metals.
B. The +3 oxidation state is the most stable oxidation state for all elements in the group 13.
C. The Lewis acidity of the boron halides increases in the order $BF_3 < BCl_3 < BBr_3 < BI_3$.
D. The tendency to form covalent compounds increases down the group.
E. Gallium has a lower melting point than aluminium.

Choose the correct answer from the options given below.

(a) A, B, and C (b) A, C, and D
(c) A, C, and E (d) A, B, and E

14. The correct order of reducing character of group 13 elements is

Ga, In, Tl, Al

(a) Ga < Al < In > Tl
(b) Al > Ga > In > Tl
(c) Al > Ga > Tl > In
(d) Ga > Al > In > Tl

15. Identify the correct statement(s) for $Al_2(CH_3)_6$ from the statements given below.

A. In $Al_2(CH_3)_6$, all Al—C bonds are equivalent.
B. In $Al_2(CH_3)_6$, there are two 3-centre-2-electron bonds.
C. $Al_2(CH_3)_6$ is a lewis acid.
D. $Al_2(CH_3)_6$ can be synthesised from $AlCl_3$ and CH_3MgBr.
E. $Al_2(CH_3)_6$ is a planar molecule.

Choose the correct answer from the options given below.

(a) (A), (B) and (C) only
(b) (B), (C) and (D) only
(c) (B) and (D) only
(d) (C) and (E) only

16. Which of the following has the regular tetrahedral structure?

(a) BF_4^- (b) B_2H_6
(c) H_3BO_3 (d) B_2O_3

17. Boron reacts with NaOH and water, then the products formed will be

(a) $Na_2B_4O_7$ and H_2
(b) Na_3BO_3 and H_2
(c) $NaBO_2$ and H_2
(d) B_2O_3 and H_2

18. H_3BO_3 and HBO_2 do not differ in

(a) oxidation number (b) basicity
(c) melting point (d) structure

19. Given below are two statements, one is labelled as Assertion (A) and the other is labelled as Reason (R).

Assertion (A) In water, orthoboric acid behaves as a weak monobasic acid.

Reason (R) In water, orthoboric acid acts as a proton donor.

In the light of the above statements, choose the correct answer from the options given below.

(a) Both (A) and (R) are true and (R) is the correct explanation of (A).
(b) Both (A) and (R) are true but (R) is not the correct explanation of (A).
(c) (A) is true but (R) is false.
(d) (A) is false but (R) is true.

20. Which of the following is the correct order of ionisation enthalpy ($\Delta_i H$ kJ mol^{-1})?

(a) B > Al > Ga > In > Tl
(b) B < Al < Ga < In < Tl
(c) B < Al > Ga < In > Tl
(d) B > Al < Ga > In < Tl

21. Which of the following is the correct structural representation of diborane ?

(a) $[BH_2]^+ + [BH_4]^-$

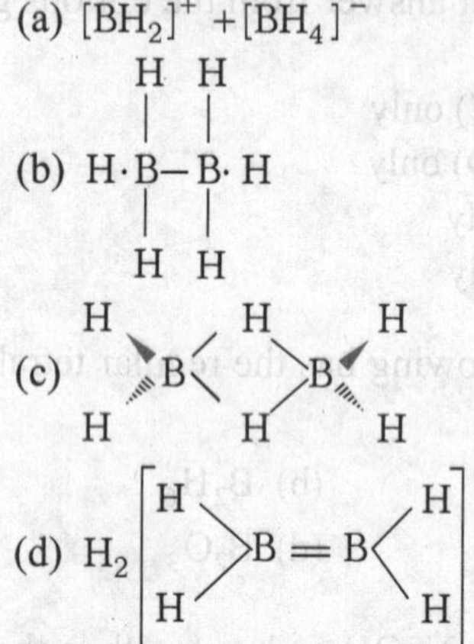

22. Match Column I with Column II.

Column I (Compound)	Column II (Use)
A. Boric acid	I. In Friedel-Craft acylation
B. Borax	II. Mild antiseptic
C. Aluminium chloride	III. Washing powder
D. Sodium peroxoborate	IV. Buffer

Choose the correct answer from the options given below.

(a) A-II, B-IV, C-I, D-III
(b) A-IV, B-III, C-II, D-I
(c) A-III, B-IV, C-II, D-I
(d) A-II, B-III, C-I, D-IV

23. Which of the following is incorrect statement(s)?

(a) BF_3 fumes strongly in moist air and is partially hydrolysed by excess of water.
(b) BF_3 is converted into the adducts $BF_3 \cdot H_2O$ and $BF_3 \cdot 2H_2O$ with small amounts of water at low temperature.
(c) H_3BO_3 is a weak acid but HBF_4 is a very strong acid.
(d) Ammonia reacts with diborane to give $B_2H_5 \cdot NH_3$.

24. The element which exists in liquid state for a wide range of temperature and can be used for measuring high temperature is

(a) B
(b) Al
(c) Ga
(d) In

25. The solution of sodium meta-aluminate on boiling with ammonium chloride gives a white precipitate of

(a) Al_2O_3
(b) $AlCl_3$
(c) $Al(OH)_3$
(d) $(NH_4)_2SO_4 \cdot Al_2(SO_4)_3$

Response Index

01	a	b	c	d	10	a	b	c	d	19	a	b	c	d
02	a	b	c	d	11	a	b	c	d	20	a	b	c	d
03	a	b	c	d	12	a	b	c	d	21	a	b	c	d
04	a	b	c	d	13	a	b	c	d	22	a	b	c	d
05	a	b	c	d	14	a	b	c	d	23	a	b	c	d
06	a	b	c	d	15	a	b	c	d	24	a	b	c	d
07	a	b	c	d	16	a	b	c	d	25	a	b	c	d
08	a	b	c	d	17	a	b	c	d					
09	a	b	c	d	18	a	b	c	d					

Performance Scanner

> 90% Excellent !	You have mastered these topics. The concepts of these topics are at your fingertips. Move on to the next test and maintain this momentum.
76-90% Very Good !	You have a good command over these topics. Revise these topics again after a few days and enhance your performance.
60-75% Good !	You have a wide scope to learn for these topics. Revise these topics again.
<60 Not Satisfactory!	You have a long way ahead of you to master these topics. Revise it thoroughly.

Test 2

Syllabus
- Electronic Configuration, General Trends in Physical and Chemical Properties of Elements
- Unique Behaviour of Carbon

For deeper insight **Scan the QR Code**

Important Instructions
- The test is of 30 minutes duration and contains 15 multiple choice questions (Four options with a single correct answer).
- Choose the correct option and fill the OMR given on the last page of test accordingly.
- At some instances you may find more than 1 option may be correct. In such circumstances, you have to judge the most appropriate answer as per conditions given in the question.

1. Choose the incorrect statement among the following.

(a) Silicon tetrachloride ($SiCl_4$) readily reacts with water.

(b) Germanium tetrahalides (GeX_4) are more stable than germanium dihalides (GeX_2).

(c) Tin(IV) fluoride (SnF_4) exhibits ionic character.

(d) Lead(IV) fluoride (PbF_4) is primarily covalent in nature.

2. Which of the following oxides exhibits amphoteric behaviour?

(a) Carbon dioxide (CO_2)

(b) Silicon dioxide (SiO_2)

(c) Germanium dioxide (GeO_2)

(d) Tin dioxide (SnO_2)

3. Consider the following statements.

A. Dry ice (solid CO_2) is used as a refrigerant for ice cream and frozen food.

B. The C_{60} fullerene molecule contains a combination of pentagonal and hexagonal carbon rings.

C. Zeolites like ZSM-5 can catalyse the conversion of methanol to gasoline.

D. Carbon monoxide (CO) is a toxic, pungent smelling gas.

E. Graphite is used in nuclear reactors.

Which of the following statements are correct?

(a) (A) and (C)

(b) (B) and (C)

(c) (C), (D) and (E)

(d) (A), (B), (C) and (E)

4. Match List-I with List-II.

	List-I (Compound)		List-II (Characteristic)
A.	Coke	I.	Carbon atoms are sp^3-hybridised
B.	Diamond	II.	Used as a dry lubricant.
C.	Fullerene	III.	Used as a reducing agent.
D.	Graphite	IV.	Cage-like molecules.

Choose the correct answer from the options given below.

(a) A-I B-II C-III D-IV

(b) A-II B-III C-I D-IV

(c) A-III B-I C-IV D-II

(d) A-IV B-III C-II D-I

5. Which of the following compounds is commonly used in cosmetic surgery due to its biocompatibility and inertness?

(a) Zeolites
(b) Silica
(c) Silicates
(d) Silicones

6. Select the incorrect statement regarding carbon monoxide (CO).

(a) It reduces the oxygen-carrying capacity of blood.

(b) Carboxyhaemoglobin (HbCO) is more stable than oxyhaemoglobin (HbO_2).

(c) It is produced through the complete combustion of carbon-containing fuels.

(d) It can lead to the formation of carboxyhaemoglobin upon inhalation.

7. Which of the following complex ions is unlikely to exist due to steric hindrance and unfavourable bonding interactions?

(a) $[GeCl_6]^{2-}$ (b) $[Sn(OH)_6]^{2-}$
(c) $[SiCl_6]^{2-}$ (d) $[SiF_6]^{2-}$

8. The compounds of group 14 elements which is expected to be most ionic in nature is

(a) $PbCl_2$ (b) $PbCl_4$ (c) $SiCl_4$ (d) CCl_4

9. Fullerene (C_{70}), an allotrope of carbon, contains.

(a) 25 hexagons and 12 pentagons
(b) 20 hexagons and 12 pentagons
(c) 12 hexagons and 25 pentagons
(d) 18 hexagons and 14 pentagons

10. Arrange the following group 14 elements in decreasing order of their tendency for catenation.

C, Si, Sn, Ge

Choose the correct answer from the options given below:

(a) C > Si > Ge > Sn (b) C > Ge > Si > Sn
(c) Sn > Ge > Si > C (d) Si > C > Ge > Sn

11. Which of the following hydrides is the most volatile?

(a) CH_4 (b) SiH_4 (c) GeH_4 (d) SnH_4

12. Among the following ions, how many are expected to behave as oxidising agents?

$Pb^{4+}, Sn^{2+}, Ge^{2+}, Ge^{+}, Pb^{2+}$

(a) 1 (b) 2 (c) 3 (d) 4

13. Given below are two statements.

Statement I SnO_2 and PbO_2 are acidic oxides, while GeO and SiO are amphoteric.

Statement II Allotropic forms of carbon arise from the ability to form long carbon chains and π-bonds between carbon and other atoms having vacant *p* or *d*-orbitals.

In the light of the above statements, choose the correct answer from the options given below.

(a) Both Statement I and Statement II are incorrect.
(b) Statement I is correct but Statement II is incorrect.
(c) Statement I is incorrect but Statement II is correct.
(d) Both Statement I and Statement II are correct.

14. Given below are two statements, one is labelled as Assertion (A) and the other is labelled as Reason (R).

Assertion (A) Carbon dioxide (CO_2) exhibits acidic properties, while carbon monoxide (CO) is neutral.

Reason (R) CO_2 reacts with water to form a weakly acidic carbonic acid (H_2CO_3), whereas CO does not show this reaction.

In the light of the above statements, choose the correct answer from the options given below.

(a) Both (A) and (R) are true and (R) is the correct explanation of (A).
(b) Both (A) and (R) are true but (R) is not the correct explanation of (A).
(c) (A) is true but (R) is false.
(d) (A) is false but (R) is true.

15. Compound *X*, a potent oxidising agent used in lead-acid batteries and exhibits amphoteric behaviour. Compound *X* is

(a) $PbCO_3$ (b) $PbSO_4$
(c) PbO (d) PbO_2

Response Index

01	(a)	(b)	(c)	(d)	10	(a)	(b)	(c)	(d)	19	(a)	(b)	(c)	(d)
02	(a)	(b)	(c)	(d)	11	(a)	(b)	(c)	(d)	20	(a)	(b)	(c)	(d)
03	(a)	(b)	(c)	(d)	12	(a)	(b)	(c)	(d)	21	(a)	(b)	(c)	(d)
04	(a)	(b)	(c)	(d)	13	(a)	(b)	(c)	(d)	22	(a)	(b)	(c)	(d)
05	(a)	(b)	(c)	(d)	14	(a)	(b)	(c)	(d)	23	(a)	(b)	(c)	(d)
06	(a)	(b)	(c)	(d)	15	(a)	(b)	(c)	(d)	24	(a)	(b)	(c)	(d)
07	(a)	(b)	(c)	(d)	16	(a)	(b)	(c)	(d)	25	(a)	(b)	(c)	(d)
08	(a)	(b)	(c)	(d)	17	(a)	(b)	(c)	(d)					
09	(a)	(b)	(c)	(d)	18	(a)	(b)	(c)	(d)					

Performance Scanner

> 90% Excellent !	You have mastered these topics. The concepts of these topics are at your fingertips. Move on to the chapter test and maintain this momentum.
76-90% Very Good !	You have a good command over these topics. Revise these topics again after a few days and enhance your performance.
60-75% Good !	You have a wide scope to learn for these topics. Revise these topics again.
<60 Not Satisfactory!	You have a long way ahead of you to master these topics. Revise it thoroughly.

Chapter Break Thru

Syllabus

- Electronic Configuration, General Trends in Physical and Chemical Properties of Elements
- Unique Behaviour of Boron

- Electronic Configuration, General Trends in Physical and Chemical Properties of Elements
- Unique Behaviour of Carbon

Important Instructions

- The test is of 1 hour duration and contains 50 multiple choice questions (Four options with a single correct answer).
- Choose the correct option and fill the OMR given on the last page of test accordingly.
- At some instances, you may find more than 1 option may be correct. In such circumstances, you have to judge the most appropriate answer as per the conditions given in the question.

1. Arrange the following oxide in decreasing order of their acidic character?

$$CO, SiO_2, Tl_2O_3, PbO_2$$

Choose the correct answer from the options given below:

(a) $CO > SiO_2 > PbO_2 > Tl_2O_3$
(b) $SiO_2 > PbO_2 > CO > Tl_2O_3$
(c) $PbO_2 > CO > SiO_2 > Tl_2O_3$
(d) $Tl_2O_3 > PbO_2 > SiO_2 > CO$

2. The most probable oxidation state of an element with the electronic configuration of $1s^2 2s^2 2p^6 3s^2 3p^1$ is

(a) +1 (b) +2
(c) +3 (d) −1

3. Which one of the following species does not exist?

(a) $[BF_6]^{3-}$
(b) $[AlF_6]^{3-}$
(c) $[GaF_6]^{3-}$
(d) $[InF_6]^{3-}$

4. The first ionisation enthalpy of aluminium is smaller that that of magnesium because

(a) atomic size of Al > Mg
(b) atomic size of Al < Mg
(c) Al has one electron in the *p*-orbital.
(d) atomic number of Al > Mg

5. Which is true for an element *R* present in group 13 of the periodic table?

(a) It is a gas at room temperature.
(b) It has oxidation state of +4.
(c) It forms R_2O_3.
(d) It forms RX_2.

6. The general trend in the properties of elements of carbon family shows that with the rise in atomic member,

(a) the tendency toward catenation increases.
(b) tendency to show +2 oxidation state increases.
(c) the metallic character decreases.
(d) the tendency to form complexes with covalency higher than four decreases.

7. Ge (II) compounds are powerful reducing agent whereas Pb (IV) compounds are strong oxidations.The reason is

(a) Pb is more electropositive than Ge
(b) ionisation potential of lead is less than that of Ge
(c) ionic radii of Pb^{2+} and Pb^{4+} are larger than those of Ge^{2+} and Ge^{4+}
(d) more pronounced inert pair effect in Pb than Ge

8. Given below are two statements.

Statement I Graphite is a good conductor of heat and electricity.

Statement II Graphite has all the electrons firmly held together in C—C σ-bonds.

In the light of the above statements, choose the correct answer from the options given below.

(a) Both Statement I and Statement II are incorrect.
(b) Statement I is correct but Statement II is incorrect.
(c) Statement I is incorrect but Statement II is correct.
(d) Both Statement I and Statement II are correct.

9. Among the halides, what is the decreasing order of Lewis acid character?

(i) BCl_3 (ii) $AlCl_3$
(iii) $GaCl_3$ (iv) $InCl_3$

(a) (i) > (ii) > (iii) > (iv)
(b) (iv) > (iii) > (ii) > (i)
(c) (iii) > (iv) > (ii) > (i)
(d) (ii) > (iii) > (iv) > (i)

10. Standard electrode potential values, $E°$ for Al^{3+} / Al is –1.66 V and that of Tl^{3+} / Tl is +1.26 V. On the basis of this data, which of the following statement is wrong?

(a) Al has higher tendency to form Al^{3+} *(aq)* ions.
(b) Tl^{3+} is not only unstable in solution but is a powerful oxidising agent also.
(c) Tl^{4+} is more stable in solution than Tl^{3+}.
(d) Aluminium is less electropositive than thallium.

11. When tin is treated with concentrated nitric acid

(a) it is converted into stannous nitrate
(b) it is converted into stannic nitrate
(c) it is converted into meta-stannic acid
(d) it becomes passive

12. White lead is formed when one of the following is added to the solution of any lead salt?

(a) Na_2CO_3 (b) Dil. HCl
(c) Dil. H_2SO_4 (d) Dil. NaOH

13. Magnesium combines with which of the following element on heating?

(a) Al (b) B
(c) Ga (d) Tl

14. The chemical formula of bauxite is

(a) Al_2O_3 (b) $Al_2O_3 \cdot 2H_2O$
(c) Na_3AlF_4 (d) Al_2Cl_6

15. Given below are two statements.

Statement I Amorphous boron and aluminium metal on heating in air form B_2O_3 and Al_2O_3 respectively.

Statement II Boron trioxide is acidic and reacts with basic oxides to form metal borates.

In the light of the above statements, choose the correct answer from the options given below.

(a) Both Statement I and Statement II are incorrect.
(b) Statement I is correct but Statement II is incorrect.
(c) Statement I is incorrect but Statement II is correct.
(d) Both Statement I and Statement II are correct.

16. The correct order of decreasing ionic character of lead dihalides is

(a) $PbF_2 > PbCl_2 > PbBr_2 > PbI_2$
(b) $PbF_2 > PbBr_2 > PbCl_2 > PbI_2$
(c) $PbF_2 > PbI_2 > PbCl_2 > PbBr_2$
(d) $PbCl_2 > PbBr_2 > PbF_2 > PbI_2$

17. Which of following statement about diamond is incorrect?

(a) Diamond is ionic in nature.
(b) It has very high melting point.
(c) It has 3-dimensional network structure involving strong C—C bonds.
(d) The bond between C-atoms are directional and difficult to break.

18. Given below are two statements, one is labelled as Assertion (A) and the other is labelled as Reason (R).

Assertion (A) The first ionisation enthalpy of Sn is greater than that of Pb.

Reason (R) The $4f$ electrons in Pb are poor at shielding the outermost electrons.

In the light of the above statements, choose the correct answer from the options given below.

(a) Both (A) and (R) are true and (R) is the correct explanation of (A).
(b) Both (A) and (R) are true but (R) is not the correct explanation of (A).
(c) (A) is true but (R) is false.
(d) (A) is false but (R) is true.

19. In which of the following pairs, both of the species are electron deficient?

(a) BCl_3, CCl_4 (b) BCl_3, AlH_3
(c) $SiCl_4, CCl_4$ (d) CCl_4, SiF_4

20. Select the correct statement.

(a) The melting point of tin is higher but boiling point is lower than that of lead.
(b) The melting point of tin is lower but boiling point is higher than that of lead.
(c) The melting and boiling point of tin are lower than that of lead.
(d) The melting and boiling point of tin are higher than that of lead.

21. The element forming neutral as well as acidic oxide is

(a) Si (b) Sn
(c) B (d) C

22. Which gas is liberated when Al_4C_3 is hydrolysed?

(a) CH_4 (b) C_2H_2
(c) C_2H_6 (d) CO_2

23. In laboratory, silicon can be prepared by which reaction?

(a) By heating carbon in electric furnace
(b) By heating potassium with potassium dichromate
(c) Silica with magnesium.
(d) None of the above

24. Which of the following is water soluble and strongly basic?

(a) $Al(OH)_3$ (b) $Ga(OH)_3$
(c) $In(OH)_3$ (d) TlOH

25. Given below are two statements, one is labelled as Assertion (A) and the other is labelled as Reason (R).

Assertion (A) It is difficult to obtain pure crystalline boron.

Reason (R) Boron is highly reactive.

In the light of the above statements, choose the correct answer from the options given below.

(a) Both (A) and (R) are true and (R) is the correct explanation of (A).
(b) Both (A) and (R) are true but (R) is not the correct explanation of (A).
(c) (A) is true but (R) is false.
(d) (A) is false but (R) is true.

26. Water gas is an equimolar mixture of

(a) CO and CH_4 (b) CO_2 and H_2
(c) CO and H_2 (d) CO and N_2

27. Atomic orbitals of carbon involved in diamond structure are

(a) *sp*-hybridised
(b) sp^2-hybridised
(c) sp^3-hybridised
(d) sp^3d-hybridised

28. The main reason that $SiCl_4$ is easily hydrolysed as compared to CCl_4 is

(a) Si can extend its coordination number beyond four.
(b) Si—Si bond is weaker.
(c) $SiCl_4$ is ionic.
(d) $SiCl_4$ is covalent.

29. The tin (IV) oxide is

(a) acidic (b) basic
(c) neutral (d) amphoteric

30. Given below are two statements.

Statement I Al and Ga have nearly same atomic radii.

Statement II Al and Ga show diagonal relationship.

In the light of the above statements, choose the correct answer from the options given below.

(a) Both Statement I and Statement II are incorrect.
(b) Statement I is correct but Statement II is incorrect.
(c) Statement I is incorrect but Statement II is correct.
(d) Both Statement I and Statement II are correct.

■ Response Index

01 ⓐ ⓑ ⓒ ⓓ	14 ⓐ ⓑ ⓒ ⓓ	27 ⓐ ⓑ ⓒ ⓓ	40 ⓐ ⓑ ⓒ ⓓ
02 ⓐ ⓑ ⓒ ⓓ	15 ⓐ ⓑ ⓒ ⓓ	28 ⓐ ⓑ ⓒ ⓓ	41 ⓐ ⓑ ⓒ ⓓ
03 ⓐ ⓑ ⓒ ⓓ	16 ⓐ ⓑ ⓒ ⓓ	29 ⓐ ⓑ ⓒ ⓓ	42 ⓐ ⓑ ⓒ ⓓ
04 ⓐ ⓑ ⓒ ⓓ	17 ⓐ ⓑ ⓒ ⓓ	30 ⓐ ⓑ ⓒ ⓓ	43 ⓐ ⓑ ⓒ ⓓ
05 ⓐ ⓑ ⓒ ⓓ	18 ⓐ ⓑ ⓒ ⓓ	31 ⓐ ⓑ ⓒ ⓓ	44 ⓐ ⓑ ⓒ ⓓ
06 ⓐ ⓑ ⓒ ⓓ	19 ⓐ ⓑ ⓒ ⓓ	32 ⓐ ⓑ ⓒ ⓓ	45 ⓐ ⓑ ⓒ ⓓ
07 ⓐ ⓑ ⓒ ⓓ	20 ⓐ ⓑ ⓒ ⓓ	33 ⓐ ⓑ ⓒ ⓓ	46 ⓐ ⓑ ⓒ ⓓ
08 ⓐ ⓑ ⓒ ⓓ	21 ⓐ ⓑ ⓒ ⓓ	34 ⓐ ⓑ ⓒ ⓓ	47 ⓐ ⓑ ⓒ ⓓ
09 ⓐ ⓑ ⓒ ⓓ	22 ⓐ ⓑ ⓒ ⓓ	35 ⓐ ⓑ ⓒ ⓓ	48 ⓐ ⓑ ⓒ ⓓ
10 ⓐ ⓑ ⓒ ⓓ	23 ⓐ ⓑ ⓒ ⓓ	36 ⓐ ⓑ ⓒ ⓓ	49 ⓐ ⓑ ⓒ ⓓ
11 ⓐ ⓑ ⓒ ⓓ	24 ⓐ ⓑ ⓒ ⓓ	37 ⓐ ⓑ ⓒ ⓓ	50 ⓐ ⓑ ⓒ ⓓ
12 ⓐ ⓑ ⓒ ⓓ	25 ⓐ ⓑ ⓒ ⓓ	38 ⓐ ⓑ ⓒ ⓓ	
13 ⓐ ⓑ ⓒ ⓓ	26 ⓐ ⓑ ⓒ ⓓ	39 ⓐ ⓑ ⓒ ⓓ	

■ Performance Scanner

> 90% Excellent !	You have mastered this chapter. The concepts of this chapter are at your fingertips. Move on to the next chapter and maintain this momentum.
76-90% Very Good !	You have a good command over this chapter. Revise the chapter again after a few days and enhance your performance.
60-75% Good !	You have a wide scope to learn for this chapter. Revise this chapter again.
<60 Not Satisfactory!	You have a long way ahead of you to master this chapter. Revise it thoroughly.

Scan for Online **Chapter Test**

Space for Rough Work

Space for Rough Work

Space for Rough Work

Space for Rough Work

Space for Rough Work

Space for Rough Work

MEDACE
NEET (UG)
SELF ASSESSMENT KIT

Test Booklet No. 3947210

Test Booklet Code CH10

Purification and Characterisation of Organic Compounds

Topics Covered

Methods of Purification

Qualitative Analysis

Quantitative Analysis

Important Instructions

- This Booklet Contains – 3 Topic Tests and One Test on Complete Chapter.
- Each question carries 4 marks.
- For each correct response the candidate will get 4 marks and for every incorrect response 1 mark will be additionally deducted from the total score.
- Use **Blue/Black** point pen only for filling the OMR.
- Rough work is to be done in the space provided for this purpose in the test booklet only.

Name of the Candidate (In Capitals)

____

Candidate's Signature __________

Invigilator's Signature __________

Facsimile signature stamp of center superintendent__________

Do not open this Booklet until you start attempting the Test

Topical Follow Thru

Test 1

Syllabus
- Crystallisation
- Sublimation
- Distillation, Differential Extraction and Chromatography-Principles and their Applications

For deeper insight **Scan the QR Code**

Important Instructions
- The test is of 30 minutes duration and contains 15 multiple choice questions (Four options with a single correct answer).
- Choose the correct option and fill the OMR given on the last page of test accordingly.
- At some instances, you may find more than 1 option may be correct. In such circumstances, you have to judge the most appropriate answer as per the conditions given in the question.

1. The condition of "mobile phase is liquid and stationary phase is solid" explains which kind of chromatography?

(a) Gas-liquid chromatography
(b) Paper chromatography
(c) Thin layer chromatography
(d) Partition chromatography

2. Separation of absolute alcohol from the rectified spirit can be done by which of the following method?

(a) Azeotropic distillation
(b) Steam distillation
(c) Fractional distillation
(d) Simple distillation

3. Given below are two statements.

Statement I The purification method used to purify essential oils is steam distillation.
Statement II Steam distillation is used to separate volatile compounds which are insoluble in water.
In the light of the above statements, choose the most appropriate answer from the options given below.

(a) Both Statement I and Statement II are incorrect.
(b) Statement I is correct but Statement II is incorrect.
(c) Statement I is incorrect but Statement II is correct.
(d) Both Statement I and Statement II are correct.

4. In the sugar factories, the raw juices are generally concentrated by

(a) sublimation
(b) steam distillation
(c) crystallisation
(d) vacuum distillation

5. The most reliable method of separating different types of sugars from each other is

(a) Fehling solution test
(b) sublimation
(c) fractional crystallisation
(d) chromatography

6. Match List-I with List-II.

	List-I (Types of distillation)		List-II (Examples)
A.	Simple distillation	I.	Spent-lye in soap industry
B.	Fractional distillation	II.	$CHCl_3$ and $PhNH_2$
C.	Steam distillation	III.	Aniline-water mixture
D.	Distillation under reduced pressure	IV.	Crude oil in petroleum

Choose the correct answer from the options given below:
(a) A-I, B-II, C-III, D-IV
(b) A-II, B-IV, C-III, D-I
(c) A-II, B-I, C-IV, D-III
(d) A-III, B-II, C-I, D-IV

7. Given below are two statements, one is labelled as Assertion (A) and the other is labelled as Reason (R).

Assertion (A) Benzene with boiling point 353 K and methanol with boiling point 338 K are separated by simple distillation.

Reason (R) To separate two liquids from their mixture when their boiling point differ by 80°C so, the separation method used is fractional distillation.

In the light of the above statements, choose the correct answer from the options given below.
(a) Both (A) and (R) are true and (R) is the correct explanation of (A).
(b) Both (A) and (R) are true but (R) is not the correct explanation of (A).
(c) (A) is true but (R) is false.
(d) (A) is false but (R) is true.

8. Firstly evolved vapours will be rich in which of the following substance, when petroleum is heated gradually
(a) diesel
(b) kerosene
(c) lubricating oil
(d) petroleum ether

9. The value of R_f of a substance does not depend on the
(a) nature of the substance
(b) concentration of the substance
(c) temperature
(d) nature of the solvent

10. The fractionating column is used in which of the following separation technique?
(a) Chromatography
(b) Sublimation
(c) Fractional distillation
(d) Crystallisation

11. Given below are two statements.

Statement I The value of retardation factor (R_f) can be measured in metre or centimeter.

Statement II The value of R_f of a compound remains constant in all solvents.

In the light of the above statements, choose the most appropriate answer from the options given below.
(a) Both Statement I and Statement II are incorrec
(b) Statement I is correct but Statement II is incorrect.
(c) Statement I is incorrect but Statement II is correct.
(d) Both Statement I and Statement II are correct.

12. For the separation of which types of compounds the fractional crystallisation method is used?
(a) Inorganic and organic solids mixed with each other.
(b) Organic solids which are highly soluble in water.
(c) Organic solids having small difference in their solubilities in preferred solvent.
(d) With the greater difference in their solubilities of different organic solids in preferred solvent.

13. Which of the following statements is/are not correct about R_f?
A. R_f value is dependent on the mobile phase.
B. R_f value depends on the type of chromatography.
C. The R_f value cannot be more than one ($R_f < 1$).
D. Low polarity compounds have higher R_f value which means higher adsorption.
E. The solute with least R_f value will come out last in the separation of mixture.

Choose the correct answer from the options given below.
(a) A, B and C
(b) Only E
(c) Only D
(d) Both B and E

14. Which compound includes the one that have high vapour pressure at a temperature below its melting point?

(a) Citric acid
(b) Salicylic acid
(c) Benzoic acid
(d) Acetic acid

15. The purification of aniline from aniline-water mixture can be done by the method of

(a) simple distillation
(b) steam distillation
(c) fractional distillation
(d) vacuum distillation

Response Index

01	a	b	c	d	10	a	b	c	d	19	a	b	c	d
02	a	b	c	d	11	a	b	c	d	20	a	b	c	d
03	a	b	c	d	12	a	b	c	d	21	a	b	c	d
04	a	b	c	d	13	a	b	c	d	22	a	b	c	d
05	a	b	c	d	14	a	b	c	d	23	a	b	c	d
06	a	b	c	d	15	a	b	c	d	24	a	b	c	d
07	a	b	c	d	16	a	b	c	d	25	a	b	c	d
08	a	b	c	d	17	a	b	c	d					
09	a	b	c	d	18	a	b	c	d					

Performance Scanner

> 90% Excellent !	You have mastered these topics. The concepts of these topics are at your fingertips. Move on to the next test and maintain this momentum.
76-90% Very Good !	You have a good command over these topics. Revise these topics again after a few days and enhance your performance.
60-75% Good !	You have a wide scope to learn for these topics. Revise these topics again.
<60 Not Satisfactory!	You have a long way ahead of you to master these topics. Revise it thoroughly.

Test 2

Syllabus • Detection of Nitrogen, Sulphur, Phosphorus and Halogens

For deeper insight **Scan the QR Code**

Important Instructions

- The test is of 30 minutes duration and contains 15 multiple choice questions (Four options with a single correct answer).
- Choose the correct option and fill the OMR given on the last page of test accordingly.
- At some instances, you may find more than 1 option may be correct. In such circumstances, you have to judge the most appropriate answer as per conditions given in the question.

1. Which compound gets precipitated in the detection of carbon and hydrogen?

(a) Copper (b) Carbon dioxde
(c) Calcium carbonate (d) Copper sulphate

2. In the estimation of N, S and halogens from Lassaigne's test, the organic compound is

(a) dissolved with sodamide
(b) fused with sodium
(c) fused with calcium
(d) extracted with sodamide

3. Which of the following compounds, does not give a positive test in Lassaigne's test for nitrogen ?

(a) Azobenzene (b) Phenyl hydrazine
(c) Glycine (d) Hydrazine

4. Match List-I with List-II.

	List-I (Elements present)	List-II (Compounds formed)
A.	Carbon and hydrogen	I. $[Fe(CN)_5NOS]^{4-}$
B.	Nitrogen	II. $[NH_4]_3PO_4 \cdot 12MoO_3$
C.	Sulphur	III. $CuSO_4 \cdot 5H_2O$
D.	Phosphorus	IV. $Fe_4[Fe(CN)_6]_3 \cdot xH_2O$

Choose the correct answer from the options given below.

(a) A-I, B-II, C-III, D-IV
(b) A-III, B-IV, C-I, D-II
(c) A-IV, B-II, C-III, D-I
(d) A-II, B-I, C-IV, D-III

5. The sodium fusion extract is boiled with conc. HNO_3 before testing for halogens is to

(a) convert Fe^{2+} into Fe^{3+}
(b) make the solution acidic
(c) make solution more clear
(d) destroy CN^- and S^{2-} ions

6. On treating sodium fusion extract with sodium nitroprusside, appearance of a violet colour indicates the presence of

(a) carbon (b) nitrogen
(c) sulphur (d) chlorine

7. Which of the following statements is/are correct?

A. When $(CH_3COO)_2Pb$ solution is added to the acidified Lassaigne's extract of an organic compound, a black precipitate of PbS is formed.
B. In Lassaigne's test for halogens, conc. HNO_3 is used to remove HCN and H_2S.
C. In Lassaigne's test, N present in the organic compound is converted into CN^- ions.
D. The formula of nitroprusside ion is $[Fe(CN)_5NOS]^{2-}$.
E. Victor Meyer's method is used for determination of molecular mass in qualitative analysis.

Choose the correct answer from the options given below.

(a) A, B and C
(b) B and D
(c) D and E
(d) C, D and E

8. Given below are two statements, one is labelled as Assertion (A) and the other is labelled as Reason (R).

Assertion (A) In Lassaigne's test, hydroxylamine (NH_2OH) contains N and hence gives prussian blue colour.

Reason (R) CN^- is not formed with Na metal, hydroxylamine does not contain C.

In the light of the above statements, choose the correct answer from the options given below

(a) Both (A) and (R) are true and (R) is the correct explanation of (A).

(b) Both (A) and (R) are true but (R) is not the correct explanation of (A).

(c) (A) is true but (R) is false.

(d) (A) is false but (R) is true.

9. The sodium extract on acidification with acetic acid and then adding lead acetate solution gives a black precipitate. The organic compound contains

(a) halogen (b) nitrogen
(c) phosphorus (d) sulphur

10. Which of the following compound gives positive test for nitrogen with Lassaigne's solution of an organic compound?

(a) $Fe(CN)_3$
(b) $Fe_4[Fe(CN)_6]_3$
(c) $Na_4[Fe(CN)_5NOS]$
(d) $K_4[Fe(CN)_6]$

11. Given below are two statements.

Statement I Ferriferrocyanide is prussian blue, but sometimes appears green due to colloidal state, if N is present in small amount.

Statement II Lassaigne's test fails in case of diazo compounds, since these lose N_2 on heating before Na has a chance to form NaCN.

In the light of the above statements, choose the most appropriate answer from the options given below.

(a) Both Statement I and Statement II are incorrect.

(b) Statement I is correct but Statement II is incorrect.

(c) Statement I is incorrect but Statement II is correct.

(d) Both Statement I and Statement II are correct.

12. The formation of which compound takes place and blood red colour is obtained in Lassaigne's test when both nitrogen and sulphur are present.

(a) $[Fe_4(Fe(CN)_6)_3]$ (b) $[Fe(CNS)_3]$
(c) $[Fe_3(CN)_6]$ (d) $K_3[Fe(CN)_6]$

13. The presence of phosphorus can be observed by the formation of

(a) white ppt. (b) yellow ppt.
(c) red ppt. (d) black ppt.

14. Presence of carbon in an organic compound can be represented by

(a) burning it with green edge flame
(b) heating it with copper which turns black
(c) heating it with copper oxide to convert it into CO_2
(d) burning it with a white flame

15. In which of the following compounds, Lassaigne's test does not confirm the presence of nitrogen?

(a) $NH_2 \cdot NH_2 \cdot H_2O$ (b) $C_6H_5NH_2$
(c) $C_6H_5NO_2$ (d) NH_2CONH_2

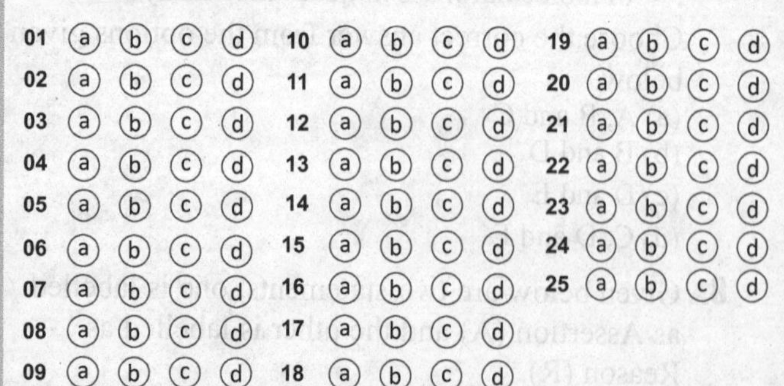

Performance Scanner

> 90% Excellent !	You have mastered these topics. The concepts of these topics are at your fingertips. Move on to the next test and maintain this momentum.
76-90% Very Good !	You have a good command over these topics. Revise these topics again after a few days and enhance your performance.
60-75% Good !	You have a wide scope to learn for these topics. Revise these topics again.
<60 Not Satisfactory!	You have a long way ahead of you to master these topics. Revise it thoroughly.

Test 3

Syllabus

- Quantitative Analysis (Basic Principles Only)
- Estimation of Carbon, Hydrogen, Nitrogen, Halogens, Sulphur, Phosphorus
- Numerical Problems in Organic Quantitative Analysis

For deeper insight **Scan the QR Code**

Important Instructions

- The test is of 30 minutes duration and contains 15 multiple choice questions. (Four options with a single correct answer).
- Choose the correct option and fill the OMR given on the last page of test accordingly.
- At some instances, you may find more than 1 option may be correct. In such circumstances, you have to judge the most appropriate answer as per conditions given in the question.

1. Kjeldahl's method is used in the estimation of which element?

(a) Nitrogen (b) Carbon
(c) Sulphur (d) Oxygen

2. How much sulphur is present in organic compound if on analysis 0.43 g of this compound gives 1.721 g of $BaSO_4$?

(a) 30% (b) 55% (c) 60% (d)80%

3. In Duma's method for determining the nitrogen content of an organic compound, the nitrogen content is determined in the form of

(a) NH_2NH_2 (b) NaCN
(c) gaseous N_2 (d) (NH_4NO_3)

4. In an experiment 0.32 g of magnesium pyrophosphate was produced from 0.2 g of an organic compound. The percentage of phosphorus in it is

(a) 34.64% (b) 66.14%
(c) 41.44% (d) 44.68%

5. Match List-I with List-II.

List-I (Characteristics)	List-II (Methods)
A. Quantitative estimation of C and H in an organic compound	I. Kjeldahl's method
B. Quantitative estimation of N in methanamine	II. Carius method
C. Quantitative estimation of halogens in organic compound	III. Liebig method
D. Quantitative estimation of N in nitrobenzene	IV. Duma's method

Choose the correct answer from the options given below.

(a) A-I, B-II, C-III, D-IV
(b) A-III, B-IV, C-II, D-I
(c) A-II, B-III, C-IV, D-I
(d) A-IV, B-II, C-I, D-III

6. In the estimation of nitrogen by Kjeldahl's method, 2.8 gm of an organic compound required 30 millimole of H_2SO_4 for the complete neutralisation of NH_3 gas evolved. The percentage of nitrogen in the sample is

(a) 20% (b) 25%
(c) 30% (d) 35%

7. In an organic compound the sulphur present is oxidised by fuming nitric acid into

(a) molecular sulphur
(b) sulphuric acid
(c) sulphur dioxide
(d) hydrogen sulphide

8. 0.2685 g of an organic substance in a quantitative analysis yielded 0.25 g of the barium sulphate. The percentage of sulphur in the substance is

(a) 18.52 % (b) 12.79 %
(c) 17.5 % (d) 15.81 %

9. 2 g of an organic compound on Kjeldahl's analysis gave enough ammonia to just neutralise 10 cm^3 of 1 M H_2SO_4. The percentage of nitrogen in the compound is

(a) 56 % (b) 28 %
(c) 42 % (d) 14 %

10. Given below are two statements, one is labelled as Assertion (A) and the other is labelled as Reason (R).

Assertion (A) Duma's method is more applicable to nitrogen containing organic compounds than Kjeldahl's method.

Reason (R) Kjeldahl's method does not give satisfactory results for compounds in which N is linked to O atom.

In the light of the above statements, choose the correct answer from the options given below.

(a) Both (A) and (R) are true and (R) is the correct explanation of (A).
(b) Both (A) and (R) are true but (R) is not the correct explanation of (A).
(c) (A) is true but (R) is false.
(d) (A) is false but (R) is true.

11. In Duma's method of estimation of nitrogen 0.25 g of an organic compound gave 75 mL of nitrogen collected at 300 K temperature and 725 mm Hg pressure. The percentage composition of nitrogen in the compound would be

(Aqueous tension at 300 K = 25 mm Hg)

(a) 14.45
(b) 15.45
(c) 31.2
(d) 17.45

12. 0.44 g of an organic compound gave 0.32 g CO_2 on complete combustion. If it contains 1.86% hydrogen then the percentage of C and O will be

(a) 19.83 and 78.31 (b) 28 and 73
(c) 22 and 66.6 (d) 22 and 82

13. In Kjeldahl's method of estimation of N, $CuSO_4$ acts as

(a) chocking agent (b) reducing agent
(c) catalytic agent (d) hydrolysing agent

14. Consider the following statements.

A. Estimation of oxygen can be determined by carius method.
B. Quantitative analysis is one which is used for separating out the specific constituents from a mixture.
C. In the estimation of sulphur, the organic compound is heated with sodium peroxide in a carius tube.
D. In Kjeldahl's method of estimation of nitrogen, the compound containing nitrogen is heated with conc. HCl.
E. Duma's method is a method of estimation of sulphur.

Choose the incorrect statements among given options.

(a) A, B and C (b) D and E
(c) B and C (d) C, D and E

15. NH_3 evolved from 0.75 g of the soil sample in the Kjeldahl's method for nitrogen estimation, neutralises 10 mL of 1 M H_2SO_4. Find the percentage of nitrogen present in the soil.

(a) 35.33 % (b) 37.33 %
(c) 18.66 % (d) 45.33 %

Response Index

01	a	b	c	d	10	a	b	c	d	19	a	b	c	d
02	a	b	c	d	11	a	b	c	d	20	a	b	c	d
03	a	b	c	d	12	a	b	c	d	21	a	b	c	d
04	a	b	c	d	13	a	b	c	d	22	a	b	c	d
05	a	b	c	d	14	a	b	c	d	23	a	b	c	d
06	a	b	c	d	15	a	b	c	d	24	a	b	c	d
07	a	b	c	d	16	a	b	c	d	25	a	b	c	d
08	a	b	c	d	17	a	b	c	d					
09	a	b	c	d	18	a	b	c	d					

Performance Scanner

> 90% Excellent !	You have mastered these topics. The concepts of these topics are at your fingertips. Move on to the chapter test and maintain this momentum.
76-90% Very Good !	You have a good command over these topics. Revise these topics again after a few days and enhance your performance.
60-75% Good !	You have a wide scope to learn for these topics. Revise these topics again.
<60 Not Satisfactory!	You have a long way ahead of you to master these topics. Revise it thoroughly.

Chapter Break Thru

Syllabus	Crystallisation, Sublimation, Distillation, Differential Extraction and Chromatography-Principles and their Applications	Detection of Nitrogen, Sulphur, Phosphorus and Halogens	Quantitative Analysis (Basic Principles Only) Estimation of Carbon, Hydrogen, Nitrogen, Halogens, Sulphur, Phosphorus Numerical Problems in Organic Quantitative Analysis

Important Instructions

- The test is of 1 hour duration and contains 30 multiple choice questions (Four options with a single correct answer).
- Choose the correct option and fill the OMR given on the last page of test accordingly.
- At some instances, you may find more than 1 option may be correct. In such circumstances, you have to judge the most appropriate answer as per the conditions given in the question.

1. Liebig's method is used for the estimation of

(a) nitrogen
(b) sulphur
(c) carbon and hydrogen
(d) halogens

2. Which of the following compound will be suitable for Kjeldahl's method for nitrogen estimation?

(a) N (pyridine)
(b) NH_2 (benzene ring)
(c) NO_2 (benzene ring)
(d) $\overset{+}{N_2}Cl$ (benzene ring)

3. An organic compound contains 69% carbon and 4.80% hydrogen, the remainder being oxygen. The mass of CO_2 and H_2O produced when 0.20 g of this substance is subjected to complete combustion are respectively.

(a) 0.506 g, 0.0864 g
(b) 0.864 g, 0.0964 g
(c) 0.76 g, 0.0864 g
(d) 0.506 g, 0.0264 g

4. Given below are two statements.

Statement I Absolute alcohol can be prepared from rectified spirit by fractional distillation.

Statement II A 95 : 5 mixture of alcohol and water is called rectified spirit.

In the light of the above statements, choose the most appropriate answer from the options given below.

(a) Both Statement I and Statement II are incorrect.
(b) Statement I is correct but Statement II is incorrect.
(c) Statement I is incorrect but Statement II is correct.
(d) Both Statement I and Statement II are correct.

5. In Duma's method for estimation of nitrogen, 0.25g of an organic compound gave 40 mL of nitrogen collected at 300K temperature and 725 mm Hg. If the aqueous tension at 300 K is 25 mm, the volume of nitrogen in the compound is (in mL)

(a) 43.52 (b) 33.53
(c) 30.52 (d) 28.52

6. For estimation of nitrogen, 1.4 g of an organic compound was digested by Kjeldahl's method and the evolved ammonia was absorbed in 60 mL of $M/10$ H_2SO_4. The unreacted acid required 20 mL of $M/10$ sodium hydroxide for complete neutralisation. The percentage of nitrogen in the compound is

(a) 25% (b) 6%
(c) 10% (d) 15%

7. 29.5 mg of an organic compound containing nitrogen was digested according to Kjeldahl's method and the evolved ammonia was absorbed in 20 mL of 0.1 M HCl solution. The excess of acid required 15 mL of 0.1 M NaOH for complete neutralisation. The percentage of nitrogen in compound is,

(a) 23.7 % (b) 27.7 %
(c) 25.7 % (d) 20.7 %

8. In the estimation of sulphur by carius method, 0.468 g of an organic sulphur compound afforded 0.688g of $BaSO_4$. The percentage of sulphur in the compound is

(a) 30.60 % (b) 28.60 %
(c) 45.20 % (d) 20.19 %

9. The working principle of paper chromatography is

(a) solubility (b) volatility
(c) adsorption (d) partition

10. The presence of carbon in an organic compound is detected by heating it with

(a) Na metal to convert into NaCN
(b) CaO to convert it into CO which burn with blue flame
(c) CuO to convert it into CO_2 which turn water milky
(d) Cu wire to give a bluish green flame.

11. During the fusion of an organic compound with Na metal, nitrogen of the compound is converted into

(a) $NaNO_2$ (b) $NaNH_2$
(c) NaCN (d) $NaNO_3$

12. Lassaigne's test (with silver nitrate) is commonly used to detect halogens such as Cl, Br and I but not useful for F because

(a) AgF formed is volatile
(b) AgF formed is explosive
(c) AgF formed is soluble in water
(d) AgF formed is in liquid

13. The method used to separate a mixture of benzene and chloroform is

(a) distillation (b) sublimation
(c) crystallisation (d) separating funnel

14. A substance which decomposes at or below its boiling point can be purified by which of method given below?

(a) Distillation under reduced pressure
(b) Steam distillation
(c) Crystallisation
(d) Sublimation

15. Aniline is insoluble in water and possess a vapour pressure of 10-15 mm Hg at 100°C. It can be purified by which of the given method.

(a) Crystallisation
(b) Chromatography
(c) Steam distillation
(d) Vacuum distillation

16. Match List-I with List-II.

	List-I (Method of purification)	List-II (Reagent used in purification)
A.	Duma's method	I. $AgNO_3$
B.	Kjeldahl's method	II. Silica gel
C.	Carius method	III. Nitrogen
D.	Chromatography	IV. Ammonium sulphate

Choose the correct match from the options given below.

(a) A-III, B-IV, C-I, D-II
(b) A-III, B-I, C-IV, D-II
(c) A-II, B-III, C-IV, D-I
(d) A-III, B-IV, C-II, D-I

17. When toluene is steam distilled, the pressure of toluene in vapour is

(a) equal to the pressure of barometer
(b) less than the pressure of barometer
(c) equal to vapour pressure of toluene in simple distillation
(d) more than the vapour pressure of toluene in simple distillation

18. Aniline in separated from aniline-water mixture by

(a) differential extraction
(b) vacuum distillation
(c) chromatography
(d) crystallisation

19. 0.16 g of an organic compound gave by Duma's method 46 cc of N_2 measured over H_2O at 15°C and at a pressure of 755 mm of Hg, what will be the %N?
(Given aqueous tension of $H_2O = 15$ mm of Hg)
(a) 33 % (b) 39 %
(c) 66 % (d) 69 %

20. Duma's method involves the determination of nitrogen content in the organic compound in which of the following form
(a) NH_3 (b) N_2
(c) NaCN (d) $(NH_4)_2SO_4$

21. Which of the following statement is correct regarding steam distillation of a mixture of *o*-nitrophenol and *p*-nitrophenol?
(a) Vapour of *o*-nitrophenol are carried by steam because of its lower boiling point due to chelation.
(b) Vapour of *o*-nitrophenol are carried by steam because of its lower boiling point and solubility in steam.
(c) Vapour of *o*-nitrophenol are carried by steam because its boiling point is reduced by steam.
(d) Vapour of *p*-nitrophenol are carried by steam because of its lower boiling point.

22. Given below are two statements.
Statement I A mixture of pigments can be separated by chromatography.
Statement II Chromatography is used to separate only coloured substance into individual compounds.
In the light of the above statements, choose the most appropriate answer from the options given below.
(a) Both Statement I and Statement II are incorrect.
(b) Statement I is correct but Statement II is incorrect.
(c) Statement I is incorrect but Statement II is correct.
(d) Both Statement I and Statement II are correct.

23. When an organic compound is present in aqueous medium and is less soluble in any organic solvent, then it is separated by
(a) continuous extraction
(b) thin layer chromatography
(c) column chromatography
(d) steam distillation

24. Given below are two statements, one is labelled as Assertion (A) and the other is labelled as Reason (R).
Assertion (A) Paper chromatography can be used to separate only polar compounds.
Reason (R) In paper chromatography, the moving phase is a liquid while the stationary phase is a solid.
In the light of the above statements, choose the correct answer from the options given below
(a) Both (A) and (R) are true and (R) is the correct explanation of (A).
(b) Both (A) and (R) are true but (R) is not the correct explanation of (A).
(c) (A) is true but (R) is false.
(d) (A) is false but (R) is true.

25. In Carius method, 0.198 g organic compound gave 0.574 g AgCl. The percentage of chlorine in the compound will be
(a) 18.4 % (b) 71.7 %
(c) 62.9 % (d) 58.7 %

26. Given below are two statements, one is labelled as Assertion (A) and the other is labelled as Reason (R).
Assertion (A) Lithium can be used in place of sodium in Lassaigne's test.
Reason (R) It generally form covalent compounds.
In the light of the above statements, choose the correct answer from the options given below
(a) Both (A) and (R) are true and (R) is the correct explanation of (A).
(b) Both (A) and (R) are true but (R) is not the correct explanation of (A).
(c) (A) is true but (R) is false.
(d) (A) is false but (R) is true.

27. During the estimation of sulphur, organic compound on treating with conc. HNO_3 is converted into which of the following compound?
(a) SO_2 (b) H_2S
(c) H_2SO_4 (d) $H_2S_2O_7$

28. In an estimation of bromine by Carius method, 1.6 g of an organic compound gave 1.88 g of AgBr. The mass percentage of bromine in the compound is
(Atomic mass, Ag = 108, Br = 80 g mol^{-1})
(a) 50 % (b) 60 % (c) 70 % (d) 80 %

29. In the sulphur estimation, 0.471 g of an organic compound gave 1.44 g of barium sulphate. The percentage of sulphur in the compound is
(Atomic mass of Ba = 137 u)
(a) 32 % (b) 42 %
(c) 22 % (d) 12 %

30. Consider the following statements about carius method for the detection of halogens.
I. In this method, nitric acid is used as a reactant.
II. The tube used is known as Carius tube.
III. During the process, C and H are oxidised to CO and H_2.
IV. Silver nitrate is used as one of the reactant.
V. Taken compound is heated with concentrated sulphuric acid.
Choose the correct answer from the options given below.
(a) I, II and IV (b) III, IV and V
(c) II and IV only (d) II, III and V

Response Index

01	ⓐ ⓑ ⓒ ⓓ	14	ⓐ ⓑ ⓒ ⓓ	27	ⓐ ⓑ ⓒ ⓓ	40	ⓐ ⓑ ⓒ ⓓ
02	ⓐ ⓑ ⓒ ⓓ	15	ⓐ ⓑ ⓒ ⓓ	28	ⓐ ⓑ ⓒ ⓓ	41	ⓐ ⓑ ⓒ ⓓ
03	ⓐ ⓑ ⓒ ⓓ	16	ⓐ ⓑ ⓒ ⓓ	29	ⓐ ⓑ ⓒ ⓓ	42	ⓐ ⓑ ⓒ ⓓ
04	ⓐ ⓑ ⓒ ⓓ	17	ⓐ ⓑ ⓒ ⓓ	30	ⓐ ⓑ ⓒ ⓓ	43	ⓐ ⓑ ⓒ ⓓ
05	ⓐ ⓑ ⓒ ⓓ	18	ⓐ ⓑ ⓒ ⓓ	31	ⓐ ⓑ ⓒ ⓓ	44	ⓐ ⓑ ⓒ ⓓ
06	ⓐ ⓑ ⓒ ⓓ	19	ⓐ ⓑ ⓒ ⓓ	32	ⓐ ⓑ ⓒ ⓓ	45	ⓐ ⓑ ⓒ ⓓ
07	ⓐ ⓑ ⓒ ⓓ	20	ⓐ ⓑ ⓒ ⓓ	33	ⓐ ⓑ ⓒ ⓓ	46	ⓐ ⓑ ⓒ ⓓ
08	ⓐ ⓑ ⓒ ⓓ	21	ⓐ ⓑ ⓒ ⓓ	34	ⓐ ⓑ ⓒ ⓓ	47	ⓐ ⓑ ⓒ ⓓ
09	ⓐ ⓑ ⓒ ⓓ	22	ⓐ ⓑ ⓒ ⓓ	35	ⓐ ⓑ ⓒ ⓓ	48	ⓐ ⓑ ⓒ ⓓ
10	ⓐ ⓑ ⓒ ⓓ	23	ⓐ ⓑ ⓒ ⓓ	36	ⓐ ⓑ ⓒ ⓓ	49	ⓐ ⓑ ⓒ ⓓ
11	ⓐ ⓑ ⓒ ⓓ	24	ⓐ ⓑ ⓒ ⓓ	37	ⓐ ⓑ ⓒ ⓓ	50	ⓐ ⓑ ⓒ ⓓ
12	ⓐ ⓑ ⓒ ⓓ	25	ⓐ ⓑ ⓒ ⓓ	38	ⓐ ⓑ ⓒ ⓓ		
13	ⓐ ⓑ ⓒ ⓓ	26	ⓐ ⓑ ⓒ ⓓ	39	ⓐ ⓑ ⓒ ⓓ		

Performance Scanner

> 90% Excellent !	You have mastered this chapter. The concepts of this chapter are at your fingertips. Move on to the next chapter and maintain this momentum.
76-90% Very Good !	You have a good command over this chapter. Revise the chapter again after a few days and enhance your performance.
60-75% Good !	You have a wide scope to learn for this chapter. Revise this chapter again.
<60 Not Satisfactory!	You have a long way ahead of you to master this chapter. Revise it thoroughly.

Scan *for Online*
Chapter Test

Space for Rough Work

Space for Rough Work

Space for Rough Work

Space for Rough Work

Test Booklet No. 3947211

Test Booklet Code CH11

MED ACE

NEET (UG)

SELF ASSESSMENT KIT

Some Basic Principles of Organic Chemistry

Topics Covered

Fundamentals of Carbon, Classification and Nomenclature

Isomerism of Organic Compounds

Bond Fission, Electron Displacement in Organic Molecules, Reagent and Reaction Intermediate

Important Instructions

- This Booklet Contains – 3 Topic Tests and One Test on Complete Chapter.
- Each question carries 4 marks.
- For each correct response the candidate will get 4 marks and for every incorrect response 1 mark will be additionally deducted from the total score.
- Use **Blue/Black** point pen only for filling the OMR.
- Rough work is to be done in the space provided for this purpose in the test booklet only.

Name of the Candidate (In Capitals) ______________________

____

Candidate's Signature ______________

Invigilator's Signature ______________

Facsimile signature stamp of center superintendent______________

Do not open this Booklet until you start attempting the Test

Topical Follow Thru

Test 1

Syllabus Tetravalency of Carbon: Shapes of Simple Molecules-Hybridisation (*s* and *p*), Classification of Organic Compounds Based on Functional Groups and those Containing Halogens, Oxygen, Nitrogen and Sulphur

For deeper insight **Scan the QR Code**

Important Instructions

- The test is of 30 minutes duration and contains 15 multiple choice questions (Four options with a single correct answer).
- Choose the correct option and fill the OMR given on the last page of test accordingly.
- At some instances, you may find more than 1 option may be correct. In such circumstances, you have to judge the most appropriate answer as per conditions given in the question.

1. The IUPAC name of the given compound is

$$CH_3—C\equiv C—\overset{\displaystyle CH_3}{\overset{|}{C}H}—\underset{\underset{\displaystyle CH_3}{|}}{C}=CH_2$$

(a) 2, 3-dimethylhex-1-en-4-yne
(b) 5-ethyl-4-methyl-1-hexa-2-yn-5-ene
(c) 3-methylene-4-methylhepta-5-yne
(d) 4-methyl-5-methylene hepta-2-yne

2. The correct increasing order of carbon-carbon bond length in the given compounds is

I. $H_2C{=}CH_2$ II. III. $H_3C—CH_3$

(a) III < II < I (b) I < II < III
(c) II < I < III (d) I < III < II

3. Given below are two statements, one is labelled as Assertion (A) and the other is labelled as Reason (R).

Assertion (A) All the carbon atoms in $CH_2{=}C{=}CH—CH{=}CH_2$ are sp^2-hybridised.

Reason (R) In this molecule, all the carbon atoms are not attached to each other by double bonds.

In the light of the above statements, choose the correct answer from the options given below.

(a) Both (A) and (R) are true and (R) is the correct explanation of (A).
(b) Both (A) and (R) are true but (R) is not the correct explanation of (A).
(c) (A) is true but (R) is false.
(d) (A) is false but (R) is true.

4. Which of the following has the least hindered rotation about carbon-carbon bond?

(a) Ethane
(b) Butene
(c) Acetylene
(d) Tetramethylethane

5. How many 2° carbon atoms are present in the given compound?

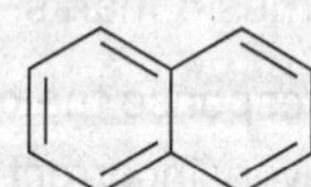

(a) 1 (b) 5
(c) 6 (d) 8

6. Ease of abstraction of hydrogen ion is greater when attached to

(a) 1° carbon (b) 2° carbon
(c) 3° carbon (d) iso-carbon

7. $Me—C\equiv C\overset{a}{—}C\equiv C\overset{b}{—}Et$

The correct relation between bond lengths a and b is

(a) $a = b$ (b) $a > b$
(c) $b > a$ (d) $a >>> b$

8. The IUPAC name of the compound is

OH, CH_3 (cyclohexene ring structure)

(a) 2-methylcyclohex-2-en-1-ol
(b) 1-methylcyclohex-1-en-2-ol
(c) 3-hydroxy-2-methylcyclohexane
(d) 1-hydroxy-2-methyl cyclohexane

9. The number of sp^2-sp^2 sigma bond in the compound given below is

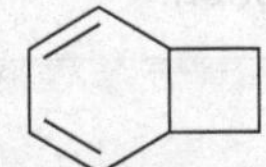

(a) 2 (b) 3 (c) 4 (d) 5

10. Bond X is made by the overlap of which type of hybridised orbitals.

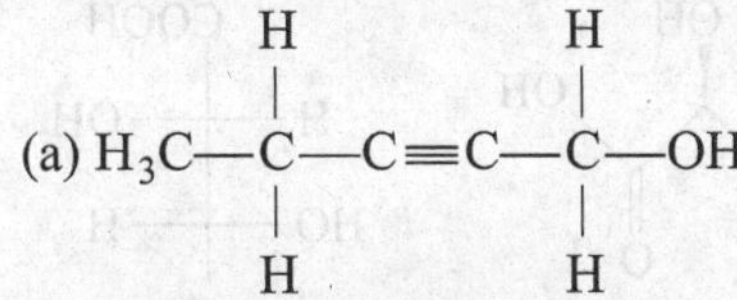

(a) sp and sp^3 (b) sp and sp^2
(c) sp^2 and sp^3 (d) sp^2 and sp^2

11. The correct order regarding the electronegativity of hybrid orbitals of carbon is

(a) $sp > sp^2 < sp^3$ (b) $sp > sp^2 > sp^3$
(c) $sp < sp^2 > sp^3$ (d) $sp < sp^2 < sp^3$

12. The correct structure of 2-amino-4-hydroxy benzoic acid is

(a) benzene ring with OH, H_2N, HOOC
(b) benzene ring with OH, H_2N, COOH
(c) benzene ring with OH, HOOC, NH_2
(d) benzene ring with OH, COOH, NH_2

13. Choose the incorrect statement from the following.

(a) Carbon is the essential elements of all organic molecules.
(b) A single bond contains only σ-bond, whereas there is one sigma bond and one π-bond in double bond.
(c) Carbon has unique property of catenation and trivalency.
(d) In CH_4 molecule, the hybridisation is sp^3.

14. The correct structure of 3,3-dimethylbutyne is

(a) $H_3C—C(H)(H)—C\equiv C—C(H)(H)—OH$
(b) $(CH_3)_3C—C\equiv CH$
(c) $H_3C—C\equiv CCH(CH_3)_2$
(d) $H_3C—C(CH_3)=C(CH_3)—OH$

15. The IUPAC name of the given compound is

$$CH_3—CH(CH_2CHO)—CH_2—CHO$$

(a) 3-(formylmethyl) hexane 1, 5-dial
(b) 3-methylpentane-1, 5-dial
(c) 2-(formylmethyl) butanal
(d) 3-(formylmethyl) pentanal

Response Index

01	a	b	c	d	10	a	b	c	d	19	a	b	c	d
02	a	b	c	d	11	a	b	c	d	20	a	b	c	d
03	a	b	c	d	12	a	b	c	d	21	a	b	c	d
04	a	b	c	d	13	a	b	c	d	22	a	b	c	d
05	a	b	c	d	14	a	b	c	d	23	a	b	c	d
06	a	b	c	d	15	a	b	c	d	24	a	b	c	d
07	a	b	c	d	16	a	b	c	d	25	a	b	c	d
08	a	b	c	d	17	a	b	c	d					
09	a	b	c	d	18	a	b	c	d					

Performance Scanner

> 90% Excellent !	You have mastered these topics. The concepts of these topics are at your fingertips. Move on to the next test and maintain this momentum.
76-90% Very Good !	You have a good command over these topics. Revise these topics again after a few days and enhance your performance.
60-75% Good !	You have a wide scope to learn for these topics. Revise these topics again.
<60 Not Satisfactory!	You have a long way ahead of you to master these topics. Revise it thoroughly.

Test 2

Syllabus **Homologous Series :** Isomerism-Structural and Stereoisomerism

For deeper insight **Scan the QR Code**

Important Instructions

- The test is of 30 minutes duration and contains 15 multiple choice questions (Four options with a single correct answer).
- Choose the correct option and fill the OMR given on the last page of test accordingly.
- At some instances, you may find more than 1 option may be correct. In such circumstances, you have to judge the most appropriate answer as per conditions given in the question.

1. Which of the following represents a *meso*-compound?

O, OH, OH, HO, HO, O (I)

COOH; H—OH; HO—H (II)

O, OH, OH, HO, HO, O (III)

(a) Only I (b) Only II

(c) Only III (d) I and II

2. What is the relationship between the following compounds?

H_3C, CH_3

(a) Constitutional isomers

(b) Diastereomers

(c) Enantiomers

(d) Conformational isomers

3. The molecular formula of third homologue in the homologous series of monocarboxylic acids is

(a) C_2H_2O

(b) $C_2H_4O_2$

(c) $C_3H_3O_3$

(d) $C_3H_6O_2$

4. Which of the following pairs of compounds are functional isomers?

(a) Ethanol and dimethyl ether

(b) Propanal and propanoic acid

(c) Butane and *iso*-butane

(d) 1-butene and 2-butene

5. Given below are two statements, one is labelled as Assertion (A) and the other is labelled as Reason (R).

Assertion (A) *Meso*-compounds are optically inactive.

Reason (R) *Meso*-compounds have a plane of symmetry.

In the light of the above statements, choose the correct answer from the options given below.

(a) Both (A) and (R) are true and (R) is the correct explanation of (A).

(a) Both (A) and (R) are true but (R) is not the correct explanation of (A).

(c) (A) is true but (R) is false.

(d) (A) is false but (R) is true.

6. The number of structural isomers possible for an organic compound with molecular formula C_5H_{12} is

(a) 3 (b) 5 (c) 4 (d) 1

7. Consider the following compound.

Cl, Cl

Number of stereoisomers possible for this compound is

(a) 2 (b) 3
(c) 4 (d) 5

8. Which of the following compounds will not exhibit geometrical isomerism?

(a) 1,2-dichloroethene
(b) But-2-ene
(c) 1,1-dichloroethene
(d) Hex-3-ene

9. The number of structural isomers possible for compound having molar mass 58 and empirical formula C_2H_5 is

(a) 2 (b) 3
(c) 4 (d) 5

10. The type of isomerism shown by pentan-2-one and 3-methylbutan-2-one is

(a) chain
(b) positional
(c) stereo
(d) functional

11. Which of the following compound will not exhibit geometrical isomerism?

(a) 2,3-dichloro-2-butene
(b) 1-chloro-1-pentene
(c) 1,2-dichloroethene
(d) 2-methyl-2-butene

12. Consider the compounds given below.

I. $CH_3—C(=O)—CH_3$ II. $CH_2=CH—OH$

III. 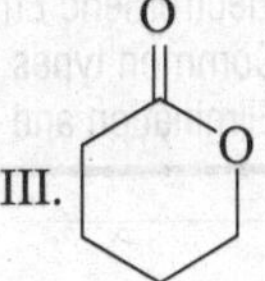

IV. 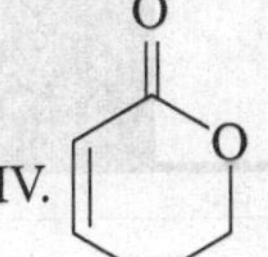

V. (O, NH)

The number of compounds that can show tautomerism is

(a) 4 (b) 5
(c) 3 (d) 2

13. Which of the following compound shows functional isomerism?

(a) C_2H_5OH (b) CH_2Cl_2
(c) C_2H_4 (d) C_4H_{10}

14. The compound that will exhibit *cis-trans* geometrical isomerism is

(a) 2-butyne (b) 2-butanol
(c) 2-butene (d) Butanol

15. Which of the following statement is correct regarding geometrical isomers?

(a) Position of functional group.
(b) Position of atoms.
(c) Spatial arrangement of atoms.
(d) Length of carbon chain.

Response Index

01	(a)	(b)	(c)	(d)	10	(a)	(b)	(c)	(d)	19	(a)	(b)	(c)	(d)
02	(a)	(b)	(c)	(d)	11	(a)	(b)	(c)	(d)	20	(a)	(b)	(c)	(d)
03	(a)	(b)	(c)	(d)	12	(a)	(b)	(c)	(d)	21	(a)	(b)	(c)	(d)
04	(a)	(b)	(c)	(d)	13	(a)	(b)	(c)	(d)	22	(a)	(b)	(c)	(d)
05	(a)	(b)	(c)	(d)	14	(a)	(b)	(c)	(d)	23	(a)	(b)	(c)	(d)
06	(a)	(b)	(c)	(d)	15	(a)	(b)	(c)	(d)	24	(a)	(b)	(c)	(d)
07	(a)	(b)	(c)	(d)	16	(a)	(b)	(c)	(d)	25	(a)	(b)	(c)	(d)
08	(a)	(b)	(c)	(d)	17	(a)	(b)	(c)	(d)					
09	(a)	(b)	(c)	(d)	18	(a)	(b)	(c)	(d)					

Performance Scanner

> 90% Excellent !	You have mastered these topics. The concepts of these topics are at your fingertips. Move on to the next test and maintain this momentum.
76-90% Very Good !	You have a good command over these topics. Revise these topics again after a few days and enhance your performance.
60-75% Good !	You have a wide scope to learn for these topics. Revise these topics again.
<60 Not Satisfactory!	You have a long way ahead of you to master these topics. Revise it thoroughly.

Test 3

Syllabus

- Covalent Bond Fission-Homolytic and Heterolytic: Free Radicals, Carbocations and Carbanions, Stability of Carbocation and Free Radicals, Electrophiles and Nucleophiles
- Electronic Displacement in Organic Molecules - Inductive Effect, Electromeric Effect, Resonance, and Hyperconjugation
- Common types of Organic Reactions - Substitution, Addition, Elimination and Rearrangement

For deeper insight **Scan the QR Code**

Important Instructions

- The test is of 30 minutes duration and contains 15 multiple choice questions (Four options with a single correct answer).
- Choose the correct option and fill the OMR given on the last page of test accordingly.
- At some instances, you may find more than 1 option may be correct. In such circumstances, you have to judge the most appropriate answer as per conditions given in the question.

1. Which of the following statements regarding resonance is incorrect?

(a) The greater the number of contributing structures, the higher is the resonance energy.

(b) Resonance structures differ in the arrangement of electrons but have the same positions of nuclei.

(c) The resonance hybrid (the actual structure of the molecule) is more stable (lower in energy) than any of its individual resonance structures.

(d) Resonance structures cannot have the same number of unpaired electrons.

2. Which of the following species is not an electrophile?

(a) Cl (b) BH_3

(c) $H_3O^{\oplus}$ (d) NH_3

3. Which of the following reactions is an elimination reaction?

(a) $CH_3CH_2CH_3 + Cl_2 \longrightarrow CH_3CH_2CH_2Cl + HCl$

(b) $(CH_3)_3CBr + KOH(aq) \longrightarrow (CH_3)_3COH + KBr$

(c) $CH_3CH{=}CH_2 + Br_2 \longrightarrow CH_3CHBrCH_2Br$

(d) $CH_3CH_2CH_2Br + KOH(alc.) \longrightarrow CH_3CH{=}CH_2 + KBr + H_2O$

4. Carbanions are capable of undergoing various reactions, except

(a) rearrangement to form a more stable carbanion

(b) combination with a cation to form a new C—C bond

(c) addition to a carbonyl group, resulting in a new C—C bond and an alkoxide

(d) elimination to form an alkene

5. Given below are two statements, one is labelled as Assertion (A) and the other is labelled as Reason (R).

Assertion (A) The inductive effect is a permanent effect.

Reason (R) It involves the displacement of sigma electrons along a carbon chain due to electronegativity differences.

In the light of the above statements, choose the most appropriate answer from the options given below.

(a) Both (A) and (R) are true and (R) is the correct explanation of (A).

(a) Both (A) and (R) are true but (R) is not the correct explanation of (A).

(c) (A) is true but (R) is false.

(d) (A) is false but (R) is true.

6. Select the correct statements from the following with respect to electron displacement in a covalent bond.

I. Inductive effect operates through π-bond.

II. Resonance effect operates through σ-bond.

III. Inductive effect operates through σ-bond.

IV. Resonance effect operates through π-bond.

V. Mesomeric effect is delocalisation of lone pair of electrons.

Choose the correct answer from the options given below.

(a) I, II and I (b) III, IV and V
(c) II, IV and V (d) I, III and V

7. Given below are two statements.

Statement I A compound with delocalised electron is more stable than that compound in which all its electrons are localised.

Statement II The extra stability that a compound gains as a result of having delocalised electrons, is called delocalisation energy.

In the light of the above statement, choose the correct answer from the options given below.

(a) Both Statement I and Statement II are incorrect.
(b) Statement I is correct, but Statement II is incorrect.
(c) Statement I is incorrect, but Statement II is correct.
(d) Both Statement I and Statement II are correct.

8. Which of the following is obtained by thermolysis of azides?

(a) Free radicals
(b) Carbocation
(c) Arene
(d) Nitrene

9. Match List-I with List-II.

List-I (Mechanism steps)	List-II (Effect)
A. 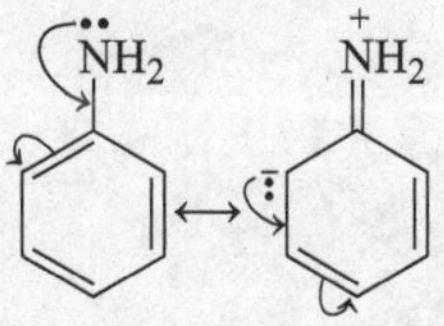 Aniline ($\ddot{N}H_2$) ↔ $\overset{+}{N}H_2$ resonance structure	I. $-E$ effect
B. 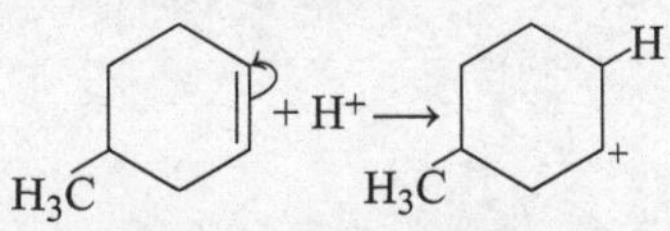 4-methylcyclohexene (H₃C) + H^+ ⟶ carbocation (H, +, H_3C)	II. $-R$ effect
C. 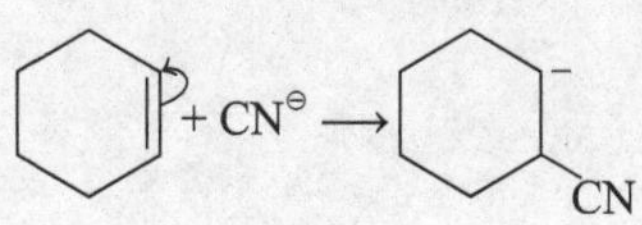 Cyclohexene + $CN^{\ominus}$ ⟶ carbanion (–, CN)	III. $+E$ effect
D. 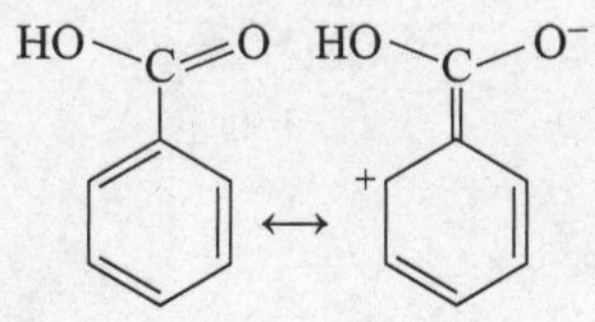 HO–C=O benzoic acid ↔ HO–C–O^- (+)	IV. $+R$ effect

Choose the correct answer from the options given below.

(a) A-IV, B-III, C-I, D-II
(b) A-IV, B-II, C-I, D-III
(c) A-II, B-III, C-I, D-IV
(d) A-I, B-II, C-IV, D-III

10. In which type of organic reaction does the attacking reagent seek electron-deficient sites?

(a) Nucleophilic substitution
(b) Electrophilic addition
(c) Elimination
(d) Free radical substitution

11. Match List-I with List-II.

List-I (Term)	List-II (Explanation)
A. Homolytic bond fission	I. Formation of ions
B. Heterolytic bond fission	II. Formation of free radicals
C. Inductive effect	III. Shifting of π electrons in a conjugated system
D. Resonance effect	IV. Polarisation of sigma bonds due to electronegativity difference

Choose the correct answer from the options given below.

(a) A-I, B-II, C-III, D-IV
(b) A-III, B-II, C-IV, D-I
(c) A-II, B-I, C-IV, D-III
(d) A-IV, B-I, C-III, D-II

12. Which of the following is incorrect regarding hyperconjugation?

(a) Like the inductive effect, it involves the delocalisation of electrons through σ-bonds adjacent to an empty *p*-orbital.
(b) Hyperconjugation involves the overlapping of filled orbitals with the empty *p*-orbital of the carbocation.
(c) Like resonance, it involves the displacement of σ or lone pair of electrons to the carbon bearing a positive charge.
(d) It is also known as no-bond resonance.

13. Consider the following carbonium ions.

$C_6H_5\overset{+}{C}H_2$, (I) p-$(CH_3O)C_6H_4\overset{+}{C}H_2$ (II)

p-$(NO_2)C_6H_4\overset{+}{C}H_2$, (III) p-$(CH_3)C_6H_4\overset{+}{C}H_2$ (IV)

The descending order of stability of the carbonium ions is

(a) IV > II > I > III
(b) II > IV > III > I
(c) II > IV > I > III
(d) IV > II > III > I

14. Order of stability of vinyl, allyl, tertiary radicals is

(a) tertiary > vinyl > allyl
(b) vinyl > tertiary > allyl
(c) tertiary > allyl > vinyl
(d) allyl > tertiary > vinyl

15. Which of the following is an electrophile?

(a) H_2O
(b) NH_3
(c) SO_3
(d) $R—O—R$

Response Index

01	(a) (b) (c) (d)		10	(a) (b) (c) (d)		19	(a) (b) (c) (d)
02	(a) (b) (c) (d)		11	(a) (b) (c) (d)		20	(a) (b) (c) (d)
03	(a) (b) (c) (d)		12	(a) (b) (c) (d)		21	(a) (b) (c) (d)
04	(a) (b) (c) (d)		13	(a) (b) (c) (d)		22	(a) (b) (c) (d)
05	(a) (b) (c) (d)		14	(a) (b) (c) (d)		23	(a) (b) (c) (d)
06	(a) (b) (c) (d)		15	(a) (b) (c) (d)		24	(a) (b) (c) (d)
07	(a) (b) (c) (d)		16	(a) (b) (c) (d)		25	(a) (b) (c) (d)
08	(a) (b) (c) (d)		17	(a) (b) (c) (d)			
09	(a) (b) (c) (d)		18	(a) (b) (c) (d)			

Performance Scanner

> 90% Excellent !	You have mastered these topics. The concepts of these topics are at your fingertips. Move on to the chapter test and maintain this momentum.
76-90% Very Good !	You have a good command over these topics. Revise these topics again after a few days and enhance your performance.
60-75% Good !	You have a wide scope to learn for these topics. Revise these topics again.
<60 Not Satisfactory!	You have a long way ahead of you to master these topics. Revise it thoroughly.

Chapter Break Thru

Syllabus	Tetravalency of Carbon: Shapes of Simple Molecules-Hybridisation (*s* and *p*) Classification of Organic Compounds Based on Functional Groups and those Containing Halogens, Oxygen, Nitrogen and Sulphur	**Homologous Series** : Isomerism- Structural and Stereoisomerism	Covalent Bond Fission, Homolytic and Heterolytic: Free Radicals, Carbocations and Carbanions, Stability of Carbocation and Free Radicals, Electrophiles and Nucleophiles Electronic Displacement in Organic Molecules - Inductive Effect, Electromeric Effect, Resonance, and Hyperconjugation Common types of Organic Reactions - Substitution, Addition, Elimination and Rearrangement

Important Instructions

- The test is of 1 hour duration and contains 50 multiple choice questions (Four options with a single correct answer).
- Choose the correct option and fill the OMR given on the last page of test accordingly.
- At some instances, you may find more than 1 option may be correct. In such circumstances, you have to judge the most appropriate answer as per the conditions given in the question.

1. In which of the following compounds, all the carbon atoms are not *sp*-hybridised ?

(a) Acetylene
(b) Vinyl acetylene
(c) 1,3-butadiyne
(d) Cyanogen

2. In 2-butene, which one of the following statements is true ?

(a) $C_1 — C_2$ bond is a $sp^3 - sp^3$, σ bond
(b) $C_2 — C_3$ bond is a $sp^3 - sp^2$, σ bond
(c) $C_1 — C_2$ bond is a $sp^3 - sp^2$, σ bond
(d) $C_4 — C_3$ bond is a $sp^2 - sp^2$, σ bond

3. Which of the following species is a nucleophile?

(a) $\overset{+}{NO_2}$ (b) $:CX_2$
(c) $:\overset{..}{\bar{N}}H_2$ (d) $\bullet CH_3$

4. Given below are two statements.

Statement I Singlet carbene has bent structure.

Statement II The carbon atom in singlet carbene is *sp*-hybridised.

In the light of the above statement, choose the correct answer from the options given below.

(a) Both Statement I and Statement II are incorrect.
(b) Statement I is correct but Statement II is incorrect.
(c) Statement I is incorrect but Statement II is correct.
(d) Both Statement I and Statement II are correct.

5. Which of the following compound show geometrical isomerism?

(a) CH_2 / CH_3
(b) CH_2 / CH_3
(c) CH—Cl / CH_3
(d) CH—Cl / CH_3

6. Given below are two statements.

Statement I Metamers can also be position or chain isomers.

Statement II Tautomerism was introduced by van Laar to explain the chemical reactivity of a substance according to two possible structures.

In the light of the above statement, choose the correct answer from the options given below.

(a) Both Statement I and Statement II are incorrect.
(b) Statement I is correct, but Statement II is incorrect.
(c) Statement I is incorrect, but Statement II is correct.
(d) Both Statement I and Statement II are correct.

7. The number of acyclic ether metamers of the compound with molecular formula C_4H_8O is

(a) 1 (b) 2
(c) 6 (d) 4

8. Positive resonance effect (+*R* effect) and negative resonance effect (–*R* effect) are respectively shown by which of the following substituents?

(a) $—NH_2, —OH$
(b) $—OH, —NO_2$
(c) $—NO_2, —CHO$
(d) $—NO_2, —COOH$

9. Alkyl group in benzene are *o*, *p*-directing because of

(a) inductive effect
(b) electromeric effect
(c) hyperconjugate effect
(d) All of the above

10. Given below are two statements, one is labelled as Assertion (A) and the other is labelled as Reason (R).

Assertion (A) ElcB reaction is favoured by stabilisation of carbanion and poor leaving group.

Reason (R) The reaction is generally first order and bimolecular.

In the light of the above statements, choose the correct answer from the options given below.

(a) Both (A) and (R) are true and (R) is the correct explanation of (A).
(b) Both (A) and (R) are true but (R) is not the correct explanation of (A).
(c) (A) is true but (R) is false.
(d) (A) is false but (R) is true.

11. Consider the following species.

I. $PhO^{\ominus}$ II. $CH_3S^{\ominus}$
III. $OH^{\ominus}$ IV. $MeO^{\ominus}$

The decreasing basic character of above species.

(a) I > II > III > IV
(b) III > IV > II > I
(c) IV > III > II > I
(d) I > II > IV > III

12. Tautomerism will be exhibited by

(a) $(CH_3)_3CNO$ (b) $(CH_3)_2NH$
(c) R_3CNO_2 (d) RCH_2NO_2

13. What type of isomerism can be exhibited by the compounds with molecular formula $C_4H_{10}O$?

(a) Chain and position
(b) Functional and position
(c) Metamerism
(d) Chain, position, functional and metamerism

14. The compound which will not show tautomerism is

(a) $PhCH{=}CHOH$
(b) $PhCH{=}CHOCH_3$
(c) $CH_2{=}\overset{+}{N}(O^-)(OH)$
(d) $PhCH{=}NOH$

15. Match List-I with List-II.

List-I (Process)	List-II (Condition)
A. Carbocation	I. SO_3
B. Resonance	II. sp^2-hybridised carbon with empty *p*-orbital
C. Hyperconjugation	III. σ-*p*-conjugation
D. Electrophile	IV. π-conjugation

Choose the correct answer from the options given below.

(a) A-I, B-II, C-III, D-IV
(b) A-IV, B-III, C-II, D-I
(c) A-II, B-IV, C-III, D-I
(d) A-II, B-IV, C-I, D-III

16. Which of the following has *sp*-hybridised carbon atoms?

(a) Cyclopropene
(b) Bicyclobutene
(c) Propadiene
(d) 1,3-butadiene

17. Match the List-I with List-II.

List-I	List-II
A. Carbocation	I. Two unshared e^- pair
B. Carbanion	II. Four unshared e^- pair
C. Chloride ion	III. One unshared e^- pair
D. Nitrene	IV. Zero unshared e^- pair

Choose the correct answer from the options given below.

(a) A-II, B-III, C-IV, D-I
(b) A-I, B-III, C-II, D-IV
(c) A-IV, B-III, C-II, D-I
(d) A-III, B-IV, C-II, D-I

18. Match the List-I with List-II.

List-I (Reactants + Reagent)	List-II (Mechanism)
A. I–$CH_2CH_2CH_2CH_2CH_2$–I + Mg (ether)	I. S_N2
B. Me–$CH_2CH_2CH_2$–Br + PMe_3	II. S_N1
C. Me_3C–Br $\xrightarrow{Aq.\ NaOH}$	III. E2
D. Me_3C–CH_2–Cl $\xrightarrow{CN^\ominus}$	IV. Intramolecular S_N2

Choose the correct answer from the options given below.

(a) A-III, B-IV, C-I, D-II
(b) A-I, B-III, C-II, D-IV
(c) A-II, B-III, C-I, D-IV
(d) A-IV, B-I, C-II, D-III

19. Which of the following is the most reactive towards electrophilic reagent?

(a) benzene ring with CH_3 and $NHCOCH_3$ (ortho)
(b) benzene ring with CH_3 and OCH_3 (ortho)
(c) benzene ring with CH_3 and OH (ortho)
(d) benzene ring with CH_3 and CH_2OH (ortho)

20. Which of the following best describes hyperconjugation?

(a) It is delocalisation of π-electrons in nearby empty orbitals.
(b) It is delocalisation of σ-electrons in nearby empty orbitals.
(c) It is the effect of alkyl groups donating a small amount of electron density into a nearby p-orbital.
(d) It is the delocalisation of σ-electrons into an adjacent p-orbital involved in π-bonding.

21. Consider the following statements about carbocation and select the correct statements.

I. It is formed by heterolytic fission of covalent bond.
II. It is electrophilic in nature.
III. It occupies the maxima in activation energy diagram.
IV. The most stable carbocation leads to the major product in a chemical reaction involving the reactive intermediate.
V. Carbocations are highly stable and reactive species.

Choose the correct answer from the options given below.

(a) I, II and IV
(b) II and IV
(c) III, IV and II
(d) III and V

22. Given below are two statements, one is labelled as Assertion (A) and the other is labelled as Reason (R).

Assertion (A) The presence of nitro group facilitates nucleophilic substitution reactions in aryl halides.

Reason (R) The intermediate carbocation is destabilised due to the presence of nitro group.

In the light of the above statements, choose the correct answer from the options given below.

(a) Both (A) and (R) are true and (R) is the correct explanation of (A).
(b) Both (A) and (R) are true but (R) is not the correct explanation of (A).
(c) (A) is true but (R) is false.
(d) (A) is false but (R) is true.

23. Give the IUPAC name of following compound.

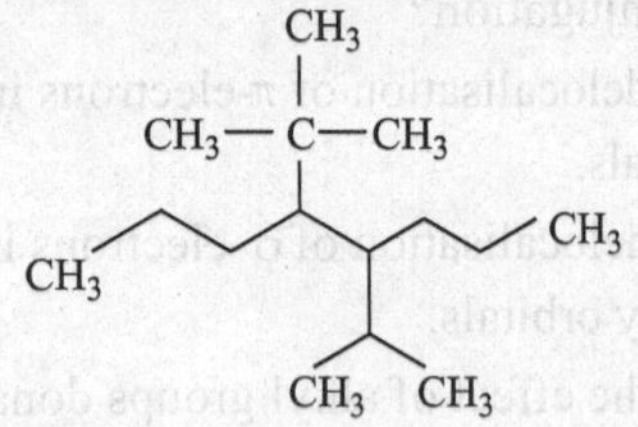

(a) 2,2-dimethyl-3-propyl-4-*iso*-propylheptane
(b) 4-*iso*-propyl-5-*tert*-butyloctane
(c) 4-*tert*-butyl-5-*iso*-propyloctane
(d) 2-methyl-3-propyl-4-*iso*-propylheptane

24. Consider the compound given below.

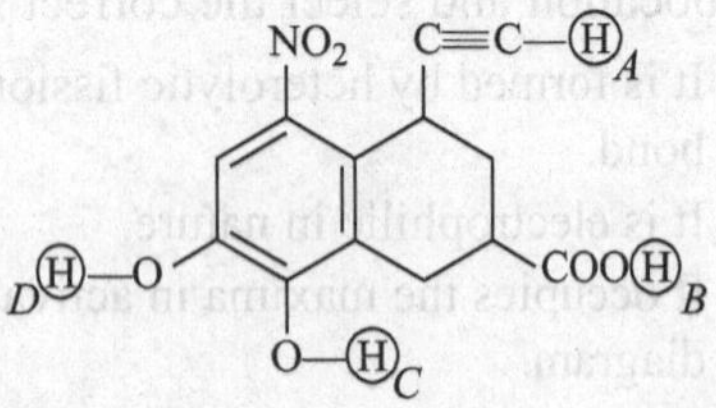

Arrange the following labelled hydrogens in decreasing order of acidity.

(a) $C > B > A > D$ (b) $B > C > D > A$
(c) $B > A > C > D$ (d) $C > B > D > A$

25. Given below are two statements, one is labelled as Assertion (A) and the other is labelled as Reason (R).

Assertion (A) $:CX_2$ acts as an electrophile.

Reason (R) It contains a lone pair of electrons.

In the light of the above statements, choose the most appropriate answer from the options given below.

(a) Both (A) and (R) are true and (R) is the correct explanation of (A).
(b) Both (A) and (R) are true but (R) is not the correct explanation of (A).
(c) (A) is true but (R) is false.
(d) (A) is false but (R) is true.

26. How many structural isomers are possible when two of the hydrogen atoms of propane are replaced by two chlorine atoms?

(a) 2 (b) 4
(c) 6 (d) 5

27. $CH_3CH_2NO_2$ and H_2NCH_2COOH are

(a) metamers
(b) functional isomers
(c) tautomers
(d) optical isomers

28. Which of the followng is the most stable carbocation?

(a) $F_3C-CH_2^+$ (b) $(CH_3)_2CH^+$
(c) CH_3^+ (d) F_3C^+

29. Which of the following intermediate does not have planar geometry about central carbon?

(a) *tert*-butyl free radical
(b) *tert*-butyl carbanion
(c) *tert*-butyl carbocation
(d) Allyl carbanion

30. Given below are two statements, one is labelled as Assertion (A) and the other is labelled as Reason (R).

Assertion (A) *Neo*-pentane and *iso*-pentane are chain isomers.

Reason (R) *Neo*-pentane contains a quaternary carbon while *iso*-pentane contains a tertiary carbon.

In the light of the above statements, choose the correct answer from the options given below.

(a) Both (A) and (R) are true and (R) is the correct explanation of (A).
(b) Both (A) and (R) are true but (R) is not the correct explanation of (A).
(c) (A) is true but (R) is false.
(d) (A) is false but (R) is true.

31. The correct IUPAC name of the following compound is

$$CH_3CH_2-\underset{OH}{\underset{|}{CH}}-CH_2CH_2-\underset{CH_3}{\underset{|}{CH}}-CH_2CH_3$$

(a) 3-methyl-6-octanol
(b) 6-methyloctan-3-ol
(c) 1,4-diethylpentan-1-ol
(d) 6-ethylpentan-3-ol

32. The IUPAC name of the compound

O

CH_2—CH—CH_2OH is

(a) 1,2-epoxy-3-prapanol
(b) 1,2-oxo-3-propanol
(c) 2,3-epoxy-1-propanol
(d) 2,3-epoxyallylalcohol

33. IUPAC nomenclature of the following compound is

(a) 1-methyl-3-propylcyclohexane
(b) 3-methyl-1-propylcyclohexane
(c) 1-(3-methylcyclohexyl) propane
(d) 3-(1-methyl cyclohexyl) propane

34. Which among the following correctly defines diastereomer?

(a) These have same magnitude but different signs of optical rotation.
(b) Non-superimposable object mirror relationship.
(c) These differ in all physical properties.
(d) Separation is very difficult.

35. Which of the following general formulae represents alkanamides?

(a) $C_nH_{2n-1}NO$
(b) $C_nH_{2n+1}NO$
(c) $C_nH_{2n+3}NO$
(d) $C_nH_{2n-3}NO$

36. The IUPAC name of an alkane containing only one methyl, one ethyl and *n* propyl group is

(a) 2,3-dimethylpentane
(b) 3-methylhexane
(c) 2,3-dimethylbutane
(d) 3-ethyl-4-methyl pentane

37. Given below are two statements.

Assertion (A) The IUPAC name for the compound $NCCH_2CH_2COOH$ is 3-cyanopropanoic acid.

Reason (R) COOH is considered as principal group while CN is considered as the substituent functional group.

In the light of the above statements, choose the most appropriate answer from the options given below.

(a) Both (A) and (R) are true and (R) is the correct explanation of (A).
(b) Both (A) and (R) are true but (R) is not the correct explanation of (A).
(c) (A) is true but (R) is false.
(d) (A) is false but (R) is true.

38. The IUPAC name of following compound is,

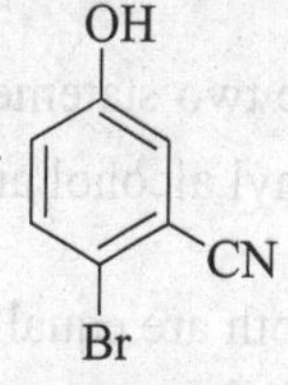

(a) 4-bromo-3-cyanophenol
(b) 2-bromo-5-hydoxybenzonitrile
(c) 2-cyano-4-hydroxybromobenzene
(d) 6-bromo-3-hydroxybenzonitrile

39. Match the List-I with List-II.

List-I (Functional group)	List-II (Generic name)
A. —SCN	I. Sulphonic acid
B. —SO_3H	II. Nitrile
C. —CN	III. Thiocyanate
D. —NCS	IV. Isothiocyanate

Choose the correct answer from the options given below.

(a) A-III, B-II, C-I, D-IV
(b) A-I, B-II, C-III, D-IV
(c) A-III, B-I, C-II, D-IV
(d) A-IV, B-I, C-II, D-III

40. Identify the chiral molecule among the following compounds.

(a) *Iso*-propyl alcohol
(b) 2-pentanol
(c) 1-bromo-3-butene
(d) *Iso*-butyl alcohol

41. During enolisation of the following compound, which of the following labelled hydrogen is involved?

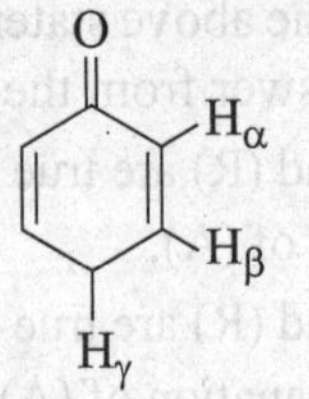

(a) H_α
(b) H_β
(c) H_γ
(d) Any of the three

42. Given below are two statements.

Statement I Vinyl alcohol and acetaldehyde are tautomers.

Statement II Both are equally stable.

In the light of the above statements, choose the most appropriate answer from the options given below.

(a) Both Statement I and Statement II are incorrect.
(b) Statement I is correct but Statement II is incorrect.
(c) Statement I is incorrect but Statement II is correct.
(d) Both Statement I and Statement II are correct.

43. Given below are two statements, one is labelled as Assertion (A) and the other is labelled as Reason (R).

Assertion (A) Methoxy propane and ethoxyethane are metamers.

Reason (R) The number of carbon atoms on either side of the functional group is different but same molecular formula.

In the light of the above statements, choose the most appropriate answer from the options given below.

(a) Both (A) and (R) are true and (R) is the correct explanation of (A).
(b) Both (A) and (R) are true but (R) is not the correct explanation of (A).
(c) (A) is true but (R) is false.
(d) (A) is false but (R) is true.

44. What is the systematic IUPAC name of the following compound?

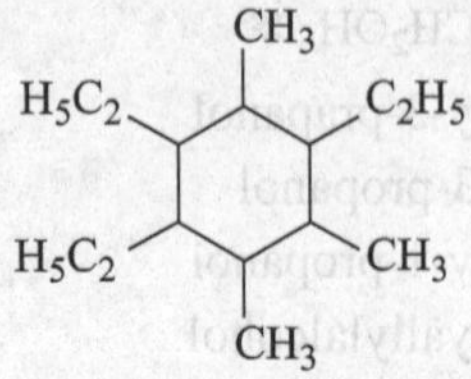

(a) 1,3,4-triethyl-2,5,6 trimethylcyclohexane
(b) 1,2,5-triethyl-3,4,6-trimethylcyclohexane
(c) 1,2,4-triethyl-3,5,6-trimethylcyclohexane
(d) 2,5,6-trimethyl -1,3,4-trimethylcyclohexane

45. Which of the following is not an isomer of allyl alcohol?

(a) 1-propanol (b) Acetone
(c) 2-methyloxirane (d) Cyclopropanol

46. Among the following, example of nucleophilic addition reaction is

(a) hydrolysis of ethyl chloride by NaOH
(b) purification of acetaldehyde by $NaHSO_3$
(c) alkylation of anisole
(d) decarboxylation of acetic acid

47. Given below are two statements.

Statement I 1,2,3,4-tetrachloro-1,3-butadiene has two non-polar stereoisomers.

Statement II Out of the four stereoisomers of 1,2,3,4-tetrachloro-1,3-butadiene, two of them are polar.

In the light of the above statements, choose the correct answer from the options given below.

(a) Both Statement I and Statement II are incorrect.
(b) Statement I is correct but Statement II is incorrect.
(c) Statement I is incorrect but Statement II is correct.
(d) Both Statement I and Statement II are correct.

48. How many different structural isomers exist for C_3H_6O in which no carbon atom is sp^2 or sp-hybridised?

(a) 2 (b) 3
(c) 4 (d) 5

49. Which of the following is not a nucleophile?

(a) Br^- (b) H^+ (c) NH_3 (d) C_6H_5

50. The inductive effect of the group $—CH_3$, COO^-, —Br, $—NH_3^+$ respectively are

(a) $+I, -I, +I, +I$

(b) $+I, +I, -I, -I$

(c) $-I, -I, +I, +I$

(d) $-I, +I, -I, +I$

■ **Response Index**

01 ⓐ ⓑ ⓒ ⓓ	14 ⓐ ⓑ ⓒ ⓓ	27 ⓐ ⓑ ⓒ ⓓ	40 ⓐ ⓑ ⓒ ⓓ
02 ⓐ ⓑ ⓒ ⓓ	15 ⓐ ⓑ ⓒ ⓓ	28 ⓐ ⓑ ⓒ ⓓ	41 ⓐ ⓑ ⓒ ⓓ
03 ⓐ ⓑ ⓒ ⓓ	16 ⓐ ⓑ ⓒ ⓓ	29 ⓐ ⓑ ⓒ ⓓ	42 ⓐ ⓑ ⓒ ⓓ
04 ⓐ ⓑ ⓒ ⓓ	17 ⓐ ⓑ ⓒ ⓓ	30 ⓐ ⓑ ⓒ ⓓ	43 ⓐ ⓑ ⓒ ⓓ
05 ⓐ ⓑ ⓒ ⓓ	18 ⓐ ⓑ ⓒ ⓓ	31 ⓐ ⓑ ⓒ ⓓ	44 ⓐ ⓑ ⓒ ⓓ
06 ⓐ ⓑ ⓒ ⓓ	19 ⓐ ⓑ ⓒ ⓓ	32 ⓐ ⓑ ⓒ ⓓ	45 ⓐ ⓑ ⓒ ⓓ
07 ⓐ ⓑ ⓒ ⓓ	20 ⓐ ⓑ ⓒ ⓓ	33 ⓐ ⓑ ⓒ ⓓ	46 ⓐ ⓑ ⓒ ⓓ
08 ⓐ ⓑ ⓒ ⓓ	21 ⓐ ⓑ ⓒ ⓓ	34 ⓐ ⓑ ⓒ ⓓ	47 ⓐ ⓑ ⓒ ⓓ
09 ⓐ ⓑ ⓒ ⓓ	22 ⓐ ⓑ ⓒ ⓓ	35 ⓐ ⓑ ⓒ ⓓ	48 ⓐ ⓑ ⓒ ⓓ
10 ⓐ ⓑ ⓒ ⓓ	23 ⓐ ⓑ ⓒ ⓓ	36 ⓐ ⓑ ⓒ ⓓ	49 ⓐ ⓑ ⓒ ⓓ
11 ⓐ ⓑ ⓒ ⓓ	24 ⓐ ⓑ ⓒ ⓓ	37 ⓐ ⓑ ⓒ ⓓ	50 ⓐ ⓑ ⓒ ⓓ
12 ⓐ ⓑ ⓒ ⓓ	25 ⓐ ⓑ ⓒ ⓓ	38 ⓐ ⓑ ⓒ ⓓ	
13 ⓐ ⓑ ⓒ ⓓ	26 ⓐ ⓑ ⓒ ⓓ	39 ⓐ ⓑ ⓒ ⓓ	

■ **Performance Scanner**

> 90% Excellent !	You have mastered this chapter. The concepts of this chapter are at your fingertips. Move on to the next chapter and maintain this momentum.
76-90% Very Good !	You have a good command over this chapter. Revise the chapter again after a few days and enhance your performance.
60-75% Good !	You have a wide scope to learn for this chapter. Revise this chapter again.
<60 Not Satisfactory!	You have a long way ahead of you to master this chapter. Revise it thoroughly.

Scan for Online **Chapter Test**

Scan for Online **Unit Test**

Space for Rough Work

Test Booklet No. **3947212**

Test Booklet Code **CH12**

MEDACE

NEET (UG)

SELF ASSESSMENT KIT

Hydrocarbons

Topics Covered

Alkanes

Alkenes

Alkynes and Aromatic Hydrocarbons

Important Instructions

- This Booklet Contains – 3 Topic Tests and One Test on Complete Chapter.
- Each question carries 4 marks.
- For each correct response the candidate will get 4 marks and for every incorrect response 1 mark will be additionally deducted from the total score.
- Use **Blue/Black** point pen only for filling the OMR.
- Rough work is to be done in the space provided for this purpose in the test booklet only.

Name of the Candidate (In Capitals) ______________________

____

Candidate's Signature ______________

Invigilator's Signature ______________

Facsimile signature stamp of center superintendent______________

Do not open this Booklet until you start attempting the Test

Topical Follow Thru

Test 1

Syllabus

Alkanes : Classification, Isomerism, IUPAC Nomenclature, General Method of Preparation, Properties and Reactions, Conformations, Sawhorse and Newman Projections (of Ethane), Mechanism of Halogenation.

For deeper insight **Scan the QR Code**

Important Instructions

- The test is of 30 minutes duration and contains 15 multiple choice questions (Four options with a single correct answer).
- Choose the correct option and fill the OMR given on the last page of test accordingly.
- At some instances, you may find more than 1 option may be correct. In such circumstances, you have to judge the most appropriate answer as per conditions given in the question.

1. The correct IUPAC name of the given compound is

(a) 3-ethyl, 1-2-dimethylpentane
(b) 4-ethyl-3-methyl hexane
(c) methyl octane
(d) 3-ethyl-4-methyl hexane

2. The product obtained by the reaction of sodium with a mixture of 1-iodo-2-methylpropane and 2-iodopropane is

(a) 2,4-dimethylpentane
(b) 1,3-dimethyhexane
(c) 2,3-dimethylhexane
(d) 1,3-dimethylpentane

3. Ethane can be best prepared by the reaction.

(a) $CH_3CH_2COONa \xrightarrow[\text{CaO, }\Delta]{\text{NaOH}}$

(b) $CH_3CH_2Br + (CH_3)_2CuLi \xrightarrow{Et_2O}$

(c) $CH_3CH_2I + CH_3I \xrightarrow[Et_2O]{Na}$

(d) $CH_3CH_2COONa + CH_3COONa \xrightarrow[\text{Electrolysis}]{H_2O}$

4. Given below are two statements, one is labelled as Assertion (A) and the other is labelled as Reason (R).

Assertion (A) Raney nickel is used as a catalyst for hydrogenation.

Reason (R) Raney nickel is obtained from reaction of a Ni-Al alloy with NaOH.

In the light of the above statements, choose the correct answer from the options given below.

(a) Both (A) and (R) are true and (R) is the correct explanation of (A).
(b) Both (A) and (R) are true but (R) is not the correct explanation of (A).
(c) (A) is true but (R) is false.
(d) (A) is false but (R) is true.

5. Alkane which is solid at room temperature is

(a) $C_{16}H_{34}$ (b) $C_{10}H_{22}$
(c) $C_{19}H_{40}$ (d) $C_{15}H_{32}$

6. Solubility order of the following alkanes in a non-polar solvent is

(a) $C_4H_{10} > C_3H_8 > C_2H_6 > CH_4$
(b) $CH_4 > C_3H_8 > C_2H_6 > C_4H_{10}$
(c) $CH_4 > C_2H_6 \approx C_3H_8 > C_4H_{10}$
(d) $CH_4 > C_2H_6 > C_3H_8 > C_4H_{10}$

7. Given below are two statements.

Statement I Boiling point of alkanes increase with decrease in molecular weight.

Statement II van der Waals' forces increases with increasing molecular weight.

In the light of the above statements, choose the correct answer from the options given below.

(a) Both Statement I and Statement II are incorrect.

(b) Statement I is correct but Statement II is incorrect.

(c) Statement I is incorrect but Statement II is correct.

(d) Both Statement I and Statement II are correct.

8. Which of the following alkanes is the least reactive towards free radical substitution reaction?

(a) CH_4 (b) $CH_3CH_2CH_3$

(c) C_2H_6 (d) $(CH_3)_3CH$

9. The total number of isomers of butane and pentane, respectively are

(a) 2, 4 (b) 2, 3 (c) 3, 4 (d) 1, 2

10. Total number of products obtained when methane is subjected to chlorination are

(a) 2 (b) 1 (c) 3 (d) 4

11. For the following reaction,

$$CH_4 + O_2 \xrightarrow[\Delta]{Mo_2O_3} Z$$

The product Z formed in the given reaction is

(a) CH_3CHO (b) $HCOOH$

(c) $HCHO$ (d) CH_3OH

12. Among the following species, number of compounds having 3° carbon atoms are

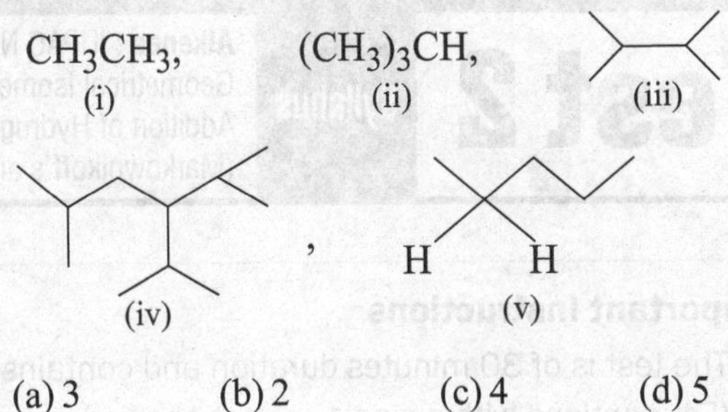

(a) 3 (b) 2 (c) 4 (d) 5

13. The correct statement regarding the comparison of staggered and eclipsed conformations of butane, is

(a) the eclipsed conformation of butane is more stable than staggered conformation due to torsional strain in staggered conformation.

(b) the eclipsed conformation of butane is more stable than staggered conformation because eclipsed conformation has torsional strain.

(c) the staggered conformation of butane is more stable than eclipsed conformation, because staggered conformation has no torsional strain.

(d) the staggered conformation of butane is less stable than eclipsed conformation, because groups on each carbon atom have high repulsion when away from each other.

14. The distance between two carbon atoms is largest in

(a) benzene (b) ethene

(c) propyne (d) ethane

15. Which of the following alkane would give only one monochlorinated product when reacted with Cl_2 in presence of light ?

(a) Propane (b) Butane

(c) *Iso*-butane (d) *Neo*-pentane

Response Index

01	a	b	c	d	10	a	b	c	d	19	a	b	c	d
02	a	b	c	d	11	a	b	c	d	20	a	b	c	d
03	a	b	c	d	12	a	b	c	d	21	a	b	c	d
04	a	b	c	d	13	a	b	c	d	22	a	b	c	d
05	a	b	c	d	14	a	b	c	d	23	a	b	c	d
06	a	b	c	d	15	a	b	c	d	24	a	b	c	d
07	a	b	c	d	16	a	b	c	d	25	a	b	c	d
08	a	b	c	d	17	a	b	c	d					
09	a	b	c	d	18	a	b	c	d					

Performance Scanner

> 90% Excellent ! You have mastered these topics. The concepts of these topics are at your fingertips. Move on to the next test and maintain this momentum.

76-90% Very Good ! You have a good command over these topics. Revise these topics again after a few days and enhance your performance.

60-75% Good ! You have a wide scope to learn for these topics. Revise these topics again.

<60 Not Satisfactory! You have a long way ahead of you to master these topics. Revise it thoroughly.

Test 2

Syllabus

Alkenes : IUPAC Nomenclature, General Method of Preparation, Geometrical Isomerism, Mechanism of Electrophilic Addition, Addition of Hydrogen, Halogens, Water, Hydrogen Halide (Markownikoff's and Peroxide Effect) Ozonolysis and Polymerisation

For deeper insight **Scan the QR Code**

Important Instructions

- The test is of 30 minutes duration and contains 15 multiple choice questions (Four options with a single correct answer).
- Choose the correct option and fill the OMR given on the last page of test accordingly.
- At some instances, you may find more than 1 option may be correct. In such circumstances, you have to judge the most appropriate answer as per conditions given in the question.

1. The correct statement regarding the geometrical isomers of 2-butene is

(a) *trans*-2-butene is more stable than *cis*-2-butene.
(b) *cis*-2-butene and *trans*-2 butene are not interconvertible at room temperature.
(c) *cis*-2-butene has less dipole moment than *trans*-2-butene.
(d) *cis*-2-butene and *trans*-2-butene are structural isomers.

2. Number of sigma and pi bonds in cyclohexa-2,5-diene are

(a) 6,2 (b) 10,4 (c) 10,2 (d) 14,2

3. Given below are two statements, one is labelled as Assertion (A) and the other is labelled as Reason (R).

Assertion (A) Treatment of bromine water with 1-butene yields 1-bromobutan-2-ol.

Reason (R) Attack of water on bromonium ion follows Markownikoff's rule and results in 1-bromobutan-2-ol.

In the light of the above statements, choose the correct answer from the options given below.

(a) Both (A) and (R) are true and (R) is the correct explanation of (A).
(b) Both (A) and (R) are true but (R) is not the correct explanation of (A).
(c) (A) is true but (R) is false.
(d) (A) is false but (R) is true.

4. When 3,3-dimethylpentan-2-ol is heated with conc. H_2SO_4, the major product obtained is

(a) 2,3-dimethyl-pent-2-ene
(b) 3,3-dimethyl-pent-2-ene
(c) 2,3-dimethyl-pent-1-ene
(d) *cis* and *trans*-isomers of 2,3-dimethyl-but-2-ene

5. The restricted rotation about carbon-carbon double bond in 2-butene is due to

(a) overlap of one *p*- and sp^2-hybridised orbitals
(b) overlap of two sp^2-hybridised orbitals
(c) overlap of two *p*- orbitals
(d) overlap of one *s* and one sp^2-hybridised orbital

6. The reaction of an alkene with cold and dilute $KMnO_4$ (Baeyer's reagent) results in the formation of

(a) a *vicinal* dihalide
(b) an epoxide
(c) a *vicinal* diol
(d) a carbonyl compound

7. Ozonolysis of 2-methyl-2-butene, followed by treatment with zinc and water, would yield

(a) acetone and acetaldehyde
(b) only acetone
(c) acetone and formaldehyde
(d) only acetaldehyde

8. Which of the following compounds shows geometrical isomerism?

(a) 2-methylbut-2-ene
(b) 3-methylpent-1-ene
(c) 4-methylpent-2-ene
(d) 2-methylpent-1-ene

9. The addition of bromine to *trans*-2-butene results in a

(a) *meso*-compound
(b) pair of enantiomers
(c) racemic mixture
(d) single achiral product

10. Match List-I with List-II.

	List-I (Reaction/Reagent)		List-II (Product/Observation)
A.	Alkene + $H_2O(H^+)$	I.	*Vicinal* dibromide
B.	Alkene + Br_2 (CCl_4)	II.	*Vicinal* diol
C.	Alkene + O_3, then Zn/H_2O	III.	Carbonyl compounds
D.	Alkene + Cold, dilute $KMnO_4$	IV.	*Syn*-addition of —OH

Choose the correct answer from the options given below.

(a) A-I, B-II, C-III, D-IV
(b) A-IV, B-II, C-I, D-III
(c) A-II, B-I, C-III, D-IV
(d) A-IV, B-I, C-III, D-II

11. Select the incorrect statements from the following.

A. Alkenes are unsaturated hydrocarbons containing at least one carbon-carbon double bond.
B. Alkenes readily undergo nucleophilic addition reactions.
C. The addition of hydrogen halides to asymmetrical alkenes always follows Anti-Markownikoff's rule.
D. The *E/Z* nomenclature is used to describe the stereochemistry of alkenes with two different groups on each carbon of the double bond.
E. The stability of alkenes increases with decreasing number of alkyl substituents on the double bond.

Choose the correct answer from the options given below.

(a) A, B and C (b) A,C and D
(c)A, D and E (d) B, C and E

12. Which of the following alkene polymerise to give *cis*-polyisoprene?

(a) $CH_3—CH=CH_2$
(b) $CH_3—CH_2—CH=CH_2$
(c) $CH_2=C(CH_3)—CH=CH_2$
(d) $CH_2=CH—CH_2—CH_3$

13. Which of the following compound has zero dipole moment?

(a) (Et)(H)C=C(H)(Me) (b) (Et)(H)C=C(Et)(H)
(c) (Et)(H)C=C(H)(Et) (d) (Me)(H)C=C(Me)(H)

14. Consider the reaction,

1-methylcyclohexene $\xrightarrow[\text{(ii) } H_2O_2,\ OH^-]{\text{(i) } B_2H_6,\ THF}$ Z

The product *Z* formed in the given reaction is

(a) 1-methylcyclohexanol
(b) *trans*-2-methylcyclohexanol
(c) 1-methyl cyclohexane-1,2-diol
(d) *cis*-1-methylcyclohexanal

15.

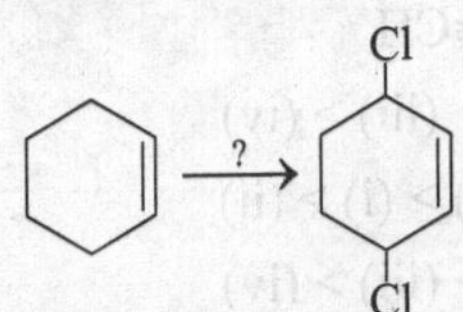

The correct choice of reagent for this transformation is

(a) HCl, $FeCl_3$ (b) HCl, $AlCl_3$
(c) Cl_2, Dark, $AlCl_3$ (d) Cl_2, UV-light

Response Index

01	(a) (b) (c) (d)	10	(a) (b) (c) (d)	19	(a) (b) (c) (d)
02	(a) (b) (c) (d)	11	(a) (b) (c) (d)	20	(a) (b) (c) (d)
03	(a) (b) (c) (d)	12	(a) (b) (c) (d)	21	(a) (b) (c) (d)
04	(a) (b) (c) (d)	13	(a) (b) (c) (d)	22	(a) (b) (c) (d)
05	(a) (b) (c) (d)	14	(a) (b) (c) (d)	23	(a) (b) (c) (d)
06	(a) (b) (c) (d)	15	(a) (b) (c) (d)	24	(a) (b) (c) (d)
07	(a) (b) (c) (d)	16	(a) (b) (c) (d)	25	(a) (b) (c) (d)
08	(a) (b) (c) (d)	17	(a) (b) (c) (d)		
09	(a) (b) (c) (d)	18	(a) (b) (c) (d)		

Performance Scanner

> 90% Excellent !	You have mastered these topics. The concepts of these topics are at your fingertips. Move on to the next test and maintain this momentum.
76-90% Very Good !	You have a good command over these topics. Revise these topics again after a few days and enhance your performance.
60-75% Good !	You have a wide scope to learn for these topics. Revise these topics again.
<60 Not Satisfactory!	You have a long way ahead of you to master these topics. Revise it thoroughly.

Test 3

Syllabus **Alkynes** : Acidic Character, Addition of Hydrogen, Halogen, Water, Hydrogen Halides and Polymerisation, Friedel-Craft's Alkylation and Acylation, Directive Influence of the Functional Group, Aromatic Hydrocarbon : Nomenclature, Benzene, Structure and Aromaticity, Mechanism of Electrophilic Substitution; Halogenation, Nitration.

For deeper insight **Scan the QR Code**

Important Instructions

- The test is of 30 minutes duration and contains 25 multiple choice questions (Four options with a single correct answer).
- Choose the correct option and fill the OMR given on the last page of test accordingly.
- At some instances, you may find more than 1 option may be correct. In such circumstances, you have to judge the most appropriate answer as per conditions given in the question.

1. The reaction of benzene with chlorine in the presence of sunlight yields

(a) chlorobenzene
(b) benzene hexachloride (BHC)
(c) 1,4-dichlorobenzene
(d) No reaction occurs

2. The correct order of reactivity of the following alkynes towards electrophilic addition reactions is

(i) $CH_3—C\equiv CH$
(ii) $HC\equiv CH$
(iii) Et-C$\equiv$CH
(iv) *t*-Bu-C$\equiv$CH

(a) (i) > (ii) > (iii) > (iv)
(b) (iv) > (iii) > (i) > (ii)
(c) (ii) > (i) > (iii) > (iv)
(d) (iii) > (iv) > (ii) > (i)

3. The major product formed in the reaction of toluene with bromine in the presence of $FeBr_3$ is

(a) *ortho*-bromotoluene
(b) *meta*-bromotoluene
(c) *para*-bromotoluene
(d) a mixture of *ortho*- and *para*-bromotoluene

4. Given below are two statements, one is labelled as Assertion (A) and the other is labelled as Reason (R).

Assertion (A) The *sp*-hybridised orbitals of carbon atoms in ethyne molecules have highest electronegativity.

Reason (R) It has maximum percentage of *s*-character.

In the light of the above statements, choose the correct answer from the options given below.

(a) Both (A) and (R) are true and (R) is the correct explanation of (A).
(b) Both (A) and (R) are true but (R) is not the correct explanation of (A).
(c) (A) is true but (R) is false.
(d) (A) is false but (R) is true.

5. Which of the following reagents can be used to convert 2-butyne to *cis*-butene?

(a) H_2/Pd-$BaSO_4$ (Lindlar's catalyst)
(b) Na/NH_3 (liq.)
(c) H_2/Pt
(d) $LiAlH_4$

6. Which of the following molecule possesses *sp* and sp^3-hybridised carbon atom?

(a) But-2-yne
(b) 1,3,5-hexatriene
(c) Buta-1,2-diene
(d) Propadiene

7. Given below are two statements.

Statement I Alkynes can easily react with CN^- nucleophile but alkenes cannot.

Statement II Alkynes are more reactive than alkene.

In the light of the above statements, choose the correct answer from the options given below.

(a) Both Statement I and Statement II are incorrect.
(b) Statement I is correct but Statement II is incorrect.

(c) Statement I is incorrect but Statement II is correct.
(d) Both Statement I and Statement II are correct.

8. When prop-1-yne reacts with two equivalents of HBr in the presence of a peroxide, the major product is

(a) $CH_3CBr_2CH_3$

(b) $CH_3CH_2CHBrCH_2Br$

(c) $CH_3CHBrCH_3$

(d) $CH_3CH_2CHBr_2$

9. Given below are two statements, one is labelled as Assertion (A) and the other is labelled as Reason (R).

Assertion (A) Friedel-Crafts acylation of benzene with acetyl chloride yields acetophenone as the major product.
Reason (R) The acyl group (—COR) is a deactivating group and *ortho/para* director.
In the light of the above statements, choose the correct answer from the options given below.
(a) Both (A) and (R) are true and (R) is the correct explanation of (A).
(b) Both (A) and (R) are true but (R) is not the correct explanation of (A).
(c) (A) is true but (R) is false.
(d) (A) is false but (R) is true.

10. The reaction of 1-butyne with $HgSO_4$ and H_2SO_4 in water produces

(a) butanone (b) butanal
(c) 2-butanone (d) butanoic acid

11. Given below are two statements.
Statement I Benzene undergoes electrophilic substitution reactions less readily than nucleophilic substitution reactions.
Statement II The electrophilic substitution reactions in benzene proceed *via* a σ-complex intermediate.
In the light of the above statements, choose the correct answer from the options given below.
(a) Both Statement I and Statement II are incorrect.
(b) Statement I is correct but Statement II is incorrect.
(c) Statement I is incorrect but Statement II is correct.
(d) Both Statement I and Statement II are correct.

12. Select the correct statements about aromatic hydrocarbons.

A. Benzene is a planar molecule with delocalised pi electrons.
B. Benzene undergoes substitution reactions rather than addition reactions.
C. The carbon-carbon bond length in benzene is exactly equal to single bond due to delocalised pi bond.
D. Benzene is more stable than its hypothetical cyclohexatriene structure.
E. Electrophilic aromatic substitution in benzene proceeds *via* a stable arenium ion intermediate.

Choose the correct answer from the options given below.

(a) A, B, C and D
(b) A, B, C and E
(c) A, B, D and E
(d) A,C and D only

13. Match List-I with List-II.

List-I (Reaction)	List-II (Product)
A. Benzene + Cl_2 + ($FeCl_3$)	I. Chlorobenzene
B. Benzene + CH_3COCl + anhy ($AlCl_3$)	II. Acetophenone
C. Benzene + HNO_3 + (H_2SO_4)	III. Nitrobenzene
D. Benzene + H_2SO_4 + (SO_3)	IV. Benzenesulphonic acid

Choose the correct answer from the options given below.

(a) A-I,B-II,C-III,D-IV
(b) A-II,B-IV,C-III,D-I
(c) A-IV,B-II,C-III,D-I
(d) A-III,B-II,C-IV,D-I

14. Choose the incorrect statement from the following.
(a) Phenol is reduced to benzene by passing its vapour over heated zinc dust.
(b) Benzene is commercially isolated from coal tar.
(c) In the presence of nickel catalyst at high temperature and pressure, cyclohexane will be formed from benzene.
(d) The —OH group deactivates the benzene ring for the attack by an electrophile.

15. What is the minimum number of C-atoms required to have four carbon-carbon double bond in a cyclic structure?
(a) Eight (b) Five
(c) Seven (d) Four

16. The number of sigma (σ) and pi (π) bonds present in hept-2,5-diyne respectively are
(a) 14 and 2 (b) 12 and 2
(c) 14 and 4 (d) 2 and 4

17. When prop-1-yne reacts with two equivalents of HBr, the major product is
(a) $CH_3CBr_2CH_3$
(b) CH_3, CH_2CHBr_2
(c) $CH_3CH_2CHBrCH_3$
(d) $CH_3CH(Br)CH_3$

18. Which of the following reactions proceeds *via* a vinyl cation intermediate?
(a) Hydroboration-oxidation of alkynes.
(b) Addition of HCl to alkynes.
(c) Ozonolysis of alkynes.
(d) Reduction of alkynes with $Na/NH_3(l)$.

19. The product(s) obtained by the oxymercuration ($HgSO_4 + aq.H_2SO_4$) of but-2-yne
(a) $CH_3CH_2CH_2CHO$
(b) $CH_3CH_2COCH_3$
(c) $CH_3CH_2CHO + HCHO$
(d) $CH_3CH_2COOH + HCOOH$

20. Which of the following statements is correct?
(a) Alkynes are more reactive than alkenes in electrophilic addition reactions but less reactive in nucleophilic addition reactions.
(b) Alkynes are more reactive than alkenes in nucleophilic addition reactions but less reactive in electrophilic addition reactions.
(c) Alkynes are less reactive than alkenes in both electrophilic and nucleophilic addition reactions.
(d) Alkynes are more reactive than alkenes in both electrophilic and nucleophilic addition reaction.

21. The major product formed on monobromination ($Br_2/FeBr_3$) of the following compound,

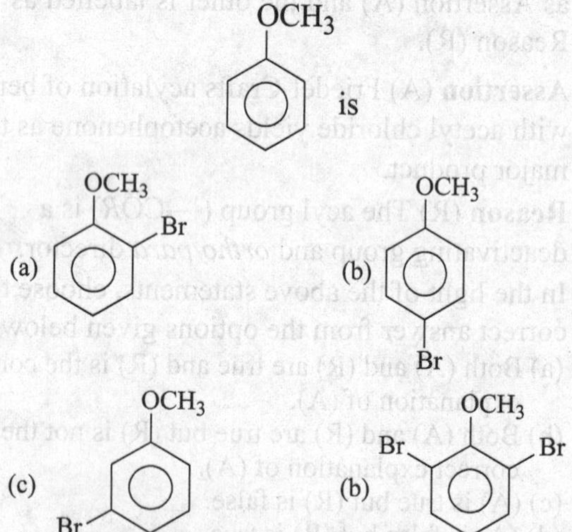

22. Which of the following isomeric compounds has the greatest dipole moment?

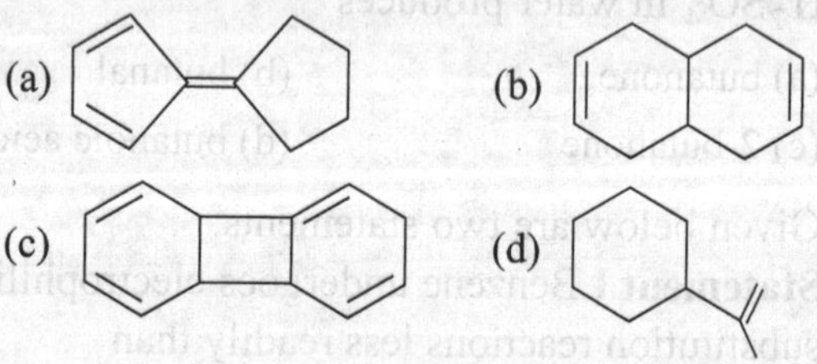

23. Which of the following is not a characteristic of aromatic compounds?
(a) Planar structure
(b) Cyclic and conjugated system
(c) Delocalised pi-electron cloud
(d) sp^3-hybridised carbon atoms

24. The major product formed in the reaction of toluene with a mixture of concentrated nitric acid (HNO_3) and concentrated sulphuric acid (H_2SO_4) at a temperature below 60°C is

(a) *o*-nitrotoluene

(b) *m*-nitrotoluene

(c) *p*-nitrotoluene

(d) a mixture of *o*- and *p*-nitrotoluene

25. Which of the following aromatic compounds is the most reactive towards electrophilic aromatic substitution?

(a) Benzene

(b) Chlorobenzene

(c) Nitrobenzene

(d) Anisole

Response Index

01	a	b	c	d	10	a	b	c	d	19	a	b	c	d
02	a	b	c	d	11	a	b	c	d	20	a	b	c	d
03	a	b	c	d	12	a	b	c	d	21	a	b	c	d
04	a	b	c	d	13	a	b	c	d	22	a	b	c	d
05	a	b	c	d	14	a	b	c	d	23	a	b	c	d
06	a	b	c	d	15	a	b	c	d	24	a	b	c	d
07	a	b	c	d	16	a	b	c	d	25	a	b	c	d
08	a	b	c	d	17	a	b	c	d					
09	a	b	c	d	18	a	b	c	d					

Performance Scanner

> 90% Excellent !	You have mastered these topics. The concepts of these topics are at your fingertips. Move on to the chapter test and maintain this momentum.
76-90% Very Good !	You have a good command over these topics. Revise these topics again after a few days and enhance your performance.
60-75% Good !	You have a wide scope to learn for these topics. Revise these topics again.
<60 Not Satisfactory!	You have a long way ahead of you to master these topics. Revise it thoroughly.

Chapter Break Thru

Syllabus		
Alkanes : Classification, Isomerism, IUPAC Nomenclature, General Method of Preparation, Properties and Reactions, Conformations, Sawhorse and Newman Projections (of Ethane), Mechanism of Halogenation.	**Alkenes** : IUPAC Nomenclature, General Method of Preparation, Geometrical Isomerism, Mechanism of Electrophilic Addition, Addition of Hydrogen, Halogens, Water, Hydrogen Halide (Markownikoff's and Peroxide Effect) Ozonolysis and Polymerisation.	**Alkynes** : Acidic Character, Addition of Hydrogen, Halogen, Water, Hydrogen Halides and Polymerisation, Friedel-Craft's Alkylation and Acylation, Directive Influence of the Functional Group, Aromatic Hydrocarbon : Nomenclature, Benzene, Structure and Aromaticity, Mechanism of Electrophilic Substitution; Halogenation, Nitration.

Important Instructions

- The test is of 1 hour duration and contains 50 multiple choice questions (Four options with a single correct answer).
- Choose the correct option and fill the OMR given on the last page of test accordingly.
- At some instances, you may find more than 1 option may be correct. In such circumstances, you have to judge the most appropriate answer as per the conditions given in the question.

1. Which of the following compound is a non-benzenoid aromatic compound?

(a) Tropolone (b) Benzoic acid
(c) Aniline (d) Anthracene

2. Consider the reaction given below.

$$CH_3CH_2CH(Br)CH_3 \xrightarrow[+Me_3\,C-OH]{(CH_3)_3COK} B \text{ (Major product)}$$

Product B is

(a) but-1-ene (b) prop-1-ene
(c) pent-2-ene (d) pent-1-ene

3. An alkene on ozonolysis produces butanone only. The alkene is

(a) but-3-ene
(b) 3,4-dimethylbut-2-ene
(c) 3,4-dimethyl hex-3-ene
(d) 3,5-dimethyl pentene

4. Given below are two statements, one is labelled as Assertion (A) and the other is labelled as Reason (R).

Assertion (A) 2-bromobutane on reaction with sodium ethanoxide in ethanol gives 1-butene as a major product.

Reason (R) 1-butene is less stable than 2-butene.

In the light of the above statements, choose the correct answer from the options given below.

(a) Both (A) and (R) are true and (R) is the correct explanation of (A).
(b) Both (A) and (R) are true but (R) is not the correct explanation of (A).
(c) (A) is true but (R) is false.
(d) (A) is false but (R) is true.

5. Which of the following products would produce a racemic mixture on monochlorination ?

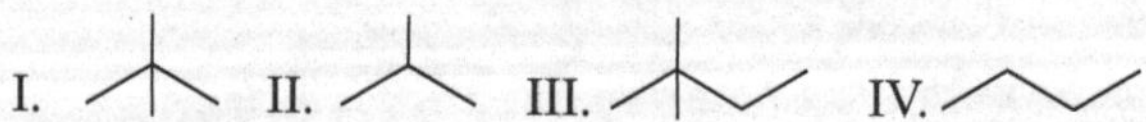

Choose the correct answer from the options given below.

(a) I and II
(b) II and III
(c) II and IV
(d) III and IV

6. Given below are two statements.

Statement I Addition of HI to vinyl chloride produces 1-chloro-1-iodo ethane.

Statement II HI adds to vinyl chlorides against Markownikoff's rule.

In the light of the above statements, choose the correct answer from the options given below.

(a) Both Statement I and Statement II are incorrect.
(b) Statement I is correct but Statement II is incorrect.
(c) Statement I is incorrect but Statement II is correct.
(d) Both Statement I and Statement II are correct.

7. In the reaction,

$$C_5H_{10}\ A \xrightarrow[\text{(ii) } H_3O^+]{\text{(i) } KMnO_4 \cdot H_2O,\ OH^{\ominus}} \text{Acetone} + \text{Acetic acid}$$

Predict the compound *A*.

(a) $CH_3—CH{=}CH—CH_2—CH_3$

(b) CH_3(H)C=C(H)$CH_2—CH_3$ [CH_3 and H on one carbon; $CH_3—CH_2$ and H on the other]

(c) CH_3(H)C=C(CH_3)($CH_2—CH_3$)

(d) (Me)(Me)C=CH—CH_3

8. Consider the following compounds.

I. Pent-1-ene
II. Pent-2-ene
III. 2-methyl-but-1-ene
IV. 2-methyl-but-2-ene

The compound which has the lowest and highest heat of combustion are respectively.

(a) IV and I (b) I and IV
(c) II and III (d) III and II

9. The product *C* formed in the given reaction sequence is

$$C_2H_2 \xrightarrow{NaNH_2} A \xrightarrow{CH_3I} B \xrightarrow[\text{Dil. } H_2SO_4,\ H_2O]{HgSO_4} C$$

(a) CH_3CHO (b) CH_3COCH_3
(c) $CH_3CH_2CH_2CHO$ (d) $CH_3CH_2CH{=}CH_2$

10. When a compound *X* is heated with soda lime, the product obtained is ethane, what is *X*?

(a) Butanoic acid (b) Propanoic acid
(c) Ethanoic acid (d) Methanoic acid

11. Complete the following reaction.

(alkene with CH_3) $\xrightarrow{NBS} B \xrightarrow{\text{Alc. KOH}} C$

Here, *B* and *C* respectively are

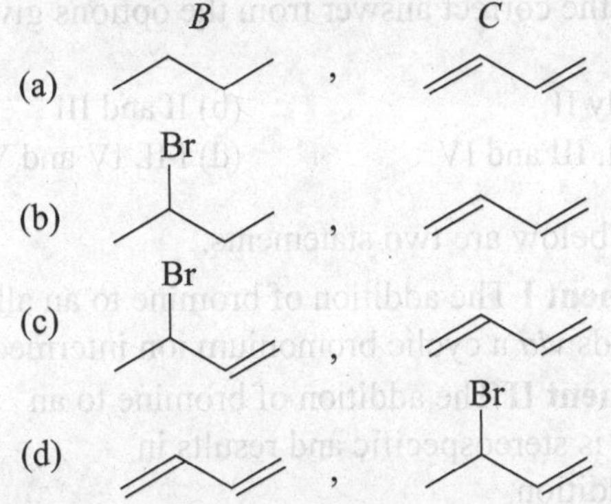

12. Given below are two statements.

Statement I Cyclopentadienyl anion is much more stable than allyl anion.

Statement II Cyclopentadienyl anion is aromatic in character.

In the light of the above statements, choose the correct answer from the options given below.

(a) Both Statement I and Statement II are incorrect.
(b) Statement I is correct but Statement II is incorrect.
(c) Statement I is incorrect but Statement II is correct.
(d) Both Statement I and Statement II are correct.

13. Which of the following statement is incorrect about oxymercuration and demercuration reaction?

(a) In this reaction, alcohol is formed by Markownikoff's addition.
(b) It is an electrophilic addition reaction.
(c) Regiospecificity of this reaction is syn.
(d) The regioselectivity in oxymercuration is due to more stable carbocation.

14. When *neo*-pentyl alcohol is treated with concentrated H_2SO_4, the product *X* is

(a) 2-methylbut-2-ene (b) 1-methylbut-1-ene
(c) *neo*-hexane (d) 2-methylhexane

15. Which of the following statements is incorrect?

I. Alkenes and alkynes decolourise alkaline $KMnO_4$ solution (Baeyer's test for unsaturation).
II. Hexane easily dissolve in conc. H_2SO_4.

III. The reactivity of alkenes depends on heat of hydrogenation.
IV. Alkynes are weakly polar in nature.
V. *Vicinal* dihalides on treatment with zinc metal lose a molecule of ZnX_2 to form an alkene.

Select the correct answer from the options given below.

(a) Only II
(b) II and III
(c) I, II, III and IV
(d) I II, IV and V

16. Given below are two statements.

Statement I The addition of bromine to an alkene proceeds *via* a cyclic bromonium ion intermediate.

Statement II The addition of bromine to an alkene is stereospecific and results in anti-addition.

In the light of the above statements, choose the correct answer from the options given below.

(a) Both Statement I and Statement II are incorrect.
(b) Statement I is correct but Statement II is incorrect.
(c) Statement I is incorrect but Statement II is correct.
(d) Both Statement I and Statement II are correct.

17. Which of the following reaction is/are the example of electrophilic substitution reaction?

I. $C_6H_6 \xrightarrow[\text{323-333 K}]{\text{HNO}_3,\ \text{Conc.H}_2\text{SO}_4} C_6H_5NO_2 + H_2O$

II. $C_6H_6 + H_2S_2O_7 \text{ (Fuming)} \longrightarrow C_6H_5SO_3H$

III. $C_6H_6 + CH_3COCl \xrightarrow{\text{Anhyd. AlCl}_3} C_6H_5COCH_3$

IV. $C_6H_6 + CH_3Cl \xrightarrow{\text{Anhyd. AlCl}_3} C_6H_5CH_3 + HCl$

V. $C_6H_6 + Cl_2 \xrightarrow{\text{Anhyd. AlCl}_3} C_6H_5Cl + HCl$
Chlorobenzene

Choose the correct option.

(a) Only III
(b) I II and III
(c) I, III and IV
(d) I, II, III, IV and V

18. Given below are two statements, one is labelled as Assertion (A) and the other is labelled as Reason (R).

Assertion (A) The energy difference between staggered and eclipsed conformations of ethylene dichloride is less than in ethylene dibromide.

Reason (R) The bond moment of C—Cl is greater than that of C—Br.

In the light of the above statements, choose the correct answer from the options given below.

(a) Both (A) and (R) are true and (R) is the correct explanation of (A).
(b) Both (A) and (R) are true but (R) is not the correct explanation of (A).
(c) (A) is true but (R) is false.
(d) (A) is false but (R) is true.

19. Given below are two statements.

Statement I Propene reacts with HBr in presence of benzoyl peroxide to yield 2-bromopropane.

Statement II In presence of peroxide, the reaction occurs through a more stable carbocation.

In the light of the above statements, choose the correct answer from the options given below.

(a) Both Statement I and Statement II are incorrect.
(b) Statement I is correct but Statement II is incorrect.
(c) Statement I is incorrect but Statement II is correct.
(d) Both Statement I and Statement II are correct.

20. At 420 K, the reaction between CH_4 and Cl_2 does not occur. Addition of which of the following will enable the reaction to happen at 420 K.

(a) CO_2
(b) $Pb(OCOCH_3)_2$
(c) $(CH_3)_4Pb$
(d) H_2SO_4

21. Final product of the reaction will be

(styrene) $\xrightarrow{NH_2\text{-}NH_2}$? is

(a) (toluene, CH_3) $+ N_2\uparrow$ (b) (ethylbenzene, C_2H_5) $+ N_2\uparrow$

(c) (ethylcyclohexane, C_2H_5) $+ N_2\uparrow$ (d) (methylcyclohexane, CH_3) $+ N_2\uparrow$

22. Consider the reaction given below,

$$\underset{\text{Ethyne}}{CH{\equiv}CH} \xrightarrow[\text{(liq.) } NH_3]{NaNH_2/} A \xrightarrow{CH_3I} B \xrightarrow{H_2 + Ni_2Br} C \xrightarrow{O_3/\text{Red.}} D \xrightarrow{LAH} \underset{\text{(Final product)}}{E}$$

The product E is
(a) methanol + ethanol (b) ethanol + propanol
(c) ethane (d) ethene

23. Consider the following reaction,

$A \xleftarrow{O_3/\text{Red}}$ (benzene) $\xrightarrow[KMnO_4]{\text{Cold alk.}} B$

(benzene) $\xrightarrow[KMnO_4]{\text{Hot alk.}} C$

Here, A, B and C are

	A	B	C
(a)	OHC–CHO (H–C(=O)–C(=O)–H)	No reaction	No reaction
(b)	H–C(=O)–C(=O)–H	COOH–COOH	H–C(=O)–C(=O)–H
(c)	COOH–COOH	COOH–COOH	COOH–COOH
(d)	COOH–COOH	CO_2	CHO–CHO

24. The smallest ketone and its next homologue are reacted with NH_2OH to form
(a) two different oximes
(b) three different oximes
(c) two oximes which are optically active
(d) two oximes which are optically inactive

25. What is the IUPAC name of compound given below ?

$CH_3-CH(C_2H_5)-CH{=}CH-CH_2-CH{=}CH-CH(CH_3)_2$

(a) 2-ethyl-8-methylnon-3,6-diene
(b) 8-ethyl-2-methylnon-3,6-diene
(c) 2,8-dimethyldeca-3,6-diene
(d) 1,3-dimethyldeca-4,7-diene

26. Select the incorrect statements.
A. The dipole moment of *cis*-2-butene is the vector sum of the CH_3—C and C—H bond dipoles.
B. sp^3-carbon is more electronegative than sp^2-carbon.
C. NBS is used for brominating alkenes at the allylic position.
D. Addition of Br_2 to alkene is not stereospecific.
E. Alkaline potassium permanganate is known as Baeyer's reagent.
(a) A, B and C (b) B and D
(c) B, D and E (d) A and C

27. An organohalogen compound X, when heated with alcoholic potassium hydroxide does not undergo dehydrohalogenation reaction. The compound X is
(a) *neo*-pentyl chloride
(b) *iso*-butyl chloride
(c) *iso*-propyl chloride
(d) tertiarybutyl chloride

28. The decreasing order of reactivity of Diels-Alder reaction of the following ?

A. (1,3-butadiene) + (ethene) $\xrightarrow{\Delta}$

B. (diene with Me) + (COOR-substituted alkene) $\xrightarrow{\Delta}$

C. (2,3-dimethyl-1,3-butadiene, Me, Me) + (COOR-substituted alkene) $\xrightarrow{\Delta}$

D. (2,3-dimethyl-1,3-butadiene, Me, Me) + (alkene with two COOR) $\xrightarrow{\Delta}$

Choose the correct option.

(a) A > B > C > D (b) D > C > B > A

(c) D > C > A > B (d) B > A > C > D

29. Consider the reaction given below,

$$Me-\equiv-\equiv-Me \xrightarrow[+\ C_2H_5OH]{Na\ +\ Liq.NH_3} B$$

Here, compound B is

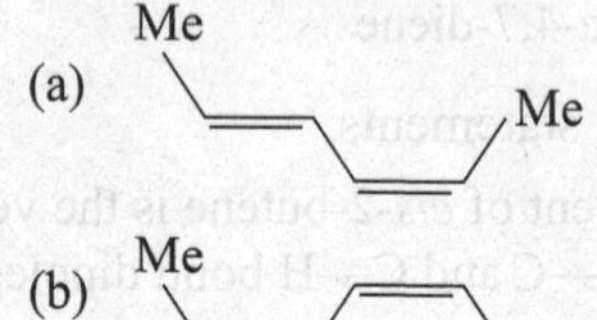

(a)

(b)

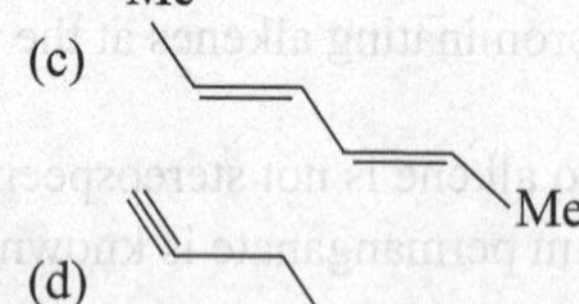

(c)

(d)

30. Consider the conformation of butane given below

(A) Staggered (B) Anti-staggered (C) *Skew* or *gauche,* (D) Eclipsed and (E) Partially eclipsed

The correct order of stability of given species is

(a) $B > A > C > E > D$

(b) $A > B > C > E > D$

(c) $C > A > B > E > D$

(d) $D > C > A > B > E$

31. Match List-I with List-II.

	List-I	List-II
A.	$CH_2{=}CH_2 + H_2 \xrightarrow{Pt/Pd/Ni}$	I. Methanol
B.	$CH_3{-}Cl + H_2 \xrightarrow{Zn/H^+}$	II. Methanal
C.	$CH_4 + O_2 \xrightarrow[\Delta]{Mo_2O_3}$	III. Methane
D.	$2CH_4 + O_2 \xrightarrow{Cu/523\ K/100atm}$	IV. Ethane

Choose the correct answer from the options given below.

(a) A-IV, B-I, C-II, D-III

(b) A-IV, B-III, C-II, D-I

(c) A-III, B-IV, C-I, D-II

(d) A-II, B-I, C-IV, D-III

32. The intermediate product during the addition of HCl to propene in the presence of peroxide is

(a) $CH_3\dot{C}HCH_2Cl$ (b) $CH_3\overset{+}{C}HCH_3$

(c) $CH_3CH_2\dot{C}H_2$ (d) $CH_3CH_2\overset{+}{C}H_2$

33. The reagent used in given reaction is

H_3C / CH_3 (1,2-dimethylcyclohexene) $\xrightarrow{Reagent}$ H, H / CH_3 CH_3

(a) H_2/Pd supported over $BaSO_4$

(b) H_2/Pt or Pd or Ni

(c) Na/liquid NH_3

(d) Zn-Hg/HCl

34. Predict the order of reactivity of the following compounds in dehydrogenation

A. CH_3–$CH_2CH_2CH_2$–Cl

B. $(CH_3)_2CH$–CH_2–Cl

C. $(CH_3)_2CH$–CH_2–Br

D. CH_3–CH(Br)–CH_2–CH_3

E. $(CH_3)_3C$–Br

is

(a) C > E > B > D > A

(b) E > C > B > D > A

(c) A > B > C > D > E

(d) E > A > B > C > D

35. When benzyl bromide reacted with monosodium acetylide, the product of reaction is

(a) 1-phenylpropyne

(b) 3-phenylpropyne

(c) 2-methylpropyne

(d) 2-methylacetylene

36. Given below are two statements.

Statement I C-atom in ethene is *sp*-hybridised while it is sp^2 in ethyne.

Statement II C—H bond in ethyne is shorter than C—H bond in ethene.

In the light of the above statements, choose the correct answer from the options given below.

(a) Both Statement I and Statement II are incorrect.
(b) Statement I is correct but Statement II is incorrect.
(c) Statement I is incorrect but Statement II is correct.
(d) Both Statement I and Statement II are correct.

37. Match List-I with List-II.

	List-I (Compounds)		List-II (Type of strains/Forces)
A.	(cyclohexane chair)	I.	Electrostatic force of attraction, torsional strain.
B.	OH F (chair)	II.	Electrostatic force of attraction, torsional strain, steric strain.
C.	OH; H, OH; H, H; H (Newman projection)	III.	Electrostatic force of attraction, torsional strain, angle strain, steric strain.
D.	CH_3; H, CH_3; H, H; H (Newman projection)	IV.	Electrostatic force of attraction, torsional strain, angle strain.

Choose the correct answer from the options given below.

(a) A-II, B-III, C-IV, D-I
(b) A-II, B-III, C-II, D-IV
(c) A-IV, B-III, C-I, D-II
(d) A-III, B-IV, C-II, D-I

38. Given below are two statements, one is labelled as Assertion (A) and the other is labelled as Reason (R).

Assertion (A) CHBr=CHCl exhibits geometrical isomerism but $CH_2Br—CH_2Cl$ does not.

Reason (R) Presence of C=C is one of the condition of geometrical isomerism.

In the light of the above statements, choose the correct answer from the options given below.

(a) Both (A) and (R) are true and (R) is the correct explanation of (A).
(b) Both (A) and (R) are true but (R) is not the correct explanation of (A).
(c) (A) is true but (R) is false.
(d) (A) is false but (R) is true.

39. On ozonolysis of pent-1,3-diene, three product are formed. Two products are formaldehyde and acetaldehyde. The third product is

(a) methanol
(b) ethanol
(c) glyoxal
(d) propionaldehyde

40. In the presence of Pd-$BaSO_4$, 2-butyne is treated with H_2. The product formed is

(a) *cis*-2-butene
(b) *trans*-2-butene
(c) 2-methylbutene
(d) 1-chlorobutene

41. Consider the following reaction;

$$2\,H—\equiv—H \xrightarrow[NH_4Cl]{CuCl} A \xrightarrow{H_2+Ni_2Br} B \xrightarrow{Br_2} \underset{(Major)}{C}$$

Here, the compound formed *C* is,

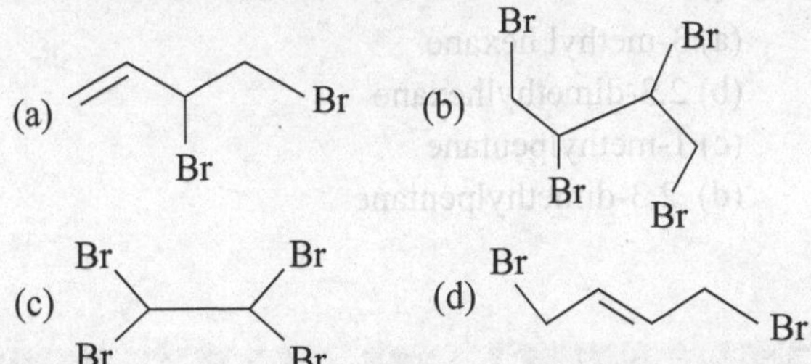

42. Consider the reaction given below.

$$CH_3—CH=CH—CH_2—C\equiv C—Me \xrightarrow{CrO_3/CH_3COOH} A + B$$

Products *A* and *B* are

	A	*B*
(a)	ethanoic acid	pent-3-yne-1-oic acid
(b)	methanoic acid	pent-3-yne-1-oic acid
(c)	propanoic acid	pent-3-yne-1-oic acid
(d)	ethanoic acid	but-3-yne-1-oic acid

43. 3-chloro-4-methylbenzene sulphonic acid is heated with super heated steam.

The major product is

(a) toluene
(b) *o*-chlorotoluene
(c) *p*-methylbenzene sulphonic acid
(d) *m*-chlorobenzene sulphonic acid.

44. At 10-20 atm pressure and 773 K, heating of n-hexane in presence of oxides of vanadium supported over alumina ultimately yields.
(a) 1-hexane
(b) benzene
(c) 3,2-dimethylbutane
(d) 1-methylpentane

45. Among the given molecules, which exhibit confirmational isomerism?
(a) CH_3OH (b) H_2O_2
(c) $NH_2—NH_2$ (d) All of these

46. From the given compounds, which has the lowest boiling point?
(a) 2-methyl propane
(b) 2-methylbutane
(c) n-butane
(d) 2,2-dimethylpropane

47. Which of the following isomeric heptanes can yield seven different monochlorinated products upon free radical chlorination?
(a) 3-methyl hexane
(b) 2,3-dimethylhexane
(c) 1-methylpentane
(d) 2,3-dimethylpentane

48. Which of the following is the correct order of reactivity towards monobromination?
(a) $C_6H_6 > C_6H_5COOH > C_6H_5CH_3 > C_6H_5NO_2$
(b) $C_6H_5CH_3 > C_6H_6 > C_6H_5COOH > C_6H_5NO_2$
(c) $C_6H_5COOH > C_6H_5CH_3 > C_6H_5NO_2 > C_6H_6$
(d) $C_6H_6 > C_6H_5CH_3 > C_6H_5NO_2 > C_6H_5COOH$

49. When a compound X is oxidised with hot $KMnO_4$, the solution becomes colourless. Name the compound X.
(a) CH_3OH
(b) $(CH_3)_3CH$
(c) C_2H_6
(d) C_3H_8

50. Consider the compounds given below,

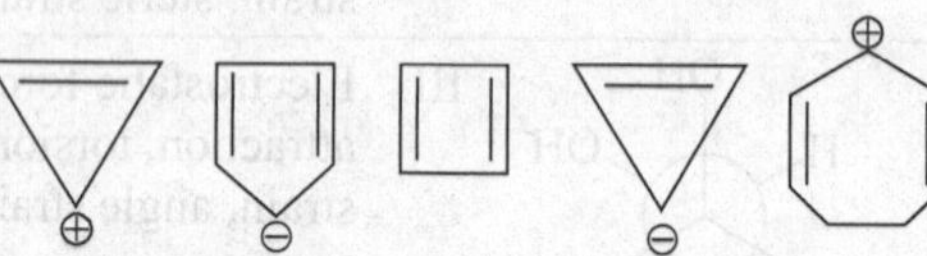

The total number of aromatic compound from the following is
(a) 4 (b) 5
(c) 2 (d) 1

■ Response Index

01 ⓐ ⓑ ⓒ ⓓ	14 ⓐ ⓑ ⓒ ⓓ	27 ⓐ ⓑ ⓒ ⓓ	40 ⓐ ⓑ ⓒ ⓓ
02 ⓐ ⓑ ⓒ ⓓ	15 ⓐ ⓑ ⓒ ⓓ	28 ⓐ ⓑ ⓒ ⓓ	41 ⓐ ⓑ ⓒ ⓓ
03 ⓐ ⓑ ⓒ ⓓ	16 ⓐ ⓑ ⓒ ⓓ	29 ⓐ ⓑ ⓒ ⓓ	42 ⓐ ⓑ ⓒ ⓓ
04 ⓐ ⓑ ⓒ ⓓ	17 ⓐ ⓑ ⓒ ⓓ	30 ⓐ ⓑ ⓒ ⓓ	43 ⓐ ⓑ ⓒ ⓓ
05 ⓐ ⓑ ⓒ ⓓ	18 ⓐ ⓑ ⓒ ⓓ	31 ⓐ ⓑ ⓒ ⓓ	44 ⓐ ⓑ ⓒ ⓓ
06 ⓐ ⓑ ⓒ ⓓ	19 ⓐ ⓑ ⓒ ⓓ	32 ⓐ ⓑ ⓒ ⓓ	45 ⓐ ⓑ ⓒ ⓓ
07 ⓐ ⓑ ⓒ ⓓ	20 ⓐ ⓑ ⓒ ⓓ	33 ⓐ ⓑ ⓒ ⓓ	46 ⓐ ⓑ ⓒ ⓓ
08 ⓐ ⓑ ⓒ ⓓ	21 ⓐ ⓑ ⓒ ⓓ	34 ⓐ ⓑ ⓒ ⓓ	47 ⓐ ⓑ ⓒ ⓓ
09 ⓐ ⓑ ⓒ ⓓ	22 ⓐ ⓑ ⓒ ⓓ	35 ⓐ ⓑ ⓒ ⓓ	48 ⓐ ⓑ ⓒ ⓓ
10 ⓐ ⓑ ⓒ ⓓ	23 ⓐ ⓑ ⓒ ⓓ	36 ⓐ ⓑ ⓒ ⓓ	49 ⓐ ⓑ ⓒ ⓓ
11 ⓐ ⓑ ⓒ ⓓ	24 ⓐ ⓑ ⓒ ⓓ	37 ⓐ ⓑ ⓒ ⓓ	50 ⓐ ⓑ ⓒ ⓓ
12 ⓐ ⓑ ⓒ ⓓ	25 ⓐ ⓑ ⓒ ⓓ	38 ⓐ ⓑ ⓒ ⓓ	
13 ⓐ ⓑ ⓒ ⓓ	26 ⓐ ⓑ ⓒ ⓓ	39 ⓐ ⓑ ⓒ ⓓ	

■ Performance Scanner

> 90% Excellent !	You have mastered this chapter. The concepts of this chapter are at your fingertips. Move on to the next chapter and maintain this momentum.
76-90% Very Good !	You have a good command over this chapter. Revise the chapter again after a few days and enhance your performance.
60-75% Good !	You have a wide scope to learn for this chapter. Revise this chapter again.
<60 Not Satisfactory!	You have a long way ahead of you to master this chapter. Revise it thoroughly.

Scan for Online Chapter Test

Scan for Online Unit Test

Test Booklet No. **3947213**

Test Booklet Code **SPT1**

MEDACE

NEET (UG)

SELF ASSESSMENT KIT

Syllabus Part Thru 1

(Half Syllabus Test)

Chapters Covered

- Some Basic Concepts of Chemistry
- Structure of Atom
- Classification of Elements and Periodicity in Properties
- Chemical Bonding
- Thermodynamics
- Chemical Equilibrium

Important Instructions

- The test is of 45 minutes duration and the Test Booklet contains 45 multiple choice questions (four options with a single correct answer) from Chemistry.
- Candidates are advised to read all questions before they start attempting the question paper.
- Each questions carries 4 marks. For each correct response, the candidate will get 4 marks. For each incorrect response, one mark will be deducted from the total scores.
- In the event of candidate marking more than one option then one mark will be deducted. The maximum marks are 180.
- Use **Blue/Black Point Pen** only for writing particular on this page/marking response on Answer Sheet.

Name of the Candidate (In Capitals) ____________________

Candidate's Signature ____________

Invigilator's Signature ____________

Facsimile signature stamp of center superintendent____________

Do not open this Booklet until you start attempting the Test

Chemistry (Q. No. 1-45)

1. The electron in the ground state of hydrogen atom absorbs 12.1 eV of energy. It will jump to which orbit?

(a) 4th (b) 6th
(c) 8th (d) 3rd

2. Match List-I with List-II.

	List-I (Law)	List-II (Scientist)
A.	Law of conservation of mass	I. Richter
B.	Law of constant composition	II. Dalton
C.	Law of multiple proportion	III. J.L. Proust
D.	Law of reciprocal proportion	IV. Antoine Lavoisier

Choose the correct answer from the options given below.
(a) A-I, B-II, C-III, D-IV
(b) A-II, B-I, C-IV, D-III
(c) A-IV, B-I, C-II, D-III
(d) A-IV, B-III, C-II, D-I

3. 12 g of an alkaline earth metal gave 14.8 g of its nitride. Atomic weight of that metal is,

(a) 40 (b) 30 (c) 25 (d) 35

4. What will be the number of atoms of each element that are present in 3.42 g of sucrose ($C_{12}H_{22}O_{11}$)?

(a) $C = 7.228 \times 10^{22}$ atoms, $H = 132.5 \times 10^{21}$ atoms, $O = 66.25 \times 10^{21}$ atoms
(b) $C = 7.228 \times 10^{22}$ atoms, $H = 13.25 \times 10^{21}$ atoms, $O = 6.625 \times 10^{21}$ atoms
(c) $C = 6.228 \times 10^{22}$ atoms, $H = 13.25 \times 10^{21}$ atoms, $O = 66.25 \times 10^{21}$ atoms
(d) $C = 6.228 \times 10^{22}$ atoms, $H = 132.5 \times 10^{21}$ atoms, $O = 66.25 \times 10^{21}$ atoms

5. The degeneracy of the level of H-atom that has energy $-\frac{R_H}{16}$ is

(a) 16 (b) 12
(c) 10 (d) 6

6. 1 g of hydrogen is found to combine with 80 g of bromine and 1 g of calcium (valency = 2) combine with 4 g of bromine. The equivalent weight of calcium is

(a) 18 (b) 20
(c) 25 (d) 60

7. Which of the following represents the correct electronic configuration of the most electropositive element?

(a) $[He]2s^1$ (b) $[Xe]6s^1$
(c) $[He]2s^2$ (d) $[Xe]6s^2$

8. What will be work done when 1 mole of an ideal gas is compressed reversibly from 1.0 bar to 4.00 bar at constant temperature of 300 K?

(a) 3.46 kJ (b) 6.92 kJ
(c) –3.46 kJ (d) –6.92 kJ

9. Match List-I with List-II.

List-I	List-II
A. $\lambda = h/p$	I. UV radiation
B. Lyman series	II. IR-radiation
C. Paschen series	III. Heisenberg's uncertainty principle
D. $\Delta x \, \Delta p \geq h/4\pi$	IV. de-Broglie's relationship

Choose the correct answer from the options given below.
(a) A-III, B-IV, C-II, D-I
(b) A-I, B-III, C-IV, D-II
(c) A-II, B-III, C-I, D-IV
(d) A-IV, B-I, C-II, D-III

10. 1.615 g of anhydrous $ZnSO_4$ was placed in moist air. After a few days, its mass was found to be 2.875 g. The molecular formula for hydrated salt is

(a) $ZnSO_4 \cdot 3H_2O$
(b) $ZnSO_4 \cdot 6H_2O$
(c) $ZnSO_4 \cdot 7H_2O$
(d) $ZnSO_4 \cdot 9H_2O$

11. If the binding energy of electrons in a metal is 250 kJ/mol, the threshold frequency of the striking photons will be

(a) $2.15 \times 10^{19}\ s^{-1}$
(b) $2.5 \times 10^{16}\ s^{-1}$
(c) $3.05 \times 10^{16}\ s^{-1}$
(d) $6.26 \times 10^{14}\ s^{-1}$

12. Given below are two statements, one is labelled as Assertion (A) and the other is labelled as Reason (R).

Assertion (A) Bond order can assume any positive value including zero.

Reason (R) Higher is the bond order, shorter is the bond length and greater is the bond energy.

In the light of the above statements, choose the correct answer from the options given below.

(a) Both (A) and (R) are true and (R) is the correct explanation of (A).
(b) Both (A) and (R) are true but (R) is not the correct explanation of (A).
(c) (A) is true but (R) is false.
(d) (A) is false but (R) is true.

13. Given below are two statements.

Statement I de-Broglie concept of dual nature of matter gave the relation between wavelength (λ) and momentum (p) of material particle.

Statement II de-Broglie concept is applicable only to macroscopic particles.

In the light of the above statements, choose the correct answer from the options given below.

(a) Both Statement I and Statement II are incorrect.
(b) Statement I is correct but Statement II is incorrect.
(c) Statement I is incorrect but Statement II is correct.
(d) Both Statement I and Statement II are correct.

14. Which of the following set of quantum numbers represents impossible arrangements?

	n	l	m_l	m_s
(a)	3	3	−2	1/2
(b)	4	0	0	1/2
(c)	3	2	−2	1/2
(d)	5	3	0	1/2

15. In two elements, ${}_{Z_1}A^{M_1}$ and ${}_{Z_2}B^{M_2}$, $M_1 \neq M_2$ and $Z_1 \neq Z_2$ but $M_1 - Z_1 = M_2 - Z_2$. These two elements are

(a) isotonic
(b) isobaric
(c) isotope
(d) isoelectronic

16. A gas expands isothermally against a constant external pressure of 1 atm from the volume of 10 dm^3 to a volume of 20 dm^3. It absorbs 800 J of thermal energy from its surrounding. Then ΔU is

(a) +213 J
(b) −213 J
(c) +328 J
(d) −328 J

17. The frequency of light emitted for the transition $n = 4$ to $n = 2$ of He^+ is equal to the transition in H-atom corresponding to which of the following?

(a) $n = 3$ to $n = 2$
(b) $n = 3$ to $n = 1$
(c) $n = 2$ to $n = 1$
(d) $n = 4$ to $n = 3$

18. Which among the given statement is correct?

(a) $FeCl_2$ is more covalent than $FeCl_3$.
(b) $FeCl_3$ is more covalent than $FeCl_2$.
(c) Both $FeCl_2$ and $FeCl_3$ are equally covalent.
(d) $FeCl_2$ and $FeCl_3$ do not have any covalent character.

19. Consider the reaction, where $K_p = 0.497$ at 500 K

$$PCl_5(g) \rightleftharpoons PCl_3(g) + Cl_2(g)$$

If the three gases are mixed in a rigid container so that the partial pressure of each gas is initially 1 atm, which is true?

(a) More PCl_5 will be produced.
(b) More PCl_3 will be produced.
(c) Equilibrium will be established when 50% reaction is complete.
(d) Equilibrium can't be predicted.

20. What will be the ΔG° for conversion of oxygen to ozone, $\frac{3}{2}O_2(g) \longrightarrow O_3(g)$ at 298 K, if $K_p = 2.47 \times 10^{-29}$?

(a) 1.63 kJ/mol
(b) 163.23 kJ/mol
(c) 0.163 kJ/mol
(d) 16.3 kJ/mol

21. Given below are two statements.

Statement I Outermost electronic configuration of most electronegative element is ns^2np^6.

Statement II Most electronegative elements are halogens.

In the light of the above statements, choose the correct answer from the options given below.

(a) Both Statement I and Statement II are incorrect.
(b) Statement I is correct but Statement II is incorrect.
(c) Statement I is incorrect but Statement II is correct.
(d) Both Statement I and Statement II are correct.

22. Which of the following is the correct order for bond dissociation enthalpy of halogen molecule?

(a) $Cl_2 > Br_2 > F_2 > I_2$
(b) $Br_2 > I_2 > F_2 > Cl_2$
(c) $F_2 > Cl_2 > Br_2 > I_2$
(d) $I_2 > Br_2 > Cl_2 > F_2$

23. Ease of formation of the cation is favoured by

(a) lower value of ionisation potential.
(b) lower value of electron affinity.
(c) higher value of electron affinity.
(d) lower value of electronegativity.

24. What will be the free energy change for the following reaction at 300 K?

$$2CuO(s) \longrightarrow Cu_2O(s) + \frac{1}{2}O_2(g)$$

Given, $\Delta H = 145.6$ kJ/mol, $\Delta S = 116\ JK^{-1}mol^{-1}$

(a) 110.8 kJ/mol (b) 210.8 kJ/mol
(c) 230 kJ/mol (d) 80.8 kJ/mol

25. Electron affinity is maximum for which of the following?

(a) Cl (b) F (c) Br (d) I

26. The equilibrium constant for the reaction at 100 K are

$$CoO(s) + H_2(g) \rightleftharpoons Co(s) + H_2O(g), K_1 = 65$$
$$CoO(s) + CO(g) \rightleftharpoons Co(s) + CO_2(g), K_2 = 500$$

The equilibrium constant for the reaction

$CO(g) + H_2O(g) \rightleftharpoons CO_2(g) + H_2(g)$ at 100 K is

(a) 7.69 (b) 5.69
(c) 8.99 (d) 76.9

27. Which among the following species has shortest bond length?

(a) O_2^{2+} (b) O_2^+
(c) O_2^- (d) O_2^{2-}

28. Given below are two statements, one is labelled as Assertion (A) and the other is labelled as Reason (R).

Assertion (A) The endothermic reactions are favoured by lower temperature and the exothermic reactions are favoured by higher temperature.

Reason (R) Change of temperature affects, the entropy factor.

In the light of the above statements, choose the correct answer from the options given below.

(a) Both (A) and (R) are true and (R) is the correct explanation of (A).
(b) Both (A) and (R) are true but (R) is not the correct explanation of (A).
(c) (A) is true but (R) is false.
(d) (A) is false but (R) is true.

29. Standard molar enthalpies of formation of $CaCO_3(s)$, $CaO(s)$ and $CO_2(g)$ are –1206.92 kJ/mol, –635.09 kJ/mol and –393.51 kJ/mol respectively. Then ΔH for decomposition of $CaCO_3(s)$ is

(a) –178.3 kJ/mol
(b) –166.8 kJ/mol
(c) +178.3 kJ/mol
(d) +166.8 kJ/mol

30. The relation between K_p and K_C for the reaction $2NO(g) + Cl_2(g) \rightleftharpoons 2NOCl(g)$ is

(a) $K_p = K_C$ (b) $K_p = K_C(RT)$
(c) $K_p = \frac{K_C}{RT}$ (d) $K_p = \frac{K_C}{(RT)^2}$

31. Given below are two statements.

Statement I Metallic character order is $K > Mg > Al > B$.

Statement II Metallic character of the elements increases along the period and decreases down the group.

In the light of the above statements, choose the correct answer from the options given below.

(a) Both Statement I and Statement II are incorrect.
(b) Statement I is correct but Statement II is incorrect.
(c) Statement I is incorrect but Statement II is correct.
(d) Both Statement I and Statement II are correct.

32. During the conversion of $NH_2OH \longrightarrow N_2O$, the equivalent mass of NH_2OH is (Mol. mass of NH_2OH is M).

(a) M (b) $\frac{M}{2}$
(c) $\frac{M}{4}$ (d) $\frac{M}{5}$

33. Which of the following are neutral oxides?

I. CO II. MnO_2 III. N_2O
IV. Al_2O_3 V. K_2O

Choose the correct answer from the options given below.

(a) I and II
(b) II and V
(c) II, III and V
(d) I and III

34. Match List-I with List-II.

List-I (Compounds)	List-II (Shape)
A. XeO_3	I. Square planar
B. NH_2^-	II. Tetrahedral
C. NH_4^+	III. Pyramidal
D. $[PtCl_4]^{2-}$	IV V shape

Choose the correct answer from the options given below.

(a) A-III, B-IV, C-II, D-I
(b) A-II, B-I, C-III, D-IV
(c) A-I, B-II, C-III, D-IV
(d) A-IV, B-I, C-II, D-III

35. Which of the following set does not contain isoelectronic species?

(a) $PO_4^{3-}, SO_4^{2-}, ClO_4^-$
(b) $SO_3^{2-}, CO_3^{2-}, NO_3^-$
(c) $BO_3^{3-}, CO_3^{2-}, NO_3^-$
(d) CN^-, N_2, C_2^{2-}

36. How many millilitres of 0.1 M H_2SO_4 must be added to 50 mL of 0.1 M NaOH to give solution that has a concentration of 0.05 M in H_2SO_4?

(a) 400 mL (b) 200 mL
(c) 100 mL (d) 500 mL

37. The energy of $\sigma 2s$-orbital is greater than $\sigma^* 1s$-orbital because

(a) $\sigma 2s$ is bigger than $\sigma^* 1s$ MO.
(b) $\sigma 2s$ is bonding whereas $\sigma^* 1s$ is an antibonding MO.
(c) $\sigma 2s$-orbital has a greater value of n than $\sigma^* 1s$ MO.
(d) $\sigma 2s$-orbital is formed only after $\sigma^* 1s$.

38. Which of the following compound has least tendency to form H-bond?

(a) HF (b) HCl
(c) H_2O (d) NH_3

39. Consider the following equilibrium,

$$2NOCl(g) \rightleftharpoons 2NO(g) + Cl_2(g)$$

For this equilibrium, the value of K_C is 3.75×10^{-4} at 1069 K. The value of K_p for the reaction at this temperature will be

(a) 0.041 (b) 0.033
(c) 0.021 (d) 0.192

40. Which statements are correct about bond angle of NCl_3, NF_3 and NH_3?

I. Bond angle of $NCl_3 > NF_3$.
II. Bond angle of $NCl_3 < NF_3$.
III. Bond angle of $NH_3 > NF_3$.
IV. Bond angle of $NH_3 < NF_3$.

Choose the correct answer from the options given below.

(a) I and II (b) I and III
(c) I, II, III (d) I, II, IV

41. Consider the following reaction at 298 K.

$$2NH_3(g) + CO_2(g) \rightleftharpoons NH_2CONH_2(aq) + H_2O(l)$$

Standard Gibbs energy change, $\Delta_r G^\ominus$ at the given temperature is -13.6 kJ mol^{-1}. Then, the value of equilibrium constant will be

(a) 2.6×10^{-4} (b) 3.4×10^{-3}
(c) 2.4×10^{2} (d) 3.2×10^{2}

42. Which graph correctly shows the energy E of a photon of light related to its wavelength (λ)?

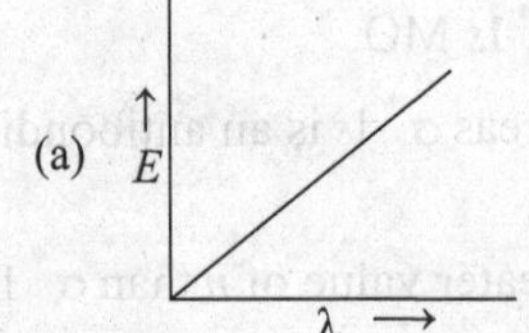

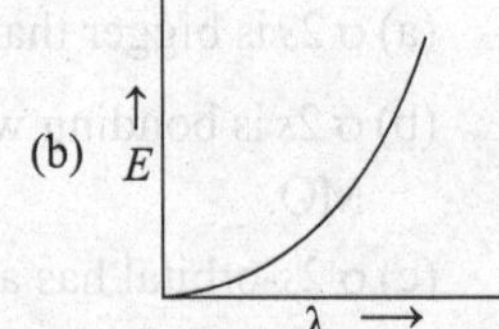

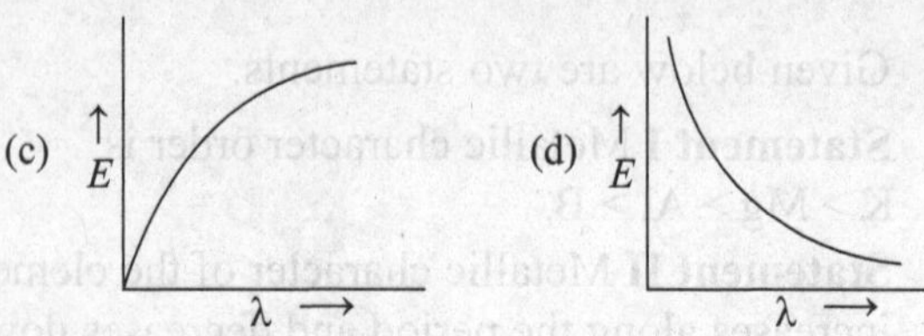

43. In a reaction,

$$CH_3Cl(g) \longrightarrow C(s) + 3H(g) + Cl(g)$$

Bond energy of C—H bond and C—Cl bond are 500 kJ and 320 kJ respectively. ΔH° of the reaction is

(a) 820 kJ (b) 320 kJ
(c) 1500 kJ (d) 1820 kJ

44. The enthalpy change when 1 L of 1 M H_2SO_4 is completely neutralised by 1 L of 1 M $Ca(OH)_2$ will be

[Given : $\Delta H_{\text{Neutralisation}} = -13.7$ kcal/mol]

(a) -13.7 kcal
(b) -27.4 kcal
(c) -137 kcal
(d) -2.74 kcal

45. Which among the following has maximum bond angle?

(a) NH_3 (b) PCl_3
(c) NH_4^+ (d) SCl_2

Response Index

01 ⓐ ⓑ ⓒ ⓓ	14 ⓐ ⓑ ⓒ ⓓ	27 ⓐ ⓑ ⓒ ⓓ	40 ⓐ ⓑ ⓒ ⓓ
02 ⓐ ⓑ ⓒ ⓓ	15 ⓐ ⓑ ⓒ ⓓ	28 ⓐ ⓑ ⓒ ⓓ	41 ⓐ ⓑ ⓒ ⓓ
03 ⓐ ⓑ ⓒ ⓓ	16 ⓐ ⓑ ⓒ ⓓ	29 ⓐ ⓑ ⓒ ⓓ	42 ⓐ ⓑ ⓒ ⓓ
04 ⓐ ⓑ ⓒ ⓓ	17 ⓐ ⓑ ⓒ ⓓ	30 ⓐ ⓑ ⓒ ⓓ	43 ⓐ ⓑ ⓒ ⓓ
05 ⓐ ⓑ ⓒ ⓓ	18 ⓐ ⓑ ⓒ ⓓ	31 ⓐ ⓑ ⓒ ⓓ	44 ⓐ ⓑ ⓒ ⓓ
06 ⓐ ⓑ ⓒ ⓓ	19 ⓐ ⓑ ⓒ ⓓ	32 ⓐ ⓑ ⓒ ⓓ	45 ⓐ ⓑ ⓒ ⓓ
07 ⓐ ⓑ ⓒ ⓓ	20 ⓐ ⓑ ⓒ ⓓ	33 ⓐ ⓑ ⓒ ⓓ	46 ⓐ ⓑ ⓒ ⓓ
08 ⓐ ⓑ ⓒ ⓓ	21 ⓐ ⓑ ⓒ ⓓ	34 ⓐ ⓑ ⓒ ⓓ	47 ⓐ ⓑ ⓒ ⓓ
09 ⓐ ⓑ ⓒ ⓓ	22 ⓐ ⓑ ⓒ ⓓ	35 ⓐ ⓑ ⓒ ⓓ	48 ⓐ ⓑ ⓒ ⓓ
10 ⓐ ⓑ ⓒ ⓓ	23 ⓐ ⓑ ⓒ ⓓ	36 ⓐ ⓑ ⓒ ⓓ	49 ⓐ ⓑ ⓒ ⓓ
11 ⓐ ⓑ ⓒ ⓓ	24 ⓐ ⓑ ⓒ ⓓ	37 ⓐ ⓑ ⓒ ⓓ	50 ⓐ ⓑ ⓒ ⓓ
12 ⓐ ⓑ ⓒ ⓓ	25 ⓐ ⓑ ⓒ ⓓ	38 ⓐ ⓑ ⓒ ⓓ	
13 ⓐ ⓑ ⓒ ⓓ	26 ⓐ ⓑ ⓒ ⓓ	39 ⓐ ⓑ ⓒ ⓓ	

Performance Scanner

> 90% Excellent !	You have mastered the first half of NEET syllabus (11th). The concepts of this syllabus are on your fingertips. Maintain this momentum.
76-90% Very Good !	You have a good command over the first half of NEET syllabus (11th). Revise it again after a few days and enhance your performance.
60-75% Good !	You have a wide scope to learn for the first half of NEET syllabus (11th). Revise it again.
<60% Not Satisfactory!	You have a long way ahead of you to master the first half of NEET syllabus (11th). Revise it thoroughly.

Scan for Online Part Test

Space for Rough Work

Space for Rough Work

MEDACE

NEET (UG)

SELF ASSESSMENT KIT

Test Booklet No. 3947214

Test Booklet Code SPT2

Syllabus Part Thru 2

(Half Syllabus Test)

Chapters Covered

Ionic Equilibrium

Redox Reactions

p-Block Elements-I

Purification and Characterisation of Organic Compounds

Some Basic Principles of Organic Chemistry

Hydrocarbons

Important Instructions

- The test is of 45 minutes duration and the Test Booklet contains 45 multiple choice questions (four options with a single correct answer) from Chemistry.
- Candidates are advised to read all questions before they start attempting the question paper.
- Each questions carries 4 marks. For each correct response, the candidate will get 4 marks. For each incorrect response, one mark will be deducted from the total scores.
- In the event of candidate marking more than one option then one mark will be deducted. The maximum marks are 180.
- Use **Blue/Black Point Pen** only for writing particular on this page/marking response on Answer Sheet.

Name of the Candidate (In Capitals) ____________________

Candidate's Signature ____________

Invigilator's Signature ____________

Facsimile signature stamp of center superintendent____________

Do not open this Booklet until you start attempting the Test

Chemistry (Q. No. 1-45)

1. The inductive effect of the groups $-CH_3, -COO^-, -NO_2, -NH_3^+$ respectively are

(a) $+I, -I, +I, +I$

(b) $-I, +I, -I, +I$

(c) $-I, -I, +I, +I$

(d) $+I, +I, -I, -I$

2. The correct stability order of the following resonance structure is,

$\underset{\text{I}}{CH_2=C=O}$, $\underset{\text{II}}{H_2\overset{-}{C}-\overset{+}{C}=O}$

$\underset{\text{III}}{H_2C=\overset{+}{C}-\overset{-}{O}}$, $\underset{\text{IV}}{H_2\overset{-}{C}-C\equiv\overset{+}{O}}$

(a) I > IV > III > II (b) I > III > II > IV

(c) IV > I > III > II (d) I > II > III > IV

3. Boron compounds behave as Lewis acid because of

(a) acidic nature

(b) covalent nature

(c) electron deficient character

(d) ionising property

4. When boron is fused with potassium hydroxide which pair of species are formed?

(a) $K_2O + B_2O_3$ (b) $KO_2 + B_2H_6$

(c) $K_3BO_3 + H_2$ (d) $K_3BO_3 + H_2O$

5. The tendency for catenation in the group 14 element is in order

(a) C <<< Si < Ge <<< Sn < Pb

(b) C >>> Si > Ge >>> Sn > Pb

(c) C <<< Si < Ge ≈ Sn < Pb

(d) C >>> Si > Ge ≈ Sn >>> Pb

6. Given below are two statements, one is labelled as Assertion (A) and the other is labelled as Reason (R).

Assertion (A) Stannous chloride is a powerful oxidising agent which oxidises mercuric chloride to mercury.

Reason (R) Stannous chloride gives grey precipitate with mercuric chloride, but stannic chloride does not do so.

In the light of the above statements, choose the correct answer from the options given below.

(a) Both (A) and (R) are true and (R) is the correct explanation of (A).

(b) Both (A) and (R) are true but (R) is not the correct explanation of (A).

(c) (A) is true but (R) is false.

(d) (A) is false but (R) is true.

7. For a cell reaction, E°_{cell} has negative value, then which of the following gives the correct relation for the values of ΔG° and K_{eq}?

(a) $\Delta G^\circ > 0, K_{eq} < 1$

(b) $\Delta G^\circ > 0, K_{eq} < 1$

(c) $\Delta G^\circ < 0, K_{eq} > 1$

(d) $\Delta G^\circ < 0, K_{eq} < 1$

8. Consider the following reaction.

$$BCl_3 + NH_4Cl \xrightarrow[C_6H_5Cl]{140°C} A \xrightarrow{NaBH_4} B$$

Identify A and B.

(a) $A = NaBO_2, B = H_3BO_3$

(b) $A = Na_2B_4O_7, B = B_2O_3$

(c) $A = BN, B = [NH_4]^+ [BCl_4]^-$

(d) $A = B_3N_3H_3Cl_3, B = B_3N_3H_6$

9. Consider the following reactions.

A. $H_2 + Br_2 \longrightarrow 2HBr$

B. $4KCN + Fe(CN)_2 \longrightarrow K_4[Fe(CN)_6]$

C. $NaBr + HCl \longrightarrow NaCl + HBr$

D. $NH_4Br + KOH \longrightarrow KBr + NH_3 + H_2O$

E. $2Cs + 2H_2O \longrightarrow 2CsOH + H_2$

Which of these do not involve oxidation-reductions?

(a) A and B (b) Only E
(c) B, C and D (d) C and D

10. In presence of peroxide, hydrogen chloride and hydrogen iodide do not give anti-Markovnikov's addition to alkene. It is because

(a) all the steps are enothermic in both the cases
(b) one of the step in endothermic in both the cases
(c) one is oxidising and the other is reducing
(d) both are highly ionic

11. Given below are two statements.

Statement I When double and triple bonds are in conjugation, addition takes place at triple bond.
Statement II When double and triple bonds are not in the conjugation, addition takes place at double bond.

In the light of the above statements, choose the correct answer from the options given below.

(a) Both Statement I and Statement II are incorrect.
(b) Statement I is correct but Statement II is incorrect.
(c) Statement I is incorrect but Statement II is correct.
(d) Both Statement I and Statement II are correct.

12. How many different structural isomers exists for C_3H_6O in which no atom is *sp*^{2} or *sp*-hybridised?

(a) 1 (b) 2
(c) 4 (d) 3

13. Anthraquinone is prepared by the oxidation of anthracene by chromic acid. The crude reaction product is usually purified by

(a) fractional crystallisation
(b) distillation
(c) steam distillation
(d) sublimation

14. Given below are two statements, one is labelled as Assertion (A) and the other is labelled as Reason (R).

Assertion (A) Pb^{4+} compounds are stronger oxidising agent than Sn^{4+} compounds.
Reason (R) The higher oxidation state of the group 14 elements are more stable for the heavier members of the group due to inert pair effect.

In the light of the above statements, choose the correct answer from the options given below.

(a) Both (A) and (R) are true and (R) is the correct explanation of (A).
(b) Both (A) and (R) are true but (R) is not the correct explanation of (A).
(c) (A) is true but (R) is false.
(d) (A) is false but (R) is true.

15. The number of electrons involved in the reduction of $Cr_2O_7^{2-}$ in acidic solution to Cr^{3+} is

(a) 1 (b) 4
(c) 3 (d) 6

16. Which of the following substance acts as an oxidising as well as reducing agent?

(a) Na_2O (b) $SnCl_2$
(c) Na_2O_2 (d) $NaNO_2$

17. $KMnO_4$ (purple) is reduced to K_2MnO_4 (green) by SO_3^{2-} in basic medium. 1 mole of $KMnO_4$ is reduced by

(a) 0.75 mole of SO_3^{2-} (b) 0.5 mole of SO_3^{2-}
(c) 1.75 mole of SO_3^{2-} (d) 2.75 mole of SO_3^{2-}

18. Solubility product of AgCl is 2.8×10^{-10} at 25°C. Calculate the solubility of the salt in 0.1 M $AgNO_3$ solution (in multiple of 10^{-9} mol/litre)

(a) 3.8 (b) 4.8 (c) 2 (d) 2.8

19. The number of S^{2-} ion present in 1 L of 0.1 M H_2S solution having $[H^+] = 0.1$ M is ($K_a = 1.1 \times 10^{-21}$)

(a) $6.625 \times 10^{+6}$ (b) 6.625×10^3
(c) 6.6×10^8 (d) 6.6×10^2

20. The dissociation constant of weak acid H*A* is 4.9×10^{-8}. After making the necessary approximation, what will be the pH of 0.1 M acid?

(a) 3.826 (b) 6.023
(c) 4.155 (d) 2.001

21. 0.1 mole of CH_3NH_2 ($K_b = 5 \times 10^{-5}$) is mixed with 0.08 mole of HCl and diluted to one litre. The $[H^+]$ in solution is

(a) 8×10^{-2} M (b) 8×10^{-11} M
(c) 8×10^{-10} M (d) 8×10^{-6} M

22. A buffer solution contains 1 mole of $(NH_4)_2SO_4$ and 1 mole of NH_4OH ($K_b = 10^{-5}$). The pH of solution will be

(a) 9 (b) 8.69
(c) 11 (d) 12.7

23. Given below are two statements.

Statement I Salting-out action of soap in presence of NaCl is based on common ion effect.

Statement II Salting-out action of soap is based on the fact that the concentration of Na^+ increases, RCOONa shows precipitation because $[RCOO^-][Na^+] > K_{sp}$.

In the light of the above statements, choose the correct answer from the options given below.

(a) Both Statement I and Statement II are incorrect.
(b) Statement I is correct but Statement II is incorrect.
(c) Statement I is incorrect but Statement II is correct.
(d) Both Statement I and Statement II are correct.

24. Benzene reacts with fuming sulphuric acid to give

(a) sodium benzene sulphonate
(b) benzene sulphonic acid
(c) sodium benzoate
(d) phenol

25. Propyne and propene can be distinguished by

(a) conc. H_2SO_4
(b) Br_2 in CCl_4
(c) Dil. $KMnO_4$
(d) $AgNO_3$ in ammonia

26. Iodination of an alkane is carried out in presence of

(a) C_2H_5OH (b) PCO_3
(c) HNO_3 or HIO_3 (d) H_2SO_4

27. For the dissociation reaction :

$$N_2O_4(g) \rightleftharpoons 2NO_2(g),$$

the equilibrium constant K_p is 0.120 atm at 298 K and total pressure of system is found to be 2 atm. The degree of dissociation of N_2O_4 is

(a) 0.101 (b) 0.131
(c) 0.151 (d) 0.121

28. A solution of HCl has pH = 5. If 1 mole of it is diluted to 1 L, what will be the pH of resulting solution?

(a) 7.12 (b) 5.16
(c) 2.16 (d) 6.98

29. Which one of the following is not true regarding electromeric effect?

(a) It results in the complete transfer of shared pair of electron.
(b) It is a permanent effect.
(c) It operates on multiple bonds.
(d) It requires an attacking reagent.

30. Consider the following equation,

$$aK_2Cr_2O_7 + bKCl + cH_2SO_4 \longrightarrow xCrO_2Cl_2 + y\,KHSO_4 + zH_2O$$

The above equation will be balanced when,

(a) $a = 2, b = 4, c = 6$ and $x = 2, y = 6, z = 3$
(b) $a = 4, b = 2, c = 6$ and $x = 6, y = 2, z = 3$
(c) $a = 6, b = 4, c = 2$ and $x = 6, y = 3, z = 2$
(d) $a = 1, b = 4, c = 6$ and $x = 2, y = 6, z = 3$

31. $AlCl_3$ is an electron deficient compound but AlF_3 is not because,

(a) atomic size of F is smaller than Cl, which makes AlF_3 more covalent.
(b) $AlCl_3$ is a covalent compound, while AlF_3 is an ionic compound.
(c) Al in $AlCl_3$ is sp^2-hybridised but in AlF_3, Al is sp^3d^2-hybridised.
(d) AlF_3 exists as dimer but $AlCl_3$ does not.

32. 0.40 g of an organic compound gave 0.3 g of silver bromide by Carius method. The percentage of bromine in the compound is

(a) 29.65% (b) 30.11%
(c) 31.91% (d) 40.11%

33. Arrange the following compounds in their decreasing order of boiling points :

I. C_8H_{18} II. $CH_3-(CH_2)_8-CH_3$
III. C_9H_{20} IV. $(CH_3)_3C-C(CH_3)_3$

(a) I > II > III > IV (b) III > I > IV > II
(c) I > III > II > IV (d) II > III > I > IV

34. Aluminium chloride exists as a dimer, (Al_2Cl_6) in solid state as well as in solution or non-polar solvents such as benzene. But when dissolved in water, it gives

(a) $Al^{3+} + 3Cl^-$
(b) $Al_2O_3 + 6HCl$
(c) $[Al(H_2O)_6]^{3+} + 3Cl^-$
(d) $[Al(OH)_6]^{3-} + 3HCl$

35. In oxidation of alkene,

$$\underset{\text{Alkene}}{R\text{—}CH{=}CH\text{—}R} \xrightarrow{[\text{Reagent}]} \underset{\text{Carboxylic acid}}{2R\text{—}COOH}$$

Which of the following reagents is not suitable for above oxidation ?

(a) Hot alkaline $KMnO_4$ followed by acidification
(b) Hot acidic $KMnO_4$ solution
(c) Hot acidic $K_2Cr_2O_7$
(d) Hot Cr_2O_3

36. Consider the following reaction,

$$\underset{|\ \ \ \ \ \ \ |}{H_2C\text{—}CH_2} + KOH \xrightarrow{\text{Alcohol}} A \xrightarrow{NaNH_2} B$$
$$Br\ \ \ \ \ \ Br$$

A and *B* of the above reaction are respectively.

	A	*B*
(a)	$H_2C{=}CHBr$	$HC{\equiv}CH$
(b)	$H_2C{=}CH_2$	$HC{\equiv}CH$
(c)	$H_2C{=}CHBr$	$H_2C{=}CH_2$
(d)	$H_2C{=}CH_2$	$HC{\equiv}CBr$

37. 64 g of an organic compound contain 24 g of carbon, 8 g of hydrogen and the rest oxygen. The empirical formula of the compound is

(a) CH_4O (b) C_2H_2O
(c) CH_3O_2 (d) $C_2H_{10}O_3$

38. Which type of isomerism is observed between I and II ?

$$\underset{\text{(I)}}{CH_3\text{—}CH_2\text{—}\overset{\displaystyle O}{\overset{\|}{C}}\text{—}OCH_3},\quad \underset{\text{(II)}}{CH_3\text{—}\overset{\displaystyle O}{\overset{\|}{C}}\text{—}OC_2H_5}$$

(a) Functional isomerism
(b) Metamerism
(c) Position isomerism
(d) Stereoisomerism

39. The major product *Y* in the given reaction is

$$EtC{\equiv}CH \xrightarrow[\text{THF}]{BD_3} X \xrightarrow{CH_3COOH} Y$$

(a) $(Et)(H)C{=}C(H)(D)$ (b) $(Et)(D)C{=}C(H)(H)$
(c) $(Et)(H)CH\text{—}\overset{O}{\overset{\|}{C}}\text{—}D$ (d) $Et\text{—}\underset{\underset{O}{\|}}{C}\text{—}CHD_2$

40. The sum of *p*, *q*, *r*, *s* and *t* in the following redox reaction is

$$pBr_2 + qOH^- \longrightarrow rBr^- + sBrO_3^- + tH_2O$$

(a) 19 (b) 18 (c) 20 (d) 17

41. An indicator has $pK_{In} = 5.3$. In a certain titration, this indicator is found to be 80% ionised in its acid form. Thus pH of the solution is

(a) 4.7 (b) 5.7 (c) 4.0 (d) 3.7

42. The number of possible structures for C_5H_8 with one triple bond is

(a) 3 (b) 5 (c) 7 (d) 4

43. The IUPAC name of the following compound is

[Skeletal structure: H_3C chain with CH_3 branch and ethyl branch (CH_3), ending in CH_3]

(a) 5-ethyl-7-methyloctane
(b) 4-ethyl-3-methyloctane
(c) 3-methyl-4-ethyloctane
(d) 2,4-diethylhetane

44. Equal volumes of three acid solutions of pH 3,4 and 5 are mixed in a vessel. What will be the H^+ ion concentration in the mixture?

(a) 3.7×10^{-3} M
(b) 7.8×10^{-3} M
(c) 78×10^{-5} M
(d) 3.7×10^{-4} M

45. The solubility product of aluminium sulphate is given by expression

(a) $4S^3$
(b) $612S^4$
(c) $4S^5$
(d) $108S^5$

Response Index

01 ⓐ ⓑ ⓒ ⓓ	14 ⓐ ⓑ ⓒ ⓓ	27 ⓐ ⓑ ⓒ ⓓ	40 ⓐ ⓑ ⓒ ⓓ
02 ⓐ ⓑ ⓒ ⓓ	15 ⓐ ⓑ ⓒ ⓓ	28 ⓐ ⓑ ⓒ ⓓ	41 ⓐ ⓑ ⓒ ⓓ
03 ⓐ ⓑ ⓒ ⓓ	16 ⓐ ⓑ ⓒ ⓓ	29 ⓐ ⓑ ⓒ ⓓ	42 ⓐ ⓑ ⓒ ⓓ
04 ⓐ ⓑ ⓒ ⓓ	17 ⓐ ⓑ ⓒ ⓓ	30 ⓐ ⓑ ⓒ ⓓ	43 ⓐ ⓑ ⓒ ⓓ
05 ⓐ ⓑ ⓒ ⓓ	18 ⓐ ⓑ ⓒ ⓓ	31 ⓐ ⓑ ⓒ ⓓ	44 ⓐ ⓑ ⓒ ⓓ
06 ⓐ ⓑ ⓒ ⓓ	19 ⓐ ⓑ ⓒ ⓓ	32 ⓐ ⓑ ⓒ ⓓ	45 ⓐ ⓑ ⓒ ⓓ
07 ⓐ ⓑ ⓒ ⓓ	20 ⓐ ⓑ ⓒ ⓓ	33 ⓐ ⓑ ⓒ ⓓ	46 ⓐ ⓑ ⓒ ⓓ
08 ⓐ ⓑ ⓒ ⓓ	21 ⓐ ⓑ ⓒ ⓓ	34 ⓐ ⓑ ⓒ ⓓ	47 ⓐ ⓑ ⓒ ⓓ
09 ⓐ ⓑ ⓒ ⓓ	22 ⓐ ⓑ ⓒ ⓓ	35 ⓐ ⓑ ⓒ ⓓ	48 ⓐ ⓑ ⓒ ⓓ
10 ⓐ ⓑ ⓒ ⓓ	23 ⓐ ⓑ ⓒ ⓓ	36 ⓐ ⓑ ⓒ ⓓ	49 ⓐ ⓑ ⓒ ⓓ
11 ⓐ ⓑ ⓒ ⓓ	24 ⓐ ⓑ ⓒ ⓓ	37 ⓐ ⓑ ⓒ ⓓ	50 ⓐ ⓑ ⓒ ⓓ
12 ⓐ ⓑ ⓒ ⓓ	25 ⓐ ⓑ ⓒ ⓓ	38 ⓐ ⓑ ⓒ ⓓ	
13 ⓐ ⓑ ⓒ ⓓ	26 ⓐ ⓑ ⓒ ⓓ	39 ⓐ ⓑ ⓒ ⓓ	

Performance Scanner

> 90% Excellent !	You have mastered the second half of NEET syllabus (11th). The concepts of this syllabus are on your fingertips. Maintain this momentum.
76-90% Very Good !	You have a good command over the second half of NEET syllabus (11th). Revise it again after a few days and enhance your performance.
60-75% Good !	You have a wide scope to learn for the second half of NEET syllabus (11th). Revise it again.
<60% Not Satisfactory!	You have a long way ahead of you to master the second half of NEET syllabus (11th). Revise it thoroughly.

Scan for Online Part Test

Space for Rough Work

Space for Rough Work

Test Booklet No. **3947215**

Test Booklet Code **NSS1**

MED ACE

NEET (UG)

SELF ASSESSMENT KIT

NEET Stepping Stones 1

(Based on Class 11th Syllabus)

Name of the Candidate (In Capitals)

____

____

____

Candidate's Signature ____________

Invigilator's Signature ____________

Facsimile signature stamp of center superintendent____________

Important Instructions

- The test is of 45 minutes duration and the Test Booklet contains 45 multiple choice questions (four options with a single correct answer) from Chemistry.
- Candidates are advised to read all questions before they start attempting the question paper.
- Each questions carries 4 marks. For each correct response, the candidate will get 4 marks. For each incorrect response, one mark will be deducted from the total scores.
- In the event of candidate marking more than one option then one mark will be deducted. The maximum marks are 180.
- Use **Blue/Black Point Pen** only for writing particular on this page/marking response on Answer Sheet.

Do not open this Booklet until you start attempting the Test

Chemistry (Q.No. 1-45)

1. 4.5 moles each of hydrogen and iodine are heated in a sealed 10 litre vessel. At equilibrium, 3 moles of HI was found. The equilibrium constant for the reaction is,

$$I_2(g)+H_2(g) \rightleftharpoons 2HI(g)$$

(a) 1 (b) 6
(c) 1.33 (d) 40

2. At 727°C and 1.23 atm of total equilibrium pressure, SO_3 partially dissociates into SO_2 and O_2 according to $SO_3(g) \rightleftharpoons SO_2(g)+\frac{1}{2}O_2(g)$.

The density of equilibrium mixture is 0.9 g/litre. The degree of dissociation is,

(a) $\frac{2}{5}$ (b) $\frac{2}{3}$
(c) $\frac{5}{3}$ (d) $\frac{3}{5}$

3. The number of sigma bond in P_4O_{10} is

(a) 5 (b) 8
(c) 14 (d) 16

4. Which of the following options with respect to increasing bond dissociation energy is correct?

(a) $He_2^+ < O_2^- < C_2 < NO$
(b) $He_2^+ < C_2 < O_2^- < NO$
(c) $O_2^- < He_2^+ < C_2 < NO$
(d) $He_2^+ < NO < C_2 < O_2^-$

5. Given below are two statements, one is labelled as Assertion (A) and the other is labelled as Reason (R).

Assertion (A) The temperature dependence of the equilibrium constant depends on the sign of ΔH for the reaction.

Reason (R) The equilibrium constant for an exothermic reaction increases as the temperature increases.

In the light of the above statements, choose the correct answer from the options given below.

(a) Both (A) and (R) are true and (R) is the correct explanation of (A).
(b) Both (A) and (R) are true but (R) is not the correct explanation of (A).
(c) (A) is true but (R) is false.
(d) (A) is false but (R) is true.

6. The reagent used for catalytic hydrogenation of an alkene as well as bring about homogeneous catalysis is

(a) Lucas reagent (b) Wilkinson's reagent
(c) DIBAL-H (d) Pd/C

7. Given below are two statements, one is labelled as Assertion (A) and the other is labelled as Reason (R).

Assertion (A) Lactic acid is optically active.
Reason (R) A symmetry in the inner structure of the organic compound causes optical activity.
In the light of the above statements, choose the correct answer from the options given below.

(a) Both (A) and (R) are true and (R) is the correct explanation of (A).
(b) Both (A) and (R) are true but (R) is not the correct explanation of (A).
(c) (A) is true but (R) is false.
(d) (A) is false but (R) is true.

8. A mixture of benzene and chloroform is separated by

(a) sublimation (b) separating funnel
(c) crystallisation (d) distillation

9. Given below are two statements.

Statement I The heat absorbed during the isothermal expansion of an ideal gas against vacuum is zero.

Statement II The volume occupied by the molecules of an ideal gas is zero.

In the light of the above statements, choose the correct answer from the options given below.

(a) Both Statement I and Statement II are incorrect.
(b) Statement I is correct but Statement II is incorrect.
(c) Statement I is incorrect but Statement II is correct.
(d) Both Statement I and Statement II are correct.

10. A gas absorbs 100 J of heat and is simultaneously compressed by a constant external pressure of thermodynamics 1.50 atm from a volume of 8 L to 2 L. ΔE will be

(a) 650 J (b) 780 J
(c) 1011 J (d) 532 J

11. The correct increasing order of size of the following species is

(a) $Mg^{2+} < Al < F^- < Na^+$
(b) $Al < F^- < Mg^{2+} < Na^+$
(c) $Mg^{2+} < Na^+ < F^- < Al$
(d) $Mg^{2+} < F^- < Na^+ < Al$

12. Given below are two statements.

Statement I He and Be have similar outer electronic configuration of the type ns^2.

Statement II He and Be both are chemically inert.

In the light of the above statements, choose the correct answer from the options given below.

(a) Both Statement I and Statement II are incorrect.
(b) Statement I is correct but Statement II is incorrect.
(c) Statement I is incorrect but Statement II is correct.
(d) Both Statement I and Statement II are correct.

13. An electron is moving with a kinetic energy of 4.55×10^{-25} J. What will be the de-Broglie wavelength for this electron?

(a) 7.28×10^{-7} m (b) 72.8×10^{-7} m
(c) 7.28×10^{-9} m (d) 7×10^{-10} m

14. If a shell is having g subshell, which is correct statement about principal quantum number n of this shell?

(a) $n < 5$ (b) $n \geq 5$
(c) $n \geq 6$ (d) $n \geq 7$

15. A gaseous hydrocarbon gives upon combustion, 0.72 g of water and 3.08 of CO_2. The empirical formula of hydrocarbon is,

(a) C_7H_8 (b) C_5H_6 (c) C_2H_5 (d) C_4H_8

16. 250 mL of sodium carbonate solution contains 2.65 g of Na_2CO_3. If 10 ml of this solution is diluted to one litre, what is the concentration of the resultant solution? (Molar mass of $Na_2CO_3 = 106$)

(a) 0.1 M (b) 10^{-3} M
(c) 10^{-5} M (d) 1 M

17. Given below are two statements.

Statement I Between $SiCl_4$ and CCl_4, only $SiCl_4$ reacts with water.

Statement II $SiCl_4$ is ionic and CCl_4 is covalent.

In the light of the above statements, choose the correct answer from the options given below.

(a) Both Statement I and Statement II are incorrect.
(b) Statement I is correct but Statement II is incorrect.
(c) Statement I is incorrect but Statement II is correct.
(d) Both Statement I and Statement II are correct.

18. Mass of KHC_2O_4 (Potassium acid oxalate) required to reduced 100 mL of 0.02 M $KMnO_4$ in acidic medium (Mn^{2+}) is x g and to neutralise 100 mL of 0.05 M $Ca(OH)_2$ is y g. Then

(a) $x = 3y$ (b) $3y = x$
(c) $x = y$ (d) $x = \frac{y}{2}$

19. Given below are two statements, one is labelled as Assertion (A) and the other is labelled as Reason (R).

Assertion (A) H_3PO_3 is a dibasic compound.

Reason (R) The two —H atom are directly attached to P.

In the light of the above statements, choose the correct answer from the options given below.

(a) Both (A) and (R) are true and (R) is the correct explanation of (A).
(b) Both (A) and (R) are true but (R) is not the correct explanation of (A).
(c) (A) is true but (R) is false.
(d) (A) is false but (R) is true.

20. The rate constant at 25°C for the reaction of NH_4^+ and OH^- to form NH_4OH is $4\times10^{10}\ M^{-1}s^{-1}$ and ionisation constant of *aq.* NH_3 is 1.8×10^{-5}. The rate constant of proton transfer to NH_3 is

(a) 7.2×10^5 (b) 4.2×10^5
(c) 9.2×10^5 (d) 2×10^5

21. What % of the carbon in the H_2CO_3-HCO_3^-, buffer solution will be in the form of HCO_3^-, so as to have neutral solution ($K_a = 4\times10^{-7}$)

(a) 30 (b) 50
(c) 90 (d) 80

22. The uncertainty in position of a dust particle with mass equal to 1 mg. (Uncertainty in its velocity is 5.5×10^{-20} m/s) is

(a) 9.6×10^{-10} m (b) 4.82×10^{-10} m
(c) 8.2×10^{-10} m (d) 6.2×10^{-10} m

23. Given below are two statements.

Statement I BCl_3 is more stable than $TlCl_3$.

Statement II The inert pair effect in B is more than Tl.

In the light of the above statements, choose the correct answer from the options given below.

(a) Both Statement I and Statement II are incorrect.
(b) Statement I is correct but Statement II is incorrect.
(c) Statement I is incorrect but Statement II is correct.
(d) Both Statement I and Statement II are correct.

24. Arrange the following elements in the increasing order of metallic character.

B, Al, Mg, K

(a) B < Al < K < Mg (b) B < Al < Mg < K
(c) K < Al < Mg < B (d) K < B < Mg < Al

25. Central atom of which of the following molecules have sp^3d^2-hybridisation?

I. BrF_5 II. XeF_4 III. IF_5
IV. SF_6 V. H_2SO_4

Choose the correct answer from the options given below.

(a) I, II, V (b) II, III, V
(c) I, IV (d) I, II, III, IV

26. In which of the following molecules, central atom contains 3 bond pairs and 2 lone pairs of electrons in its valence shell?

(a) Boron trifluoride
(b) Phosphorus trichloride
(c) Chlorine trifluoride
(d) Xenon trioxide

27. The correct IUPAC name of the following compound.

```
                               Cl
                               |
                          CH2—CH—CH3
                          |
CH3—CH2—CH2—CH2—C—CH2—CH2—CH2—CH3
                          |
                         CH3
```

is

(a) 4-butyl-2-chloro-4-methyloctane
(b) 5-(2-chloropropyl)-5-methylnonane
(c) 4,4-dibutyl-2-chloropentane
(d) None of the above

28. Given below are two statements.

Statement I The pK_a of weak acid becomes equal to pH of the solution at the mid point of its titration.

Statement II The molar concentration of proton acceptor and proton donor becomes equal at mid point of a weak acid.

In the light of the above statements, choose the correct answer from the options given below.

(a) Both Statement I and Statement II are incorrect.
(b) Statement I is correct but Statement II is incorrect.
(c) Statement I is incorrect but Statement II is correct.
(d) Both Statement I and Statement II are correct.

29. For the reaction, $N_2(g)+3H_2(g) \rightleftharpoons 2NH_3(g)$, the value of K_p is $3.6\times10^{-2}\ atm^{-2}$ at 500 K. The value of K_C for the reaction at same temperature will be

(a) $62.15\ M^{-2}$
(b) $60.66\ M^{-2}$
(c) $51.98\ M^{-2}$
(d) $52.98\ M^{-2}$

30. Which among the given compounds will exhibit geometrical isomerism?

(a) 2-pentene
(b) 2-butyne
(c) 2-methyl propene
(d) 2-butanol

31. Given below are two statements, one is labelled as Assertion (A) and the other is labelled as Reason (R).

Assertion (A) Trichloroacetic acid is more acidic than acetic acid.

Reason (R) Due to electron releasing group acidic nature increases.

In the light of the above statements, choose the correct answer from the options given below.

(a) Both (A) and (R) are true and (R) is the correct explanation of (A).
(b) Both (A) and (R) are true but (R) is not the correct explanation of (A).
(c) (A) is true but (R) is false.
(d) (A) is false but (R) is true.

32. The IUPAC name of the given compound is

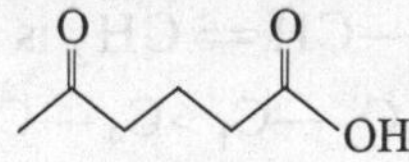

(a) 2-keto hexanoic acid
(b) 5-keto hexanoic acid
(c) 5-oxohexanoic acid
(d) hexa-2, 6-dienone-6-ol

33. Product of the following reaction is

$$CH \equiv CH \xrightarrow[\Delta,\ \text{High pressure}]{Ni(CN)_2} \text{Product}$$

(a) benzene
(b) cyclobuta-1,3-diene
(c) cyclooctatetraene
(d) cyclohexene

34. Isomers X and Y react with HBr

X: $(CH_3)_2C{=}CBr_2$ (CH$_3$, CH$_3$ on one carbon; Br, Br on the other)

Y: $CH_3(Br)C{=}C(Br)CH_3$ (Br and CH$_3$ on each carbon)

A mixture of X and Y is treated with HBr. The correct option representing the structures of three different possible products of the reaction is

(a) $(CH_3)_2CHCBr_3$, $(CH_3)_2CBrCHBr_2$, $CH_3CHBrCHBrCH_3$
(b) $(CH_3)_2CHCBr_3$, $(CH_3)_2CBrCHBr_2$, $CH_3CBr_2CHBrCH_3$
(c) $(CH_3)_2CBrCBr_3$, $(CH_3)_2CHCBr_3$, $CH_3CBr_2CHBrCH_3$
(d) $(CH_3)_2CBrCHBr_2$, $CHBr_2CBr(CH_3)CH_3$, $CH_3CHBrCBr_2CH_3$

35. Select the suitable set of reagents for the following reaction.

$$CH_3—CH_2—CH_2—CH{=}CH_2 \xrightarrow[?]{?} CH_3—CH_2—CH_2—CH_2—CH_2—OH$$

(Major or 100%)

(a) $BH_3 + H_2O_2/\bar{O}H$ or $HBr / C_6H_5CO_3H + aq.\ KOH$
(b) $BH_3 + H_2O_2/\bar{O}H$ or $HBr + aq.\ KOH$
(c) $HBr/C_6H_5CO_3H + aq.\ KOH$ or $HBr + H_2O_2$
(d) $HBr + aq.\ KOH$ only

36. $2CH_2{=}CH_2 \xrightarrow{\Delta}$ cyclobutane ($CH_2—CH_2$ / $CH_2—CH_2$ ring)

For this reaction, $\Delta H = -49$ kJ/mol, $\Delta S = -40.0$ J/K/mol. The lowest temperature above which the forward reaction will be spontaneous is

(a) 952°C (b) 1080°C
(c) 1219°C (d) 1225°C

37. For the redox reaction,

$$MnO_4^- + C_2O_4^{2-} + H^+ \longrightarrow Mn^{2+} + CO_2 + H_2O$$

The correct set of coefficients of the reactants for the balanced reaction is

	MnO_4^-	$C_2O_4^{2-}$	H^+
(a)	2	5	16
(b)	16	5	2
(c)	5	16	2
(d)	2	16	5

38. Consider the following species.

NO_2^-, CN^-, $(CH_3CO)_2\bar{C}H$, SiF_4, HCl

The number of species that acts as ambident nucleophile is

(a) 1 (b) 2
(c) 3 (d) 4

39. For which of the following compound, heterolytic bond dissociation energy of C—Cl bond is minimum?

(a) CH_3Br (b) CH_3CH_2Br

(c) $(CH_3)_3CBr$ (d) $(CH_3)_2CHBr$

40. Choose the incorrect statement from the following.

(a) Bonds that project upward out of the plane of the paper are indicated by a wedge (Δ).

(b) Bonds that lie behind the plane are indicated with a dashed wedge (|||||).

(c) Bonds that lie in the plane of the page are indicated by a line (—).

(d) For tetrahedral C atoms, the bond angle is approximately 90°.

41. Choose the correct order of behaviour of Lewis acid in decreasing order.

(a) $BBr_3 > BCl_3 > BF_3$

(b) $BCl_3 > BBr_3 > BF_3$

(c) $BF_3 > BBF_3 > BCl_3$

(d) $BF_3 > BCl_3 > BBr_3$

42. For a closed system, under which condition, the relation $\Delta H = \Delta U + p\Delta V$ is valid

(a) constant pressure

(b) constant temperature

(c) constant pressure and temperature

(d) constant composition

43. Which of the following statement regarding steam distillation is based on the fact that?

(a) Water and organic liquid both undergo distillation.

(b) Vaporisation of organic liquids takes place at lower temperature than its boiling point.

(c) Vaporisation of organic liquids takes place at higher temperature than its boiling point.

(d) Vaporisation of organic liquids takes place at its boiling point

44. $H\overset{\alpha}{—}C\equiv C—\underset{\underset{H}{|}}{CH}—\underset{\underset{H}{|\beta}}{C}=\underset{\underset{H}{|\gamma}}{C}—H$

The order of bond energy of C—H bonds represented by α, β and γ for the compound given above is

(a) $\alpha > \beta > \gamma$ (b) $\alpha > \gamma > \beta$

(c) $\beta > \alpha > \gamma$ (d) $\gamma > \beta > \alpha$

45. The length of carbon-carbon bond in decreasing order for the given molecule

$\overset{4}{C}H_3—\overset{3}{C}H_2—\overset{2}{C}H=\overset{1}{C}H_2$ is

(a) $C_3—C_2 > C_2—C_1 > C_4—C_3$

(b) $C_4—C_3 > C_3—C_2 > C_2—C_1$

(c) $C_2—C_1 > C_4—C_1 > C_3—C_2$

(d) are equal

Response Index

01	ⓐ ⓑ ⓒ ⓓ	14	ⓐ ⓑ ⓒ ⓓ	27	ⓐ ⓑ ⓒ ⓓ	40	ⓐ ⓑ ⓒ ⓓ
02	ⓐ ⓑ ⓒ ⓓ	15	ⓐ ⓑ ⓒ ⓓ	28	ⓐ ⓑ ⓒ ⓓ	41	ⓐ ⓑ ⓒ ⓓ
03	ⓐ ⓑ ⓒ ⓓ	16	ⓐ ⓑ ⓒ ⓓ	29	ⓐ ⓑ ⓒ ⓓ	42	ⓐ ⓑ ⓒ ⓓ
04	ⓐ ⓑ ⓒ ⓓ	17	ⓐ ⓑ ⓒ ⓓ	30	ⓐ ⓑ ⓒ ⓓ	43	ⓐ ⓑ ⓒ ⓓ
05	ⓐ ⓑ ⓒ ⓓ	18	ⓐ ⓑ ⓒ ⓓ	31	ⓐ ⓑ ⓒ ⓓ	44	ⓐ ⓑ ⓒ ⓓ
06	ⓐ ⓑ ⓒ ⓓ	19	ⓐ ⓑ ⓒ ⓓ	32	ⓐ ⓑ ⓒ ⓓ	45	ⓐ ⓑ ⓒ ⓓ
07	ⓐ ⓑ ⓒ ⓓ	20	ⓐ ⓑ ⓒ ⓓ	33	ⓐ ⓑ ⓒ ⓓ	46	ⓐ ⓑ ⓒ ⓓ
08	ⓐ ⓑ ⓒ ⓓ	21	ⓐ ⓑ ⓒ ⓓ	34	ⓐ ⓑ ⓒ ⓓ	47	ⓐ ⓑ ⓒ ⓓ
09	ⓐ ⓑ ⓒ ⓓ	22	ⓐ ⓑ ⓒ ⓓ	35	ⓐ ⓑ ⓒ ⓓ	48	ⓐ ⓑ ⓒ ⓓ
10	ⓐ ⓑ ⓒ ⓓ	23	ⓐ ⓑ ⓒ ⓓ	36	ⓐ ⓑ ⓒ ⓓ	49	ⓐ ⓑ ⓒ ⓓ
11	ⓐ ⓑ ⓒ ⓓ	24	ⓐ ⓑ ⓒ ⓓ	37	ⓐ ⓑ ⓒ ⓓ	50	ⓐ ⓑ ⓒ ⓓ
12	ⓐ ⓑ ⓒ ⓓ	25	ⓐ ⓑ ⓒ ⓓ	38	ⓐ ⓑ ⓒ ⓓ		
13	ⓐ ⓑ ⓒ ⓓ	26	ⓐ ⓑ ⓒ ⓓ	39	ⓐ ⓑ ⓒ ⓓ		

Performance Scanner

> 90% Excellent !	You have mastered the NEET syllabus (11th). The concepts of this entire syllabus are at your fingertips. Maintain this momentum.
76-90% Very Good !	You have a good command over the entire NEET syllabus (11th). Revise it again after a few days to enhance your performance.
60-75% Good !	You have a wide scope to learn for the entire NEET syllabus (11th). Revise it again.
<60% Not Satisfactory!	You have a long way ahead of you to master the NEET syllabus (11th). Revise it thoroughly.

Space for Rough Work

Space for Rough Work

Test Booklet No. 3947216

Test Booklet Code NSS2

MEDACE
NEET (UG)
SELF ASSESSMENT KIT

NEET Stepping Stones 2

(Based on Class 11th Syllabus)

Name of the Candidate (In Capitals)

____

____

____

Candidate's Signature ______________

Invigilator's Signature ______________

Facsimile signature stamp of center superintendent______________

Important Instructions

- The test is of 45 minutes duration and the Test Booklet contains 45 multiple choice questions (four options with a single correct answer) from Chemistry.
- Candidates are advised to read all questions before they start attempting the question paper.
- Each questions carries 4 marks. For each correct response, the candidate will get 4 marks. For each incorrect response, one mark will be deducted from the total scores.
- In the event of candidate marking more than one option then one mark will be deducted. The maximum marks are 180.
- Use **Blue/Black Point Pen** only for writing particular on this page/marking response on Answer Sheet.

Do not open this Booklet until you start attempting the Test

Chemistry (Q. No. 1-45)

1. If the shortest wavelength of H-atom in Lyman series is x. Then longest wavelength in Balmer series of He^+ is

(a) $\frac{36x}{5}$ (b) $\frac{9x}{5}$ (c) $\frac{5x}{9}$ (d) $\frac{5x}{3}$

2. What will be the ratio of coefficients of HNO_3, $Fe(NO_3)_2$ and NH_4NO_3 in the balanced form of following redox reaction?

$Fe + HNO_3 \longrightarrow Fe(NO_3)_2 + NH_4NO_3 + H_2O$

(a) 10 : 1 : 4 (b) 10 : 4 : 1
(c) 1 : 10 : 4 (d) 4 : 1 : 10

3. According to molecular orbital theory, the correct statements are

I. C_2^{2-} is expected to be diamagnetic.
II. O_2^{2+} is expected to have a longer bond length than O_2.
III. N_2^+ and N_2^- have the same bond order.
IV. He_2^+ has the same energy as two isolated He atoms.
V. O_2 and N_2^{2-} will have same bond order.

(a) I, II, III and IV (b) I, III and V
(c) I and IV (d) II and V

4. Arrange in decreasing order, the energy of 2s orbital in the following atoms H, Li, Na, K

(a) $E_{2s}(H) > E_{2s}(Li) > E_{2s}(Na) > E_{2s}(K)$
(b) $E_{2s}(H) > E_{2s}(Na) > E_{2s}(Li) > E_{2s}(K)$
(c) $E_{2s}(H) > E_{2s}(Na) = E_{2s}(K) > E_{2s}(Li)$
(d) $E_{2s}(K) > E_{2s}(Na) > E_{2s}(Li) > E_{2s}(H)$

5. For the reaction, $H_2S + H_2O_2 \longrightarrow S + 2H_2O$

(a) H_2S is an acid and H_2O_2 is a base.
(b) H_2S is a base and H_2O_2 is acid.
(c) S is an oxidising agent and H_2O_2 is a reducing agent.
(d) H_2S is a reducing agent and H_2O_2 is an oxidising agent.

6. Given below are two statements, one is labelled as Assertion (A) and the other is labelled as Reason (R).

Assertion (A) $H_2C{=}CH^-$ is a better nucleophile than $HC{\equiv}C^-$.

Reason (R) The carbon carrying the negative charge is sp^2-hybridised in $H_2C{=}CH^-$ and sp-hybridised in $HC{\equiv}C^-$.

In the light of the above statements, choose the correct answer from the options given below.

(a) Both (A) and (R) are true and (R) is the correct explanation of (A).
(b) Both (A) and (R) are true but (R) is not the correct explanation of (A).
(c) (A) is true but (R) is false.
(d) (A) is false but (R) is true.

7. Styrene can be purified by

(a) simple distillation
(b) fractional distillation
(c) chromatography
(d) distillation under reduced pressure

8. Consider the reaction given in equations (i) and (ii) with equilibrium constants K_1 and K_2 respectively.

$$SO_2(g) + \frac{1}{2}O_2(g) \overset{K_1}{\rightleftharpoons} SO_3(g) \quad \ldots \text{(i)}$$

$$2SO_3(g) \overset{K_2}{\rightleftharpoons} 2SO_2(g) + O_2(g) \quad \ldots \text{(ii)}$$

K_1 and K_2 are related as

(a) $2K_1 = K_2^2$ (b) $K_1^2 = \frac{1}{K_2}$
(c) $K_2^2 = \frac{1}{2}K_1$ (d) $K_2 = \frac{2}{K_1^3}$

9. Choose the incorrect statement from the following.

(a) An element which has high electronegativity always has high electron gain enthalpy.
(b) Electron gain enthalpy is the property of an isolated atom.

(c) Electronegativity is the property of a bonded atom.

(d) Both electronegativity and electron gain enthalpy are usually directly related to nuclear charge and inversely related to atomic size.

10. Given that, $C + O_2 \longrightarrow CO_2$; $\Delta H = -x$ kJ

$2CO + O_2 \longrightarrow 2CO_2$; $\Delta H = -y$ kJ

The enthalpy of formation of CO will be

(a) $y - 2x$ (b) $\frac{2x - y}{2}$

(c) $\frac{y - 2x}{2}$ (d) $2x - y$

11. Select the incorrect statements from the following.

A. The greater the disorder in an isolated system, the lower is the entropy.

B. The entropy change can be attributed to rearrangement of atoms or ions from one pattern in the reactants to another (in the product).

C. Decrease of regularity in structure would mean increase in entropy.

D. The gaseous state is the state of highest entropy.

E. Entropy change is directly proportional to the temperature.

Choose the correct answer from the options given below.

(a) B, C and E

(b) A and E

(c) A, B and C

(d) B, C, D and E

12. Consider the following compounds/species.

$PF_5, N_2O_5, CO_2, CH_4, PCl_5$

The number of compounds having equal covalency and oxidation number is

(a) 2 (b) 3 (c) 4 (d) 5

13. For the reaction at 298 K, $2A + B \longrightarrow C$, $\Delta H = 400$ kJ/mole, $\Delta S = 0.2$ kJ. $K^{-1}mol^{-1}$. The temperature at which the reaction becomes spontaneous is (consider ΔH and ΔS to be constant over the temperature range)

(a) 2000 K (b) 1500 K

(c) 2050 K (d) 1700 K

14. The electronic configuration of singly positive nitrogen molecular ion is

(a) $\sigma 1s^2 \sigma^* 1s^2 \sigma 2s^2 \sigma^* 2s^2 \pi 2p_x^2 = \pi 2p_y^2 \sigma 2p_z^2$

(b) $\sigma 1s^2 \sigma^* 1s^2 \sigma 2s^2 \sigma^* 2s^2 \sigma 2p_z^2 \pi 2p_x^2 = \pi^* 2p_y^1$

(c) $\sigma 1s^2 \sigma^* 1s^2 \sigma 2s^2 \sigma^* 2s^2 \sigma 2p_z^1 \pi 2p_x^2 = \pi 2p_y^1$

(d) $\sigma 1s^2 \sigma^* 1s^2 \sigma 2s^2 \sigma^* 2s^2 \sigma 2p_z^2 \pi 2p_x^2$

15. Given below are two statements, one is labelled as Assertion (A) and the other is labelled as Reason (R).

Assertion (A) According to common ion effect, the solubility of HgI_2 is expected to be less in an aqueous solution of KI than in water.

Reason (R) Iodide ion (I^-) is highly polarisable.

In the light of the above statements, choose the correct answer from the options given below.

(a) Both (A) and (R) are true and (R) is the correct explanation of (A).

(b) Both (A) and (R) are true but (R) is not the correct explanation of (A).

(c) (A) is true but (R) is false.

(d) (A) is false but (R) is true.

16. If an ore sample containing Mn is treated with 50 mL of 0.2750 M $Na_2C_2O_4$ and the unreacted $Na_2C_2O_4$ required 18.28 mL of 0.1232 M $KMnO_4$ in acidic medium, the number of moles of Mn in the ore is

(a) 4.12×10^{-2}

(b) 3.72×10^{-3}

(c) 6.41×10^{-2}

(d) 8.12×10^{-3}

17. In a saturated solution of calcium phosphate, the concentration of PO_4^{3-} ions is 6.6×10^{-7} M. The K_{sp} of $Ca_3(PO_4)_2$ will be

(a) 4.356×10^{-34}

(b) 4.356×10^{-31}

(c) 4.356×10^{-33}

(d) 4.356×10^{-32}

18. For the given compounds,

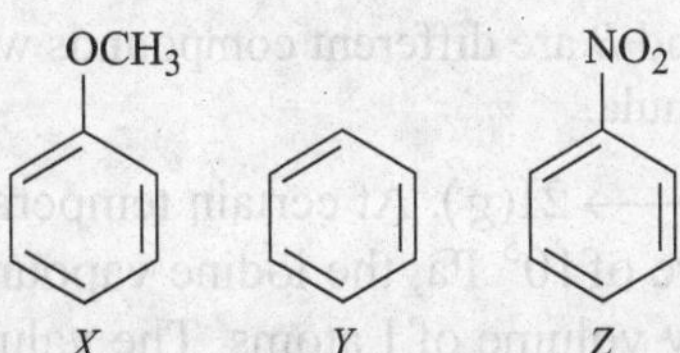

The correct order of reaction with electrophile is

(a) $Y > Z > X$ (b) $Z < X < Y$

(c) $X > Y > Z$ (d) $X \approx Y > Z$

19. 12.825 g of a sample of $Ba(OH)_2$ is dissolved in 10 ml of 0.5 N HCl solution. The excess of HCl is titrated with 0.2 N NaOH. The volume of NaOH used is 10 cc. Then the percentage of $Ba(OH)_2$ is the sample will be

(a) 6 (b) 8 (c) 4 (d) 2

20. Which of the following compounds will show aromatic character?

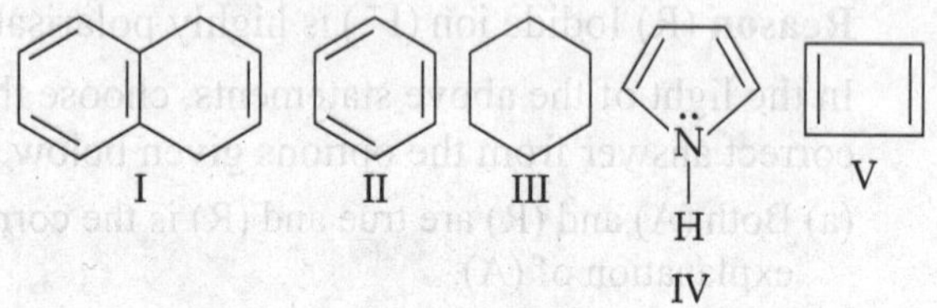

(a) II and IV (b) I, II and IV
(c) II and III (d) I and V

21. Given below are two statements.

Statement I The heat of combustion found by using bomb calorimeter gives the value of internal energy change ΔU and not enthalpy change ΔH.

Statement II In a closed vessel, $\Delta U > \Delta H$ only if pressure inside the calorimeter remains constant.

In the light of the above statements, choose the most appropriate answer from the options given below.

(a) Both Statement I and Statement II are incorrect.
(b) Statement I is correct but Statement II is incorrect.
(c) Statement I is incorrect but Statement II is correct.
(d) Both Statement I and Statement II are correct.

22. Consider the reaction given below.

$$C_2H_2 \xrightarrow[Hg^{2+}/H^+]{H_2O} A; \ CH_2=CH_2 \xrightarrow[200\text{–}400°C]{1/2\,O_2,\,Ag} B$$

(a) A and B have different molecular formula with same functional group.
(b) A and B are unsaturated compounds.
(c) A and B are isomers.
(d) A and B are different compounds with different formula.

23. $I_2(g) \longrightarrow 2I(g)$. At certain temperature and total pressure of 10^5 Pa, the iodine vapour contains 40% by volume of I atoms. The value of K_p at the temperature is

(a) 2.67×10^4 (b) 2.67×10^6
(c) 4×10^3 (d) 6×10^3

24. Which of the following statement are incorrect?

A. Al_2O_3 can be used as adsorbent in thin layer chromatography.
B. Column chromatography involves in the separation of a mixture over a column of adsorbent.
C. The mixture adsorbed on adsorbent is placed below the top of adsorbent.
D. In paper chromatography, the mobile phase is solid and stationary phase is liquid.
E. Mixture of naphthalene and benzophenone can be separated by sublimation method.

Choose the most appropriate answer from the options given below.

(a) A, B and D
(b) B, C and E
(c) A, B and E
(d) C and D

25. Match List-I with List-II.

	List-I (Atoms)		List-II (Properties)
A.	He	I.	High electron affinity
B.	Cl	II.	Most electropositive element
C.	Ca	III.	Strong reducing agent
D.	Li	IV.	Highest ionisation energy

Choose the correct answer from the options given below.

(a) A-IV, B-I, C-II, D-III
(b) A-IV, B-I, C-III, D-II
(c) A-IV, B-II, C-I, D-III
(d) A-IV, B-II, C-III, D-I

26. The equilibrium constant K_p at 27°C for a homogeneous gaseous reaction is 10^{-8}. Then, the standard free energy change $\Delta G°$ for the reaction (using $R = 2$ cal K^{-1} mol^{-1}) will be

(a) 11.05 kcal (b) – 1.8 kcal
(c) 3.72 kcal (d) – 3.72 kcal

27. Given below are two statements.

Statement I The dipole moment helps to predict whether a molecule is polar or non-polar.

Statement II The dipole moment helps to predict geometry of molecules.

In the light of the above statements, choose the correct answer from the options given below.

(a) Both Statement I and Statement II are incorrect.
(b) Statement I is correct but Statement II is incorrect.
(c) Statement I is incorrect but Statement II is correct.
(d) Both Statement I and Statement II are correct.

28. Which of the following is true?

(a) *tert*-butoxide is a stronger base as well as stronger nucleophile than ethoxide.
(b) *tert*-butoxide is weaker base but stronger nucleophile than ethoxide.
(c) *tert*-butoxide is stronger base but weaker nucleophile than ethoxide.
(d) *tert*-butoxide and ethoxide are equally strong bases as well as strong nucleophiles.

29. Given below are two statements.

Statement I Volume of a gas is inversely proportional to the number of moles of gas.

Statement II The ratio by volume of gaseous reactants and products is in agreement with their molar ratio.

In the light of the above statements, choose the correct answer from the options given below.

(a) Both Statement I and Statement II are incorrect.
(b) Statement I is correct but Statement II is incorrect.
(c) Statement I is incorrect but Statement II is correct.
(d) Both Statement I and Statement II are correct.

30. The atomic number of vanadium (V), chromium (Cr), manganese (Mn) and iron (Fe) are respectively 23, 24, 25 and 26. Which of the following element is expected to have the highest second ionisation enthalpy?

(a) Cr (b) V
(c) Fe (d) Mn

31. In the following sequence the product *D* is

$$CH\equiv CH \xrightarrow{HBr} A \xrightarrow{HBr} B \xrightarrow{Alc.KOH} C \xrightarrow{NaNH_2} D$$

(a) ethanol (b) ethane
(c) ethyne (d) ethanol

32. Match List-I with List-II.

	List-I		List-II
A.	Energy of ground state of He^+	I.	-6.04 eV
B.	Potential energy of first orbit of H-atom	II.	-27.2 eV
C.	The energy of second excited state of He^+	III.	8.71×10^{-18} J
D.	Ionisation potential of He^+	IV.	-54.4 eV

Choose the correct answer from the options given below.

(a) A-I, B-II, C-III, D-IV (b) A-I, B-III, C-II, D-IV
(c) A-II, B-III, C-I, D-IV (d) A-IV, B-II, C-I, D-III

33. Consider the following compounds/species.

(i) N_2O_5 (ii) Al_2O_3 (iii) ZnO (iv) Cl_2O_7
(v) N_2O (vi) SO_3 (vii) P_4O_6

The number of compounds/species which are acidic oxide is

(a) 5 (b) 6 (c) 3 (d) 4

34. Match List-I and List-II.

	List-I (Atomic number)		List-II (Symbol)
A.	105	I.	Uun
B.	107	II.	Uns
C.	109	III.	Unp
D.	110	IV.	Une

Choose the correct answer from the options given below.

(a) A-III, B-II, C-IV, D-I
(b) A-I, B-III, C-II, D-IV
(c) A-IV, B-III, C-II, D-I
(d) A-II, B-III, C-I, D-IV

35. Which of the following statement is incorrect?

(a) Bonding molecular orbitals possess less energy than combining atomic orbitals.
(b) Bonding molecular orbitals are denoted by σ^*, π^* etc.
(c) Energy of electron in bonding molecular orbitals contributes to attraction between atoms.
(d) Bonding molecular orbital contributes towards stability of molecule.

36. The enthalpy of vaporisation of liquid water using the data.

$$H_2(g)+\frac{1}{2}O_2(g)\longrightarrow H_2O(l);$$
$$\Delta H = -285.77 \text{ kJ/mol} \quad \ldots \text{(i)}$$
$$H_2(g)+\frac{1}{2}O_2(g)\longrightarrow H_2O(g);$$
$$\Delta H = -241.84 \text{ kJ/mol} \quad \ldots \text{(ii)}$$

(a) + 43.93 kJ/mol (b) – 43.93 kJ/mol
(c) 86.72 kJ/mol (d) – 86.72 kJ/mol

37. Select the correct statements regarding quantum numbers from the following.

A. Electron in the same orbital must have different spin quantum numbers.
B. The azimuthal quantum number (l) defines the shape of the orbital within a given principal energy level (n).
C. In case of multielectron system, electron with same principal quantum number (n) do not experience same energies within an atom.
D. Effective nuclear charge decreases as one moves from left to right across a period in the periodic table.
E. Sum of the principal quantum number (n) and the azimuthal quantum number (l), is equal to the total number of nodes in an orbital.

Choose the correct answer from the options given below.

(a) A, B and C (b) B, C and D
(c) C and E only (d) C, D and E

38. Which one of the following has tetrahedral structure?

(a) SO_2 (b) SO_3
(c) SO_4^{2-} (d) SO_3^{2-}

39. Which of the following has maximum dipole moment?

(a) NCl_3 (b) NBr_3
(c) NH_3 (d) NI_3

40. The bond dissociation energies for Cl_2, I_2 and ICl are 242.3, 151.0 and 211.3 kJ/mole respectively. The enthalpy of sublimation of iodine is 62.8 kJ/mole. The standard enthalpy of formation of ICl (g) nearly equal to

(a) – 211.3 kJ/mole (b) – 14.6 kJ/mole
(c) 16.8 kJ/mole (d) 33.5 kJ/mole

41. The value of $\Delta G°$ for the phosphorylation of glucose in glycolysis is 14.4 kJ /mol. The value of K_C at 298 K will be

(a) 2.42×10^{-3} (b) 1.44×10^{-3}
(c) 2.99×10^{-3} (d) 3.81×10^{-3}

42. Electrophilic substitution of compound X will be fastest at which position?

Cl–(biphenyl, positions 1, 2 on the first ring and 3, 4 on the second ring, top and bottom)–CH_3

(a) 1 (b) 2 (c) 4 (d) 3

43. For the given redox reaction below, what is the sum of x, y, m and n?

$$xMnO_4^- + yH_2C_2O_4 + 6H^+ \longrightarrow mMn^{2+} + nCO_2 + 8H_2O$$

(a) 18 (b) 15
(c) 19 (d) 20

44. Which has highest nucleophilicity?

(a) F^- (b) OH^-
(c) CH_3^- (d) NH_2^-

45. Emission transitions in the Paschen series to orbit $n = 3$ from orbit n can be represented as

$$\nu = 3.29\times10^{15}\ (\text{Hz})\left[\frac{1}{(3)^2}-\frac{1}{n^2}\right]$$

Thus, value of 'n' if the transition is observed at 1285 nm (wavelength) is

(a) 10 (b) 5
(c) 8 (d) 7

Response Index

01 ⓐ ⓑ ⓒ ⓓ	14 ⓐ ⓑ ⓒ ⓓ	27 ⓐ ⓑ ⓒ ⓓ	40 ⓐ ⓑ ⓒ ⓓ
02 ⓐ ⓑ ⓒ ⓓ	15 ⓐ ⓑ ⓒ ⓓ	28 ⓐ ⓑ ⓒ ⓓ	41 ⓐ ⓑ ⓒ ⓓ
03 ⓐ ⓑ ⓒ ⓓ	16 ⓐ ⓑ ⓒ ⓓ	29 ⓐ ⓑ ⓒ ⓓ	42 ⓐ ⓑ ⓒ ⓓ
04 ⓐ ⓑ ⓒ ⓓ	17 ⓐ ⓑ ⓒ ⓓ	30 ⓐ ⓑ ⓒ ⓓ	43 ⓐ ⓑ ⓒ ⓓ
05 ⓐ ⓑ ⓒ ⓓ	18 ⓐ ⓑ ⓒ ⓓ	31 ⓐ ⓑ ⓒ ⓓ	44 ⓐ ⓑ ⓒ ⓓ
06 ⓐ ⓑ ⓒ ⓓ	19 ⓐ ⓑ ⓒ ⓓ	32 ⓐ ⓑ ⓒ ⓓ	45 ⓐ ⓑ ⓒ ⓓ
07 ⓐ ⓑ ⓒ ⓓ	20 ⓐ ⓑ ⓒ ⓓ	33 ⓐ ⓑ ⓒ ⓓ	46 ⓐ ⓑ ⓒ ⓓ
08 ⓐ ⓑ ⓒ ⓓ	21 ⓐ ⓑ ⓒ ⓓ	34 ⓐ ⓑ ⓒ ⓓ	47 ⓐ ⓑ ⓒ ⓓ
09 ⓐ ⓑ ⓒ ⓓ	22 ⓐ ⓑ ⓒ ⓓ	35 ⓐ ⓑ ⓒ ⓓ	48 ⓐ ⓑ ⓒ ⓓ
10 ⓐ ⓑ ⓒ ⓓ	23 ⓐ ⓑ ⓒ ⓓ	36 ⓐ ⓑ ⓒ ⓓ	49 ⓐ ⓑ ⓒ ⓓ
11 ⓐ ⓑ ⓒ ⓓ	24 ⓐ ⓑ ⓒ ⓓ	37 ⓐ ⓑ ⓒ ⓓ	50 ⓐ ⓑ ⓒ ⓓ
12 ⓐ ⓑ ⓒ ⓓ	25 ⓐ ⓑ ⓒ ⓓ	38 ⓐ ⓑ ⓒ ⓓ	
13 ⓐ ⓑ ⓒ ⓓ	26 ⓐ ⓑ ⓒ ⓓ	39 ⓐ ⓑ ⓒ ⓓ	

Performance Scanner

> 90% Excellent !	You have mastered the NEET syllabus (11th). The concepts of this entire syllabus are at your fingertips. Maintain this momentum.
76-90% Very Good !	You have a good command over the entire NEET syllabus (11th). Revise it again after a few days to enhance your performance.
60-75% Good !	You have a wide scope to learn for the entire NEET syllabus (11th). Revise it again.
<60% Not Satisfactory!	You have a long way ahead of you to master the NEET syllabus (11th). Revise it thoroughly.

Space for Rough Work

Test Booklet No. **3947217**

Test Booklet Code **NSS3**

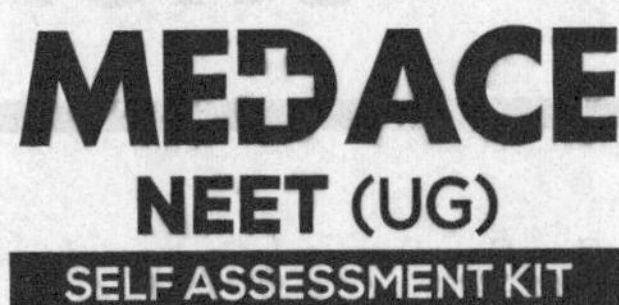

NEET (UG)

SELF ASSESSMENT KIT

NEET Stepping Stones 3

(Based on Class 11th Syllabus)

Name of the Candidate (In Capitals)

____

____

____

Candidate's Signature ____________

Invigilator's Signature ____________

Facsimile signature stamp of center superintendent____________

Important Instructions

- The test is of 45 minutes duration and the Test Booklet contains 45 multiple choice questions (four options with a single correct answer) from Chemistry.
- Candidates are advised to read all questions before they start attempting the question paper.
- Each questions carries 4 marks. For each correct response, the candidate will get 4 marks. For each incorrect response, one mark will be deducted from the total scores.
- In the event of candidate marking more than one option then one mark will be deducted. The maximum marks are 180.
- Use **Blue/Black Point Pen** only for writing particular on this page/marking response on Answer Sheet.

Do not open this Booklet until you start attempting the Test

Chemistry (Q. No. 1-45)

1. If S_1, S_2, S_3 and S_4 are the solubilities of AgCl in water, in 0.01 M $CaCl_2$, in 0.01 M NaCl and in 0.05 M $AgNO_3$ respectively at a certain temperature, the correct order of solubilities is

(a) $S_1 > S_2 > S_3 > S_4$ (b) $S_1 > S_3 > S_2 > S_4$

(c) $S_1 > S_2 = S_3 > S_4$ (d) $S_1 > S_3 > S_4 > S_2$

2. From the given data below,

$NH_3(g) + 3Cl_2(g) \longrightarrow NCl_3(g) + 3HCl(g); \; -\Delta H_1$ ...(i)

$N_2(g) + 3H_2(g) \longrightarrow 2NH_3(g); \; -\Delta H_2$ ...(ii)

$H_2(g) + Cl_2(g) \longrightarrow 2HCl(g); \; \Delta H_3$ ...(iii)

The heat of formation of $NCl_3(g)$ in term of ΔH_1, ΔH_2 and ΔH_3 is

(a) $\Delta H_f = -\Delta H_1 - \frac{\Delta H_2}{2} - \frac{3}{2}\Delta H_3$

(b) $\Delta H_f = \Delta H_1 + \frac{\Delta H_2}{2} - \frac{3}{2}\Delta H_3$

(c) $\Delta H_f = \Delta H_1 - \frac{\Delta H_2}{2} + \frac{3}{2}\Delta H_3$

(d) $\Delta H_f = \Delta H_1 + \frac{\Delta H_2}{2} + \frac{3}{2}\Delta H_3$

3. The hybridisation of atomic orbitals of nitrogen in NO_2^+, NO_3^- and NH_4^+ are

(a) sp, sp^2 and sp^3 respectively

(b) sp, sp^3 and sp^2 respectively

(c) sp^2, sp and sp^3 respectively

(d) sp^2, sp^3 and sp respectively

4. Select the correct statement regarding crystallisation from the following.

A. Crystallisation technique is based on the difference in solubilities of compound and the impurities in a suitable solvent.

B. The impure compound is dissolved in a solvent in which it is sparingly soluble at higher temperature.

C. The solution is diluted to get a nearly saturated solution.

D. On cooling the solution, the impure compound crystallises out.

E. For the purification of solid organic compounds, the crystallisation technique can be used.

Choose the correct answer from the options given below

(a) A, B and C (b) B, C and E

(c) A, B and E (d) C, D and E

5. Which of the following statement given below is true for reaction?

$2Al(s) + 6HCl(aq) \longrightarrow 2Al^{3+}(aq) + 6Cl^-(aq) + 3H_2(g)$

(a) 11.2 L $H_2(g)$ at STP is produced for every mole HCl (aq) consumed.

(b) 6 L HCl (aq) is consumed for every 3L $H_2(g)$ produced.

(c) 33.6 L $H_2(g)$ is produced regardless of temperature and pressure for every mole of Al that reacts.

(d) 67.2L $H_2(g)$ at STP is produced for every mole of Al that reacts.

6. Match List-I with List-II.

List-I (Element)		List-II (Position in periodic table)	
A.	Tl	I.	*s*-block
B.	Ra	II.	*p*-block
C.	Re	III.	*d*-block
D.	Es	IV.	*f*-block

Choose the correct answer from the options given below.

(a) A-II, B-I, C-III, D-IV

(b) A-II, B-I, C-IV, D-III

(c) A-I, B-II, C-III, D-IV

(d) A-I, B-II, C-IV, D-III

7. Which of the following reaction is an example of disproportionation reaction?

(a) $Cl_2(g) + H_2O(l) \longrightarrow HCl(aq) + HClO(aq)$

(b) $2NaCl(s) \longrightarrow 2Na(s) + Cl_2(g)$

(c) $2H_2O(l) \longrightarrow 2H_2(g) + O_2(g)$

(d) $Zn(s) + 2HCl(aq) \longrightarrow ZnCl_2(aq) + H_2(g)$

8. Which of the following statements are incorrect about element X, Y and Z having atomic number 19, 37 and 55 respectively?

A. Their ionisation potential would increases with increasing atomic number.

B. Y would have an ionisation potential between those X and Z.

C. Z would have highest ionisation potential.

D. X would have the highest negative value of $\Delta_{eg}H$.

E. X would have high electronegativity value on pauling scale than Y.

Choose the correct answer from the options given below

(a) C, D and E only

(b) A, B and C only

(c) A, C and E only

(d) B, C and D only

9. Select the incorrect statements from the following.

A. In the hydrocarbons, $CH_2{=}C{=}CH{-}CH_3$ total 8σ and 2π-bonds are present.

B. 2, 4-dimethylhexane has 4 primary, 2-secondary and 2-tertiary carbon atom.

C. The state of hybridisation of C_2 and C_3 carbon in the hydrocarbon $CH_2{=}C{=}CHCH_3$ is sp^2 and sp.

D. The ratio of π to σ bond in benzene is 1 : 4.

E. The compound of $C_4H_{10}O$ shows metamerism.

Choose the correct answer from the options given below:

(a) A and C (b) B, D and E

(c) A, B and D (d) D and E

10. Consider the properties given below.

(i) Heat (ii) Entropy

(iii) Enthalpy (iv) Work

(v) Gibb's free energy

The total number of functions that depend upon the initial and final state of the system is

(a) 3 (b) 2

(c) 5 (d) 4

11. Match List-I with List-II.

	List-I		List-II
A.	Sodium nitrite	I.	$pH = \frac{1}{2}[pK_w - pK_b - \log C]$
B.	Anilinium chloride	II.	$pH = \frac{1}{2}[pK_w + pK_a - pK_b]$
C.	Ammonium cyanide	III.	$pH = \frac{1}{2}[pK_w + pK_a + \log C]$
D.	Hydrogen cyanide	IV.	$pH = \frac{1}{2}[pK_a - \log C]$

Choose the correct answer from the options given below.

(a) A-I, B-II, C-III, D-IV

(b) A-IV, B-I, C-II, D-III

(c) A-III, B-I, C-II, D-IV

(d) A-II, B-IV, C-III, D-I

12. The two electrons have the following set of quantum numbers

$X: 3, 2, -2, +1/2$

$Y: 3, 0, 0, +1/2$

Which of the following is true?

(a) X and Y have same energy.

(b) X has greater energy than Y.

(c) X has less energy than Y.

(d) X and Y represent same electron.

13. Given data,

Bond	Bond enthalpy
N≡N	945 kJ mol^{-1}
H—H	436 kJ mol^{-1}
N—H	391 kJ mol^{-1}

The enthalpy change of the reaction will be

$$N_2(g) + 3H_2(g) \longrightarrow 2NH_3(g)$$

(a) – 89 kJ/mol (b) – 93 kJ/mol

(c) – 105 kJ/mol (d) 105 kJ/mol

14. Which of the following is the most likely product of the reaction between ethene and bromine in the presence of a non-aqueous solvent?

(a) Ethyl bromide (b) 1, 2-dibromoethane

(c) Bromine water (d) Ethene dibromide

15. 40 mL of 0.1 M ammonium hydroxide is mixed with 20 mL of 0.1 M HCl. Then the pH of the mixture is

(pK_b of ammonia solution is 4.74)

(a) 926×10^{-2} (b) 926×10^{-3}

(c) 926×10^{-4} (d) 926×10^{-1}

16. The ionisation potential of the ground state of hydrogen atom is -2.17×10^{-11} ergs per atom. The wavelength (Å) of the photon that is emitted when an electron in 3rd Bohr orbit returns to 1st orbit in a hydrogen atom will be

(a) 1842 (b) 372

(c) 912 (d) 1029

17. Select the incorrect statement from the following.

(a) One gram atom of carbon contains Avogadro's number of atoms.

(b) One mole of oxygen gas contains Avogadro's number of molecules.

(c) One mole of hydrogen contains Avogadro's number of atoms.

(d) One mole of electrons stands for 6.02×10^{23} electrons.

18. Number of molecules in 100 mL of each O_2, NH_3 and CO_2 at STP condition are

(a) in the order $CO_2 < O_2 < NH_3$.

(b) the same.

(c) $NH_3 = CO_2 < O_2$.

(d) in the order $NH_3 < O_2 < CO_2$.

19. Match List-I and List-II.

	List-I		List-II
A.	$\Delta H < 0, \Delta S < 0$	I.	Reaction is spontaneous at all temperatures.
B.	$\Delta H > 0, \Delta S > 0$	II.	Non-spontaneous at low temperature but spontaneous at high temperature.
C.	$\Delta H < 0, \Delta S > 0$	III.	Spontaneous at low temperature but non-spontaneous at high temperature.
D.	$\Delta H > 0, \Delta S < 0$	IV.	Non-spontaneous at all temperatures.

Choose the correct option given below.

(a) A-III, B-II, C-I, D-IV

(b) A-I, B-II, C-III, D-IV

(c) A-IV, B-II, C-I, D-III

(d) A-III, B-I, C-II, D-IV

20. The density of 3 M solution of NaCl is 1.25 g/mL. What is the molality of solution?

(a) 2.5 m (b) 2.8 m

(c) 2.0 m (d) 2.6 m

21. Select the incorrect statements from the following.

A. First law of thermodynamics does not tell anything about the spontaneity of a process.

B. A spontaneous process is a process which does not take place by itself.

C. First law of thermodynamics deals only with different form of energy.

D. A spontaneous process may not be instantaneous.

E. For a reaction to be spontaneous at constant temperature and pressure the following condition should be satisfied; $\Delta H > 0$ and $\Delta S < 0$.

Choose the correct answer from the options given below.

(a) A, B and C

(b) A, C and D

(c) B and E

(d) C and E

22. Using the Gibb's free energy change, $\Delta G° = +63.3$ kJ.

For the reaction,

$$Ag_2CO_3 \longrightarrow 2Ag^+(aq) + CO_3^{2-}(aq)$$

The K_{sp} of $Ag_2CO_3(s)$ in water at 25°C is

(a) 2.9×10^{-5} (b) 8.0×10^{-12}

(c) 7.4×10^{-26} (d) 6.4×10^{-12}

23. Solubility product of a salt AB is 1×10^{-8} M^2 in a solution in which the concentration of A^+ ions is 10^{-3} M. The salt will be precipitate when the concentration of B^- ions is kept

(a) between 10^{-8} M to 10^{-12} M

(b) between 10^{-12} M to 10^{-8} M

(c) $> 10^{-5}$ M

(d) $< 10^{-8}$ M

24. The entropy value, (in JK^{-1}/mol) of $H_2(g)=130.6$, $Cl_2(g)=223.0$ and $HCl(g)=186.7$ at 298 K and 1 atm pressure. Then entropy change of reaction is $H_2(g)+Cl_2(g) \longrightarrow 2HCl(g)$ is

(a) + 540.3 J/K mol (b) + 73.4 J/K mol
(c) – 29.3 J/K mol (d) + 19.8 J/K mol

25. A 0.02 M solution of pyridinium hydrochloride has pH = 3.44. The ionisation constant of pyridine is

(a) 1.5×10^{-7} (b) 1.5×10^{-9}
(c) 15×10^{-11} (d) 1.5×10^{-8}

26. Choose the incorrect statement for an electron that has the quantum numbers $n=4$ and $m=2$?

(a) The electron may have the quantum number, $s=+\frac{1}{2}$.
(b) The electron may have the quantum number, $l=2$
(c) The electron may have the quantum number, $m=-2$
(d) The electron may have the quantum number, $l=0, 1, 2$

27. For which of the following process given in the graph, $q=\Delta U$?

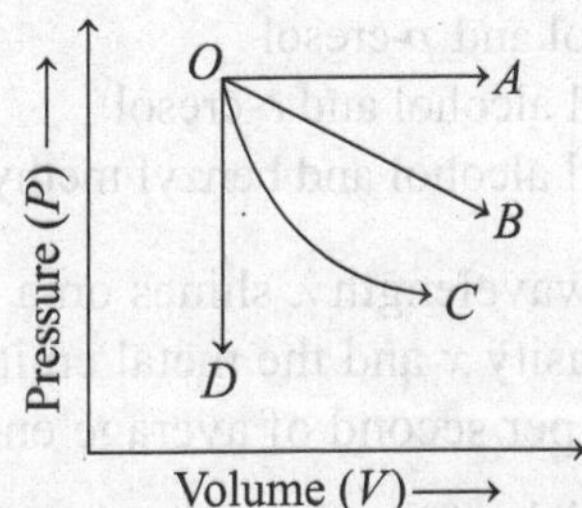

(a) $O\to A$ (b) $O\to B$
(c) $O\to D$ (d) $O\to C$

28. The reaction quotient, Q_C is useful in predicting the direction of the reaction.
Which of the following is incorrect statement?

(a) If $Q_C>K_C$, net reaction goes from right to left.
(b) If $Q_C<K_C$, net reaction goes from left to right.
(c) If $Q_C=K_C$, no net reaction occurs.
(d) If $Q_C>K_C$, net reaction goes from left to right.

29. Which of the following order with respect to ionisation energy is correct?

(a) N > O > F (b) N < O < F
(c) N > O < F (d) N < O > F

30. Among the following, the molecules/ions that have same bond order are

(a) CO and O_2^{2-} (b) O_2^- and CO
(c) O_2^{2-} and B_2 (d) CO and N_2^+

31. 1.0 g of Ca and 1.63 g of a metal *M* when treated with an acid in excess separately, produces the same amount of hydrogen. If equivalent weight of Ca is 20.0, what is equivalent weight of metal *M*?

(a) 8.2 (b) 135.4 (c) 32.6 (d) 65.2

32. Match List-I with List-II.

	List-I (Mixture)		List-II (Property use to distinguished)
A.	1-butyne, 2-butyne	I.	Zinc dust distillation
B.	C_6H_6, $CH_2{=}CH_2$	II.	Tollen's reagent
C.	C_6H_6, C_6H_{14}	III.	Baeyer's reagent
D.	Benzene, Phenol	IV.	Sooty flame test

Choose the correct answer from the options given below:

(a) A-II, B-III, C-IV, D-I
(b) A-II, B-III, C-I, D-IV
(c) A-III, B-II, C-IV, D-I
(d) A-II, B-IV, C-III, D-I

33. For the energy levels in an atom, which one of the following statement is correct?

(a) There are seven principal electron energy levels.
(b) The second principal energy level has four sub energy level and contains a maximum of six electrons.
(c) The principal energy level *N* can have a maximum of 32 electrons.
(d) The 4*s* sub-energy level has higher energy than 3*d* sub-energy level.

34. Select the incorrect statement from the following.

(a) Stability of triphenyl methyl carbocation can be explained only by resonance effect.
(b) *p*-methoxybenzyl carbocation is more stable than *p*-nitrobenzyl carbocation.
(c) Singlet carbene does not acts as a electrophile.
(d) The central carbon atom of a carbanion possesses octet of electrons.

35. Given below are two statements.

Statement I Rotation about C—C single bond in ethane is completely free.

Statement II There are weak repulsive interactions between bonds adjacent to C—C bond.

In the light of the above statements, choose the correct answer from the options given below.

(a) Both Statement I and Statement II are incorrect.
(b) Statement I is correct but Statement II is incorrect.
(c) Statement I is incorrect but Statement II is correct.
(d) Both Statement I and Statement II are correct.

36. 0.30 g of a hydrocarbon on combustion gave 0.66 g CO_2. The percentage of hydrogen in the hydrocarbon is about

(a) 25% (b) 15% (c) 40% (d) 20%

37. The element that exists in liquid state for a wide range of temperature that can be used for measuring high temperature is

(a) In (b) Ga (c) Al (d) B

38. Consider the reaction given below.

Element, $M + N_2 \xrightarrow{\Delta} X \xrightarrow{H_2O} NH_3$

The element that belongs to group 13 can be

(a) Mg or B (b) Ga or Al
(c) B or Al (d) Mg, Al or B

39. Consider the following species.

$R\bar{C}H_2$ (I), (II), (III), (IV)

The order of stability of the following carbanions is

(a) I > II > III > IV (b) I > III > II > IV
(c) IV > III > II > I (d) III > IV > I > II

40. Major organic product formed from the following sequence of reactions is

$\xrightarrow[\text{Light}]{Br_2} \xrightarrow[CH_3CH_2OH]{Na\overset{+}{O}\overset{-}{C}H_2CH_3} \xrightarrow[\text{(ii) } H_2O_2, OH^-]{\text{(i) } B_2H_6}$

(a) Br ... OH (b) Br ... OH
(c) OH (b) OH

41. In the following case,

R–(pyridinium)N–H $\rightleftharpoons$ R–(pyridine)N + H^+

pK_a is maximum when R is

(a) H (b) NH_2
(c) CN (d) CH_3

42. Provide a sequence of reactions to carry out the following change

(methylcyclohexane, CH_3) $\longrightarrow$ (1-methylcyclohexanol, CH_3, OH)

(a) $\xrightarrow[\Delta]{\text{Conc. } H_2SO_4} \xrightarrow[OH^-]{B_2H_6, H_2O_2}$

(b) $\xrightarrow[\Delta]{\text{Conc. } H_2SO_4} \xrightarrow{H_3O^+}$

(c) $\xrightarrow[\Delta]{\text{Conc. } H_2SO_4} \xrightarrow{Hg(OOCCH_3)_2}$

(d) $\xrightarrow[\Delta]{\text{Conc. } H_2SO_4} \xrightarrow{MnO_4^-, OH^-}$

43. Which of the following pairs of compound is both i.e functional isomer and position isomer?

(a) Benzyl alcohol and methoxybenzene
(b) *o*-cresol and *p*-cresol
(c) Benzyl alcohol and *o*-cresol
(d) Benzyl alcohol and benzyl methyl ether

44. Light of wavelength λ shines on a metal surface with intensity x and the metal emits y electrons per second of average energy, z.

Then, which of the following statement is true if x is doubled?

(a) y will be doubled and z will becomes half.
(b) y will remain same and z will be doubled.
(c) Both y and z will be doubled.
(d) y will be doubled but z will remain same.

45. If electron, hydrogen, helium and neon nuclei all are moving with the velocity of light, then the correct order of wavelength is

(a) electron > hydrogen > helium > neon
(b) electron > helium > hydrogen > neon
(c) electron < hydrogen < helium < neon
(d) neon < hydrogen < helium < electron

Response Index

01 ⓐ ⓑ ⓒ ⓓ	14 ⓐ ⓑ ⓒ ⓓ	27 ⓐ ⓑ ⓒ ⓓ	40 ⓐ ⓑ ⓒ ⓓ
02 ⓐ ⓑ ⓒ ⓓ	15 ⓐ ⓑ ⓒ ⓓ	28 ⓐ ⓑ ⓒ ⓓ	41 ⓐ ⓑ ⓒ ⓓ
03 ⓐ ⓑ ⓒ ⓓ	16 ⓐ ⓑ ⓒ ⓓ	29 ⓐ ⓑ ⓒ ⓓ	42 ⓐ ⓑ ⓒ ⓓ
04 ⓐ ⓑ ⓒ ⓓ	17 ⓐ ⓑ ⓒ ⓓ	30 ⓐ ⓑ ⓒ ⓓ	43 ⓐ ⓑ ⓒ ⓓ
05 ⓐ ⓑ ⓒ ⓓ	18 ⓐ ⓑ ⓒ ⓓ	31 ⓐ ⓑ ⓒ ⓓ	44 ⓐ ⓑ ⓒ ⓓ
06 ⓐ ⓑ ⓒ ⓓ	19 ⓐ ⓑ ⓒ ⓓ	32 ⓐ ⓑ ⓒ ⓓ	45 ⓐ ⓑ ⓒ ⓓ
07 ⓐ ⓑ ⓒ ⓓ	20 ⓐ ⓑ ⓒ ⓓ	33 ⓐ ⓑ ⓒ ⓓ	46 ⓐ ⓑ ⓒ ⓓ
08 ⓐ ⓑ ⓒ ⓓ	21 ⓐ ⓑ ⓒ ⓓ	34 ⓐ ⓑ ⓒ ⓓ	47 ⓐ ⓑ ⓒ ⓓ
09 ⓐ ⓑ ⓒ ⓓ	22 ⓐ ⓑ ⓒ ⓓ	35 ⓐ ⓑ ⓒ ⓓ	48 ⓐ ⓑ ⓒ ⓓ
10 ⓐ ⓑ ⓒ ⓓ	23 ⓐ ⓑ ⓒ ⓓ	36 ⓐ ⓑ ⓒ ⓓ	49 ⓐ ⓑ ⓒ ⓓ
11 ⓐ ⓑ ⓒ ⓓ	24 ⓐ ⓑ ⓒ ⓓ	37 ⓐ ⓑ ⓒ ⓓ	50 ⓐ ⓑ ⓒ ⓓ
12 ⓐ ⓑ ⓒ ⓓ	25 ⓐ ⓑ ⓒ ⓓ	38 ⓐ ⓑ ⓒ ⓓ	
13 ⓐ ⓑ ⓒ ⓓ	26 ⓐ ⓑ ⓒ ⓓ	39 ⓐ ⓑ ⓒ ⓓ	

Performance Scanner

> 90% Excellent !	You have mastered the NEET syllabus (11th). The concepts of this entire syllabus are at your fingertips. Maintain this momentum.
76-90% Very Good !	You have a good command over the entire NEET syllabus (11th). Revise it again after a few days to enhance your performance.
60-75% Good !	You have a wide scope to learn for the entire NEET syllabus (11th). Revise it again.
<60% Not Satisfactory!	You have a long way ahead of you to master the NEET syllabus (11th). Revise it thoroughly.

Space for Rough Work

Test Booklet No. 3947218

Test Booklet Code NSS4

MEDACE

NEET (UG)

SELF ASSESSMENT KIT

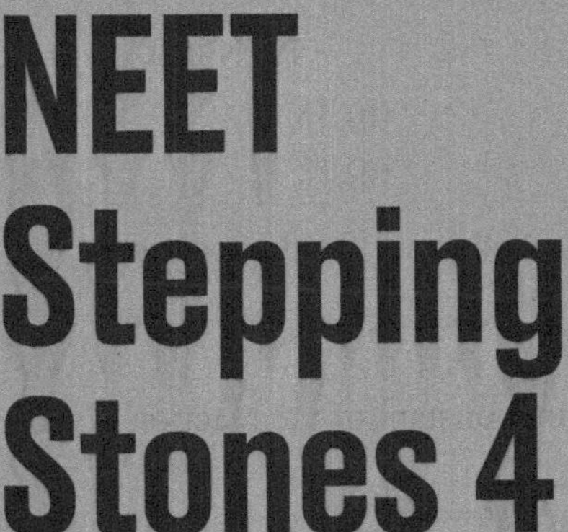

NEET Stepping Stones 4

(Based on Class 11th Syllabus)

Name of the Candidate (In Capitals)

____

____

____

Candidate's Signature ________________

Invigilator's Signature ________________

Facsimile signature stamp of center superintendent________________

Important Instructions

- The test is of 45 minutes duration and the Test Booklet contains 45 multiple choice questions (four options with a single correct answer) from Chemistry.
- Candidates are advised to read all questions before they start attempting the question paper.
- Each questions carries 4 marks. For each correct response, the candidate will get 4 marks. For each incorrect response, one mark will be deducted from the total scores.
- In the event of candidate marking more than one option then one mark will be deducted. The maximum marks are 180.
- Use **Blue/Black Point Pen** only for writing particular on this page/marking response on Answer Sheet.

Do not open this Booklet until you start attempting the Test

Chemistry (Q. No. 1-45)

1. pH of a saturated solution of $Ca(OH)_2$ is 8. The solubility product (K_{sp}) of $Ca(OH)_2$ is

(a) 0.5×10^{-16} (b) 0.5×10^{-18}

(c) 0.5×10^{-15} (d) 0.5×10^{-21}

2. Given below are two statements

Statement I Reaction of *tert*-butylchloride with Na/dry ether, Δ gives 2,2,3,3-tetramethyl butane.

Statement II Tertiary butyl chloride on Wurtz reaction gives alkene.

In the light of the above statements, choose the correct answer from the options given below.

(a) Both Statement I and Statement II are incorrect.

(b) Statement I is correct but Statement II is incorrect.

(c) Statement I is incorrect but Statement II is correct.

(d) Both Statement I and Statement II are correct.

3. Among the given statements, choose the incorrect one.

(a) CuCl is more covalent than NaCl.

(b) HBr has higher boiling point than HCl.

(c) HF is less polar than HBr.

(d) MCl_2 is more ionic than MCl_4.

4. Given below are two statements, one is labelled as Assertion (A) and other is labelled as Reason (R).

Assertion (A) PbI_4 is a stable compound.

Reason (R) Pb^{2+} ion with concentrated solution of KI form a soluble complex.

In the light of above statements, choose the correct answer from the options given below.

(a) Both (A) and (R) are true and (R) is the correct explanation of (A).

(b) Both (A) and (R) are true but (R) is not the correct explanation of (A).

(c) (A) is true but (R) is false.

(d) (A) is false but (R) is true.

5. In the given redox reaction, what is the value of $2(x+y+z)$?

$$x\text{MnO} + y\text{PbO}_2 + z\text{HNO}_3 \longrightarrow \text{HMnO}_4 + \text{Pb(NO}_3)_2 + 4\text{H}_2\text{O}$$

(a) 17 (b) 36

(c) 34 (d) 18

6. The equilibrium constant for the reaction,

$SO_2(g) + \frac{1}{2}O_2(g) \rightleftharpoons SO_3(g)$ is 4×10^{-3} atm

The equilibrium constant of the reaction given below will be

$$2SO_3(g) \rightleftharpoons 2SO_2(g) + O_2(g)$$

(a) 6.25×10^8 atm (b) 6.25×10^6 atm

(c) 6.25×10^4 atm (d) 0.625×10^4 atm

7. 0.5 g of an organic compound of Kjeldahl's analysis gave enough ammonia to just neutralise 10 cm^3 of 1 M H_2SO_4. The percentage of nitrogen in the compound is

(a) 50 (b) 56

(c) 62 (d) 68

8. In the following reaction (unbalanced), equivalent weight of As_2S_3 is related to molecular weight M by

$$As_2S_3 + H^+ + NO_3^- \longrightarrow NO + H_2O + AsO_4^{3-} + SO_4^{2-}$$

(a) $\frac{M}{28}$ (b) $\frac{M}{14}$

(c) $\frac{M}{7}$ (d) $\frac{M}{6}$

9. The reaction $A(g) + B(g) \rightleftharpoons 2C(g)$ occurs by mixing of 3 moles of A and 1 mole of B in one litre container. If α of B is $\frac{1}{3}$, then K_C for the reaction is

(a) 0.25 (b) 2.5

(c) 0.77 (d) 0.125

10. Given below are two statements, one is labelled as Assertion (A) and the other is labelled as Reason (R).

Assertion (A) *p*-nitrophenol is less volatile than *o*-nitrophenol.

Reason (R) In *p*-nitrophenol, intermolecular hydrogen bonding occurs.

In the light of above statements, choose the correct answer from the options given below.

(a) Both (A) and (R) are true and (R) is the correct explanation of (A).
(b) Both (A) and (R) are true but (R) is not the correct explanation of (A).
(c) (A) is true but (R) is false.
(d) (A) is false but (R) is true.

11. ΔH_f° for $CO_2(g)$, $CO(g)$ and $H_2O(g)$ are –393.5, –110.5 and –241.8 kJ/mol respectively. Standard enthalpy change for the reaction given below is

$$CO_2(g) + H_2(g) \longrightarrow CO(g) + H_2O(g)$$

(a) – 4.12 kJ/mol
(b) 41.2 kJ/mol
(c) 8.26 kJ/mol
(d) –8.26 kJ/mol

12. The entropy change involved in the isothermal reversible expansion of 2 moles of an ideal gas from a volume of 10 dm^3 to a volume of 100 dm^3 at 27°C is (in J/mol K)

(a) 38.3 (b) 28.3
(c) 35.2 (d) 41.3

13. The angular momentum of an electron in a Bohr's orbit of He^+ is 3.1652×10^{-34} kg m^2 / sec. What is the wave number in terms of R of the spectral line emitted when an electron fall from this level to the first excited state?

(a) $\frac{3R}{9}$ (b) $\frac{5R}{9}$
(c) $\frac{9R}{5}$ (d) $5R$

14. Given below are two statements.

Statement I The bond angle in molecules depend upon electronegativity of central atom and multiplicity of bonds.

Statement II Among the two O—H bonds in H_2O molecule, the energy required to break the first O—H bond and the other O—H bonds is the same.

In the light of the above statements, choose the correct answer from the options given below.

(a) Both Statement I and Statement II are incorrect.
(b) Statement I is correct but Statement II is incorrect.
(c) Statement I is incorrect but Statement II is correct.
(d) Both Statement I and Statement II are correct

15. Which of the following is the correct order of electron affinity?

(a) $C > N < O < F$ (b) $C > N > O > F$
(c) $C < N < O < F$ (d) $C < N > O > F$

16. What will be the amount of $CO_2(g)$ produced by combustion of 16 g of oxygen?

(a) 44 g (b) 17 g
(c) 22 g (d) 11 g

17. The molarity of a solution obtained by mixture of 750 mL of 0.5 M HCl and 250 mL of 2 M HCl will be

(a) 0.875 M (b) 1.875 M
(c) 0.555 M (d) 1.525 M

18. The ratio of radii of third and fourth Bohr orbits of hydrogen atom is

(a) 16 : 25 (b) 25 : 16
(c) 9 : 16 (d) 16 : 9

19. Which of the following compound exhibit sp^3d^2-hybridisation?

(a) ClF_3 (b) SF_6
(c) PCl_5 (d) PCl_3

20. For a reaction where the enthalpy change is ΔH and the reaction is reversed, then the enthalpy change will

(a) remain same (b) become negative
(c) become positive (d) become zero

21. What concentration of acetic acid is needed to give a hydrogen ion concentration of 3.5×10^{-4} M? ($K_\alpha = 1.8 \times 10^{-5}$)

(a) 5.2×10^{-3} M (b) 7.8×10^{-3} M
(c) 6.8×10^{-3} M (d) 6×10^{-3} M

22. The pH of 0.02 M $NH_4Cl(aq)$ ($pK_b = 4.73$) is
(a) 3.98 (b) 5.48
(c) 5.0 (d) 6.26

23. Given below are two statements.
Statement I On passing HCl(g) through a saturated solution of $BaCl_2$, a white turbidity appears.
Statement II The common ion effect is responsible for white turbidity in above statement.
In the light of the above statements, choose the correct answer from the options given below.
(a) Both Statement I and Statement II are incorrect.
(b) Statement I is correct but Statement II is incorrect.
(c) Statement I is incorrect but Statement II is correct.
(d) Both Statement I and Statement II are correct.

24. The power of halides of boron to act as Lewis acid in decreasing order is
(a) $BBr_3 > BCl_3 > BF_3$
(b) $BBr_3 > BF_3 > BCl_3$
(c) $BCl_3 > BBr_3 > BF_3$
(d) $BF_3 > BBr_3 > BCl_3$

25. MnO_4^- is a good oxidising agent in different medium changing to
$$MnO_4^- \longrightarrow Mn^{2+} \longrightarrow MnO_4^{2-} \longrightarrow MnO_2 \longrightarrow Mn_2O_3$$
Change in oxidation number respectively w.r.t. MnO_4^-, are
(a) 1, 3, 4, 5 (b) 5, 4, 3, 2
(c) 5, 1, 3, 4 (d) 2, 6, 4, 3

26. The enolic form of acetone contains
(a) 9σ bond, 1π bond and 2 lone pairs
(b) 6σ bond, 2π bond and 0 lone pair
(c) 9σ bond, 2π bond and 1 lone pair
(d) 4σ bond, 4π bond and 2 lone pairs

27. Given below are two statements, one is labelled as Assertion (A) and the other is labelled as Reason (R).
Assertion (A) Addition of bromine on *trans*-2-butene yields *meso*-2, 3-dibromobutane.
Reason (R) Br_2 show electrophilic addition on alkene.
In the light of above statements, choose the correct answer from the options given below
(a) Both (A) and (R) are true and (R) is the correct explanation of (A).
(b) Both (A) and (R) are true but (R) is not the correct explanation of (A).
(c) (A) is true but (R) is false.
(d) (A) is false but (R) is true.

28. The correct order of sequence of increasing number of π-bonds in the structures of the following molecules.
I. $H_2S_2O_6$ II. H_2SO_3 III. $H_2S_2O_5$
(a) I, II, III (b) III, II, I
(c) II, III, I (d) II, I, III

29. The reaction that defines ΔH_f° is
(a) $H_2(g) + I_2(g) \longrightarrow 2HI(g)$
(b) $N_2(g) + 3H_2(g) \longrightarrow 2NH_3(g)$
(c) $\frac{1}{2}H_2(g) + \frac{1}{2}F_2(g) \longrightarrow HF(g)$
(d) $CO(g) + \frac{1}{2}O_2(g) \longrightarrow CO_2(g)$

30. The heat of combustion of benzoic acid is -2546 kJ mol^{-1} at 25°C and 1 atm. The ΔE is
(a) -1555.6 kJ mol^{-1} (b) -2244.7 kJ mol^{-1}
(c) -2544.76 kJ mol^{-1} (d) -2868.66 kJ mol^{-1}

31. $\frac{K_p}{K_C}$ for the given reaction is
$$CO(g) + \frac{1}{2}O_2(g) \longrightarrow CO_2(g)$$
(a) RT^3 (b) $\frac{4}{RT}$
(c) $\frac{1}{\sqrt{RT}}$ (d) $\frac{RT}{3}$

32. The correct stability order of the given carbanions is

(I) o-nitrobenzyl carbanion ($\bar{C}H_2$, NO_2) (II) m-nitrobenzyl carbanion ($\bar{C}H_2$, NO_2) (III) p-nitrobenzyl carbanion ($\bar{C}H_2$, NO_2) (IV) benzyl carbanion ($\bar{C}H_2$)

(a) I > II > III > IV (b) I > II > IV > III
(c) I > III > II > IV (d) IV > III > II > I

33. Match List-I with List-II.

	List-I		List-II
A.	Beilstein test	I.	Sulphur
B.	Sodium nitroprusside	II.	Carbon
C.	Liebig's method	III.	Nitrogen
D.	Kjeldahl's method	IV.	Chlorine

(a) A-III, B-IV, C-II, D-I
(b) A-IV, B-II, C-I, D-III
(c) A-III, B-II, C-IV, D-I
(d) A-IV, B-I, C-II, D-III

34. The number of correct statement regarding use of sodium metal in Lassaigne's test is

I. It is very reactive.
II. Its melting point is low.
III. Its compounds are soluble in water.
IV. It can detect the presence of iodine.
V. It converts all the elements present into covalent form.

(a) 1 (b) 2 (c) 3 (d) 4

35. Choose the number of incorrect statement regarding SF_4 molecule.

(A) It has *see-saw* shape.
(B) Geometry is trigonal bipyramidal.
(C) Central atom has two lone pair.
(D) It has 4 bonding pairs.
(E) Hybridisation is sp^2d^2.

(a) 1 (b) 2 (c) 3 (d) 4

36. 1.16 g of hydrocarbon on combustion gave 1.8 g water. The percentage of carbon is about

(a) 63.43 (b) 82.76
(c) 16.24 (d) 92.75

37. For reaction, $PCl_3(g) + Cl_2(g) \rightleftharpoons PCl_5(g)$ the value of K_C at 230°C is 13. The value of K_p at this temperature will be

(a) 0.315 (b) 0.810 (c) 0.217 (d) 0.412

38. Consider the following species.

$$NO_3^-, CO_3^{2-}, ClO_3^-, SO_3, NH_4^+$$

The number of species that are isoelectronic and isostructural is

(a) 1 (b) 2 (c) 3 (d) 4

39. Choose the correct statement about two diastereoisomers, i.e. I and II of *trans*-3, 6-dimethyloct-4-en.e

(I): $CH_3CH_2-C^*(H)(Me)-CH=CH-C^*(H)(Me)-CH_2CH_3$ (carbons numbered 1–8) and (II): $Et-C^*(H)(Me)-CH=CH-C^*(H)(Me)-Et$

Which statement is true about (I) and (II)?

(a) (I) is optically active and (II) is not.
(b) (II) is optically active and (I) is not.
(c) Both are optically active.
(d) Both are optically inactive due to the presence of centre of symmetry.

40. Which of the following is non-aromatic in nature?

(a) Azulene (b) [10]-Annulene
(c) Furan (d) Pyrrole

41. Consider the following statements.

Statement I Equilibrium is dynamic in nature.
Statement II At the stage of equilibrium $\Delta G < 0$.

In the light of the above statements, choose the most appropriate answer from the options given below

(a) Both Statement I and Statement II are incorrect.
(b) Statement I is correct but Statement II is incorrect.
(c) Statement I is incorrect but Statement II is correct.
(d) Both Statement I and Statement II are correct.

42. What will be the molarity of the solution in which 0.1825 g of HCl gas is dissolved in 100 mL of solution?

(a) 5×10^{-2} (b) 5×10^{-4}
(c) 5×10^{-3} (d) 5×10^{-6}

43. Match List-I with List-II.

	List-I (Orbital)		List-II (Radial nodes)
A.	4*s*	I.	5
B.	3*p*	II.	4
C.	5*s*	III.	1
D.	6*s*	IV.	3

Choose the correct answer from the options given below

(a) A-IV, B-II, C-III, D-I
(b) A-II, B-I, C-III, D-IV
(c) A-III, B-IV, C-I, D-II
(d) A-IV, B-III, C-II, D-I

44. How much volume of 10 M HCl should be diluted with water to prepare 2.00 L of 5 M HCl?

(a) 2 L (b) 1.0 L
(c) 3.5 L (d) 4.0 L

45. The percentage ionic character in certain bond $A—B$ is 76.81% and the bond length $A—B$ is given as 159.6 pm. What is the dipole moment of AB molecule? (1D $= 3.335 \times 10^{-30}$ Cm)

(a) 4.61 D (b) 2.89 D
(c) 5.01 D (d) 5.88 D

■ Response Index

01	a	b	c	d	14	a	b	c	d	27	a	b	c	d	40	a	b	c	d
02	a	b	c	d	15	a	b	c	d	28	a	b	c	d	41	a	b	c	d
03	a	b	c	d	16	a	b	c	d	29	a	b	c	d	42	a	b	c	d
04	a	b	c	d	17	a	b	c	d	30	a	b	c	d	43	a	b	c	d
05	a	b	c	d	18	a	b	c	d	31	a	b	c	d	44	a	b	c	d
06	a	b	c	d	19	a	b	c	d	32	a	b	c	d	45	a	b	c	d
07	a	b	c	d	20	a	b	c	d	33	a	b	c	d	46	a	b	c	d
08	a	b	c	d	21	a	b	c	d	34	a	b	c	d	47	a	b	c	d
09	a	b	c	d	22	a	b	c	d	35	a	b	c	d	48	a	b	c	d
10	a	b	c	d	23	a	b	c	d	36	a	b	c	d	49	a	b	c	d
11	a	b	c	d	24	a	b	c	d	37	a	b	c	d	50	a	b	c	d
12	a	b	c	d	25	a	b	c	d	38	a	b	c	d					
13	a	b	c	d	26	a	b	c	d	39	a	b	c	d					

■ Performance Scanner

> 90% Excellent !	You have mastered the NEET syllabus (11th). The concepts of this entire syllabus are at your fingertips. Maintain this momentum.
76-90% Very Good !	You have a good command over the entire NEET syllabus (11th). Revise it again after a few days to enhance your performance.
60-75% Good !	You have a wide scope to learn for the entire NEET syllabus (11th). Revise it again.
<60% Not Satisfactory!	You have a long way ahead of you to master the NEET syllabus (11th). Revise it thoroughly.

Space for Rough Work

Space for Rough Work

MED+ACE

NEET (UG)

SELF ASSESSMENT KIT

Exactly as per the Latest Pattern of NTA

Released on 25 Jan 2025

CHEMISTRY - XIth

Hints, Solutions & Mind Maps Booklet

MED ACE

NEET (UG)

SELF ASSESSMENT KIT

Exactly as per the Latest Pattern of NTA

Released on 25 Jan 2025

CHEMISTRY - XI th

Hints, Solutions & Mind Maps Booklet

Authors

Pooja Yadav, Swati Chauhan

ARIHANT PRAKASHAN (SERIES), MEERUT

卐 **Administrative & Production Offices**

Regd. Office

'Ramchhaya' 4577/15, Agarwal Road, Darya Ganj, New Delhi -110002
Tele: 011- 47630600, 43518550

卐 **Head Office**

Kalindi, TP Nagar, Meerut (UP) - 250002
Tel: 0121-7156203, 7156204

卐 **Sales & Support Offices**

Agra, Ahmedabad, Bengaluru, Bareilly, Chennai, Delhi, Guwahati, Hyderabad, Jaipur, Jhansi, Kolkata, Lucknow, Nagpur & Pune.

卐 **PRICE** ₹1000.00

卐 **PO No :** TXT-59-T063623-03-25

Published by Arihant Publications (India) Ltd.

For further information about the books published by Arihant, log on to www.arihantbooks.com or e-mail at info@arihantbooks.com

CHEMISTRY XIth

CONTENT LIST

MEDACE

NEET (UG)

SELF ASSESSMENT KIT

HINTS & SOLUTIONS

Hints & Explanations

Ch-1 Some Basic Concepts of Chemistry

Topical Follow Thru

Test-1

1. (c) Option (c) is incorrect because the components completely mix with each other in any state form a mixture.

The substances in a mixture can be elements, compounds or both and they can be in any proportion and state.

2. (d) Both Statement I and Statement II are correct because glucose contains carbon, hydrogen and oxygen in fixed ratio and has fixed composition.

The constituents of pure substance cannot be separated by simple physical method.

3. (b)

	List-I (Physical quantity)	List-II (Derived unit)
A.	Frequency (ν) $\left(\nu = \frac{1}{t}\right)$	s^{-1}
B.	Energy (E) $[E = mc^2]$	$kg\ m^2\ s^{-2}$
C.	Electrical resistance (R) $\left[R = \frac{V}{I}\right]$	VA^{-1}
D.	Electric current	A

Hence, the correct match is A-II, B-I, C-IV, D-III.

4. (a)

Multiple	Prefix	Symbol
10^{24}	yotta	Y
10^{6}	mega	M
10^{3}	kilo	k
10^{2}	hecto	h

So, the correct increasing order is

hecto < kilo < mega < yotta

5. (d) Except V, all the given statements are correct because zeros are not significant when they are the leading digits in a number hence, 0.003 has 1 significant figure and 0.300 has 3 significant figures as zeros come at the end of number are significant.

While statements I, II, III, IV are factually correct statements.

6. (c) (A) is true but (R) is false because zeroes at the end or right of a number are significant provided, they are on the right side of the decimal point.

So, option (c) is correct.

7. (d) Statement (d) is incorrect. The correct form is :

The relative number and kinds of atoms in a given compound remains constant.

8. (b) We use conversion factor

$$1 = \frac{1\,\text{carat}}{3.168\,\text{grains}} = \frac{3.168\,\text{grains}}{1\,\text{carat}}$$

$$1 = \frac{1\,\text{gram}}{15.4\,\text{grains}} = \frac{15.4\,\text{grains}}{1\,\text{gram}}$$

$$0.500\,\text{carat} = 0.500\,\text{carat} \times \frac{3.168\,\text{grains}}{1\,\text{carat}} \times \frac{1\,\text{grams}}{15.4\,\text{grains}} = 0.1\,\text{grams}$$

Total mass of the ring

$$= 7.00 + 0.10\,\text{g}$$

$$= 7.10\,\text{g} \times \frac{1\,\text{kg}}{1000\,\text{g}} = 0.0071\,\text{kg}$$

Thus, option (b) is correct.

9. (b) Gay Lussac concluded a law which states that "the volume of gas (at fixed temperature and pressure) is proportional to the number of moles (or molecules of gas present) hence, option (b) is correct.

10. (c) Statement I is incorrect but Statement II is correct.

1 L of O_2 and 1 L of O_3 contains the same number of moles and hence same number of molecules but not atoms. Number of atoms in O_3 will be 1.5 times than that in O_2.

11. (a) Mass of $KClO_3$ taken = 4.90 g

Total mass at the product ($KCl + O_2$)

$$= 2.96 + 1.92 = 4.88\,\text{g}$$

Difference between the mass of the reactants and the total mass of the product = 4.90 − 4.88 = 0.02 g

This small difference may be due to experimental error.

Thus, law of conservation of mass holds goods with in experimental error.

12. (b) 6.62×10^{-34} has three significant figures.

0.72 has two significant figures.

8.35 has three significant figures.

0.0075 has two significant figures.
$\frac{22}{7} = 3.1428(\ldots)$ has infinite number of significant figures.
So, two value has significant number = 2.

13. (b)

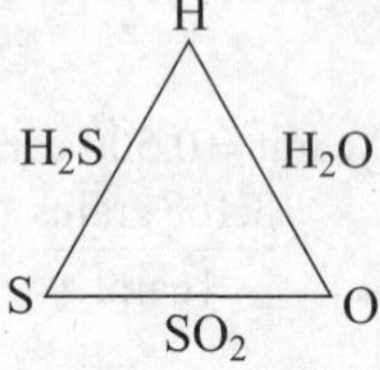

In H_2S, 5.89 g of H combine with = 94.11 g S
Hence, 1 g H combine with = 16 g S
In SO_2, 50 g oxygen combine with = 50 g S
Hence, 1 g O combine with 1 g S
In H_2O, 11.11 g H combine with = 88.89 g O
1 g H combine with = 8 g O
In the two compounds H_2S and H_2O, the weights of S and O that combine with the fixed weight of 1 g of H are with ratio of 16 : 8 or 2 : 1 (Ratio I)
In SO_2, the ratio of weight of S and O is 1 : 1 (Ratio II)
Ratio I and Ratio II are 2 : 1 and this is in accordance with the law of reciprocal proportion.

14. (b) Statements I, II and III are incorrect.

I. Law of constant proportion is not applicable if the elements exist in different isotopes which may be involved in the formation of compound.
II. At 1 atm 25°C, molar volume is 22.7L.
III. Molecular weight is twice of vapour density.

Hence, option (b) is correct.

15. (a) The number of H atoms or the weighs of H that combine with one atom or 12 parts by weight of carbon in the three cases bear a simple ratio of 4 : 2 : 1. Hence, the law of multiple proportion is illustrated.

Test-2

1. (d) Given,
Atomic mass of chlorine = 34.97 g / mol and 36.97 g/mol
Relative abundance = 0.755 and 0.245
Average atomic mass
$= (34.97 \times 0.755) + (36.97 \times 0.245)$
$= 35.46\,g$
So, option (d) is correct.

2. (c) Consider, the percentage of isotope with atomic weight (A) $10.01 = x$
The percentage of isotopes with atomic weight $(B) 11.01 = 100 - x$
Average atomic weight
$$= \frac{10.01x + (100 - x) \times 11.01}{100}$$
$$10.81 = \frac{10.01x + 1101 - 11.01x}{100}$$
$$10.81 = \frac{1101 - x}{100}$$
or $1101 - x = 1081$
or $x = 1101 - 1081 = 20$
% of isotope with atomic weight 10.01 = 20%
% of isotope with atomic weight 11.01 = 80%
Hence, option (c) is correct.

3. (d) (A) is false but (R) is true.
The molecular formula of ethene is C_2H_4 and its empirical formula is CH_2.
Molecular mass
$= 2 \times$ Empirical mass,
Molecular formula
$= (\text{Empirical formula})_2$.

4. (c) Statements (a), (b) and (d) are correct but (c) is incorrect because average atomic mass depends upon the atomic mass of different isotopes and their fractional abundances.

5. (c) A is true but R is false. It is because an atom of sodium is 23 times heavier than $\frac{1}{12}$ th of the mass of an atom of C-12 isotope.

6. (a) Morphine $= \frac{14}{285.34} \times 100$
$= 4.9\%$
(Molecular mass of morphine = 285.34)
LSD $= \frac{3 \times 14}{323} \times 100 = 13\%$
(Molecular mass of LSD = 323)
Phencylidine $= \frac{14}{243} \times 100 = 5.76\%$
(Molecular mass of phencylidine = 243)
Heroine $= \frac{14}{369} \times 100 = 3.79\%$
Thus, LSD has maximum percentage of nitrogen by mass.
Hence, option (a) is correct.

7. (b) Compound equivalent mass $\left(E = \frac{M}{n}\right)$
HBr $(n = 1) \longrightarrow \frac{80.91}{1} \simeq 80.91$
NaCl $(n = 1) \longrightarrow \frac{58.5}{1} = 58.5$
NH_3 $(n = 1) \longrightarrow \frac{17}{1} = 17$
KOH $(n = 1) \longrightarrow \frac{56.10}{1} \approx 56.10$
So, correct match is A-II, B-III, C-IV, D-1.

8. (d) Both Statement I and Statement II are correct.

9. (d) All statements are correct.
I. n-factor = 6 $[Ca_3(PO_4)_2]$
$\therefore$ Eq. wt. = Mol. wt /6
II. n-factor = 3 $[Na_3(PO_4)]$
$\therefore$ Eq. wt. = Mol. wt. /3
III. n-factor = 2$[K_2SO_4]$
$\therefore$ Eq. wt. = Mol. wt. /2
IV. n-factor = 8$[K_2SO_4Al_2(SO_4)_3]$
$\therefore$ Eq. wt. = Mol. wt. /8
V. n-factor = 5$[KMnO_4$ in acidic medium]
Hence, option (d) is correct.

10. (b) Weight of oxide
$= 0.2075 - 0.1475$
$= 0.06\,g$

Mole of Co $= \frac{0.1475}{59} = 0.0025$

Mole of O $= \frac{0.06}{16} = 0.00375$

Simplest ratio of Co $= \frac{0.0025}{0.0025} = 1.0$

Simplest ratio of O $= \frac{0.00375}{0.0025} = 1.5$

Ratio of Co : O

1 : 1.5

or 2 : 3

So, the formula of the compound is Co_2O_3

11. (b) $\mathbf{Al_2(SO_4)_3}$, Valency factor = 6

Equivalent mass $= \frac{\text{Molecular weight}}{6}$

$\mathbf{BaSO_4}$, Valency factor = 2

Equivalent mass $= \frac{\text{Molecular weight}}{2}$

$\mathbf{AlCl_3}$, Valency factor = 3

Equivalent mass $= \frac{\text{Molecular weight}}{3}$

$\mathbf{H_3PO_4}$, (structure: P with oxidation state +3, double-bonded O (−2), and three OH groups, H +1, O −1)

Valency factor = 3

Equivalent mass $= \frac{\text{Molecular weight}}{3}$

$\mathbf{H_2O}$, Valency factor = 1

Equivalent mass $= \frac{\text{Molecular weight}}{1}$

Hence, two species (H_3PO_4, $AlCl_3$) have valency factor = 3

12. (c)

	C	H	O
Moles	$\frac{9}{12}$	$\frac{1}{1}$	$\frac{3.5}{14}$
	$\frac{3}{4}$	1	$\frac{1}{4}$
Simplest whole number	3	4	1

Empirical formula (E.F) = C_3H_4N

Empirical formula mass = 54

Molecular formula mass

= Empirical formula mass × n

$n = \frac{108}{54} = 2$

So, molecular formula

$= (C_3H_4N)_2 = C_6H_8N_2$

Thus, option (c) is correct.

13. (a) Percentage yield of 1st step = 70%

That means, the formation of $CaCO_3$ is 70% of $CaCl_2$.

Percentage yield of second step = 65%

That means the formation of CaO is 65% of $CaCO_3$.

The overall percentage yield for producing CaO from $CaCl_2$.

$= 0.7 \times 0.65 \times 100$

$= 45.5\%$

Hence, option (a) is correct.

14. (a) Molar mass of $K_2SO_4 \cdot Al_2(SO_4)_3 \cdot 24H_2O = 948$ g

Mass % of $K_2SO_4 = \frac{174}{948} \times 100$

$= 18.35\%$

Mass % of $Al_2(SO_4)_3 = \frac{342}{948} \times 100$

$= 36.07\%$

Mass % of $H_2O = \frac{432}{948} \times 100$

$= 45.56\%$

Mass % of $SO_4^{2-} = \frac{384}{948} \times 100$

$= 40.50\%$

Hence, the correct match is A-IV, B-III, C-II, D-I.

15. (a)

Element	%	Moles	Mole ratio
C	70.6	$\frac{70.6}{12} = 5.88$	$\frac{5.88}{0.84} = 7$
H	4.2	$\frac{4.2}{1} = 4.2$	$\frac{4.2}{0.84} = 5$
N	11.8	$\frac{11.8}{14} = 0.84$	$\frac{0.84}{0.84} = 1$
O	13.4	$\frac{13.4}{16} = 0.837$	$\frac{0.837}{0.84} = 0.99 \approx 1$

Thus, the formula is C_7H_5NO.

Test-3

1. (d)

$MgCO_3(s) \longrightarrow MgO(s) + CO_2(g)$

Moles of $MgCO_3 = \frac{40}{84} = 0.476$ mol

From the above equation, 1 mole of $MgCO_3$ gives 1 mole of MgO

$\therefore$ 0.476 mole of $MgCO_3$ = 19.04 g of MgO

Practical yield of MgO = 16 g MgO

$\therefore$ % Purity $= \frac{16}{19.04} \times 100 = 84\%$

2. (d) 16 mL of CH_3OH is dissolved in 100 mL of solution.

Volume and mass of

$H_2O = 100 - 16 = 84$ mL

$= 84$ g

(since, $d_{H_2O} = 1$ g/mL)

Mass of solution $= V_{sol} \times d_{sol}$

$= 100 \times 0.9 = 90$ g

Mass of weight of solute

$(W_2) = W_{sol} - W_1 = 90 - 84 = 6$ g

Molar mass of $CH_3OH = 32$ g/mol

$\therefore M = \frac{W_2 \times 1000}{MW_2 \times V_{sol}} = \frac{6 \times 1000}{32 \times 100}$

$= 1.875$ M

$\therefore m = \frac{W_2 \times 1000}{MW_2 \times W_1} = \frac{6 \times 1000}{32 \times 84}$

$= 2.232$ m

Hence, option (d) is correct.

3. (b) $n_{H_2} = \frac{64}{2} = 32$ mol

$n_{O_2} = \frac{64}{32} = 2$ mol

1 mole of O_2 requires = 2 moles of H_2

2 mole of O_2 requires = 4 moles of H_2

Since, H_2 is present in excess, therefore O_2 is the limiting reagent.

2 moles of O_2 = 4 moles of $H_2O = 4 \times 18 = 72$ g H_2O

Moles of H_2 left = 32 − 4

= 28 mol = 28 × 2

= 56 g H_2

So, II and III statements are correct.

Hence, option (b) is correct.

4. (a) The correct match is
A-III, B-IV, C-I, D-II.

A. $\underset{1.0\text{ g}}{2H_2} + \underset{1.0\text{ g}}{O_2} \longrightarrow 2H_2O$

$\frac{1}{4}$ mol $\frac{1}{32}$ mol

O_2 is the limiting reagent.

1 mole of O_2 = 2 mole of H_2O

$\frac{1}{32} = \frac{x}{36}$

$\Rightarrow x = 1.125$ g

B. $\underset{1.0\text{ g}}{N_2} + \underset{1.0\text{ g}}{3H_2} \longrightarrow 2NH_3$

$\frac{1}{28}$ mol $\frac{1}{6}$ mol

N_2 is the limiting reagent

$\frac{1}{28}$ mol of $N_2 = \frac{x}{34}$ mol of NH_3

$x = \frac{34}{28} = 1.214$ g

C. $\underset{1.0\text{ g}}{CaCO_3} \xrightarrow{\Delta} CaO + CO_2$

$\frac{1}{100}$ mol $\frac{1}{56}$ mol $\frac{1}{44}$ mol

$\frac{1}{100} = \frac{x}{56}$

$\Rightarrow \quad x = 0.56$ g

D. $\underset{1.0\text{ g}}{C} + \underset{1.0\text{ g}}{2H_2} \longrightarrow CH_4$

$\frac{1}{12}$ mol $\frac{1}{4}$ mol

C is the limiting reagent.

$\therefore \frac{1}{12}$ mol of $C = \frac{x}{16}$ mol of CH_4

$x = \frac{16}{12} = 1.333$ g

5. (a) We know that,

$$\text{Molality} = \frac{\text{moles of solute}}{\text{mass of solvent (in kg)}}$$

The given solution is 0.5 molal, that means 1000 g H_2O has 0.5 moles (41 g) of sodium acetate.

Total mass of solution = 1041 g

Thus, 0.5 mol of sodium acetate is in 1041 g solution.

Hence, 0.150 mol of sodium acetate is in $= \frac{1041}{0.5} \times 0.15$

$= 312.3$ g solution

6. (c) Molality and mole fraction involves only mass and do not depend upon volume.

So, these are independent of temperature. Rest other quantities are temperature dependent.

Hence, option (c) is correct.

7. (c) I. 1 molecule of $O_2 = \frac{32}{6.023 \times 10^{23}}$

$= 5.313 \times 10^{-23}$ g

II. 1 atom of $N_2 = \frac{14}{6.023 \times 10^{23}}$

$= 2.32 \times 10^{-23}$ g

III. 1 mole of $H_2O = 18$ g

IV. Weight of Fe = 10^{-10} g

So, the correct order is

II < I < IV < III

8. (d) Specific gravity = 1.12 g/mL

Specific gravity

$= \frac{\text{Density of NaCl}}{\text{Density of } H_2O}$

Density of NaCl = Specific gravity × Density of H_2O

$= 1.12 \times 1 = 1.12$ g/mL

50% $\left(\frac{w}{V}\right)$ NaCl soluton

= 50 g NaCl in 100 mL solution

58.5 g NaCl

$= \frac{100 \times 58.5}{50}$ mL solution

= 117 mL solution

$$\text{Density} = \frac{\text{Mass}}{\text{Volume}}$$

Mass = Density × Volume

$= 1.12 \times 117 = 131.04$ g

Therefore, in ppm

$= \frac{\text{Mass of solute} \times 10^6}{\text{Mass of solution}}$

$= \frac{58.5 \times 10^6}{131.04} = 0.445 \times 10^6$

$= 4.45 \times 10^5$ ppm

Hence, option (d) is the correct answer.

9. (a) 106 g Na_2CO_3 = 1 mole

= 1 g atom C

12 g C = 1 g atom of C

1 g C contains = 6.023×10^{23} carbon atoms.

So, both A and R are true and R is the correct explanation of A.

10. (d) Calculation of O_2 gas required to burn 112 L of CO.

$$\underset{\substack{1\text{ mol}\\=22.4\text{ L}}}{CO} + \underset{0.5\text{ mol}}{\frac{1}{2}O_2} \longrightarrow \underset{1\text{ mol}}{CO_2}$$

22.4 L of CO at NTP require O_2

= 0.5 mol

112 L of CO at NTP will require

$O_2 = \frac{0.5}{22.4} \times 112 = 2.5$ mol

This O_2 is to be obtained by heating $KClO_3$.

$$\underset{2\text{ mol}}{2KClO_3} \longrightarrow 2\,KCl + \underset{3\text{ mol}}{3O_2}$$

$2(39 + 35.5 + 3 \times 16) = 245$ g

3 mole of O_2 are produced from $KClO_3 = 245$ g

2.5 moles of O_2 will be produced from $KClO_3$.

$= \frac{245 \times 2.5}{3} = 204.1679 \approx 204$ g

11. (a)

$$\underset{\substack{2\text{ mol}\\2\times 22400\text{ cm}^3}}{2C_2H_2} + \underset{\substack{5\text{ mol}\\5\times 22400\text{ cm}^3}}{5O_2} \rightarrow \underset{\substack{4\text{ mol}\\4\times 22400\text{ cm}^3}}{4CO_2} + 2H_2O$$

$\therefore 2 \times 22400$ cm^3 of acetylene require O_2 for complete combustion = 5×22400 cm^3

200 cm^3 of acetylene will require O_2 for complete combustion

$= \frac{5 \times 22400}{2 \times 22400} \times 200$

= 500 cm^3 at STP

Further, 2×22400 cm^3 of acetylene produce CO_2

$= 4 \times 22400$ cm^3

200 cm^3 of acetylene will produce

$CO_2 = \frac{4 \times 22400}{2 \times 22400} \times 200$

= 400 cm^3 at STP.

12. (d) Four species, i.e. 7 g CO, 11 g CO_2, 8 g O_2 and 16 g SO_2 have same number of moles

$8 \text{ g } O_2 = \frac{8}{32} \text{ mol} = 0.25 \text{ mol}$

$7 \text{ g CO} = \frac{7}{28} \text{ mol} = 0.25 \text{ mol}$

$14 \text{ g } N_2 = \frac{14}{28} = 0.5 \text{ mol}$

$11 \text{ g } CO_2 = \frac{11}{44} = 0.25 \text{ mol}$

$16 \text{ g } SO_2 = \frac{16}{64} = 0.25 \text{ mol}$

13. (a) For the given condition, the balanced chemical equation is

$$\underset{24\text{ g}}{Mg} + \underset{16\text{ g}}{\frac{1}{2}O_2} \longrightarrow \underset{40\text{ g}}{MgO}$$

As 24 g Mg reacts with 16g O_2

2.0 g Mg reacts with $\frac{16 \times 2}{24}$ g O_2

which is equal to 1.33 g .

But, only 0.65g of O_2 is available.

Thus, O_2 is the limiting reagent.

16 g of O_2 react with 24g of Mg.

$\because$ 0.65 g of O_2 will react with Mg

$= \frac{24}{16} \times 0.65 = 0.975$ g.

Amount of Mg left unreacted

$= 2.0 - 0.975 = 1.025$ g Mg

Hence, Mg is present in excess and 1.025 g Mg is left behind unreacted.

14. (a) As we know that,

Normality = Molarity × Valence factor (n)

Valence factor (n) of $H_2SO_4 = 2$

Molarity, $(M) = \frac{0.02}{2} = 0.01$ M

Moles of $H_2SO_4 = \frac{0.01 \times 250}{1000}$

$= 2.5 \times 10^{-3}$ mol

$\left[\text{As, molarity} = \frac{\text{Number of moles of solute}}{\text{Volume of solution (mL)}} \times 1000\right]$

Number of molecules in 250 mL of 0.02 N H_2SO_4

$= 2.5 \times 10^{-3} \times N_A$

$= 2.5 \times 10^{-3} \times 6.023 \times 10^{23}$

$= 15.0575 \times 10^{20}$ molecules

15. (a) Among the given statements I, III and IV are incorrect.

Their correct statements are

I. Sum of mole fraction of all components of mixture is always equal to 1.

III. In molality amount of solvent are measured in terms of mass (kg).

IV. Formality is the concentration term used particulary for ionic compounds.

Chapter Break Thru

1. (d) Statements (a), (b), (c) are correct but (d) is incorrect.

We know that,

I pound $= 454 \times 10^{-3}$ kg

Unit factor $= \frac{454 \times 10^{-3}}{1 \text{pound}}$ kg

$10 \text{ pound} = \frac{10 \text{pound} \times 454 \times 10^{-3}}{1 \text{pound}}$

$= 454 \times 10^{-2}$ kg

$= 4.54$ kg

So, In S.I unit 10 pounds is equal to 4.54 kg.

2. (b) II and III statements are incorrect because

- The SI unit of measurement of volume of liquid is cubic meter.
- The unit of work done is represented by kg m^2s^{-2}.

3. (d) Dry ice is compound. Air, aerated drink, brass and diesel are mixture. So, four species are mixture.

Hence, option (d) is correct.

4. (c) II and III have same number of significant number as 3.

$6.023 \times 10^{23} = 4$ (significant figures)

$7.70 \times 10^{-20} = 3$ (significant figures)

7.50 = 3 (significant figures)

0.75 = 2 (significant figures)

0.92 = 2 (significant figures)

Hence, option (c) is correct.

5. (c) MgO and $Mg(OH)_2$ do not follow the law of multiple proportion because $Mg(OH)_2$ contains a hydrogen atom in addition to Mg and O-atoms.

For multiple proportion law to apply, types of atoms in the molecules must be same.

6. (d)

	First oxide	Second oxide
Sulphur	50 %	40 %
Oxygen	50 %	60 %

In first oxide, 1 part oxygen combine with sulphur 50/50 = 1

Similarly, for second oxide

$\frac{40}{60} = 0.67$

So, the ratio is 1 : 0.67 or 3 : 2

7. (b) $X = 50$ % $\quad Y = 50$ %

$X : Y = 5 : 2.5$

Hence, the simplest ratio is 2 : 1.

So, the formula of compound is X_2Y.

So, option (b) is correct.

8. (c) 0.1653 g of Al reacts with 0.652 g of chlorine

$27 \text{ g of Al} = \frac{0.652}{0.1653} \times 27$

= 106.49 g of chlorine

Moles of chlorine

$= \frac{106.49}{35.5} = 2.999 \approx 3$

Thus, simplest formula is $AlCl_3$.

Molecular mass is 267 g mol^{-1}.

Empirical formula weight of $AlCl_3$.

$= 27 + 3 \times 35.5 = 133.5$

$n = \frac{\text{Molecular mass}}{\text{Empirical formula mass}}$

$= \frac{267}{133.5} = 2$

So, molecular formula $= (AlCl_3)_2$

$= Al_2Cl_6$

Thus, option (c) is correct.

9. (d) Molecular formula of zinc phosphate is $Zn_3(PO_4)_2$

$= 65.38 \times 3 + 2(31 + 16 \times 4)$

$= 196.14 + 2 \times 95 = 386.14$

$\% \text{ of Zn} = \frac{196.14 \times 100}{386.14} = 50.80\%$

$\% \text{ of P} = \frac{62 \times 100}{386.14} = 16.05\%$

$\% \text{ of O} = \frac{128 \times 100}{386.14} = 33.15\%$

So, option (d) is correct.

10. (c) Balance the equation,

$$\underset{1\text{ mmol}}{BrO_3^-} + \underset{5\text{ mmol}}{5Br^-} \longrightarrow \underset{3\text{ mmol}}{3Br_2} + 3H_2O$$

$50 \times 0.1 = 5$ mmol $30 \times 0.5 = 15$ mmol

Here, Br^- is the limiting reagent.

5 mmol of Br^- gives 3 mmol of Br_2.

15 mmol of Br^- gives

$\frac{3 \times 15}{5} = 9$ mmol

$= 9 \times 10^{-3}$ mol.

11. (b) Statement I is correct but Statement II is incorrect because volume of a gas is directly proportional to its moles at a particular temperature and pressure.

12. (b) From the reaction,

$CaCO_3 + 2HCl \longrightarrow CaCl_2 + CO_2 + H_2O$

100 g $CaCO_3$ requires 73 g HCl

10 g $CaCO_3$ requires 7.3 g HCl

Mass of HCl left unreacted

$= 10 - 7.3 = 2.7$ g

Hence, $CaCO_3$ is the limiting reagent, since it is completely consumed in the reaction and $CaCO_3$ will decide the amount of product formed.

100 g $CaCO_3$ gives 44 g CO_2.

So, 10 g $CaCO_3$ gives 4.4 g CO_2.

Thus, option (b) is correct.

13. (c) Statements (a), (b) and (d) are correct but statement (c) is incorrect because one atomic mass unit is equal to $\frac{1}{12}$th of the mass of an atom of carbon-12 isotopes.

14. (d) All statements I, II, III, IV and V are correct.

I. Mass of $KClO_3 = 4.90$ kg

Total mass of product ($KCl + O_2$)

$= 2.96 + 1.92 = 4.88$ g

Difference of mass

$= 4.90 - 4.88 = 0.02$ g

Illustrate law of conservation of mass.

II. $\underset{17.0\text{ g}}{AgNO_3} + \underset{5.85\text{ g}}{NaCl} \longrightarrow \underset{14.35\text{ g}}{AgCl} + \underset{8.5\text{ g}}{NaNO_3}$

Mass of reactant = Mass of product

$= 22.85$ g

Illustrate law of conservation of mass

III. $\underset{4.2\text{ g}}{NaHCO_3} + \underset{10.0\text{ g}}{CH_3COOH} \longrightarrow \underbrace{CH_3COONa + H_2O}_{12.0\text{ g}} + \underset{2.2\text{ g}}{CO_2}$

Mass of reactant = Mass of product

$= 14.2$ g

So, illustrate law of conservation of mass.

Statements IV and V are facts of law of conservation of mass.

15. (c) In (a), number of atoms

$= \frac{0.5}{63.5} \times 6.023 \times 10^{23}$

$= 4.742 \times 10^{21}$ atoms of Cu

In (b) number of atoms

$= \frac{0.635}{63.5} \times 6.023 \times 10^{23}$

$= 6.023 \times 10^{21}$ atoms of Cu

In (c) number of atoms

$= 0.25 \times 6.023 \times 10^{23}$

$= 1.506 \times 10^{23}$ atoms of Cu

In (d) number of atoms

$= \frac{1}{63.5} \times 6.023 \times 10^{23}$

$= 0.016 \times 6.023 \times 10^{23}$

$= 9.63 \times 10^{21}$ atoms of Cu

So, 0.25 moles of Cu has largest number of atoms.

Thus, option (c) is correct.

16. (b) 3.2 g of $O_2 = \frac{3.2}{32} = 0.1$ mole

$= 0.1 \times 6.023 \times 10^{23}$ molecules

$= 6.023 \times 10^{22}$ molecules

$= 6.023 \times 10^{22} \times 16$ electrons

$= 9.635 \times 10^{23}$ electrons.

17. (d) 1 electron has weight

$= 9.108 \times 10^{-31}$ kg

1 mole of electrons

$= 9.108 \times 10^{-31} \times 6.023 \times 10^{23}$ kg of electrons

1 kg of electrons

$= \frac{1}{9.108 \times 6.023} \times 10^8$ mole

18. (b) Both (A) and (R) are true but (R) is not the correct explanation of (A). The correct explanation is based on law of constant proportion.

So, option (b) is correct.

19. (d) Limiting reagent is F_2

$2NH_3 + 5F_2 \longrightarrow N_2F_4 + 6HF$

190 g NH_3 give 104 g N_2F_4

8 gram will give $= \frac{104}{190} \times 8$

$= 4.379$ g of N_2F_4

$\% \text{ yield} = \frac{3.56}{4.379} \times 100 = 81.30\%$

So, option (d) is correct.

20. (a) $\frac{\text{Eq. wt. of metal hydroxide}}{\text{Eq. wt. of metal oxide}}$

$= \frac{\text{wt. of metal hydroxide}}{\text{wt. of metal oxide}}$

$\frac{E + 17}{E + 8} = \frac{7.4}{5.6}$

$(E + 17) \times 5.6 = (E + 8)\, 7.4$

or $\quad 1.8E = 36$

or $\quad E = 20$

21. (d) Number of moles of H_3PO_4

$= \frac{\text{Mass}}{\text{Molar mass}} = \frac{196}{98} = 2$

Gram equivalent $= 2 \times 3$ (due to tribasic acid) $= 6$

So, number of moles and gram equivalent in 196 g of H_3PO_4 are 2 and 6 respectively.

22. (a) $\frac{(29.2 - 20.2)(1.79 \times 10^5)}{1.37}$

$= \frac{9.0 \times 1.79 \times 10^5}{1.37}$

As least precise term 9.0 has only two significant figures, hence the result will also contain two significant figures.

23. (d) Both Statement I and Statement II are correct.

24. (a) n-factor for $O_2 = 4$

Volume strength of $H_2O_2 = \frac{24}{4} = 6$

6 volume strength (V.S) of $H_2O_2 = 1N\, H_2O_2$

6 VS of H_2O_2 × Vol. of H_2O_2 = Vol. of O_2

VS of $H_2O_2 \times 100\ cm^3 = 3\ dm^3$

VS of $H_2O_2 \times 0.1 dm^3 = 3 dm^3$

VS of $H_2O_2 = 30 dm^3$ or L

6 VS of $H_2O_2 = 1N$

$30\ VS\ of\ H_2O_2 = \frac{1\times 30}{6} = 5N$

Molarity (M) of $H_2O_2 = \frac{5}{2} = 2.5\,M$

[$\because$ Normality $= n \times$ Molarity]

25. (d) We know that,

Molality and mole fraction relationship given by,

$$m = \frac{x_2 \times 1000}{(1-x_2)\times MW_1}$$

$$3 = \frac{x_2 \times 1000}{(1-x_2)\times 18}$$

So, $x_2 = 0.05$

Hence, option (d) is correct.

26. (b) All statements about Dalton's atomic theory are correct except (V) because all atoms of a given element always have identical properties.

Hence, option (b) is correct.

27. (c) We know that,

$M_1V_1 = M_2V_2$

$$\left(M_1 = \frac{\text{Mass\%} \times 10 \times d}{\text{Molecular mass}}\right)$$

$$V_1 \times \frac{90\times 10\times 1.8}{98} = 0.2\times 1L$$

So, $V_1 = 0.012\ L = 12\ mL$

28. (a) In given reaction (I),

$X + 2Y \longrightarrow XY_2$

0.1 mole of $XY_2 = 10\,g$

1 mole of $XY_2 = 100\,g$ or $\frac{10}{0.1}$

In given reaction (II),

$3X + 2Y \longrightarrow X_3Y_2$

0.05 mole of $X_3Y_2 = 9\,g$

1 mole of $X_3Y_2 = \frac{9}{0.05} = 180\,g$

$\therefore X + 2Y = 100$

$3X + 2Y = 180$

M. wt. of $XY_2 = 100$

M. wt. of $X_3Y_2 = 180$

Solve for X and Y

$X = 40\,g$ and $Y = 30\,g$

Hence, option (a) is correct.

29. (a) Both (A) and (R) are correct and (R) is the correct explanation of (A) because equal number of molecules are present when moles are same, for the same mass the molecular weight has to be same.

Hence, molecular weight of N_2 = Molecular weight of CO = 28 g

Molecular weight of N_2O = Molecular weight of CO_2 = 44 g

30. (d)

Element	%	At. mass	Relative no. of atoms	Simplest ratio
C	38.71	12	$\frac{38.71}{12} = 3.22$	$\frac{3.22}{3.22} = 1$
H	9.67	1	$\frac{9.67}{1} = 9.67$	$\frac{9.67}{3.22} = 3$
O	51.62	16	$\frac{51.62}{16} = 3.22$	$\frac{3.22}{3.22} = 1$

Hence, empirical formula is CH_3O.

31. (c) Equal volume of different gases contain equal number of molecule at STP.

500 mL of CO_2 at STP will contain $= 6.00 \times 10^{23}$ molecule

100 mL of CO_2 at STP will contain

$$= \frac{6.00\times 10^{23}}{500} \times 100$$

$= 1.2 \times 10^{23}$ molecule

Thus, option (c) is correct.

32. (b) $H_2 + \frac{1}{2}O_2 \longrightarrow H_2O$

2g 16 g 18 g

10 g H_2 require $O_2 = 80\,g$ which is not present

64 g O_2 contains 8 g of H_2 and H_2 left = 2g

Thus, O_2 is the limiting reactant and H_2 is excess reactant.

Hence, H_2O formed from 64 g of O_2

$= \frac{18}{16} \times 64 = 72\,g = \frac{72}{18}$ mol

$= 4$ mol

Thus, option (b) is correct.

33. (d) Mass of product = Mass of reactant. Hence, mass will remain same.

So, option (d) is correct.

34. (b) According to law of reciprocal proportions, if certain masses of two different element A and B combines separately with a fixed mass of another element C, then the ratio of those certain masses of A and B is either, one or a simple multiple of the ratio of the masses of A and B combining with each other.

Carbon and oxygen combine to form CO_2. They also combine separately with H to form CH_4 and H_2O respectively.

Ratio of masses of C to O in CO_2

$= \frac{12}{32} = 3:8$ (C:O)

Ratio of masses in CH_4

$= \frac{12}{4} = 3:1$ (C:H)

Ratio of the masses of O and H combining with fixed mass in H_2O.

$= 16:2 = 8:1$

Ratio of C and O in CH_4 and H_2O

$= \frac{3:1}{8:1} = 3:8$

This is same to the ratio of C and O in CO_2.

35. (d) Statements (B), (C), (D) are incorrect.

$$nP_4 = \frac{1.24}{31\times 4} = 0.01\ \text{mole}$$

$$nO_2 = \frac{8}{32} = 0.25\ \text{moles}$$

In reaction (I), moles of O_2 required

$= 0.01$ mol of $P_4 \times \frac{5 \text{ mole } O_2}{\text{Mole of } P_4}$

$= 0.01 \times 5 = 0.05$ mole

Since, there is more O_2 present than required.

Therefore, P_4 is the limiting quantity. Hence, statement B is incorrect.

Molecular weight of $P_4O_{10} = 284$ g/mol

So, P_4O_{10} in terms of mass

$= n \times$ mol. wt.

$= 0.01 \times 284 = 2.84$ g

Hence, (C) is incorrect.

Molecular weight of $P_4O_6 = 220$ g/mol

So, P_4O_6 in terms of mass

$= n \times$ mol. wt.

$= 0.01 \times 220 = 2.2$ g

Hence, (B), (C), (D) are incorrect.

36. (b) Molecular weight of $CaCO_3 = 40 + 12 + 48 = 100$ g

Moles of 10 g $CaCO_3 = \frac{10}{100}$

0.1 mole = 0.1 g atom

Thus, option (b) is correct.

37. (b) Formula of M_2O_3 is

First oxide	Second oxide
O = 32%	O = 51.2%
M = 68%	M = 48.8%

Let the atomic weight of the metal $= M$ g

$(2M + 51.2)$ g of M_2O_3 contains $= 2M$ g of metal 100 g of M_2O_3 contains

$$= \left(\frac{2M}{2M + 51.2}\right) \times 100 = 68$$

$200M = (2M + 51.2) \times 68$

$M = 54.4$

Therefore, in second oxide,

$$O = \frac{51.2}{16} = 3.2 \approx 3$$

$$M = \frac{54.4}{48.8} = 1.11 \approx 1$$

Therefore, the formula of the second oxide is $= MO_3$.

38. (b) We know that,

Specific heat × Atomic weight $= 6.4$

$$\text{Atomic weight} = \frac{6.4}{\text{specific heat}}$$

$$= \frac{6.4}{0.25} = 25.6$$

Atomic weight = Eq.wt. × Valency $= 25.6$

$$\text{Valency} = \frac{\text{Atomic weight}}{\text{Eq. wt.}} = \frac{25.6}{12}$$

$= 2.13 \approx 2$

(Valency is always a whole number)

39. (d) $M = \frac{\% \text{ by weight} \times 10 \times d}{MW_2}$

$$= \frac{36.5 \times 10 \times 1.2}{36.5} = 12 \text{ M}$$

$$m = \frac{36.5 \times 1000}{36.5 \times (100 - 36.5)}$$

$$= \frac{1000}{63.5} = 15.7 \text{ m}$$

40. (a) $C_3H_8 + 5O_2 \longrightarrow 3CO_2 + 4H_2O$

$C_4H_{10} + 6\frac{1}{2}O_2 \longrightarrow 4CO_2 + 5H_2O$

Consider propane $= x$ L

Then, butane $= (3 - x)$ L

1 L C_3H_8 gives 3 L of CO_2 and 1 L C_4H_{10} gives 4 L of CO_2

Hence, CO_2 produced

$= 3x + 4(3 - x)$

$12 - x = 10$ (given)

Hence, $x = 2$ L (propane)

butane = 1 L

Hence, option (a) is correct.

41. (c) Time taken $= \frac{6.023 \times 10^{23}}{10,00,000}$

$= 6.023 \times 10^{17}$ s

$$= \frac{6.023 \times 10^{17}}{60 \times 60 \times 24 \times 365} \text{ years}$$

$= 1.9089 \times 10^{10}$ years

42. (d) Both Statement I and Statement II are correct. Calomel is a chemical with formula Hg_2Cl_2. Hg_2Cl_2. Atomic weight of Hg and Cl are = 200.59 u and 35.5 u respectively.

∴ Ratio of weight of Hg and Cl

$$= \frac{2 \times 200.59}{2 \times 35.5} = 5.6$$

43. (b) Relative number of moles of Fe in iron oxide

$$= \frac{69.9}{56} = 1.25$$

Relative no. of moles of oxygen in iron oxide.

$$= \frac{30.1}{16} = 1.88$$

Simplest molar ratio of

Fe : O = 1.25 : 1.88 = 1 : 1.5 = 2 : 3

∴ Empirical formula = Fe_2O_3

44. (a) Let mass of metal combined $= wg$

equivalent mass of oxygen = 8

equivalent of oxygen $= \frac{0.200}{8}$

Equivalent of halogen of

equivalent mass $(E) = \frac{3.17}{E}$

$$\therefore \quad \frac{0.200}{8} = \frac{3.17}{E}$$

$$E = \frac{3.17 \times 8}{0.200}$$

$= 126.8 \text{ g eq}^{-1} \approx 127 \text{ g eq}^{-1}$

45. (a) The correct match is A-I, B-IV, C-II, D-III.

A. $\overset{+7}{Mn}O_4^- \longrightarrow Mn^{+2}$

$n = 5$ So, eq.wt. $= \frac{M}{5}$

M = Molar mass

B. $H_3PO_2 \longrightarrow H_2PO_2^- + H^{\oplus}$

$n = 1$, So, eq. wt. $= \frac{M}{1} = M$

C. $2H_2\overset{-1}{O_2} \longrightarrow 2H_2O + \overset{(0)}{O_2}$

$n = 2$, So, eq. wt. $= \frac{M}{2}$

D. $\overset{(0)}{N_2} + 3H_2 \longrightarrow 2\overset{-3}{N}H_3$

$n = 6$, So, eq. wt. $= \frac{M}{6}$

46. (d) $\underset{0.112\,dm^3}{X} + O_2 \longrightarrow CO_2 + H_2O$

No. of moles of $X = \frac{0.112}{22.4}$

$= 5\times10^{-3}$ moles

No. of moles of $CO_2 = \frac{0.88}{44}$

$= 0.02$ moles

No. of atoms of C in 1 molecule of

$X = \frac{0.02}{5\times10^{-3}} = 4$

47. (a) $M = \frac{W_2 \times 1000}{MW_2 \times V_{sol}}$

$= \frac{410.3\times1000}{98\times1000} = 4.186\,M$

$m = \frac{W_2 \times 1000}{MW_2 \times (V\times d - W_2)}$

$= \frac{410.3\times1000}{98\times(1000\times1.243-410.3)}$

$= \frac{410.3\times1000}{98\times832.7}$

$= 5.027$ m

Hence, option (a) is correct.

48. (c) Mass of NaCl in 10 g salt

$= 10\times\frac{95}{100} = 9.5\,g$

Number of molecules of NaCl

$= \frac{9.5}{58.5}\times6.023\times10^{23}$

$= 9.78\times10^{22} \approx 10\times10^{22} \approx 10^{23}$

49. (a) Both (A) and (R) are true and (R) is the correct explanation of (A).

50. (a) From given,

$N_2 \equiv 2NH_3 \equiv 3H_2 \equiv 6H$

Equivalent weight of

$N_2 = \frac{x_2}{6} = y_2$

Equivalent weight of

$NH_3 = \frac{2x_1}{6} = y_1$

$\therefore y_1 - y_2 = \left(\frac{2x_1}{6} - \frac{x_2}{6}\right)$

$= \frac{2x_1 - x_2}{6}$

Thus, option (a) is correct.

Ch-2 Structure of Atom

Topical Follow Thru

Test-1

1. (b) The charge to mass ratio (e/m) of the particles in the cathode is independent of the nature of gas taken in the discharge tube or the nature of the cathode.

Thus, option (b) is incorrect statement.

2. (b) Sulphide ion can be represented as S^{2-}

Number of protons = 16
Number of electrons = 18
Number of neutrons = 16

So, option (b) is correct.

3. (c) R. A Millikan advised a method known as oil drop experiment to determine the charge on the electrons.

So, Statement I is incorrect but Statement II is correct.

4. (c) Statement given in option (c) is incorrect. Its correct form is they travel in mutually perpendicular planes.

5. (b) Among the given statements only II, III, IV and V are correct but Statement I is incorrect because most of α-particles ($\approx$ 99%) passed through the gold foil are undeflected. A small fraction of the α-particles was deflected by small angle but not a hyperbolic curve deflection.

So, option (b) is correct answer.

6. (b) We know that,

$E = \frac{nhc}{\lambda} = nhc\bar{\nu}$

Where symbols have their usual meanings $\left(\because \bar{\nu} = \frac{1}{\lambda}\right)$

$\therefore\ 10 = nhc\bar{\nu}$ [$\because$ Given]

or $n = \frac{10}{hc\bar{\nu}}$

Hence, option (b) is correct.

7. (b) Among the given radiations only two, i.e. cosmic rays and γ-rays have lower wavelength than the visible light whereas infrared, microwave and radiowave have higher wavelength than the visible light.

So, option (b) is corrrect.

8. (c) Among the given statement only statements IV and V are incorrect. Their corrected form are as:

IV. Proton is a fundamental particles of an atom carrying one unit positive charge and having mass nearly equal to the mass of an atom of hydrogen.

V. For anode rays, e/m ratio is maximum when hydrogen gas used in the discharge tube.

So, option (c) is correct.

9. (d) The correct match is A- IV, B-III, C-II, D-I.

Isobar = ${}^{14}_{6}C$, ${}^{14}_{7}N = 14$ (Mass number same)

Isotone = ${}^{14}_{6}C$, ${}^{16}_{8}O = 8$ (Neutrons are same)

Isotope = ${}^{14}_{6}C$, ${}^{13}_{6}C = 6$ (Protons are same)

Isoelectronic = ${}_{8}O^{2-}$, ${}_{9}F^{-} = 10$ (Electrons are same)

10. (d) Among the given statements, only statements I, II, III and V are correct but statement IV is incorrect. The corrected form of statement IV is as follows,

The velocity of X-ray is same as that of microwave because the velocity of all the electromagnetic waves in a given medium is same.

So, option (d) is correct.

11. (c) KE = (Energy of radiation – Work function)

$$=\left(h\times\frac{c}{\lambda}-4.2\right)$$

$$=\frac{6.6\times10^{-34}\times3\times10^{8}}{2000\times10^{-10}}-(4.2\times1.602\times10^{-19})$$

$$=(9.9\times10^{-19})-(6.7\times10^{-19})$$

$$=3.2\times10^{-19}\text{ J}$$

12. (c) Incorrect statement is given in option (c). Its correct form is atomic models helps to understand the origin and nature of the characteristic of electromagnetic radiation absorbed or emitted by atom.

13. (c) By using $c = \nu\lambda$

where, c is speed of light, ν is the frequency and λ is wavelength.

$$\frac{\nu_1}{\nu_2}=\frac{\lambda_2}{\lambda_1}$$

$$\frac{\nu_1}{\nu_2}=\frac{6.56\times10^{-5}}{4.1\times10^{-5}}=1.6:1$$

Hence, option (c) is correct.

14. (a) We know that,

$$E=\frac{hc}{\lambda}\text{ or }E\propto\frac{1}{\lambda}$$

So, graph between energy of photon and wavelength is hyperbolic.

Hence, option (a) is correct.

15. (a) All radiation in vacuum travel with the same speed $= 3\times10^8$ m/s

Distance travelled from mars to earth 8×10^7 km.

$$=8\times10^7\times10^3\text{ m}$$

$$\text{Time taken}=\frac{8\times10^7\times10^3}{3\times10^8}$$

$$=2.66\times10^2\text{ s}$$

$$=4\text{ min }26\text{ s}$$

So, option (a) is correct.

Test-2

1. (b) H_α line of Balmer series means first line of Balmer series.

$n_1 = 2, n_2 = 3.$

$$\frac{1}{\lambda_\alpha}=R\left(\frac{1}{2^2}-\frac{1}{3^2}\right)=\frac{5R}{36}$$

$$\frac{1}{X}=\frac{5R}{36}$$

$$R=\frac{36}{5X}\quad\text{...(i)}$$

H_β line of Balmer series means second line of Balmer series,

$n_1 = 2, n_2 = 4$

$$\bar{\nu}=\frac{1}{\lambda_\beta}=R\left(\frac{1}{2^2}-\frac{1}{4^2}\right)=\frac{3R}{16}$$

$$\lambda_\beta=\frac{16}{3R}\quad\text{...(ii)}$$

Substituting the value of R from Eq. (i) to Eq. (ii) we get;

$$\lambda_\beta=\frac{16\times5}{3\times36}\times(X)\Rightarrow\lambda_\beta=\frac{80}{108}X\text{Å}$$

Thus, option (b) is correct.

2. (b) Potential energy (P.E.)

$$=-\frac{Ze^2}{r_n}$$

$$\text{Kinetic energy (K.E.)}=\frac{1}{2}\frac{Ze^2}{r_n}$$

$$E_{\text{Total}}=\frac{-Ze^2}{r_n}+\frac{1}{2}\frac{Ze^2}{r_n}=\frac{-Ze^2}{2r_n}$$

$$E_{\text{Total}}=\frac{1}{2}\text{ P.E.}$$

$$\text{K.E.}=-\frac{1}{2}\text{P.E.}$$

$$\frac{\text{K.E.}}{\text{P.E.}}=\frac{1}{2}\frac{Ze^2}{r_n}\Big/-\left(\frac{Ze^2}{r_n}\right)=-\frac{1}{2}$$

So, option (b) is correct.

3. (c) (A) is true but (R) is false as Bohr's theory successfully explain the hydrogen spectrum. It also explain the spectrum of some other one electron system (H like species) such as He^+, Li^{2+}, Be^{3+} etc. Its applicability diminishes for complex atoms, such as carbon and nitrogen due to additional electron-electron interactions.

So, option (c) is correct.

4. (d) We know that,

$$\bar{\nu}_{H_2^+}=k\left(\frac{1}{n_1^2}-\frac{1}{n_2^2}\right)$$

$$\bar{\nu}_{H_2^+}=15200\text{ cm}^{-1}\quad\text{(Given)}$$

$$\bar{\nu}_{Li^{2+}}=?$$

$$\bar{\nu}_{Li^{2+}}=kZ^2\left(\frac{1}{n_1^2}-\frac{1}{n_2^2}\right)$$

$$=3^2\times15200$$

$$=136800\text{ cm}^{-1}$$

So, option (d) is correct.

5. (c) The radius of a hydrogen like atom is given by

$$r=a_0n^2/Z$$

Given that, $a_0 = 5.29\times10^{-11}$ m; $Z = 1, n = 2$

$$r=\frac{(5.29\times10^{-11})\times4}{1}$$

$$r=21{\cdot}16\times10^{-11}\text{ m}$$

6. (b) The correct match is A-II, B-IV, C-I, D-III.

7. (c) We know that,

$$r_n=n^2r_1$$

$$\text{So, }E_n=\frac{-ke^2}{2r_n}=\frac{-ke^2}{2n^2r_1}$$

Thus, E_n is inversely proportional to n^2.

As, r_n increases with n^2, the magnitude of E_n decreases because, $E_n\propto\frac{1}{r_n}$.

So, as r_n increases, $|E_n|$ decreases.

8. (a) We know that,

$$E_n\text{ for }H_2^+=\frac{E_1\times Z^2\text{eV}}{n^2}$$

where, n takes only integer value.

For the first Bohr orbit, $n = 2$

$$E_1=-13.6\text{eV}$$

For H-atom, $n = 2, 3, 4$

$$Z=1$$

$$\text{Thus, }E_2=\frac{-13.6}{4}=-3.4\text{ eV}$$

So, the value is only – 3.4 eV.

Hence, option (a) is correct.

9. (d) Both statement I and Statement II are correct.

We know that,

$$\frac{1}{\lambda}=R_HZ^2\left[\frac{1}{n_1^2}-\frac{1}{n_2^2}\right]$$

For Lyman series, $n_1 = 1$ and $n_2 = 2$ ($\because$ for maximum λ, transition is from very next level)

$$\therefore \frac{1}{\lambda} = 109678 \times (1)^2 \left[\frac{1}{(1)^2} - \frac{1}{(2)^2}\right]$$

$$\frac{1}{\lambda} = \frac{109678 \times 3\,\text{cm}^{-1}}{4}$$

$$\lambda = \frac{4}{3 \times 109678} = 121.56 \times 10^{-7}$$

$$\lambda = 121.56\,\text{nm}$$

10. (d) Energy of nth Bohr orbit (E_n)

$$= -R_H (1/n^2)$$

The energy of second Bohr orbit of hydrogen atom is – 328 kJ/mol.

$$E_2 = -328 = \frac{-R_H}{(2)^2}\,\text{kJ/mol}$$

$$R_H = 1312$$

$$\therefore \quad E_n = \frac{1312}{n^2}\,\text{kJ/mol}$$

For $n = 3$,

$$\therefore \quad E_3 = \frac{-1312}{(3)^2} = -145.8\,\text{kJ/mol.}$$

11. (a) We know that,

$$\Delta E = hc \cdot R_H \left[\frac{1}{n_1^2} - \frac{1}{n_2^2}\right]$$

For lowest energy of spectral line in the Lyman series, $n_1 = 1, n_2 = 2$

Hence, $\Delta E = hc \cdot R_H \left[\frac{1}{1^2} - \frac{1}{2^2}\right]$

$$= \frac{3hcR_H}{4}$$

12. (c) Among the given statements only statement III is correct.
It is because, the Bohr's model is applicable only to hydrogen atom and hydrogen like species, i.e. to one electron system, thus Bohr's model can easily explain the spectrum of any atom or ion containing one electron only.

13. (d) $\frac{1}{\lambda} = \bar{\nu}_H = R_H \left[\frac{1}{n_1^2} - \frac{1}{n_2^2}\right]$

$$= 1.097 \times 10^7 \left[\frac{1}{1^2} - \frac{1}{\infty^2}\right]$$

$$\therefore \quad \lambda = \frac{1}{1.097 \times 10^7} = 9.11 \times 10^{-8}\,\text{m}$$

$$= 91.1 \times 10^{-9}\,\text{m}$$

$$= 91.1\,\text{nm} \approx 91\,\text{nm}$$

$$(\because 1\,\text{nm} = 10^{-9}\,\text{m})$$

14. (b) Ionisation energy of H

$$= 2.18 \times 10^{-18}\ \text{J atom}^{-1}$$

$\therefore E_1$ (energy of Ist orbit of H-atom)

$$= -2.18 \times 10^{-18}\ \text{J atom}^{-1}$$

$$\therefore E_n = \frac{-2.18 \times 10^{-18}}{n^2}\ \text{J atom}^{-1}\ \text{as}$$

$Z = 1$ for H -atom

$$\Delta E = E_3 - E_1$$

$$= \frac{-2.18 \times 10^{-18}}{3^2} - \frac{-2.18 \times 10^{18}}{1^2}$$

$$= -2.18 \times 10^{-18} \times \left[\frac{1}{3^2} - \frac{1}{1^2}\right]$$

$$\Delta E = h\nu = -2.18 \times 10^{-18} \times \left(\frac{-8}{9}\right)$$

$$1.94 \times 10^{-18}\,\text{J/atom}$$

$$\therefore \quad \nu = \frac{\Delta E}{h} = \frac{1.94 \times 10^{-18}\,\text{J/atom}}{6.625 \times 10^{-34}\,\text{Js}}$$

$$= 2.93 \times 10^{15}\,\text{s}^{-1}$$

15. (b) In first excited state, E_n is given by

$$= \frac{1}{2}mv^2 + \left[-\frac{Ze^2}{r}\right]$$

$$= +\frac{1}{2}\frac{Ze^2}{r} - \frac{Ze^2}{r} = -\frac{1}{2}\frac{Ze^2}{r}$$

$$\therefore \text{KE} = \frac{1}{2}\frac{Ze^2}{r} = +6.8\,\text{eV}$$

Test-3

1. (d) Among the given statements only statement (d) is incorrect because spin quantum number does not give the orientation of electronic cloud.

2. (a) Among the given statements, only I, II and III are correct but IV and V are incorrect. Their corrected form are

IV. An orbital can accommodate a maximum two electron with opposite spin.

V. The energies of the various subshell in the same shell are in the order $s < p < d < f$.

So, option (a) is correct.

3. (b) The correct match is A-II, B-IV, C-III, D-I.

Orbit angular momentum $= \frac{nh}{2\pi}$

Orbital angular momentum $= \sqrt{l(l+1)}\,\hbar$

Spin angular momentum $= \sqrt{s(s+1)}\,\hbar$

Magnetic momenta (spin only formula) $= \sqrt{n(n+2)}$

4. (a) Kinetic energy is inversely proportional to mass of particles
Mass of particles – electron < proton < α-particle
So, energy of particles electron (E_1) > proton (E_3) > α-particle (E_2)
Thus, option (a) is correct.

5. (d) Option (d) is correct.
IV. $3d_{x^2-y^2}$; V. $3d_{z^2}$ are degenerate orbitals.
II. 2s; III. 2p assumed to have same energies in the absence of magnetic and electric field.

6. (b) Principal quantum number gives size, azimuthal gives shape and magnetic quantum number gives orientation.
So, option (b) is correct.

7. (b) Statement I is correct but Statement II is incorrect because Heisenberg's uncertainty principle is not due to limitation of the measuring instrument. It is on account of the fact that microscopic particles cannot be seen even under a microsope. Their position and velocity cannot be changed without disturbing them by hitting with photons.

8. (b) Both (A) and (R) are true but (R) is not the correct explanation of (A). The corrected form of (R) is:

The de-Broglie equation has been shown to apply to elementry particles, neutral atoms and molecules. So, it has significance for any microscopic or submicroscopic particles.

As per de-Broglie wavelength

$$\lambda = \frac{h}{mv}$$

9. (d) Given, $m = 10^{-10}$ g $= 10^{-13}$ kg

$$\Delta v = \frac{0.0001}{100} \times 10^{-6} \times 10^{-2} \text{ m/s}$$

$$= 10^{-14} \text{ m/s}$$

So, $\Delta x \cdot \Delta p = \frac{h}{4\pi}$ $[\because \Delta p = m \cdot \Delta v]$

$$\Delta x = \frac{6.62 \times 10^{-34}}{4 \times 3.14 \times 10^{-13} \times 10^{-14}}$$

$$\Delta x = \frac{6.62 \times 10^{-34}}{12.56 \times 10^{-27}}$$

$$\Delta x = 5.2 \times 10^{-8} \text{ m}$$

So, option (d) is correct.

10. (b) All the energy states in which n is greater than 1 are called excited states.

11. (a) The electronic configuration of the element will be $1s^2, 2s^2 2p^6, 3s^2 3p^6, 4s^2, 3d^{10}, 4p^1$ thus the total number of electron is 31.

Hence, atomic number will be 31.

12. (c) Statement I is incorrect but Statement II is correct. The corrected form of Statement I is: 2s- and 2p-orbital are not degenerate orbitals. In an atom, degenerate atoms are those that have same energy level.

13. (a) One element has unpaired electron = 2

- ${}_7N = 1s^2, 2s^2 2p^3$
  Unpaired electron = 3
- ${}_{24}Cr = 1s^2, 2s^2 2p^6, 3s^2 3p^6 3d^5, 4s^1$
  Unpaired electron = 6
- ${}_{34}Se = 1s^2, 2s^2 2p^6, 3s^2 3p^6, 3d^{10} 4s^2 4p^4$
  Unpaired electron = 2
- ${}_{36}Kr = 1s^2, 2s^2 2p^6, 3s^2 3p^6 3d^{10}, 4s^2 4p^6$
  Unpaired electron = 0
- ${}_5B = 1s^2, 2s^2 2p^1$
  Unpaired electron = 1

So, option (a) is correct.

14. (d) (A) is false but (R) is true.

Cr^{+3} and Sc have same number of electron = 21 but their electronic configuration is not same.

$Sc = [Ar]\, 3d^1 4s^2$

$Cr^{3+} = [Ar] 3d^3 4s^0$

15. (b)

Quantum number	Notation
$n = 5, l = 2$	5d
$n = 6, l = 3$	6f
$n = 4, l = 0$	4s
$n = 5, l = 3$	5f

So, option (b) is correct.

16. (d) Hund's rule states that electrons fill degenerate orbitals singly before pairing up, which minimises electron-electron repulsion and stabilises the atom. Thus, option (d) is the correct answer.

17. (a) $n + l = 7$

$7 + 0 = 7s$
$6 + 1 = 6p$
$5 + 2 = 6d$
$4 + 3 = 4f$

Order of energy is

$$4f < 5d < 6p < 7s.$$

So, option (a) is correct.

18. (d) According to Hund's rule, electron will occupy degenerate orbitals before pairing up. Thus, option (d) is correct answer.

19. (d) The correct match is A-IV, B-III, C-II, D-I.

Angular nodes $= l$ (Azimuthal quantum number)

Spherical nodes $= n - l - 1$

$3p = 1, 1$ $\quad 3d = 2, 0$
$2s = 0, 1$ $\quad 3s = 0, 2$

So, option (d) is correct.

20. (d) Statement (d) is incorrect because ψ represents atomic orbital and ψ^2 represents probability density of finding an electron.

21. (b) Graph between radial probability $R^2(r)$ and finding the electron at a distance r from the nucleus for $2p$ subshell is

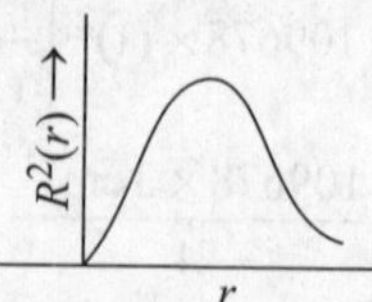

All the graphs has one planar node, The $2p$ radial distribution function show no radial nodes.

Hence, option (b) is correct.

22. (a) Statement (a) is false because. YZ plane is a nodal plane for $3d_{xy}$ orbital. The electron density is only in XY plane. So, probability of finding an electron is not equal to zero for XY plane.

So, option (a) is correct.

23. (d) p_z orbital located along the axis and $d_{x^2-y^2}$ orbital located on the axis. So, option (d) is correct.

24. (a) Radii of maximum probability of electron is smaller for orbital having higher value of 'l' for given same value of n.

So, $(r_{max})_{3s} > (r_{max})_{3p} > (r_{max})_{3d}$ is the correct order.

25. (c) Radial nodes $(n - l - 1) = 2$

$l = 0, n = 3$

So, orbital is 3s.

Hence, option (c) is correct.

Chapter Break Thru

1. (b) α-particles does not pass through the nucleus, it is due to the fact that same charges repel each other.

2. (c) The correct match is A-III, B-IV, C-II, D-I.

	(Outermost configuration)	(Inner orbit)	(Atomic number)
A.	$3s^1$	$1s^2 2s^2 2p^6$	$10 + 1 = 11$
B.	$2p^3$	$1s^2 2s^2$	$4 + 3 = 7$
C.	$3p^5$	$1s^2 2s^2 2p^6 3s^2$	$12 + 5 = 17$
D.	$3d^6$	$1s^2 2s^2 2p^6 3s^2 3p^6 4s^2$	$20 + 6 = 26$

3. (a) A black body absorbs and emits radiation of all frequencies. The frequency distribution of the emitted radiation depends only on the temperature of the black body. As the temperature increases, the emitted radiation shifts towards shorter wavelengths and higher frequencies.

Hence, both Statement I and Statement II are incorrect.

4. (b) Among the given options, only (b) is incorrect.

(a) $\Delta E = \Delta E_1 + \Delta E_2$ (correct)

(c) $h\nu = h\nu_1 + h\nu_2$

$\nu = \nu_1 + \nu_2$ (correct)

(d) $\frac{hc}{\lambda} = \frac{hc}{\lambda_1} + \frac{hc}{\lambda_2}$

$\frac{1}{\lambda} = \frac{1}{\lambda_1} + \frac{1}{\lambda_2}$ (correct)

5. (a) Both (A) and (R) are true and (R) is the correct explanation of (A).

The magnitude of an electron's spin angular momentum cannot be changed.

Spin angular momentum is an intrinsic property of an electron, similar to its charge and rest mass. The spin quantum number of an electron is fixed and can be either half-integer or integer, such as 1/2, 3/2, 0, or 1.

Although the direction of the particle's spin can be changed.

6. (d) Both Statement I and Statement II are correct because number of spherical nodes in any orbital $= n - l - 1$.

For p-orbitals, $l = 1$

So, no. of spherical nodes for $2p$-orbital

$= n - 1 - 1$ or $2 - 2 = 0$

7. (b) Both $d_{x^2-y^2}$ and d_{z^2} have electronic density along the axis. $d_{x^2-y^2}$ has electron density along the x- and y-axis and d_{z^2} has electron density along the z-axis as shown in figures.

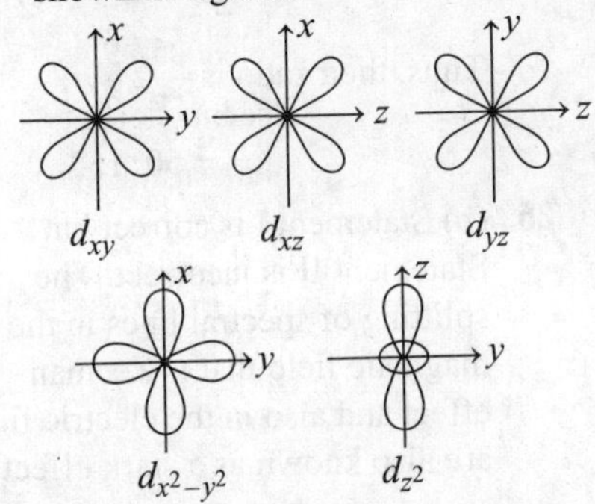

8. (c) The set of quantum number II, III, IV and V are not permitted.

II. The set of quantum numbers are not permitted as value of s cannot be zero.

IV. The set of quantum numbers are not permitted because value of m cannot be greater than l.

III & V. The set of quantum number are not permitted because n value cannot be equal to l.

So, option (c) is correct.

9. (c) According to the Aufbau principle, electrons are filled in various atomic orbitals in the increasing order of energy.

$1s < 2s < 2p < 3s < 3p < 4s < 3d < 4p < 5s < 4d < 5p < 6s < 4f < 5d < 6p < 7s$

10. (d) The correct match is A-II, B-IV, C-III, D-I.

- Magnetic quantum number (m_l) informs about the orientation of the orbital.
- Spin quantum number (m_s) informs about the orientation of the spin of an electron.
- Azimuthal quantum number (l) informs about the shape of an orbital.
- Principal quantum number (n) informs about the size of the orbital.

11. (c) Orbitals with the same shells and sub-shells are known as degenerate orbitals.

From the given options, the options that represent degenerate orbitals due to the same shell, i.e. $n = 3$ are ($3d_{xy}, 3d_{yz}, 3d_{z^2}$) and $n = 4$ are ($4d_{xy}, 4d_{yz}, 4d_{z^2}$).

12. (b) Statement I is correct but Statement II is incorrect because the kinetic energy of the ejected electron is proportional to the frequency of the electromagnetic radiation.

13. (c) Statement I is incorrect but Statement II is correct because the effect of Heisenberg's Uncertainty principle is significant only for motion of microscopic objects and is negligible for that of macroscopic objects.

14. (b) Higher is the mass, and shorter is the wavelength. So, being the heaviest among others, an alpha particle has the shortest wavelength.

15. (b) The correct match is A-III, B-I, C-IV, D-II.

Radio frequency region around 10^6 Hz, used for broadcasting.

Microwave region around 10^{10} Hz used for radar.

Infrared region around 10^{13} Hz used for heating.

Ultraviolet region around 10^{16} Hz, a component of the sun's radiation.

16. (b) $\lambda(A) = 300 \text{ nm} = 300 \times 10^{-9}$ m or 3×10^{-7} m;

$\lambda(B) = 300 \times 10^{-6}$ m $= 3 \times 10^{-4}$ m

$\lambda(C) = 3 \times 10^{-9}$ m,

$\lambda(D) = 30 \times 10^{-10}$ m $= 3 \times 10^{-9}$ m

As energy is inversely proportional to wavelength. Hence, the increasing order of energies is $(B) < (A) < (C) = (D)$.

17. (b) We know that,

Angular momentum $= \sqrt{l(l+1)}\,\frac{h}{2\pi}$

For d-electron, $l = 2$

Angular momentum

$= \sqrt{2(2+1)}\,\frac{h}{2\pi} = \sqrt{6}\cdot\frac{h}{2\pi}$

where, $\hbar = \frac{h}{2\pi}$

So, angular momentum is $\sqrt{6}\,\hbar$.

Thus, option (b) is correct.

18. (b) For $4p, n = 4, l = 1$

Radial nodes
$= (n - l - 1) = (4 - 1 - 1) = 2$

19. (c) Atoms of different elements that have the same mass number but different atomic number are called isobars.

20. (d) The region in which there is a maximum probability of finding an electron is called orbital.

21. (a) According to the Aufbau principle a new electron enters the orbitals when $(n+1)$ is minimum. For example, 4*s* orbital filled first then the 3*d* orbital.

22. (b) Let energy of first excited state $= E_1$

$\therefore$ E_1 for $Li^{2+} = E_1$ for $H \times Z_{Li}^2$
$= E_1$ for $H \times 9$

E_1 for $He^+ = E_1$ for $H \times Z_{He}^2$
$= E_1$ for $H \times 4$

or E_1 for $Li^{2+} = \frac{9}{4} E_1$ for He^+
$= 19.6 \times 10^{-18} \times \frac{9}{4}$
$= 44.1 \times 10^{-18}$ J/atom

23. (d) In this effect, a thin foil (thickness 100 nm) made up of gold and coated with fluorescent ZnS screen which is circular around it. α-particles mostly move through the gold foil having zero deflection, a small fraction is deflected and one in twenty thousand turns 180°.

24. (b) The atomic radius of an atom is given by the formula,

$$r_n = \frac{52.9n^2}{Z} \text{ pm}$$

where, r_n is the radius of *n*th orbit of an atom and *Z* is the atomic number of that atom.
The ratio of the atomic radius of the 5th orbit in chlorine atom and 3rd orbit in helium atom is

$$r_5 = \frac{52.9 \times (5)^2}{17} = \frac{52.9 \times 25}{17}$$

$$r_3 = \frac{52.9 \times (3)^2}{2} = \frac{52.9 \times 9}{2}$$

Thus, their ratio is $\frac{25}{17} : \frac{9}{2}$
$= 50 : 153$.

25. (b) Statement I is correct but Statement II is incorrect. The splitting of spectral lines in the magnetic field that is Zeeman effect and also in the electric field are also known as a stark effect.

26. (c) de-Broglie gave the relation between momentum and wavelength as

$$\lambda = \frac{h}{p}$$

Here, *h* is Planck's constant, whose value is 6.626×10^{-34} J/s.

$$\text{Wavelength} = \frac{h}{mc}$$
$$= \frac{6.626 \times 10^{-34} \text{kg m}^2\text{s}^{-1}}{(3.31 \times 10^{-34} \text{ kg} \times 3 \times 10^8 \text{ m/s})}$$
$= 67$ Å.

27. (d) The range of magnetic quantum number of an orbital is from $-(l-1)$ to $+(l-1)$. For 2*p* orbital, there are 3 magnetic quantum numbers namely –1, 0 and 1. For $2p_z$ orbital is 0, taken that *z* is the internuclear axis.

28. (b) The set of quantum number $n = 1, l = 2, m = 0, s = -\frac{1}{2}$, is not valid because the value of azimuthal quantum number should lie only in between 0 and $n - 1$, where *n* is principal quantum number.

29. (d) Given,

$\lambda = 3.6$ Å $= 3.6 \times 10^{-10}$ m

Velocity of photon = Velocity of light

$$m = \frac{h}{\lambda v}$$
$$= \frac{6.626 \times 10^{-34} \text{ kg m}^2\text{s}^{-1}}{3.6 \times 10^{-10} \text{ m} \times 3 \times 10^8 \text{ m/s}}$$
$= 6.135 \times 10^{-33}$ kg

30. (a) Fact given in I, II and V are correct but III and IV are incorrect.
Number of spectral lines
$= \frac{n(n-1)}{2}$
(from n^{th} level to the first level)
If $n = 4$, then spectral lines
$= \frac{4(4-1)}{2} = 6$
If $n = 5$, then spectral lines
$= \frac{5(5-1)}{2} = 10$
If $n = 6$, then spectral lines
$= \frac{6(6-1)}{2} = 15$

31. (c) The wave number is the reciprocal or the inverse of wavelength.

Wave number = 1/wavelength. Its units is cm^{-1}. The wavelength of violet colour is 400 nm as seen in the electromagnetic spectrum.

Wave number $= \frac{1}{400 \text{ nm}}$
$= \frac{1}{400 \times 10^{-7} \text{cm}}$
$= 2.5 \times 10^{-3} \times 10^7 \text{ cm}^{-1}$
$= 25 \times 10^3 \text{ cm}^{-1}$

32. (c) Speed's uncertainty is $10 \times \frac{5}{100} = 0.5$ m/s.

According to Heisenberg's uncertainty principle, i.e.

$$\Delta x \cdot \Delta p \geq \frac{h}{4\pi}$$
$$\Delta x = \frac{h}{2m\pi} \text{ m/s}$$

Therefore, uncertainty in position
$$= \frac{6.626 \times 10^{-34} \text{ kg m}^2\text{s}^{-1}}{2 \times 6 \text{ kg} \times 3.1416}$$
$= 0.176 \times 10^{-34}$ m.

33. (c) The number of orbitals within an orbit is n^2. But as each orbital can accommodate 2 electrons,the number of electrons that can exist with the '*n*' as the principal quantum number is $2n^2$. So, here $2n^2 = 2(4)^2 = 2(16) = 32$

34. (b) Both (A) and (R) are true but (R) is not the correct explanation of (A).

According to Bohr's postulate, angular momentum is quantised and this is given by the expression $m_e vr = \frac{nh}{2\pi}, (n = 1, 2, 3, \dots)$. $m_e vr$ is the angular momentum and h is the Planck's constant. Movement of an electron can only be possible in orbits whose angular momentum is the integral multiple of $\frac{h}{2\pi}$.

35. (d) The statement that does not form of Bohr's model of the hydrogen atom is "the position and velocity of the electrons in the orbit cannot be determined simultaneously". This statement is actually given by Heisenberg's in his uncertainty principle.

36. (c) From de-Broglie relation,

$$\lambda = \frac{h}{mv}$$

For CH_4, $\lambda_{CH_4} = \frac{h}{m_{CH_4} \times v_{CH_4}}$

For O_2, $\lambda_{O_2} = \frac{h}{m_{O_2} \times v_{O_2}}$

If wavelength of CH_4 and O_2 are equal, then,

$$\frac{h}{m_{CH_4} \times v_{CH_4}} = \frac{h}{m_{O_2} \times v_{O_2}}$$

$$\frac{v_{CH_4}}{v_{O_2}} = \frac{m_{O_2}}{m_{CH_4}} = \frac{32}{16} = 2$$

so, $v_{CH_4} = 2v_{O_2}$

The velocity of CH_4 molecule is two times the velocity of O_2 molecule.

37. (c) Work function = Threshold energy

$$h\nu_o = \frac{hc}{\lambda_o}$$

Given, $\lambda_o = 330\,\text{nm} = 330 \times 10^{-9}$ m

$$= \frac{6.6 \times 10^{-34}\ \text{Js} \times 3 \times 10^{8}\ \text{m/s}}{330 \times 10^{-9}\ \text{m}}$$

$$= 0.06 \times 10^{-17} = 6 \times 10^{-19}\,\text{J}$$

38. (b) Among the given statements, only I, III and IV are incorrect while the statements given in II and V are correct.

I. No two electrons in an atom can have the same value of all the four quantum numbers n, l, m_l and m_s.

III. Since, velocity is $v \propto \frac{1}{n}$.

IV. From the expression of energy, $E \propto -\frac{1}{n^2}$.

Thus, option (b) is correct.

39. (a) According to Bohr's atomic model,

$$r \propto \frac{n^2}{Z}$$

For 3rd orbit of Li^{2+}, $n_1 = 3$

$$Z_1 = 3$$

For 2nd orbit of Be^{3+}, $n_2 = 2$

$$Z_2 = 4$$

From the above equation,

$$\frac{(r_2)_{Be^{3+}}}{(r_3)_{Li^{2+}}} = \frac{n_2^2 \times Z_1}{n_1^2 \times Z_2}$$

$$(r_2)_{Be^{3+}} = \frac{154.2 \times 2 \times 2 \times 3}{3 \times 3 \times 4}$$

$$= 51.4\ \text{pm}$$

Hence, the radius of second Bohr orbit of Be^{3+} is 51.4 pm.

40. (b)

	Quantum number	Notation
(a)	$n = 5, l = 2$	$5d$
(b)	$n = 6, l = 3$	$6f$
(c)	$n = 4, l = 0$	$4s$
(d)	$n = 5, l = 4$	$5g$

Thus, option (b) is correct.

41. (a) As we know that,

$$\Delta p = m \times \Delta v$$

$$\Delta p = 9.1 \times 10^{-28} \times 3 \times 10^4 \times \frac{0.001}{100}$$

$$= 2.73 \times 10^{-28}\ \text{kg ms}^{-1}$$

Hence, from Heisenberg's principle, $\Delta x = \frac{h}{\Delta p \times 4\pi}$

$$= \frac{6.626 \times 10^{-27}}{2.73 \times 10^{-28} \times 4 \times 3.14}$$

$$= 1.93\ \text{cm}$$

42. (d) According to Bohr's model

$$mvr = \frac{nh}{2\pi}$$

From de-Broglie equation

$$\because \quad \lambda = \frac{h}{mv}$$

$$2\pi r = \frac{nh}{mv} = n\lambda$$

where, symbols have their usual meaning.

Also, $r = \frac{a_0 n^2}{Z}$

Where, a_0 = Bohr radius = 45.3 pm and Z = Atomic number

On substituting the value of r from Eq. (ii) to Eq. (i), we get

$$n\lambda = \frac{2\pi n^2 a_0}{Z}$$

$$\lambda = \frac{2\pi n a_0}{Z} \quad [\because n = 4, Z = 1]$$

$$\lambda = \frac{2\pi \times 4 \times 54.3}{1} = 434.4\,\pi\ \text{pm}$$

43. (c) Statement I is incorrect but Statement II is correct. The velocity of the electron, according to Bohr's model is given by

$$v_n = 2.18 \times 10^6 \times \left(\frac{Z}{n}\right) \text{ms}^{-1} \quad \text{...(i)}$$

So, as Z decreases, v_n also decreases.

Hence, velocity of the electron increases as the positive charge increases.

Thus, Statement I is incorrect.

From equation (i), As the value of n decreases, velocity will increase accordingly.

44. (b) Statements I, III, IV and V are correct but statement II is incorrect. It is because Zeeman effect, splitting of spectral line in presence of magnetic field could not be explained by Bohr's model. So, option (b) is correct.

45. (a) Total number of spectral lines given by

$$\frac{1}{2}[n-1]\times n = 15$$

$$\Rightarrow \quad n^2 - n = 30$$

$$\therefore \quad n = 6$$

Thus, electron are excited upto 6th energy level from ground state. Therefore,

$$\frac{1}{\lambda} = R_H\left[\frac{1}{1^2} - \frac{1}{n^2}\right]$$

$$\Rightarrow \frac{1}{\lambda} = 109737\times\left[\frac{1}{1^2} - \frac{1}{6^2}\right]$$

$$\frac{1}{\lambda} = 109737\times\frac{35}{36}$$

$$\lambda = 9.373\times10^{-6}\text{ cm}$$

$$= 937.3\text{ Å}$$

46. (a) For a given orbital with principal quantum number n and the azimuthal quantum number l the number of radial nodes $= n-l-1$

For $3s = 3-0-1 = 2$ is the number of radial node.

For $2p = 2-1-1 = 0$ is the number of radial node.

47. (d) Total number of nodes is given by the formula $= (n-l-1)$

For $3s$ orbital, total nodes = 2

48. (c) The order of the given frequency is as follows :

Radiation from FM radio < microwaves<amber colour < X-rays < cosmic rays.

49. (c) The ideal body, which emits and absorbs radiation of all frequencies, is called a black body and the radiation emitted by them is called black body radiation. The exact frequency distribution of the emitted radiation from a black body depends only on its temperature. At a given temperature, intensity of radiation emitted increases with decrease of wavelength, reaches a maximum value at a given wavelength and then starts decreasing with further decrease of wavelength. Thus, (A) is true but (R) is false.

50. (b) X-rays have frequencies in the range of 10^{16} to 10^{20} Hz.

UV rays have frequencies in the range of 10^{14} to 10^{16} Hz.

Microwaves have frequencies in the range of 10^8 and 10^{10} Hz.

So, correct order is X-rays > UV rays > microwaves.

Thus, order given in option (b) is incorrect.

Ch-3 Classification of Elements and Periodicity in Properties

Topical Follow Thru

Test-1

1. (c) The element with atomic number 119 belongs to alkali metal in IA group. It will have only one electron in the valence shell, i.e. $8s^1$, therefore it's oxide form is of type M_2O.

So, statement given in option (c) is incorrect.

2. (b) The correct match is A-IV, B-I, C-II, D-III.

A. In (Indium) is an element which is present in group 13 and 5th period.

B. Cs (Caesium) is a highly reactive metal in 6th period.

C. I (Iodine) is present in 5th period and 17th group.

D. Xe (Xenon) is a noble gas which is similar to argon (atomic no. 18) and having atomic number 54.

3. (d) Considering Statement I, Elements of groups IB and IIB are transition elements such as copper and zinc respectively.

Considering Statement II, Elements of VB group can be a metalloids, e.g. arsenic.

Hence, both Statement I and Statement II are correct.

4. (c) The element with $Z = 114$ will have electronic configuration [Rn] $5f^{14}6d^{10}7s^2 7p^2$.

Thus, the element belongs to the p-block as its valence electron enters in p-orbital and total number of e^- in 7th orbital is 4. So, the group number is $10+4 = 14$.

5. (c) Elements in the same group have similar chemical properties and physical properties due to repeatition of valence shell electronic configuration.

Elements having same number of electrons are termed as isoelectronic. Thus, elements of same group are not isoelectronic. Hence, (A) is true but (R) is false.

6. (d) The elements in which electrons are progressively filled in $4f$-orbital are called lanthanoids.

7. (a) A. Unq (Unnilquadium) – 104

B. Uns (Unnilseptium) – 107

C. Unt (Unniltrium) – 103

D. Uub (Ununbium) – 112

Hence, the correct match is A-II, B-IV, C-I, D-III.

8. (c) Electronic configuration reveals that p-orbital of element is not complete. Therefore, it is a p-block element. Moreover, the atomic number of the element is 34 (Se). Thus, it is more considered as a metalloid.

9. (d) The electronic configuration of Lu is [Xe] $4f^{14}5d^1 6s^2$. The last electron in Lu goes into $5d$-orbital but it is studied in the f-block of the

periodic table because the chemistry of Lu is dominated by 4 *f*-electrons.
Hence, both Statements I and II are correct.

10. (a) The elements A and B have same electron in their valence orbital, i.e. 1. Hence, they belong to same group that is group 13.

11. (d) Cu (copper) belongs to group 11 and K belongs to group 1. Hence, statement (d) is incorrect.

12. (b) The element with five electrons in outer subshell is having $ns^2 np^5$ configuration. Only halogen family members have this electronic configuration.

13. (a) Zn, Cd and Hg are *d*-block elements which are not considered as transition elements because the *d*-orbitals in these elements are completely filled.
Therefore, on the basis of properties, all transition elements are *d*-block elements but on the basis of electronic configuration, all *d*-block elements are not transition elements.
Hence, both (A) and (R) are true and (R) is the correct explanation of (A).

14. (a) Periods are the horizontal rows which represents the highest principal quantum number of the atoms in the period.

15. (b) Statement I is correct but Statement II is incorrect. It is because the 3*d*-transition series starts with scandium and ends with zinc.

Test-2

1. (b) The correct order of increasing radius of given atoms/ions is

$$Na^+ < Ne < O^{2-} < Cl^-.$$

On, going from left to right in a period, atomic or ionic radius decreases while it increases on moving down the groups. However, cations are smaller than anions in size.

2. (c) $Na^+ = 10$ electrons $= 1s^2 2s^2 2p^6$
$\rightarrow 0$ unpaired electron
$B = 5$ electrons $= 1s^2 2s^2 2p^1$
$\rightarrow 1$ unpaired electron
$N = 7$ electrons $= 1s^2 2s^2 2p^3$
$\rightarrow 3$ unpaired electrons
$O^{2-} = 10$ electrons $= 1s^2 2s^2 2p^6$
$\rightarrow 0$ unpaired electron

3. (d) Both Statement I and Statement II are correct.

4. (c) As we move from Cl to I, the electron gain enthalpy (i.e. energy released in electron gain) become less and less negative due to a corresponding increase in the atomic size.
However, the electron gain enthalpy of F is less negative than that of Cl due to its small size.
Thus, the negative electron gain enthalpy follows the order

$$F < Cl > Br > I$$

5. (c) [He] $2s^2 2p^3$ configuration belongs to nitrogen. Being smallest in size and with stable electronic configuration, element (nitrogen) has maximum ionisation energy.

6. (b) Statement I is correct but Statement II is incorrect. Correct statement II is the first ionisation enthalpy of 5*d*-elements is actually higher than that of 3*d* and 4*d*-elements. This is because 5*d*-elements have a greater effective nuclear charge and weaker shielding of valence electrons.

7. (b) Among the given statements, the statement (b) is incorrect because halogens have high electron affinities. This is due to their strong tendency to gain an additional electron to change into the stable $ns^2 np^6$ configuration.

8. (b) While moving across a period from left to right, electronegativity increases. So, the increasing order of given element regarding electronegativity is $C < N < O < F$.

9. (a) The given configuration are of alkali metals, alkaline earth metals, transition element and bromine.
Among these alkali metals and alkaline earth metal are more metallic than transition metal. Br is a non-metal (halogen).
So, the correct order is

$$III < I < II < IV.$$

10. (d) The large rise between IE_{III} and IE_{IV} suggests that the element has three valence electrons, i.e. the element is Al.
Thus, option (d) is correct.

11. (a) Electron gain enthalpy values of noble gases are positive because they have stable electronic configuration and hence, they have no tendency to take additional electron.
Thus, both (A) and (R) are true and (R) is the correct explanation of (A).

12. (a) A-IV, B-III, C-II, D-I

A. Chlorine (Cl) has the maximum electron affinity among all the elements, due to its high effective nuclear charge and small atomic size.
B. Fluorine (F) is the most electronegative element in the modern periodic table. It has a high electronegativity due to its small atomic size, high nuclear charge and low number of electrons in its outer shell.
C. Helium (He) has the maximum ionisation enthalpy among all the elements. This is due to the strong nuclear attraction and the stable electronic configuration of helium, making it difficult to remove an electron.
D. Caesium (Cs) has the maximum metallic character among all the elements. Being an alkali metal, it has a low ionisation energy and a high atomic radius, making it easily lose electrons to form a positive ion. this results in a high metallic character.

13. (c) The non-metallic character increases along a period and decreases down the group, therefore, non-metallic character increases in the order

$$P < S < N < O.$$

14. (d) The heaviest alkali metal is the most electropositive element, i.e. Cs, ([Xe] $6s^1$). Hence, among the given electronic configuration, [Xe] $6s^1$ represents most electropositive element.

15. (a) Strongest reducing agent among the halide ions is I^-.
Large sized iodide ion has maximum tendency to lose electrons and has maximum reducing power. On the other hand, fluoride ion is smaller in size and has low reducing power.
Hence, the correct order of reducing power is

$$F^- < Cl^- < Br^- < I^-$$

Test-3

1. (a) Pb^{4+} salts are better oxidising agent as they can be easily reduced to Pb^{2+}.

2. (b) Smaller the ionic radii, greater the magnitude of charge leads to higher lattice energy.
So in case of NaCl and LiF, NaCl have low lattice energy than LiF as the size of Li^+ is smaller than Na^+.
Rest of the other options are correct.
$AlF_3 > MgF_2$ [charge on cation]
$Li_3N > Li_2O$ [charge on anion]
$MgF_2 > NaF$
[charge on cation and anion]

3. (c) The chemical reactivity increases in alkali metals down the group because with increase in atomic number, atomic size increases which makes it easier to lose electrons and make element more reactive but in case of halogens, with increase in atomic number, atomic size increases which makes it harder for halogens to gain electrons. This leads to decrease in chemical reactivity.

4. (a) Ionic oxides are usually basic in nature and basic oxides are formed by metals. Hence, *X* belongs to left side of periodic table having lowest atomic number.
In case of *Y*, it forms amphoteric oxide which means it belongs to middle side of periodic table. So, the atomic number of *Y* is greater than that of *X*.
As *Z* form giant molecule of its oxide, it belongs to right side of periodic table because the ionic radii increases.

5. (a) Lithium chloride (LiCl) is hydrated because Li has a high polarising power. Li^+ is smaller in size and has high charge density. Hence, it forms hydrated compound. On the other hand, NaCl is anhydrous because sodium has a low polarising power as compared to lithium.
Hence, both (A) and (R) are true and (R) is the correct explanation of (A).

6. (a) Lattice energy increases as the charge on the ion increases and the size decreases. Hydration energy increases as the size of the ion decreases and charges on it increases.
Since, the hydration enthalpy decreases down a group, thus the first element in group 2, i.e. Mg will be more soluble or will have more hydration enthalpy than lattice enthalpy.

7. (c) Among the given reactions, only option (c) involves absorption of energy because the negatively charged species of oxygen gains electrons by absorption of energy.

$$O^-(g) + e^- \longrightarrow O^{2-}(g)$$

In other reaction, all neutral electronegative atoms absorbed electron and releases energy. So, this process does not involve the absorption of energy.

8. (b) Amphoteric oxides are oxides that have both acidic and basic properties and can neutralise both acids and bases.
Al_2O_3, ZnO and PbO are the examples of amphoteric oxides.

9. (d) Valence electron in $A = 3$
Valence electron in $B = 6$
Thus, *A* is electropositive and B is electronegative. '*A*' can lose three electrons and '*B*' can gain two electrons to attain a stable configuration.
Thus, '*A*' exists as A^{3+} and *B* as B^{2-}.
Hence, the compound is A_2B_3.

10. (a) Both (A) and (R) are true and (R) is the correct explanation of (A).
In P_4O_{10}, oxidation of P is +5 and in P_4O_6, oxidation of P is +3.
Hence, P_4O_{10} is more acidic than P_4O_6.

11. (d) Both Statement I and Statement II are correct.

12. (d) As we move from left to right in a period, nuclear charge increases and hence atomic radius decreases. Therefore, atomic radius of Be = 111, C = 77, O = 66, B = 88 pm.
Thus, the correct match is
A-IV, B-II, C-I, D-III

13. (c) Group 16 elements are O, S, Se, Te.
Due to inert pair effect, stability of +4, +6 oxidation state decreases on moving down the group. Hence, Te^{4+} is more stable than Te^{6+}. Hence, TeO_2 will act as an oxidising agent not a reducing agent.

14. (d) On moving down the group, first ionisation enthalpy decreases. Therefore, order of first ionisation enthalpy for group 13 elements is

$$B > Al > Ga > Tl > In.$$

15. (b)

X	*Y*	*Z*
Amphoteric	Basic	Acidic

On moving left to right along the same period, acidic nature of oxide increases. Basically, basic nature of oxides changes from amphoteric to acidic on moving along a period. Hence, the correct order is $Y < X < Z$.

Chapter Break Thru

1. (a) During addition of electron in O_2 to form O_2^-, the additional π-molecular electrons is added to the less stable antibonding orbital. Therefore, it is easier to remove an electron from O_2^- ions to form neutral O_2. Hence, it has lowest first ionisation enthalpy.

2. (a) In option (a), the first electron is removed from $3s^1$, which is easily removed, but to remove the 2nd electron more energy is required because of stable configuration. Hence, the difference will be maximum between two ionisation enthalpy.

3. (b) Ionisation potential $\propto \dfrac{1}{\text{Atomic size}}$

As the atomic size increases down the group, but decreases in period, the ionisation potential will decreases down the group.
The correct order is,

$$Ca > K > Rb > Cs$$

4. (a) On going down the group both the atomic size and atomic mass increase but the increase in atomic mass compensates the bigger atomic size, As a result, the density of metals increase from Li to Cs potassium is, however, lighter than sodium.
Thus, the correct order of density is

$$Li < K < Na < Rb.$$

5. (d) Among the given statements A, B and C are correct while rest statements are incorrect.
The correct statement of D and E are as follows
Lothar-Meyer's curve is plotted between atomic weight and atomic volume and he find out that elements with similar properties occupied the similar positions on the graph.
The most strongly electropositive alkali metals occupy the position of the graph.

6. (a) The correct match is A-II, B-I, C-IV, D-III.

7. (d) The element with atomic number 118 is Ununoctium with atomic symbol Uuo. This element belongs to noble gas family, i.e. 18 th group and 7 th period. Its given electronic configuration is correct.

8. (b) Among the given statements, B, C and D are correct while statements A and E are incorrect.

- Group VIII consist of three triads such as Fe, Co, Ni, Ru, Rh, Pd and Os, Ir, Pt arranged in 4 th, 5 th and 6 th period respectively. This group is not divided into A and B parts.
- Also, no place is alloted to lanthanoids and actinoids in this table.

9. (c) The ionisation potential increases across the period but the second ionisation potential of oxygen is highest among given element because after removal of 1st electron, the 2nd electron has to be removed from stable half-filled orbital.
Hence, correct order is

$$O > F > N > C.$$

10. (d) Among given statement, option (d) is incorrect. The correct form is,
In any period, the atomic radius of noble gases is the largest.

11. (a) The correct match is
A-II, B-III, C-IV, D-I.
44 $\rightarrow$ *d*-block
83 $\rightarrow$ *p*-block
62 $\rightarrow$ *f*-block
55 $\rightarrow$ *s*-block

12. (b) Both A and R are true but R is not the correct explanation of A.
The correct explanation is,
Lattice energy of Na_2SO_4 is less than its hydration energy but lattice energy of $BaSO_4$ is more than its hydration energy.

13. (c) Metallic character increases down the group and decreases from left to right across a period in the periodic table. Since, Si is a metalloid and P is a non-metal. Thus, the correct order is

$$P < Si < Be < Mg < Na.$$

14. (a) The element with the configuration $3s^2\,3p^5$ represents Cl and will have the maximum electron affinity among the given.

15. (c) A is true, but R is false. The correct form of R is,
Additional electrons are repelled more efficiency by $2p$ electrons in F atom than by $3p$ electrons in Cl atom.

16. (d) Both Statement I and Statement II are correct.

17. (c) The second ionisation energy of Na will be higher than that of Mg. Since, in case of Na the second electron will be removed from $2p^6$ configuration.

18. (b) Statement I is correct but Statement II is incorrect. The correct form of Statement II is,
Chlorine is better oxidising agent than fluorine.

19. (d) Screening effect is the decrease in the effective nuclear charge on valence electron as a result of variation in the force of attraction acting on the electrons.
Order of screening effect for a given shell is

$$s > p > d > f.$$

20. (a) As the atomic number increases, the energy of orbital decreases.
Therefore, the correct order of decreasing order is

$$H > Li > Na > K.$$

21. (b) Atomic radii increase from top to bottom in a group and decreases from left to right across periods.
Hence, the correct increasing order of atomic radii is, F < Si < Li < Na.

22. (d) A cation is always smaller than its atom and also on moving from left to right in a period atomic and ionic size decreases. Therefore Mg has larger size than Al and Mg^{2+} will have larger size than Al^{3+}.
Largest = Mg,
Smallest = Al^{3+}

23. (c) (A) is true but (R) is false.
IUPAC name of this element is ununbium in which un and bi are used for 1 and 2 respectively in latin words.

24. (a) Metal form basic oxides. Non-metals form acidic oxide. Metallic character decreases from Na to Cu. Hence, the decreasing order of basic character of oxides is

$Na_2O > Al_2O_3 > CuO.$

25. (c) On moving from left to right in periodic table, acidic nature of oxide increases.
So, metallic oxides are basic, non-metallic oxides are acidic and BeO is amphoteric.

26. (a) The correct match is
A-IV, B-III, C-II, D-I.
- Zn, Be, Sn, Pb, Sb and Al form amphoteric oxides.
- Oxides of non-metals are acidic in nature and form acids on hydrolysis.
- However, N_2O, NO, CO and H_2O are neutral oxides.
- Oxides of metals for basic oxides.

27. (c) Electron affinity increases across a period. Element of second period have less negative electron affinity than those of corresponding element of 3rd period.
Hence, the correct order is,
N < Al < O < Cl

28. (d) Isoelectronic species are those, which have same number of electrons.
$O^{2-} = 8 + 2 = 10e^-$, $Zn^{2+} = 28e^-$,
Mg = 12, K = 19
$Mg^{2+} = 12 - 2 = 10$
$N^{3-} = 10e^-, F^+ = 8e^-, Mg^+ = 11e^-$
$Na = 11e^-$, $Ca = 20e^-$,
$Na^+ = 10e^-$ $Mg^{2+} = 10e^-$
Hence, O^{2-} and Mg^{2+} are isoelectronic.

29. (a) Tenth element in periodic table is a member of noble gases (group 18). The atomic number of other elements of noble gases are 2—He, 18—Ar, 36—Kr, Xe—54.

30. (a) The magnitude of ionic radius of Al^{3+} is less than that of Na^+ because the effective nuclear charge of outer shell electrons in Al^{3+} is greater than in Na^+.
Hence, both (A) and (R) are true and (R) is the correct explanation of (A).

31. (a) The group of elements in which the differentiating electron enters in the antipenultimate (inner to the penultimate shell, i.e. $n - 2$) shell is called *f*-block or inner transition elements.

32. (b) Henry Moseley gave a modern periodic law.
He showed that atomic number is more fundamental property of an element than its atomic mass.

$$\sqrt{\nu} = a(Z - b)$$

Z = atomic number, ν = frequency
a = proportionality constant,
b = constant

33. (a) Group 6 is a part of *d*-block element. Since, these elements have a total six electrons in the *ns* and $(n - 1)$ *d* subshells, therefore in accordance to extra stability of exactly half-filled *d*-orbital, the general configuration is $(n-1)d^5 4s^1$.

34. (a) The electron gain enthalpy becomes more and more negative from left to right across the period due to increasing nuclear charge and less negative from top to bottom due to increasing atomic size.

35. (b) Number of electrons in each species
$N_2 = 14$, $CN^- = 14$, $C_2^{2-} = 14$,
$NO^+ = 14$, $O_2^{2-} = 18$, $CO = 14$,
$NO = 15$
Hence, same number of electrons are present in group (b) only.
∴ It is an isoelectronic group.

36. (b) On moving from left to right in a period, acidic character of the normal oxides of the element goes on increasing with increase in electronegativity. Thus, the correct order is

$CO_2 > B_2O_3 > BeO > Li_2O$

37. (b) Statement given in option (b) is incorrect it is because group 17 elements have very high negative electron gain enthalpies because they can attain stable noble gas electronic configuration by picking up an electron.

38. (c) Statements II, III and IV are incorrect. Their correct statements are as follows
II. Elements like Zn, Cd, Hg are diamagnetic in nature.
III. The maximum number of elements are present in 6th and 7th period.
IV. Every period start with alkali group except 1st period (H).
Thus, option (c) is correct.

39. (b) The correct match is
A-IV, B-III, C-II, D-I.
A. Transition element (*d*-block) = Mn (25)
B. Noble gases (Inert gases) = Kr (36)
C. Lanthanoids = Ce (58)
D. Actinoids = Th (90)
Hence, option (b) is corrrect.

40. (d) I, II and V are correctly matched while III and IV are incorrectly matched. Their correct term is
III → B < C < O < N as N > O due to half-filled subshell in N.
IV → $Al^{3+} < Mg^{2+} < Na^+ < F^-$

41. (c) (A) is true but (R) is false. The correct form of (R) is metallic character decreases along the period but increases down the group.

42. (a) The order of electronegativity is $F > O > Cl > S > C > P$.

43. (a) Li^+ has $1s^2$ configuration which is the configuration of He atom (i.e. noble gas). Hence, it possess highest ionisation potential value.

44. (b) An ionic compound dissolves in water if and only if its hydration energy overcomes the lattice energy.

45. (a) The negative ion (anion) is greater in size than its neutral atom. This is because the negative ion is having more electrons than neutral atom as these electrons repel each other in penultimate shell and increases the size.

46. (d) The atomic number of Ununennium is 119. Here, un is written for 1 and enn is written for 9.

47. (d) Statement (d) is incorrect because the ionisation energy increases gradually with increase in atomic number is applied in period not for group.

48. (b) No. of electrons in NO_3^-

$= 7 + 8 \times 3 + 1 = 32$

No. of electrons in CO_3^{2-}

$= 6 + 8 \times 3 + 2 = 32$

No. of electrons in SO_2

$= 16 + 8 \times 2 = 32$

Number of electrons in ClO_3^-

$= 17 + (3 \times 8) + 1 = 42$

Therefore, option (b) is correct.

49. (b) As the charge on the atom increases, the ionisation energy increases or nuclear charge increases.

Hence, 3rd ionisation enthalpy will be the largest.

50. (a) From the electronic configuration (ns^2, np^1) it can be predicted that the element belongs to the 3rd group of periodic table and is a metal. The oxide formed by the metals are basic.

Ch-4 Chemical Bonding and Molecular Structure

Topical Follow Thru

Test-1

1. (c)

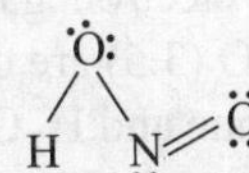

In HNO_2 molecule, polar covalent bond is present between O and H and non-polar covalent bond is present between N and O.

2. (b) Ionic character depends upon electronegativity difference between cation and anion of compound. More electronegativity difference means stronger ionic interactions hence more ionic character. Also, as the cation becomes larger and anion becomes smaller ionic character increases. Hence, CsF has the most ionic character.

3. (a) $H^+ + H_2O$ is best explained by the co-ordinate covalent bond. In H_2O, O-atom will donate electron pair to H^+ forming H_3O^+

Coordinate bond

$H_2\ddot{O} + H^+ \longrightarrow [H_2O \rightarrow H]^+$ Acceptor

Donor

4. (a) CH_4 has symmetrical tetrahedral structure. Due to this, the dipole moment in each bond cancel out another. Hence, overall dipole moment is zero.

In NF_3, the EN difference between N and F is less as compared to EN difference between N and H. Therefore, NF_3 will have a lower dipole moment than NH_3.

In H_2O, the EN difference between H and O is high, therefore it will have a maximum dipole moment.

So, the increasing order of dipole moment is

$CH_4 < NF_3 < NH_3 < H_2O$.

5. (c) SO_3 will be non-polar due to $\mu_{net} = 0$, whereas all other are polar. Thus, it has least dipole moment.

6. (c) (A) is true but (R) is false.

Correct Reason is bond breaking occur due to the collisions of the another molecules or by supplying high energy to break the electrostatic interaction between them.

7. (c) From Fajans' rule, bigger the anion, more is the polarisability. From periodic table, atomic size increases down the group as shown below.

$I^- > Br^- > Cl^- > F^-$

I^- is most polarised followed by Br^-, Cl^- and F^-

Thus, the order of polarisability is $I^- > Br^- > Cl^- > F^-$.

8. (d) Bond length $\propto \dfrac{1}{\text{Bond order}}$

The O—O bond order varies as O_2 (2.0), O_3(1.5) and H_2O_2 (1.0).

Hence, the correct order of bond length is $O_2 < O_3 < H_2O_2$.

9. (a) Statement given in option (a) is correct regarding bond angles whereas all other are incorrect.

10. (c) Lattice energy $= \frac{kq_1q_2}{r}$

where, q_1 and q_2 are the charges on the ions and r is the shortest distance between the centre of cations and anions.

So, lattice energy is proportional to the charge and inversely proportional to the size of ions.

Lattice energy of $CaCl_2$ is greater than KCl. Anion is same in both the compounds.

So, the deciding factor here becomes the charge.

11. (a) Two statements, i.e. II and III are correct.

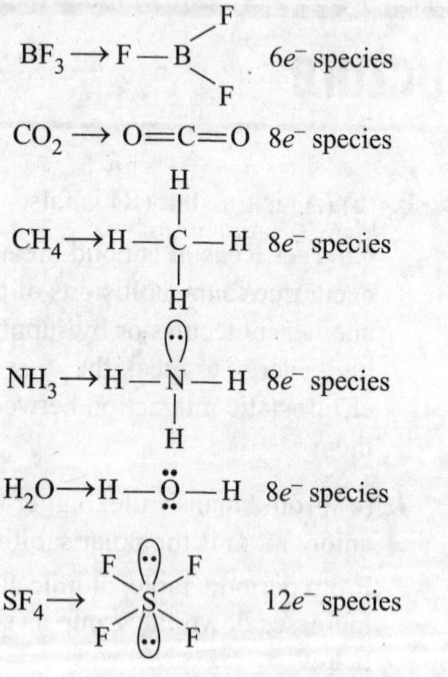

$BF_3 \rightarrow$ F—B(F)(F) $6e^-$ species

$CO_2 \rightarrow$ O=C=O $8e^-$ species

$CH_4 \rightarrow$ H—C(H)(H)—H $8e^-$ species

$NH_3 \rightarrow$ H—N(H)—H $8e^-$ species

$H_2O \rightarrow$ H—Ö—H $8e^-$ species

$SF_4 \rightarrow$ S(F)(F)(F)(F) $12e^-$ species

12. (a) Among the given compounds, KCl is the only ionic compound. While all other compound contains covalent bonds.

13. (c) KCN ionises as K^+ and CN^- ions, which shows that KCN has an ionic bond. In the CN^- ion, the carbon and nitrogen are covalently bonded $[C \equiv N]^-$.

K— C≡N

Ionic bond between potassium and cyanide ions $K^+[C \equiv N]^-$.

Covalent bond between carbon and nitrogen in cyanide ions.

14. (c) Ionic compound are generally soluble in polar solvents like water but insoluble in non-polar solvents like benzene.

15. (b) Among the given compounds H_2O_2 and HNO_3 follows octet rule whereas $BeCl_2$, $AlCl_3$, SO_3, H_2SO_4 and PCl_5 does not follow octet rule as $BeCl_2$, $AlCl_3$ are electron deficient whereas

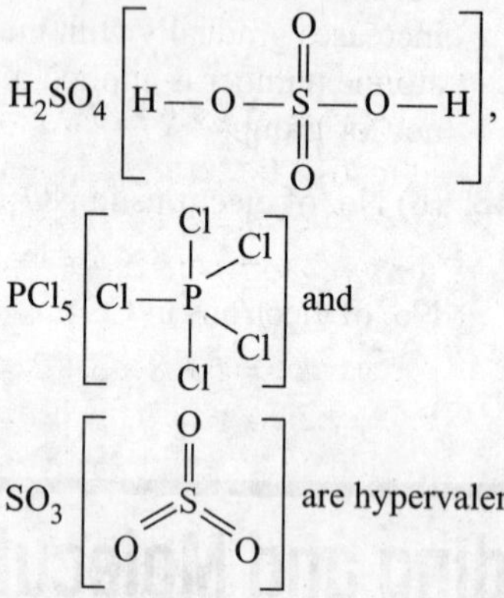

H_2SO_4 [H—O—S(=O)(=O)—O—H],

PCl_5 [Cl—P(Cl)(Cl)(Cl)(Cl)] and

SO_3 [S(=O)(=O)=O] are hypervalent.

16. (c) Bond angles are $H_2O = 104.5°$, F_2O or $OF_2 = 105°$, $Cl_2O = 110°$, $H_2S = 92.1°$ (In Br_2O, Bond angle $> 110°$). In Cl_2O, since oxygen is more electronegative than chlorine the bonding electrons lie closer to oxygen atom and hence there is a large repulsion making angle greater than 109.5°.

17. (c)

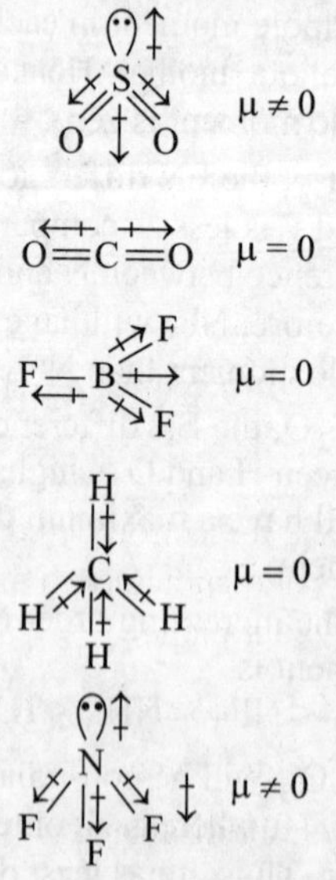

SO_2: $\mu \neq 0$

O=C=O $\mu = 0$

BF_3: $\mu = 0$

CH_4: $\mu = 0$

NF_3: $\mu \neq 0$

18. (b) BF_3 is trigonal planar and B_2H_6 is a dimer of trigonal planar molecule (BH_3), therefore both of these have zero dipole moment. NH_3 and NF_3, on the other hand have pyramidal structure and thus have dipole moments.

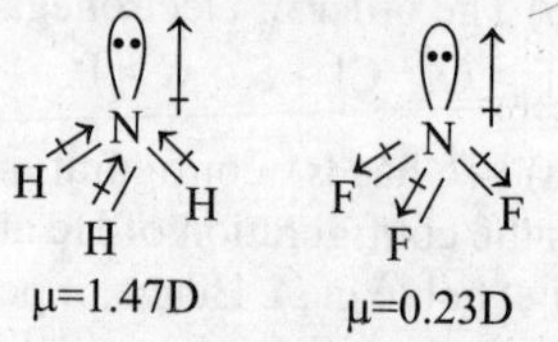

μ=1.47D μ=0.23D

In NH_3, the dipole moment of the three N—H bonds reinforce the dipole moment due to lone pair of electrons. But in NF_3, the dipole moments of the three N—F bonds oppose the dipole moment due to lone pair of electron. As a result, dipole moment of NH_3 ($\mu = 1.47$ D) is higher than that of NF_3 ($\mu = 0.23$ D).

19. (a) The bond angles depend upon electronegativity of the central atom and number of lone pair of electrons. Greater the electronegativity and the more the number of lone pairs, smaller the angle.

Since, the electronegativities of N (3.0) and O (3.5) are close, but NH_3 has one and H_2O has two lone pair of electron, therefore bond angle in NH_3 is larger (107°) than in H_2O (104.5°). Similarly, the electronegativities of P (2.1) and S (2.5) are close but PH_3 has one while H_2S has two lone pair of electrons therefore, bond angle in PH_3 (93°) is little more that in H_2S (92.2°). Thus, the actual order is $NH_3 > H_2O > PH_3 > H_2S$.

20. (b) NO is an odd electron species as N has 5 valence electrons and O has 6 valence electrons. Thus overall 1 electron on N remain unpaired. Since, H_2SO_4 has an expanded octet thus H_2SO_4 is an and expanded octet molecule.

21. (c) BF_3 is an electron deficient ($6e^-$) compound. So, it accepts $2e^-$ to attain stable configuration.

$H_3N: \longrightarrow BF_3$ (co-ordinate bond)

22. (d) Lattice energy $= \frac{q_1 q_2}{r}$

where, q_1 and q_2 are charge on ions and r is the distance between them. Since, interionic distance in CaO and NaCl are similar, (larger cation has smaller anion and *vice versa*). Therefore, r is almost the same. Therefore, lattice energy depend only on charge.

Since, the magnitude of charge on Na^+ and Cl^- ions is unity and that on Ca^{2+} and O^{2-} ions is 2 each, therefore the lattice energy of CaO is four times the lattice energy of NaCl, i.e. 4u.

23. (b) Due to larger size of potassium it has least degree of polarisation so it has maximum ionic character.

24. (a) PF_3 is a trigonal pyramidal. So, it has net dipole moment. Thus, PF_3 is polar molecules. Rest of the compounds have symmetrical shape. Thus, they are non-polar.

25. (d) High charge and small size of the cations increase polarisation. As the size of the given cation decrease as

$K^+ > Ca^{+2} > Mg^{+2} > Be^{+2}$

Hence, polarising power decrease as

$K^+ < Ca^{+2} < Mg^{+2} < Be^{+2}$

Test-2

1. (a) A sigma bond is formed by the overlap of *s-s, s-p*, p_x - p_x, *s-d* orbitals. Therefore, rotation around a sigma bond is possible without any restriction according to VBT theory.

2. (d) Among the given options, $[Co(NH_3)_6]^{3+}$ is incorrectly matched with its hybridisation. Its actual hybridisation is d^2sp^3 instead of sp^3d^2.

3. (c) SO_4^{2-} is sp^3-hybridised with perfectly tetrahedral shape.

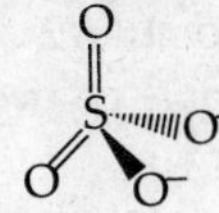

4. (a) At large distance, the energy is zero, means that there is no interaction.

As the two H-atoms approach each other, the force of attraction between the nucleus of one and the electron of other and *vice-versa* comes into play.

Similarly, repulsive forces between the two nuclei and between the two atoms electrons also exist. The distance at which the repulsive forces are exactly balanced by attractive forces is bond length. Here, the energy is minimum. If the two atoms are further brought closer to each other, repulsive forces become more dominant and energy increases. This is best explained by graph (a).

5. (b) (1) sp^3d is MX_5 kind of geometry in which two are at axial positions. Hence, no. of *X—M—X* bonds of 180° are = 1.

(2) In sp^3d^2, it is octahedral type geometry. Hence, there would be 3 bonds with straight 180°.

6. (b) There are 3 number of bonds of F—S—F at 180° in regular octahedral molecule.

7. (c) BrF_5 has distorted octahedral structure. Bromine in BrF_5 undergoes sp^3d^2 hydridisation giving square pyramidal shape.

8. (b) SF_4 molecule does not have sp^3 hybridisation. It has sp^3d hybridisation while all others have sp^3 hybridisation.

9. (b) The π-electron cloud lies in a plane perpendicular to the molecular plane.

10. (c) XeF_4 has sp^3d^2 hybridisation and square planar structure. I_3^- is sp^3d hybridised and is linear in shape. Its lone pair of electrons use the equatorial plane and the axial plane is occupied by bond pairs. Therefore the bond pairs are present in the same plane. Thus, this is also a planar molecule.

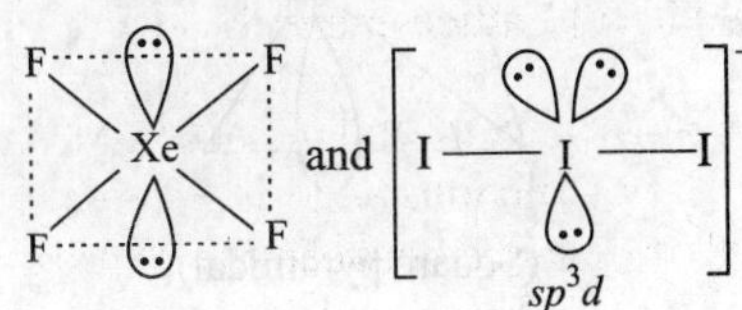

11. (b) Statement I is correct but Statement II is incorrect. The correct form of statement II :

In H_2O, there is sp^3 hybridisation but in $SnCl_2$ the hybridisation is sp^2.

12. (c) No. of hybrid orbital formed $(X) = \frac{1}{2}$ valence electron of central atom (VE) + No. of monovalent atoms/groups (NA) – charge on polyatomic cation (c) + charge on polyatomic anion.

For SF_2, $X = \frac{1}{2}(6+2-0) = 4$, hybridisation $= sp^3$

For SF_4, $X = \frac{1}{2}(6+4-0) = 5$, hybridisation $= sp^3d$

For SF_6, $X = \frac{1}{2}(6+6-0) = 6$, hybridisation $= sp^3d^2$

Thus, the correct set of hybridisation of sulphur atom respectively is sp^3, sp^3d and sp^3d^2.

13. (c) I atom has 7 electron in the valence shell, 5 of these are shared with 5F atoms. One lone pair is present. Thus, around I there are 5 bond pairs and one lone pair. Hence, shape is square pyramidal. As there are total 6 electron pairs around I, hybridisation is sp^3d^2.

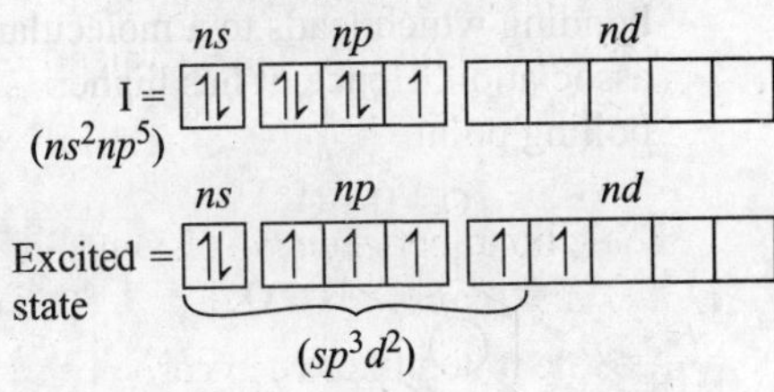

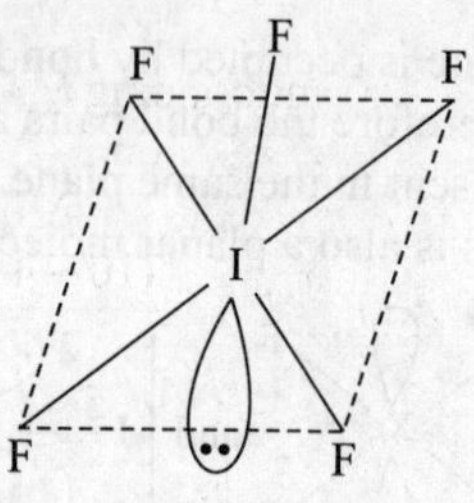

(Square pyramidal)

14. (c) Among the given molecules, XeF_2, I_3^- and ICl_2^- has linear shape while NO_2^- and H_2S has bent shape.

	B.P. + L.P	Shape
H_2S	2 + 2	Bent
XeF_2	2 + 3	Linear
NO_2^-	2 + 1	Bent
I_3^-	2 + 3	Linear
ICl_2^-	2 + 3	Linear

15. (c) Isostructural compound have same type of hybridisation.
In NF_3, N is sp^3 hybridised. (3 b.p. + 1 l. p.)
In NO_3^-, N is sp^2 hybridised.
In BF_3, B is sp^2 hybridised.
In H_3O^+, O is sp^3 hybridised.
In HN_3, central nitrogen is sp hybridised.
From this, we find that NF_3 and H_3O^+ are isostructural and BF_3 and NO_3^- are isostructural.

Test-3

1. (b) *Ortho*-nitrophenol has a lower boiling point than *meta*-nitrophenol due to intramolecular hydrogen bonding. While *para*-nitrophenol has intermolecular hydrogen bonding which leads to a molecular association. Hence, it has higher boiling point.

O—H--O
N=O

Further, benzene and nitrobenzene do not show hydrogen bonding, thus will have lower boiling point.

2. (c) Metallic bonds are formed by attraction between metal ions and delocalised or free e^- whereas ionic bond are formed by transfer of e^- from one atom to another and in covalent bond sharing of e^- takes place.

3. (b) Methanol and ethanol contain polar covalent O—H bond. Hence, they can form hydrogen bonds. Due to their hydrogen bonding character, they are miscible with water.

4. (d) There will be eight lobes and two nodal planes in $\pi^* 3d_{xy}$

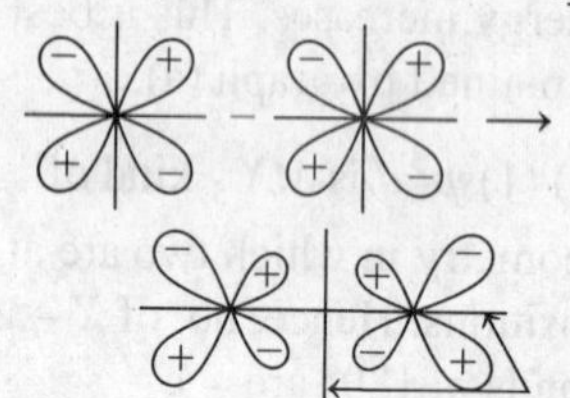

ABMO Nodal planes = 2

5. (b) Since, the BMOs are formed by attraction, therefore, their energy is lower than atomic orbitals as well as the ABMOs which are formed by repulsion. Greater is the electron density in the BMOs, higher will be the bond order and thus smaller will be the bond length.

6. (b) The electronic configuration of N_2 is $\sigma 1s^2 \sigma^* 1s^2 \sigma 2s^2$, $\sigma^* 2s^2 \pi 2p_x^2 = \pi 2p_y^2 \sigma 2p_z^2$.
Therefore, $\sigma 2p_z^2$ represents HOMO while $\pi^* 2p_x$ and $\pi^* 2p_y$, represents LUMO.

7. (c) An incoming electron will go to $\pi^* 2p_z$ orbital since it is half-filled. The filling of electrons in M.O. of O_2 is shown as

$$\sigma 1s^2 \sigma^* 1s^2 \sigma 2s^2 \sigma^* 2s^2 \sigma 2p_z^2$$
$$(\pi 2p_x^2 = \pi 2p_y^2)(\pi^* 2p_x^1 = \pi^* 2p_y^1)$$

The filling of electrons in MO of O_2^- is shown as

$$\sigma 1s^2 \sigma^* 1s^2 \sigma 2s^2 \sigma^* 2s^2$$
$$\sigma 2p_z^2 (\pi 2p_x^2 = \pi 2p_y^2)$$
$$(\pi^* 2p_x^2 = \pi^* 2p_y^1)$$

8. (c) The peroxide ion O_2^{2-} has 18 electrons arranged in the following manner;

$$\sigma 1s^2 \sigma^* 1s^2 \sigma 2s^2 \sigma^* 2s^2 \sigma 2p_z^2 \begin{bmatrix} \pi 2p_x^2 \\ \pi 2p_y^2 \end{bmatrix} \begin{bmatrix} \pi^* 2\pi_x^2 \\ \pi^* 2p_y^2 \end{bmatrix}$$

All the electrons are paired. Thus, O_2^{2-} ion is diamagnetic. The bond order may be calculated as (bonding− antibonding)/2, that is $(10-8)/2 = 1$.

9. (a) According to MO theory, the bond orders for F_2, NO, C_2 and CN^- are 1, 2.5, 2 and 3 respectively. Also the bond length is inversely proportional to the bond order thus, the bond length of F_2 is largest as its bond order is lowest.

10. (c) Mercurous ion is represented as Hg_2^{2+}. It is evidenced by the fact that, its $\mu = 0$, i.e. it is diamagnetic. It is possible only when there is presence of metallic bond.

Cl—Hg—Hg—Cl

11. (a) The molecular orbital electronic configuration of B_2 molecule is

$$\sigma 1s^2 \sigma^* 1s^2 \sigma 2s^2 \sigma^* 2s^2$$
$$(\pi 2p_x^1 = \pi 2p_y^1)$$

If however, the Hund's rule is violated then the configuration would be

$$\sigma 1s^2 \sigma^* 1s^2 \sigma 2s^2 \sigma^* 2s^2 \pi 2p_x^2$$

$$\therefore \text{B.O.} = \frac{6-4}{2} = 1$$

Since, all the electrons are paired up and the molecule is diamagnetic.

12. (c) Among the given species N_2 and O_2^{-2} show diamagnetism.

$N_2 : \sigma 1s^2 \sigma^* 1s^2 \sigma 2s^2 \sigma^* 2s^2$
$\pi 2p_x^2 = \pi 2p_y^2 \; \sigma 2p_z^2$
$O_2^{2-} : \sigma 1s^2 \sigma^* 1s^2 \sigma 2s^2 \sigma^* 2s^2 \sigma 2p_z^2$
$(\pi 2p_x^2 = \pi 2p_y^2)(\pi^* 2p_x^2 = \pi^* 2p_y^2)$

13. (b) Statement I is correct but Statement II is incorrect. The correct form is :

In $O_2, \sigma(2p_z)$ is filled before $\pi(2p_x)$ and $\pi(2p_y)$ while in N_2^{-2} $\pi(2p_x)$ and $\pi(2p_y)$ are filled first. So, they don't have same molecular orbital configuration.

14. (d) Total no. of electrons in CN^- $= 6+7+1 = 14$

Total no. of electrons in O_2^- $= 8+8+1 = 17$

Total no. of electrons in NO^+ $= 7+8-1 = 14$

Total no. of electrons in CN^+ $= 6+7-1 = 12$

As CN^- and NO^+ contain the same total no. of electron their MO electronic configuration will be same.

Thus, CN^- and NO^+ have the same bond order.

15. (a) Bond order

$$= \frac{\text{Bonding molecular orbital electron} - \text{Antibonding molecular orbital electron}}{2}$$

$O_2^{2-} = 1.0$ — Diamagnetic

$O_2^+ = 2.5$ — Paramagnetic

$N_2^+ = 2.5$ — Paramagnetic

$N_2^- = 2.5$ — Paramagnetic

16. (a) The electron configuration and the bond order of these species are as follows

(NO has $7+8 = 15$ electrons)

$NO: \sigma 1s^2\ \sigma^* 1s^2\ \sigma 2s^2\ \sigma^* 2s^2$ $\sigma 2p_z^2\ (\pi 2p_x^2 = \pi 2p_y^2)\ \pi^* 2p_x^1$

$KK\sigma 2s^2\sigma^* 2s^2\sigma 2pz^2(\pi 2p_x^2 = \pi 2p_y^2)$ $\pi^* 2p_x^1$

Bond order $= \frac{1}{2}(8-3) = 2.5$

NO^+; one electron is removed from $\pi^* 2p_x$,

Bond order $= \frac{1}{2} = (8-2) = 3$

NO^{+2} ; one electron is removed from $\pi^* 2p_x$ and one electron is removed from $\pi 2p_y$

Bond order $= \frac{1}{2}(7-2) = 2.5$

NO^- ; one electron is added to $\pi^* 2p_y$ of NO,

Bond order $= \frac{1}{2}(8-4) = 2$

Thus, NO^+ has the highest bond order and therefore the, shorter bond length. The correct order of bond length will be

$NO^+ < NO \approx NO^{+2} < NO^-$

17. (c) F—H ...... F bonding is strongest because of maximum electronegativity and smallest size of fluorine atom.

18. (b) The water (H_2O) molecules are tetrahedrally oriented with respect to each other. In this arrangement each oxygen atom is surrounded tetrahedrally by four hydrogen atom. Therefore, one water molecule is capable of forming 4 hydrogen bond.

19. (d) Total no. of electrons in the given species are as follows

$NO = 7+8 = 15$

$NO_2 = 7+2\times 8 = 23$

$ClO_2 = 17+2\times 8 = 33$

$ClF_2^- = 17+2\times 9+1 = 36$

Only ClF_2^- has even number of electrons and equal to inert gas configuration hence, it is not paramagnetic.

20. (a) Both He_2 and H_2^{+2} have zero bond order and hence do not exist.

21. (d) Molecular orbital configuration of

$B_2 \rightarrow \sigma 1s^2\sigma^* 1s^2\sigma 2s^2\sigma^* 2s^2(\pi 2p_x^1 = \pi 2p_y^1)$ (Paramagnetic)

$C_2^- \rightarrow \sigma 1s^2\sigma^* 1s^2\sigma 2s^2\sigma^* 2s^2(\pi 2p_x^2 = \pi 2p_y^2)\sigma 2p_z^1$ (Paramagnetic)

$O_2^+ \rightarrow$ $\sigma 1s^2\sigma 1s^2\sigma 2s^2\sigma^* 2s^2\sigma 2p_z^2(\pi 2p_x^2 = \pi 2p_y^2)(\pi^* 2p_x^2 = \pi^* 2p_y^1)$ (Paramagnetic)

$He_2^+ \rightarrow \sigma 1s^2\sigma^* 1s^1$ (Paramagnetic)

22. (b) In an antibonding M.O., electron density is minimum between the two nuclei of the molecule.

23. (b) B.O. in $N_2 = \frac{(10-4)}{2} = 3.0$

B.O. in $N_2^- = \frac{(10-5)}{2} = 2.5$

B.O. in $O_2 = \frac{(10-6)}{2} = 2.0$

B.O. in $O_2^- = \frac{(10-7)}{2} = 1.5$

Statements (a), (c), (d) are correct but (b) is wrong.

24. (c) $\sigma 2s$ and $\pi^* 2p_x$ are gerade while $\sigma^* 2s$ and $\pi 2p_x$ are ungerade.

25. (b) The distribution of electrons in the O_2 molecule is $\sigma 1s^2\sigma^* 1s^2$ $\sigma 2s^2\sigma^* 2s^2\sigma 2p_z^2$. $(\pi 2p_x^2\pi 2p_y^2), (\pi^* 2p_x^1\pi^* 2p_y^1)$

Chapter Break Thru

1. (d) Statements A, B and C are correct about Kössel-Lewis approach and covalency. While statements D and E are incorrect their correct statements are

- The negative and positive ions are stabilised by electrostatic attraction.
- Covalency of Ca is two while that of chlorine is seven.

Thus, option (d) is correct.

2. (b) PH_3, O_2, B_2H_6 and H_2SO_4 have covalent bonds. Their structures are as follows

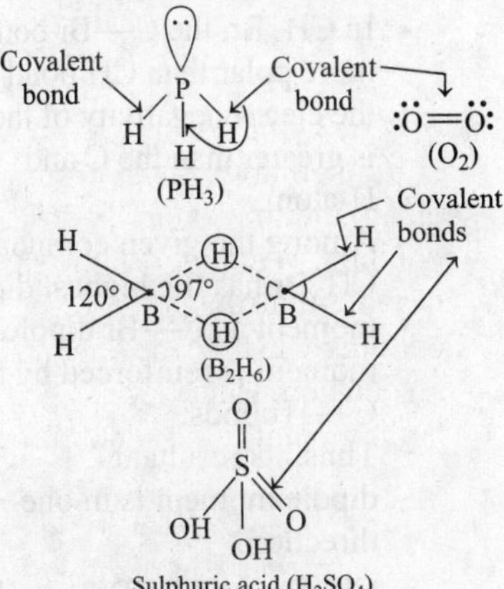

[Covalent bond between S, O and also between H and O].

3. (a) The correct match is

A-II, B-I, C-IV, D-III.

A. CH_4 molecule is tetrahedral in shape.

H C H H H 109.5°

B. $XeOF_4$ molecule is square pyramidal in shape.

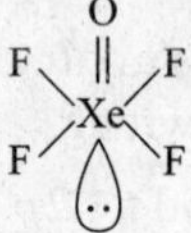

C. $H_2O \rightarrow$ V-shape

H H 104.45°

D. $NH_3 \rightarrow$ Trigonal pyramidal

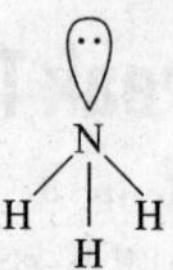

Hence, option (a) is correct.

4. (b) The correct reason is that BeF_2 molecule is linear as it is *sp*-hybridised.

While H_2O is bent due to lone pair-lone pair repulsion. It is sp^3 hybridised.

5. (b) • In CBr_4 the dipole moment is zero because four C—Br bond dipoles cancel each other.

• In CH_3Br, the C—Br bond is more polar than CH bond as the electronegativity of the Br is greater than the C and H-atom.

Among the given compounds, CH_3Br has the highest dipole moment as C—Br dipole moment is reinforced by three C—H bonds.

Thus, its resultant dipole moment is in one direction.

• CH_2Br_2 and $CHBr_3$ also have some dipole moment but less than CH_3Br. Also $CHBr_3$ has a lower dipole moment than CH_2Br_2.

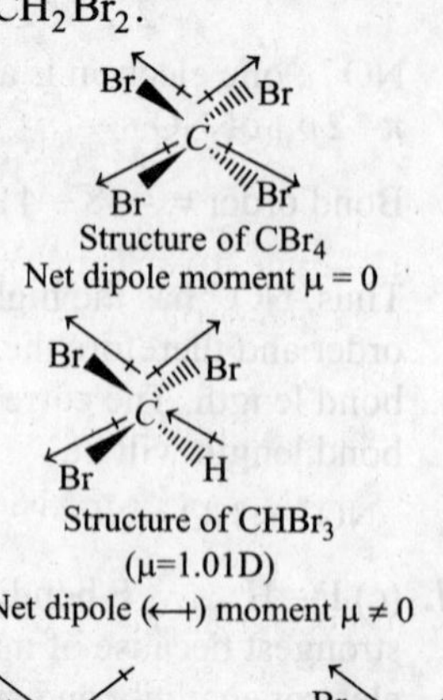

Structure of CBr_4

Net dipole moment $\mu = 0$

Structure of $CHBr_3$

(μ=1.01D)

Net dipole ($\leftrightarrow$) moment $\mu \neq 0$

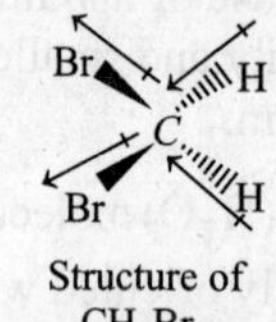

Structure of CH_2Br_2

(Net dipole moment $\mu \neq 0$)

Structure of CH_3Br (1.8D)

Therefore, the decreasing order of dipole moment (μ) is as follows

$CH_3Br > CH_2Br_2 > CHBr_3 > CBr_4$

6. (a) Among the given orbitals (vi) and (vii) show zero overlapping

• (i), (iii) and (iv) show positive or in phase overlap.

• (ii) and (v) shows negative or out of phase overlap.

7. (c) The structure of $CuSO_4 \cdot 5H_2O$ is as follows

H—O, H—O, Cu, O—H, O—H, $\delta+$, $\delta-$, H---O, H---O, S, O^-, O^-

The bonds involved are as follows

Ionic bond (i.e. electrovalent bond) between Cu^{2+} and SO_4^{2-}.

Covalent bond in H_2O and SO_4^{2-} molecule.

Coordinate covalent bond between Cu and four water (H_2O) molecules.

Hydrogen bond between H and O of H_2O and SO_4^{2-}.

8. (a) Lithium (Li) has the smallest size in the alkali group. So, its polarising power is very high.

Thus, it has a covalent character and covalent molecule is more soluble in non-polar solvent.

Therefore, it gives maximum solubility in non-polar solvent.

9. (b) Statements III and IV are correct.

The charge and size of Cu and Na is almost same, but the electronegativity difference in Cu and Cl is less.

Moreover, Cu has pseudo noble gas configuration, i.e. having 18 electrons in the outermost shell, has greater polarising power than a cation with noble gas configuration, i.e. having 8 electrons.

Thus, CuCl is covalent and NaCl is ionic.

10. (c) Given that dipole moment of HBr $= 2.6 \times 10^{-30}$ Cm

Interatomic distance

$$= 1.14 Å = 1.14 \times 10^{-10} \text{ m}$$

Percent ionic character

$$= \frac{\text{Observed dipole moment}}{\text{Theoretical dipole moment}} \times 100$$

$$= \frac{2.6 \times 10^{-30} \text{ Cm}}{1.6 \times 10^{-19} \text{ C} \times 1.14 \times 10^{-10} \text{ m}} \times 100$$

$$= \frac{2.6 \times 10^{-30} \times 100}{1.824 \times 10^{-19} \times 10^{-10}}$$

$$= 14.25\%$$

11. (c) Statements A, D are correct.

• Bond angle increases with increasing EN of central atom.

• Also, as the size of central atom increases, bond angle decreases.

Thus, option (c) is correct.

12. (a) Both (A) and (R) are true and (R) is the correct explanation of (A).

13. (d) Statements (a), (b), (c) are correct but statement (d) is incorrect because .

Overlapping of two distinct atomic orbital, each having an unpaired electron formed a covalent bond.

14. (b)

Structure of molecule	Shape and hybridisation
$[PCl_4]^+$ (Cl, P, Cl, Cl, Cl)	Tetrahedral (sp^3)
$[PCl_4]^-$ (Cl, Cl, P, Cl, Cl)	*See-saw* (sp^3d)
Cl, Cl, Cl—As, Cl, Cl	Trigonal bipyramidal (sp^3d)

Hence, option (b) is correct.

15. (d) Hybridisation of SO_4^{2-}

$\Rightarrow \frac{1}{2}(6+0+2)=4=sp^3$

and is tetrahedral.

Hybridisation of ClO_4^-

$\Rightarrow \frac{1}{2}(7+0+1)=4=sp^3$

and is tetrahedral.

16 (a) In T-shaped structure, $3bp$ and $2\,lp$ are present.

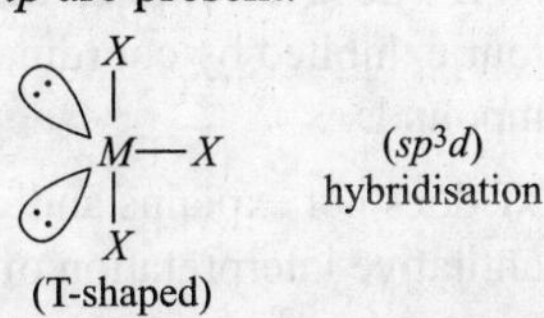

Thus, option (a) is correct.

17. (b) In sp^3d-hybridisation (trigonal bipyramidal structure), possible atomic orbital involved to form three equatorial bonds and two equally strong axial bonds are $d_{z^2}, s, p_x, p_y, p_z$. Thus, in sp^3d hybridisation d_{z^2} orbital is involved.

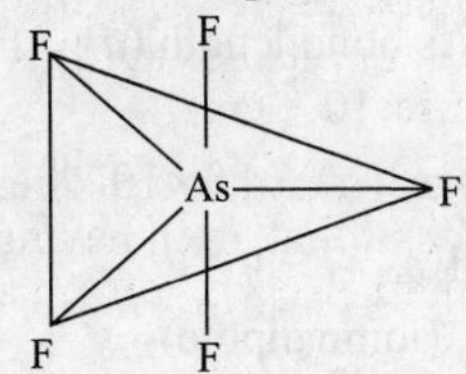

So, option (b) is correct.

18. (d) H_2SO_4 has zero, XeO_3 has 1 lone pair, XeF_4 has 2 lone pairs, XeF_2 has 3 lone pairs. So, the correct decreasing order is $XeF_2 > XeF_4 > XeO_3 > H_2SO_4$.

19. (d) All the given statements about molecular orbital (MO) theory are true.

Thus, option (d) is correct.

20. (b) Isoelectronic species have same bond order.

Number of electrons in the given species are as follows

I. $O_2^- = 8+8+1 = 17e^-s$

II. $CN^- = 6+7+1 = 14\,e^-s$

III. $NO^{\oplus} = 7+8-1 = 14e^-s$

IV. $CN^{\oplus} = 6+7-1 = 12e^-s$

Hence, CN^- and NO^+ have identical bond order. Thus, option (b) is correct.

21. (b) We know that,

bond dissociation energy $\propto$ bond order.

The bond order (BO) of the given species are as follows

BO. of $O_2 = \frac{1}{2}(8-4) = 2$

BO. of $O_2^- = \frac{1}{2}(8-5) = 1.5$

BO. of $O_2^{2-} = \frac{1}{2}(8-6) = 1$

BO. of $O_2^+ = \frac{1}{2}(8-3) = 2.5$

So, BO. $\longrightarrow O_2^{2-} < O_2^- < O_2 < O_2^{\oplus}$

Same order is followed by bond energy.

Thus, option (b) is correct.

22. (b) Except (b) all are correctly matched.

$CO^+ < CO$ (Bond strength)
2.5 3

Bond strength $\propto$ Bond order

Bond order $\propto$ Bond energy

23. (d) All the given statements are correct regarding MOT.

24. (c) Statement I is incorrect but Statement II is correct.

The species that have different number of electron will likely have different bond order.

CO and NO have different number of electrons. Hence, they will have different bond order.

Number of electrons in CO $= 6+8 = 14$

Number of electrons in NO $= 7+8 = 15$

The bond order of NO = 2.5 and CO = 3.

NO_2^- and BF_3 have same hybridisation, i.e. sp^2.

$NO_2^- \Rightarrow 2\sigma + 1\,lp = 3$, i.e. sp^2 - hybridised.

$BF_3 \Rightarrow 3\sigma + 0\,lp = 3$, i.e. sp^2 - hybridised.

25. (d) Intermolecular hydrogen bonding is present in concentrated acetic acid, H_2O_2 and HCN, while cellulose and salicylic acid has intramolecular hydrogen bonding.

Hydrogen peroxide (H_2O_2)

Concentrated acetic acid (CH_3COOH)

Hydrogen cyanide (HCN)

$\overset{\delta-}{H—C\equiv N}...\overset{\delta+}{H}—C\equiv \overset{\delta-}{N}$

Cellulose

Salicylic acid

In all the above structure, the dotted line represented the hydrogen bonding.

26. (b) Statement I is correct but Statement II is incorrect.

There is high difference between the electronegativites of Li and Cl. Hence, option (b) is correct.

27. (b) The nitrate ion, NO_3^- has following resonance structure.

28. (a) In *trans*-1,2-dichloroethylene, the four bond dipoles cancel each other

trans-1,2-dichloroethylene
($\mu_{net}=0$)

Other compounds have a net dipole moment,

cis-1,2-dichloroethylene ($\mu_{net} \neq 0$) 1. 1-dichloroethylene ($\mu_{net} \neq 0$)

trans-1, 2-dichloropent-2-ene ($\mu_{net} \neq 0$)

29. (d) Among the given species, $SnCl_2$ and O_3 has identical shape i.e. (bent shape).

30. (c) CaC_2, Al_4C_3 and Be_2C are ionic carbide and easily hydrolysed but SiC is covalent hydride which can not be hydrolysed.

31. (d) We assume that the z-axis is the internuclear axis, $\sigma 2s$ has no nodal plane. $\sigma^* 2p_x$ and $\pi 2p_y$ both have one nodal plane. $\pi^* 2p_y$ has two nodal planes: one along the internuclear axis while the other perpendicular to the internuclear axis.

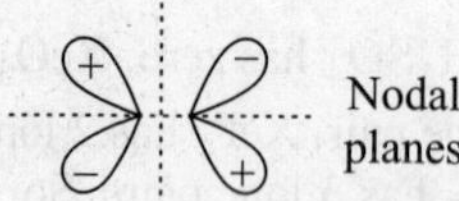

32 (d) As hydrogen bonding increased, boiling point increases except (d) all other are correct. In (d) CH_3N_3 has lower boiling points than N_3H due to H-bonding in later.

33. (c) Among the given species, only

- PCl_3 (sp^3, 1 lone pair) trigonal pyramidal [Non-planar]
- NH_2^- (sp^3, 2 lone pairs) bent [Non-planar]
- BrF_3 (sp^3d, 2 lone pairs) T-shape [Non-planar]
- XeO_2F_2 (sp^3d, 2 lone pairs) T-shape [Non-planar]
- XeF_4 (sp^3d^2, 2 lone pair) square [Planar]
- SiO_2 (sp, 0 lone pair) linear [Planar]
- CO_2 (sp, 0 lone pair) linear [Planar]
- SF_4 (sp^3d, 1 lone pair) *see-saw* [Non-planar]

34. (a) Both (A) and (R) are true and (R) is the correct explanation of (A).

35. (c) Hydrogen bond is written as

$$A—H\cdots B \text{ or } A—H\cdots A$$

A and B represent O, N or F. A—H is one molecule or part of a molecule and B is a part of another molecule. The dotted line represents the hydrogen bond. As we can see, H-atom is sandwiched between two highly electronegative atoms.

Thus, its largest coordination number is two.

36. (a) Greater is the oxidation state of the cation higher will be its polarising power and thus greater will be the covalent character (or lower will be the ionic character).

37. (a) The ground state electronic configuration of Hg is [Xe] $4f^{14}5d^{10}6s^2$. Therefore, the Hg-atom has two valence electrons (the 6s electrons). Steric number of Hg is $2+0=2$ which is confirmed by its Lewis structure.

There are no lone pair on the Hg-atom. The molecule has linear geometry. So, we conclude that Hg is sp-hybridised because it has the geometry of the two sp-hybrid orbitals.

38. (c) $sp^3d^3 : ns + np_x + np_y + np_z + nd_{x^2-y^2} + nd_{xy} + ndz^2$

39. (d) Lattice energy $= \dfrac{Kq_1q_2}{d^2}$, where

q_1q_2 are the charge on ions and d is the distance of separation.

So, the lattice energy depends upon the charge and size of the ions.

40. (d) The Lewis structure of C_2H_6 is

```
    H   H
    |   |
H—C—C—H
    |   |
    H   H
```

Every C-atom is sp^3-hybridised as it forms 4 σ-bonds. Thus, the C—C bond is sp^3—sp^3 sigma bond while the C—H bonds are sp^3—s sigma bond.

41. (d) VBT does not explain the colour exhibited by coordination compounds.

VBT does not explains and gives quantitative interpretation of magnetic data.

VBT does not distinguish between weak field ligand and strong field ligand.

42. (c) In N_2 molecule, (N≡N) triple bond has highest bond strength. Hence, it needs more amount of energy to break this bond, so has highest bond energy.

43. (c) As bond length (d) = 1.257 Å $= 1.257 \times 10^{-8}$ cm.

Charge, $(q) = 4.8 \times 10^{-10}$ esu

$$\mu_{(ionic)} = q \times d$$

μ_{ionic} (ionic dipole)

$$= 4.8 \times 10^{-10} \times 1.275 \times 10^{-8} \text{ esu cm}$$

Observed dipole moment $\mu_{observed} = 1.032\,D$

$$\%\text{ ionic character} = \frac{\mu_{observed}}{\mu_{ionic}} \times 100\%$$

$$= \frac{1.032}{6.12} \times 100\%$$

$$= 16.86\%$$

44. (c) The strength of a bond is dependent on the extent of overlapping sigma (σ) bond is created by the "end to end" overlap of the atomic orbitals or we can say that overlapping of orbitals takes place to a larger extent.

While in π bond the extent of overlapping occurs to a smaller extent. As in this case the overlap of atomic orbitals occurs along the direction perpendicular to the internuclear axis.

Due to the geometry of the overlapping orbitals, rotation of an atom is not possible around π-bond.

45. (a) The electronic configuration of N_2 is

$\sigma(1s)^2, \sigma^*(1s)^2$
$(\sigma 2s)^2 (\sigma^* 2s)^2 (\pi 2p_x^2 = \pi 2p_y^2)$
$(\sigma 2p_z)^2$

$$N_2, BO = \frac{10-4}{2} = 3$$

$$N_2^-, BO = \frac{10-5}{2} = 2.5$$

$$N_2^{2-}, BO = \frac{10-6}{2} = 2$$

Thus, the correct order of increasing BO is $N_2^{2-} < N_2^- < N_2$.

46. (c) In NH_3 and NF_3, the central nitrogen has three σ-bond and one lone pair.

Hence, both are sp^3-hybridised and possess trigonal pyramidal shape. The dipole moment vector do not cancel out each other.

Hence, both molecules have non-zero dipole moment. NH_3 has larger dipole moment than NF_3 because in NH_3 the dipole moment vector of the bond and the lone pair are in the same direction but in NF_3, these are in the opposite direction.

47. (d) Statement given in option (d) is incorrect. Its correct form is the number of molecular orbital formed is equal to the number of combining atomic orbitals.

48. (b) Rb^+ has the lowest polarising power among the given species and thus will form most ionic compound whereas Be^{2+} has the highest polarising power, thus it will form the least ionic or covalent compound.

49. (c) The steric number of Be in $BeCl_2$ is 2. Therefore, it is linear with *sp*-hybridisation. The steric number of B in BCl_3 is 3. Therefore it is trigonal planar with sp^2-hybridisation.

50. (c)

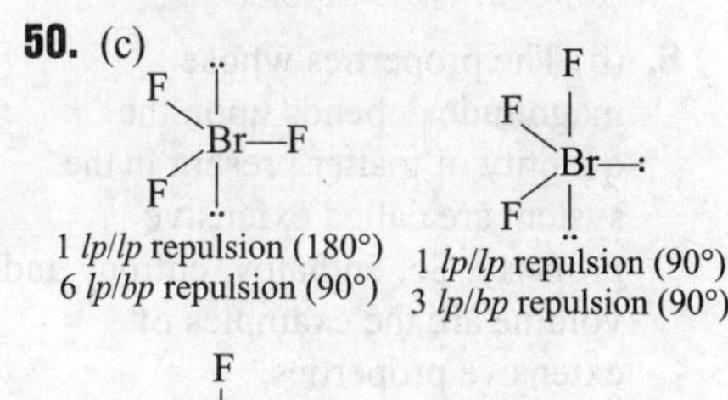

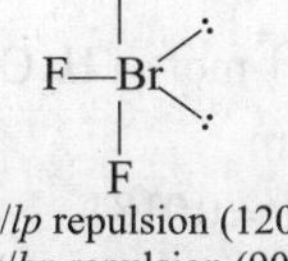

0 *lp*/*lp* repulsion (120°)
4 *lp*/*bp* repulsion (90°)

These factors indicate that arrangement (3) is the most probable as it minimizes lone pair-lone pair and lone pair-bond pair repulsions.

Ch-5 Thermodynamics

Topical Follow Thru

Test-1

1. (c) In isolated system, neither the exchange of matter nor the exchange of energy is possible with the surrounding. Dessicator will not allow the exchange of matter and energy with the surrounding. Hence, it is an example of an isolated system.

2. (b) Expansion work,

$$W = -p_{ext}\Delta V$$
$$= -p_{ext}(V_{final} - V_{initial})$$
$$p_{ext} = 1\,atm$$

$V_{initial}$ = Volume of 8g O_2 at STP

$$\text{Now, moles of } O_2 = \frac{8}{32} = \frac{1}{4}$$
$$= 0.25\,mol$$

$$V_{initial} = 22.4 \times 0.25 = 5.6\,L$$
$$V_{final} = 5.6 \times 2 = 11.2\,L$$

Thus,

$$\Delta V = 5.6\,L$$
$$W = -(1\,atm \times 5.6\,L)$$
$$= -5.6\,L\,atm$$

3. (b) In an isolated system, there is no exchange of energy as heat or as work, i.e. $W = 0$ and $Q = 0$.

4. (b) Since, work done is equal to the area under *pV*-curve between initial and final volume.

As seen from the figure, this area is maximum for adiabatic process, less for isothermal and least for isobaric process.

$$W_{adiabatic} > W_{isothermal} > W_{isobaric}$$

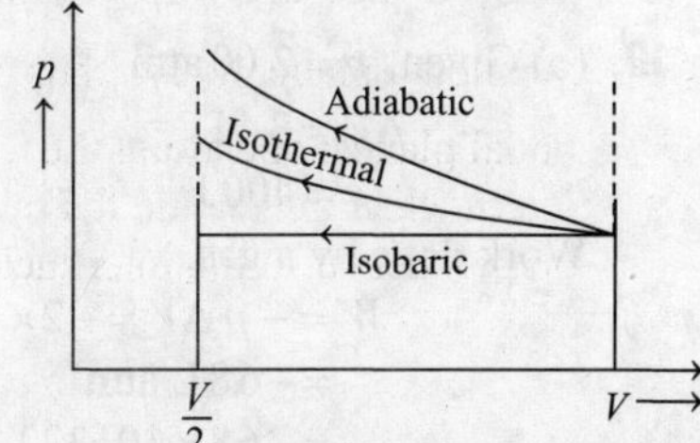

5. (c) According to first law of thermodynamics,

$$\Delta U = q + W$$

where, ΔU is the change in internal energy.

In the cyclic process,

$$\Delta U = 0$$

but $W + q = \Delta U$

$$W_{cyc} + q_{cyc} = 0 \quad \ldots(i)$$

$$q_{cyc} = [14.7 - 25.2 - 3.56 + 31.5] \text{ kJ} \quad \ldots(ii)$$

Putting (ii) in (i), we get

$W_{cyc} = -17.44$ kJ.

6. (b) The properties whose magnitude depends upon the quantity of matter present in the system are called extensive property. So, enthalpy, entropy and volume are the examples of extensive properties.

7. (c) Volume of 1 mol of H_2O at 373 K and 1 atm

$(V_1) = 18 \text{ cm}^3 = 0.018 \text{ L}$

Volume of 1 mole of H_2O vapour at 373 K and 1 atm ($pV = RT$)

$$V = \frac{RT}{p} = \frac{0.0821 \times 373}{1} = 30.62 \text{ L}$$

$$W = -p(V_2 - V_1)$$
$$= -1(30.62 - 0.018)$$
$$= -30.6 \text{ L atm} = -30.6 \times 101.3$$
$$\approx -3100 \text{ J}$$

8. (c) Using the formula

$$W = -2.303 nRT \log \frac{p_1}{p_2}$$

On substituting the given values

$$W = -2.303 \times 1 \times 2 \times 27 \times \log \frac{10}{1}$$

$$W = -124.4 \text{ cal}$$

9. (b) As ΔH remains same by different paths, it is a state function. As q changes by different paths, it is a path function.

10. (b) Given, $p = 2.00$ atm

$$\Delta V = 3.4 \text{ L}$$
$$q = 400 \text{ J}$$

Work done by a gas,

$$W = -p\,\Delta V = -2 \times 3.4$$
$$= -6.8 \text{ L atm}$$
$$= -6.8 \times 101.32 \text{ J}$$
$$= -688.976 \text{ J}$$
$$\Delta U = q + (-W)$$
$$= 400 + (-688.976)$$
$$= -288.976 \approx -289 \text{ J}$$

11. (b) State function depends upon initial and final state of the system and does not depend upon path of the system. So, heat and work are not state function.

12. (b) $q = 250$ J

$$W = -p(V_2 - V_1)$$
$$= -0.5(10 - 1) = -4.5 \text{ L atm}$$
$$= -4.5 \times 101 \text{ J} = -454.5 \text{ J}$$
$$\Delta U = q + W$$
$$= 250 - 454.5 = -204.5 \text{ J}$$

13. (a) $H = U + pV$

$\therefore \Delta H = \Delta U + p\,\Delta V + V\,\Delta p$

If p is constant, i.e. $\Delta p = 0$ only then

$$\Delta H = \Delta U + p\,\Delta V$$

14. (a) Given, $q = 80$ cal

$$W = 500 \text{ cal}$$
$$\Delta U = ?$$

Using the formula,

$$q = \Delta U + W$$
$$80 = \Delta U + 500$$
$$-500 + 80 = \Delta U$$
$$\Delta U = -420 \text{ cal}$$

15. (d) As $\Delta H = \Delta U + \Delta n_g RT$

ΔH value is less than or greater than ΔU depending on the value of Δn_g which is the change in number of moles of the gaseous components.

As a result, (a) and (b) cannot be true.

$\Delta U < \Delta H$ when $\Delta n_g < 0$

Hence, (c) is also false and only (d) is correct.

16. (c)

I. In Adiabatic process, total heat of the system remains constant, i.e. $q = 0$. So, A-I.

II. In Isothermal process, temperature remains constant, i.e. $\Delta T = 0$. So, B-III.

III. In Isobaric process, pressure remains constant, i.e. $\Delta p = 0$. So, C-IV.

IV. In Isochoric process, volume remains constant, i.e. $\Delta U = 0$. So, D-II.

17. (a) The closed vessel made of conducting material allows heat transfer but mass transfer is restricted so it follows the definition of a closed system that if there is no exchange of matter but exchange of energy is possible between the system and the surroundings in a closed system.

Hence, both (A) and (R) are correct and (R) is the correct explanation of (A).

18. (b) From work equation,

$$\int dW = \int -p \cdot dV$$

$$W = -\int 20 \cdot \frac{dV}{V} = -20 \ln \frac{V_2}{V_1}$$

$$= -20 \ln \frac{10}{1} = -20 \times 2.303$$

$$W = -46.06 \text{ L-atm}$$
$$W = -4666.8 \text{ J}$$

From internal energy equation,

$$\Delta U = q + W$$
$$\Rightarrow 500 = q - 4666.8$$
$$q = 5166.8 \text{ J}$$

19. (a) The correct match is A-IV, B-I, C-II, D-III.

A. Reversible process is carried out infinitesimally slowly.

B. An adiabatic process is the one in which heat transfer does not take place.

C. When $\Delta G = 0$, then reaction is at equilibrium.

D. In cyclic process, internal energy change and enthalpy change equal to zero.

20. (b) Total work done (W)

$$= W_{AB} + W_{BC} + W_{CA}$$
$$= -p\Delta V + 0 + 2.303\, nRT \log \frac{V_C}{V_A}$$
$$= -1 \times 20 + 2.303 \times 2 \times 0.082 \times 121.95 \log 2$$
$$\left(T = \frac{pV}{nR} = \frac{1 \times 20}{2 \times 0.082} = 121.95 \text{ K} \right)$$
$$= -20 + 13.864 = -6.136 \text{ L atm}$$
$$= -6.136 \times 101.3 \text{ J}$$
$$\approx -621.58 \text{ J}$$

21. (a) $\Delta U = q + W$

$\Rightarrow \quad -1455\,J = 812\,J + W$

$\Rightarrow \quad W = -2267\,J$

Negative values of work done indicates that work is done by the system.

22. (d) For an isothermal expansion of an ideal gas, $\Delta U = 0$

Since, p_{ext} is zero in vacuum.

$W = -p_{ext} \cdot \Delta V = 0$

$W = 0$

$\therefore \quad q = 0$

23. (b) According to the first law of thermodynamics,

$\Delta U = q + W$

For adiabatic process, $q = 0$

Thus, $\Delta U = W$

For expansion into vacuum $(p_{ext} = 0) W = -p\Delta V = 0$

Thus, $\Delta U = q$

For cyclic process $(V_f - V_i)$,

$\Delta U = 0$ Thus, $q = -W$

For isothermal process $(\Delta T = 0)$ involving an ideal gas, $\Delta U = 0$.

Thus, $q = -W$.

24. (b) Although neither heat nor work is a state function, their sum $(q + W)$ is equal to ΔU and ΔU is a state function. Similarly, q_V is a state function as it is equal to ΔU. Further, temperature (T) is also a state function. Moreover, by specifying the exact path, we give the path function an exact value.

25. (c) Statement I is incorrect but Statement II is correct. The corrected form of Statement I is : If the value of the property of a system is equal to the sum of values for the parts of the system, then such property is called an extensive property.

Test-2

1. (c) During the phase change of a substance the temperature change is zero. As we know that specific heat capacity $= q/C\Delta T$ which is zero; specific heat capacity becomes infinity, so during the process of conversion of ice into the water, the specific heat capacity is infinity.

2. (d) Hess's law cannot be used for the determination of entropy.

3. (b) In polyatomic molecules such as H_2O, bond enthalpy (better called average bond enthalpy) is the average of the bond dissociation enthalpies. Thus,

$$\Delta_{O-H} H^\circ = \frac{502 + 427}{2} = 464.5\,kJ$$

4. (c) The calorific value (CV) of a fuel or food is the standard enthalpy of combustion per gram of the substance, i.e. the amount of heat released when one gram of the substance undergoes complete combustion. Thus,

$$C.V.(C_6H_{12}O_6) = \frac{-2802}{180} = -15.6\,kJ\,g^{-1}$$

$$C.V.(CH_4) = \frac{-890}{16} = -55.6\,kJ\,g^{-1}$$

$$C.V.(CO) = \frac{-283}{28} = -10.1\,kJ\,g^{-1}$$

$$C.V.(H_2) = \frac{-285}{2} = -142.5\,kJ\,g^{-1}$$

Hence, $CO(g)$ has minimum calorific value.

5. (d) $\Delta_a H^\circ$ is the enthalpy change when one mole of the substance in its standard state dissociates into isolated atoms in the gas phase. The standard state of bromine is Br_2 (liquid) and it does not involve enthalpy of atomisation as it convert its state into solid. In case of $H_2(g)$, the enthalpy of atomisation is the same as bond dissociation enthalpy. In $CH_4(g)$, it is just the enthalpy of atomisation and in Na(s), the enthalpy of atomisation is associated to convert it into Na(g).

6. (d) There are many compounds that cannot be directly synthesised from their elements.

In some cases, the reaction proceeds too slowly, or side reactions may produce substances other than the desired compound. In these cases, $\Delta_f H^\circ$ can be determined by an indirect approach, which is based on Hess's law of heat summation (or simply Hess's law). It is used to calculate enthalpy of combustion, neutralisation, ionisation, etc.

7. (b) $M^+X^-(s) \xrightarrow{\Delta_{Lattice}H^\circ} M^+(g) + X^-(g)$

8. (b) The Born-Haber cycle traces the formation of sodium chloride through five steps : (i) sublimation of solid Na, (ii) dissociation of Cl_2 molecule, (iii) ionisation of Na atoms, (iv) formation of Cl^- ions, and (v) formation of solid NaCl from ions.

9. (c) $S + O_2 \longrightarrow SO_2$,

$\Delta H_f = -4.6\,kJ$

$\because$ 0.5 g of sulphur on burning produce 1g of SO_2

$\therefore$ 32g of sulphur on burning produce $= \frac{32 \times 1}{0.5} = 64$ g of SO_2

$\therefore \Delta H = -4.6 \times 64$

$= -294.4\,kJ$

10. (b) During combustion, C is oxidised to CO_2 and H is oxidised to H_2O. Thus, saturated hydrocarbons have higher calorific values than the corresponding unsaturated hydrocarbons. More the number of C and H atoms, greater is the calorific value.

Hence, C_4H_{10} has maximum standard enthalpy of combustion per gram than others.

11. (b) $\Delta H_{fusion} = -1.435\,kcal\,mol^{-1}$

$= 1435\,cal\,mol^{-1}$

$\Delta S = 5.26\,cal\,mol^{-1}K^{-1}$

$$\Delta S = \frac{\Delta H_{fusion}}{T}$$

$$T = \frac{\Delta H_{fusion}}{\Delta S} = \frac{1435}{5.26}\,K$$

$= 272.81 \approx 0°C$

12. (b) The enthalpy of vaporisation is given by,

$$T = \frac{\Delta_{vap} H}{\Delta S}$$

$$= \frac{30000 \text{ J mol}^{-1}}{75 \text{ JK}^{-1} \text{ mol}^{-1}} = 400 \text{ K}$$

13. (b) In a combustion reaction, sum of enthalpies of reactants is greater than the sum of the enthalpies of products. Therefore, combustion of all organic compounds is an exothermic reaction.

Also, enthalpies of all elements in their standard state are zero.

So, both (A) and (R) are true but (R) is not the correct explanation of (A).

14. (b) $\Delta_f H°$ is the enthalpy change when 1 mole of the substance is formed from its elements in the standard state, i.e. in reaction (b). Reaction (a) does not represent $\Delta_f H°$ because standard state of carbon is graphite and not diamond. In (c), 2 moles of NH_3 are produced and in (d), $CO(g)$ is not in standard state.

15. (b) $CuSO_4(s) + 5H_2O(l) \longrightarrow CuSO_4 \cdot 5H_2O(s)$

$\Delta H = \Delta H_1$

$CuSO_4(s) + aq \longrightarrow CuSO_4(aq),$

$\Delta H = \Delta H_2$

$CuSO_4 \cdot 5H_2O + aq \longrightarrow CuSO_4(aq) + 5H_2O,$

$\Delta H = \Delta H_3$

Then, $\Delta H_2 = \Delta H_1 + \Delta H_3$

$-15.89 = -18.69 + \Delta H_3$

or $\Delta H_3 = 18.69 - 15.89$

$= +2.80$ kcal

16. (c) Since, both HCl and KOH are strong acid and strong base respectively. Thus, 57.3 kJ heat will be released.

17. (d) (i)

$P_4(\text{Yellow}) + 5O_2 \longrightarrow 2P_2O_5,$

$\Delta H_1 = -9.91 \text{ kJ mol}^{-1}$

(ii) $P_4(\text{Red}) + 5O_2 \longrightarrow 2P_2O_5,$

$\Delta H_2 = -8.78 \text{ kJ mol}^{-1}$

Eq. (i) – Eq. (ii) gives the required result

$-9.91 + 8.78 = -1.13$ kJ

18. (b) $C + O_2 \longrightarrow CO_2;$

$\Delta H°_f = -393.5 \text{ kJ mol}^{-1}$

$CO_2 \longrightarrow C + O_2;$

$\Delta H° = 393.5 \text{ kJ mol}^{-1}$ ...(i)

$C + \frac{1}{2}O_2 \longrightarrow CO;$

$\Delta H = -110.5$ ...(ii)

$H_2 + \frac{1}{2}O_2 \longrightarrow H_2O;$

$\Delta H = -241.8 \text{ kJ mol}^{-1}$ ...(iii)

(i) + (ii) + (iii)

$CO_2 + H_2 \longrightarrow CO + H_2O;$

$\Delta H = 393.5 + (-110.5) + (-241.8)$

$= 41.2$ kJ

19. (b) $\Delta_r H = \Sigma \Delta H°_f$ (product) $- \Sigma \Delta H°_f$ (reactant)

$\Delta H = [2 \times (-34.7) + 0] - [(-48.4 + 0)]$

$= -69.4 + 48.4 \text{ kJ} = -21.00$ kJ

20. (c) Among the given reaction, option (c) represents the reaction that provide enthalpy of formation of CH_3Cl.

$C(s) + \frac{3}{2}H_2(g) + \frac{1}{2}Cl_2(g) \longrightarrow CH_3Cl(g)$

21. (b) Benzene is more stable than cyclohexene.

Theoretically, benzene has structure of 3C=C in closed ring. So, its theoretical hydrogenation energy $= 3q_2$ and calculated hydrogenation energy of benzene $= q_1$.

Therefore, resonance energy should be

= Theoretical value – Calculated value

$= 3q_2 - q_1$

22. (b) In combustion, energy release. Hence, it is exothermic and negative.

23. (c) For one mole energy change is

C (graphite) $\longrightarrow$ C (diamond),

$\Delta H = -1.9$ kJ

For combustion of 6 g of diamond and 6 g of graphite.

$C_{diamond} \longrightarrow C_{graphite}$

i.e. For $\frac{1}{2}$ mol, $\Delta H = \frac{-1.9}{2} = -0.95$ kJ

[**Note** Consider the magnitude]

24. (c) $\Delta H°_{reaction}$

$= \Delta_f H°_{(C_6H_6)} - 3\Delta_f H°_{(C_2H_2)}$

$= 85 - 3(230)$

$= -605 \text{ kJ mol}^{-1}$

25. (a) The involved reaction is

$\underset{\text{Ethylene}}{CH_2{=}CH_2} + H_2 \rightarrow CH_3{-}CH_3$

or H—C(H)=C(H)—H + H—H ⟶ H—C(H)(H)—C(H)(H)—H

$\Delta H_{reaction} = \Sigma BE_{(Reactants)} - \Sigma BE_{(Products)}$

$= [BE_{(4C-H)} + BE_{(C=C)} + BE_{(H-H)}] - (BE_{(6C-H)} + BE_{(C-C)}]$

$= BE_{(C=C)} + BE_{(H-H)} - 2BE_{(C-H)} - BE_{(C-C)}$

$= 600 + 400 - 2 \times 410 - 350$ kJ

$= 1000 - 1170 = -170 \text{ kJ mol}^{-1}$

Test-3

1. (d) After freezing, the molecules attain an ordered packing and, therefore, entropy decreases.

Rest of the process involved in reactions are as follows

(a) Here, one molecule gives two atoms, i.e. the number of particles increases leading to a more disordered situation.

(b) The reactant ($NaHCO_3$) is a solid and it has low entropy. Among products, there are one solid and two gases. Therefore, the products represent a condition of high entropy.

(c) At 0 K, the constituent particles are static and the entropy is minimum. If the temperature is raised to 115 K, the particles begin to move and oscillate about their equilibrium positions in the lattice and the system becomes disordered. Therefore, entropy increases.

2. (b) The connectivity between entropy and the spontaneity of a reaction is expressed by the second law of thermodynamics.

The entropy of the universe (system + surroundings) increases in a spontaneous process and remains unchanged in equilibrium process.

3. (d) $C_2H_2(g)+\frac{5}{2}O_2(g)\longrightarrow 2CO_2(g)+H_2O(l);$

$\Delta G^\circ = -1234$ kJ ...(i)

$C(s)+O_2(g)\longrightarrow CO_2(g);$

$\Delta G^\circ = -394$ kJ ...(ii)

$H_2(g)+\frac{1}{2}O_2(g)\longrightarrow H_2O(l);$

$\Delta G^\circ = -237$ kJ ...(iii)

$H_2(g)+2C(s)\longrightarrow C_2H_2(g);$

$\Delta G^\circ = ?$

By 2× Eq. (ii) + Eq. (iii) − Eq. (i)

$$\Delta G^\circ = 2\times(-394)+(-237)-(-1234)$$
$$= -788+(-237)+1234$$
$$= -1025+1234 = +209 \text{ kJ}$$

4. (c) Gibbs-Helmholtz equation is as follows,

$$\Delta G = \Delta H - T\Delta S$$

From Gibbs-Helmholtz equation, it is clear that ΔG will always be negative, if ΔH is negative and $T\Delta S$ is positive.

5. (c) Statement (c) is incorrect about entropy because it is an extensive property of the system. Its value increases with an increase in the number of particles in system.

6. (d) "Reversible" under strict thermodynamic sense is a special way of carrying out a process such that the system is at all times in perfect equilibrium with its surroundings.
So, in a reversible process the total change in entropy is always zero.

$$\Delta S_{sys} + \Delta S_{surr} = 0$$

7. (c) $\Delta H = \Delta U + \Delta n_g RT$

$\Rightarrow \Delta H = 2000 + 2\times 2\times 300$

$[\because \Delta n_g = 2-0=2,\ R = 2 \text{ cal K}^{-1}\text{mol}^{-1}]$

$$= 3200 \text{ cal}$$
$$\Delta G = \Delta H - T\Delta S$$
$$= 3200-(300\times 40)$$
$$= -8800 \text{ cal}$$

8. (d) ΔS for the isothermal reversible expansion of an ideal gas is given as

$$\Delta S = 2.303\, nR \log\left(\frac{V_2}{V_1}\right)$$
$$= (2.303)(2)(2)\log\frac{20}{2}$$
$$= (9.212)\log 10$$
$$= 9.2 \text{ cal K}^{-1}\text{ mol}^{-1}\ (\log 10 = 1)$$

9. (d) According to the thermodynamics,

$$\Delta G = \Delta H - T\Delta S$$

A reaction is non-spontaneous at every temperature, if ΔG is positive at all temperatures.
Only condition (ii) shows spontaneous process while conditions (i), (iii) and (iv) shows non-spontaneous process.
In condition (v), ΔH and ΔS shows no role in spontaneity of a reaction as their value is zero.

10. (a) The standard Gibbs free energy change, ΔG°, for a reaction is related to its equilibrium constant, K, by the equation $\Delta G^\circ = -RT\ln K$. This equation can be used to predict the ratio of the products to reactants at equilibrium for a given reaction.
If $\Delta G^\circ > 0$, then $K<1$ and the reaction is reactant-favoured at equilibrium.

11. (d) Second law of thermodynamics states that in a cyclic process, heat cannot be completely converted into work.

12. (a) Using the formula of entropy change,

$$\Delta S = 2.303 nR \log\left(\frac{V_2}{V_1}\right)$$

On substituting the given value, we will get

$$= 2.303\times 5\times 8.314\log\frac{100}{10}$$
$$= 95.7 \text{ JK}^{-1}$$

13. (d) We know that,

$$\Delta G^\circ = -RT\ln K$$

or $\ln K = \frac{-\Delta G^\circ}{RT}$ or $K = e^{-\Delta G^\circ/RT}$

So, the relation between ΔG° and K is given in option (d).

14. (a) Using formula

$$\Delta H = \Delta U + \Delta n_g RT$$
$$= -5+(-1\times 2.0\times 298) \text{ cal}$$
$$= -601 \text{ cal}$$

Now, substitute the value of ΔH in the formula,

$$\Delta G = \Delta H - T\,\Delta S$$
$$= -601-298(-10)$$
$$= 2379 \text{ cal}$$

15. (b) Both (A) and (R) are true but (R) is not the correct explanation of (A).
In this process, one molecule of hydrogen gives two atoms, i.e. number of gaseous particle increase leading to more disordered state.

Chapter Break Thru

1. (c) $C(s)+O_2(g)\longrightarrow CO_2(g)$

$$\Delta S^\circ = \Sigma S^\circ_{(\text{Product})} - \Sigma S^\circ_{(\text{Reactant})}$$
$$\Delta S^\circ = 213.5 - 5.690 - 205$$
$$= 2.81 \text{ J K}^{-1}$$

2. (b) In given reaction,

I. $2NH_3(g)\longrightarrow N_2(g)+3H_2(g)$

$\Delta n_g = n_{\text{products}} - n_{\text{reactants}}$

$\Delta n_g = 4-2 = 2\,(+\text{ve})$

II. $NH_4Cl(s)\longrightarrow NH_3(g)+HCl(g)$

$\Delta n_g = 2-0 = 2\,(+\text{ve})$

III. $Ag^+(aq)+Cl^-(aq)\longrightarrow AgCl(s)$

$\Delta n_g = 0$

IV. $N_2(g)+O_2(g)\longrightarrow 2N_2O(g)$

$\Delta n_g = 2-3 = -1$

V. $PCl_3(g)+Cl_2(g) \longrightarrow PCl_5(g)$

$\Delta n_g = 1-2 = -1$

In I, II reactions, n_g value is +ve is So, positive entropy change attained.

3. (b) Work done $= -p \times \Delta V$

$= 1 \times (2.5 - 2.0) = -0.5$ L-atm

$= -0.5 \times 101.3$ J $= -50.65$ J

From the first law of thermodynamics,

$\because \quad q = \Delta U - W$

$300 = \Delta U + 50.65$

$\therefore \Delta U = 249.35$ J

4. (d) $C_p - C_V = R$

$$C_p = R + \frac{3}{2}R = \frac{5}{2}R$$

$\left(\frac{\Delta H}{\Delta T}\right) = C_p$ (for 1 mole of gas)

$$\Delta H = C_p \Delta T = \frac{5}{2}R(373-298)$$

$$= \frac{5}{2} \times R \times 75 \text{ cal mol}^{-1}$$

$(R = 2$ cal/K mol$)$

$= 375 \text{ cal mol}^{-1}$

5. (c) The enthalpy change of a reaction does not depend upon the nature of intermediate reaction steps. This is according to Hess's law.

6. (a) Tendencies of reactions to occur in the forward direction and effect of temperature are as follows

ΔH	ΔS	ΔG	Nature
–	+	–	Spontaneous (at all T)
–	–	(– at low T)	Spontaneous
–	–	(+ at high T)	Non-spontaneous
+	–	+	Non-spontaneous (at all T)

7. (d) For any gas, $C_p - C_V = R$, which is the gas constant. Hence, its value for any gas hydrogen or nitrogen is same. Here, for ideal gas $C_p - C_V = R/M$, where M is the mass of one mole of gas.

Mass of one mole of hydrogen $M = 2g$ and that of nitrogen is $M = 28$ g

$a = C_p - C_V = \frac{R}{2}$ (For hydrogen)

$b = C_p - C_V = \frac{R}{28}$ (For nitrogen)

$\Rightarrow \quad a = 14$ b

8. (a) For adiabatic change,

$$T_2 = T_1\left(\frac{V_1}{V_2}\right)^{\gamma-1}$$

$$= 300\left(\frac{1}{8}\right)^{1.33-1}$$

$$= 300\left(\frac{1}{8}\right)^{1/3} = 150 \text{ K}$$

$w = -nC_V(T_2 - T_1) \quad [\because n = 1]$

$= -1 \times 3 \times 2(150 - 300)$

$= 900$ cal

[**Note** For NH_3, $C_V = 3R = 3 \times 2$ cal]

9. (d) Work involved in heating of gas

$W = -p \cdot \Delta V$

$= -p(V_2 - V_1)$

$$= -p\left[\left(\frac{nRT_2}{p}\right) - \left(\frac{nRT_1}{p}\right)\right]$$

$= -nR(T_2 - T_1)$

$= -1 \times 8.314\ (373 - 273)$

$= -831.4$ J

10. (c) Statement I is incorrect but Statement II is correct because a compound is formed from its elements if $\Delta_r G°$ and $\Delta_f G°$ are negative.

11. (d) According to Kelvin-Planck statement, no process is possible whose sole result is the absorption of heat from a reservoir and complete conversion of the heat into work.

According to Clausius statement, no process is possible whose sole result is the transfer of heat from a colder object to a hotter object.

Hence, both statements I and II are correct.

12. (b) For combustion of 1 mole of benzene, $\Delta n_g = -1.5$

$$\Delta H = \Delta U + \Delta n_g RT$$

$$\Rightarrow -3271 = \Delta U - \frac{1.5 \times 8.314 \times 300}{1000}$$

$\Rightarrow \quad \Delta U = -3267.25$ kJ

For 1.5 mole of combustion of benzene,

$\Delta U = -3267.25 \times 1.5$

$= -4900.89$ kJ

13. (a) $\Delta G = \Delta H - T\Delta S$,

For process to be spontaneous ΔG should be –ve which will be so when $\Delta H =$ + ve, $\Delta S =$ + ve and $T\Delta S > \Delta H$.

14. (c) Enthalpy of ionisation depends upon the size of molecules. Larger the size, lesser will be ionisation energy. So, the correct order is

$$\Delta H_3 > \Delta H_4 > \Delta H_1 > \Delta H_2.$$

15. (b) At 298 K, the standard enthalpy of formation is taken as zero for elementary substance in the normal physical state in which it exists.

As Cl_2 exists in the gaseous state but Br_2 exist in the liquid state, hence it is zero for $Cl_2(g)$.

16. (b) For an isothermal process,

$$\Delta S = nR \ln \frac{V_2}{V_1}$$

$V_1 = 2\text{ dm}^3, V_2 = 20\text{ dm}^3$,

$n = 2$ mol, $R = 8.314$ JK^{-1} mol^{-1}

$$\therefore \Delta S = (2\text{ mol}) \times (8.314 \text{ JK}^{-1}\text{mol}^{-1}) \times 2.303 \log \frac{20\text{ dm}^3}{2\text{ dm}^3}$$

$= 38.294$ JK^{-1}

17. (c) $W = -2.303nRT \log \frac{V_2}{V_1}$

$$= -2.303 \times 2 \times 2 \times 300 \log \frac{50}{15}$$

$= -2763.6\ (\log 10 - \log 3)$

$= -2763.6\ (1 - 0.4771)$

$= -2763.6 \times 0.5229$

$= -1445$ cal

18. (d) $\Delta S = \Sigma n\, \Delta S$ (Products) $- \Sigma n\, \Delta S$ (Reactants)
In option (d), change in entropy is negative. Because at higher temperature, degree of randomness is high.

19. (c) The enthalpy of neutralisation for the following reaction is

$$H^{\oplus}(aq) + \overset{\ominus}{O}H(aq) \longrightarrow H_2O(l)$$

$\Delta H^{\ominus} = -57.32 \text{ kJ mol}^{-1}$

$\Delta H^{\ominus}_{\text{reaction}} = \Sigma$ Heat of formation of products $- \Sigma$ Heat of formation of reactants

$= \Delta_f H^{\ominus} H_2O - (\Delta_f H^{\ominus} H^{\oplus} + \Delta_f H^{\ominus} OH^{\ominus})$

$-57.32 = -285.84 - (0 + x)$

$x = -285.84 + 57.32 = -228.52 \text{ kJ}$

Thus, the enthalpy of formation of hydroxylation is $-228.52 \text{ kJ mol}^{-1}$.

20. (a) From the first law of thermodynamics, $\Delta U = q + W$
For adiabatic change, $q = 0$
$\therefore \quad \Delta U = W_{\text{ad.}}$
Hence, both (A) and (R) are true and (R) is the correct explanation of (A).

21. (d) The properties that do not depend upon the quantity of matter present in the system or size of the system are called intensive properties. So temperature, pressure and dipole moment are the examples of intensive properties.

22. (b) $\Delta H = \Delta U + \Delta n_g RT$
Here, $\Delta n_g = 1, T = 967 + 273 = 1240 \text{ K}$

$$176 = \Delta U + \left(\frac{1 \times 8.314 \times 1240}{1000}\right) \text{kJ}$$

$176 = \Delta U + 10.309 \text{ kJ}$
$\Delta U = 176 - 10.309 \text{ kJ} = 165.69 \text{ kJ}$

23. (a) $\Delta G = \Delta H - T\,\Delta S$
$= -2.5 \times 10^3 - 25 \times 74$
$=$ negative
So, the reaction is spontaneous.

24. (a) $W = -10 \text{ J}, q = 40 \text{ J}$
From the first law,
$\Delta U = q + W$
$= 40 - 10 = 30 \text{ J}$

25. (b) $W = -p_{\text{ext}} \Delta V$
$= -2.5 \text{ atm} \times (6 - 4) \text{ dm}^3$
$= -5 \text{ L atm} = -5 \times 101.3 \text{ J}$
$= -506.5 \text{ J}$

For isothermal expansion of ideal gas, $\Delta U = 0$
$\therefore \quad q = -W = 506.5 \text{ J}$
This heat is used to heat up 1 mole of water (18 g of water)
$q = m \times c \times \Delta T$
$506.5 = 18 \times 4.2 \times \Delta T$
or $\Delta T = 6.7$
$\therefore$ Final temperature of water
$= 20°\text{C} + 6.7°\text{C} = 26.7°\text{C}$

26. (a) $\Delta G = \Delta H - T\,\Delta S$
For spontaneous reaction at all temperature,
$\Delta H = -\text{ve}$
$\Delta S = +\text{ve}$
So, $\Delta G = -\text{ve}$

27. (b) If a refrigerator door is kept open, then room will become hot, because the refrigerator exhausts more heat into the room than earlier. In this way, temperature of the room increases and room become hot. No refrigerator is efficient. Thus, it exhausts more heat into the room than it extracts from it.

28. (a) As, reaction is carried out in a closed vessel (bomb calorimeter), no expansion or compression can take place.
So, work done, $(W = 0)$. Hence, by first law of thermodynamics $\Delta U = q$. But q is $-$ve, i.e. < 0 because the given reaction is exothermic (being redox reaction). Hence, $\Delta U < 0$.

29. (a) For adiabatic process, $q = 0$ and hence ΔS (system) $= 0$.
Irreversible process is accompanied by increase of entropy, therefore ΔS (surrounding) is positive.

30. (b) We know, $\log K = \dfrac{-\Delta_r G^{\ominus}}{2.303RT}$

$$= -\frac{(-13.6 \times 10^3 \text{ J mol}^{-1})}{2.303\,(8.314 \text{ JK}^{-1} \text{ mol}^{-1})\,(298 \text{ K})}$$

$= 2.38$
Hence, $K = \text{antilog } 2.38$
$= 2.398 \times 10^2$

31. (d) $\Delta S^{\ominus} = \Sigma S^{\ominus}_{\text{(products)}} - \Sigma S^{\ominus}_{\text{(reactants)}}$

$$= [S^{\ominus}_{CO_2}] - \left[S^{\ominus}_{CO} + \frac{1}{2} S^{\ominus}_{O_2}\right]$$

$$= 213.8 - \left[197.9 + \frac{1}{2} \times 205\right]$$

$= -86.6 \text{ JK}^{-1}$

According to Gibb's-Helmholtz equation

$\Delta G^{\ominus} + \Delta H^{\ominus} - T\,\Delta S^{\ominus}$
$= -282.84 - 298 \times (-86.6 \times 10^{-3})$
$= -282.84 + 25.87$
$= -257.033 \text{ kJ}$

32. (c) $\Delta S_{\text{Reaction}} = \Sigma S_{\text{Product}} - \Sigma S_{\text{Reactants}}$
$= 2 \times S_{H_2O} - [2 \times S_{H_2} + S_{O_2}]$
$= 2 \times 68 - [2 \times 126.6 + 201.20]$
$\Delta S = -318.4 \text{ JK}^{-1}$

33. (a) The volume occupied by water is very small and the volume change is equal to the volume occupied by 1 mole of water vapour.
$(V_1 = 18 \text{ mL})$
From ideal gas equation,
$pV_2 = nRT$
$R =$ gas constant
$= 0.0821$ L-atm/mol/K
$T = 413 \text{ K}; \quad p = 1.0 \text{ atm}$

$$V_2 = \frac{nRT}{p}$$

$$V_2 = \frac{1.0 \times 0.0821 \times 413}{1.0} = 33.90 \text{ L}$$

Work done, $W = -p_{\text{ext}} \times \Delta V$
$= -(1.0) \times (33.90)$ L-atm
$= -33.9 \times 101.3 \text{ J} = -3434.8 \text{ J}$

34. (d) Both Statement I and Statement II are correct because entropy of all elements and compounds decrease with decrease of temperature and becomes zero at 0 K.

35. (d) From reaction of ammonia formation

$$\frac{1}{2}N_2(g)+\frac{3}{2}H_2(g)\longrightarrow NH_3(g)$$

$$\Delta H^{\ominus}_{298\,K}=\sum H^{\circ}_{f\,(\text{Product})}-\sum H^{\circ}_{f\,(\text{Reactant})}$$

$$=-13.00\,\text{kcal/mol}-0$$

$$=-13.00\,\text{kcal/mol}$$

For calculation $\Delta H_{773\,K}$

$$\frac{\Delta H_2-\Delta H_1}{T_2-T_1}=\Delta C_p$$

$$\frac{\Delta H_2-(-13.0)}{773-298}=\left(8.0-\frac{1}{2}\times 7.0-\frac{3}{2}\times 6.0\right)\times 10^{-3}$$

$$\frac{\Delta H_2+13}{475}=(8-3.5-9)\times 10^{-3}$$

$$=-4.5\times 10^{-3}\times 475$$

$$\Delta H_2+13=-2137.5\times 10^{-3}$$

$$\Delta H_2=-2.1375-13$$

$$=-15.1375\,\text{kcal/mol}$$

36. (a) Dissolution of KNO_3 in water is endothermic.

$$\Delta H_{sol}=35.8\,\text{kJ mol}^{-1}$$

∴Heat absorbed when 0.06 mole of KNO_3 is dissolved

$$=35.8\times 0.06\,\text{kJ}$$

$$=2148\,\text{J}$$

$$q=m\times c\times \Delta T$$

$$\therefore\ 2148=100\times 4.184\times \Delta T$$

or $\Delta T=5.13\,\text{K}$

As dissolution is endothermic, $\Delta T=5.13\,\text{K}$ is fall in temperature.

Hence, temperature of solution $=298-5.13=292.8\,\text{K}\approx 293\,\text{K}$

37. (b) The reaction is

$$NH_3+\frac{3}{2}CuO\longrightarrow \frac{1}{2}N_2+\frac{3}{2}H_2O+\frac{3}{2}Cu$$

$$\Delta_r H^{\circ}=\Sigma H^{\circ}_{\text{Products}}-\Sigma H^{\circ}_{\text{Reactants}}$$

$$=\left[\frac{1}{2}H^{\circ}_{N_2}+\frac{3}{2}H^{\circ}_{H_2O}+\frac{3}{2}H^{\circ}_{Cu}\right]-\left[H^{\circ}_{NH_3}+\frac{3}{2}H^{\circ}_{CuO}\right]$$

$$=\left[0+\frac{3}{2}(-285)+0\right]-\left[-46+\frac{3}{2}(-155)\right]=-149\,\text{kJ}$$

Heat evolved from 17g NH_3 $=149\,\text{kJ}$

∴ Heat evolved from 8.5 g NH_3

$$=\frac{149}{2}\,\text{kJ}=74.5\,\text{kJ}$$

38. (a) Solids and liquids do not show significant change in the volume when heated. Thus, ΔV is insignificant.

$$\Delta H=\Delta U+p\,\Delta V$$

$$=\Delta U+p\times 0 \text{ or } \Delta H=\Delta U$$

Hence, (A) and (R) are true and (R) is the correct explanation of (A).

39. (a) **Intensive property** The properties that do not depend upon the quantity of matter present in the system or size of the system are called intensive property,

e.g. Temperature, heat capacity, concentration.

Extensive property The property whose magnitude depend upon the quantity of matter present in the system are called extensive property. e.g. Enthalpy, entropy, volume, free energy.

40. (a) (i) $2C(s)+2H_2(g)\longrightarrow C_2H_4(g)$

$$\Delta H=12.5\,\text{kcal}$$

(ii) $C(s)\longrightarrow C(g),\ \Delta H=171\,\text{kcal}$

(iii) $\frac{1}{2}H_2(g)\longrightarrow H(g),$ $\Delta H=52.1\,\text{kcal}$

Calculate ΔH for

$$CH_2{=}CH_2(g)\longrightarrow 2C(g)+4H(g)$$

2× Eq. (ii) + 4 × Eq. (iii) − Eq. (i)

Therefore,

$$\Delta H=537.9\,\text{kcal}$$

Hence,

$$4BE(C{-}H)+BE(C{=}C)=537.9$$

$$4\times 99.3+x=537.9$$

or $x=140.7\,\text{kcal}$

41. (b) $C(s)+\frac{1}{2}O_2(g)\longrightarrow CO(g)$

$$\Delta H-\Delta U=\Delta n_g RT$$

$$=\frac{1}{2}\times 8.314\times 298=1238.78\,\text{mol}^{-1}\,\text{J}$$

42. (c) $\Delta H=\Delta(U+pV)$

$$=\Delta U+\Delta(RT)=\Delta U+R\,\Delta T$$

For isothermal expansion of ideal gas, $\Delta U=0$

$(\because \Delta U=C_V\,\Delta T \text{ and } \Delta T=0)$

$\therefore\ \Delta H=0+0=0$

43. (c) $A\to C;\ \Delta H=q_1$

$C\to D;\ \Delta H=q_2$

$D\to 2B;\ \Delta H=q_3\times 2$

Adding all three equations, we get

$A\to 2B;\ \Delta H=q_1+q_2+2q_3$

44. (d) According to I[st] law of thermodynamics,

$$\Delta U=q+W$$

For isothermal process, $\Delta U=0$

Hence, $q=-W$

For cyclic process, $\Delta U=0$

Hence, $q=-W$

For isochoric process, $\Delta V=0$

Hence, $W=p\,\Delta V=0$

$$\Delta U=q$$

For adiabatic process, $q=0$

Hence, $\Delta U=W$

For expansion into vacuum, $W=0$

Hence, $\Delta U=q$

Thus, only (d) is incorrect.

45. (a) The heat of reaction is basically ΔH at constant pressure and ΔU at constant volume. Their relation is given by

$$\Delta H=\Delta U+\Delta n_g RT$$

Here, $\Delta n_g=12-15=-3$

Thus,

$$\Delta H-\Delta U=-3\times 8.314\times 10^{-3}\times 298$$

$$=-7.43\,\text{kJ}$$

46. (b) Heat absorbed by water

$$=m\times s\times \Delta t$$

$$=18940\,\text{g}\times 0.998\,\text{cal g}^{-1}\,\text{deg}^{-1}\times 0.632^{\circ}\text{C}$$

$$=11946.14\,\text{cal}$$

∴ Heat produced on combustion of 1.89 g of benzoic acid

$$=11946.14\,\text{cal}$$

Molar mass of benzoic acid $(C_6H_5COOH) = 122\,g$

$\therefore$ Molar heat of combustion

$$= \frac{11946.14}{1.89} \times 122\,cal$$

$$= 771126.5\,cal = 771.12\,kcal$$

47. (c) A reaction that is spontaneous and favourable is known as an exergonic reaction. It releases energy into the surroundings.

Hence, from the options given, only photosynthesis is not a type of exergonic reaction.

48. (c) From the given data in the problem we can write

$$\Delta S_T = nR \ln \frac{V_2}{V_1}$$

$$= 2.303 nR \log \frac{V_2}{V_1}$$

$$= 2.303 \times 1 \times 8.314 \times \log \frac{20}{2}$$

$$= 2.303 \times 8.314 \times 1$$

$$= 19.15\,J\,mol^{-1}\,K^{-1}$$

49. (a) Isothermal reversible process,

$$W = -\int_{V_1}^{V_2} nRT \frac{dV}{V}$$

$$W = -nRT \ln \frac{V_2}{V_1}$$

$$W = -2.303 nRT \log \frac{V_2}{V_1}$$

From first law of thermodynamics

$$\Delta U = q + W$$

For isothermal process

$$\Delta T = 0 \text{ then } \Delta U = 0$$

So $q = -W$

$$q = 2.303 nRT \log \frac{V_2}{V_1}$$

50. (b) Enthalpy of neutralisation of oxalic acid by strong base

$$= -25.4\,kcal\,mol^{-1}$$

As oxalic acid is dibasic, so heat of neutralisation

$$= 2 \times -13.7$$

$$= -27.4\,kcal$$

$\therefore$ Enthalpy of dissociation of oxalic acid

$$= -25.4 - (-27.4)$$

$$= 2.0\,kcal\,mol^{-1}$$

Ch-6 Chemical Equilibrium

Topical Follow Thru

Test-1

1. (a) In the reaction,

$$2C(s) + O_2(g) \rightleftharpoons 2CO_2(g)$$

Equilibrium constant is given by

$$K_p = K_C (RT)^{\Delta n_g}$$

$\Delta n_g \neq 0$ for the reaction

Thus, $K_p \neq K_C$

While in other reactions, $\Delta n_g = 0$, hence, $K_p = K_C$.

2. (b) For the reaction,

$$SO_2(g) + \frac{1}{2}O_2(g) \rightleftharpoons SO_3(g)$$

Equilibrium constant,

$$K_1 = \frac{[SO_3]}{[SO_2][O_2]^{1/2}} \quad ...(i)$$

For the reaction,

$$2SO_3(g) \rightleftharpoons 2SO_2(g) + O_2(g)$$

Equilibrium constant,

$$K_2 = \frac{[SO_2]^2 [O_2]}{[SO_3]^2} \quad ...(ii)$$

On squaring both sides in Eq. (i),

$$K_1^2 = \frac{[SO_3]^2}{[SO_2]^2 [O_2]} \quad ...(iii)$$

On multiplying Eq. (ii) and Eq. (iii),

$$K_1^2 \times K_2 = 1$$

$$\Rightarrow \quad K_2 = \frac{1}{K_1^2}$$

$$\Rightarrow \quad K_1^2 = \frac{1}{K_2}$$

3. (b) Amongst the given options (b) is correct i.e. except C and D other statements are correct. The corrected form of these statements are as follows

C. For dissolution of solids in liquids, the solubility remains constant at a given temperature.

D. For dissolution of gases in liquids, the concentration of a gas in liquid is directly proportional to the pressure of the gas over the liquid.

4. (b) The correct match is

A-III, B-I, C-IV, D-II

5. (b) The given equations are

$$N_2 + O_2 \rightleftharpoons 2NO \quad ...(i)$$

$$\frac{1}{2}N_2 + \frac{1}{2}O_2 \rightleftharpoons NO \quad ...(ii)$$

Equilibrium constant for reaction (i) is

$$K_1 = \frac{[NO]^2}{[N_2][O_2]}$$

Equilibrium constant for reaction (ii) is

$$K_2 = \frac{[NO]}{[N_2]^{\frac{1}{2}} [O_2]^{\frac{1}{2}}}$$

Hence, the relation between both K_1 and K_2 is

$$\therefore \quad K_1 = K_2^2$$

$$\text{or} \quad K_2 = \sqrt{K_1}$$

6. (a) $2KClO_3 \xrightarrow{\Delta} 2KCl + 3O_2$

and $2Pb(NO_3)_2 \rightarrow 2PbO + O_2 + 4NO_2$

Above reactions are the examples of thermal decomposition. $KClO_3$ is decomposed into KCl and O_2 but KCl and O_2 cannot be converted into $KClO_3$. Similarly in $Pb(NO_3)_2$, it decomposes into PbO, O_2 and NO_2 but they cannot be converted back into the $Pb(NO_3)_2$. Hence, these are the examples of irreversible reactions.

7. (d) (A) is false but (R) is true. The correct statement of (A) is as follows

A. $N_2 + 3H_2 \rightleftharpoons 2NH_3$

$$K_p = \frac{(p_{NH_3})^2}{(p_{N_2})(p_{H_2})^3}$$

So, unit of K_p should be,

$$= \frac{(atm)^2}{(atm)(atm)^3} = (atm)^{-2}$$

8. (d) It is the characteristic of reaction. Hence, no reason for lower value.

9. (b) Except A and E all options are correct. The corrected form of A and E are as follows

- Equilibrium is possible only in a closed system at a given temperature.
- The magnitude of such quantities at any stage indicates the extent to which the physical process has proceeded before reaching equilibrium.

10. (b) The equilibrium constant for the first reaction is

$$H_3PO_4 \overset{K_1}{\rightleftharpoons} H^+ + H_2PO_4^-$$

$$K_1 = \frac{[H^+][H_2PO_4^-]}{[H_3PO_4]}$$

The equilibrium constant for the second reaction is

$$H_2PO_4^- \overset{K_2}{\rightleftharpoons} H^+ + HPO_4^{2-}$$

$$K_2 = \frac{[H^+][HPO_4^{2-}]}{[H_2PO_4^-]}$$

The equilibrium constant for the third reaction is

$$HPO_4^{2-} \overset{K_3}{\rightleftharpoons} H^+ + PO_4^{3-}$$

$$K_3 = \frac{[H^+][PO_4^{3-}]}{[HPO_4^{2-}]};$$

Multiplying these three,

$$K_1 \times K_2 \times K_3 = \frac{[H^+]^3[PO_4^{3-}]}{[H_3PO_4]}$$

11. (a) All the given options are correct except B and C. The corrected form of B and C are as follows

- The value of equilibrium constant is independent of initial concentrations of the reactants and products.
- Equilibrium constant is temperature dependent having one unique value for a particular reaction represented by a balanced equation at a given temperature.

12. (d) The law of mass action states that the rate of a chemical reaction is directly proportional to the product of the molar concentration of the reactants raised to their stoichiometric coefficient.

13. (a) The stability of oxide depends on the value of equilibrium constant.

Greater is the value of K, more will be the tendency to give forward reaction. Hence, as K value increases the stability of reactant decreases, so only option (a) is correct.

14. (c) Option (c) is incorrect among all the options. Its correct form is as follows

All the measurable properties of the system remain constant.

15. (a) Among the given reactions, (i) and (ii) are homogeneous reactions while (iii), (iv) and (v) are heterogeneous reaction as the reactants and products are in different phases.

16. (c) (A) is true but (R) is false.

17. (a) α-D-glucose $\rightleftharpoons$ β-D-glucose

At equil. $1-x$ $\quad x$

$$K_C = \frac{x}{1-x} = 1.8$$

$\Rightarrow \quad x = 1.8 - 1.8x$

$\Rightarrow \quad 2.8x = 1.8$

$\therefore \quad x = \frac{1.8}{2.8} = 0.643$

$\Rightarrow \quad (1-x) = 1 - 0.643 = 0.357$

Percentage of α-D-glucose

$= 0.357 \times 100 = 35.7\%$

18. (d) Both Statement I and Statement II are correct.

19. (a) For the equilibrium reaction,

$$I_2 \rightleftharpoons 2I^-$$

Initial conc. 1.0 $\quad$ 0

Eq. conc. $1-x \quad 2x$

The equilibrium constant for the reaction is

$$K_C = \frac{[I^-]^2}{[I_2]} = \frac{4x^2}{1-x}$$

$4x^2 + 10^{-6}x - 10^{-6} = 0$

we get $x \simeq 5 \times 10^{-4}$

$[I_2] = 1 - x = 1 - 5 \times 10^{-4} = 0.9995\,M$

$[I^-] = 2x = 2(5 \times 10^{-4}) = 1 \times 10^{-3}\,M$

Hence, $[I_2(g)] > [I^-(g)]$

20. (a) The equilibrium reaction is given as

$$2AB_2(g) \rightleftharpoons 2AB(g) + B_2(g)$$

At equil. 1 $\quad$ 0 $\quad$ 0

$(1-x)p \quad (x)p \quad (x/2)p$

The equilibrium constant for this

$$K_p = \frac{(xp)^2 \times \left(\frac{x}{2}p\right)}{[p(1-x)]^2}$$

$$\therefore K_p = \frac{x^2 \cdot x}{2(1-x)^2}\left[\frac{p^3}{p^2}\right]^1$$

$$= \frac{x^3 \cdot p}{2}$$

$(1 - x = 1,$ since $x << 1)$

or $x = 3\sqrt{\frac{2K_p}{p}}$

Also can be written as

$$x = \left(\frac{2K_p}{p}\right)^{1/3}$$

21. (c) Given the values of

$A_2 = 3.0 \times 10^{-3}$ M,

$B_2 = 4.2 \times 10^{-3}$ M,

$AB = 2.8 \times 10^{-3}$ M

$A_2(g) + B_2(g) \rightleftharpoons 2AB(g)$

So, the equilibrium constant (K_C) for the above reaction is

$$K_C = \frac{[AB]^2}{[A_2][B_2]}$$

$$K_C = \frac{(2.8 \times 10^{-3})^2}{3 \times 10^{-3} \times 4.2 \times 10^{-3}} = 0.62$$

22. (b) The value of $K (K = 1.6 \times 10^{12})$ is very high which means reaction proceeds almost towards completion, i.e. system will proceed more towards forward reaction and thus will contain mostly products at equilibrium.

23. (a) The reaction is given as

	A +	$2B \rightleftharpoons$	$2C$ +	D
Initial conc.	a	$1.5a$	0	0
At equil.	$(a-x)$	$(1.5a - 2x)$	$2x$	x

Given, $a - x = 1.5a - 2x$

$\therefore \quad x = 0.5a$

Now,

$[A] = 0.5a, [B] = 0.5a, [C] = a,$
$[D] = 0.5a$

$$K_C = K_p = \frac{(a)^2 (0.5a)}{(0.5a)(0.5a)^2} = 4$$

24. (c) When the reaction can be expressed as the sum of two other reactions , the equilibrium constant of the overall reaction is equal to the product of equilibrium constants of individual reactions, so 20 units × 30 units = 600 units.

25. (d) $NH_4HS(s) \rightleftharpoons NH_3(g) + H_2S(g)$

At $t = 0$	0	0.5	0
At $t =$ eq.	$1-x$	$0.5 + p$	p

$p_T = 0.5 + p + p = 0.75$

$\therefore p = 0.125$ atm

$K_p = p_{NH_3} \times p_{H_2S}$

$= (0.5 + 0.125) \times 0.125$

$= 0.078 \text{ atm}^2$

Test-2

1. (b) $A + B \rightleftharpoons C + D$

	A	B	C	D
Concentration at $t = 0$	1	1	1	1
Concentration at eq.	$1-x$	$1-x$	$1+x$	$1+x$

$$\because K_C = \frac{[C][D]}{[A][B]} = \frac{(1+x)^2}{(1-x)^2} = 100$$

or $\quad \dfrac{1+x}{1-x} = 10$

or $\quad 1 + x = 10 - 10x$

$\therefore \quad x = \dfrac{9}{11}$

Now $[D] = 1 + x = 1 + \dfrac{9}{11} = 1.818$

Thus, its value w.r.t. initial concentration increases

2. (b) For the given reaction

$$2A \rightleftharpoons B + C$$

$$Q = \frac{[B][C]}{[A]^2} = \frac{2 \times \frac{1}{2}}{\left(\frac{1}{2}\right)^2} = 4$$

$\Delta G° = -2.303RT \log K_C$

$2249.5 = -2.303 \times 8.314 \times 200 \log K_C$

$\log K_C = -0.587$

$\therefore K_C = 0.259$

$\because \quad Q > K_C$

Therefore, reaction shifts in reverse direction.

3. (b) The reaction is

$CO_2 + C \text{ (graphite)} \rightleftharpoons 2CO$

p_{initial}	1.0 atm	0
p_{final}	$(1.0 - x)$ atm	$2x$ atm

Total p at equilibrium,

$1.5 = 1.0 - x + 2x$

$1.5 = 1.0 + x$

$x = 0.5$ atm

Now $\quad K_p = \dfrac{(p_{CO})^2}{(p_{CO_2})}$

$$K_p = \frac{(2 \times 0.5)^2}{(1.0 - 0.5)} = \frac{1.0}{0.5} = 2 \text{ atm}$$

4. (b) K_p and K_C values do not change with the presence of catalyst. Both forward and backward reaction rates are affected equally so, the value of equilibrium constant remains same as before, i.e. 2×10^{-4}.

5. (a) Both the statements are incorrect.

The corrected form of both statements are as follows

Statement I The reaction is spontaneous and proceeds in the forward direction, if $\Delta G < 0$ (–ve).

Statement II The reaction is non-spontaneous and the products of the forward reaction shall be converted to the reactant, if $\Delta G > 0$ (+ve).

6. (b) According to Le-Chatelier principle on increasing pressure equilibrium will shift to that side which has lesser number of gaseous moles.

$$2NH_3(g) \rightleftharpoons N_2(g) + 3H_2(g)$$

Number of moles on left sides are lesser than right side.

So, equilibrium will shift to left side on increasing the pressure of the system.

7. (c) Statement II is correct but Statement I is incorrect because according to Le-Chatelier's principle, the endothermic reactions are favoured at higher temperature and the exothermic reactions are favoured at lower temperature.

8. (d) The reaction is given as

$$H_2S \rightleftharpoons H^+ + HS^-$$

The equilibrium constant for H_2S,

$$K = \frac{[H^+][HS^-]}{[H_2S]}$$

It is clear from the above relation that an increase in $[H^+]$ will show a decrease in $[HS^-]$ to maintain constant K value.

9. (a) If a forward reaction is exothermic, it means that higher energy is released during forward reaction. In case of backward reactions they has higher activation energy than the forward reaction. This means that more energy is required for the backward reaction to occur compared to the forward reaction.

10. (d) When the concentration of the reactants are changed, the concentration of the products are also changed in such a way that the overall value of the equilibrium constant (K_C) remains the same because equilibrium constant depends only upon the temperature, not upon the concentration of reactant.

Thus, on doubling concentration, equilibrium constant remains the same.

11. (b) The equilibrium reaction is as

$$2NO + O_2 \rightleftharpoons 2NO_2$$

In this reaction,
Number of moles of gaseous reactants, $n_r = 3$
Number of moles of gaseous products, $n_p = 2$
Since, n_p is less than n_r, according to Le-Chatelier principle, when we increase the pressure then the equilibrium shifts in forward direction, i.e. where the fewer number of moles of gas are present.
The reaction given above is exothermic in nature as it is combustion reaction.
So, (A) and (R) are true but (R) is not the correct explanation of (A).

12. (b) All the other options are correct except (b).
For the reaction,

$$CH_4(g) + 2O_2(g) \rightleftharpoons CO_2(g) + 2H_2O(l)$$

$$\Delta_r H = -170.8 \text{ kJ mol}^{-1}$$

$$K_C = \frac{[CO_2]}{[CH_4][O_2]^2} \quad ...(i)$$

Here, $K_C = K_p$ because H_2O is in liquid form

$$\text{and } K_p = \frac{p_{CO_2}}{p_{CH_4} \times p_{O_2}^2} \quad ...(ii)$$

Thus, the number of moles of H_2O and CO_2 are not equal at equilibrium so the concentration is also different.
The equilibrium constant,

$$(K_p) = \frac{[CO_2]}{[CH_4][O_2]} \text{ is not correct.}$$

13. (b) For $2A + B \rightleftharpoons C + D$

$$K_C = \frac{(0.1)(0.1)}{(0.1)^2 (0.1)} = 10$$

From $\Delta G° = -RT \ln K_C$.

$$\Delta G° = -8.314 \times 300 \ln 10$$
$$= -8.314 \times 300 \times 2.303$$
$$= -5744.14 \text{ J/mol}$$

14. (c) When $NaNO_3$ is heated in a closed vessel, it decomposes as

$$NaNO_3(s) \rightleftharpoons NaNO_2(s) + \frac{1}{2}O_2(g); \Delta H = +\text{ve}$$

So, this reaction is an endothermic reaction.
Also $K_p = (p_{O_2})^{1/2}$ and thus addition of $NaNO_3$ or $NaNO_2$ has no effect.
Hence, only the increase in temperature favours forward direction reaction.

15. (a) According to Le-Chatelier's principle, if a system at equilibrium is subjected to change of concentration, pressure or temperature, the equilibrium shifts in the direction that tends to undo the effect.
Here, only option (a) is following the Le-Chatelier's principle.

16. (a) According to Le-Chatelier's principle, on increasing pressure, volume decreases. Hence, the reaction will move in the direction where there are less number of moles.

$$\underbrace{2SO_2 + O_2}_{(2+1) \text{ moles}} \rightleftharpoons \underbrace{2SO_3}_{2 \text{ moles}}$$

Hence, the equilibrium will move towards right, to overcome change.

17. (a) Ice $\rightleftharpoons$ Water, increase in pressure leads to melting of ice and favours the change showing decrease in volume.

$$\text{Solid} \rightleftharpoons \text{Liquid}$$
$$V_L > V_S$$

18. (c) According to Le-Chatelier's principle, addition of KCNS favours forward reaction.

$$Fe^{3+}(aq) + SCN^-(aq) \longrightarrow [Fe(SCN)]^{2+}(aq)$$

$$K_{eq} = \frac{[\text{Product}]}{[\text{Reactant}]} = \frac{[Fe(SCN)]^{2+}}{[Fe^{3+}][SCN^-]}$$

So, if we increase more SCN^- ions so the equilibrium will shift towards the right.

19. (c) The exothermic reaction is given as

$$CoCl_4^{2-}(aq) + 6H_2O(l) \rightleftharpoons [Co(H_2O)_6]^{2+} + 4Cl^-$$

$$K_C = \frac{[Co(H_2O)_6]^{2+}[Cl^-]^4}{[CoCl_4]^{2-}} \text{ as}$$

solvents have constant concentration. On adding water, the concentration of aqueous solution of $[CoCl_4]^{2-}$ will decrease.

20. (d) For the reaction

$$2NO(g) + O_2(g) \rightleftharpoons 2NO_2(g)$$

The standard free energy of formation will be,

$$\Delta G_f^\circ = 2 \times \Delta G°_{NO_2} - [2 \times \Delta G°_{NO} + \Delta G°_{O_2}]$$

$$\Delta G_f^\circ = 2\Delta G°_{NO_2} - 2\Delta G°_{NO} \quad [\Delta G°_{O_2} = 0]$$

$$\Delta G_f^\circ = -RT \ln K_p$$

$$\therefore \Delta G°_{NO_2} = \frac{1}{2}\Delta G°_f + \Delta G°_{NO}$$

$$= \frac{1}{2}[-RT \ln K_p] + G°_{NO}$$

$$= \frac{1}{2}[-R \times 298 \ln (1.6 \times 10^{12})] + 86600$$

$$= 0.5[-R \times 298 \ln (1.6 \times 10^{12}) + 2 \times 86600]$$

21. (b) Given: $\frac{K_{p_1}}{K_{p_2}} = \frac{1}{8}$ and $\alpha_X = \alpha_Z = \alpha$

$$\begin{array}{ccc} X & \rightleftharpoons & 2Y \\ 1 & & 0 \\ 1-\alpha & & 2\alpha \end{array}$$

$$K_{p_1} = \frac{\left[(p_1)\frac{2\alpha}{1+\alpha}\right]^2}{p_1\frac{(1-\alpha)}{(1+\alpha)}}$$

$$\therefore K_{p_1} = \frac{(2\alpha)^2}{(1-\alpha)} \times \left[\frac{p_1}{1+\alpha}\right]^1$$

$$\begin{array}{ccccc} Z & \rightleftharpoons & P & + & Q \\ 1 & & 0 & & 0 \\ 1-\alpha & & \alpha & & \alpha \end{array}$$

$$K_{p_2} = \frac{\left[(p_2)\left(\frac{\alpha}{1+\alpha}\right)\right]^2}{\left(\frac{1-\alpha}{1+\alpha}\right)p_2}$$

$$\therefore K_{p_2} = \frac{(\alpha)^2}{(1-\alpha)^2} \times \left[\frac{p_2}{1+\alpha}\right]^1$$

Given, $\frac{K_{p_1}}{K_{p_2}} = \frac{1}{8}$

$$\therefore \frac{\frac{4\alpha^2 p_1}{1-\alpha^2}}{\frac{\alpha^2 p_2}{1-\alpha^2}} = \frac{1}{8}$$

$$\Rightarrow \frac{4p_1}{p_2} = \frac{1}{8}$$

$$\frac{p_1}{p_2} = \frac{1}{32}$$

22. (b) If more amount of *trans*-2-butene is added then its concentration in right hand side will increases. So, in order to maintain the equilibrium constant k, the equilibrium is shifted in backward direction.

Therefore, more *cis*-2-pentene will be formed.

23. (b) The correct option is (b).

Initially on increasing temperature, rate of reaction increases, so % yield also increases with time. But at equilibrium % yield at high temperature (T_2) would be less than at T_1 as reaction is exothermic so the graph is

% Yield vs Time (T_1, T_2)

24. (a) $SrCO_3(s) \rightleftharpoons SrO(s) + CO_2(g)$;

$K_p = p_{CO_2} = 0.8$ atm

The reaction should favour the forward direction as $Q < K_p$, but since $SrCO_3$ is not taken initially, reaction cannot take place in forward direction.

$SrO(s) + CO_2(g) \rightleftharpoons SrCO_3$;

$$K_p = \frac{1}{0.8} = 1.25 \text{ atm}$$

Thus, on increasing pressure, volume of container will decrease till p_{CO_2} becomes 0.8 atm having same mole of CO_2. The reaction will attain equilibrium till $p = 1.25$. By using ideal gas equation,

$$pV = nRT$$

$$\therefore \text{Initial mole of } CO_2 = \frac{pV}{RT}$$

$$= \frac{0.2 \times 10}{RT} = \frac{2}{RT}$$

$$\text{At eq. } V = \frac{nRT}{p} = \frac{2}{RT} \times \frac{RT}{0.8} = \frac{5}{2}$$

$$= 2.5 \text{ litre}$$

Thus, when the pressure of CO_2 will be maximum, i.e. 1.6 atm, the volume will be 2.5 L.

$$V = 2.5 \text{ litre}$$

25. (d) The production of NO will be favoured by high concentration of N_2. Pressure is not considered here because the number of moles are the same on both sides and the catalyst does not affect the equilibrium of the reaction.

Chapter Break Thru

1. (a) The given reaction is,

$$N_2O_4(g) \rightleftharpoons 2NO_2(g)$$

	N_2O_4	NO_2
Initial mole	1.0	0
Moles at equi.	1 − 0.2	0.4

Total = 0.8 + 0.4 = 1.2

Initially $p_1 V = n_1 RT_1$

or $1 \times V = 1 \times RT_1$ or $V = 300R$ ...(i)

At equilibrium,

$$p_2 V = n_2 RT_2 \text{ or } p_2 = \frac{n_2 RT_2}{V}$$

$$\Rightarrow \frac{1.2R \times 600}{300R} \Rightarrow p_2 = 2.4 \text{ atm}$$

2. (a) The given reaction is,

$$PCl_5(g) \rightleftharpoons PCl_3(g) + Cl_2(g)$$

	PCl_5	PCl_3	Cl_2
Initial conc.	1	0	0
Equil. conc.	1 − α	α	α

Total = 1 + α

$$\text{At equilibrium, } p_{PCl_5} = \frac{1-\alpha}{1+\alpha} p.$$

$$p_{PCl_3} = \frac{\alpha}{1+\alpha} p, \; p_{Cl_2} = \frac{\alpha}{1+\alpha} p$$

$$K_p = \frac{\left(\frac{\alpha}{1+\alpha} p\right)\left(\frac{\alpha}{1+\alpha} p\right)}{\left(\frac{1-\alpha}{1+\alpha}\right) p} = \frac{\alpha^2 p}{1-\alpha^2}$$

3. (c) Statement I is incorrect, but Statement II is correct. The correct form is,

Addition of inert gas at constant volume does not change the partial pressure or the molar concentration of the substance involved in the reaction.

Hence, equilibrium remains undisturbed.

4. (b) The vapour density is directly proportional to the molar mass of gas molecules. When thermal dissociation of gas takes place, the molar mass decreases.

Hence, the vapour density of gas will decrease.

5. (c) The given reaction is,

$$N_2 + 3H_2 \rightleftharpoons 2NH_3$$

$$28 \text{ g} \quad 6 \text{ g} \quad 2 \times 17 = 34 \text{ g}$$

340 g of mixture will contain

$$N_2 = \frac{28}{34} \times 340 = 280 \text{ g}$$

and $H_2 = 60$ g

6 g of H_2 will theoretically produce $NH_3 = 34$ g

$\therefore$ 60 g of H_2 will produce $NH_3 = 340$ g

As yield is 20%, actual yield is

$$= \frac{20}{100} \times 340 = 68 \text{ g}$$

6. (b) Gibbs free energy is given by the formula,

$$\Delta G° = -2.303RT \log K_C$$

$$= -2.303 \times 8.314 \times 300 \times \log(2 \times 10^{13})$$

$$= -5744.14 \times 13.3010$$

$$= -76402.8 \text{ J/mol}$$

$$= -7.64 \times 10^4 \text{ J/mol}$$

7. (c) The reaction involved is

$$PCl_5(g) \rightleftharpoons PCl_3(g) + Cl_2(g)$$

Compressing the equilibrium mixture means increasing pressure. Increase of pressure shifts the equilibrium to the side in which number of gaseous moles is less, i.e. backward direction which means that PCl_3 and Cl_2 will combine to form PCl_5.

8. (d) At equilibrium, individual molecules are continually reacting, even though the overall composition of the reaction mixture does not change because the rates of forward and backward reactions are equal.

9. (c) In the third reaction, all the reactants and products are water-soluble strong electrolytes. They exist in the form of ions only, which can be exchanged in the forward as well as in backward direction.

10. (c) $A + 2B \rightleftharpoons C + \text{Heat}$,

The equation shows, that it is an exothermic reaction. Since, the heat is released in the reaction, so the reaction is favoured in forward reaction at low temperature.

$$\Delta n = 1 - (2 + 1) = -2$$

Since, the number of moles decreases, the forward reaction is favoured at high pressure.

11. (a) $CO(g) + 2H_2(g) \rightleftharpoons CH_3OH(g)$

$$K_C = \frac{[CH_3OH]}{[CO]\,[H_2]^2}$$

$$\Rightarrow \quad 10.5 = \frac{[CH_3OH]}{(0.25)\,(0.12)^2}$$

$$\Rightarrow [CH_3OH] = 0.0378$$

12. (c) Given reaction is

$$NH_3(g) \rightleftharpoons \frac{1}{2}N_2(g) + \frac{3}{2}H_2(g)$$

Δn = change in number of moles of gaseous species

$$= \left(\frac{3}{2} + \frac{1}{2}\right) - 1 = 2 - 1 = 1$$

Given, $K_C = 4$

Now, we have $K_p = K_C (RT)^{\Delta n_g}$

(Temperature) $T = 527 + 273$
$= 800\,K$

$\therefore K_p = 4 \times (800R)^1$

Now, for the reaction

$$N_2(g) + 3H_2(g) \rightleftharpoons 2NH_3(g)$$

$$K_p' = \left(\frac{1}{K_p}\right)^2 = \left(\frac{1}{4 \times 800R}\right)^2$$

13. (a) Solid liquid equilibrium is established only at the melting point or freezing point of the substance.

14. (c) $CH_4(g) + 2S_2(g) \rightleftharpoons CS_2(g) + 2H_2S(g)$

Since, the number of moles of gaseous reactants and product are same ($\Delta n_g = 0$), the reaction will not affected by changing the pressure.

15. (d) When a catalyst is added to a reversible, it increases the speed of forward as well as backward reaction to the same extent. Hence, equilibrium is not disturbed but attained quickly.

16. (c) As the synthesis of ammonia by Haber's process is carried out in closed vessel, volume remains constant.
Hence, addition of inert gas has no effect on equilibrium.

17. (b) Both A and R are true but R is not the correct explanation of A.
At equilibrium, there is no free energy change,
i.e. $\Delta G = 0$
The correct explanation is that when $Q_C = K_C$, concentration are same as that at equilibrium.

18. (d) The reaction is,

$$\frac{1}{2}H_2 + \frac{1}{2}I_2 \rightleftharpoons HI;\ K = 50$$

For dissociation,

$$HI \rightleftharpoons \frac{1}{2}H_2 + \frac{1}{2}I_2,$$

$$K' = \frac{1}{K} = \frac{1}{50} = 0.02$$

19. (b) With the increase in temperature, equilibrium constant of a reaction increases if reaction is endothermic and decrease if reaction is exothermic.

20. (d) For given reaction,

$$K_p = \frac{p_{N_2} \times (p_{H_2})^3}{p_{NH_3}^2};$$

where p = pressure

$$K_p = \frac{(\text{atm})^4}{(\text{atm})^2} \Rightarrow K_p = (\text{atm})^2$$

21. (a) Equilibrium constant at constant temperature is constant. Hence, it does not depend on volume.
Therefore, it will be 300.

22. (c) A is true but R is false.
The correct form of R is :
The value of K is not independent of the stoichiometry of reactant and product at equilibrium.

23. (b) $\dfrac{p_{H_2O}}{p_{H_2}} = \dfrac{60}{40} = \dfrac{3}{2} = 1.5$

$$K_p = \frac{p_{H_2O}^2}{p_{H_2}^2} = \left(\frac{p_{H_2O}}{p_{H_2}}\right)^2$$

$$= (1.5)^2 = 2.25$$

24. (a) The reaction is

$$N_2O_4(g) \rightleftharpoons 2NO_2(g)$$

Since, the number of moles of both N_2O_4 and NO_2 are same,

$$\therefore p_{N_2O_4} = p_{NO_2} = \frac{20}{2} = 10\text{ bar}$$

$$Q_p = \frac{[p_{NO_2}]^2}{p_{N_2O_4}}$$

$$= \frac{(10)^2}{10} = 10\text{ bar}$$

K_p of the reaction can be calculated as

$$\Delta G^\circ = -2.303RT \log K_p$$

and $\Delta G^\circ_{\text{reaction}} = 2\Delta G^\circ_f(NO_2) - \Delta G^\circ_f(N_2O_4)$

$\Delta G^\circ = 0$ at equilibrium.

$$\therefore \Delta G = \Delta G^\circ - 2.303RT \log Q_p$$

$$\Delta G = 0 - 2.303 \times 8.314 \times 298 \log 10$$

$$\Delta G = -5705\text{ J}$$

Since, ΔG is negative, the reaction will be spontaneous and proceeds in forward direction.

25. (c) (A) is true but (R) is false. Tthe correct form of (R) is :
The expression for Q_C and equilibrium constant is same but the concentration used in Q_C are not necessarily the equilibrium values.

26. (a) Both (A) and (R) are correct and (R) is the correct explanation of (A).

We have the relation,
$$K_p = K_C (RT)^{\Delta n}$$
where, Δn = number of moles of gaseous products – number of moles of gaseous reactants

However if, $(RT)^{\Delta n} > 1, K_p > K_C$

$(RT)^{\Delta n} < 1, K_p < K_C$

$(RT)^{\Delta n} = 0, K_p = K_C$

27. (a) The reaction is,
$$PCl_5 \rightleftharpoons PCl_3 + Cl_2$$
Initial conc. of $PCl_5 = \frac{5}{5} = 1$

conc. at equilibrium $= 1 - \frac{40}{100} = 0.6$
$$\therefore K_C = \frac{[PCl_3][Cl_2]}{[PCl_5]} = \frac{0.4 \times 0.4}{0.6}$$
$$= 0.266\,M$$

28. (a) The given reaction is,
$$A(g) + B(g) \rightleftharpoons 2C(g)$$
Initial conc. 3 1

At equi. $3 - 0.75$ $1 - 0.75$ 1.5

$= 2.25$ $= 0.25$
$$K = \frac{[C]^2}{[A][B]} = \frac{(1.5)^2}{(2.25)(0.25)} = 4.0$$

29. (b) Statement I is correct but Statement II is incorrect because when the initial concentrations of the reactants increase in a reaction, the equilibrium constant remains the same.

30. (c) The given reaction is,
$$XY_2(g) \rightleftharpoons XY(g) + Y(g)$$
Initial conc. 600 mm 0 0

At equi. $600 - p$ p p

Total $600 + p = 800$ or $p = 200$ mm

Actual value 400 200 200
$$K_p = \frac{[XY][Y]}{[XY_2]} = \frac{200 \times 200}{400} = 100$$

31. (b) The given reaction is,
$$2G + J \rightleftharpoons D + 2T$$
$$K = \frac{[D][T]^2}{[G]^2[J]}$$
$$\Rightarrow 1.5 \times 10^{-3} = \frac{(0.5)(T)^2}{(1)^2(2)}$$
$$[T] = 0.077\,M$$

32. (d) The given reaction is,
$$C(s) + CO_2(g) \rightleftharpoons 2CO(g)$$
$$K_p = \frac{p_{CO}^2}{p_{CO_2}} \text{ or } 63 = \frac{(10p_{CO_2})^2}{p_{CO_2}}$$
$$\Rightarrow p_{CO_2} = \frac{63}{100} = 0.63 \text{ atm}$$
$$p_{CO} = 10p_{CO_2}$$
$$= 10 \times 0.63 = 6.3 \text{ atm}$$
$$p_{Total} = p_{CO} + p_{CO_2}$$
$$= 0.63 + 6.3 = 6.93 \text{ atm}$$

33. (d) The given reaction is,
$$AB(g) \rightleftharpoons A(g) + B(g)$$
Initial 1 0 0

At equil. $\frac{2}{3}$ $\frac{1}{3}$ $\frac{1}{3}$

Total $= \frac{2}{3} + \frac{1}{3} + \frac{1}{3} = \frac{4}{3}$
$$K_p = \frac{p_A p_B}{p_{AB}} = \frac{\left(\frac{1/3}{4/3}p\right)\left(\frac{1/3}{4/3}p\right)}{\left(\frac{2/3}{4/3}p\right)}$$
$$= \frac{1/3 \times 1/3 p}{4/3 \times 2/3}$$
or $K_p = \frac{1}{8}p$

or $p = 8K_p$

34. (d) Both Statement I and Statement II are correct.

35. (a) As number of mole of product ≠ number of moles of reactant; pressure will affect the equilibrium amount of X_3Y. Further, equilibrium constant changes with temperature.
Hence, option (a) is correct.

36. (c) Dilution with water means adding water, which is one of the reactants. Hence, equilibrium will shift forward, thereby decreasing the equilibrium concentration of $CoCl_4^{2-}$.

37. (b) The correct match is
A-I, B-II, C-IV, D-III
$$K_p = K_C [RT]^{\Delta n_g}$$
$$\frac{K_p}{K_C} = [RT]^{\Delta n_g}$$
For (A), $\Delta n_g = -2, \frac{K_p}{K_C} = (RT)^{-2}$

(B), $\Delta n_g = 0, \frac{K_p}{K_C} = (RT)^0$

(C), $\Delta n_g = -\frac{3}{2}, \frac{K_p}{K_C} = (RT)^{-3/2}$

(D), $\Delta n_g = \frac{1}{2}, \frac{K_p}{K_C} = (RT)^{1/2}$

38. (b) Standard free energy is given by $\Delta G° = -2.303RT \log K_p$
When $\Delta G° < 0$ (given), i.e. –ve, $\log K$ is +ve i.e. K is greater than one.

39. (b) The reaction according to data is, $Na_2SO_4(s)$ + Water $\rightleftharpoons$ $Na_2SO_4(aq)$ + Heat

On increasing the temperature equilibrium will shift backward, i.e. some solid Na_2SO_4 will precipitate out of solution.

40. (c) For gaseous substances, active mass can be expressed in terms of molar concentration (molarity)
$$M = \frac{n_{NH_3}}{V_L} = \frac{1.7 \text{ g}/17 \text{ g mol}^{-1}}{2 \text{ L}}$$
$$= 0.05\,M$$

41. (a) The concentration of X and Y are increasing, hence there are products, while concentration of Z decreases, therefore it is reactant. The concentration of Y increases less than X means production of Y is less than X. Hence, Y must be O_2 and X must be NO because 2 moles of NO_2 produces 2 moles of NO and 1 mole of O_2.
Therefore,
$$X = NO, Y = O_2, Z = NO_2$$
Thus, option (a) is correct.

42. (b) $SO_2 + \frac{1}{2}O_2 \overset{K_1}{\rightleftharpoons} SO_3$
$$K_1 = \frac{[SO_3]}{[SO_2][O_2]^{1/2}}$$
$$2SO_3 \overset{K_2}{\rightleftharpoons} 2SO_2 + O_2;$$
$$K_2 = \frac{[SO_2]^2[O_2]}{[SO_3]^2}$$

or $\dfrac{K_1}{K_2} = \dfrac{[SO_3]}{[SO_2][O_2]^{\frac{1}{2}}} \Big/ \dfrac{[SO_2]^2[O_2]}{[SO_3]^2}$

or $K_1 = \dfrac{1}{\sqrt{K_2}}$

43. (d) $\ln K = \dfrac{-\Delta H^\circ}{RT} + \dfrac{\Delta S^\circ}{R}$

Considering that $\dfrac{\Delta S^\circ}{R} = 0$ and

ΔH = negative for exothermic.
Comparing it with line quation,

$y = c + mx$

Therefore, the slope is positive.

44. (c) $\alpha = 50\% = \dfrac{50}{100} = 0.5$

$$N_2 + 3H_2 \rightleftharpoons 2NH_3$$

	N_2	$3H_2$	$2NH_3$
Initial	1	3	0
Final	$1-\alpha$	$3-3\alpha$	2α

Total moles $= 1-\alpha+3-3\alpha+2\alpha$
$= 4-2\alpha$
$= 4-2\times 0.5 = 3$

45. (c) $N_2O_4(g) \rightleftharpoons 2NO_2(g)$

Molecular mass of $N_2O_4 = 28 + 64$
$= 92$ g/mol

Vapour density, $D = \dfrac{92}{2} = 46$

Let the degree of dissociation be x. Given, observed density, $d = 30$

Applying the equation,

$$x = \frac{D-d}{d} = \frac{46-30}{30} = \frac{16}{30} = 0.533$$

Degree of dissociation = 53.3%.

46. (a) The correct match is
A-IV, B-III, C-II, D-I.

A. At equilibrium, $Q = K$.

B. When $Q < K$, reaction proceeds in forward direction.

C. When $Q > K$, reaction proceeds in backward direction.

D. When $K >> 1$, reaction about to complete.

47. (b) $CaCO_3(s) \overset{Kp}{\rightleftharpoons} CaO(s) + CO_2(s)$

$$K_p = p_{CO_2}$$

We know that, $\Delta G^\circ = -RT \ln K_p$

$\Rightarrow \ln K_p = \dfrac{-\Delta G^\circ}{RT}$

$$\ln K_p = \frac{-83.14\times 10^3 \text{ J/mol}}{8.314 \text{ J/K/mol}\times 700 \text{ K}}$$

$$2.303 \log K_p = \frac{-83.14\times 10^3 \text{ J/mol}}{8.314\times 700 \text{ J/mol}}$$

$$\log K_p = \frac{-14.28}{2.303}$$

$$\log K_p = -6.20$$

$$K_p = 10^{-6.2} = 6.3\times 10^{-7} \text{ atm}$$

48. (c) (A) is true but (R) is false because the equilibrium constant is temperature dependent and its value is different at different temperatures for a same chemical reaction.

49. (b) It is an endothermic equilibrium (in the forward direction). Thus, a temperature increase favours the formation of NO. The pressure change at constant volume is possible by adding and inert gas.
Similarly, the volume change at constant pressure can be achieved by adding an inert gas.
For this system, there is no effect of the adding of inert gas at constant volume or at constant pressure because Δn_g is zero for this system, i.e. there is no change in the total number of moles of gases in a reaction.

50. (d) Chemical equilibrium can be attained from either direction, i.e. from the direction of the reactants taking N_2 and H_2 and getting NH_3 as well as from the direction of the products (taking NH_3 and decomposing it into N_2 and H_2).

Ch-7 Ionic Equilibrium

Topical Follow Thru

Test-1

1. (c) Conjugate acids of given bases are :
H_2O, HCl, ROH and CH_3COOH.
Their acidic strength is in the following order:
$HCl > CH_3COOH > H_2O > ROH$
Hence, basic strength of the conjugate bases will be in the order :

$$RO^- > OH^- > CH_3COO^- > Cl^-$$

2. (b) As a general rule, the greater the number of terminal oxygens in the Lewis structure of oxyacid, the greater is its acidity.
Thus, the correct order of trend of acidic strength is

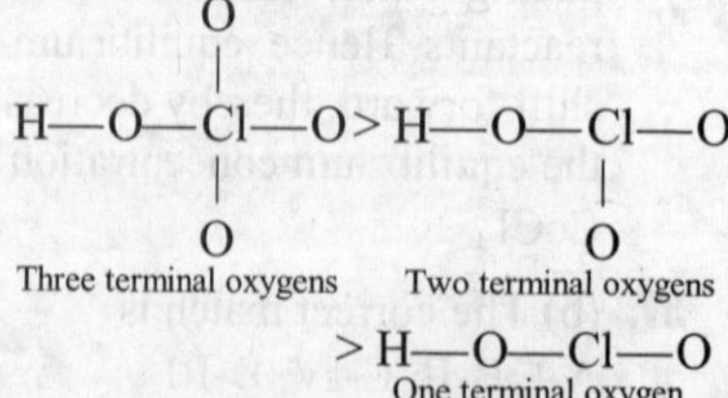

3. (d) Every acid has its conjugate base. Cl^- and NO_3^- are the conjugate bases of HCl and HNO_3 respectively or HCl and HNO_3 are conjugate acids of Cl^- and NO_3^- respectively.

4. (c) CH_3COOH can behave as strong acid than NH_3 because NH_3 has negligible tendency to dissociate while CH_3COOH can dissociate partially in aqueous solution.

5. (b) Since, HNO_2 ionises to give H^+ ion in this reaction

$$HNO_2(aq) \rightleftharpoons H^+(aq) + NO_2^-(aq)$$

Hence, it is an Arrhenius acid.
Therefore, statement I is correct.

In reaction,

$$HNO_2(l) + H_2O(aq) \rightleftharpoons H_3O^+(aq) + NO_2^-(aq)$$

HNO_2 donates a proton hence, it is a Bronsted-Lowry acid and changes to NO_2^- (conjugate base)

Therefore, statement II is incorrect.

6. (d) H_2O in $[Al(H_2O)_6]^{3+}$ is a source of H^+.

Thus, proton is accepted by HCO_3^-.

Thus, $[Al(H_2O)_6]^{3+}$ is proton donor and HCO_3^- is proton acceptor which converted into H_2CO_3 (acid).

Thus, Bronsted-Lowry acids are $[Al(H_2O)_6]^{3+}$ and H_2CO_3.

7. (d) $H_2PO_3^-$ is proton acceptor as well as proton donor.

$$H_3PO_3 \rightleftharpoons H_2PO_3^- + H^+$$
$$H_2PO_3^- \rightleftharpoons HPO_3^{2-} + H^+$$
$$HPO_3^{2-} \rightleftharpoons \text{No ionisation}$$

Hence, $H_2PO_3^-$ is an amphiprotic species but HPO_3^{2-} is not because it only accepts proton.

In case of HCO_3^-

$$H_2CO_3 \rightleftharpoons H^+ + HCO_3^-$$
$$HCO_3^- \rightleftharpoons H^+ + CO_3^{2-}$$

HCO_3^- is proton donor as well as proton acceptor.

Hence, it is an amphiprotic.

Thus, (A) is false but (R) is true.

8. (d) In the mixture of strong acids.

$$\text{Total } [H_3O^+] = \frac{N_1V_1 + N_2V_2}{V_1 + V_2}$$

$1\text{ M HCl} = 1\text{ N HCl}, N_1V_1 = 100$

$2\text{ M HCl} = 2\text{N HCl}, N_2V_2 = 100$

$$\therefore [H_3O^+] = \frac{100+100}{100+50} = 1.33\text{ M}$$

9. (a) The equilibrium moves in the direction of formation of weaker acid and weaker base because the strong acid donates a proton to the stronger base.

Hence, in the reaction A and B, weaker acids and weaker bases are formed. Therefore, the reactions A and B will proceed in forward direction.

10. (a) Greater is the value of ionisation constant (K_b) of a base, greater is the basic strength.

Hence, the order of their basic strength is

$$A > D > C > B$$

11. (b) $H_2SO_4 \longrightarrow H^+ + HSO_4^-$

H_2SO_4 behaves as strong acid in this reaction.

Hence, $[H^+] = [HSO_4^-] = 0.2\text{M}$

$$HSO_4^- \rightleftharpoons H^+ + SO_4^{2-}, \quad K_a = 1.3 \times 10^{-2}$$

$$\begin{array}{ccc} C & 0 & 0 \\ C(1-\alpha) & C\alpha & C\alpha \end{array}$$

$C = 0.2\text{M}$

$\therefore \text{Total } [H^+] = 0.2 + 0.2\alpha$

$= 0.2(1+\alpha)$

$[SO_4^{2-}] = 0.2\alpha, [HSO_4^-] = 0.2(1-\alpha)$

By Ostwald's dilution law,

$$K_a = \frac{[H^+][SO_4^{2-}]}{[HSO_4^-]}$$

$$\Rightarrow 1.3 \times 10^{-2} = \frac{0.2(1+\alpha) \times 0.2\alpha}{0.2(1-\alpha)}$$

$$\Rightarrow \frac{(1+\alpha)\alpha}{(1-\alpha)} = 0.065$$

$$\Rightarrow \alpha^2 + 1.065\alpha - 0.065 = 0$$

$$\Rightarrow \alpha = 0.058$$

$\therefore \quad [H^+] = 0.2116\text{M}$

$[SO_4^{2-}] = 0.0116\text{M}$

$[HSO_4^-] = 0.1884\text{ M}$

12. (b) $HA + H_2O \rightleftharpoons H_3O^+ + A^-$

$$K_a = 1.0 \times 10^{-6}$$

Given reaction is the reverse of ionisation of HA. Thus

$$K = \frac{1}{K_a} = 1.0 \times 10^6$$

13. (c) By Ostwald's dilution law,

$[(CH_3)_3NH^+] = [OH^-]$

$= \sqrt{K_bC} = \sqrt{6.2 \times 10^{-5} \times 1.02}$

$= 7.95 \times 10^{-3}\text{ M}$

14. (d) Considering statement I,

$$HA + HA \rightleftharpoons H_2A + A^-$$

$[H_2A^-] = [A^-]$

$K = [H_2A^-][A^-] = 4 \times 10^{-8}$

$[H_2A^-]^2 = [A^-]^2 = 4 \times 10^{-8}$

$\therefore [A] = 2 \times 10^{-4}$

Hence, statement I is correct.

In case of statement II, the autoprotolysis constant of NH_3 is $[NH_4^+][NH_2^-]$, which is correct.

Thus, both statement I and statement II are correct.

15. (b) NH_4^+ is the conjugate acid of NH_3.

$$NH_4OH \rightleftharpoons NH_4^+ + OH^-$$

$$K_b = \frac{[NH_4^+][OH^-]}{[NH_4OH]}$$

$$NH_4^+ + H_2O \rightleftharpoons NH_4OH + H^+$$

$$K_a = \frac{[NH_4OH][H^+]}{[NH_4^+]} = 5.55 \times 10^{-10}$$

$$\therefore K_b \cdot K_a = [H^+][OH^-] = 1 \times 10^{-14}$$

$$\therefore K_b = \frac{1 \times 10^{-14}}{K_a} = \frac{1 \times 10^{-14}}{5.55 \times 10^{-10}}$$

$$= 1.8 \times 10^{-5}$$

Or

Since, $K_aK_b = K_w$

$$K_b = \frac{K_w}{K_a} = \frac{1 \times 10^{-14}}{5.55 \times 10^{-10}} = 1.8 \times 10^{-5}$$

Test-2

1. (b) $BaSO_4 \rightleftharpoons Ba^{2+} + SO_4^{2-}$

$K_{sp} = [Ba^{2+}][SO_4^{2-}]$

$1 \times 10^{-5} = [0.1][SO_4^{2-}]$

$[SO_4^{2-}] = 1 \times 10^{-4}\text{ M}$

2. (a) Being amphoteric in nature, $Al(OH)_3$ reacts with both NaOH and HCl.

In the presence of NaOH, (a strong base), the molar solubility of $Al(OH)_3$ increases due to the formation of a soluble complex ion $Al(OH)_4^-$.

Similarly, in the presence of HCl, a strong acid, the molar solubility of $Al(OH)_3$ increases due to formation of a soluble complex ion ($AlCl_4^-$).

Hence, both (A) and (R) are true and (R) is the correct explanation of (A).

3. (b) In aqueous solution,

$$Ca(OH)_2 \rightleftharpoons Ca^{2+} + 2OH^-$$

Let the solubility of $Ca(OH)_2$ be S mol L^{-1}

$$\therefore K_{sp} = [Ca^{2+}][OH^-]^2$$
$$= S(2S)^2 = 4S^3$$

Given, solubility, $S = \sqrt{3}$

$$\therefore K_{sp} = 4 \times (\sqrt{3})^3$$
$$= 4 \times 3\sqrt{3} = 12\sqrt{3}$$

4. (b) In case of statement I, the solution is said to be supersaturated if $Q > K_{sp}$ and results in the formation of precipitate.

In case of statement II.

$$PbI_2(s) \rightleftharpoons Pb^{2+}(aq) + 2I^-(aq)$$
$$K_{sp} = [Pb^{2+}][I^-]^2$$
$$= (S)(2S)^2 = 4S^3$$

Hence, statement I is correct but statement II is incorrect.

5. (d) $CaSO_4 \rightleftharpoons Ca^{2+} + SO_4^{2-}$

$$K_{sp} = [Ca^{2+}][SO_4^{2-}] = \sqrt{9 \times 10^{-6}}$$
$$= 3 \times 10^{-3} \text{ M}$$
$$\therefore [CaSO_4] = 3 \times 10^{-3} \text{ mol L}^{-1}$$
$$= 3 \times 10^{-3} \times 136 \text{ g L}^{-1}$$
$$= 0.408 \text{ g L}^{-1}$$

$\therefore$ Volume of water to dissolve 1g

$$CaSO_4 = \frac{1\text{g}}{0.408 \text{ g L}^{-1}} = 2.45 \text{ L}$$

6. (a) A. $Ag_2CrO_4 \rightleftharpoons 2Ag^{2+} + CrO_4^{2-}$

$$K_{sp} = [Ag^{2+}]^2[CrO_4^{2-}]$$
$$= (2S)^2(S) = 4S^3$$

B. $Fe(OH)_3 \rightleftharpoons Fe^{3+} + 3OH^-$

$$K_{sp} = [Fe^{3+}][OH^-]^3$$
$$= (S)(3S)^3 = 27S^4$$

C. $BaCrO_4 \rightleftharpoons Ba^{2+} + CrO_4^{2-}$

$$K_{sp} = [Ba^{2+}][CrO_4^{2-}]$$
$$= (S)(S) = S^2$$

D. $Ca_3(PO_4)_2 \rightleftharpoons 3Ca^{2+} + 2PO_4^{3-}$

$$K_{sp} = [Ca^{2+}][PO_4^{3-}]^2$$
$$= (3S)^3(2S)^2 = 108S^5$$

Thus, the correct match is A-II, B-IV, C-III, D-I.

7. (c) $Mg(OH)_2 \rightleftharpoons Mg^{2+} + 2OH^-$

$$pH = 12, \ pOH = 2$$
$$\therefore \quad [OH^-] = 10^{-2} \text{ M}$$
$$\therefore \quad K_{sp} = [Mg^{2+}][OH^-]^2$$
$$1.8 \times 10^{-11} = (S)(10^{-2})^2$$
$$S = 1.8 \times 10^{-7} \text{ M}$$

8. (b) Among the given statements, only statement (b) is incorrect. The solubility of Ag_2CrO_4 is decreased by $AgNO_3$ instead of AgCl because AgCl is sparingly soluble salt. Hence, it is not effective in decreasing solubility of Ag_2CrO_4.

9. (d) $Ca(OH)_2 \rightleftharpoons Ca^{2+} + 2OH^-$

$$K_{sp} = [Ca^{2+}][OH^-]^2$$
$$5.5 \times 10^{-6} = (S)(2S)^2 = 4S^3$$
$$\therefore \quad S = 0.011$$
$$\therefore [OH^-] = 2S = 2 \times 0.011 = 0.022$$
$$[\because pOH = -\log[OH^-]]$$
$$\therefore pOH = 1.65 \text{ and } pH = 12.35$$

10. (d) Solubility is directly related to square root of K_{sp}. Larger the value of K_{sp}, higher will be solubility. So, the order of solubility of given sulphides is CuS > CdS > HgS.

11. (b)

CuS	8×10^{-37}	$K_{sp} = S^2$	8.94×10^{-19} M
MnS	7×10^{-16}	$K_{sp} = S^2$	2.64×10^{-8} M
Bi_2S_3	1×10^{-70}	$K_{sp} = 108S^5$	3.92×10^{-15} M
Ag_2S	6×10^{-51}	$K_{sp} = 4S^3$	1.14×10^{-17} M
FeS	1×10^{-16}	$K_{sp} = S^2$	1×10^{-4} M

Thus, CuS, Bi_2S_3 and Ag_2S have solubility in range of 10^{-14} to 10^{-20} M.

12. (a) $Ag_2CrO_4 \rightleftharpoons 2Ag^+ + CrO_4^{2-}$

$$K_{sp} = 1.1 \times 10^{-12}$$
$$\therefore \quad K_{sp} = [Ag^+]^2[CrO_4^{2-}]$$
$$1.1 \times 10^{-12} = 4S^3$$
$$S = 6.51 \times 10^{-5} \text{ M}$$
$$AgBr \rightleftharpoons Ag^+ + Br^-$$
$$K_{sp} = [Ag^+][Br^-]$$
$$5.0 \times 10^{-13} = S^2$$
$$\therefore \quad S = 7.07 \times 10^{-7} \text{ M}$$

The ratio of their solubilities is

$$\frac{(S)_{Ag_2CrO_4}}{(S)_{AgBr}} = \frac{6.51 \times 10^{-5}}{7.07 \times 10^{-7}} = \frac{92.1}{1} \approx \frac{92}{1}$$
$$\therefore \quad (S)_{Ag_2CrO_4} : (S)_{AgBr} = 92 : 1$$

13. (a) When two or more solutions are mixed, their resultant concentrations are affected.

$\Rightarrow$ Total volume = 0.25 L

$$[Pb^{2+}]_{mix} = [Pb(NO_3)_2]_{mix}$$
$$= \frac{0.15 \times 0.10}{0.25} = 0.06 \text{ M}$$
$$[Cl^-]_{mix} = [NaCl]_{mix}$$
$$= \frac{0.1 \times 0.20}{0.250} = 0.08 \text{ M}$$

Precipitation of $PbCl_2$ occurs if $[Pb^{2+}][Cl^-]^2 > K_{sp}$

$$\therefore [Pb^{2+}][Cl^-]^2 = (0.06)(0.08)^2$$
$$= 3.84 \times 10^{-4} > 1.2 \times 10^{-5}$$

Since, ionic product

$$[Pb^{2+}][Cl^-]^2 > K_{sp}$$

Hence, $PbCl_2$ precipitates.

14. (d) Both Statement I and Statement II are correct.

15. (a) In 0.01 M $CaCl_2$, there are two chloride ions common to AgCl but in $AgNO_3$, only one silver ion common to AgCl.

So, due to common ion effect, the solubility of AgCl decreases. Hence, option (a) is correct.

Test-3

1. (a) $(CH_3COO)_2Ca \rightleftharpoons 2CH_3COO^- + Ca^{2+}$

$CH_3COO^- + H_2O \rightleftharpoons CH_3COOH + OH^-$

Solution is alkaline due to hydrolysis of CH_3COO^-.

$C = [CH_3COO^-] = 0.05 \times 2 = 0.10\,M$

$\therefore pH = 7 + \frac{pK_a}{2} + \frac{\log C}{2}$

$= 7 + 2.37 + \left(\frac{-1}{2}\right) = 8.87$

$C = 0.1$ $[\because \log 0.1 = -1]$

2. (c) $[H^+] = 0.1 \times \frac{0.1}{100} = 10^{-4}\,M$

$\therefore pH = -\log[H^+]$

$= -\log(10^{-4}) = 4$

3. (d) Both Statement I and Statement II are correct.
   - Dilution of buffer solution does not affect its pH because the ratio of salt and acid/base concentration remains unchanged.
   - In qualitative analysis, pH of 8 to 10 is required for precipitation of cations IIIA group. It is maintained with $NH_4Cl + NH_4OH$ buffer.

4. (c) $Al(OH)_3(s) \rightleftharpoons Al^{3+}(aq) + 3OH^-(aq)$

$K_{sp} = [Al^{3+}][OH^-]^3$

$2.7 \times 10^{-11} = (S)(3S)^3 = 27S^4$

$S = 1 \times 10^{-3}\ mol\ L^{-1}$

$= 0.001\ mol\ L^{-1}$

$\therefore$ Solubility of $Al(OH)_3$ in $g\ L^{-1}$

$= 1 \times 10^{-3} \times 78\ g\ L^{-1}$

$= 7.8 \times 10^{-2}\ g\ L^{-1}$

Now, for pH of solution

$S = 1 \times 10^{-3}\ mol\ L^{-1}$

$[OH^-] = 3S = 3 \times 1 \times 10^{-3} = 3 \times 10^{-3}$

$\therefore pOH = 3 - \log 3$ $\{\because pOH = -\log[OH^-]\}$

$\therefore pH = 14 - pOH$

$= 14 - (3 - \log 3) = 11.47$

Hence, Statement (c) is incorrect.

5. (c) KNO_3 is a salt of strong acid (HNO_3) and strong base (KOH). Hence, its aqueous solution is neutral; pH = 7

NH_4Cl is a salt of strong acid (HCl) and weak base (NH_4OH). Hence, its aqueous solution is acidic; pH < 7.

CH_3COONa is a salt of weak acid (CH_3COOH) and strong base (NaOH). Hence, its aqueous solution is basic; pH > 7.

Na_2CO_3 is a salt of weak acid (H_2CO_3) and strong (NaOH). Hence, its aqueous solution is basic; pH > 7.

Also, acetic acid is more acidic than carbonic acid. Hence, pH of $CH_3COONa <$ pH of Na_2CO_3.

The correct order is

$NH_4Cl < KNO_3 < CH_3COONa < Na_2CO_3$.

6. (c) $\underset{(0.01\ M)}{(NH_4)_2SO_4} \rightleftharpoons \underset{(0.02\ M)}{2NH_4^+} + SO_4^{2-}$

$\therefore [NH_4^+] = 0.02, [NH_4OH] = 0.02\,M$

$\therefore pOH = pK_b + \log\frac{[NH_4^+]}{[NH_4OH]}$

$= pK_b + \log 1$

$= 14 - pK_a$ $[\because \log 1 = 0]$

$= 14 - 9.26 = 4.74$

$\therefore$ pH = 14 − pOH

$= 14 - 4.74 = 9.26$

7. (a) pH = 3 means $[H^+]_1 = 10^{-3}\,M$

pH = 6 means $[H^+]_2 = 10^{-6}\,M$

$\therefore \frac{[H^+]_1}{[H^+]_2} = \frac{10^{-3}}{10^{-6}} = 10^3$

= 1000 times.

8. (a) The reaction between acetic acid and ammonium hydroxide is given as :

$CH_3COOH + NH_4OH \longrightarrow CH_3COONH_4 + H_2O$

$pH = 7 + \frac{1}{2}(pK_a - pK_b)$

Given, $K_a = K_b = 1.8 \times 10^{-5}$

Now, $pK_a = -\log K_a$

$= -\log(1.8 \times 10^{-5})$

$= -[\log 1.8 + (-5)\log 10]$

$= -0.255 + 5 = 4.745$

Similarly, $pK_b = 4.745$

$\therefore pH = 7 + \frac{1}{2}(4.745 - 4.745)$

$pH = 7 + \frac{1}{2}(0)$

pH = 7

$\therefore$ pH of $CH_3COONH_4 = 7$

9. (c) $K_a(HA) = \frac{K_w}{K_h} = \frac{10^{-14}}{10^{-9}} = 10^{-5}$

$K_a(HB) = \frac{K_w}{K_h} = \frac{10^{-14}}{10^{-6}} = 10^{-8}$

$K_a(HC) = 10^{-3}$ (Given)

Greater the value of dissociation constant, more is the acidic strength.

Hence, the order of acidic strength of these acids will be $HC > HA > HB$.

10. (a) Both (A) and (R) are true and (R) is the correct explanation of (A).

11. (b) 0.1 M HCl = 100 mL

$\therefore N_1V_1$ (acid) = 10

0.1 M NaOH = 50 mL

$\therefore N_2V_2$ (base) = 5

$\therefore$ Thus, $N_1V_1 > N_2V_2$

Resultant mixture is acidic

$\therefore$ Resultant $[H^+] = \frac{N_1V_1 - N_2V_2}{V_1 + V_2}$

$= \frac{10 - 5}{100 + 50} = \frac{5}{150} = \frac{1}{30}$

$\therefore pH = -\log[H^+]$

$= -\log\left(\frac{1}{30}\right) = 1.48$

12. (d) At the equivalence point, CH_3COONa is formed.

$\therefore [CH_3COONa] = \frac{0.1}{2}\,M = 0.05$

CH_3COONa is a salt of weak acid and strong base.

$\therefore$ The formula to be used for pH of salt is

$pH = \frac{1}{2}[\log K_w + \log K_a - \log C]$

$= -\frac{1}{2}[\log 10^{-14} + \log(2 \times 10^{-5}) - \log(5 \times 10^{-2})]$

$= -\frac{1}{2}[-14 + \log 2 + (-5)$

$\log 10 - \log 5 + 2\log 10]$

$= -\frac{1}{2}[-14 + 0.3 - 5 - 0.69 + 2]$

$pH = -\frac{1}{2}(-17.39) = 8.695$

13. (b) Among the given statements I and II, the statement II is incorrect because the pH of an acidic buffer remains the same if the concentration of both salt and acid are doubled.

14. (c) H_2S = weak acid
H_2SO_4 = strong acid
NaCl = neutral
$NaNO_2$ = basic
∴ The order will be
$NaNO_2 < NaCl < H_2S < H_2SO_4$.
i.e. $C < D < A < B$

15. (d) We know that

$pH + pOH = 14$

$[H_3O^+] = 10^{-pH}\ mol\ L^{-1}$

$= 10^{-5}\ mol\ L^{-1}$

∴ $pH = 5$

⇒ $pOH = 14 - pH$

$pOH = 14 - 5 = 9$

Chapter Break Thru

1. (d) The stronger is the acid, the weaker is its conjugate base. Similarly, the weaker is the acid, the stronger is its conjugate base. The correct order of acidic strength is

$HF > HCOOH > HCN > H_2O$.

Thus, HF (the strongest acid) has the weakest conjugate base (F^-).

2. (b) Any species that can play the dual role of a proton donor as well as of a proton acceptor can act both as a Bronsted acid as well as a Bronsted base.

$\underset{\text{Acid}}{HCO_3^-} \rightleftharpoons H^+ + CO_3^{2-}$

$\underset{\text{Base}}{HCO_3^-} + H^+ \rightleftharpoons H_2CO_3$

3. (b) On dilution, the degree of dissociation increases with a decreases in concentration.

At infinite dilution, i.e. $C \to 0$, the degree of dissociation is around unity.

When α^2 is plotted against $\frac{1}{C}$ for $\alpha < 0.05$, a straight line with slope equal to dissociation constant of weak electrolyte is obtained.

$$K_a = C\alpha^2 \text{ or } \alpha^2 = \frac{K_a}{C}$$

Option (iv) is the incorrect form of option (iii).

The corrected form of option (v) is given in option (ii).

4. (a) Both (A) and (R) are true and (R) is the correct explanation of (A).

5. (b) We know,

$pH = \frac{1}{2}pK_w + \frac{1}{2}(pK_a + \log C)$

$HA + OH^- \rightleftharpoons H_2O + A^-$

Now,

$K_{eq} = \frac{K_a}{K_w}$

$K_a = K_{eq} \times K_w$

$= 10^9 \times 10^{-14} = 10^{-5}$

We get, $K_a = 10^{-5}$

$(\because \log 0.1 = -1)$

$pH = 7 + \frac{1}{2}(5 + \log 0.1) = 9$

6. (a) The correct match is
A-III, B-I, C-II, D-IV.

A. $NaNO_3$ is a salt of weak acid strong base.

$pH = \frac{1}{2}[pK_w + pK_a + \log C]$

B. $C_6H_5NH_3^+Cl$ is salt of weak base and strong acid.

$pH = \frac{1}{2}[pK_w - pK_b - \log C]$

C. NH_4CN is a salt of weak acid and weak base.

$pH = \frac{1}{2}[pK_w + pK_a - pK_b]$

D. HCN is a weak acid.

$pH = \frac{1}{2}[pK_a - \log C]$

7. (c) We know that,

$pH = pK_a + \log\frac{[Salt]}{[Acid]}$.

$5 = -\log(1.0 \times 10^{-4}) + \log\frac{[Salt]}{[0.04\ M]}$

$5 = 4 + \log\frac{[Salt]}{[0.04\ M]}$

$1 = \log\frac{[Salt]}{[0.04\ M]}$

$10 = \frac{[Salt]}{[0.04\ M]}$

$[Salt] = 0.4\ M$

$[\text{Formic acid}] = 0.4\ M$

8. (d) Weakest acid has the strongest conjugate base.

The corresponding acids of the given ions are HNO_3, HCl, H_2SO_4 and CH_3COOH. CH_3COOH is the weakest acid. Hence, (CH_3COO^-) is the strongest conjugate base.

9. (d) The pH value of a basic buffer is always greater than 7.

Among the given options, $NH_4OH + NH_4Cl$ is the only mixture which consists of a mixture of a weak base and its conjugated salt and thus has a pH greater than 7.

10. (a) Given, $K_a = 1.74 \times 10^{-5}$

$C = 0.05 \text{ or } 5 \times 10^{-2}\ M$

By Oswald's dilution law

$\alpha = \sqrt{\frac{K_a}{C}} \Rightarrow \sqrt{\frac{1.74 \times 10^{-5}}{5 \times 10^{-2}}}$

$\alpha = 1.86 \times 10^{-2}$

11. (c) We know that,

$pH = -\log[H^+] = -\log x$

[where, x is concentration of H^+]

Now, $[H^+]$ increase by 100 times.

$pH = -\log[100x]$

$= -\log x - \log 100$

$[\log ab = \log a + \log b]$

$= -\log x - 2$

i.e. $pH = x - 2$ decreases by 2.

12. (c) The reaction involved is,

$$\underset{S}{Ag_2SO_4} \longrightarrow \underset{2S}{2Ag^+} + \underset{S}{SO_4^{2-}}$$

$$K_{sp} = (2S)^2(S) = 4S^3$$

$$S = 2.5 \times 10^{-2}\ M$$

$$K_{sp} = 4 \times (2.5 \times 10^{-2})^3$$

$$\Rightarrow \quad K_{sp} = 62.5 \times 10^{-6}$$

13. (a) $[H^+] = \text{Conc. of solution} \times \alpha$

$\because$ Conc. of solution = 0.1

and $\alpha = \frac{2}{100} = 0.02$

$\therefore \quad [H^+] = 0.1 \times 0.02 = 2 \times 10^{-3}\ M$

Now, $[OH^-] = \frac{\text{Ionic product of water}}{[H^+]}$

$$= \frac{1 \times 10^{-14}}{2 \times 10^{-3}} = 5 \times 10^{-12}\ M$$

14. (b) The reaction involved is

$$\underset{(S)}{HgCl_2} \rightleftharpoons \underset{(S)}{Hg^{2+}} + \underset{2(S)}{2Cl^-}$$

$$K_{sp} = (S)(2S)^2 = 4S^3$$

$$S = \left[\frac{K_{sp}}{4}\right]^{1/3}$$

$$\Rightarrow \left[\frac{4 \times 10^{-15}}{4}\right]^{1/3} = 10^{-5}\ M$$

$$\therefore \quad [Cl^-] = (2S) = 2 \times 10^{-5}\ M$$

15. (c)

$$\underset{C-x}{HCOOH} \rightleftharpoons \underset{x+0.01}{H^+} + \underset{x}{HCOO^-}$$

$$K_a = \frac{(x + 0.01)x}{0.01 - x}$$

Neglect x w.r.t 0.01 due to common ion effect

$\because \quad K_a = x$

$$x \cong [HCOO^-] = 1.8 \times 10^{-4}$$

16. (b) Let initially the concentration of H^+ ions

$[H^+] = 10^{-x}$ so that $pH = x$

On increasing $[H^+]$ 10 times, now $[H^+] = 10 \times 10^{-x} = 10^{-(x-1)}$

$\therefore$ $pH = x - 1$ i.e. decrease by one.

17. (d) Given,

K_α formic acid $= 3.54 \times 10^{-4}$;

K_α acetic acid $= 3.50 \times 10^{-5}$

$$\frac{\text{Strength of formic acid}}{\text{Strength of acetic acid}} = \sqrt{\frac{K_\alpha \text{ (formic acid)}}{K_\alpha \text{ (acetic acid)}}}$$

$$\Rightarrow \sqrt{\frac{3.54 \times 10^{-5}}{3.50 \times 10^{-4}}} = 0.3180$$

18. (b) H_3PO_2 (Hypophosphorus acid) is monobasic. Its salt, NaH_2PO_2 does not contain acidic hydrogen. Hence, NaH_2PO_2 is not an acid salt.

(Structure: P with =O, H, OH and H attached)

19. (b)

Compounds	NaCl	NH_4Cl
Nature	Neutral salt	Acidic
salt pH :	7	< 7
	NaCN	HCl
	Basic salt	Pure acid
	> 7	< 7

$\therefore$ Their pH will be in order

$NaCN > NaCl > NH_4Cl > HCl$

20. (b) NH_4Cl solution is acidic in nature, its $pH < 7$. $NaNO_3$ solution is neutral, its $pH = 7$, CH_3COOK and Na_2CO_3 are basic solutions, their $pH > 7$.

As Na_2CO_3 is more basic than CH_3COOK, therefore pH of Na_2CO_3 is greater than that of CH_3COOK.

21. (a) The given solution will form acidic buffer for which pH is given by

$$pH = pK_a + \log\frac{[Salt]}{[Acid]}$$

$$6 = 5 + \log\frac{[Salt]}{[Acid]}$$

$$\log\frac{[Salt]}{[Acid]} = 1$$

$$\frac{[Salt]}{[Acid]} = 10$$

Initially 10 mmoles each of salt and acid was present when x mmoles of NaOH is added.

$$10 = \frac{0.1 + x}{0.1 - x}$$

$$1 - 10x = 0.1 + x$$

$$x = 0.0818$$

The amount of NaOH added to the solution

$$w = \frac{40 \times 0.0818}{10}$$

$$\Rightarrow \quad w = 0.327\ g$$

22. (b) pH of buffer solution is given by

$$pH = pK_a + \log\frac{[Salt]}{[Acid]}$$

$$(\because pK_a = -\log K_a)$$

$$pH = -\log(6.2 \times 10^{-10}) + \log\left(\frac{0.2}{0.1}\right)$$

$$= 9.509$$

$$-\log[H^+] = 9.509$$

$$[H^+] = 3.09 \times 10^{-10}$$

23. (b) Ammonium formate is a salt of weak acid and weak base.

$$pK_a = 3.8,\ pK_b = 4.8$$

$$pH = 7 + \frac{1}{2}pK_a - \frac{1}{2}pK_b$$

$$= 7 + \frac{1}{2} \times 3.8 - \frac{1}{2} \times 4.8$$

$$= 7 + 1.9 - 2.4 = 6.5$$

24. (c) Hydrolysis constant is given by the formula.

$$K_h = \frac{K_w}{K_a K_b} \quad \text{... (i)}$$

Substitute the values

$$K_h = \frac{10^{-14}}{1.8 \times 10^{-5} \times 4 \times 10^{-10}}$$

$$\Rightarrow K_h = 1.4$$

25. (a) The given reaction is

$$HA + NaOH \rightleftharpoons NaA + H_2O, \quad k = 10^9$$

For the reverse reaction

$$NaA + H_2O \rightleftharpoons NaOH + HA,$$

$$K' = \frac{1}{k} = \frac{1}{10^9} = 10^{-9}$$

$A^- + H_2O \rightleftharpoons OH^- + HA$

$K' = C\alpha^2$ or $\alpha = \sqrt{\frac{K'}{C}}$

$[OH^-] = C\alpha = C\sqrt{\frac{K'}{C}} = \sqrt{K'C}$

$[OH^-] = \sqrt{10^{-9} \times 10^{-1}} = 10^{-5}$ M

pOH = 5 or pH = 14 − 5

pH = 9

26. (d) For conjugate acid-base pair

$$K_\alpha = \frac{K_w}{K_b}$$

where, $K_w = 10^{-14}$ (water)

$K_b = 1.77 \times 10^{-5}$ (base)

$$K_\alpha = \frac{10^{-14}}{1.77 \times 10^{-5}}$$

$\Rightarrow K_\alpha = 5.64 \times 10^{-10}$

27. (c) As an acid indicator is a weak acid, it dissociates as

$$HIn \rightleftharpoons H^+ + In^-$$

Colour A Colour B

$$K_{In} = \frac{[H^+][In^-]}{HIn}$$

The indicator, HIn will show a colour change at mid point, i.e. point at which $[In^-] = [HIn]$

Hence, $K_{In} = [H^+] = 10^{-5}$ or pH = 5

28. (b) Buffer solutions have reserved acid to yield unionised base and reserved base to yield unionised acid.

29. (c) Statement I is incorrect but statement II is correct. The correct form of I is :

- HCO_3^- is a strong conjugate base but a weak acid.

CO_3^{2-} is a weak base.

$$\underset{\text{Weak acid}}{H_2CO_3} \xrightarrow{-H^+} \underset{\substack{\text{Strong base}\\\text{(weak acid)}}}{HCO_3^-} \xrightarrow{-H^+} \underset{\substack{\text{Weak}\\\text{base}}}{CO_3^{2-}}$$

30. (d) $H_3PO_4 \rightleftharpoons H_2PO_4^- + H^+, K_1$

$H_2PO_4^- \rightleftharpoons HPO_4^{2-} + H^+, K_2$

$HPO_4^{2-} \rightleftharpoons PO_4^{3-} + H^+, K_3$

Higher order ionisation constants (K_2, K_3) are smaller than the lower order ionisation constant (K_1) of a polyprotic acid. It is more difficult to remove a positively charged proton from a negative ion $(H_2PO_4^-, HPO_4^{2-})$ due to electrostatic attraction.

Hence, the order is $K_3 < K_2 < K_1$.

31. (b) Acid = 0.1 mol

Salt = 0.2 mol

∴ For buffer

$$pH = pK_a + \log\frac{[Salt]}{[Acid]}$$

$[\because pK_a = -\log K_a]$

$= 5 - \log 2 + \log\frac{0.2/V}{0.1/V}$

$= 5 - \log 2 + \log 2$

pH = 5

32. (b) Statement I is correct but statement II is incorrect. The correct form of Statement II is : HCl acid is stronger than acetic acid, hence from equimolar solution, H^+ ions produced from HCl acid is more than acetic acid.

33. (c) (A) is true but (R) is false. The corrected form of (R) is, Phenolphthalein is a weak acid, which dissociates as

$$HPh \rightleftharpoons H^+ + Ph^-$$

NH_4OH, being a weak base, given small amount of OH^- ions, which are insufficient to shift the equilibrium toward right.

34. (c) NaZ is a salt of weak acid and strong base.

$\therefore$ pH $= \frac{1}{2}(pK_w + pK_a + \log C)$

$\Rightarrow 8.90 \times 2 = 14 + pK_a + \log 0.1$

$\Rightarrow 17.8 = 14 + pK_a - 1$

$pK_a = 4.8$

$-\log K_a = (-4.8)$

$= 1.585 \times 10^{-5}$

$\approx 1.6 \times 10^{-5}$

35. (c) $BOH \rightleftharpoons B^+ + OH^-$;

$(K_b = 2.5 \times 10^{-6})$

$H^+ + OH^- \rightleftharpoons H_2O \left(K = \frac{1}{K_w}\right)$

$BOH + H^+ \rightleftharpoons B^+ + H_2O \quad K' = ?$

$$K' = K_b \times \frac{1}{K_w} = \frac{2.5 \times 10^{-6}}{10^{-14}}$$

$= 2.5 \times 10^8$

36. (a) $CaCl_2 + Na_2SO_4 \longrightarrow CaSO_4 + 2NaCl$

Millimoles 0.02 M 0.0004 M 0 0

Suppose V mL of both are mixed.

$$[Ca^{+2}] = \frac{0.02}{2} = 10^{-2} \text{ M}$$

$$[SO_4^{2-}] = \frac{0.0004}{2} = 2 \times 10^{-4} \text{ M}$$

Thus, $[Ca^{+2}][SO_4^{2-}]$ in solution $< K_{sp}$

$\Rightarrow 2 \times 10^{-4} \times 10^{-2}$

$= 2 \times 10^{-6} < 2.4 \times 10^{-5}$

∴ $CaSO_4$ will not precipitate.

37. (b) Statement I is correct but statement II is incorrect. The correct form of statement II is, $[H^+] = 10^{-7}$ M obtained from H_2O cannot be neglected in comparison to 10^{-8} M from HCl.

38. (a) The hydrolysis constant is given by formula

$$K_h = \sqrt{\frac{K_w}{K_\alpha C}} \quad \text{...(i)}$$

Substituting the values

$$K_h = \sqrt{\frac{10^{-14}}{1.3 \times 10^{-9}(1/80)}}$$

$= 2.48 \times 10^{-2}$

$K_h = 2.48\%$

39. (b) At the half neutralisation point of an acid,

$$pH = pK_a$$

Hence, value of pH = 5.4

40. (c) The given reaction will be,

$$CH_3COOH \rightleftharpoons CH_3COO^- + H^+$$

Initial conc.	C	0	0
At conc.	$C(1-\alpha)$	$C\alpha$	$C\alpha$

K_α can be given as

$$K_\alpha = \frac{C\alpha \cdot C\alpha}{C(1-\alpha)} = \frac{C\alpha^2}{1-\alpha} \text{ as } \alpha <<< 1$$

$K_\alpha \approx C\alpha^2$

$$\Rightarrow \alpha = \sqrt{\frac{K_\alpha}{C}} \quad \text{...(i)}$$

Substituting the values

$$\alpha=\sqrt{\frac{1\times10^{-5}}{0.1}}=10^{-2}$$

41. (a) Among the given statements, only statements II and V are correct but I, III, IV are incorrect. The correct form of I, III and IV are as

I. Due to common ion effect, AgCl is not soluble in concentrated solution of NaCl.

III. The formula is valid for acidic salts as well as for zwitter ion molecule.

IV. $NaCN + HCl \longrightarrow NaCl + HCN$

	NaCN	HCl	NaCl	HCN
	0.5	1	0	0
	0	(1 − 0.5) = 0.5	0.5	0.5

It becomes a mixture HCN + NaCl + HCl, which is not a buffer.

42. (d) PO_4^{3-} and $C_2O_4^{2-}$ are the two Bronsted bases.

Bronsted bases are proton (H^+) acceptor.

$$PO_4^{3-}+H^+\longrightarrow HPO_4^{2-}$$
$$C_2O_4^{2-}+H^+\longrightarrow HC_2O_4^-$$

HPO_4^{2-} and $HC_2O_4^-$ are Bronsted acids as they are proton (H^+) donor.

43. (b) Bronsted Lowry theory can not explain the acidic nature of CO_2 because it has no protons. Lewis concept cannot explain the acidic nature of H_2SO_4 because as per Lewis, acid is one which accepts electron pair.

H_2SO_4 and $HClO_4$ can act as conjugate base.

44. (c) The dissociation constant of weak acid and its conjugate base are related by an expression.

$$\Rightarrow \quad pK_a + pK_b = pK_w$$
$$\Rightarrow \quad pK_a + 10.83 = 14$$
$$\Rightarrow pK_a = 14 - 10.83 = 3.17$$
$$\Rightarrow K_a = \text{antilog } (-3.17)$$
$$= 6.76\times10^{-4}$$

45. (b) Statement I is correct but statement II is incorrect because Ostwald's dilution law is applicable for weak electrolytes like H_3PO_4, H_2CO_3.

$$\text{Degree of dissociation } (\alpha)=\sqrt{\frac{K_a}{C}}$$

46. (b) Among the given compounds (a), (b), (c) and (d) number of ions given in solution are 3, 2, 5 and 4 respectively. K_{sp} is proportional to number of ions in solution.

Hence, $CaSO_4$ will have the lowest K_{sp}.

$$Ba(OH)_2 \rightleftharpoons Ba^{2+}+2OH^-$$
$$CaSO_4 \rightleftharpoons Ca^{2+}+SO_4^{2-}$$
$$Al_2(SO_4)_3 \rightleftharpoons 2Al^{3+}+3SO_4^{2-}$$
$$Na_3PO_4 \rightleftharpoons 3Na^+ + PO_4^{3-}$$

47. (d) An acidic buffer contains equimolar quantities of weak acid and its salt with strong base. A basic buffer contains equimolar quantities of weak base and its salt with strong acid. Sodium acetate is a salt with strong base but sodium propionate is not weak acid, it is also a salt.

48. (a) The concentration of cation will be decided by the solubility of the sulphide. If two or more compounds have the same ion ratio, the one with the larger K_{sp} value will have the higher molar solubility.

For each given sulphide,

$$S=\sqrt{K_{sp}}$$

Thus, MnS with the maximum K_{sp} has the maximum solubility and, hence, provides the maximum concentration of cations.

49. (b) According to the Henderson equation, pH of the acidic buffer is given as

$$pH = pK_a + \log\frac{[Salt]}{[Acid]}$$

On dilution (addition of more of solvent, H_2O), the value of K_a does not change and the ratio [salt]/[acid] remains unchanged as both [salt] and [acid] will change to the same extent. Thus, the pH of buffer does not change on dilution.

50. (a) **Common ion effect** The degree of dissociation of a weak electrolyte is supressed by the addition of another electrolyte containing the common ion.

So, addition of HCl(*aq*) to HCOOH(*aq*) decreases the ionisation of HCOOH(*aq*) due to common ion effect of H^+ ion.

Hence, both (A) and (R) are true and (R) is the correct explanation of (A).

Ch-8 Redox Reactions

Topical Follow Thru

Test-1

1. (b) SO_2 (O.N of sulphur = +4) can act both as an oxidising agent and as a reducing agent. This is because S can increase its O.N to 6 (in H_2SO_4) or decrease it to 0 (as in its elemental form).

2. (a) Let the oxidation state of iron in $[Fe(H_2O)_5NO]SO_4$ be *x*. The complex ion is $[Fe(H_2O)_5NO]^{+2}$.

$$x+5\times0+1=+2$$

or $\quad x=+1$

3. (a) In reaction (a) N gets oxidised. In $\overset{+}{NH_4}$, oxidation state of N is −3 while in N_2 it is 0. Hence, N is oxidised from −3 to 0.

4. (a) (A) $\mathbf{N_2O_5}$

Oxidation state of oxygen $= -2$

So, oxidation state of nitrogen $= +5$

$$2x + (-2 \times 5) = 0$$
$$2x = 10$$
$$x = 5$$

(B) $\mathbf{NaN_3}$

Oxidation state of sodium $= +1$

So oxidation state of nitrogen

$$= \frac{-1}{3}$$

$$NaN_3 \longrightarrow Na^+ N_3^-$$
$$3x = -1$$
$$x = \frac{-1}{3}$$

(C) **NO**

Oxidation state of oxygen $= 2$

So, oxidation state of nitrogen

$$= +2$$
$$x + (-2) = 0$$
$$x = 2$$

(D) $\mathbf{N_2H_4}$

Oxidation state of hydrogen $= +1$

So, oxidation state of nitrogen $= -2$.

$$2x + (+1 \times 4) = 0$$
$$2x = -4$$
$$x = -2$$

5. (c) (i) NH_4^+

$$x + 1 \times 4 = +1$$
$$x = -3$$

(ii) N_2H_4

$$2x + 4 \times (1) = 0$$
$$2x + 4 = 0$$
$$x = -2$$

(iii) NH_2OH

$$x + 1 \times 2 + (-2) + 1 = 0$$
$$x + 2 - 2 + 1 = 0 \Rightarrow x = -1$$

(iv) N_2O

$$2x + (-2) = 0$$
$$x = +1$$

6. (a) Oxidation number of S in S_8 is zero; in S_2F_2, it is +1
$(2x - 2 = 0 \text{ or } x = +1)$
and in H_2S, it is -2
$(+2 + x = 0 \text{ or } x = -2)$

7. (a) For $K_2O: 2x - 2 = 0$

$\Rightarrow \quad x = +1$

For $K_2O_2: 2x - 2 = 0$

$\Rightarrow x = +1$

(in peroxide, the O.S. of oxygen is -1)

For $KO_2: x - 2 \times \frac{1}{2} = 0 \Rightarrow x = +1$

(in superoxide, the O.S. of oxygen is $-\frac{1}{2}$)

8. (b) Oxidation number of P in $HP_2O_7^-$ is

$$2x + (+1 \times 1) + (-2 \times 7) = -1$$
$$2x = 12$$
$$x = +6$$

9. (d) The oxidation number of Mn in given species are as follows

(a) MnO_2

$$x + (-2 \times 2) = 0$$
$$x = 4$$

(b) $MnCl_2$

$$x + (-1 \times 2) = 0$$
$$x = +2$$

(c) $MnSO_4$

$$x + (-2 \times 1) = 0$$
$$x = +2$$

(d) $KMnO_4$

$$x + (-2 \times 4) = -1$$
$$x = +7$$

10. (c) Since, F has always an oxidation number of -1, therefore, O has positive oxidation number, i.e. +2 in OF_2.

11. (d) $\overset{x}{C_{12}}\ \overset{+1}{H_{22}}\ \overset{-2}{O_{11}}$

$$\therefore 12x + 22 \times (+1) + 11 \times (-2) = 0$$
$$x = 0$$

12. (b) $\overset{-2}{O} = \overset{+2}{C} = \overset{0}{C} = \overset{+2}{C} = \overset{-2}{O}$

In C_3O_2, the two carbon atoms linked with oxygen atoms are present in +2 oxidation state and central carbon has zero oxidation state. So, the average oxidation state of $C = \frac{2+0+2}{3} = \frac{+4}{3}$

13. (c) The structure of CrO_5 is

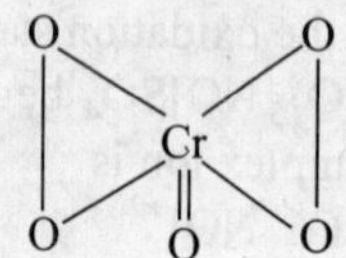

i.e. it has two peroxide bonds each O having an O.N. of -1 and one double bond in which O.N. of O is -2.

Therefore, the O.N. of Cr in CrO_5 is $x + 4 \times (-1) + 1 \times (-2) = 0$

or $\quad x = +6$

14. (d) The O.N. of C increase from +3 in $(COOH)_2$ to +4 in CO_2, therefore, it acts as a reducing agent.

$$\overset{+3}{(COOH)_2} \longrightarrow \overset{+4}{2CO_2}$$

In all the remaining compound, one element has already the maximum possible O.N. i.e. N has +5 in HNO_3, Mn has +7 in $KMnO_4$ and S has +6 in H_2SO_4 and they cannot further increase their O.N. and hence cannot act as reducing agent.

15. (a) $2\overset{+1}{H}\overset{-1}{I} + \overset{+1}{H_2}\overset{+6}{S}\overset{-2}{O_4} \longrightarrow \overset{0}{I_2} + \overset{+4}{S}\overset{-2}{O_2} + 2\overset{+1}{H_2}\overset{-2}{O}$

Ist half reaction :

$$2H\overset{-1}{I} \longrightarrow \overset{0}{I_2}$$

In this reaction, oxidation number of I increase by one thus, this is an oxidation reaction and HI behave as a reducing agent.

IInd half-reaction :

$$H_2\overset{+6}{S}O_4 \longrightarrow \overset{+4}{S}O_2$$

In this reaction, oxidation number of S decrease by two, thus this is a reduction reaction and H_2SO_4 behaves as an oxidising agent.

16. (a) Writing the oxidation number of Cr, Cl and Mn on each species in the four set of ions, then,

(a) $\overset{+3}{Cr}O_2^-, \overset{+5}{Cl}O_3^-, \overset{+6}{Cr}O_4^{2-}, \overset{+7}{Mn}O_4^-$

(b) $\overset{+5}{Cl}O_3^-, \overset{+6}{Cr}O_4^{2-}, \overset{+7}{Mn}O_4^-, \overset{+3}{Cr}O_2^-$

(c) $\overset{+3}{Cr}O_2^-, \overset{+5}{Cl}O_3^-, \overset{+7}{Mn}O_4^-, \overset{+6}{Cr}O_4^{2-}$

(d) $\overset{+6}{Cr}O_4^{2-}, \overset{+7}{Mn}O_4^-, \overset{+3}{Cr}O_2^-, \overset{+5}{Cl}O_3^-$

Only in the arrangement (a), the oxidation number of central atom increases from left to right, therefore, option (a) is correct.

17. (a) O_2^{2-} (peroxide)

$$2x = -2 \Rightarrow x = -1$$

18. (c) Fe_3O_4 is a mixed oxide.

$FeO \cdot Fe_2O_3$
$\uparrow$ 2 $\uparrow$ +3

Fe_3O_4
$\uparrow$
$3x - 8 = 0$
$x = \frac{8}{3}$

19. (b) NH_4NO_3 is actually NH_4^+ and NO_3^-. It is an ionic compound.
The oxidation number of nitrogen in the two species is different as shown below.
Let, oxidation number of N in $\overset{+}{N}H_4$ is x.

$x + (4 \times 1) = +1$
or $x + 4 = +1$
or $x = -3$

Let, oxidation number of N in NO_3^- is x.

$x + (3 \times -2) = -1$
or $x - 6 = -1$
or $x = +5$

20. (b)

I. Ca^{2+} $\langle$ $Cl^- \leftarrow -1$; $OCl^- \leftarrow +1$

II. +6 both in S
III. 0 and 5
IV. −2, −1
V. NH_4^+ and NO_3^- ($\uparrow$ −3, $\uparrow$ +5)

21. (a) Oxidation number of hydrogen is always +1 is a wrong rule since, it is +1 in hydrogen halides, −1 in hydrides and zero in H_2 molecule.
All the other three statements (b), (c) and (d) are correct.

22. (b) $NH_4^+ + NO_2^- \longrightarrow N_2 + 2H_2O$
($\uparrow$ −3, $\uparrow$ +3, $\uparrow$ 0)
Reduction
Oxidation

23. (d)
(a) $\underline{Mn}O_4^{2-} \Rightarrow$ O.N. of Mn = 6
(b) $\underline{Cr}O_5 \Rightarrow$ O.N. of Cr = 6 (two peroxide linkages)
(c) $\underline{Cr}O_2Cl_2 \Rightarrow$ O.N. of Cr = 6

24. (c) Let the oxidation number of Cr in $K_2Cr_2O_7$ be x.
Oxidation number of O = −2, K = +1

$2 \times 1 + 2x + 7(-2) = 0$
$2x = 12; x = +6$

25. (c) Write the balanced equation for this reaction. The reaction must be balanced with respect to charge.

$M^{3+} - 3e^- \longrightarrow M^{6+}$

$\therefore$ After removing 3 electrons from M^{3+}, its oxidation state will be +6.

Test-2

1. (b) $2\overset{+5\ -2}{KClO_3} \xrightarrow{\Delta} 2K\overset{-1}{Cl} + 3\overset{0}{O_2}$

Here, one element of $KClO_3$ is oxidised ($\overset{-2}{O} \longrightarrow \overset{0}{O_2}$) while the other is reduced ($\overset{+5}{Cl} \longrightarrow \overset{-1}{Cl}$) and hence, it is an example of intramolecular redox reaction.

2. (c) The given reaction is a redox reaction since here the oxidation state of N in NO_3^- is +5 and in NO, the oxidising state of N is +2. Since, oxidising state of N is changing by 3 units, thus the number of electron required to balance the equation is 3.

3. (b) $8Al + 3Fe_3O_4 \longrightarrow 4Al_2O_3 + 9Fe$
In the above reaction, Al is reductant while Fe is an oxidant.
Oxidation no. of Al in an elementary state = 0
Oxidation no. of Al in Al_2O_3 = +3
$\therefore$ No. of electron transferred by 1 Al atom = 3
No. of electrons transferred by 8Al atoms = 8 × 3 = 24 electrons
Hence, 24 electrons are transferred from reductant to oxidant.

4. (d) In Fe_3O_4, the average oxidation number of Fe is $\frac{8}{3}$.
For 3Fe atoms of Fe_3O_4, the total oxidation number is 8.
On the reactant side, the oxidation number of Fe is 0.
Hence, during the reaction, the oxidation number of Fe changes by 8.
Hence, the reaction involve 8 electrons.

5. (a) $MnO_4^- \longrightarrow Mn^{+2}$

$MnO_4^- + H^+ \longrightarrow Mn^{+2} + H_2O$
$MnO_4^- + 8H^+ \longrightarrow Mn^{+2} + 4H_2O$
$MnO_4^- + 8H^+ + 5e^- \longrightarrow Mn^{+2} + 4H_2O$ ...(i)
$C_2O_4^{-2} \longrightarrow 2CO_2 + 2e^-$ ...(ii)

For balancing the reaction 2× equation (i) + 5 × equation (ii), we get

$2MnO_4^- + 5C_2O_4^{-2} + 16H^+ \longrightarrow 2Mn^{+2} + 10CO_2 + 8H_2O$

6. (c) The unbalanced redox equation is as follows

$N_2O_4 + BrO_3^- \xrightarrow[H_2O]{H^+} NO_3^- + Br^-$

Balance all atoms other than H and O

$N_2O_4 + BrO_3^- \xrightarrow[H_2O]{H^+} 2NO_3^- + Br^-$

The oxidation number of N changes from +4 to +5. The changes in the oxidation number of N is 1.
Total change in the oxidation number for 2N atom is 2.
The oxidation number of Br changes from +5 to −1. So, the change in the oxidation number of Br is 6.
The increase in the oxidation number is balanced with decrease in the oxidation number by multiplying N_2O_4 and NO_3^- with 3.

$3N_2O_4 + BrO_3^- \xrightarrow[H_2O]{H^+} 6NO_3^- + Br^-$

O atoms are balanced by adding 3 water molecules on LHS

$$3N_2O_4 + BrO_3^- + 3H_2O \longrightarrow 6NO_3^- + Br^-$$

Hydrogen atoms are balanced by adding $6H^+$ atoms on RHS

$$3N_2O_4 + BrO_3^- + 3H_2O \xrightarrow[H_2O]{H^+} 6NO_3^- + Br^- + 6H^+$$

This is the balanced chemical equation.

7. (b)

$$H_2O + \overset{0}{Br_2} \longrightarrow \overset{+1}{HOBr} + \overset{-1}{HBr}$$

(Oxidation: Br 0 → +1; Reduction: Br 0 → −1)

In the given reaction, since Br is oxidised as well as reduced thus, it is a disproportionation reaction.

8. (b) The balanced equation is

$$2H_2O_2 + 2ClO_2 + 2OH^- \longrightarrow 2Cl^- + 5O_2 + 6H_2O$$

Hence, the values of x and y are 2 and 5 respectively.

9. (a) $IO_3^- + aI^- + bH^+ \longrightarrow cH_2O + dI_2$

***Step* I** $I^- \longrightarrow I_2$ (oxidation)

$IO_3^- \longrightarrow I_2$ (reduction)

***Step* II** $2IO_3^- + 12H^+ \longrightarrow I_2 + 6H_2O$

***Step* III** $2IO_3^- + 12H^+ + 10e \longrightarrow I_2 + 6H_2O$

$2I^- \longrightarrow I_2 + 2e$

***Step* IV** $2IO_3^- + 12H^+ + 10e^- \longrightarrow I_2 + 6H_2O$

$[2I^- \longrightarrow I_2 + 2e^-] \times 5$

***Step* V** $2IO_3^- + 10I^- + 12H^+ \longrightarrow 6I_2 + 6H_2O$

$IO_3^- + 5I^- + 6H^+ \longrightarrow 3I_2 + 3H_2O$

On comparing,

$a = 5, b = 6, c = 3, d = 3.$

10. (c) (a) The reaction of H_2SO_4 with NaOH.

$$H_2SO_4 + 2NaOH \longrightarrow Na_2SO_4 + H_2O$$

Thus, it is acid-base neutralisation reaction.

(b) In atmosphere, formation of O_3 from O_2 by lightening $3O_2 \longrightarrow 2O_2$ changes in one allotrope of O to another. Thus it is allotropic formation.

(c) Formation of oxides of nitrogen from nitrogen and oxygen by lightening

$$N_2 + O_2 \longrightarrow 2NO$$

Here in N_2, N has oxidation number 0 and in NO, it is +2. Thus, N_2 is reduced and similarly oxidation number of O changes from 0 to −2 and thus O_2 is oxidised.

(d) Evaporation of H_2O

$$H_2O(l) \longrightarrow H_2O(g)$$

States changes only

Thus, the formation of oxides of nitrogen from nitrogen and oxygen by lightening is the redox reaction where oxidation, as well as reduction takes place, simultaneously.

11. (c) In disproportionation reaction, an element in one oxidation state is simultaneously oxidised and reduced.

$$2\overset{+1}{Cu}Br \longrightarrow \overset{+2}{Cu}Br_2 + \overset{0}{Cu}$$

(Reduction: Cu +1 → 0; Oxidation: Cu +1 → +2)

12. (c) In the given reaction

$$MnO_4^- + 4H^+ + 3e^- \longrightarrow MnO_2 + 2H_2O$$

Mn change its oxidation state from +7 to +4.

Hence, it undergoes only reduction and not disproportionation.

13. (a) In $X + YZ \longrightarrow XZ + Y$; X is oxidised while Y is reduced.

'X' had an oxidation state of 0. In a displacement reaction, when metals react to form a salt, it loses electrons to non-metal and oxidised. So, here the oxidaition state 'X' is positive when it form a salt, XZ.

'Y' on the othe side, displaced by X, the oxidation state of Y becomes zero. Its oxidation state has decreased, means it gained electron(s) and reduced.

14. (d) In all these reactions, the same substance is reduced as well as oxidised.

15. (b) The total balanced reaction is given by

$$6BrO_3^- + 10Cr^{+3} + 22H_2O \longrightarrow 3Br_2 + 10CrO_4^{-2} + 44H^+$$

$\therefore x, y, z$ are 6, 10, 22 respectively.

Chapter Break Thru

1. (b) The two sulphur atoms in $Na_2S_2O_3$ have −2 and +6 oxidation states. The sulphur in the middle have made 6 bonds hence it has +6 oxidation state, while other sulphur shows −2 oxidation state.

$$NaO^- - \underset{\underset{O}{\|}}{\overset{\overset{S}{\|}}{S}} - O^- Na$$

2. (a) The oxidation number of HCN and HNC can be calculated as follows

(i) $\overset{+1}{H}\overset{x}{C}\overset{-3}{N}$

$x + (+1 \times 1) + (-3 \times 1) = 0$

$x = +2$

(ii) $\overset{+1}{H}\overset{-3}{N}\overset{x}{C}$

$x + (1 \times 1) + (-3 \times 1) = 0$

$x = +2$

3. (a) Oxidation number of Cr in $K_2Cr_2O_7$ is

$2 \times (+1) + 2x - (2 \times 7) = 0$

or $x = +6$

Similarly, oxidation number of Cr in K_2CrO_4 is

$2 \times (+1) + x - (2 \times 4) = 0$ or $x = +6$

So, there is no change in oxidation number of chromium.

4. (a) $\overset{+2}{Fe}SO_4 \longrightarrow \overset{+3}{Fe_2}(SO_4)_3$

$FeSO_4$ present in Mohr's salt gets converted into $Fe_2(SO_4)_3$. This is an one-electron change and hence equivalent weight of Mohr's salt is equal to its molecular weight.

5. (c) The balanced equation is

$$2MnO_4^- + 5H_2S + 6H^+ \longrightarrow 5S + 2Mn^{+2} + 8H_2O$$

Thus, the coefficients of *x*, *y* and *z* are 2, 5, 6 respectively.

6. (b) $\overset{0}{Fe} + H\overset{+5}{N}O_3 \longrightarrow \overset{+2}{Fe}(NO_3)_2 + \overset{-3}{N}H_4NO_3 + H_2O$

Half-reactions are

(i) $\overset{0}{Fe} \longrightarrow \overset{+2}{Fe}(NO_3)_2 \uparrow 2$

(ii) $H\overset{+5}{N}O_3 \longrightarrow \overset{-3}{N}H_4NO_3 \downarrow 8$

To make increase in O.N. = decrease, multiply. Eq. (i) by 4 and add Eq. (ii). Hence,

$4Fe + HNO_3 \longrightarrow 4Fe(NO_3)_2 + NH_4NO_3$

To balance N atoms on the two sides, multiply HNO_3 by 10. Hence,

$4Fe + 10HNO_3 \longrightarrow 4Fe(NO_3)_2 + NH_4NO_3$

To balance O-atoms, add $3H_2O$ on RHS. Hence,

$4Fe + 10HNO_3 \longrightarrow 4Fe(NO_3)_2 + NH_4NO_3 + 3H_2O$

H-atoms are automatically balanced.

Hence, the correct ratio is 10 : 4 : 1.

7. (c)

(a) $\overset{+6}{Xe}\overset{-1}{F_6} + 2\overset{+1}{H_2}\overset{-2}{O} \longrightarrow \overset{+6}{Xe}\overset{-2}{O}\overset{-1}{F_4} + 2\overset{+1}{H}\overset{-1}{F}$

No change in oxidation number, hence no redox reaction occurs.

(b) $\overset{+6}{Xe}\overset{-1}{F_6} + 2\overset{+1}{H_2}\overset{-2}{O} \longrightarrow \overset{+6}{Xe}\overset{-2}{O_2}\overset{-1}{F_2} + 4\overset{+1}{H}\overset{-1}{F}$

No change in oxidation numbers hence no redox reaction occurs.

(c) $\overset{+4}{Xe}\overset{-1}{F_4} + \overset{+1}{O_2}\overset{-1}{F_2} \longrightarrow \overset{+6}{Xe}\overset{-1}{F_6} + \overset{0}{O_2}$

Increase O.N (Oxidation)

Hence, it is a redox reaction.

(d) $\overset{+2}{Xe}\overset{-1}{F_2} + \overset{+5}{P}\overset{-1}{F_5} \longrightarrow [\overset{+2}{Xe}\overset{-1}{F}] + \overset{+5}{P}\overset{-1}{F_6}$

No change in oxidation number, hence no redox reaction occurs.

8. (b) Reducing property means gain of electron that means reduction.

(i) $Cl_2 + \overset{+4}{S}O_2 \longrightarrow \overset{+6}{S}O_2Cl_2$

Oxidation

(ii) $2H_2\overset{-2}{S} + \overset{+4}{S}O_2 \longrightarrow 3\overset{0}{S} + 2H_2O$

Reduction

(iii)

$2FeCl_3 + \overset{+4}{S}O_2 + 2H_2O \longrightarrow 2FeCl_2 + H_2\overset{+6}{S}O_4 + 2HCl$

Oxidation (reducing agent)

(iv) $\overset{+4}{S}O_2 + H_2O \longrightarrow H_2\overset{+4}{S}O_3$

No reduction or oxidation

9. (c) I. $C_6H_{12}O_6$

$\Rightarrow 6x + (+1 \times 12) + (-2 \times 6) = 0$

$\Rightarrow x = 0$

II. H_2SO_4

$\Rightarrow x + (+1 \times 2) + (-8) = 0$

$\Rightarrow x = +6$

III. $CrO_5 \Rightarrow x + 4(-1) + (-2) = 0$

$x = +6$

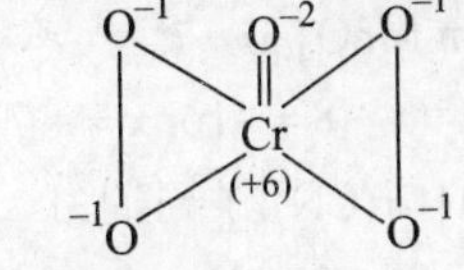

IV. Mn_2O_3

$\Rightarrow 2x + (-2 \times 3) = 0$

$\Rightarrow x = 3$

V. MnO_4^-

$\Rightarrow x + (-2 \times 4) = -1$

$\Rightarrow x = +7$

10. (d) Hydrogen can have oxidation number of both, i.e. –1 and +1. –1 in metal hydrides, *M*H, zero in H_2 and +1 in halogen acids.

11. (b) A reaction in which two atoms or molecules combine together to form a third molecule is called a combination reaction.

e.g. $A + B \longrightarrow C$

Either *A* or *B* or both *A* and *B* must be in the elemental form for such a reaction to be a redox reaction.

So, I, II and IV are examples of combination reaction and V is an example of decomposition reaction.

12. (d) In CN^-, oxidation of C is +2, and it changes to +4 oxidation state in CO_2. So, C is also oxidised. Thus, statement in option (d) is not correct.

13. (c) In H_2SO_5, oxidation state of S will be +6. This is evident from the structure of H_2SO_5 and only one oxygen atom is present in form of peroxide and two oxygen atoms are present in form of oxide.

$$H-O-\underset{\underset{O^{-2}}{\|}}{\overset{\overset{O^{-2}}{\|}}{S}}-\overset{-1}{O}-\overset{-1}{O}-H$$

S = +6

Consider the other statements.

(a) $(NH_4)_2S_2O_8 \longrightarrow 2NH_4^+ + S_2O_8^{-2}$

$$O^- - \underset{\underset{O^{-2}}{\|}}{\overset{\overset{O^{-2}}{\|}}{S}} - \overset{-1}{O} - \overset{-1}{O} - \underset{\underset{O^{-2}}{\|}}{\overset{\overset{O^{-2}}{\|}}{S}} - O^-$$

+6 +6

(b) Oxidation no. of Os in OsO_4 is $x + 4(-2) = 0, x = +8$

(d) Oxidation no. of O in KO_2 is $-\frac{1}{2}$ (when oxygen reacts with alkali metal, alkali metals have positive oxidation state).

14. (b) $BaO_2 + H_2SO_4 \longrightarrow BaSO_4 + H_2O_2$

The most electronegative atom is O. It appears in SO_4^{-2} where its O.N. is –2 and in H_2O_2 where it is –1. Therefore, option (b) is correct.

15. (a) Correct answer is

A. $H_2O_2 \xrightarrow{\Delta} 2H_2O + O_2$ is a disproportionation and redox reaction.

B. $2NaH \xrightarrow{\Delta} 2Na + H_2$ is a decomposition redox reaction.

C. $V_2O_5 + 5Ca \xrightarrow{\Delta} 2V + 5CaO$ is a metal displacement redox reaction.

D. $CaCO_3 \xrightarrow{\Delta} CaO + CO_2$ is a decomposition reaction.

16. (c) The match given in (c) option is correct while other are incorrect and their correct match are as follows

$2H_2O \xrightarrow{\Delta} 2H_2 + O_2$ is a decomposition reaction.

$CuSO_4 + Zn \longrightarrow Cu + ZnSO_4$ is a metal displacement reaction.

$Zn + 2HCl \longrightarrow ZnCl_2 + H_2$ is a non-metal displacement reaction.

17. (d) In BrO_4^-, Br is in maximum oxidation state, i.e. +7 so, it can only reduce itself.

18. (a)

$$\overset{+6}{3Mn}\overset{2-}{O_4} + 4\overset{+}{H} \longrightarrow 2\overset{+7}{Mn}O_4^- + 2H_2O + \overset{+4}{Mn}O_2$$

(Oxidation: $MnO_4^{2-} \to MnO_4^-$; Reduction: $MnO_4^{2-} \to MnO_2$)

MnO_4^{2-} is oxidised as well as reduced. Therefore, it is a disproportionation reaction.

19. (c) $2\overset{+1}{H_2}\overset{-2}{O} \xrightarrow{\Delta} 2\overset{0}{H_2} + \overset{0}{O_2}$

Here, hydrogen is reduced. Thus, option (c) is correct regarding given decomposition reaction.

20. (a)

I. $Ni(CO)_4$

$\Rightarrow x + (0 \times 4) = 0$

$\Rightarrow \quad x = 0$

II. H_2SO_4

$\Rightarrow x + (+1 \times 2) + (-2 \times 4) = 0$

$\Rightarrow \quad x = +6$

III. Cl_2O_7

$\Rightarrow 2x + (-2 \times 7) = 0$

$\Rightarrow \quad x = +7$

IV. HNO_3

$\Rightarrow x + (+1 \times 1) + (-2 \times 3) = 0$

$\Rightarrow \quad x = +5$

21. (b) $NH_4NO_3 \rightleftharpoons NH_4^+ + NO_3^-$

In NH_4^+,

$x + 4 = +1$

$\Rightarrow \quad x = -3$

In NO_3^-,

$x - 6 = -1 \Rightarrow x = +5$

22. (d) Oxidation state of hydrogen $= +1$

Oxidation state of oxygen $= -2$

In orthophosphoric acid (H_3PO_4), phosphorus has the oxidation state of +5.

In pyrophosphoric acid ($H_4P_2O_7$), phosphorus has the oxidation state +5.

In metaphosphoric acid (HPO_3), phosphorus has the oxidation state +5.

In phosphorus acid (H_3PO_3), phosphorus has the oxidation state of +3.

23. (a) In metal displacement reaction, a metal in the compound is displaced by some other metal in the uncombined or elemental state.

So, I, II, III and IV are metal displacement reaction but V is decomposition reaction.

24. (d) Oxidation number of the given species are as follows

Mn in MnO_4^- is +7.

$(x - 8 = -1 \text{ or } x = +7)$

Cr in $[Cr(CN)_6]^{-3}$ is +3.

$(x - 6 = -3 \text{ or } x = +3)$

Ni in NiF_6^{-2} is +4.

$(x - 6 = -2 \text{ or } x = +4)$

Cr in CrO_2Cl_2 is +6.

$(x + 2 \times (-2) + 2 \times (-1) = 0$

or $\quad x - 4 - 2 = 0 \text{ or } x = +6)$

25. (b) Let the oxidation state of nitrogen be x.

$HNO_3 \Rightarrow +1 + x + 3(-2) = 0$

$\Rightarrow \quad x - 5 = 0$

$\Rightarrow \quad x = +5$

$NO \Rightarrow x + 1(-2) = 0 \Rightarrow x = +2$

$NH_4Cl \Rightarrow x + 4(+1) + (-1) = 0$

$\Rightarrow \quad x + 4 - 1 = 0$

$\Rightarrow \quad x = -3$

$N_2 \Rightarrow 2x = 0$

$\Rightarrow \quad x = 0$

Decreasing order of oxidation state is

$\underset{+5}{HNO_3}, \underset{+2}{NO}, \underset{0}{N_2}, \underset{-3}{NH_4Cl}$

26. (b) Correct answer is A-IV, B-I, C-III, D-II.

In reaction (I) Au (sol) is formed by reduction of $AuCl_3$, so the chemical method of preparation is "Reduction".

In reaction (II) As_2S_3 (sol) is formed by double decomposition, so the chemical method of preparation is "Double decomposition".

In reaction (III) S (sol) is formed by oxidation of H_2S, so the chemical method of preparation is "Oxidation"

In reaction (IV) $Fe(OH)_3$ (sol) is formed by hydrolysis of $FeCl_3$, so the chemical method of preparation is "Hydrolysis".

27. (c) (A) is true but (R) is false because the precipitate reaction is possible due to double decomposition.

28. (a) O.N. of S in SO_3^{-2}

$x + 3 \times (-2) = -2$

or $x - 6 = -2$ or $x = +6 - 2 = +4$

O.N. of S in $S_2O_4^{-2}$

$2x + 4 \times (-2) = -2$

or $\quad 2x - 8 = -2$

or $\quad 2x = +8 - 2 = +6$

$\therefore \quad x = +3$

O.N. of S in $S_2O_6^{-2}$

$2x + 6 \times (-2) = -2$

or $\quad 2x - 12 = -2$

or $\quad 2x = +12 - 2 = +10$

$\therefore \quad x = +5$

Thus, the order is

$S_2O_4^{-2}(+3) < SO_3^{-2}(+4) < S_2O_6^{-2}(+5)$

29. (c) None of the element in reaction (c) undergoes a change in O.N. therefore, it is not a redox reaction.

$$\overset{+1}{Ag}\overset{+5}{N}\overset{-2}{O_3} + \overset{+1}{Na}\overset{-1}{Cl} \longrightarrow \overset{+1}{Ag}\overset{-1}{Cl} + \overset{+1}{Na}\overset{+5}{N}\overset{-2}{O_3}$$

Infact, it is a double decomposition reaction.

30. (d) Both Statement I and Statement II are correct.

Ch-9 p-Block Elements-I

Topical Follow Thru

Test-1

1. (c) The correct order of increasing. ionisation energy is aluminium < gallium < boron Ionisation energy decreases down the group due to increasing atomic size and shielding effect but not smoothly. The observed discontinuity in the ionisation enthalpy value between Gallium and aluminium is due to inability of *d*- and *f*-electrons, which have low screening effect, to compensate the increase in nuclear charge. Therefore, boron has the highest ionisation energy, followed by gallium and then aluminium.

2. (a) Covalency: 4, Oxidation state: + 3

In $[BF_4]^-$, boron forms four covalent bonds with four fluorine atoms (covalency = 4) and has a formal charge of + 3 (oxidation state = + 3).

3. (d) Both Statement I and Statement II are correct.

4. (a) Gallium has a melting point of 29.76 °C, which is below the boiling point of water (100 °C).

5. (b) The correct order is $BF_3 < BCl_3 < BBr_3 < BI_3$ This order can be explained on the basis of the capacity of the halogen atom to back-donate its lone pair of electrons to empty *p*-orbital of the boron atom through $p\pi - p\pi$ bonding. Being highly electronegative, F makes BF_3 a relatively weak Lewis acid. On the other hand, I makes BI_3 a strongest Lewis acid.

6. (c) Aluminium forms six coordinate bonds with water molecules in the $[Al(H_2O)_6]^{3+}$ complex and its hybridisation is sp^3d^2. This hybridisation is a result of need of aluminium atom to accomodate six water molecules which requires a coordination number of six.

7. (d) Boron, being the lightest and smallest, has relatively high ionisation energy. Due to non-availability of *d*-orbitals, boron is unable to expand its octet. This makes it difficult to accomodate six fluoride ions to make MF_6^{3-}.

8. (b) Boric acid acts as a Lewis acid by accepting a hydroxide ion from water. This leaves behind a proton (H^+), making the solution acidic.

9. (a) The addition of KF provides fluoride ions that coordinate with AlF_3 to form the soluble complex ion $[AlF_6]^{3-}$, which is stabilised by the K^+ cations.

10. (a) The stability of the +1 oxidation state increases down the group due to the inert pair effect. This is where the *s*-electrons become less involved in bonding, leading to a preference for losing only the *p*-electrons.
Hence, the correct order is Al < Ga < In < Tl.

11. (a) Boron nitride (BN) has a hexagonal layered structure similar to graphite, with alternate boron and nitrogen atoms.

12. (b) Diborane (B_2H_6) is electron-deficient, meaning it doesn't have enough electrons to form the typical two-center, two-electron bonds for all the atoms. It has unique three-center, two-electron bonds.

13. (c) The correct option is (c). Except A, C and E all other statements are incorrect. Their correct form is

(B) While the + 3 oxidation state is common for group 13 elements, the stability of the +1 oxidation state increases down the group (due to the inert pair effect).

(D) The tendency to form covalent compounds decreases down the group due to the increasing metallic character of the elements.

14. (b) Reducing character of the boron family decreases down the group from Al to Tl because of the increase in electrode potential value for M^{3+}/M. Thus, the correct order is : Al > Ga > In > Tl.

15. (b) Correct statements are B, C and D only. Correct form of A and E are

- In $Al_2(CH_3)_6$, there are two types of Al—C bonds: terminal bonds (stronger) and bridging bonds (weaker).
- $Al_2(CH_3)_6$ has a non-planar, bridged dimeric structure.

16. (a) Among the given option, structure BF_4^- has regular tetrahedral.

17. (b) When boron reacts with fused sodium hydroxide and water, then sodium metaborate and H_2 gas is evolved.

$$2B + 6NaOH \longrightarrow 2Na_3BO_3 + 3H_2\uparrow$$

18. (a) H_3BO_3 and HBO_2 both have same oxidation number of (+3). So, both of them cannot differ in oxidation number.

19. (c) (A) is true but (R) is false. The corrected form of (R) is
In water, orthoboric acid does not act as a proton donor, it functions as a Lewis acid by accepting electron pair from water.

20. (d)
- On moving from B to Al, all the ionisation enthalpies decrease as expected and this decrease is due to an increase in atomic size and shielding effect.
- On moving from Al to Ga, the ionisation enthalpy increases slightly, because on moving from Al to Ga, both nuclear charge and shielding effect increase but due to poor shielding by *d*-electron in Ga, effective nuclear charge on valence electron increases resulting in *d*-block contraction, that's why ionisation enthalpies increases.
- On moving from Ga to In, again there is slight decrease in ionisation enthalpies due to increased shielding effect by additional ten 4*d* electrons, which outweighs the effect of increased nuclear charge.
- On moving from In to Tl, ionisation enthalpies show the increase again because fourteen 4*f* electrons shield valence electron poorly (order of shielding effect s > p > d > f) and so effective nuclear charge increases, consequently ionisation enthalpies increase.

Thus, the correct order of ionisation enthalpy is

$$B > Al < Ga > In < Tl.$$

21. (c) The correct structural representation of diborane is

$$H_2B(\mu\text{-}H)_2BH_2$$

22. (a) The correct match is A-II, B-IV, C-I, D-III.

23. (d) Reaction of ammonia with diborane gives $B_3N_3H_6$, known as inorganic benzene.

$$3B_2H_6 + 6NH_3 \xrightarrow{\Delta} 2B_3N_3H_6 + 12H_2$$

24. (c) In gallium, the crystal structure is different, suggesting that Ga consists of almost discrete Ga_2 molecule, that's why its melting point is lowest. Ga exists as liquid from 30°C upto 2000°C and hence, it is used in high temperature thermometry.

25. (c) Solution of sodium meta aluminate on boiling with NH_4Cl gives a white precipitate of $Al(OH)_3$.

$$NH_4Cl + H_2O \longrightarrow NH_4OH + HCl$$

$$NaAlO_2 + HCl + H_2O \longrightarrow NaCl + \underset{\text{White ppt}}{Al(OH)_3} \downarrow$$

Test - 2

1. (d) PbF_4 is predominantly ionic due to the large electronegativity difference between lead and fluorine.

2. (d) Amphoteric oxides can react with both acids and bases. SnO_2 can react with acids to form salts like $SnCl_4$, and with bases to form stannates.

3. (d) Except D, all statements are correct. Correct form of D is CO is toxic but colourless and odourless.

4. (c) The correct match is A-III B-I C-IV D-II.

5. (d) Silicones are biocompatible polymers used in various cosmetic and medical applications.

6. (c) CO is produced due to incomplete combustion of carbon-contain materials when there is insufficient oxygen is used in the fuel during burning process.

7. (c) Silicon's relatively small size makes it difficult to accommodate six large chloride ions around it due to steric hindrance.

8. (a) Most ionic character will be in $PbCl_2$, because Pb is in +2 oxidation state, while in all other option the charge on non-metal is +4. Since, $PbCl_2$, has low charge on cation, therefore, it will have the most ionic character.

9. (a) The distribution of 25 hexagons and 12 pentagons is involved in the C_{70} fullerene structure.

10. (a) The correct order of tendency of group 14 elements for catenation is

$$C > Si > Ge > Sn$$

Catenation is the ability of an element to form chains or rings by bonding with itself. This tendency decreases down group 14 due to the increasing atomic size and weaker bond strength.

11. (a) All the given hydrides are covalent hydrides consisting of discrete molecules which are held together by the weak van der Waals' forces. The magnitude of these forces is directly related to the molecular mass, which increases as we move down the group.
Thus, the order of volatility is $CH_4 > SiH_4 > GeH_4 > SnH_4$.
Therefore, CH_4 is the most volatile among these compounds.

12. (c) Pb^{2+}, Pb^{4+} and Sn^{2+} can act as oxidising agents. Pb^{4+} and Sn^{2+} can be reduced to lower oxidation states (Pb^{2+} and Sn). However, Pb^{2+} has a higher reduction potential thus, acts as an oxidising agent.

13. (c) Statement I is incorrect but Statement II is correct.

The correct form of statement I is SnO_2 and PbO_2 are amphoteric oxides while GeO and SiO are acidic.

14. (a) Both (A) and (R) are true and (R) is the correct explanation of (A).

15. (d) PbO_2 (Lead dioxide) is a strong oxidising agent and displays amphoteric properties. It is the primary component of the positive electrode in lead-acid batteries.

$PbCO_3$ (Lead carbonate) is not amphoteric and is not involved in lead-acid batteries.

$PbSO_4$ (Lead sulphate) is a product of the discharge reaction in lead-acid batteries but is not the oxidising agent itself.

PbO (Lead monoxide) Is amphoteric but it is not a strong oxidising agent as PbO_2.

Chapter Break Thru

1. (b) The correct decreasing order of acidity is

$$SiO_2 > PbO_2 > CO > Tl_2O_3$$

SiO_2 is an acidic oxide and reacts with alkalies to form salt.

$$SiO_2 + 2NaOH \xrightarrow{\Delta} Na_2SiO_3 + H_2O$$

CO is a neutral oxide and will not react with acids and bases.

PbO_2 is an amphoteric oxide as it reacts with both acid as well as base.

$$PbO_2 + 2NaOH \longrightarrow Na_2PbO_2 + H_2O$$

$$2PbO_2 + 2H_2SO_4 \longrightarrow 2PbSO_4 + 2H_2O + O_2$$

Tl_2O_3 is a basic oxide and reacts with acids to form salts.

$$Tl_2O_3 + 6HCl \longrightarrow 2TlCl_3 + 3H_2O$$

2. (c) In valence shell, there is 3 electrons. Hence, the oxidation state is +3.

3. (a) Boron cannot expand its covalence beyond four as it lacks *d*-orbitals and hence $[BF_6^{3-}]$ anion is not possible.

4. (c) In case of Al, the electron is to be removed from less penetrating *p*-orbital as compared to Mg where the electron is to be removed from more penetrating and completely filled *s*-orbital.

Hence, IE_1 of Al is smaller than that of Mg.

5. (c) An element *R* present in group 13 of the periodic table form an oxide of R_2O_3.

- *R* belongs to group 13, thus it will have +3 oxidation state.
- No element in group 13 is in gaseous form. All the elements are solids at room temperature.
- *R* will form RX_3 (trihalide).

6. (b) With the rise in atomic number, the tendency to show +2 oxidation state increases in case of the elements of the carbon family.

7. (d) Inert pair effect is more pronounced in heavier member like Pb.

Due to this Pb (IV) compounds are strong oxidising agent and are reduced to more stable Pb(II).

8. (b) Statement I is correct but statement II is incorrect. The correct form of statement II is,

Each carbon of graphite has one free electron which makes it a good conductor of heat and electricity.

9. (a) As the size of the element increases from B to Al and downward the group, the tendency to accept a lone pair of electron from Lewis base decreases, hence Lewis acid character decreases.

Option (a) is correct.

10. (d) The negative value of $E°$ for Al^{3+} / Al suggests that Al has a strong tendency to form Al^{3+} ions. On other hand positive value of Tl^{3+} / Tl indicates that Tl does not have high tendency to form Tl^{3+} ions. Hence, Al is more electropositive than Tl.

11. (c) Tin is oxidised to meta-stannic acid when it is treated with nitric acid.

$$Sn + 4HNO_3 \longrightarrow \underset{\text{Meta-stannic acid}}{H_2SnO_3} + 4NO_2 + H_2O$$

12. (a) White lead is also called as basic lead carbonate.

It is formed by below reaction.

$$\underset{\text{Lead salt}}{3Pb(NO_3)_2} + 3Na_2CO_3 + H_2O \longrightarrow \underset{\text{White lead}}{Pb(OH)_2 \cdot 2PbCO_3} + 6NaNO_3 + CO_2$$

13. (b) Magnesium combines with boron to give magnesium boride on heating.

$$3Mg + 2B \xrightarrow{\Delta} Mg_3B_2$$

14. (b) The chemical formula for bauxite ore (which is an aluminium ore) is $Al_2O_3 \cdot 2H_2O$.

15. (d) Both Statement I and Statement II are correct.

16. (a) The correct decreasing order is

$PbF_2 > PbCl_2 > PbBr_2 > PbI_2$.

Ionic character decreases as the size of halogen increases from top to bottom in halogen family.

17. (a) Statement given in option (a) is incorrect. Its correct form is,

Diamond is a covalent and not ionic in nature.

18. (d) (A) is false but (R) is true.

The correct form of (A) is,

The first ionisation enthalpy of Sn is less than that of Pb because the 4*f* electrons in Pb are poor at shielding the outermost electrons experience a greater effective nuclear charge and it is more difficult to remove them.

19. (b) Species in which the central atom does not have eight electrons in the valence shell one called electron deficient molecules.

In BCl_3 and AlH_3 the central atom have only 6 electrons and thus, they is an are electron deficient molecules.

20. (b) The melting point of tin is lower but boiling point is higher than lead is correct statement among the given.

21. (d) Carbon form neutral as well as acidic oxides.

$$C + \frac{1}{2}O_2 \longrightarrow CO \text{ (neutral oxide)}$$

$$C + O_2 \longrightarrow CO_2 \text{ (acidic oxide)}$$

22. (a) The complete reaction is as follows,

$$Al_4C_3 + 12H_2O \longrightarrow 4Al(OH)_3 + \underset{\text{Methane}}{3CH_4} \uparrow$$

23. (c) Si can be prepared by reaction of silica with Mg.

$$\underset{\text{(Silica)}}{SiO_2} + 2Mg \xrightarrow{\Delta} Si + 2MgO$$

24. (d) Among the given, TlOH is water soluble and strongly basic. Since, TlOH is water soluble ionic compound and it readily dissociates into Tl^+ ions and OH^- ions, making it a strong base.

25. (c) (A) is true but (R) is false.

The correct form of (R) is :

Boron is less reactive. Melting point of pure boron is very high and it is corrosive in liquid state. Pure boron is produced with difficulty because of contamination of carbon or other element that resist removal.

26. (c) Water gas is a mixture of equimolar of CO and H_2.

27. (c) In diamond, carbon atoms are sp^3-hybridised.

28. (a) Carbon due to its smaller size and non-availability of *d*-orbitals, cannot extend its covalency more than 4, while Si due to presence of vacant *d* orbitals can extend its covalency beyond four.

Due to this, $SiCl_4$ is easily hydrolysed but CCl_4 not.

$$SiCl_4 + 2H_2O \xrightarrow{\Delta} H_4SiO_4$$

29. (d) SnO_2 is an amphoteric, it forms both acidic as well as basic oxides.

$$SnO_2 + 2NaOH \longrightarrow \underset{\text{Basic}}{NaSnO_3} + H_2O$$

$$SnO_2 + 2H_2SO_4 \xrightarrow{\Delta} \underset{\text{Acidic oxide}}{Sn(SO_4)_2} + 2H_2O$$

30. (b) Statement I is correct but Statement II is incorrect.

The correct form of statement II is : Al and Be show a diagonal relationship.

Ch-10 Purification and Characterisation of Organic Compounds

Topical Follow Thru

Test - 1

1. (c) In thin layer chromatography, mobile phase is liquid and stationary phase is solid. Liquid phase moves through the stationary phase by capillary action.

2. (a) Absolute alcohol is the much pure form of alcohol which forms an azeotropic mixture with water so, only azeotropic distillation can be used for its separation from rectified spirit.

3. (d) Both Statement I and Statement II are correct.

The purification technique used to separate the essential oils from water is steam distillation because essential oils are volatile and are insoluble in water.

4. (d) If the raw juices have to be concentrated then the water content should be very low in the sugar solution so, at low pressure boiling point is lowered and evaporation of water becomes more fast.

For this process vacuum distillation is the most preferable technique.

5. (d) Among the given options, the best method for separating different sugars from each other is chromatography.

6. (b) The correct match is

A-II, B-IV, C-III, D-I.

7. (c) To separate two liquids which differ in their boiling points widely, the technique used is simple distillation. So, the assertion is true.

The correct form of Reason is, fractional distillation is used to separate the two liquids which differ in their boiling points by 10° C or so.

8. (d) On the process of distillation of petroleum the first distillation product is prepared as petroleum ether.

It is being noticed that natural gases comes out first during extraction of petroleum.

9. (b) The value of R_f doesn't depend on the concentration of the substance. Except concentration R_f depends on all the given options as

(i) nature of substance

(ii) nature of solvent

(iii) nature of filter paper used

(iv) temperature

10. (c) In fractional distillation the fractionating column is used as two liquids have a difference in their boiling point $\approx 5°C$, the fractionating column is used here. The lower boiling point liquid comes down when it passes through this column.

11. (a) Both Statement I and Statement II are incorrect.

R_f is used to compare and help identify compounds.

Thus, R_f is dimensionless.

R_f value will be different for same compounds at different solvent because it depends on the solubility and polarity with solvent.

12. (c) From the principle of fractional crystallisation, the method is used for the organic solids which are having small difference in their solubilities in preferred solvents.

13. (c) Among the given statements, only statement D is incorrect. Its correct form is :

Low polarity compounds are weakly adsorbed and has greater R_f value.

14. (c) Among the given options only benzoic acid has high vapour pressure at temperature below its melting point.

15. (b) Aniline can be separated from aniline-water mixture by using steam-distillation method.

- In simple distillation, a similar liquid mixture is boiled.
- In fractional distillation, a mixture of liquids is boiled and vapours come out through a glass tube known as fractionating column.
- Vacuum distillation, is performed under reduced pressure, which permits the purification of compounds not readily distilled at ambient pressures.

Test - 2

1. (c) Calcium carbonate ($CaCO_3$) gets precipitated during the detection of carbon and hydrogen. Firstly carbon will react with copper (II) oxide to form copper and carbon dioxide. Then, hydrogen will react with the same copper (II) oxide to form copper and water. After this, the presence of carbon dioxide is tested by reacting it with calcium hydroxide and the product obtained is calcium carbonate, which gets precipitated.

2. (b) The preparation of sodium extract is done by fusing organic compounds with Na and then extracting them with water in Lassaigne's test.

3. (d) Hydrazine ($NH_2—NH_2$) does not contain carbon atom. On fusion with Na metal, it cannot form NaCN.

So, hydrazine does not show Lassaigne's test.

4. (b) The correct match is A-III, B-IV, C-I, D-II.

5. (d) If nitrogen and sulphur are present in solution already, they will hinder in test of $AgNO_3$, HNO_3. Thus, in order to remove CN^- and S^{2-}, sodium fusion extract are boiled with concentrated HNO_3.

6. (c) On the treatment of sodium fusion extract with sodium nitroprusside, appearance of violet colour indicates the presence of sulphur.

$$S^{2-} + [Fe(CN)_5NO]^{2-} \longrightarrow \underset{\text{Violet}}{[Fe(CN)_5NOS]^{4-}}$$

7. (c) Among all statements only D and E are incorrect while other are correct. The correct form of D and E is

- The formula of sodium nitroprusside ion is $[Fe(CN)_5NO]^{2-}$
- Victor meyer's method is used for the process of determination of molecular mass in quantitative analysis.

8. (d) (A) is false but (R) is true. Correct form of (A) is Lassaigne's test does not give positive test for N, since it does not contain C. So CN^- ion is not obtained which is an essential condition for the test for N.

9. (d) The organic compound contains sulphur because a black ppt. of PbS is formed.

$$S^{2-} + Pb^{2+} \longrightarrow \underset{\text{Black}}{PbS}$$

10. (b) The sodium fusion extract is boiled with iron (II) sulphate and then acidified with concentrated H_2SO_4.

The formation of prussian blue colour confirms the presence of N.

$$6CN^- + Fe^{2+} \longrightarrow [Fe(CN)_6]^{4-}$$

$$3[Fe(CN)_6]^{4-} + 4Fe^{3+} \xrightarrow{xH_2O} Fe_4[Fe(CN_6)_3]\cdot xH_2O$$

11. (d) Both Statement I and Statement II are correct.

12. (b) In Lassaigne's test when both N and S are present, blood red colour obtained is due to the formation of

$$3NaCNS + FeCl_3 \longrightarrow \underset{\text{(Red)}}{Fe(CNS)_3} + 3NaCl$$

13. (b) When the organic compound is heated with an oxidising agent (Na_2O_2), then the phosphorus present in the compound is oxidised to phosphate.

When is boiled with HNO_3 and then treated with ammonium molybdate, a yellow colouration or ppt. indicates the presence of phosphorus.

$$Na_3PO_4 + 3HNO_3 \longrightarrow H_3PO_4 + 3NaNO_3$$

$$H_3PO_4 + \underset{\text{Ammonium molybdate}}{12(NH_4)_2MoO_4} + 21HNO_3 \longrightarrow$$

$(NH_4)_3PO_4 \cdot 12MoO_3 + 21NH_4NO_3 + 12H_2O$
Ammonium phosphomolybdate

14. (c) Carbon present in the compound is oxidised to carbon dioxide (tested by lime-water, which develops turbidity).

$$\text{Organic compound} + CuO \xrightarrow{\Delta} CO_2 + 2Cu$$

Hence, CO_2 will release if carbon is present.

15. (a) Positive Lassaigne's test is given by compounds containing both C and N.

$NH_2—NH_2 \cdot H_2O$ (Does not contain C). So, it does not give lassaigne's test.

Test- 3

1. (a) Kjeldahl's method is used in the estimation of nitrogen therefore, option (a) is correct.

While other elements like carbon is estimated with Liebig's method, Sulphur is estimated with Carius method.

2. (b) Percentage of sulphur

$$= \frac{32}{233} \times \frac{\text{Mass of } BaSO_4}{\text{Mass of organic compound}} \times 100$$

$$= \frac{32}{233} \times \frac{1.721}{0.43} \times 100$$

$= 55\%$

3. (c) The N_2 in gaseous form is evolved during the Duma's process and is measured at desired p and T.

4. (d) $P\% = \frac{62}{222} \times \frac{w_{pp}}{w} \times 100$

where, w_{pp} = mass of magnesium pyrophosphate

w = mass of organic compound

$$= \frac{62}{222} \times \frac{0.32}{0.2} \times 100$$

$= 44.68\%$

5. (b) The correct match is given in option (b).

A-III, B-IV, C-II, D-I

6. (c) Percentage of

$$N = \frac{1.4 \times \text{mEq. of } H_2SO_4 \text{ used to neutralise } NH_3}{\text{Weight of compound}}$$

m moles of $H_2SO_4 = 30$

mEq. of $H_2SO_4 = 30 \times 2 = 60$

Percentage of $N = \frac{1.4 \times 60}{2.8} = 30\%$

7. (b) The given method known as carius method for the estimation of sulphur in which it oxidised to H_2SO_4.

8. (b) % of S

$$= \frac{32}{233} \times \frac{\text{wt. of } BaSO_4}{\text{wt. of organic compound}} \times 100$$

$$= \frac{32}{233} \times \frac{0.25}{0.2685} \times 100$$

$= 12.79\%$

9. (d) $\% N = \frac{1.4 \times M \times V \times B}{\text{Mass of substance taken}}$

$$= \frac{1.4 \times 1 \times 10 \times 2}{2} = 14\%$$

where, M, V and B are the molarity, volume and basicity of the acid used.

10. (b) Both (A) and (R) are correct but (R) is not the correct explanation of (A).

Correct explanation of (A) is : Kjeldahl's method is not applicable to compounds containing azo group or having nitrogen directly attached to the ring systems, hence Duma's method is preferred.

11. (c) $p_{N_2} = 725 - 25 = 700$ mm Hg

$V = 75$ mL

$\therefore \quad pV = \frac{w}{m}RT$

$$\frac{700}{760} \times \frac{75}{1000} = \frac{w_{N_2}}{28} \times 0.0821 \times 300$$

$w_{N_2} = 0.078$ g

$$\therefore \quad \%N = \frac{0.078}{0.25} \times 100 = 31.2\%$$

12. (a) Given that

Mass of substance = 0.44 g

Mass of $CO_2 = 0.32$ g

% of H = 1.86%

% of C

$$= \frac{12}{44} \times \frac{\text{Mass of } CO_2}{\text{Mass of substance}} \times 100$$

$$= \frac{12}{44} \times \frac{0.32}{0.44} \times 100 = 19.83\%$$

$C\% = 19.83$, $H\% = 1.86$

Total O%

$= 100 - (19.83 + 1.86) = 78.31\%$

13. (c) Kjeldahl's method depends on the fact that most of the organic compounds containing nitrogen are quantitatively decomposed to give $(NH_4)_2SO_4$ when heated strongly with conc. H_2SO_4. In this method, $CuSO_4$ acts as catalytic agent.

14. (b) Among all the statements, only D and E are incorrect rest all are correct. The correct form is

- In Kjeldahl's method estimation of N, the compound containing nitrogen is heated with H_2SO_4.
- Duma's method is a method of estimation of nitrogen.

15. (b) Percentage of

$$N = \frac{1.4 \times \text{m.eq. of } H_2SO_4 \text{ used to neutralised } NH_3}{\text{Weight of compound}}$$

m.eq. of $H_2SO_4 = 2 \times 10$ m.eq.

$$\% \text{ of } N = \frac{1.4 \times 10 \times 2}{0.75} = 37.33\%$$

Chapter Break Thru

1. (c) Liebig's method is basically used for the estimation of carbon and hydrogen, in which the mass of organic compound is heated in presence of pure oxygen after that the carbon dioxide and water formed are collected and weighed and percentage of carbon and hydrogen are calculated.

2. (b) Kjeldahl's method is not applicable to compound containing nitro groups such as nitrobenzene and compound containing nitrogen in the ring such as pyridine because during digestion these compound are not completely converted into $(NH_4)_2SO_4$. Furthermore, diazonium salts on heating decomposes to lose N_2 much before they are able to react with molten Na metal to form NaCN. Thus, only aniline (b) can be suitable for the estimation of nitrogen.

3. (a) % C

$$= \frac{12}{44} \times \frac{\text{Mass of } CO_2 \text{ formed}}{\text{Mass of substance}} \times 100$$

Substituting the values

$$69 = \frac{12}{44} \times \frac{\text{Mass of } CO_2 \text{ formed}}{0.2} \times 100$$

Mass of CO_2 formed = 0.506 g

% H

$$= \frac{2}{18} \times \frac{\text{Mass of } H_2O \text{ Formed}}{\text{Mass of substance}} \times 100$$

$$4.8 = \frac{2}{18} \times \frac{\text{Mass of } H_2O \text{ formed}}{0.2} \times 100$$

Mass of H_2O formed = 0.0864 g

4. (c) Statement II is correct but statement I is incorrect.

The correct form of Statement I is, Absolute alcohol can be prepared from rectified spirit by azeotropic distillation.

5. (b) Given :

$V_1 = 40\,\text{mL}, V_2$ at NTP = ?

$p_1 = 725 - 25 = 700\,\text{mm},$

$p_2 = 760\,\text{mm}$

$T_1 = 300\,\text{K}, T_2 = 273\,\text{K}$

Applying ideal gas equation,

$$\frac{p_1V_1}{T_1} = \frac{p_2V_2}{T_2}$$

$$\Rightarrow \quad V_2 = \frac{p_1V_1T_2}{p_2T_1}$$

$$\Rightarrow V_2 = \frac{700 \times 40 \times 273}{760 \times 300}$$

$= 33.53\,\text{mL}$

6. (c) 20 mL of $\frac{M}{10}$ NaOH = 10 mL of $M/10\ H_2SO_4$

Volume of $M/10\ H_2SO_4$ left unused = 10 mL

$\therefore$ Volume of $\frac{M}{10}\ H_2SO_4$ used will be

$60 - 10 = 50\,\text{mL}$

$$\therefore \quad \%\,N = \frac{1.4 \times M \times B \times V}{\text{Mass of substance}}$$

$$= \frac{1.4 \times 1 \times 2 \times 50}{1.4 \times 10} = 10$$

7. (a) Mass of substance taken $= 29.5 \times 10^{-3}$ g

Volume of acid taken = 20 mL of 0.1 M HCl

Now 15 mL of 0.1 M NaOH = 15 mL of 0.1 M HCl

$\therefore$ Volume of acid used 20-15 = 5 mL of 0.1 M HCl

$$\%\,N = \frac{1.4 \times M \times B \times V}{\text{Mass of substance}}$$

$$\Rightarrow \frac{1.4 \times 0.1 \times 1 \times 5}{29.5 \times 10^{-3}} = 23.7\%$$

8. (d) % of sulphur

$$= \frac{32}{233} \times \frac{\text{Mass of } BaSO_4}{\text{Mass of substance}} \times 100$$

32 = molar mass of sulphur

233 = molar mass of $BaSO_4$

$$\%\,S = \frac{32}{233} \times \frac{0.688}{0.468} \times 100$$

$\%\,S = 20.19\%$

9. (d) In paper chromatography, separation of components of a mixture depends upon their partitioning (distribution) between water held in stationary phase (i.e. paper) and liquid present in liquid phase.

10. (c) When C is heated with CuO it get converted into CO_2.

$$C + 2CuO \xrightarrow{\Delta} CO_2 + 2Cu$$

11. (c) During the fusion, N of the organic compound is converted into NaCN.

The reaction involved is as follow

$$\underset{\text{From organic compound}}{C + N} + Na \xrightarrow{\Delta} NaCN$$

12. (c) AgF formed by Lassaigne's test is highly soluble in water and does not form precipitate. Hence, it cannot detect F.

13. (a) A mixture of benzene and chloroform is separated by distillation method.

14. (a) Distillation under reduced pressure decreases the boiling point and hence the liquid can be distilled without decomposition.

15. (c) A liquid which is insoluble in water and has a vapour pressure of 10-15 mm Hg at 100°C can be purified by steam distillation method.

16. (a) The correct match is A-III, B-IV, C-I, D-II.

17. (b) In steam distillation, the mixture distills when the vapour pressure of toluene + water becomes equal to the atmospheric pressure, the vapour pressure of toluene is itself less than the pressure of barometer, i.e. atmospheric pressure.

18. (a) Aniline being more soluble in organic solvent than in water. Hence, it can separated using differential extraction method.

19. (a) Given, $w = 0.16\,\text{g}, V_1 = 46\,\text{mL}$

$T_1 = 15°\text{C}, p = 755\,\text{mm of Hg}$

$= 288\,\text{K}, \ p_1 = 15\,\text{mm of Hg}$

$$\frac{(p - p_1)V_1}{T_1} = \frac{p_2V_2}{T_2}$$

$$\frac{(755 - 15) \times 46}{288} = \frac{760 \times V_2(\text{mL})}{273}$$

$V_2(\text{mL}) = 42.46$

$$\%\text{ of N} = \frac{28}{22400} \times \frac{V_2(\text{mL})}{w} \times 100$$

$$= \frac{28}{22400} \times \frac{42.46}{0.16} \times 100$$

$\approx 33\%$

20. (b) In Duma's method, the reaction involved is as follows

$$C_xH_yN_z + \left(2x + \frac{y}{2}\right)CuO \longrightarrow xCO_2 + \frac{y}{2}H_2O + \frac{z}{2}N_2 + \left(2x + \frac{y}{2}\right)Cu$$

So, nitrogen exists as N_2.

21. (a) Only *o*-nitrophenol is capable of forming intramolecular H-bonding (chelation) which leads to its lower boiling point (less than 100°C) and also lower solubility in water (steam). Thus, option (a) is the correct answer.

22. (b) Statement I is correct but statement II is incorrect.
The correct form of statement II is chromatography can be used to separate both colourless and coloured substances.

23. (a) The organic compounds that are present in aqueous medium and is less soluble in any organic solvents can be separated by using continuous extraction.

24. (c) (A) is true but (R) is false. The correct form of (R) is :
In paper chromatography both the moving and stationary phase are liquid.

25. (b) % of chlorine

$$= \frac{35.5}{143.5} \times \frac{\text{Mass of AgCl}}{\text{Mass of substance}} \times 100$$

$$= \frac{35.5}{143.5} \times \frac{0.574}{0.198} \times 100$$

$$= 71.71\%$$

26. (d) (A) is false but (R) is true. The correct form of (A) is :
In Lassaigne's test for nitrogen, sodium cannot be replaced by lithium, because NaCN will not be formed if sodium is not present.

27. (c) During carius method, sulphur of organic compound is converted into H_2SO_4.

$$S + H_2O + 3O \xrightarrow[HNO_3]{\Delta} \underset{\text{Sulphuric acid}}{H_2SO_4}$$

28. (a) According to carius method,

$$\% \text{ of Br} = \frac{\text{Mass of AgBr}}{\text{Molar mass of AgBr}} \times \frac{\text{Mass of Br}}{\text{Weight of organic compound}} \times 100$$

$$= \frac{1.88 \times 80 \times 100}{188 \times 1.6} = 50\%$$

29. (b) Given mass of organic compound = 0.471 g
Mass of $BaSO_4$ = 1.44 g
Molar mass of $BaSO_4$ = 233 g/mol

$$\% \text{ S} = \frac{\text{Molar mass of S}}{\text{Molar mass of BaSO}_4} \times \frac{\text{Mass of BaSO}_4}{\text{Mass of organic compound}} \times 100$$

$$= \frac{32}{233} \times 1.44 \times \frac{1}{0.471} \times 100$$

$$\approx 42\%$$

30. (a) Statements I, II and IV are correct while III and V are incorrrect. Their correct form is
- During the process, C and H are oxidised to CO_2 and H_2O.
- Taken compound is heated with fuming nitric acid.

Ch-11 Some Basic Principles of Organic Chemistry

Topical Follow Thru

Test-1

1. (a) $\overset{6}{H_3C}-\underset{5}{C}\equiv\underset{4}{C}-\underset{3}{CH}(CH_3)-\overset{2}{C}(CH_3)=\overset{1}{CH_2}$

The IUPAC name of the given compound is
2,3-dimethyl hex-1-en-4-yne.

2. (b) Benzene π-bonds have partial double bond character which is somewhere between single and double bond due to resonance. Hence, their bond lengths are greater than π-bonds but lesser than single bonds.
The order of bond length is single bond > partial double bond > double bond.
So, the correct order is I < II < III.

3. (d) (A) is false but (R) is true.
Correct form of (A) is except for the second carbon atom from left, all others are sp^2-hybridised. This carbon atom is *sp*-hybridised.

4. (a) Ethane has the least hindered rotation among the given option, as substituents in ethane are all H atoms which are small in size.

5. (d) There are a total 8 carbon atoms which are secondary as each is bonded to two other adjacent carbon atoms.

[Naphthalene structure with positions numbered 1–8]

6. (a) From primary carbon, ease of abstraction of H ion is greatest as the anion is more stable when no electron donating group is present. Stability order is

$$\underset{1°}{CH_3-\bar{C}H_2} > \underset{2°}{CH_3-\bar{C}H-CH_3} > \underset{3°}{CH_3-\bar{C}(CH_3)-CH_3}$$

7. (c) As the bond (a) is formed between overlap of *sp-sp* hybrid orbitals while (b) is formed by overlap of *sp-sp*^{3} hybrid orbitals hence the bond length of (b) > (a).

8. (a) The IUPAC name of the given compound is
2-methylcyclohex-2-en-1-ol.

9. (b) π-bonds are formed by sideways overlapping of vacant *p*-orbitals. The carbon atom occupies the sp^2-hybridisation state. Hence, there are four carbon atom is sp^2 hybridised, so three sp^2-sp^2 sigma bonds are present in the given compound.

10. (c) Bond X is formed by overlap of sp^2-and sp^3-hybrid orbitals.

11. (b) As *s*-character (%) increases, electronegativity increases.
So, the correct order is
$sp > sp^2 > sp^3$

12. (b) The correct structure of 2-amino-4-hydroxybenzoic acid is given in option (b).

13. (c) Statement given in option (c) is incorrect. Its correct form is carbon has unique property of catenation and tetravalency.

14. (b) The correct structure of 3,3-dimethylbutyne is given in option (b).

$$\overset{4}{H_3C}-\overset{3}{C}(CH_3)_2-\overset{2}{C}\equiv\overset{1}{CH}$$

15. (b) $\overset{3}{CH_3}-\overset{}{CH}(\overset{2}{CH_2}\overset{1}{CHO})-\overset{4}{CH_2}-\overset{5}{CHO}$
IUPAC name of the compound is 3-methylpentane-1, 5-dial.

Test-2

1. (a) *Meso*-compounds are those compounds having minimum of two stereogenic carbon atoms but are not chiral due to plane of symmetry. Therefore, only compound I is of *meso*- compound.

2. (b) First compound is *trans*-1, 2-dimethylcyclohexane while second compound is *cis*-1,2-dimethylcyclohexane. Hence, these are diastereomers.

3. (d) The molecular formula of third homologue in the homologous series of mono-carboxylic acid is CH_3CH_2COOH, i.e. $C_3H_6O_2$.

4. (a) Ethanol and dimethyl ether are functional isomers having the same molecular formula C_2H_6O.
CH_3-CH_2-OH and
CH_3-O-CH_3

5. (a) Both (A) and (R) are true and (R) is the correct explanation of (A).

6. (a) Total three structural isomers of C_5H_{12} are possible, i.e. *iso*-pentane, *neo*-pentane and *n*-pentane.

$CH_3-CH(CH_3)-CH_2-CH_3$
iso-pentane

$CH_3-CH_2-CH_2-CH_2-CH_3$
n-pentane

$CH_3-C(CH_3)_2-CH_3$
neo-pentane

7. (c) As there are only two chiral centres (*) present in the compound, hence total number of stereoisomers will be 2^n where n is number of chiral carbon atoms.
Hence, correct answer is 4.

8. (c) Correct option is 1,1-dichloroethene. Each carbon around the double bond should have different substituents to show geometrical isomerism which is not true for the given compound.

9. (a) Empirical formula (E.F.) is C_2H_5.
Empirical formula mass = 29 g/mol
Molar mass = 58 g/mol

$$n = \frac{\text{Molar mass}}{\text{Empirical mass formula}} = \frac{58}{29} = 2$$

∴ Molecular formula = $(E.F)_n$
$= (C_2H_5)_2 = C_4H_{10}$
The molecular formula is C_4H_{10} and the isomers are two (chain isomers) in number.
$CH_3-CH_2-CH_2-CH_3$, $CH_3-CH(CH_3)-CH_3$

10. (a) Pentan-2-one and 3-methylbutan-2-one are chain isomers because they differ in carbon skeleton.
$CH_3CH_2CH_2COCH_3$ (Pentan-2-one), $CH_3CH(CH_3)COCH_3$ (3-methylbutan-2-one)

11. (d) Geometrical isomerism is exhibited by only those compounds which have at least one double bond and different groups at double bonded carbon atoms. Since, 2-methyl-2-butene. $(CH_3)_2C=CH-CH_3$ contains same group at double bonded carbon atoms, it does not exhibit geometrical isomerism.

12. (a) Compounds given in option I, II, III and V will exhibit tautomerism while IV will not

I. $CH_3-C(=O)-CH_3$ (Keto form) $\xrightleftharpoons{\text{Tautomerism}}$ $CH_3-C(OH)=CH_2$ (Enol form)

II. $CH_2{=}CH{-}OH \xrightleftharpoons{\text{Tautomerism}} CH_3{-}\underset{H}{C}{=}O$
Enol form → Keto form

III. 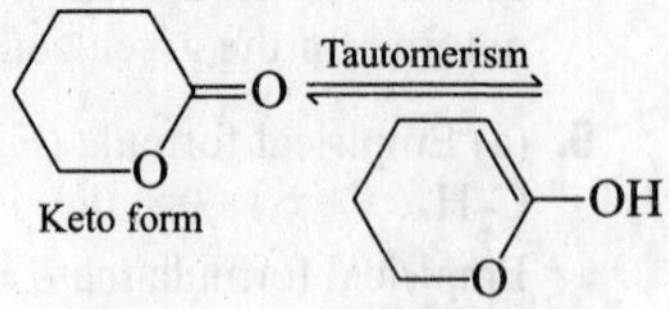 Keto form $\xrightleftharpoons{\text{Tautomerism}}$ Enol form

IV. 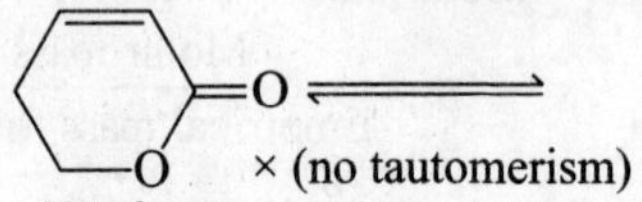 Keto form $\rightleftharpoons$ × (no tautomerism)

V. 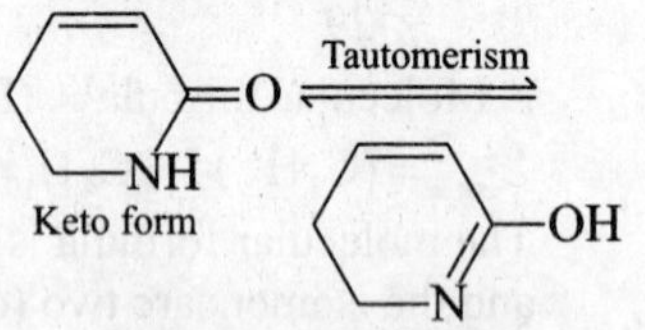 Keto form $\xrightleftharpoons{\text{Tautomerism}}$ Enol form

13. (a) Ethyl alcohol (C_2H_5OH) shows functional isomerism with dimethyl ether.

C_2H_5OH; $CH_3{-}O{-}CH_3$
Alcohol; Dimethyl ether

14. (c) 2-butene can exhibit geometrical isomerism. Its isomers are as follows

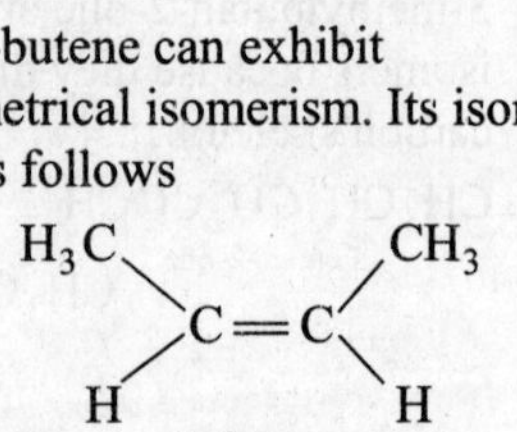

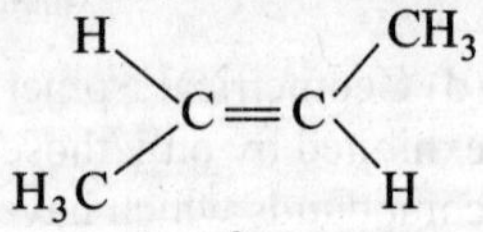

$H_3C(H)C{=}C(H)CH_3$ — *cis*-form

$H(H_3C)C{=}C(CH_3)H$ — *trans*-form

15. (c)

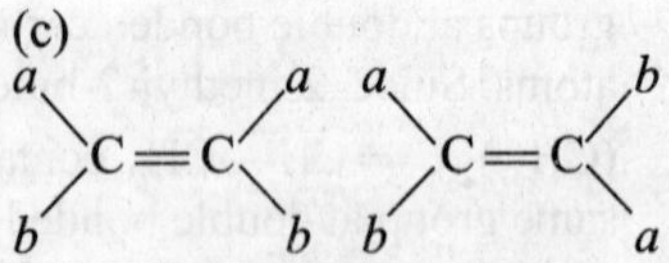

$(a)(b)C{=}C(a)(b)$ — *cis*; $(a)(b)C{=}C(b)(a)$ — *trans*

Thus, geometrical isomers differ in spatial arrangement of atoms only.

Test-3

1. (d) The incorrect statement is (d). Resonance structures can have same numbers of unpaired electrons.

2. (d) Electrophiles are electron-deficient species that are attracted to electron-rich centres. They can be positively charged or neutral species with vacant orbitals. So, Cl, BH_3 and H_3O^+ are electrophiles while NH_3 being electron rich is a nucleophile.

3. (d) Among the given options, reaction given in option (d), i.e.

$$CH_3CH_2CH_2Br + KOH(alc.) \longrightarrow CH_3CH{=}CH_2 + KBr + H_2O$$

is an elimination reaction which involves the removal of two substituents from a molecule often resulting in the formation of a double bond (alkene).

4. (d) While carbanions can undergo rearrangement, combinaiton with cations, an addition to carbonyl groups, they do not typically undergo elimination reactions to form alkenes directly.

Elimination reactions generally involve the removal of a leaving group and a proton from adjacent carbon atoms.

5. (a) Both (A) and (R) are true and (R) is the correct explanation of (A).

6. (b) Statements given in III, IV and V are correct while other statements are incorrect.

Inductive effect is a permanent effect that operates through σ-bond while resonance operates through π-bond.

7. (d) Both Statement I and Statement II are correct.

8. (d) Nitrenes are obtained by the thermolysis of azides. They are neutral monovalent nitrogen species in which nitrogen atom has 2 and shared pair of electrons with a monovalent atom or group attached and they are as reactive as carbenes.

9. (a) The correct match is A-IV, B-III, C-I, D-II.

10. (a) In nucleophilic substitution, the attacking reagent, i.e., nucleophile, seeks an electrophilic site to attack on.

11. (c) The correct match is A-II, B-I, C-IV, D-III.

12. (c) Statement given in option (c) is incorrect regarding no-bond resonance.

Resonance involves delocalisation of π-electrons, while hyperconjugation involves delocalisation of sigma electrons.

13. (c) Stability of carbocations is enhanced by

(i) presence of conjugation

(ii) presence of groups having $+I$ effect.

So, the correct order is

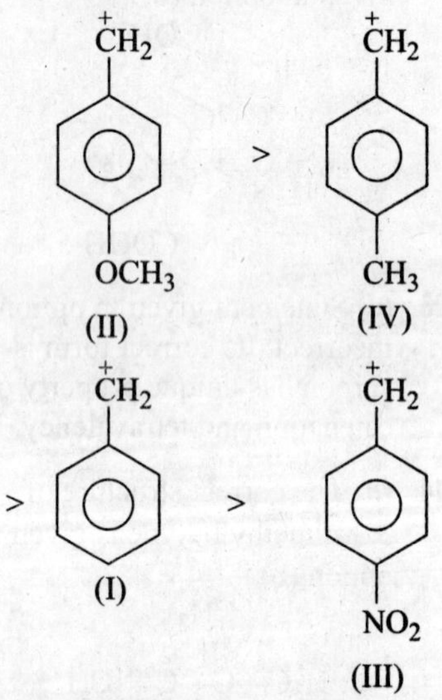

$\overset{+}{C}H_2$–C_6H_4–OCH_3 (II) > $\overset{+}{C}H_2$–C_6H_4–CH_3 (IV) > $\overset{+}{C}H_2$–C_6H_5 (I) > $\overset{+}{C}H_2$–C_6H_4–NO_2 (III)

14. (d) The stability of alkyl free radicals is not influenced by inductive effect because they have no charge (difference from carbonium and carbanions). So, they are stabilised by hyperconjugation (no bond resonance).

The relative order of stability of given free radicals is

allyl > tertiary > vinyl.

15. (c) The species which are electron deficient and accept a pair of electron are called electrophiles. Hence, SO_3 is an electrophile as it contains an electron deficient centre. While H_2O, NH_3 and $R—O—R$ are nucleophiles.

Chapter Break Thru

1. (b) In vinyl acetylene, all carbon atoms are not *sp*-hybridised.

$$\overset{sp^2}{CH_2}=\overset{sp^2}{CH}—\overset{sp}{C}\equiv\overset{sp}{CH}$$

2. (c) Statement (c) is correct.

$$\underset{sp^3}{\overset{1}{CH_3}}—\underset{sp^2}{\overset{2}{CH}}=\underset{sp^2}{\overset{3}{CH}}—\underset{sp^3}{\overset{4}{CH_3}}$$

σ-bond

3. (c) $:\ddot{N}H_2^-$ has eight electrons in the valence shell. It has also two lone pairs of electrons so, it can easily donate and hence it acts as a nucleophile. However $:CX_2$ also has one lone pair of electron but it has 6 electrons in the valence shell. Hence, it is an electrophile.

4. (b) Statement I is correct but Statement II is incorrect. Its correct form is :

The carbon atom in singlet carbene is sp^2-hybridised.

5. (d) Compound (d) shows geometrical isomerism.

Its isomers are shown below.

E-isomer Z-isomer

6. (d) Both Statement I and Statement II are correct.

7. (d) There are total 4 acyclic ethers metamers of compound with molecular formula C_4H_8O.

These are

$CH_2=CH—O—CH_2CH_3$ or

$CH_2=CH—CH_2—O—CH_3$

or $CH_2=C(CH_3)—O—CH_3$

or $CH_3—CH=CH—O—CH_3$

8. (b) Due to presence of a lone pair of electrons on O atom, OH group has $+R$ effect, while due to presence of the positive charge on N atom of NO_2 group has $-R$ effect.

9. (c) Due to hyperconjugation effect, the electron density increases at *o* and *p*-position.

When alkyl group are attached to an unsaturated system like double bond or a benzene ring, the $+I$ effect is reversed. This is called as hyperconjugation.

10. (c) (A) is true but (R) is false.

Correct (R) is : The reaction is unimolecular and of first order.

11. (b) $PhO^{\ominus}$ is most stable because the negative charge on oxygen is stabilised by resonance.

In between $CH_3S^{\ominus}$ and $MeO^{\ominus}$ size of S is greater than O. SO, $CH_3S^{\ominus}$ is more stable than $MeO^{\ominus}$. $OH^{\ominus}$ is the least stable among all.

Acidity:

$PhOH > CH_3SH > MeOH > H_2O$

Basicity:

$\bar{O}H > \bar{O}Me > CH_3S^- > OPh$

Hence the anwer is (b).

12. (d) Only RCH_2NO_2 has α-hydrogen atoms and hence show tautomerism.

$$R—CH_2—\overset{+}{N}(=O)—O^- \rightleftharpoons R—CH=\overset{+}{N}(OH)—O^-$$

13. (d) Degree of unsaturation in

$$C_4H_{10}O = \frac{(2n_C+2)-n_H}{2} = \frac{10-10}{2} = 0$$

So, unsaturation is absent in $C_4H_{10}O$ hence, it should be alcohol or ether.

(a) Alcohol and ether are functional isomers.

(b) Alcohol shows position and chain isomerism.

(c) Ether shows position isomerism and metamerism.

So, the compound ($C_4H_{10}O$) shows chain, position, functional group isomerism and metamerism.

14. (b) In $PhCH=CHOCH_3$, there is no H-atom on the electronegative atom (oxygen) which can migrate to give corresponding keto form. Hence, it will not show tautomerism.

15. (c) The correct match is A-II, B-IV, C-III, D-I

16. (c) In propadiene, $H_2\overset{3}{C}=\overset{2}{C}=\overset{1}{C}H_2$, C-2 has *sp*-hybridisation while other two carbon atoms has sp^2-hybridisation.

17. (c) The correct match is A-IV, B-III, C-II, D-I.

A. Carbocation is positively charged species and it has zero unshared pair of electron with sp^2-hybridisation.

e.g. $H—\overset{\oplus}{C}H_2$

B. Carbanions is negatively charged species and contain one unshared pair of electron with sp^3- hybridisation.

e.g. $[H—\ddot{C}H_2]^-$

C. Chloride ion is negatively charged species with four unshared pair of electrons.

$[:\ddot{Cl}:]^-$

D. Nitrene is a neutral species and it has two unshared pair of electrons.

$R-\ddot{N}:$

18. (d) The correct match is A-IV, B-I, C-II, D-III.

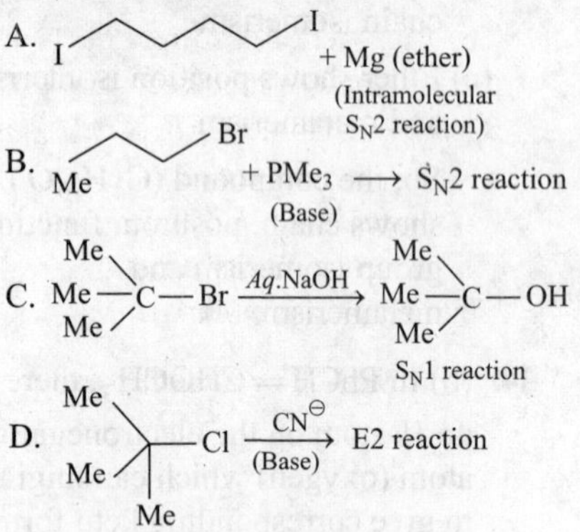

A. I–(CH₂ chain)–I + Mg (ether) (Intramolecular S_N2 reaction)

B. Me–CH₂CH₂–Br + PMe_3 ⟶ S_N2 reaction (Base)

C. $Me_3C-Br \xrightarrow{Aq.NaOH} Me_3C-OH$ S_N1 reaction

D. $Me_3C-Cl \xrightarrow[(Base)]{CN^{\ominus}}$ E2 reaction

19. (c) As $+R$ effect of OH > OCH_3.

Hence, (o-cresol: benzene ring with CH_3 and OH) is more reactive towards electrophilic reagent.

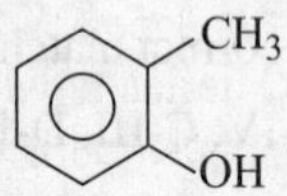

20. (d) In hyperconjugation, σ-electrons are delocalised into *p*-orbital of α-carbon involved in π-bonding.

21. (a) The Statements I, II and IV are correct while III and V are incorrect because carbocation is a reactive intermediate, not present at maxima of the activation energy diagram and it occupies one of the minima.

22. (c) (A) is true but (R) is false. Correct (R) is : Nitro group is an electron withdrawing group ($-I$ groups). It stabilises the carbanion because it disperse the negative charge on the carbon by attracting electrons or negative charge.

23. (c) Option (c) is correct.

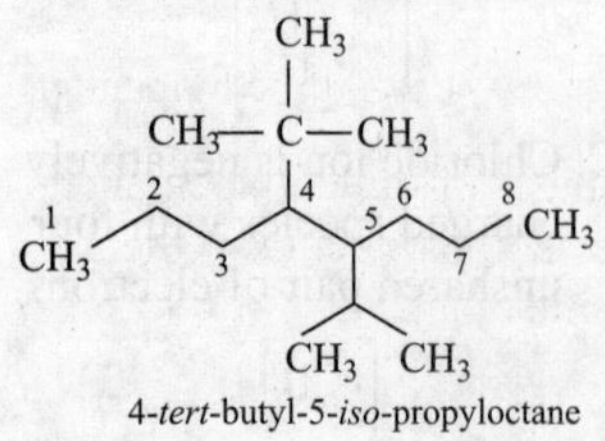

CH_3–C(CH_3)₂– at C-4; CH_3 CH CH_3 at C-5 (octane chain numbered 1–8)

4-*tert*-butyl-5-*iso*-propyloctane

24. (b) Carboxylic acids (—COOH) (*B*) are stronger from phenolic —OH group (*C* and *D*). Phenolic —OH (*C*) experiences stronger *R*-effect of —NO_2 group being placed at *para*-position to (*C*), whereas phenolic —OH (*D*) enjoys comparatively weaker electron withdrawing, $-I$ effect of the —NO_2 group from *meta*-position.

So, acidic strength

$$C > D \text{ or } B > C > D.$$

The H-atom (*A*) attached with *sp*-carbon ($s\,\% = 50$) is also acidic but lesser acidic than H-atoms (*B*, *C* and *D*) who are attached with more electronegative O-atom.

∴Electronegative: $O\,(sp^3) > C\,(sp)$

Hence, the order of acidity:

$$B > C > D > A$$

25. (b) Both (A) and (R) are true but (R) is not the correct explanation of (A). The correct explanation is: Carbon in $:CX_2$ has 6 electrons in the valence shell and hence needs two more electrons to complete the octet.

Therefore, it acts as an electrophile.

26. (b) There are total 4 isomers possible when two of the hydrogen atoms of propane are replaced by two chlorine atoms.

$ClCH_2CH_2CH_2Cl$,
$ClCH_2-CHCl-CH_3$,
$Cl_2CHCH_2CH_3$ and
$CH_3CCl_2CH_3$

27. (b) $CH_3-CH_2-NO_2$ and H_2NCH_2COOH have different functional groups but same molecular formula and hence are functional isomers.

28. (b) $(CH_3)_2CH^+$ is the most stable carbocation.

Due to $-I$ effect of the F-atom, carbocation $F_3C-CH_2^+$ and F_3C^+ are less stable than carbocation, CH_3^+ and $(CH_3)_2CH^+$, but due to stronger $+I$ effect of the two CH_3 groups, $(CH_3)_2CH^+$ carbocation is most stable.

29. (b) Simple alkyl carbanion are pyramidal, i.e. *tert*-butyl carbanion.

While allyl carbanion is planar since it is stabilised by resonance. *tert*-butyl free radical and carbocation are also planar.

30. (b) Both (A) and (R) are true but (R) is not the correct explanation of (A). The correct explanation is Both have the same molecular formula of C_5H_{12} and differ only in the arrangement of carbon atoms.

31. (b) The correct IUPAC name is 6-methyloctan-3-ol.

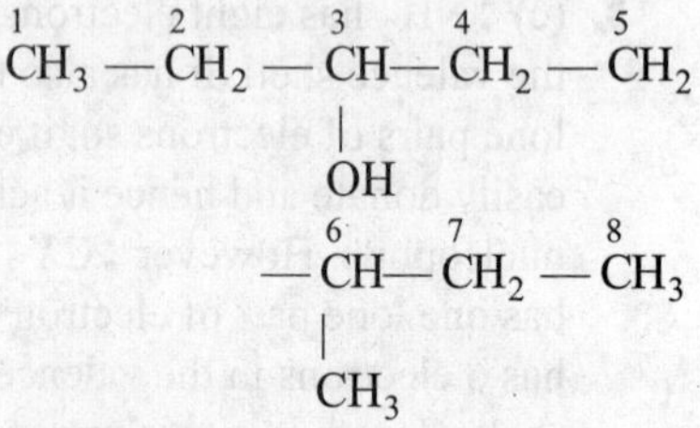

$$\overset{1}{CH_3}-\overset{2}{CH_2}-\overset{3}{CH}(OH)-\overset{4}{CH_2}-\overset{5}{CH_2}-\overset{6}{CH}(CH_3)-\overset{7}{CH_2}-\overset{8}{CH_3}$$

32. (c) The correct IUPAC name is 2,3-epoxy-1-propanol.

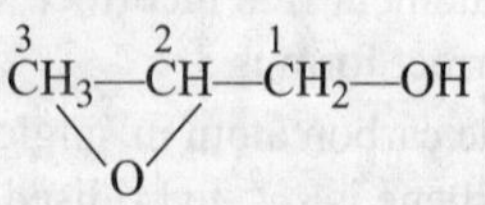

$$\overset{3}{CH_2}-\overset{2}{CH}-\overset{1}{CH_2}-OH \text{ (C-3 and C-2 bridged by O)}$$

33. (a) The correct IUPAC name is 1-methyl-3-propylcyclohexane.

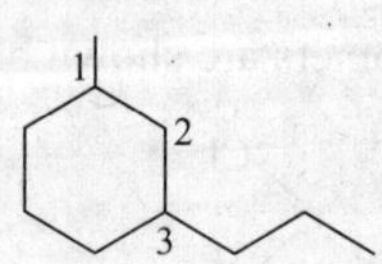

(cyclohexane ring with methyl at C-1 and propyl at C-3)

34. (c) Diastereomers differ in all physical properties.

The rest of the statements are related to enantiomers.

35. (b) Consider, for example, acetamide, i.e. CH_3CONH_2 or C_2H_5NO

Putting, $n = 2$ we have $C_nH_{2n+1}NO$

36. (b) The correct IUPAC name is 3-methylhexane.

$\overset{1}{CH_3}-\overset{2}{CH_2}-\overset{3}{CH}(CH_3)-\overset{4}{CH_2}-\overset{5}{CH_2}-\overset{6}{CH_3}$

Ethyl, n propyl, Methyl

37. (a) Both (A) and (R) are true and (R) is the correct explanation of (A). COOH is the principal functional group while CN is the substitute group and hence, $NCCH_2CH_2COOH$ is 3-cyanopropanoic acid.

38. (b) The correct IUPAC name is 2-bromo-5-hydroxybenzonitrile.

(Structure: benzene ring with OH at C-5, CN at C-1, Br at C-2)

39. (c) The correct match is A-III, B-I, C-II, D-IV.

40. (b) Chirality is the condition for a molecule to be optically active and here 2-pentanol is the only compound which is optically active and hence it is the chiral molecule.

41. (c) H_γ being located on a saturated carbon is more labile than H_α and H_β and hence is involved in enolisation.

(Structure: cyclohexanone with H_γ, H_β, H_α ⇌ enol with $O-H_\gamma$, H_β, H_α)

42. (b) Statement I is correct but Statement II is incorrect.

The correct form of statement II is Vinyl alcohol is less stable and 1, 3-migration of α-hydrogen to oxygen atom of acetaldehyde gives vinyl alcohol.

43. (a) Both (A) and (R) are true and (R) is the correct explanation of (A).

44. (c) The correct IUPAC name of given compound is 1,2,4-triethyl -3,5,6-trimethyl cyclohexane.

45. (a) Allyl alcohol have structural formula $CH_2=CH-CH_2-OH$ and molecular formula C_3H_6O. Acetone, 2-methyloxirane and cyclopropanol have same molecular formula (C_3H_6O) so, they are isomers of allyl alcohol while 1-propanol is C_3H_8O. Therefore, it is not an isomer of allyl alcohol.

46. (b) Addition of sodium hydrogen sulphite to acetaldehyde is an example of nucleophilic addition reaction.

Bisulphite addition compound (crystalline) is formed.

47. (b) Statement I is correct but Statement II is incorrect. Out of four stereoisomers *EE*, *ZZ*, *EZ* and *ZE*, *EZ* and *ZE* are identical here counted as one -*EZ* and *ZE* are polar, hence, not two but one stereoisomer is polar.

48. (b) It must be cyclic ether or alcohol.

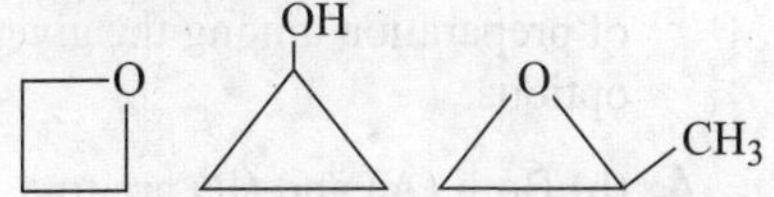

49. (b) H^+ is an electrophile because it is electron deficient while all others are nucleophiles as they are electron rich species.

50. (b) Methyl group ($-CH_3$) and carboxylate group ($-COO^-$) both are electron donating and show $+I$-effect while $-Br$ and $-\overset{+}{N}H_3$ are electron withdrawing and show $-I$ effect.

Ch-12 Hydrocarbons

Topical Follow Thru

Test-1

1. (d) The correct IUPAC name of the given compound will be 3-ethyl-4-methyl hexane.

(Skeletal structure numbered 1–6)

2. (a) The complete reaction sequence if as follows

$$H_3C-CH(CH_3)-CH_2I + ICH(CH_3)_2 \xrightarrow[\text{(Wurtz reaction)}]{\text{Na dry ether}} H_3C-CH(CH_3)-CH_2-CH(CH_3)-CH_3$$

2,4-dimethyl pentane

$+ (CH_3)_2CH-CH(CH_3)_2$

2,3-dimethylbutane

$+ H_3C-CH(CH_3)CH_2-CH(CH_3)_2$

2,4-dimethylpentane

Thus, 2,4-dimethylpentane is the formed product from the given options.

3. (a) Sodium propanoate upon reaction with soda lime give ethane.

$$CH_3CH_2COONa \xrightarrow[CaO,\ \Delta]{NaOH} CH_3-CH_3 + Na_2CO_3$$

$$CH_3CH_2Br + (CH_3)_2CuLi \xrightarrow{Et_2O} CH_3CH_2CH_3 + CuCH_3 + LiBr$$

$$CH_3CH_2I + CH_3I \xrightarrow[Et_2O]{Na} CH_3CH_2CH_3$$

$$CH_3CH_2COONa + CH_3COONa \xrightarrow[Electrolysis]{H_2O} CH_3COOH + CH_3CH_2OH + CO_2$$

Hence, option a is the best method of preparation among the given options.

4. (b) Both (A) and (R) are true but (R) is not the correct explanation of (A).

5. (c) Alkanes having carbon atoms greater than 18 are solids at room temperature.

6. (d) The solubility order of the alkanes in water is influenced by their increasing molecular size and hydrophobic character. As the number of C-atoms in alkane increases, its solubility in water decreases. Thus, the correct order of their solubility is

$$CH_4 > C_2H_6 > C_3H_8 > C_4H_{10}.$$

7. (c) Statement I is incorrect but Statement II is correct. The corrected form of statement I is Boiling point of alkanes increase with increase in molecular weight.

8. (a) Among the given options, CH_4 is least reactive towards free radical substitution reaction due to formation of unstable intermediate free radical.

9. (b) The total number of isomers of butane and pentane are 2, 3 respectively.

- Butane has only two isomers, *n*-butane and *iso*-butane.
- Pentane has three isomers, *n*-pentane, *iso*-pentane and *neo*-pentane.

10. (d) Total products formed are 4.

$$CH_4 \xrightarrow[h\nu]{Cl_2} CH_3Cl + HCl$$
$$CH_4 \xrightarrow[h\nu]{Cl_2} CH_2Cl_2 + HCl$$
$$CH_4 \xrightarrow[h\nu]{Cl_2} CHCl_3 + HCl$$
$$CH_4 \xrightarrow[h\nu]{Cl_2} CCl_4 + HCl$$

11. (c) The given reaction is a catalytic oxidation of methane. It yields methanal.

$$CH_4 + O_2 \xrightarrow{Mo_2O_3} \underset{(Z)}{HCHO} + H_2O$$

12. (a) Among the given species only (ii), (iii) and (iv) have tertiary carbon atoms others have primary and secondary carbon atoms only.

13. (c) Torsional strain is the resistance to rotation of bonds due to steric hindrance. It is more dominant in eclipsed configuration. Hence, staggered conformation is more stable as substituents are placed far and away from each other because it has no torsional strain.

14. (d) As ethane only contains saturated carbon atoms having sp^3-hybridisation, the C—C bond distance is maximum in ethane among the given species.

15. (d) Due to the symmetrical geometry of *neo*-pentane, it will give only one monochlorinated product. Because it has only one type of hydrogen atom, so replacing any hydrogen atom with chlorine will result in the same product.

Test-2

1. (b) Correct option is (b). *cis* and *trans*-isomers are not interconvertible at room temperature as it requires an energy barrier to be crossed and energy has to be given for *trans* to convert into *cis* due to higher energy in this state. The corrected form of (a), (c) and (d) are

(a) *cis*-2-butene is more stable than *trans*-2-butene.

(c) *cis*-2-butene has more dipole moment than *trans*-2-butene.

(d) *cis*-2-butene and *trans*-2-butene are geometrical isomers.

2. (d) In cyclohexa-2,5-diene, there are 8 C—H bonds and 6 single C—C bonds while there are two C—C pi bonds. Hence, total sigma bonds are 14 while pi bonds are 2.

[Structure: cyclohexa-2,5-diene ring with positions 1–6 numbered]

3. (a) Both (A) and (R) are true and (R) is the correct explanation of (A).

4. (a) The reaction takes place as,

3, 3-dimethylpentan-2-ol $\xrightarrow[H_2SO_4]{Conc.}$ (protonated alcohol, $\overset{+}{OH_2}$) $\xrightarrow{-H_2O}$ carbocation $\xrightarrow{\text{1,2-methyl shift}}$ carbocation $\xrightarrow{HSO_4^{\ominus}}$ (2, 3-dimethyl-pent-2-ene)

5. (c) The restricted rotation about C—C double bond in 2-butene is possible due to sideways overlap of two *p*-orbital.

6. (c) Reaction of an alkene with cold and dil. $KMnO_4$ gives a vicinal diol. If conditions are hot then rigorous oxidation takes place and further oxidation might occur.

$$CH_2{=}CH_2 + H_2O + \xrightarrow[{[O]}]{Dil.\ KMnO_4} \underset{OH}{CH_2}-\underset{OH}{CH_2}$$

Ethane-1,2-diol (Glycol) (*Vicinal*)

7. (a) 2-methyl-2-butene $\xrightarrow[Zn/H_2O]{O_3}$ Acetone + CH_3CHO (Acetaldehyde)

Hence, correct option is (a).

8. (c) Compound (c) shows geometrical isomerism. It is because in this pi bond is internal and not terminal. Also both carbons sharing the pi bond have different substituents on each other hence, exists in *cis/trans*- forms.

9. (a) The addition of bromine to *trans*-2-butene proceeds *via* anti-addition, resulting in a *meso* compound.

10. (d) The correct match is A-IV,B-I,C-III,D-II.

- Alkene with cold and dil. $KMnO_4$ yields a *vicinal* diol.
- Ozonolysis followed by hydrolysis yields carbonyl compounds like aldehyde or ketones.
- Acidic hydrolysis of alkene follows Markownikoff's addition and yields an alcohol.
- Alkene reacts with bromine in presence of CCl_4 yields vicinal dibromide.

11. (d) Among the given statements only statement B, C and E are incorrect. Their corrected forms are

- Alkenes undergo electrophilic addition reactions, not nucleophilic addition.
- The addition of hydrogen halides generally follows Markownikoff's rule, it can be reversed in the presence of peroxides (Kharasch effect).
- The stability of alkenes increases with an increase in number of alkyl substituents due to hyperconjugation.

12. (c) Isoprene polymerise to give polyisoprene.

$$nCH_2{=}\overset{CH_3}{\overset{|}{C}}{-}CH{=}CH_2 \longrightarrow \left(CH_2{-}\overset{CH_3}{\overset{|}{C}}{=}CH{-}CH_2\right)_n$$

Isoprene; *cis*-polyisoprene

13. (c) Alkenes in *trans* form having same groups on both side of double bond show zero dipole moment.

14. (b) The complete reaction sequence is as follows

1-methylcyclohexene $+ BH_3 \longrightarrow$ (H, CH_3; BH_2, H) $\xrightarrow[\text{Oxidation}]{H_2O_2/OH^-}$ (H, CH_3; OH, H)

trans-2-methylcyclohexan1-ol

15. (d) In the presence of light, allylic substitution takes place and Cl groups are attached at allylic carbon.

$$\text{cyclohexene} \xrightarrow{Cl_2,\ h\nu} \text{dichlorocyclohexene (Cl, Cl)}$$

Test-3

1. (b) Benzene reacts with chlorine in the presence of sunlight to form benzene hexachloride (B. C) *via* a free radical addition mechanism.

2. (c) Correct option is (c). The reactivity of alkyne decreases with increase in steric hindrance around the triple bond.

3. (c) Toluene undergoes electrophilic aromatic substitution primarily at the *ortho* and *para* positions but the major product is formed at *p*-position i.e., *p*-bromotoluene.

4. (a) Both (A) and (R) are true and (R) is the correct explanation of (A).

5. (a) Lindlar catalyst as well as $Na(liq.NH_3)$ both can reduce alkynes to alkenes but both have selectivity. Lindlar catalyst predominantly give a *cis*-alkene while Na (in liq NH_3) give *trans*-alkene. Hence, correct option is (a).

6. (a) Only but-2-yne possess *sp* and sp^3-hybridised carbon atom.

$$\underset{sp^3}{CH_3}{-}\underset{sp}{C}{\equiv}\underset{sp}{C}{-}\underset{sp^3}{CH_3}$$

7. (d) Both statement I and statement II are correct.

Alkynes have *sp*-hybridised carbon atom.

Since, *sp*-hybridised carbon in alkynes is more electronegative than sp^2-hybridised carbon in alkenes, therefore nucleophiles can attack *sp*-hybridised carbon more easily than sp^2-hybridised carbon in alkenes.

8. (d) $CH_3{-}C{\equiv}CH \xrightarrow[H_2O_2]{H-Br} CH_3{-}CH{=}CHBr \xrightarrow{H-Br} CH_3{-}CH_2{-}CHBr_2$

In presence of peroxide, Kharasch effect takes place.

9. (b) Both (A) and (R) are true but (R) is not the correct explanation of (A).

The major product in Friedel-Crafts acylation is due to the steric hindrance caused by the acyl group.

10. (c) $CH_3{-}CH_2{-}C{\equiv}CH \xrightarrow[H_2SO_4]{HgSO_4} CH_3{-}CH_2{-}\underset{OH}{\underset{|}{C}}{=}CH_2 \longrightarrow CH_3{-}CH_2{-}\overset{O}{\overset{||}{C}}{-}CH_3$

(enol form) (because keto form is more stable than enol) (keto form)

11. (c) Statement I is incorrect but statement II is correct. Correct form of statement I is Benzene undergoes electrophilic substitution reactions more readily than nucleophilic substitution reactions due to being electron rich.

12. (c) Except C, all statements are correct. Correct form of C is, the carbon-carbon bond length is nearly average of C-C single bond and C=C bond.

13. (a) The correct match is A-I,B-II,C-III,D-IV.

14. (d) Incorrect statement is given in option (d).

Its correct form is —OH group activates the benzene ring for the attack by an electrophile.

15. (a) The minimum number of C-atoms required to have four carbon-carbon double bond in a cyclic structure is eight.

16. (c) There are total 14 σ and 4 π bonds are present hept-2,5-diyne

$H_3C-C\equiv C-CH_2-C\equiv C-CH_3$ (bonds labelled σ and π)

17. (a) When prop-1-yne reacts with two equivalents of hydrogen bromide, it undergoes halogenation reaction to form di-bromoalkane.

$$CH_3C\equiv CH + 2HBr \longrightarrow CH_3CBr_2CH_3$$

18. (b) Addition of HCl to alkynes proceeds *via* vinyl cation intermediate. Addition in unsymmetrical alkynes takes place according to Markovnikov's rule.

$$R-C\equiv CH + HCl \longrightarrow R-\overset{\oplus}{C}=C(H)-H$$

The cation formed is vinyl cation.

19. (b) $CH_3C\equiv C-CH_3 \xrightarrow{HgSO_4,\ H_2SO_4} CH_3-C(H)=C(OH)-CH_3 \longrightarrow CH_3CH_2\overset{O}{\overset{\|}{C}}CH_3$ (Ketone)

20. (b) Statement (b) is correct. Alkynes are more reactive in nucleophilic addition reaction due to their greater electron density and less reactivity in electrophilic addition reaction due to the decreased availability of the π-electrons and high electronegativity of *sp*-hybridiseed carbon.

21. (b) OCH_3 is an *ortho-para* directing group.

The product formed is (b) due to steric repulsion at *ortho*-position.

Anisole $\xrightarrow[FeBr_3]{Br_2}$ (arenium ion with $\overset{\oplus}{O}CH_3$, H, Br) $\xrightarrow{-H^+}$ p-bromoanisole

22. (a) Compound (cyclopentylidene-cyclopentadiene) has the greatest dipole moment, due to high charge separation.

23. (d) So, sp^3 hybridised carbon atoms is not a characteristic of aromatic compound. Aromatic compounds have a cyclic and planar structure with sp^2-hybridised carbon atoms.

24. (d) A mixture of *o*- and *p*-nitrotoluene. The methyl group in toluene is an activating and *ortho/para*-directing group in electrophilic aromatic substitution reactions.

25. (d) The $—OCH_3$ group in anisole is a strong activating group due to resonance, making it highly reactive towards electrophilic aromatic substitution.

Chapter Break Thru

1. (a) Non-benzenoid aromatic compound are chemical compounds with conjugated pi-electron system with 5-7 membered ring. Tropolone is a non-benzenoid aromatic compound as it has 7 carbon atom.

(Tropolone structure: seven-membered ring with C=O and OH)

2. (a) In the given reaction, $(CH_3)_3CO\overset{-}{}\overset{+}{K}$ acts as a base, therefore it produces alkene on treating with alkyl halide.

$$\underset{\text{(2-bromobutane)}}{CH_3CH_2CH(Br)CH_3} \xrightarrow[+(CH_3)_3C-OH]{(CH_3)_3COK} \underset{\text{But-1-ene}}{CH_3CH_2CH=CH_2}$$

3. (c) Among the given options, 3,4-dimethyl hex-3-ene produces butanone only.

$$\underset{\text{3,4-dimethyl hex-3-ene}}{CH_3CH_2C(CH_3)=C(CH_3)CH_2CH_3} \xrightarrow{O_3} CH_3CH_2-\underset{CH_3}{C}=O + O=C(CH_3)-CH_2-CH_3$$

4. (d) (A) is false but (R) is true. The correct form of (A) is, 2-bromobutane on reaction with sodium ethoxide in ethanol gives 2-butene as major product.

5. (d) Among the given products only III and IV on halogenation gives chiral carbon, which is responsible for the racemisation. III and IV give racemic mixture on monochlorination.

Thus, only option (d) is correct.

6. (b) Statement I is correct but statement II is incorrect.

The correct form of statement II is, HI adds to vinyl chloride according to Markovnikov's rule.

7. (d) In the given reaction, product is formed by the oxidative cleavage of the double bond.

When terminal alkene is heated with $KMnO_4$, KOH solution, C = C bond cleaved and a ketone and an acid is formed.

To get the structure of the given alkene. At first, we write the structure of the product formed with their functional groups pointing to each other.

$(CH_3)_2C{=}O$ (Acetone) ; HOOC—CH_3 (Acetic acid)

↓ Process reverse ; ↓ Proceed reverse

$(CH_3)_2C{=}$; $=CH—CH_3$

Join the double bond to get compound (A).

$(CH_3)_2C{=}CH—CH_3$

2-methyl but -2-ene (A)

Hence, option (d) is correct.

8. (a) More stable or more substituted alkene has the lowest (more negative) ΔH°_C, $\Delta H_{formation}$ and ΔH°_h.

$(CH_3)_2C{=}CH(CH_3)$ 2-methyl-but-2-ene (More substituted) > $(CH_2CH_3)(CH_3)C{=}CH_2$ 2-methyl-but-1-ene (Unsymmetrical alkene) > $CH_3—CH_2—CH{=}CH—CH_3$ Pent-2-ene > $CH_3—CH_2—CH_2—CH{=}CH_2$ Pent-1-ene

Hence, the order of stability of alkene IV > III > II > I.

So, the lowest ΔH°_C is of IV and the highest is of I.

9. (b) The complete reaction sequence involved is as follows

$$HC{\equiv}CH \xrightarrow[\text{(Due to acidic H)}]{NaNH_2} HC{\equiv}C^{\ominus}Na^{\oplus}\ (A)$$
Acetylene

$$\xrightarrow[-NaI]{CH_3I} HC{\equiv}CCH_3\ (B) \xrightarrow{\text{(i) } HgSO_4 \text{ (ii) Dil. } H_2SO_4,\ H_2O} CH_3—\underset{\|}{C}—CH_3\ (C)$$
(C = O)

Thus, the compound C is CH_3COCH_3

10. (b) The complete reaction is as follows

$$CH_3CH_2COOH \xrightarrow{NaOH/CaO} CH_3CH_3 + CO_2\uparrow$$

When propanoic acid is treated with soda lime ethane and carbon dioxide is obtained.

11. (c) Complete reaction is as follows,

But-1-ene (Allylic-C-atom) $\xrightarrow[\text{Allylic substitution}]{NBS}$ 3-bromo but-1-ene (B) $\xrightarrow[-HBr]{\text{Alc. KOH}}$ Buta-1,3-diene (C)

12. (d) Both Statement I and Statement II are correct.

13. (c) Statements (a) and (b) are correct but statement (c) is incorrect. Regiospecificity of this reaction is anti.

In oxymercuration-demercuration reaction, alkenes react with mercuric acetate, $Hg(OAc)_2$ in the presence of tetrahydrofuran (THF) and water to yield hydroxy alkyl mercurial compounds which on reduction in aqueous sodium hydroxide with sodium borohydride ($NaBH_4$) produce alcohols.

14. (a) The complete reaction is as follows,

$$CH_3—C(CH_3)_2—CH_2OH \xrightarrow[-H_2O]{H^+} CH_3—C(CH_3)_2—\overset{+}{C}H_2$$
neo-pentylalcohol ; 1° carbocation

$$\xrightarrow{\text{1,2-methyl shift}} CH_3—\overset{+}{C}(CH_3)—CH_2CH_3$$
3° carbocation

$$\xrightarrow{-H^+ \text{ Saytzeff rule}} CH_3—C(CH_3){=}CHCH_3$$
2-methylbut-2-ene (Major)

15. (a) Among the given statements, only II is incorrect while all other are correct.

Hexane is non-polar solvent so, it is insoluble in conc. H_2SO_4.

16. (d) Both Statement I and Statement II are correct.

17. (d) All the given reactions, are the examples of electrophilic substitution reaction.

18. (b) Both (A) and (R) are true but (R) is not the correct explanation of (A). The correct explanation is,

Because of steric hindrance between big sized Br atoms, the energy difference between staggered and eclipsed forms of ethylene dibromide is more than that of ethylene dichloride.

19. (a) Both Statement I and Statement II are incorrect, their correct forms are

Statement I Propene reacts with HBr in presence of benzoyl peroxide gives 1-bromopropane.

Statement II In presence of peroxide, the reaction occurs through free radical mechanism.

20. (c) At 420 K, Cl_2 does not produce and hence no reaction occurs. However at this temperature $(CH_3)_4Pb$ decompose to produce $\dot{C}H_3$ which help in formation of $\dot{C}l$ which in turn, propagate the free radical chain reaction.

$$(CH_3)_4Pb \xrightarrow{\Delta} 4\dot{C}H_3 + Pb$$

$$\dot{C}H_3 + Cl_2 \longrightarrow CH_3Cl + \dot{C}l$$

$$\dot{C}l + CH_4 \longrightarrow \dot{C}H_3 + HCl$$

21. (b) The final product of the given reaction is ethyl benzene.

Styrene $\xrightarrow[\text{Reduction of double bond}]{NH_2—NH_2}$ Ethyl benzene $+ N_2\uparrow$

Thus, option (b) is correct.

22. (a) In the reaction,

$$\underset{\text{Ethyne}}{CH\equiv CH} \xrightarrow[\text{liq. } NH_3]{NaNH_2} \underset{(A)}{CH\equiv C—Na}$$

$$\xrightarrow{CH_3I} \underset{\text{Prop-1-yne } (B)}{CH\equiv C—CH_3} \xrightarrow{H_2+Ni_2Br} \underset{\text{Prop-1-ene } (C)}{\overset{1}{C}H_2=\overset{2}{C}H—\overset{3}{C}H_3}$$

$$\xrightarrow{O_3/\text{Red.}} \underset{\text{Ethanal } (D)}{CH_3—CH=O} + \underset{\text{Formaldehyde}}{CH_2=O} \xrightarrow{LAH} \underset{\text{Ethanol}}{CH_3—CH_2—OH} + \underset{\text{Methanol}}{CH_3OH} \; (E)$$

Thus, option (a) is correct.

23. (a)

$$\text{Benzene} + 3O_3 \xrightarrow[\text{Reduction}]{Zn/H_2O} 3\underset{\text{Glyoxal}}{\begin{matrix} CHO \\ | \\ CHO \end{matrix}} \; (A)$$

$$\text{Benzene} \xrightarrow[\text{or Hot alc. } KMnO_4]{\text{Cold alc. } KMnO_4} \text{No reaction } (B) \text{ and } (C)$$

24. (b) The smallest acyclic ketone is acetone which being symmetrical forms only one oxime. The next higher homologue, i.e. 2-butanone being unsymmetrical forms two oximes, i.e. *cis* and *trans*.

Thus, in all three different oximes are formed.

25. (c) The correct IUPAC name of the given compound is 2,8-dimethyldeca-3,6-diene.

26. (b) Statement given in option B and D are incorrect while A, C and E are correct. The corrected form of statement B and D are

- sp^2-carbon is more electronegative than sp^3-carbon.
- Addition of Br_2 to alkene is stereoselective/ stereospecific.

27. (a) *Neo*-pentyl chloride does not have β-hydrogen and hence does not undergo dehydrohalogenation.

$$CH_3—\overset{\beta}{\underset{CH_3}{\overset{CH_3}{C}}}—\overset{\alpha}{C}H_2Cl \xrightarrow[\Delta]{KOH} \text{No dehydrohalogenation}$$

28. (b) The Diels-Alder reaction proceeds faster, when dienophile have e^- withdrawing groups (EWG) and dienes have e^- donating group (EDG).

So, reaction (D) gives more reactivity towards Diels-Alder reaction and (A) reaction gives least reactivity.

Thus, option (b) is correct.

29. (c) Birch reduction converts $(C\equiv C)$ to $(C=C)$ in anti-addition of H_2,

So the stereochemistry around both the double bond should be *trans*.

Hence, option (c) is correct and reaction is as follows

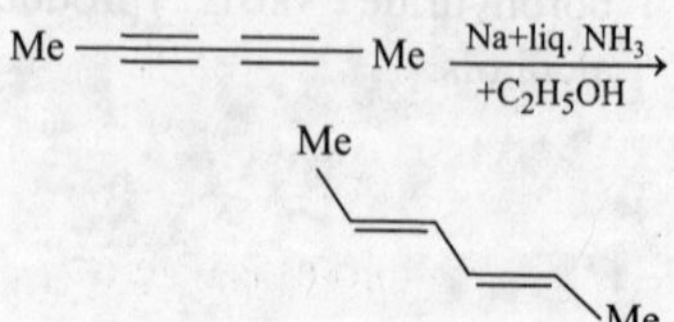

30. (a) Stability order of different conformer of butane is Anti-staggered > Staggered > Skew or gauche > Partially eclipsed > Fully eclipsed.

In anti-staggered both methyl group lies at opposite side. Therefore, repulsion decreases. Hence, it is most stable.

- Minimum repulsion present between the groups in staggered form, therefore, it is less stable than anti-staggered.
- *Skew* forms have less repulsion due to torsional strain than partially eclipsed form, therefore, it is more stable than partially eclipsed.
- Partially eclipsed forms have less repulsion than eclipsed. Therefore, it gives more stability than eclipsed form.

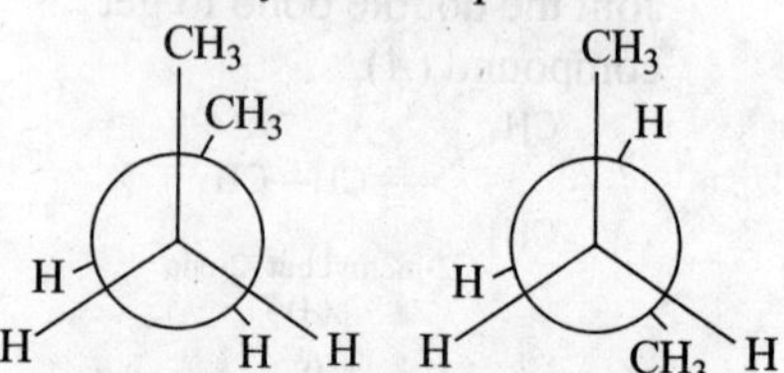

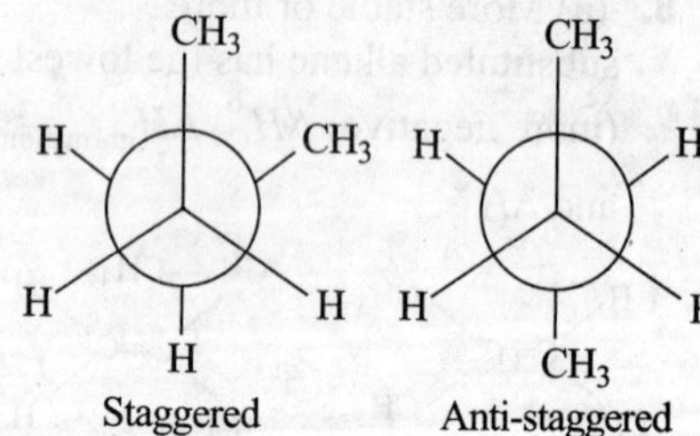

Between these conformations, all conformations are *skew* or *gauche*.

31. (b) The correct match is A-IV, B-III, C-II, D-I.

A. $CH_2=CH_2 + H_2 \xrightarrow{Pt/Pd/Ni} \underset{\text{Ethane}}{CH_3—CH_3}$

B. $CH_3—Cl + H_2 \xrightarrow{Zn, H^+} \underset{\text{Methane}}{CH_4} + HCl$

C. $CH_4 + O_2 \xrightarrow[\Delta]{Mo_2O_3} \underset{\text{Methanal}}{HCHO} + H_2O$

D. $2CH_4 + O_2 \xrightarrow{Cu/523K/100atm} \underset{\text{Methanol}}{2CH_3OH}$

32. (b) Peroxide effect is not observed in case of HCl, i.e. the reaction does not occur by radical mechanism. Instead it occurs by carbocation mechanism. Therefore, first addition of H^+ to propane occurs to give the more stable 2° carbocation (I) as the intermediate.

33. (b) When 1,2-dimethylcyclohexene is treated with H_2 gas in presence of Pt catalyst, the double bond in the cyclohexene ring is reduced to a single bond.

1, 2-dimethylcyclohexene $\xrightarrow[H_2]{Pt/Pd/Ni}$ 1, 2-dimethylcyclohexane

34. (b) Stability of carbocation $\rightarrow 3° > 2° > 1°$

Ease of formation of carbocation $\rightarrow 3° > 2° > 1°$

Thus, reactivity

A. 1-chlorobutane $\xrightarrow{-Cl^{\ominus}}$ (1°$C^{\oplus}$) $\xrightarrow{\text{1, 2-hydride shift}}$ (2°$C^{\oplus}$)

B. 1-chloro-2-methylpropane $\xrightarrow{-Cl^-}$ 1° carbocation $\xrightarrow{\text{1, 2-hydride shift}}$ (3°$C^{\oplus}$)

C. 1-bromo-2-methylpropane $\xrightarrow{-Br^-}$ 1° carbocation $\rightarrow$ (3°$C^{\oplus}$)

Reactivity due to the leaving group $\rightarrow I^{\ominus} > Br^{\ominus} > Cl^{\ominus} > F^{\ominus}$

Reactivity of $RX \rightarrow R—I > R—Br > R—Cl$

Thus, option (b) is correct.

35. (b) The complete reaction is as follow,

$$HC{\equiv}C^-Na^+ + C_6H_5CH_2Br \xrightarrow[-NaBr]{S_N2} HC{\equiv}C—CH_2C_6H_5$$

3-phenylprop-1-yne

36. (c) Statement I is incorrect but II is correct.

The correct form of statement I is, carbon atom in ethene is sp^2-hybridised while in ethyne it is sp-hybridised.

37. (c) The correct match is A-IV, B-III, C-II, D-I.

The four types of strain *viz.* (a) electrostatic force of attraction, (b) torsional strain, (c) angle strain and (d) steric strain are responsible for the stability or energy barriers of conformers. In cyclic compounds, all type of strain may present like.

Compound	Type of strains/ forces
A. (cyclohexane chair)	IV. $a+b+c$
B. (chair with OH and F)	III. $a+b+c+d$

In open chain compounds, angle strain (c) is absent.

Compound	Type of strains/ forces
D. (Newman projection: CH_3, H, CH_3, H, H, H)	II. $a+b+d$
C. (Newman projection: OH, H, OH, H, H, H)	I. $a+b$

Thus, option (c) is correct.

38. (a) Both (A) and (R) are true and (R) is the correct explanation of (A).

39. (c) The complete ozonolysis reaction is

$$\underset{\text{Pent-1,3-diene}}{CH_2{=}CH—CH{=}CHCH_3} \xrightarrow{\text{Ozonolysis}} \underset{\text{Formaldehyde}}{CH_2{=}O} + \underset{\text{Acetaldehyde}}{O{=}CHCH_3} + \underset{\text{Glyoxal}}{O{=}CH—CH{=}O}$$

40. (a) Alkynes in presence of Lindlar's catalyst (H_2/Pd-$BaSO_4$) gives *cis*-alkenes.

$$\underset{\text{But-2-yne}}{CH_3—C{\equiv}CCH_3} \xrightarrow[\text{Lindlar's catalyst}]{H_2/Pd-BaSO_4} \underset{\textit{cis}\text{-2-butene}}{(CH_3)HC{=}CH(CH_3)}$$

41. (d)

$$2H—C{\equiv}C—H \xrightarrow[NH_4Cl]{CuCl} \underset{(A)}{CH_2{=}C(H)—C{\equiv}CH} \xrightarrow{H_2 + Ni_2Br} \underset{(B)}{CH_2{=}CH—HC{=}CH_2} \xrightarrow[\text{1, 4-addition}]{Br_2} \underset{(C)}{\text{1, 4-dibromobut-2-ene}}$$

So, option (d) is correct.

42. (a) Oxidation of alkyne is slower than alkene.

With CrO_3 (in CH_3COOH), oxidative cleavage of alkene takes place without affecting the oxidation of alkynes.

Hept-2-en-5-yne $\xrightarrow{CrO_3/CH_3COOH}$ $\underset{\text{Ethanoic acid (A)}}{CH_3—COOH}$ + Pent-3-yne-1-oic acid (B)

43. (b) Sulphonation is a reversible reaction. Therefore, when heated with super heated steam, sulphonic acid undergo desulphonation.

CH_3, Cl, SO_3H (ring) $+ H_2O \longrightarrow$ CH_3, Cl (ring) $+ H_2SO_4$

o-chlorotoluene

44. (b) Cyclisation (dehydrogenation) of *n*-hexane first gives cyclohexane which upon further dehydrogenation (aromatisation) gives benzene.

$$\underset{n\text{-hexane}}{CH_3(CH_2)_4CH_3} \xrightarrow[\text{773 K } (-H_2)]{V_2O_5/Al_2O_3} \text{Cyclohexane}$$

Dehydrogenation

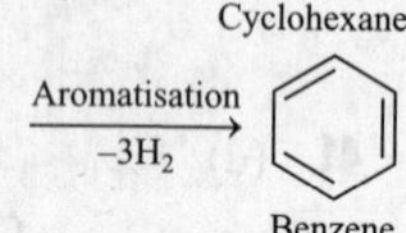

Benzene

45. (d) All the three exhibit confirmational isomerism due to rotation about C—O bond in CH_3OH, O—O bond in H_2O_2 and N—N bond in $NH_2—NH_2$.

46. (a) Boiling point increases with number of carbon atoms and decreases with branching. From the options, 2-methylpropane and *n*-butane have the least of carbon atoms, i.e. 4.

Since, 2-methylpropane has one branch but *n*-butane has none, therefore boiling point of 2-methylpropane is least.

47. (a) 3-methylhexane has seven type of different hydrogens and hence forms seven different monochlorinated product.

$$\overset{1}{C}H_3—\overset{2}{C}H_2—\overset{3}{C}H(CH_3)—\overset{4}{C}H_2—\overset{5}{C}H_2—\overset{6}{C}H_3$$

48. (b) Monobromination of the aromatic compound is an electrophilic substitution reaction.

The electron donating group (like $—CH_3$) will increase the reactivity of ring while electron withdrawing groups decreases the reactivity of the ring.

Hence, among the given aromatic compounds, the reactivity $C_6H_5CH_3$ is highest. Between C_6H_5COOH and $C_6H_5NO_2$, electron withdrawing power of $—NO_2$ group is higher than —COOH. So, the reactivity of C_6H_5COOH is higher than $C_6H_5NO_2$. Thus, the decreasing reactivity order of ring towards monobromination is

$$C_6H_5CH_3 > C_6H_6 > C_6H_5COOH > C_6H_5NO_2$$

49. (b) As 3° H-atom is most easily oxidised. The compound *X* is $(CH_3)_3CH$.

$$(CH_3)_3CH + [O] \xrightarrow[KMnO_4]{Hot} (CH_3)_3COH$$

50. (c) Among the given compounds,

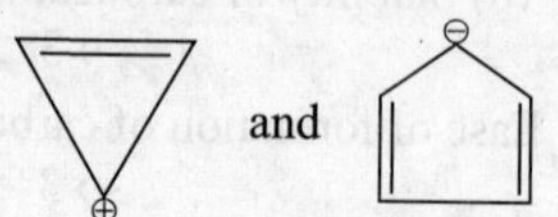

follows Huckel's rule, i.e. $(4n+2)\pi$ electrons and planar structure.

SPT1 Syllabus Part Thru

1. (d) Energy in the ground state is given by

$$E_n = -\frac{13.6}{n^2}\text{ eV}$$

$$E_1 = -13.6\text{ eV}$$

After absorbing 12.1 eV, now energy will be

$$= -13.6 + 12.1 = -1.5\text{ eV}$$

$$\therefore\ -\frac{13.6}{n^2} = -1.5$$

or $n^2 = 9, n = 3$

2. (d) The correct match is

A-IV, B-III, C-II, D-I

3. (a) $\frac{\text{Weight of alkaline earth metal}}{\text{Weight of its nitrite}}$

$$= \frac{\text{Eq. weight of metal}}{\text{Eq. weight of metal} + \text{Eq. weight of } N^{3-} \text{ ions}}$$

$$\frac{12}{14.8} = \frac{E}{E + \frac{14}{3}}$$

$$\Rightarrow 12E + 56 = 14.8E$$

$$2.8E = 56 \Rightarrow E = 20$$

Valency of alkaline earth metal = 2

$\therefore$ Atomic weight $= 2 \times 20 = 40$

4. (a) Molecular weight of sucrose $C_{12}H_{22}O_{11}$

$$= 12 \times 12 + 1 \times 22 + 16 \times 11$$

$$= 342\text{ g/mol}$$

1 mole of sucrose = 342 g

342 g/mol of sucrose contains 12 moles of C

$$\therefore 3.42\text{ g} = \frac{12}{342} \times 3.42$$

$$= 0.12\text{ mole of C}$$

$$= 0.12 \times 6.023 \times 10^{23}\text{ atoms}$$

$$= 7.228 \times 10^{22}\text{ atoms of C}$$

3.42 g of sucrose $= \frac{22}{342} \times 3.42$ moles of H

$$= 0.22\text{ mole of H}$$

$$= 0.22 \times 6.023 \times 10^{23}\text{ atoms of H}$$

$$= 132.5 \times 10^{21}\text{ atoms of H}$$

342 g/mol of sucrose = 11 moles of O

$$= 11 \times 6.023 \times 10^{23}\text{ atoms of O}$$

3.42 g of sucrose

$$= \frac{11 \times 6.023 \times 10^{23}}{342} \times 3.42$$

$$= 66.25 \times 10^{21}\text{ atoms of O}$$

5 (a) Energy of any state is given by,

$$E_n = -\frac{R_H}{n^2}$$

$$\frac{-R_H}{n^2} = -\frac{R_H}{16}$$

$$\Rightarrow n = 4$$

For $n = 4, l = 0, 1, 2, 3$ i.e. $4s, 4p, 4d, 4f$ levels.

Total number of orbital $= 1 + 3 + 5 + 7 = 16$

Degeneracy = 16

6. (b) As 1 g H_2 combines with 80 g Br_2.

Equivalent weight of $Br_2 = 80$

4 g Br_2 combines with 1 g Ca

$\therefore$ 80 g Br_2 combines with

$$\text{Ca} = \frac{1}{4} \times 80\text{ g} = 20\text{ g}$$

Hence, equivalent weight of Ca = 20

7. (b) Group I element with ns^1 configuration are more electropositive than group 2 (ns^2) configuration. Moreover, electropositive character decreases along the period.

8. (a) Work done in compression (reversible process) is given by

$$W = -2.303 nRT \log \frac{p_1}{p_2}$$

Substituting the values,

$$W = -2.303 \times 1 \times 8.314 \times 300 \log \frac{1}{4}$$

$$W = 3458.3\text{ J}$$

$$\Rightarrow\ W \approx 3.46\text{ kJ}$$

9. (d) The correct match is

A-IV, B-I, C-II, D-III.

A. According to de-Broglie equation, $\lambda = h/p$

B. The spectral lines for atomic hydrogen is Lyman series which lies in UV spectral region.

C. Paschen series lies in IR spectral region.

D. According to Heisenberg uncertainty principle, $\Delta x \Delta p \geq h/4\pi$.

10. (c) Molecular mass of anhydrous $ZnSO_4 = 65.38 + 32 + 64 = 161.38$

1.618 g of anhydrous $ZnSO_4$ combines with H_2O

$$= 2.875 - 1.615 = 1.26\text{ g}$$

$\therefore$ 161.38 g anhydrous $ZnSO_4$ will combine with 125.9 g of water

$$= \frac{125.9}{18} \simeq 7 \text{ moles of water}$$

Hence, molecular formula is $ZnSO_4 \cdot 7H_2O$.

11. (d) Binding energy of 1 mole of electrons = 250 kJ/mol

Binding energy of 1 electron

$$= \frac{250}{6.022 \times 10^{23}}$$

$$= 4.15 \times 10^{-22}\text{ kJ}$$

$$= 4.15 \times 10^{-19}\text{ J}$$

Binding energy $= h\nu_0$.

Where ν_0 = threshold frequency.

$$4.15 \times 10^{-19} = 6.62 \times 10^{-34} \times \nu_o$$

$$\nu_0 = 6.26 \times 10^{14}\text{ s}^{-1}$$

12. (b) Both (A) and (R) are true, but (R) is not the correct explanation of (A). The correct explanation is:

Bond order depends upon the number of electrons present in the bonding and anti-bonding molecular orbitals.

Bond order $= \frac{1}{2}(N_b - N_a)$

So, the value of B.O. can be positive fractional or zero.

13. (b) Statement I is correct but Statement II is incorrect. The correct form of statement II is, de-Broglie concept is applicable to microscopic as well as macroscopic particle but has significance only for microscopic particle.

14. (a) l cannot be equal to n so, $n = 3$ and $l = 3$ is not possible.

Thus, option (a) is correct.

15. (a) According to the question,

M_1 = Mass number of first element,

Z_1 = Atomic number of first element

M_2 = Mass number of second element,

Z_2 = Atomic number of second element

In isotones (isoneutronic elements)

$$M_1 - Z_1 = M_2 - Z_2$$

In isobars, $M_1 = M_2$ and in isotopes

$$Z_1 = Z_2$$

In isotope, $M_1 \neq M_2$ but $Z_1 = Z_2$

In isoelectronic, only number of electrons are same.

16. (b) For isothermal expansion of ideal gas, against constant pressure, work done is given by

$W = -p(V_2 - V_1)$

$= -1\,\text{atm}\,(20-10)\,\text{L} = -10\,\text{L atm}$

$= -10 \times 101.3\,\text{J} = -1013\,\text{J}$

Heat absorbed, $q = +800\,\text{J}$

From Ist law,

$\Delta U = q + W = 800 + (-1013)\,\text{J}$

$= -213\,\text{J}$

17. (c) The wave number is given by formula

$$\bar{\nu} = R\left[\frac{1}{n_1^2} - \frac{1}{n_2^2}\right] Z^2$$

$$\nu = \frac{c}{\lambda} = c\bar{\nu} \text{ or } \bar{\nu} = \frac{\nu}{c}$$

where ν is frequency

$$\therefore \quad \frac{\nu}{c} = R\left[\frac{1}{n_1^2} - \frac{1}{n_2^2}\right] Z^2$$

$$\Rightarrow \quad \nu = R'\left[\frac{1}{n_1^2} - \frac{1}{n_2^2}\right] Z^2 \quad \text{...(i)}$$

where $R' = Rc$

For He^+, transition is from $n = 4$ to $n = 2$ and $Z = 2$

$$\nu = R'\left[\frac{1}{2^2} - \frac{1}{4^2}\right](2)^2$$

$$= R'\left[\frac{1}{1^2} - \frac{1}{2^2}\right] \quad \text{...(ii)}$$

For H-atom, $Z = 1$, therefore same value of frequency, transition will happen from $n = 2$ to $n = 1$.

18. (b) Among the given statements, option (b) is correct. The correct form is,

$FeCl_3$ is more covalent than $FeCl_2$ because Fe^{3+} ion has greater charge and smaller size than Fe^{2+} ions and hence a greater polarising power.

19. (a) The reaction is

$$PCl_5 \rightleftharpoons PCl_3 + Cl_2$$

$$Q_p = \frac{p_{PCl_3} \times p_{Cl_2}}{p_{PCl_5}}$$

$$= \frac{1\,\text{atm} \times 1\,\text{atm}}{1\,\text{atm}} = 1\,\text{atm}$$

As $Q_p > K_p$, equilibrium will shift backward. Hence, more PCl_5 will be produced.

20. (b) Free energy is given by,

$\Delta G° = -2.303RT \log K_p$

$\Delta G° = -2.303 \times 8.314 \times 298 \log (2.47 \times 10^{-29})$

$\Delta G° = 163228.93$ J/mol

$\Delta G° = 163.23$ kJ/mol

21. (c) Statement I is incorrect but statement II is correct. The corrected form of statement I is;

Outermost electronic configuration of most electronegative elements is ns^2np^5 which belongs to halogens. This is because halogen are most electronegative elements.

22. (a) As the size increases, bond dissociation enthalpy becomes lower. But the bond dissociation enthalpy of fluorine is however lower than those of the chlorine and bromine because of interelectronic repulsion present in small atom of fluorine.

Hence, the correct order is

$Cl_2 > Br_2 > F_2 > I_2$.

23. (a) **Ionisation enthalpy** is defined as the minimum energy required to remove an electron from an isolated gaseous atom (Y) in its ground state.

$$Y(g) \longrightarrow Y^+(g) + e^-, \Delta_i H = +\text{ve}$$

Hence, lower value of ionisation energy indicate that formation of cation is more favoured.

24. (a) Given $\Delta H = 145.6$ kJ/mol

$\Delta S = 116\,\text{J K}^{-1}\,\text{mol}^{-1}$

Gibb's free energy is given by

$\Delta G = \Delta H - T\Delta S$

$= 145.6 - 300 \times \frac{116}{1000}$

$= 110.8$ kJ/mol.

25. (a) Electron affinity generally decreases down the group and increases in a period.

However, the electron affinity of Cl is more than F because of the smaller size of F, due to which there is a larger repulsion between the incoming electrons and electrons present in valence shell of F atom which makes the addition of electron to F less favourable.

26. (a) For 1st reaction,

$$K_1 = \frac{[H_2O]}{[H_2]} = 65$$

For 2nd reaction,

$$K_2 = \frac{[CO_2]}{[CO]} = 500$$

For overall reaction,

$$K = \frac{[CO_2][H_2]}{[CO][H_2O]} = \frac{K_2}{K_1} = \frac{500}{65} = 7.69$$

27. (a) Bond order $= \frac{N_b - N_a}{2}$

where, N_b = bonding electrons

N_a = antibonding electrons

$O_2^+ = \frac{10-5}{2} = 2.5$

$O_2^- = \frac{10-7}{2} = 1.5$

$O_2^{2-} = \frac{10-8}{2} = 1$

$O_2^{2+} = \frac{10-4}{2} = 3$

As we know that,

Bond order $\propto \frac{1}{\text{Bond length}}$

Hence, O_2^{2+} has highest bond order, therefore it has shortest bond length.

28. (d) (A) is false but (R) is true. The corrected form of (A) is :

The endothermic reactions are favoured at higher temperature while exothermic reactions are favoured at lower temperature.

29. (c) The reaction involved is as follows,

$CaCO_3(s) \longrightarrow CaO(s) + CO_2(g)$, $\Delta H = ?$

$\Delta_r H° = \Sigma \Delta H°_{(Product)} - \Sigma \Delta_f H°_{(Reactant)}$

$= \Delta_f H°_{(CaO)} + \Delta_f H°_{(CO_2)} - \Delta_f H°_{(CaCO_3)}$

$= -635.09 - 393.51 - (-1206.92)$

$= 178.32$ kJ/mol

30. (c) For the given reaction,

$\Delta n = 2 - 3 = -1$

The relation between K_p and K_C is

$K_p = K_C (RT)^{\Delta n} = K_C (RT)^{-1}$

$K_p = \frac{K_C}{RT}$

31. (b) Metallic character decreases along the period but increases down the group. That's why the order given in statement I is correct.

Hence, Statement I is correct but Statement II is incorrect.

32. (b) In NH_2OH, oxidation state of $N = -1$

In N_2O, oxidation state of $N = +1$

Change in oxidation state = 2

$\therefore$ Equivalent mass $= \frac{M}{2}$

33. (d) Al_2O_3 and MnO_2 are amphoteric oxides, while CO and N_2O are neutral and K_2O is basic oxide.

34. (a) The correct matching is A-III, B-IV, C-II, D-I.

A. XeO_3 – Pyramidal structure

B. NH_2^- (sp^2) – V-shape

C. NH_4^+ (sp^3) – Tetrahedral

D. $[PtCl_4]^{2-}$ (dsp^2) – Square planar

Hence, option (a) is correct.

35. (b) Species having equal number of electrons are called isoelectronic species.

The number of electrons involved in the given species are as follows

	Species	No. of electrons
(a)	PO_4^{3-}	$15 + (8 \times 4) + 3 = 50e^-$
	SO_4^{2-}	$16 + (8 \times 4) + 2 = 50e^-$
	ClO_4^-	$17 + (8 \times 4) + 1 = 50e^-$
(b)	SO_3^{2-}	$6 + (8 \times 3) + 2 = 32e^-$
	CO_3^{2-}	$7 + (8 \times 3) + 1 = 32e^-$
	NO_3^-	$16 + (8 \times 3) + 2 = 42e^-$
(c)	BO_3^{3-}	$5 + (8 \times 3) + 3 = 32e^-$
	CO_3^{2-}	$6 + (8 \times 3) + 2 = 32e^-$
	NO_3^-	$7 + (8 \times 3) + 1 = 32e^-$
(d)	CN^-	$6 + (7 + 1) = 14e^-$
	N_2	$7 \times 2 = 14e^-$
	C_2^{2-}	$6 \times 2 + 2 = 14e^-$

36. (c) Let volume of H_2SO_4 is x mL,

n-factor for $H_2SO_4 = 2$

Using, $N_1V_1 - N_2V_2 = N(V_1 + V_2)$

where, N = Molarity × n-factor

$x \times 0.1 \times 2 - 50 \times 0.1$

$= (x + 50) \times 0.05 \times 2$

$x = 100$ mL

37. (c) Energy of molecular orbital is directly proportional to 'n' value.

Since, $\sigma 2s$, orbital has greater value of n than $\overset{*}{\sigma} 1s$ MO.

Thus, energy of $\sigma 2s$ is greater than $\overset{*}{\sigma} 1s$.

38. (b) More electronegative element with small size forms H-bonds. So, F, O and N being most electronegative form H-bonds, Cl does not.

39. (b) The given equilibrium

$2NOCl(g) \rightleftharpoons 2NO(g) + Cl_2(g)$

We know that,

$K_p = K_C \cdot (RT)^{\Delta n}$

$\Delta n = (2 + 1) - 2$

$\Delta n = 1$

$K_p = 3.75 \times 10^{-4} \times 0.0831 \times 1069$

$K_p = 0.033$

40. (b) Bond angle for NB_3 molecule $\propto \frac{1}{\text{EN of atom } B}$

Electronegativity of Cl is less than F therefore, bond angle of NCl_3 is greater than NF_3.

Hence, statement (I) is correct.

Also, electronegativity of H is less than F.

So, bond angle of NH_3 is greater than NF_3.

Hence, statement (III) is also correct.

41. (c) The given reaction is

$2NH_3(g) + CO_2(g) \rightleftharpoons NH_2CONH_2(aq.) + H_2O(l)$

We know that,

$$\log K = \frac{-\Delta_r G^\ominus}{2.303RT}$$

$$\log K = \frac{-(-13.6\times 10^3 \text{ J mol}^{-1})}{2.303\times 8.314 \text{JK}^{-1}\text{mol}^{-1}\times 298 \text{ K}}$$

$$\log K = 2.38$$

$$K \approx 2.4\times 10^2$$

Thus, the value of equilibrium constant is 2.4×10^2.

42. (d) $E = \frac{hc}{\lambda}$

So, $E \propto \frac{1}{\lambda}$

Thus, it shows a hyperbolic curve.

43. (d) $H—\underset{Cl}{\overset{H}{C}}—H(g) \longrightarrow C(s) + 3H(g) + Cl(g)$

$\Delta H° =$ Sum of bond energy of reactants − Sum of bond energy of products $= [3\times (\text{C—H}) + 1\times (\text{C—Cl})] - 0$

(All the products have free atoms)

$= (3\times 500) + (320)$ kJ

$= 1500 + 320 = 1820$ kJ

44. (b) 1 L of 1 M H_2SO_4 gives 2 moles of H^+ ions.

1 L of 1 M $Ca(OH)_2$ gives 2 moles of OH^- ions. Hence, for complete neutralisation of 2 moles of H^+ ions by 2 moles of OH^- ions.

$$\Delta H = 2\times -13.7 = -\ 27.4 \text{ kcal}$$

45. (c) NH_4^+ has perfect tetrahedral symmetry, no lone pairs is present so, there will be no repulsion and the angle is nearly 109.5°. While in PCl_3, NH_3 and SCl_2 bond angle decreases from 109.5° due to presence of lone pair of electron. Hence, ammonium ion has the maximum bond angle.

SPT2 Syllabus Part Thru

1. (d) $+I$ effect is shown by methyl group (—CH_3) and carboxylate group (—COO^-) as they both are electron donating groups while —NO_2 and —NH_3^+ are electron withdrawing groups hence, show $-I$ effect.

2. (a) I is the most stable resonating structure because it is neutral. IV has complete octet on each atoms, II and III both have incomplete octet at C-atom bearing positive charge but in III structure negative charge is present on more electronegative atom i.e. oxygen and the structure with a $-ve$ charge on more electronegative atom will be more stable. Hence, the correct order is

$$\text{I} > \text{IV} > \text{III} > \text{II}$$

3. (c) Boron compounds behaves as Lewis acid because boron have only three electrons in its valence shell. Thus, its octet is incomplete and electron deficient. So, it accepts electron-pair from donor molecule and acts as Lewis acid.

4. (c) The complete reaction is as follows,

$$2B(s) + 6KOH(s) \xrightarrow{\text{Fuse}} 2K_3BO_3 + 3H_2$$

5. (d) In group 14, down the group, the size of an element increases and the strength of bonding decreases.

Thus, the tendency for catenation decreases. The correct order of catenation is

$$C >>> Si > Ge \approx Sn > Pb$$

6. (d) (A) is false but (R) is true. The correct form of (A) is Stannous chloride is a strong reducing agent not an oxidising agent that reduces mercuric chloride to mercury.

7. (b) Relation between $\Delta G°$, $E°$ and K_{eq} is

$$\Delta G° = -RT \ln K_{eq}$$

Thus, if E°_{cell} is − ve, then $\Delta G°$ is + ve, i.e. $\Delta G° > 0$ and in this case, K_{eq} would be negative and less than 1, i.e. $K_{eq} < 1$.

8. (d) $BCl_3 + 3NH_4Cl \xrightarrow[C_6H_5Cl]{140°C} \underset{(A)}{B_3N_3H_3Cl_3} \xrightarrow{NaBH_4} \underset{\text{Borazine/Inorganic Benzene } (B)}{B_3N_3H_6}$

9. (c) In B, C and D reactions, there is no change in oxidation state of reactant and products.

10. (b) Peroxide effect is not observed in case of HCl and HI as for reaction to occur, both the propagation step must be exothermic. But one of the step (reaction of HCl with carbon radical) is endothermic in both the cases.

11. (d) Both Statement I and Statement II are correct.

12. (d) There are three structural isomers of C_3H_6O.

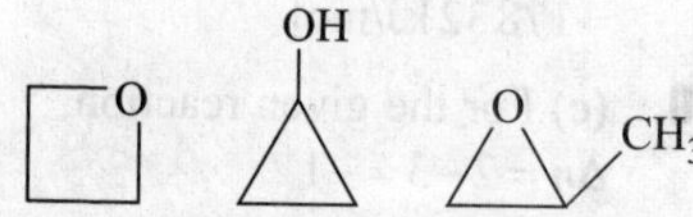

13. (d) Anthraquinone is prepared by the oxidation of anthracene by chromic acid.

The crude anthracene, being sublimable can be separated from anthraquinone by sublimation.

14. (c) (A) is true but (R) is false. The correct form of (R) is,

Due to inert pair effect, the higher oxidation states for the group 14 elements are less stable for the heavier members of the group and have a tendency to reduce to lesser oxidation state. So, they are stronger oxidation agent.

15. (c) The redox reaction involved is as follows,

$$\overset{6+}{Cr_2O_7^{2-}} + 3e^- \longrightarrow Cr^{3+}$$ (Reduction)

In this reaction, three electrons are required for the reduction of $Cr_2O_7^{2-}$ into Cr^{3+}.

16. (d) $NaNO_2$ acts as both oxidising and reducing agent because in $NaNO_2$, N atom is in +3 intermediate oxidation state.

Oxidising property

$$2NaNO_2 + 2KI + 2H_2SO_4 \longrightarrow Na_2SO_4 + K_2SO_4 + 2NO + 2H_2O + I_2$$

Reducing property

$$H_2O_2 + NaNO_2 \longrightarrow NaNO_3 + H_2O$$

17. (b) The redox reaction involved is as follows,

$$\overset{+7}{MnO_4^-} + \overset{+4}{SO_3^{2-}} \longrightarrow \overset{+6}{SO_4^{2-}} + \overset{+6}{MnO_4^{2-}}$$ ($-2e^-$; $+e^-$)

Cross-multiply by change in oxidation state.

$$2MnO_4^- + SO_3^{2-} \rightarrow SO_4^{2-} + 2MnO_4^{2-}$$

Thus, $2MnO_4^-$ is reduced by $1\ SO_3^{2-}$.

$\therefore$ $1\ MnO_4^-$ is reduced by $0.5\ SO_3^{2-}$.

18. (d) In 0.1 M $AgNO_3$, the reaction is

$$AgNO_3 \rightleftharpoons Ag^+ + NO_3^-$$

$$AgCl \rightleftharpoons Ag^+ + Cl^-$$

$$K_{sp} = [Ag^+][Cl^-]$$

Now $[Ag^+]$ can be taken as $[AgNO_3]$ while $[Cl^-]$ is the solubility of AgCl

$$\therefore [Cl^-] = \frac{K_{sp}}{[Ag^+]} = \frac{2.8 \times 10^{-10}}{0.1}$$

$\therefore$ Solubility of AgCl

$$= 2.8 \times 10^{-9} \text{ mol/L}$$

19. (b) The reaction involved is as follows,

$$H_2S \rightleftharpoons 2H^+ + S^{2-}$$

$$K_a = 1.1 \times 10^{-21} = \frac{[H^+]^2[S^{2-}]}{[H_2S]}$$

$$= \frac{10^{-2} \times [S^{2-}]}{0.1}$$

$$[S^{2-}] = 1.1 \times 10^{-20}$$

$\therefore$ Number of S^{2-} ions

$$= 1.1 \times 10^{-20} \times 6.023 \times 10^{23}$$

$$= 6.625 \times 10^3$$

20. (c) For weak acid (*HA*), K_a is given by

$$K_a = \alpha^2 C$$

where, α is degree of dissociation

$$\alpha = \sqrt{\frac{K_a}{C}}$$

$$\Rightarrow \sqrt{\frac{4.9 \times 10^{-8}}{0.1}} = 7.0 \times 10^{-4}$$

$$pH = -\log H^+ = -\log \alpha C$$

$$pH = -\log [7.0 \times 10^{-4} \times 10^{-1}]$$

$$pH = 4.155$$

21. (c) The reaction involved is as follows,

$$CH_3NH_2 + HCl \longrightarrow CH_3NH_3^+Cl$$

CH_3NH_2	HCl	$CH_3NH_3^+Cl$
0.1 mole	0.08 mole	0
0.02	0	0.08

This is basic buffer solution

$$[OH^-] = K_b \times \frac{[Base]}{[Salt]}$$

$$\Rightarrow 5 \times 10^{-5} \times \frac{0.02}{0.08} = 1.25 \times 10^{-5}$$

$$\therefore \quad [OH^-] = 1.25 \times 10^{-5}$$

$$\therefore [H^+] = \frac{10^{-14}}{[OH^-]}$$

$$\Rightarrow [H^+] = \frac{10^{-14}}{1.25 \times 10^{-5}}$$

$$= 8 \times 10^{-10} M$$

22. (b) pOH of buffer solution is given by

$$pOH = pK_b + \log \frac{[Salt]}{[Base]}$$

Or

$$pOH = pK_b + \log \frac{[Cation]}{[Base]}$$

Also, given

$$[NH_4^+] = 2 \times \text{mole of} (NH_4)_2SO_4$$

$$\therefore pOH = 5 + \log 2 = 5.3$$

$$pH = 14 - pOH$$

$$= 14 - 5.3 = 8.7$$

23. (c) Statement I is incorrect but statement II is correct.

The correct form of statement I is,

Salting-out action of soap in presence of NaCl is based on the principle of solubility product not based on common ion effect

$$RCOONa \longrightarrow RCOO^- + Na^+$$

In presence of NaCl,

$[Na^+]$ increases and

$[RCOO^-][Na^+]$ exceeds than K_{sp} of *R*COONa.

24. (b) The reaction involved is as follows,

$$\text{Benzene (C}_6\text{H}_5\text{H)} \xrightarrow{H_2SO_4 \text{ fuming}} \text{Benzene sulphonic acid (C}_6\text{H}_5\text{SO}_3\text{H)}$$

25. (d) Terminal alkyne gives white precipitate with silver nitrate in ammonia.

$$CH_3—C{\equiv}CH + NH_3 + AgNO_3 \xrightarrow{} CH_3—C{\equiv}C—Ag + NH_4NO_3$$
Propyne; Silver acetylide (White ppt.)

$$CH_3—CH{=}CH_2 + NH_3 + AgNO_3 \longrightarrow \text{No reaction}$$
Propene

26. (c) Iodination of an alkane is carried out in presence of HNO_3 or HIO_3.

$$HIO_3 + 5HI \longrightarrow 3I_2 + 3H_2$$
$$CH_4 + I_2 \rightleftharpoons CH_3I + HI$$

27. (d) For the reaction,

$$N_2O_4(g) \rightleftharpoons 2NO_2(g)$$
Moles at equil, $1-\alpha$ 2α

Let α be the degree of dissociation and p is the total pressure, then

Total number of moles $= 2\alpha + 1 - \alpha = 1 + \alpha$

$$\therefore p_{N_2O_4} = \text{Moles of } N_2O_4 \times p_{\text{total}} = \left(\frac{1-\alpha}{1+\alpha}\right)p$$

and $p_{NO_2} = \left(\frac{2\alpha}{1+\alpha}\right)p$

$$K_p = \frac{p^2_{NO_2}}{p_{N_2O_4}} = \frac{\left[\left(\frac{2\alpha}{1+\alpha}\right)p\right]^2}{\left(\frac{1-\alpha}{1+\alpha}\right)p}$$

$$= \frac{4\alpha^2p^2}{(1+\alpha)^2} \times \frac{1+\alpha}{(1-\alpha)p}$$

$$= \frac{4\alpha^2 p}{1-\alpha^2}$$

Given, $K_p = 0.120$ atm, $p = 2$ atm

$$0.120 = \frac{4\alpha^2(2)}{1-\alpha^2} = \frac{8\alpha^2}{1-\alpha^2}$$

$$\Rightarrow 0.120(1-\alpha^2) = 8\alpha^2$$
$$\alpha^2 = 0.0147$$
$$\alpha = 0.121$$

28. (d) $HCl = 10^{-5}$ M $[\because pH = 5]$

$$M_1V_1 = M_2V_2$$
$$10^{-5} \times 1\,mL = M_2 \times 1000\,mL$$
$$M_2 = \frac{10^{-5}}{1000} = 10^{-8}\text{ M}$$

HCl is acid therefore, pH would be less than 7.

In such case, the concentration of H_3O^+ from water has to be taken.

Let H_3O^+ from water be x M in the presence of 10^{-8} M HCl.

$$2H_2O \rightleftharpoons \underset{x\,M}{H_3O^+} + \underset{x\,M}{OH^-}$$

$$HCl + H_2O \rightleftharpoons \underset{10^{-8}\,M}{H_3O^+} + \underset{10^{-8}\,M}{Cl^-}$$

At equilibrium, $[H_3O^+] = x + 10^{-8}$

$[OH^-] = x$

$$K_w = [H_3O^+][OH^-]$$
$$\Rightarrow 10^{-14} = (x + 10^{-8})(x)$$
$$\Rightarrow x^2 + 10^{-8}x - 10^{-14} = 0$$

From quadratic equation,

$$x = 9.51 \times 10^{-8}\text{ M}$$
$$[H_3O^+] = 1 \times 10^{-8} + 9.51 \times 10^{-8} = 1.05 \times 10^{-7}$$
$$\Rightarrow \quad pH = -\log(1.05 \times 10^{-7}) = 6.98$$

29. (b) Among the given statements, (b) is not true. Its correct statement is :

Electromeric effect is a temporary effect.

30. (d) The balanced equation is

$$K_2Cr_2O_7 + 4KCl + 6H_2SO_4 \longrightarrow 2CrO_2Cl_2 + 6KHSO_4 + 3H_2O$$

So, $a = 1, b = 4, c = 6,$

$x = 2, y = 6, z = 3$

Thus, option (d) is correct.

31. (b) Electron deficient compounds are those in which central metal atom have incomplete octet.

Mostly, covalent compounds are electron deficient while ionic compounds are electron rich.

$AlCl_3$ is a covalent compound, while AlF_3 is an ionic compound.

The atomic size of F is smaller than Cl which makes AlF_3 more ionic. Thus, option (b) is correct.

32. (c) Given, mass of organic compound = 0.40 g

Now, 188 g of AgBr contains = 80 g of Br.

0.3 g of AgBr contains

$$= \frac{80}{188} \times 0.3\text{ g of Br}$$
$$= 0.12765\text{ g}$$

The percentage of Br in the organic compound

$$= \frac{0.12765}{0.40} \times 100$$
$$= 31.91\%$$

Alternative method

$$\Rightarrow \%\,Br = \frac{80 \times w_{AgBr} \times 100}{188 \times w_{\text{substance}}}$$
$$= \frac{80 \times 0.3 \times 100}{188 \times 0.40}$$
$$= 31.91\ \%$$

33. (d) The correct order of boiling point is II > III > I > IV.

The given compounds are all alkanes.

The order is based on the fact that greater the number of carbon atoms, higher is the boiling point due to higher molecular mass.

For the same number of carbon atoms, branching reduces the boiling point.

34. (c) When $AlCl_3$ is dissolved in water, then it forms hydrated compounds.

The reaction involves is as follows

$$AlCl_3 + 6H_2O \longrightarrow [Al(H_2O)_6]^{3+} + 3Cl^-$$

Thus, option (c) is correct.

35. (d) $R—CH{=}CH—R \xrightarrow[\text{(Oxidative cleavage)}]{\text{Reagent}} 2R—COOH$

Following reagent can be used during oxidative cleavage of alkene.

(a) Hot alkaline $KMnO_4$ followed by acidification.

(b) Hot acidic $KMnO_4$ solution.

(c) Hot acidic $K_2Cr_2O_7$ solution.

(d) But hot Cr_2O_3 cannot be used where Cr is present in + 3 oxidation state.

36. (a) *Vicinal*-dihalides on treatment with alcoholic KOH undergo dehydrohalogenation.

One molecule of hydrogen halide is eliminated to form alkenyl halide which on treatment with sodamide gives alkyne.

The given reaction is as follows

$$\underset{\text{Br}\quad\text{Br}}{H_2C—CH_2} + KOH \xrightarrow[-KBr, -H_2O]{\text{Alcohol}} \underset{(A)\ \text{(Bromoethene)}}{H_2C{=}CH(Br)}$$

$$\xrightarrow[-NaBr, -NH_3]{NaNH_2} \underset{(B)\ \text{(Ethyne)}}{HC{\equiv}CH}$$

The correct option is (a).

37. (a)

Elements	Number of moles	Simple ratio
C (24 g)	$\frac{24}{12}=2$	1
H (8 g)	$\frac{8}{1}=8$	4
O (32 g)	$\frac{32}{16}=2$	1

Empirical formula is CH_4O.

38. (b) Metamerism is observed between I and II.

Ester $—\overset{O}{\overset{\|}{C}}—O—$ has different alkyl groups in both sides of I and II compound.

39. (b) The complete reaction is as follows :

$$EtC{\equiv}CH \xrightarrow[THF]{BD_3} \underset{(X)}{(Et)(D)C{=}C(H)(BD_2)}$$

$$\xrightarrow{CH_3COOH} \underset{\text{Product } (Y)}{(Et)(D)C{=}C(H)(H)}$$

40. (b) The complete (balanced) redox reaction is,

$$3Br_2 + 6OH^- \longrightarrow 5Br^- + BrO_3^- + 3H_2O$$

$p=3, q=6, r=5, s=1, t=3$

$p+q+r+s+t=18$

41. (a) The reaction involved is,

$$\underset{\text{Acid form}}{HIn} \rightleftharpoons H^+ + In^-$$

Acid form $[HIn] = 0.80$ M

$[In^-] = 0.20$ M

$$pH = pK_{In} + \log\frac{[In^-]}{[HIn]}$$

$$= 5.3 + \log\frac{(0.20)}{(0.80)}$$

$$= 5.3 + \log\left(\frac{1}{4}\right)$$

$$= 5.3 - 0.60 = 4.7$$

$\therefore$ pH of solution = 4.7

42. (a) There are three possible structures of C_5H_8 with one triple bond

(i) $CH_3—CH_2—CH_2—C{\equiv}CH$
pent-1-yne

(ii) $CH_3—CH_2—C{\equiv}C—CH_3$
pent-2-yne

(iii) $CH_3—CH(CH_3)—C{\equiv}C—H$
3-methylbut-1-yne

43. (b) $\overset{1}{C}H_3$–$\overset{2}{C}H_2$–$\overset{3}{C}H(CH_3)$–$\overset{4}{C}H(CH_2CH_3)$–$\overset{5}{C}H_2$–$\overset{6}{C}H_2$–$\overset{7}{C}H_2$–$\overset{8}{C}H_3$

4-ethyl-3-methyloctane

44. (d) $pH = -\log[H^+]$

or $[H^+] = 10^{-pH}$;

$[H^+]$ of solution $1 = 10^{-3}$

$[H^+]$ of solution $2 = 10^{-4}$;

$[H^+]$ of solution $3 = 10^{-5}$

After the mixing,

Total volume = (1+1+1) = 3 L

For solution 1,

Moles $= M \times V$

$= 10^{-3} \times 1 = 10^{-3}$ moles

For solution 2,

Moles $= 10^{-4} \times 1 = 10^{-4}$ moles

For solution 3,

Moles $= 10^{-5} \times 1 = 10^{-5}$ moles

$\therefore$ Total moles

$= (10^{-3} + 10^{-4} + 10^{-5})$

$= 1.11 \times 10^{-3}$ moles

So, H^+ ion concentration in mixture of equal volume of these acid solution $= \frac{1.11 \times 10^{-3}}{3}$

$= 3.7 \times 10^{-4}$ M

45. (d) $Al_2(SO_4)_3 \rightleftharpoons \underset{2S}{2Al^{3+}} + \underset{3S}{3SO_4^{2-}}$

$K_{sp} = (2S)^2(3S)^3 = 4S^2 \times 27S^3$

$= 108S^5$

NSS1 NEET Stepping Stones

1. (a) The given reaction is

$$H_2(g)+I_2(g) \rightleftharpoons 2HI(g)$$

	H_2	I_2	HI
Initial conc.	4.5	4.5	0
At equil.	$4.5-x$	$4.5-x$	$2x$

Given, $2x = 3$ moles then $x = 1.5$ moles

So, concentration at equilibrium = 3 moles of each H_2 and I_2.

$$K=\frac{[HI]^2}{[H_2][I_2]}$$

$$\Rightarrow \quad K=\frac{3\times 3}{3\times 3}=1$$

2. (b)

$$SO_3(g) \rightleftharpoons SO_2(g)+\frac{1}{2}O_2(g)$$

	SO_3	SO_2	O_2
At equil.	$1-\alpha$	α	$\frac{\alpha}{2}$

$$M_{mix}=\frac{0.9\times 0.082\times 1000}{1.23}=60 \quad ...(i)$$

$$\text{Also, } M_{mix}=\frac{\alpha M_{SO_2}+\frac{\alpha}{2}M_{O_2}+(1-\alpha)M_{SO_3}}{1+\frac{\alpha}{2}}$$

$$\Rightarrow \quad 1+\frac{\alpha}{2}=\frac{80}{60} \Rightarrow \alpha=\frac{2}{3}$$

3. (d) The structure of P_4O_{10} is

(Structure of P_4O_{10}: O‖ → $p\pi$-$p\pi$ bond)

$\therefore$ Number of σ-bond = 16

4. (a) Bond dissociation energy $\propto$ Bond order

$$\text{Bond order}=\frac{N_b-N_a}{2}$$

$$He_2^+ \text{; B.O}=\frac{2-1}{2}=0.5$$

$$C_2 \text{; B.O}=\frac{8-4}{2}=2$$

$$O_2^- \text{; B.O}=\frac{10-7}{2}=1.5$$

$$NO \text{; B.O}=\frac{10-5}{2}=2.5$$

Hence, the correct order is,

$He_2^+ < O_2^- < C_2 < NO$.

5. (c) (A) is true but (R) is false. The correct form of (R) is. The equilibrium constant for an exothermic reaction decreases as temperature increases.

6. (b) Wilkinson's reagent $[(Ph_3P)_3RhCl]$ brings about homogeneous catalysis as it is soluble in reaction medium.

All other bring about heterogeneous catalysis as catalyst and reactants remain in different phase.

7. (c) (A) is true but (R) is false. The correct form of (R) is. Lactic acid is a chiral molecule because it has a chiral carbon atom and therefore, optically active.

8. (d) A mixture of benzene and chloroform is separated by distillation method.

9. (d) Both Statement I and Statement II are correct.

10. (c) Given,

$\Delta H = 100\,J$, $p = 1.5$ atm

$\Delta V = 2-8 = -6\,L$.

Work done is given by,

$$W = p\Delta V$$

$$=1.5(-6) \quad ...(i)$$

Now this work done is in litre atm. To obtain in Joules, multiply by 8.314 and divide by 0.0821.

$$\therefore \quad \Delta H = \Delta E + p\Delta V \quad ...(ii)$$

$$100=\Delta E+\frac{1.5\times(-6)}{0.0821}\times 8.314$$

$$\Delta E \simeq 1011\,J$$

11. (c) F^- has bigger size than Mg^{2+} and Na^+ due to small nuclear charge.

Further, size of Al is greater than F^- because on moving from left to right in a period atomic size decreases.

Hence, the correct increasing order of size is,

$$Mg^{2+} < Na^+ < F^- < Al.$$

12. (b) Statement I is correct but statement II is incorrect. Its correct form is :

Only He is chemically inert due to inert gas configuration, but Be does not have inert gas configuration as $2p$-subshell is vacant.

13. (a) Given, $KE=\frac{1}{2}mv^2$

$$=4.55\times 10^{-25}\,J \quad ...(i)$$

$$v^2=\frac{2\times 4.55\times 10^{-25}}{9.1\times 10^{-31}}$$

$$\Rightarrow v = 10^3\ m/s \quad ...(ii)$$

de-Broglie wavelength is given by,

$$\lambda=\frac{h}{mv} \quad ...(iii)$$

Substitute the values in Eq. (iii)

$$\lambda=\frac{6.626\times 10^{-34}}{9.1\times 10^{-31}\times 10^3}$$

$$\lambda = 7.28\times 10^{-7}\ m$$

14. (b) The maximum number of possible subshell associated with a particular shell is equal to principal quantum number $n \geq 5$.

15. (a) 18 g H_2O contains 2g H.

$\therefore$ 0.72 g H_2O contain 0.08 g H.

44 g CO_2 contains 12 g C.

3.08 g of CO_2 contain 0.84 g of C

$$\therefore C:H = \frac{0.84}{12} : \frac{0.08}{1}$$

$$= 0.07 : 0.08 = 7 : 8$$

Empirical formula = C_7H_8

16. (b) Molarity

$$= \frac{w(g) \times 1000}{\text{Molar mass} \times V\text{(mL)}}$$

$$= \frac{2.65 \times 1000}{106 \times 250} = 0.1\text{M}$$

10 mL of this solution is diluted to 1000 mL $M_1V_1 = M_2V_2$

$10 \times 0.1 = 1000 \times x$

$x = 0.001\text{M}$ or 10^{-3} M

17. (b) Statement I is correct but statement II is incorrect. Its correct form is :

Both $SiCl_4$ and CCl_4 are covalent.

Hydrolysis of $SiCl_4$ is due to presence of *d*-orbital.

18. (c) Equivalent weight of $KMnO_4$ = Equivalent weight of KHC_2O_4

$$\therefore 100 \times 10^{-3} \times 0.02 \times 5 = \frac{x}{\frac{128}{1}}$$

$$\Rightarrow x = 1.28\text{ g} \quad ...(i)$$

Eq. wt. of KHC_2O_4 = Eq. wt. of $Ca(OH)_2$

$$\Rightarrow \frac{y}{\frac{128}{1}} = 100 \times 10^{-3} \times 0.05 \times 2$$

$$\Rightarrow y = 1.28\text{ g} \quad ..(ii)$$

Hence, $x = y$

19. (c) (A) is true but (R) is false. The correct form of (R) is : Only one H-atom is directly attached to P in H_3PO_3.

```
     OH
     |
  H—P=O
     |
     OH
```

20. (a) The reaction involved is,

$$NH_4^+ + OH^- \xrightarrow{k_1} NH_4OH; \quad k_1 = 4 \times 10^{10}$$

$$NH_4OH \underset{K_b}{\overset{K_f}{\rightleftharpoons}} NH_4^+ + OH^-$$

$$K_{eq} = \frac{K_f}{K_b}$$

$$\Rightarrow 1.8 \times 10^{-5} = \frac{K_f}{4 \times 10^{10}}$$

$$\Rightarrow K_f = 7.2 \times 10^5$$

21. (d) The pH of buffer solution is given by

$$pH = pK_a + \log \frac{[HCO_3^-]}{[H_2CO_3]} \quad ...(i)$$

$$7 = 7 - \log 4 + \log \frac{[HCO_3^-]}{[H_2CO_3]}$$

$$\Rightarrow \frac{HCO_3^-}{[H_2CO_3]} = 4 \quad ...(ii)$$

% of carbon in the form of HCO_3^-

$$= \frac{[HCO_3^-]}{[HCO_3^-] + [H_2CO_3]} \times 100$$

$$\Rightarrow \frac{4}{1+4} \times 100 = 80\%$$

22. (a) Mass of the particle, $m = 1$ mg

$$= 10^{-6}\text{ kg}$$

Uncertainty in velocity,

$$\Delta v = 5.5 \times 10^{-20}\text{ m/s}$$

$$\Rightarrow \Delta x . m \Delta v = \frac{h}{4\pi}$$

$$\Rightarrow \Delta x = \frac{h}{4\pi . m\Delta v}$$

$$= \frac{6.626 \times 10^{-34}\text{ kg m}^2/\text{s}}{4 \times 3.14 \times 10^{-6}\text{ kg} \times 5.5 \times 10^{-20}\text{ ms}^{-1}}$$

$$= 9.6 \times 10^{-10}\text{ m}$$

Hence, option (a) is correct.

23. (b) Statement I is correct but Statement II is incorrect.

Because boron exibits only +3 oxidation state, so it forms BCl_3 (a stable compound).

On moving down the group, the inert pair effect becomes more and more pronounced therefore, in thallium +1 oxidation state is more stable than +3 oxidation state. Thats why BCl_3 is more stable than $TlCl_3$.

24. (b) Metallic character increases on moving down the group and decreases on going across a period from left to right in perodic table.

Hence, correct order is

B < Al < Mg < K.

25. (d) $SF_6 \Rightarrow$ Bond pair = 6

Lone pair = 0

sp^3d^2, octahedral

$IF_5 \Rightarrow$ Bond pair = 5

Lone pair = 1

sp^3d^2, square pyramidal

$BrF_5 \Rightarrow$ Bond pair = 5

Lone pair = 1

sp^3d^2, square pyramidal

$XeF_4 \Rightarrow$ Bond pair = 4

Lone pair = 2

sp^3d^2, square planar

Thus, option (d) is correct.

H_2SO_4, sp^3.

26. (c)

BF_3 (3 *bp* and no *lp*)

PCl_3 (3 *bp* and 1 *lp*)

ClF_3 (3 *bp* and 2 *lp*)

XeO_3 (3 *bp* and 1 *lp*)

From the structures, we can see that ClF_3 contains 3*bp* and 2*lp*.

27. (b)

$CH_3CH_2-CH_2-CH_2-C(CH_3)(CH_2-CH(Cl)-CH_3)-CH_2-CH_2-CH_2-CH_3$

5-(2-chloropropyl)-5-methylnonane

28. (d) Both Statement I and Statement II are correct.

The pK_a of weak acid becomes equal to pH of the solution at the mid point of its titration because the molar concentration of proton acceptor and proton donor becomes equal at mid point of a weak acid.

29. (b)

$$N_2(g) + 3H_2(g) \rightleftharpoons 2NH_3(g)$$

$$\Rightarrow \quad \Delta n = n_P - n_R$$

$$\Delta n = 2 - (1+3)$$

$$\Delta n = -2$$

$$\Rightarrow \quad K_p = K_C \times (RT)^{\Delta n}$$

$$K_C = \frac{K_p}{(RT)^{\Delta n}}$$

$$= \frac{3.6 \times 10^{-2}}{(0.0821 \times 500)^{-2}}$$

$$= 3.6 \times 10^{-2} \times (0.0821 \times 500)^2$$

$$= 60.66\,M^{-2}$$

30. (a) 2-pentene can show geometrical isomerism due to the presence of different groups on each double bonded carbon atoms.

$(CH_3)(H)C=C(H)(CH_2CH_3)$

31. (c) (A) is true but (R) is false.

Trichloroacetic acid is more acidic than acetic acid as, the electron withdrawing group increases the acidic strength.

32. (c)

$CH_3-CO-CH_2-CH_2-CH_2-COOH$ (carbons numbered 6, 5, 4, 3, 2, 1)

IUPAC name 5-oxohexanoic acid

33. (c) Four molecules of acetylene polymerise under high pressure in presence of nickel cyanide.

$$4\,CH\equiv CH \xrightarrow[\text{At higher pressure}]{Ni(CN)_2} \text{Cyclooctatetraene}$$

Thus, option (c) is correct.

34. (b) Reation mechanism is as follows.

$$(CH_3)_2C=C(Br)_2 + HBr \longrightarrow$$
(*X*)

$$H-C(CH_3)_2-C(Br)_2-Br + Br-C(CH_3)_2-C(Br)_2-H$$

$$(Br)(CH_3)C=C(Br)(CH_3) + HBr \longrightarrow$$
(*Y*)

$$Br-C(Br)(CH_3)-C(Br)(CH_3)-H$$

Hence, correct option is (b).

35. (a) Reagents given in option (a) are suitable for reaction conversion.

I. $CH_3-CH_2-CH_2-CH=CH_2$ (Pent-1-ene)

$$+ BH_3 \longrightarrow CH_3-CH_2-CH_2-CH_2-CH_2-BH_2 \xrightarrow[OH^-]{H_2O_2}$$

$$CH_3-CH_2-CH_2-CH_2-CH_2-OH$$

1-pentanol (100%)

II. $CH_3-CH_2-CH_2-CH=CH_2$ (Pent-1-ene)

$$+ HBr \xrightarrow{C_6H_5CO_3H} CH_3-CH_2-CH_2-CH_2-CH_2Br$$

1-bromopentane (major)

$$\xrightarrow{Aq.\ KOH} CH_3-CH_2-CH_2-CH_2-CH_2-OH$$

1-pentanol (major)

Thus, option (a) is correct.

36. (a) For spontaneous reaction $\Delta G = \Delta H - T\Delta S$ (should be negative)

$$\therefore \quad T > \frac{\Delta H}{\Delta S}$$

$$T > \frac{49 \times 1000\ J/mol}{-40.0J/mol/K}$$

$$T > 1225\ K \text{ or } 952°C$$

37. (a) The balanced equation is

$$2MnO_4^- + 5C_2O_4^{2-} + 16H^+ \longrightarrow 2Mn^{2+} + 10CO_2 + 8H_2O$$

38. (c) Ambident nucleophiles are those nucleophiles that have two nucleophilic sites shown by arrows but one of them is used during reaction.

So, among the given options, NO_2^-, CN^- and $(CH_3CO_2)\overset{-}{C}H$ acts as an ambident nucleophile.

39. (c) The amount of energy needed to form various types of carbocations decreases in following order $[\overset{+}{C}H_3 > 1° > 2° > 3°]$ because the more stable the carbocation, the lesser the energy required to form the carbocation.

40. (d) Statement given in option (d) is incorrect. It is because bond angle is approximately 109°.

41. (a) Due to $p\pi$-$p\pi$ back bonding between the completely filled $n\pi$ orbital of halogens and vacant $2p$ orbital of boron the correct order of acidic strength will become

$BBr_3 > BCl_3 > BF_3$.

42. (a) At constant pressure, i.e. $\Delta p = 0$, the relation $\Delta H = \Delta U + p\Delta V$ is valid.

43. (b) Organic compounds which are volatile in steam can be purified by steam distillation. It is based on the fact that vaporisation of organic liquid takes place at lower temperature than its boiling point.

44. (b) As bond length decreases, bond strength increases.

Order of bond length is

$\alpha < \gamma < \beta$.

Hence, bond energy or bond strength order:

$\alpha > \gamma > \beta$

45. (b) $C_3—C_2$ bond is shorter than $C_4—C_3$ due to hyperconjugation while $C_2—C_1$ bond is the shortest.

NSS2 NEET Stepping Stones

1. (b) Using the formula for wavelength

$$\bar{v}_{max} = \frac{1}{\lambda_{min}}$$

$$= R_H Z^2 \left[\frac{1}{n_1^2} - \frac{1}{n_2^2}\right]$$

For the shortest wavelength of Lyman series.

$\because Z = 1, n_1 = 1, n_2 = \infty, \frac{1}{x} = R_H$

For the first line of Balmer series,

$n_1 = 2, n_2 = 3$

$$\bar{v} = \frac{1}{\lambda_{max}} = R_H Z^2 \left[\frac{1}{2^2} - \frac{1}{3^2}\right]$$

$$= \frac{1 \times 4}{x}\left[\frac{5}{36}\right]$$

$$\lambda_{max} = \frac{9x}{5}$$

Hence, option (b) is correct.

2. (b) The balanced redox equation is

$$4Fe + 10HNO_3 \longrightarrow 4Fe(NO_3)_2 + NH_4NO_3 + 3H_2O$$

Thus, the correct ratio of coefficients of HNO_3, $Fe(NO_3)_2$ and NH_4NO_3 respectively is 10 : 4 : 1.

3. (b) Statements given in I, III and V are correct while II and IV are incorrect.

I. C_2^{2-} (14) : $KK(\sigma 2s^2)(\sigma^* 2s^2)$ $(\pi 2p_x^2 = \pi 2p_y^2)\sigma 2p_z^2$

It is diamagnetic.

II. O_2 (16): $KK(\sigma 2s^2)(\sigma^* 2s^2)$ $(\sigma 2p_z^2)(\pi 2p_x^2 = \pi 2p_y^2)$

$(\pi^* 2p_x^1 = \pi^* 2p_y^1)$

$$\text{B.O.} = \frac{1}{2}(8-4) = \frac{4}{2} = 2$$

O_2^{2+} (14): $KK(\sigma 2s^2)(\sigma^* 2s^2)$ $(\sigma 2p_z^2)(\pi 2p_x^2 = \pi 2p_y^2)$

$$\text{B.O} = \frac{1}{2}(8-2)$$

$$= \frac{6}{2} = 3$$

As bond order of O_2^{2+} is greater than that of O_2 so, O_2^{2+} is expected to have a shorter bond length than O_2.

III. N_2^+ (13): $KK(\sigma 2s^2)(\sigma^* 2s^2)$ $(\pi 2p_x^2 = \pi 2p_y^2)\sigma 2p_z^1$

$$\text{B.O.} = \frac{1}{2}(7-2) = \frac{5}{2} = 2.5$$

N_2^- (15): $KK(\sigma 2s^2)(\sigma^* 2s^2)$ $(\pi 2p_x^2 = \pi 2p_y^2)\sigma 2p_z^2$

$(\pi^* 2p_x^1 = \pi^* 2p_y)$

$$\text{B.O.} \frac{1}{2}[8-3] = \frac{5}{2} = 2.5$$

Thus, N_2^+ and N_2^- have the same bond order.

IV. He_2^+ has lesser energy than two isolated He atoms as some energy is released during formation of He_2^+.

V. As, O_2 and N_2^{2-} have same number of electrons thus, they will have same bond order.

4. (a) The correct order (decreasing) of energy of 2s orbital for given atom is

$$E_{2s}(\text{H}) > E_{2s}(\text{Li}) > E_{2s}(\text{Na}) > E_{2s}(\text{K})$$

The reason is that as atomic number (nuclear charge) increase, all the orbitals are pulled closer to the nucleus. Thus, less will be its energy.

5. (d) The complete reaction is as follows,

Reduction (oxidising agent)

$$\underset{-2}{H_2S} + \underset{-1}{H_2O_2} \longrightarrow \underset{0}{S} + \underset{-2}{2H_2O}$$

Oxidation (reducing agent)

Hence, option (d) is correct.

6. (a) Both (A) and (R) are true and (R) is correct explanation of (A).

7. (d) At high temperature, styrene is liable to undergo polymerisation. Therefore to avoid polymerisation styrene is purified by distillation under reduced pressure.

Hence, option (d) is correct.

8. (b) $K_1 = \frac{[SO_3]}{[SO_2][O_2]^{1/2}}$,

$K_2 = \frac{[SO_2]^2 [O_2]}{[SO_3]^2}$

From above equations,

$K_2 = \frac{1}{K_1^2}$

or $K_1^2 = \frac{1}{K_2}$

Hence, option (b) is correct.

9. (a) Elements with high electronegativity usually have negative electron gain enthalpies.

For example, both N and Cl have an electronegativity of 3.0 but the electron gain enthalpy of N is positive while that of Cl is the highest with negative sign of electron gain enthalpy in the periodic table.

10. (c) $C + O_2 \longrightarrow CO_2$;

$\Delta H = -x$ kJ ...(i)

$2CO + O_2 \longrightarrow 2CO_2$;

$\Delta H = -y$ kJ ...(ii)

Formation of CO can be written as;

$C + \frac{1}{2}O_2 \longrightarrow CO;\ \Delta H = ?$

... (iii)

Divide Eq. (ii) by 2 because heat of formation is calculated for one mole of CO.

$CO + \frac{1}{2}O_2 \longrightarrow CO_2; \Delta H = -\frac{y}{2}$ kJ

... (iv)

On subtracting Eq. (iv) from (i) we get,

Thus, $\Delta H = -x - \left(\frac{-y}{2}\right) = \frac{y}{2} - x$

$\Rightarrow \frac{y - 2x}{2}$

Hence, option (c) is correct.

11. (b) Among the given statements, statement A and E are incorrect whereas B, C and D are correct.

The correct form of incorrect statements are,

- The greater the disorder in an isolated system, the higher is the entropy.
- The entropy change is inversely proportional to the temperature.

12. (c) Only 4 compounds among the given have same values of covalency and oxidation number.

PF_5, $PCl_5 \longrightarrow$ Covalency = 5,
Oxidation number = 5

$CO_2 \longrightarrow$ Covalency = 4,
Oxidation number = 4

$CH_4 \longrightarrow$ Covalency = 4,
Oxidation number = 4

$N_2O_5 \longrightarrow$ Covalency = 4
Oxidation state = 5

Hence, option (c) is correct.

13. (c) From the relation,

$T = \frac{(\Delta H - \Delta G)}{\Delta S}$

Assuming reaction is at equilibrium

$T = \frac{\Delta H}{\Delta S} = \frac{400}{0.2} = 2000$ K

For the reaction to be spontaneous, ΔG must be negative.

So, for the given reaction to be spontaneous T should be greater than 2000 K.

14. (a) The electronic configuration of N_2^+ is given by

N_2^+ (13 electrons) :

$\sigma 1s^2 \sigma^* 1s^2 \sigma 2s^2 \sigma^* 2s^2 \pi 2p_x^2$

$= \pi 2p_y^2 \sigma 2p_z^1$

15. (b) Both (A) and (R) are true but (R) is not the correct explanation of (A). It is because HgI_2 combines with KI to form the soluble complex, K_2HgI_4.

16. (d) The reaction sequence involved is

$MnO_2 + 2e^- \longrightarrow Mn^{2+}$

n-factor = 2

Eq. wt. of $MnO_2 = \frac{\text{molecular mass}}{2}$

Excess of $C_2O_4^{2-} = 18.28$

$\times 0.1232 \times 5$ mEq of MnO_4^-

$= 11.26$ meq of $C_2O_4^{2-}$

Total $C_2O_4^{2-} = 50 \times 0.2750 \times 2$

mEq = 27.5 mEq

Reacted $C_2O_4^{2-} = 27.5 - 11.26$

$= 16.24$ mEq of $C_2O_4^{2-}$

or = 16.24 mEq of

$MnO_2 = 16.24 \times 10^{-3}$ eq of MnO_2

Moles of $MnO_2 = \frac{16.24 \times 10^{-3}}{2}$

$= 8.12 \times 10^{-3}$ mol

17. (b) $[PO_4^{3-}] = 6.6 \times 10^{-7}$ M

$[Ca^{2+}] = \frac{3}{2} \times [PO_4^{3-}]$

$= \frac{3}{2} \times 6.6 \times 10^{-7}$

$= 9.9 \times 10^{-7}$ M

$\approx 10 \times 10^{-7}$ M

$K_{sp}[Ca_3(PO_4)_2]$

$= [Ca^{2+}]^3 [PO_4^{3-}]^2$

$\Rightarrow K_{sp} = (10 \times 10^{-7})^3\ (6.6 \times 10^{-7})^2$

$K_{sp} = 4.356 \times 10^{-31}$

18. (c) Activating groups like $-OCH_3$, $-OH$ etc, activates the benzene ring towards electrophilic substitution while deactivating groups like NO_2, COOH etc deactivates the benzene ring towards electrophilic substitution.

Thus, the order of reaction with electrophile is as follows.

OCH_3-benzene (X) > benzene (Y) > NO_2-benzene (Z)

19. (d) Using law of dilution

(HCl) $V_1N_1 = V_2N_2$ (NaOH)

$V_1 \times 0.5 = 10 \times 0.2$

$V_1 = 4$ mL

Vol. of HCl reacted with $Ba(OH)_2 = 10 - 4 = 6$ ml

$$\underset{\text{of }Ba(OH)_2}{\text{Volume}} \times \underset{(HCl)}{\text{Normality}} = \frac{W}{E}$$

$$\frac{6}{1000} \times 0.5 = \frac{W}{85.5} \Rightarrow W = \frac{51.3}{200}$$

$$\% \text{ of } Ba(OH)_2 = \frac{51.3}{200 \times 12.825} \times 100 = 2\%$$

20. (a) The compounds that follow Huckel's rule is $(4n+2)\pi e^-$ will show aromatic character.

Benzene: $(4n+2)\pi e^- = 6$, $n = 1$, Aromatic

Pyrrole (N–H): $(4n+2)\pi e^- = 6$, $n = 1$, Aromatic

21. (b) Statement I is correct but statement II is incorrect. The correct form of statement II is,

In a closed vessel, $\Delta U = \Delta H$ if pressure inside the calorimeter remains constant.

Hence, option (b) is correct.

22. (c) The complete reaction involved is as follows

$$C_2H_2 \xrightarrow[Hg^{2+}/H^+]{H_2O} \underset{(A)}{CH_3CHO}$$

$$CH_2{=}CH_2 \xrightarrow[200-400°C]{\frac{1}{2}O_2,\ Ag} \underset{(B)}{CH_2{-}CH_2 \text{ (epoxide, bridged by O)}}$$

Thus, compound *A* and *B* are isomers of each other.

23. (a) $K_p = \dfrac{(p_I)^2}{p_{I_2}}$

$$= \frac{\left(10^5 \times \dfrac{40}{100}\right)^2}{\dfrac{60}{100} \times 10^5}$$

$$= 2.67 \times 10^4$$

24. (d) Among the given statements only A, B and E are correct. Statements C and D are incorrect.

The correct form of these statements are

- The mixture adsorbed on adsorbent is placed on the top of adsorbent.
- In paper chromatography, both mobile phase and stationary phase are liquid.

Hence, option (d) is correct.

25. (a) The correct match is A-IV, B-I, C-II, D-III.

- He has highest ionisation energy due to inert gas configuration.
- Cl has highest electron affinity among the given atoms.
- Li is strongest reducing agent among the given atoms.
- Ca is the most electropositive element among the given atoms.

26. (a) Using formula

$\Delta G° = -2.303\,RT \log K_p$

$\Delta G° = -2303 \times 2 \times 300 \times \log 10^{-8}$

On solving, we get

$\therefore \Delta G° = 11054.4$ cal $= 11.05$ kcal

27. (d) Both Statement I and Statement II are correct. The linear triatomic molecules of the type $B{-}A{-}B$ e.g. CO_2 have no dipole moment, not because the individual C=O bonds are non-polar but because the two bond moments (polarity) cancel each other.

Therefore, geometry of molecules can be predicted by the value of dipole moment.

28. (c) *tert*-butoxide is stronger base, but weaker nucleophile than ethoxide.

29. (c) We know that from the reaction $H_2 + Cl_2 \longrightarrow 2HCl$, the ratio of the volume of gaseous reactants and products is in agreement with their molar ratio.

The ratio of $H_2 : Cl_2 : HCl$ volumes is 1 : 1 : 2 which is the same as their molar ratio.

Thus, volume of gas is directly related to the number of moles.

Therefore, the statement I is incorrect but statement II is correct.

30. (a) Among the given elements, Cr has $[Ar]3d^5, 4s^1$ configuration and thus second electron is removed from 3*d*-subshell. Hence, it will have the highest second ionisation enthalpy.

31. (c) When ethyne reacts with 2HBr, it forms ethyne bromide followed by 1, 1-dibromoethane as a product when this product react with alc. KOH followed by $NaNH_2$, it undergoes elimination reaction to form ethyne as product.

$$H{-}C{\equiv}C{-}H + H{-}Br \longrightarrow \underset{[A]}{H_2C{=}CHBr} + H{-}Br \longrightarrow \underset{[B]}{CH_3{-}CHBr_2} \xrightarrow{\text{Alc. KOH}} \underset{[C]}{H_2C{=}CHBr} \xrightarrow{NaNH_2} \underset{\substack{[D]\\ \text{Ethyne}}}{H{-}C{\equiv}C{-}H}$$

32. (d) The correct match is A-IV, B-II, C-I, D-III.

33. (d) Among the given compounds, only 4 compounds namely N_2O_5, Cl_2O_7, SO_3 and P_4O_6 are acidic oxide.

Al_2O_3 and ZnO are amphoteric and N_2O is neutral oxide.

Hence, option (d) is correct.

34. (a) The correct match is A-III, B-II, C-IV, D-I.

Atomic number	Symbol
105	Unp
107	Uns
109	Une
110	Uun

Hence, option (a) is correct.

35. (b) Among the given statements, Statement (b) is incorrect, while all others are correct.

The correct form of statement (b) is, Bonding molecular orbitals are denoted by σ, π etc.

36. (a) Enthalpy of vaporisation of liquid water can be calculated by Equation (2) – equation (1)

$\Delta H = -241.84 - (-285.77)$

$= 43.93 \text{ kJ mol}^{-1}$

Hence, option (a) is correct.

37. (a) Among the given statements A, B and C are correct while D and E are incorrect. Their correct form is

- Effective nuclear charge generally increases as one moves left to right across a period in the periodic table.
- The total number of nodes in an orbital is the sum of angular nodes and radial nodes present in the atomic orbital.

Hence, option (a) is correct.

38. (c) SO_4^{2-} has sp^3 hybridisation with tetrahedral structure.

Hence, option (c) is correct.

39. (c) Electronegativity difference between N (3.0) and Cl (3.0) is zero and hence N—Cl bonds are non-polar.

As a result, the overall dipole moment of NCl_3 molecule and its direction is just the dipole moment of the lone pair of electrons.

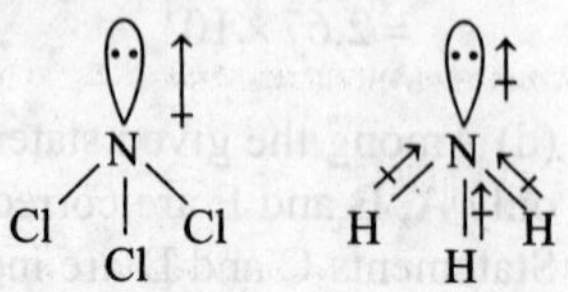

On the other hand, N—Br (3.0 – 2.8), N—I (3.0 – 2.5) and N—H (3.0 – 2.1) are polar and hence contribute towards the overall dipole moment of the respective molecules.

Since, the E.N. difference is highest in case of N—H bonds, therefore, NH_3 has the highest dipole moment.

40. (c) The given reaction is as follows,

$$\frac{1}{2}I_2(s) + \frac{1}{2}Cl_2(g) \longrightarrow ICl(g)$$

We are given

(i) $Cl_2(g) \longrightarrow 2Cl(g)$; $\Delta H = 242.3 \text{ kJ/mol}$

(ii) $I_2(g) \longrightarrow 2I(g)$; $\Delta H = 151 \text{ kJ/mol}$

(iii) $ICl(g) \longrightarrow I(g) + Cl(g)$; $\Delta H = 211.3 \text{ kJ/mol}$

(iv) $I_2(s) \longrightarrow I_2(g)$; $\Delta H = 62.8 \text{ kJ/mol}$

$\frac{1}{2}$(ii) + $\frac{1}{2}$(i) – (iii) + $\frac{1}{2}$(iv) gives the required equation.

$$\therefore \Delta H = \frac{1}{2}(151) + \frac{1}{2}(242.3) - 211.3 + \frac{1}{2}(62.8)$$

$$\Delta H \approx 16.8 \text{ kJ/mol}$$

41. (c) $\Delta G^\circ = 14.4 \text{ kJ/mol}$

$= 14.4 \times 10^3 \text{ J/mol}$

$\Delta G^\circ = -RT \ln K_C$

$\ln K_C = -14.4 \times 10^3 \text{ J/mol} / (8.314 \text{ J mol}^{-1} \text{K}^{-1} \times 298 \text{ K})$

$\ln K_C = -5.812$

$\log K_C = \frac{-5.812}{2.303}$

$\log K_C = -2.524$

$K_C = 2.99 \times 10^{-3}$

42. (c) Since $-I$ effect of —Cl is stronger than its $+R$ effect, therefore, it deactivates the ring towards electrophilic substitution.

However, due to $+I$ and hyperconjugation effect of the —CH_3 group, electron density increases at *o*-positions.

Therefore, electrophilic substitution will be the fastest at position 4.

43. (c) The half reaction are

(i) $MnO_4^- + 8H^+ + 5e^- \longrightarrow Mn^{2+} + 4H_2O$ (Reduction)

(ii) $H_2C_2O_4 \longrightarrow 2CO_2 + 2H^+ + 2e^-$ (Oxidation)

To get balanced net reaction, multiply (i) by 2 and (ii) by 5, then on adding, we get

$2MnO_4^- + 5H_2C_2O_4 + 6H^+ \longrightarrow 2Mn^{2+} + 10CO_2 + 8H_2O$

Thus,

$x = 2, y = 5, m = 2, n = 10$

$x + y + m + n = 2 + 5 + 2 + 10$

∴ Sum of x, y, m and n is 19.

44. (c) Lower the electronegativity, higher is the tendency of the atom/group to donate its pair of electrons and hence higher is nucleophilicity. Now among F(4.0), O (3.5), N (3.0) and C (2.5), C has the lowest electronegativity and hence CH_3^- has highest nucleophilicity.

45. (b) The wavelength is given by

$\lambda = \frac{c}{\nu}$ then $\nu = \frac{c}{\lambda}$

$$3.29 \times 10^{15}\left[\frac{1}{(3)^2} - \frac{1}{n^2}\right] = \frac{3 \times 10^8}{\lambda}$$

$$\Rightarrow \frac{3.29 \times 10^{15}}{3 \times 10^8}\left[\frac{1}{9} - \frac{1}{n^2}\right] = \frac{1}{\lambda}$$

[Given, $\lambda = 1285\,\text{nm}$]

$$\left[\frac{1}{9} - \frac{1}{n^2}\right] = \frac{3 \times 10^8}{1285 \times 10^{-9} \times 3.29 \times 10^{15}}$$

$$\frac{1}{9} - \frac{1}{n^2} = 0.0709$$

$$\frac{1}{n^2} = \frac{1}{9} - 0.0709$$

$$\frac{1}{n^2} = 0.04 \Rightarrow n^2 = 25$$

$$n = 5$$

Hence, the value of 'n' is 5.

NSS3 NEET Stepping Stones

1. (b) The correct order is

$S_1 > S_3 > S_2 > S_4$

Solubility in water is highest due to high dielectric constant of water. In $CaCl_2$, solubility is lesser than that in NaCl. This is due to common ion effect. $CaCl_2$ gives 0.02 M Cl^- ions while NaCl gives 0.01 M Cl^- ions.

Hence, solubility in NaCl is higher. Finally in $AgNO_3$, solubility is the least as $AgNO_3$ reacts with AgCl to give back AgCl hence concentration of Cl^- remains constant.

The common ion effect results in the decreased solubility of a salt in a solution that contains one of the salt's constituent ions.

2. (a) $\frac{1}{2}N_2 + \frac{3}{2}Cl_2 \longrightarrow NCl_3$

Operate :

$\frac{1}{2}$ Eq. (ii) + Eq. (i) $- \frac{3}{2}$ Eq. (iii)

We get $\Delta H_f = \frac{1}{2}[-\Delta H_2] + [-\Delta H_1] - \frac{3}{2}[\Delta H_3]$

$$\Delta H_f = -\Delta H_1 - \frac{\Delta H_2}{2} - \frac{3}{2}\Delta H_3$$

Hence, option (a) is correct.

3. (a) The shape of NO_2^+, NO_3^- and NH_4^+ are linear, trigonal planar and tetrahedral respectively.

Thus, the hybridisation of atomic orbitals of nitrogen in these species are sp, sp^2 and sp^3 respectively.

4. (c) Among the given statements, only A, B and E are correct, while C and D are incorrect. Their correct forms are

- The solution is concentrated to get a nearly saturated solution.
- On cooling the solution, the pure compound crystallises out.

5. (a) $2Al(s) + 6HCl(aq) \longrightarrow 2Al^{3+}(aq) + 6Cl^-(aq) + 3H_2(g)$

Thus, 6 moles of HCl produced $3H_2$ at STP $= 3 \times 22.4$ L

$\therefore$ 1 mole of HCl will produce H_2 at STP $= \frac{3 \times 22.4}{6} = 11.2$ L

Hence, option (a) is correct.

6. (a) The correct match is : A-II, B-I, C-III, D-IV.

7. (a) A disproportionation reaction is a type of redox reaction where a single substance is simultaneously oxidised and reduced.

In the given reaction of chlorine with water, chlorine undergoes both oxidation and reduction.

8. (c) Among the given statements only A, C and E are incorrect, while B and D are correct.

The corrected form of A, C and E are

- As we move down the group ionisation potential decreases as the atomic number increases.
- Z with atomic number 55 has the lowest ionisation potential.
- X and Y with atomic number are 19 and 37 have equal electronegativity value on Pauling scale i.e. (0.8).

9. (a) Among the given statements, B, D and E are correct, while A and C are incorrect. Their corrected from are as

- In the hydrocarbon, $CH_2 = C = CHCH_3$ total 9σ and 2π bonds are present.
- The state of hybridisation of C_2 and C_3 carbon in the hydrocarbon $\underset{1}{CH_2} = \underset{2}{C} = \underset{3}{CH} — \underset{4}{CH_3}$ is sp and sp^2. Hence, option (a) is correct.

10. (a) Among the given functions, only 3 functions mainly entropy, enthalpy and Gibbs free energy, depend upon the initial and final state of the system i.e., they are state function.

Hence, option (a) is correct.

11. (c) The correct match is, A-III, B-I, C-II, D-IV

(A) $NaNO_2$ is a salt of weak acid and strong base

$$pH = \frac{1}{2}[pK_w + pK_a + \log C]$$

(B) $C_6H_5NH_2^+ \bar{C}l$ is a salt of weak base and strong acid.

$$pH = \frac{1}{2}[pK_w - pK_b - \log C]$$

(C) NH_4CN is a salt of weak acid and weak base.

$$pH = \frac{1}{2}[pK_w + pK_a - pK_b]$$

(D) HCN is a weak acid

$$pH = \frac{1}{2}[pK_a - \log C]$$

Hence, option (c) is correct.

12. (b) X is $3d$ and Y is $3s$. Due to this, the energy of $3s < 3d$. Hence, option (b) is correct.

13. (b) From the reaction,

$$\begin{array}{lccc} & N_2 & + \; 3H_2 \longrightarrow & 2NH_3 \\ \text{B.E} & N \equiv N & 3H—H & 6N—H \\ \text{kJ mol}^{-1} & 945 & 3 \times 436 & 6 \times 391 \end{array}$$

$$\Delta H = \Sigma \text{B.E}_{(\text{Reactant})} - \Sigma \text{B.E}_{(\text{Product})}$$
$$= 945 + 3(436) - 6(391)$$
$$= -93 \text{ kJ/mol}$$

Hence, option (b) is correct.

14. (b) Ethene reacts with bromine to form 1, 2-dibromoethane.

$$\underset{\text{Ethene}}{C_2H_4} + Br_2 \xrightarrow[\text{solvent}]{\text{Non-aqueous}} \underset{\text{1, 2-dibromoethane}}{H—\overset{Br}{\underset{H}{C}}—\overset{Br}{\underset{H}{C}}—H}$$

15. (a) Since, Ammonium hydroxide is 50% neutralised, hence [Salt] = [Base]

$$pOH = pK_b + \log_{10}\left[\frac{\text{Salt}}{\text{Base}}\right]$$
$$= 4.74 + \log_{10}[1] = 4.74$$
$$pH = 14 - pOH$$
$$= 14 - 4.74 = 9.26$$
$$= 926 \times 10^{-2}$$

16. (d) Given, $E_1 = -2.17 \times 10^{-11}$ ergs per atom

$$= -2.17 \times 10^{-18} \text{ J/atom}$$
$$E_n = \frac{E}{n^2}$$
$$E_3 = \frac{-2.17 \times 10^{-18}}{3^2} \text{ J/atom}$$
$$\Delta E = E_3 - E_1$$
$$\Rightarrow \frac{-2.17 \times 10^{-18}}{9} - (-2.17 \times 10^{-18})$$
$$= 1.93 \times 10^{-18} \text{ J/atom}$$
$$\Delta E = \frac{hc}{\lambda}$$
$$\Rightarrow \lambda = \frac{hc}{\Delta E}$$
$$= \frac{6.626 \times 10^{-34} \times 3 \times 10^8}{1.93 \times 10^{-18}}$$
$$= 10.29 \times 10^{-8} \text{ m}$$
$$= 1029 \text{ Å}$$

17. (c) 1mole of H_2 contains $= N_A$ molecules or $2 \times N_A$ atoms.

18. (b) At STP condition, equal volume of all gases contain equal number of molecules.

Hence, number of moles

$CO_2 = O_2 = NH_3$

Hence, option (b) is correct.

19. (a) The correct match is A-III, B-II, C-I, D-IV.

(A) $\Delta H < 0$, i.e. – ve (favours)
$\Delta S < 0$, i.e. – ve (opposes)

$\Delta G = \Delta H - T\Delta S$. If T is low, $\Delta G = -$ ve (spontaneous)

If T is high, $\Delta G = +$ ve (non-spontaneous).

(B) $\Delta H > 0$, i.e. + ve (opposes), $\Delta S > 0$, i.e. + ve (favours)

ΔG will be – ve at high temperature but + ve at low temperature.

(C) $\Delta H < 0$, i.e. – ve (favours), $\Delta S > 0$, i.e., + ve (favours)

Hence, reaction is always spontaneous.

(D) $\Delta H > 0$, i.e. + ve (opposses), $\Delta S < 0$, i.e. – ve (opposes)

Hence, reaction is non-spontaneous at all temperature.

20. (b) Molality of solution

$$= \frac{\text{Mass of solute}}{\text{Mass of solvent (kg)}}$$

3 M NaCl solution means 3 moles of NaCl are present in 1 L of the solution.

Mass of 1 L of the solution
$$= \text{Volume} \times \text{Density}$$
$$= 1000 \times 1.25$$
$$= 1250 \text{ g}$$

Mass of 3 mole of NaCl (solute)
$$= 3 \times 58.5 \text{ g} = 175.5 \text{ g}$$

$\therefore$ Mass of solvent
$$= 1250\ 175.5$$
$$= 1.0745 \text{ kg}$$
$$\therefore \text{Molality} = \frac{3 \text{ mol}}{1.0745 \text{ kg}}$$
$$= 2.79 \text{ mol kg}^{-1}$$
$$\simeq 2.8 \text{ m}$$

21. (c) Among the given statements, A, C and D are correct whereas B and E are incorrect. Their correct form is;

A spontaneous process is a process which takes place by itself.

Spontaneous reaction occurs at constant temperature and pressure, so that $\Delta H < 0$ and $\Delta S > 0$.

Hence, option (c) is correct.

22. (b) $Ag_2CO_3(s) \rightleftharpoons 2Ag^+(aq) + CO_3^{2-}(aq)$

$K_{sp} = [Ag^+]^2 [CO_3^{2-}] = K$ for the reaction

($\because Ag_2CO_3$ is solid)

$$\Delta G = -2.303RT \log K$$
$$= -2.303RT \log K_{sp}$$
$$63300 = -2.303 \times 8.314 \times 298 \times \log K_{sp}$$
$$K_{sp} = 8.12 \times 10^{-12} \simeq 8 \times 10^{-12}.$$

23. (c) For $AB \rightleftharpoons \underset{10^{-3}\,M}{\underset{S}{A^+}} + \underset{S}{B^-}$

$K_{sp} = [A^+][B^-] = 10^{-8} M^2$

$[A^+] = S = 10^{-3}$ M

$[B^+] = S = 10^{-5}$ M

Therefore, when B^- ions concentration is greater than 10^{-5} M. AB will precipitate out.

Hence, option (c) is correct.

24. (d) $H_2(g) + Cl_2(g) \longrightarrow 2HCl(g)$

$\Delta S = \Sigma S_{(product)} - \Delta S_{(reactant)}$

$= 2 \times S\,(HCl) - [S(H_2) + S(Cl_2)]$

$= 2 \times 186.7 - (130.6 + 223.0)$

$= 19.8$ J/K mol

Hence, option (d) is correct.

25. (b) Pyridinium hydrochloride is a salt of weak base and strong acid.

Hence, $pH = -\frac{1}{2}[\log K_w - \log K_b + \log C]$

i.e. $3.44 = -\frac{1}{2}[-14 - \log K_b + \log(2 \times 10^{-2})]$

or $\log K_b = -8.82$

$K_b = 1.5 \times 10^{-9}$

26. (d) When $m = 2$, l cannot be 0 or 1. Thus, the statement given in option (d) is incorrect.

Hence, option (d) is correct answer.

27. (c) The process at $O \rightarrow D$ completed at constant volume so $\Delta V = 0$.

Work done,

$W = p\Delta V = 0$,

Then, $\Delta U = q - W$

$\Delta U = q - 0$

$\Delta U = q$

Hence, option (c) is correct.

28. (d) Statement given in *a*, *b* and *c*. are correct while *d* is incorrect.

29. (c) Ionisation energy is the energy required to remove an electron from the outer shell of an atom.

Since, on moving from left to right in a period, size decreases, thus larger amount of energy is required to remove an electron. i.e. ionisation energy increases.

Although, the size of O atom is smaller as compared to N but the ionisation energy of N is higher.

This is because in case of N, the electron is to be removed from stable half filled $2p^3$-orbital.

Hence, the correct order is

$N > O < F$.

30. (c) $O_2^{2-}(18\,e^-)$:

$KK\sigma\, 2s^2 \sigma^* 2s^2 \sigma 2p_z^{\,2}$
$(\pi 2p_x^{\,2}\, \pi 2p_y^{\,2})(\pi^* 2p_x^{\,2}\, \pi^* 2p_y^{\,2})$

$\text{Bond order (B.O)} = \frac{8-6}{2} = 1$

$B_2\,10e^-$: $KK\sigma\, 2s^2\ \sigma^* 2s^2\ (\pi 2p_x^1\ \pi 2p_y^{\,1})$

$\text{B.O.} = \frac{4-2}{2} = 1$

Therefore, O_2^{2-} and B_2 have identical bond order.

The bond order of rest of molecules or ions like, CO, O_2^- and N_2^+ is 3, 1.5 and 2.5 respectively.

31. (c) Equal number of equivalents produces the same amount of hydrogen.

$\frac{1.0}{20.0} = \frac{1.63}{\text{Equivalent weight of } M}$

Equivalent weight of M

$= \frac{1.63 \times 20.0}{1.0}$

$= 32.6$

Hence, equivalent weight of M is 32.6.

Option (c) is correct.

32. (a) The correct match is
A-II, B-III, C-IV, D-I.

33. (c) For principal energy level N, $n = 4$ maximum number of electrons accommodate in an energy level.

$= 2n^2 = 2 \times 4^2 = 32$

Hence, option (c) is correct.

34. (c) Statements given in a, b and d are correct, while option (c) is incorrect statement. It's correct form is, Singlet carbene acts as a electrophile.

35. (c) Statement I is incorrect but statement II is correct. The correct form of statement I is,

Rotation about C—C single bond in ethane is not completely free. There is a small energy barrier which is to be overcome for this rotation. Hence, option (c) is correct.

36. (c) Percentage of C

$= \frac{12}{44} \times \frac{\text{Weight of } CO_2}{\text{Weight of compound}} \times 100$

$= \frac{12}{44} \times \frac{0.66}{0.30} \times 100 = 60\%$

$\therefore$ Percentage of H = 100 − Percentage of C

$= 100 - 60 = 40\%$

37. (b) In gallium, the crystal structure is different suggesting that Ga consist of discrete Ga_2 molecule.

Thus, its melting point is lowest. It exists as liquid, from 30°C upto 2000°C and hence is used at high temperature.

38. (c) $M + \frac{1}{2}N_2 \xrightarrow{\Delta} MN \xrightarrow{3H_2O} M(OH)_3 + NH_3$

Mg is of group 2.

Thus, B and Al can be the possible element.

39. (d) III and IV are resonance stabilised as negative charge is in conjugation with double bond, also 1° carbanion is more stable than 2° carbanion.

40. (c)

$$\text{2-methylbutane} \xrightarrow[\text{Light}]{Br_2} \text{2-bromo-2-methylbutane}$$

$$\xrightarrow{\overset{+}{Na}\overset{-}{O}CH_2CH_3/CH_3CH_2OH} \text{2-methylbut-2-ene}$$

$$\xrightarrow[\text{(ii) } H_2O_2, OH^-]{\text{(i) } B_2H_6} \text{3-methylbutan-2-ol (OH)}$$

41. (b) $pK_a = -\log K_a$

pK_a is maximum means least acidic or maximum basic. Thus, —NH_2 group.

42. (a) Hydration takes place such that OH-group goes to least substituted carbon.

Addition is *trans* with $B_2H_6/H_2O_2, OH^-$.

43. (c) Among the given options, Benzyl alcohol and *o*-cresol are functional and positional isomer of each other.

$C_6H_5CH_2—OH$ and $o\text{-}CH_3C_6H_4OH$

44. (d) The energy of an individual photon depends only on its frequency and not on the intensity of the light beam. Thus, as only intensity is doubled keeping wavelength constant thus, number of photons (y) will be doubled and energy (z) will remain same.

45. (a) $\lambda = \frac{h}{mv}$; when v is same

$$\lambda \propto \frac{1}{m}$$

Thus, the order of wavelength is electron > hydrogen > helium > neon.

NSS4 NEET Stepping Stones

1. (b) For the reaction,

$$Ca(OH)_2(s) \rightleftharpoons \underset{S}{Ca^{2+}(aq)} + \underset{2S}{2OH^-(aq)}$$

(where, S = solubility)

$$K_{sp} = [Ca^{2+}][\bar{O}H]^2 = S(2S)^2 \quad \dots \text{(i)}$$

Given, pH = 8

We know that, pH + pOH = 14

$\therefore$ pOH = 14 − 8 = 6

$$pOH = -\log[\bar{O}H]$$

$$6 = -\log[\bar{O}H]$$

or $[\bar{O}H] = 10^{-6}$

From above equation,

$[OH^-] = 2S = 10^{-6}$

$$\therefore \quad S = \frac{10^{-6}}{2}$$

On substituting the value of 'S' in Eq. (i), we get

$$K_{sp} = 4S^3 = 4\left(\frac{10^{-6}}{2}\right)^3$$

$$= \frac{4}{8} \times 10^{-18}$$

$$K_{sp} = 0.5 \times 10^{-18}$$

2. (c) Statement I is incorrect but Statement II is correct. The correct form of statement I is Reaction of *tert*-butyl chloride with Na gives 2-methyl prop-1-ene.

$$(CH_3)_3CCl \xrightarrow[\text{Dry ether}/\Delta]{Na} (CH_3)_2C{=}CH_2$$

3. (c) Among the given statements, option (c) is incorrect while other are correct.

HF is more polar than HBr as electronegativity of F is more than that of Br.

4. (d) (A) is false but (R) is true. The correct form of (A) is

PbI_4 is not a stable compound. It is highly reactive and decomposes easily.

$$Pb^{4+} \xrightarrow{+2e^-} Pb^{2+} \text{ (due to inert pair effect)}$$

$$2I^- \xrightarrow{-2e^-} I_2 \text{ (I^- acts as reducing agent)}$$

5. (c) The balanced chemical equation is,

$$2MnO + 5PbO_2 + 10HNO_3 \longrightarrow 2HMnO_4 + 5Pb(NO_3)_2 + 4H_2O$$

$$x = 2, y = 5, z = 10$$

$$\Rightarrow x + y + z = 17$$

$$2(x + y + z) = 17 \times 2 = 34$$

6. (c) $SO_2(g) + \frac{1}{2}O_2(g) \rightleftharpoons SO_3(g)$; $K_p = 4 \times 10^{-3}$ atm

$$SO_3 \rightleftharpoons SO_2(g) + \frac{1}{2}O_2(g);$$

$$K'_p = \frac{1}{K_p} = \frac{1}{4 \times 10^{-3}} \text{ atm}$$

For reaction,

$$2SO_3 \rightleftharpoons 2SO_2 + O_2(g)$$

$$K''_p = (K'_p)^2$$

$$\Rightarrow \left[\frac{1}{4 \times 10^{-3}}\right]^2 = 6.25 \times 10^4 \text{ atm}$$

7. (b) % N is given by formula

$$\% N = \frac{1.4 \times M \times V \times B}{\text{Mass of substance taken}}$$

where, M = molarity, V = volume, B = Basicity of acid

$$= \frac{1.4 \times 1 \times 10 \times 2}{0.5}$$

$\% N = 56$

8. (a) Given,

$As_2S_3 + H^+ + NO_3^- \longrightarrow NO + H_2O + AsO_4^{3-} + SO_4^{2-}$

On balancing the As_2S_3 part of reaction,

O.S O.S — O.S — O.S
+3 −2 — +5 — +6

$$As_2S_3 \longrightarrow 2AsO_4^{3-} + 3SO_4^{2-}$$

$$\text{Equivalent weight} = \frac{\text{Molecular mass}}{\text{Valency factor}}$$

Valency factor = 2× change in oxidation state of As + 3× change in oxidation state of S

$$= 2 \times (5-3) + 3 \times [6-(-2)]$$
$$= 2 \times 2 + 3 \times 8 = 28$$

$$\text{Equivalent weight} = \frac{M}{28}$$

9. (a) $A(g) + B(g) \rightleftharpoons 2C(g)$

	$A(g)$	$B(g)$	$2C(g)$
Initial conc.	3 M	1 M	0
At infinity	$3-\alpha$	$1-\alpha$	2α
	$3-\frac{1}{3}$	$1-\frac{1}{3}$	$\frac{2}{3}$

$$K_C = \frac{[C]^2}{[A][B]}$$

$$\Rightarrow K_C = \frac{(2/3)^2}{(8/3)(2/3)} = 0.25$$

10. (c) (A) is true but (R) is false. The correct form of (R) is

Due to intramolecular hydrogen bonding in *o*-nitrophenol, it is more volatile than *p*-nitrophenol.

11. (b) From the Hess's law

$$\Delta H_{\text{reaction}} = \Sigma \Delta H_{\text{product}} - \Sigma \Delta H_{\text{reactant}} \quad ...(i)$$

$$\Delta H_{\text{reaction}} = [\Delta H_f^\circ(CO) + \Delta H_f^\circ(H_2O)] - [\Delta H_f^\circ(CO_2) + \Delta H_f^\circ(H_2)]$$

$$= [-110.5 + (-241.8)] - [-393.5 + 0]$$

$$= 41.2 \text{ kJ/mol}$$

12. (a) Entropy change n moles of ideal gas in isothermal expansion is given by

$$\Delta S = 2.303 nR \log \frac{V_2}{V_1} \quad ...(i)$$

Substituting the values,

$n = 2$

$V_2 = 100 \text{ dm}^3$

$V_1 = 10 \text{ dm}^3$

$$\Delta S = 2.303 \times 2 \times 8.314 \times \log \left[\frac{100}{10}\right]$$

$$\Delta S = 38.3 \text{ J/mol K}$$

13. (b) According to Bohr's postulate, angular momentum is given by

$$l = \frac{nh}{2\pi} \quad ...(i)$$

$$3.1652 \times 10^{-34} = \frac{n \times 6.626 \times 10^{-34}}{2\pi}$$

$$\Rightarrow \quad n = 3 \quad ...(ii)$$

Thus, the electron is transitioning from energy level 3.

Now, wave number is given by

$$\bar{\nu} = RZ^2 \left[\frac{1}{n_1^2} - \frac{1}{n_2^2}\right] \quad ...(iii)$$

For $n_1 = 2$ and $n_2 = 3, Z = 2$

$$\bar{\nu} = RZ^2 \left[\frac{1}{2^2} - \frac{1}{3^2}\right]$$

$$\bar{\nu} = \frac{5}{9} R$$

14. (b) Statement I is correct but Statement II is incorrect. The correct form of statement II is

The bond enthalpies of the two O—H bonds in H—O—H are not equal. This is becuase electronic environment around O is not same after breakage of one O—H bonds.

15. (a) Electron affinity usually increases from left to right in a periodic table. But electron affinity of N is less than both C and O because N have half-filled electronic configuration. Hence, it oppsses the addition of incoming electron.

Thus, the correct order will be $C > N < O < F$.

16. (d) The balanced chemical equation is given by

$$CH_4(g) + 2O_2(g) \longrightarrow CO_2(g) + H_2O(g)$$

So, 2 moles or 64 g of O_2 gives 44 g of CO_2

$\therefore$ 16 g O_2 will produce 11 g of CO_2

17. (a) The molarity of solution after mixing is obtained by formula

$$\text{Molarity} = \frac{M_1V_1 + M_2V_2}{V_1 + V_2} \quad ...(i)$$

Given that $V_1 = 750 \text{ mL}$, $V_2 = 250 \text{ mL}$

$M_1 = 0.5 \text{ M}, M_2 = 2 \text{ M}$

Substituting the values in Eq. (i)

$$\text{Molarity} = \frac{750 \times 0.5 + 250 \times 2}{750 + 250}$$

$$= \frac{875}{1000}$$

$$\text{Molarity} = 0.875 \text{ M}$$

18. (c) We know that $r \propto \frac{n^2}{Z}$ for hydrogen $Z = 1$ as $r \propto n^2$

$$\therefore \quad r_1 \propto n_1^2, r_2 \propto n_2^2$$

$$\frac{r_1}{r_2} = \frac{n_1^2}{n_2^2} = \frac{(3)^2}{(4)^2} = \frac{9}{16}$$

19. (b) Among the given compounds, SF_6 has sp^3d^2-hybridisation, leading to an octahedral geometry with six bonding pairs around the central sulphur atom.

While PCl_5, ClF_3 and PCl_3 have sp^3d, sp^3d and sp^3-hybridisation respectively.

20. (b) Enthalpy change will become negative by reversing a reaction. If ΔH is the enthalpy change for the forward reaction, then $-\Delta H$ is the enthalpy change for the reverse reaction.

21. (c) The reaction involved is

$$CH_3COOH \rightleftharpoons CH_3COO^- + H^+$$
$$C - C\alpha \quad C\alpha \quad C\alpha$$

Let the concentration of acetic acid is C.

$$K_\alpha = 1.8 \times 10^{-5}$$
$$= \frac{C\alpha \times C\alpha}{C(1-\alpha)} = C\alpha^2 \text{ (as } 1 >>> \alpha)$$
$$\text{or } C\alpha = \sqrt{K_\alpha C} \quad \text{...(i)}$$
$$C\alpha = [H^+] = 3.5 \times 10^{-4} \text{ M}$$

From Eq. (i),

$$\sqrt{C} = \frac{C\alpha}{\sqrt{K_\alpha}}$$
$$= \frac{3.5 \times 10^{-4}}{\sqrt{1.8 \times 10^{-5}}} \quad \text{...(ii)}$$

Simplifying Eq. (ii),

$$C = 6.80 \times 10^{-3} \text{ M}$$

22. (b) The pH of weak acid is given by formula

$$pH = \frac{1}{2}[pK_w - pK_b - \log C]$$
$$pH = \frac{1}{2}[14 - 4.73 - \log 0.02]$$
$$= \frac{1}{2}[14 - 4.73 + 1.698] = 5.48$$

23. (b) Statement I is correct but Statement II is incorrect. The correct form of statement II is

The common ion effect is not responsible for white turbidity when HCl is added to $BaCl_2$. Instead, white turbidity typically results from the precipitation of $BaSO_4$, when sulphate ion are present in the solution.

24. (a) Order of Lewis acid strength of boron halide is

$$BI_3 > BBr_3 > BCl_3 > BF_3.$$

This order is explained on basis of $p\pi$- $p\pi$ back bonding opposite to expected order due to electronegativity.

25. (c) $\overset{+7}{MnO_4^-} \longrightarrow Mn^{2+}$ change in oxidation number 5

$\longrightarrow \overset{+6}{MnO_4^{2-}}$ change in oxidation number 1

$\longrightarrow \overset{+4}{MnO_2}$ change in oxidation number 3

$\longrightarrow \overset{+3}{Mn_2O_3}$ change in oxidation number 4

26. (a)

$CH_3—C(=O)—CH_3$

Acetone (Keto form)

$\rightleftharpoons$

$H_2C=C(OH)—CH_3$ (bonds labelled σ, π)

9σ bond, 1π bond, 2 lone pairs (Enol form)

27. (b) Both (A) and (R) are true but (R) is not the correct explanation of (A). The correct explanation is Addition of Br_2 on *trans*-2-butene gives *meso*-2, 3-dibromobutane. This is due to *anti* addition of cyclic bromonium ion intermediate.

28. (c) $H_2S_2O_6$:

HO—S(=O)(=O)—S(=O)(=O)—OH 4π-bonds

H_2SO_3 : HO—S(=O)—OH 1π-bonds

$H_2S_2O_5$:

HO—S(=O)—S(=O)(=O)—OH 3π-bonds

From the given structure it is clear that the correct order of increasing π-bonds is II, III, I.

29. (c) The reaction that involves formation of products from its elemental form will define ΔH°_f.

Thus, $\frac{1}{2}H_2 + \frac{1}{2}F_2 \longrightarrow HF$ will give ΔH°_f.

30. (c) $C_6H_5COOH(s) + 7.5O_2(l) \longrightarrow 7CO_2(g) + 3H_2O(l)$

$$\Delta n_g = -0.5$$
$$\Delta H = \Delta E + \Delta n_g RT$$
$$-2546 = \Delta E - 0.5 \times 8.314 \times 10^{-3} \times 298$$
$$\Delta E = -2544.76 \text{ kJ mol}^{-1}$$

31. (c) Δn_g for the given reaction is calculated by using

$$\Delta n_g = n_p - n_r = 1 - \frac{3}{2}$$
$$\Delta n_g = \frac{-1}{2}.$$

Hence, $K_p = K_C(RT)^{-1/2}$

$$\frac{K_p}{K_C} = \frac{1}{(RT)^{1/2}} = \frac{1}{\sqrt{RT}}$$

32. (c) As $-M$ and $-I$ effect increases, stability of carbanion increases. $-M$ effect is possible only at *ortho* and *para* positions and $-I$ effect is more pronounced at *ortho*-position.

Thus, correct order of stability is

$\bar{C}H_2$ with NO_2 at ortho (I) Both $-I$ and $-M$, $-I$ more pronounced > $\bar{C}H_2$ with NO_2 at para (III) Both $-I$ and $-M$, $-I$ less pronounced

$\bar{C}H_2$ with NO_2 at meta (II) Only $-M$ > $\bar{C}H_2$ benzyl (IV)

33. (d) The correct match is A-IV, B-I, C-II, D-III.

34. (d) Statement given in I, II, III and IV are correct regarding use of sodium metal in Lassaigne's test. The corrected form of statement V is Na converts all the elements present into ionic form.

35. (b) The number of incorrect statements are two, i.e. given in (C) and (E). Their correct form are : Central atom has one lone pair and its hybridisation is sp^3d.

36. (b) Percentage of H

$$=\frac{2}{18}\times\frac{1.8}{1.16}\times 100 = 17.24\%$$

$\therefore$ Percentage of C

$= 100 -$ Percentage of H

$= 100 - 17.24 = 82.76\%$

37. (a) Applying, $K_p = K_C(RT)^{\Delta n_g}$

$PCl_3(g) + Cl_2(g) \rightarrow PCl_5(g)$;

$\Delta n_g = 1-(1+1) = -1$

$\therefore\ K_p = K_C(RT)^{-1}$

$T = 230°C$

$= (230+273)\,K = 503\,K$

$$K_P = \frac{13}{0.0821\times 503} = 0.315$$

38. (c) Number of valence electrons in $NO_3^- = (5+3\times 6+1) = 24$

Number of valence electrons in $CO_3^{2-} = (4+3\times 6+2) = 24$

Number of valence electrons in $ClO_3^- = (7+3\times 6+1) = 26$

Number of valence electrons in $SO_3 = (6+3\times 6) = 24$

The number of valence electrons in $NH_4^+ = (5+4\times 1-1) = 8$

Therefore, NO_3^-, CO_3^{2-} and SO_3 are iso-electronic.

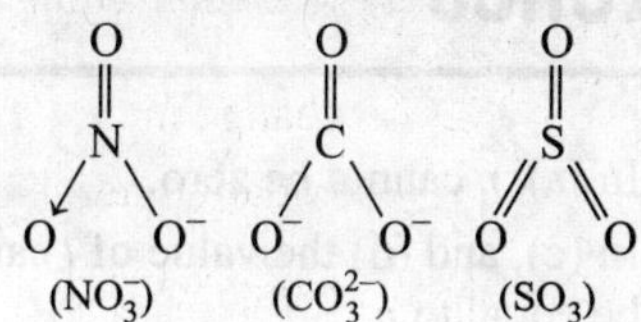

Thus, NO_3^-, SO_3 and CO_3^{2-} are iso-structural.

39. (a) The correct statement about I and II is given in option (a) i.e. I is optically active due to absence of an element of symmetry and II is not as it contains a centre of symmetry.

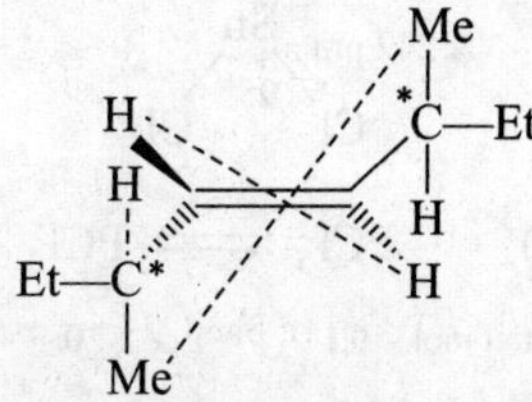

40. (b) Among the given compounds only [10]-Annulene is non-aromatic in nature, while azulene furan and pyrolle are aromatic in nature.

For a molecule to be aromatic, it must be planar, cyclic conjugation and follow Huckel rule. In case of [10]-Annulene, the ring is not perfectly planar due to angle strain and steric hindrance.

41. (b) Statement I is correct but Statement II is incorrect. The correct form of Statement II is

At the stage of equilibrium, $\Delta G = 0$.

42. (a) Molecular mass of HCl $= 36.5$ amu

No. of gram moles in 0.1825g of HCl

$$=\frac{0.1825}{36.5} = 5\times 10^{-3}$$

Volume of solution in L

$$=\frac{100}{1000} = 0.1\,L$$

$$\text{Molarity} = \frac{n}{V\,(\text{in L})} = 5\times 10^{-3}$$

$$=\frac{5\times 10^{-3}}{0.1}$$

$= 5\times 10^{-2}$ M

43. (d) The correct match is A-IV, B-III, C-II, D-I

Use the formula radial node $= (n-l-1)$

44. (b) In dilution the following equation is applicable.

$$M_1V_1 = M_2V_2$$
(10 M HCl) (5 M HCl)

$\Rightarrow\ 10\times V_1 = 5\times 2.00$

$\Rightarrow\ V_1 = \frac{5\times 2.00}{10}$

$\Rightarrow\ V_1 = 1.00$ L

45. (d) $d = 159.6\,\text{pm} = 1.596$Å

$\Rightarrow$ Now, % ionic character

$$=\frac{\mu_{obs}}{\mu_{Ion}}\times 100$$

$$\therefore \mu_{obs} = \frac{\text{Ionic character}\times\mu_{Ion}}{100}$$

$\mu_{ion} = q\times d$

$= 1.6\times 10^{-19}\times 1.596\times 10^{-10}$ m

$= 2.554\times 10^{-29}$ Cm

$$=\frac{76.81\times 2.554\times 10^{-29}}{100}$$

$= 1.96\times 10^{-29}$ Cm

$$=\frac{1.96\times 10^{-29}}{3.335\times 10^{-30}} = 5.88\,D$$

NSS5 NEET Stepping Stones

1. (b) The given equation are

$$Zn + 2HCl \longrightarrow ZnCl_2 + H_2\uparrow$$
$$3H_2 + N_2 \longrightarrow 2NH_3\uparrow$$

From the equation, it is clear that, 2 moles of NH_3 require = 3 moles of H_2

1 mole of H_2 requires = 2 moles of HCl.

Thus, 2 moles of NH_3 require

$= 3\times 2$ moles of HCl

$= 3\times 2\times 36.5$ g of HCl

$\therefore$ 4 moles of NH_3 required

$$= \frac{3\times 2\times 36.5\times 4}{2}$$

$= 438$ g HCl

2. (a) For isoelectronic species, more negatively charged species have larger size, whereas more positively charged species have smaller size.

Thus, S^{2-} has larger ionic radii and Ca^{2+} has smaller ionic radii.

So, correct order is

$$S^{2-} > Cl^- > K^+ > Ca^{2+}.$$

3. (a) O_2^+ is paramagnetic due to the presence of unpaired electron.

$O_2^+ = \sigma 1s^2 \overset{*}{\sigma} 1s^2 \sigma 2s^2 \overset{*}{\sigma} 2s^2$
$\sigma 2p_z^2 \pi 2p_x^2 \approx \pi 2p_y^2 \overset{*}{\pi} 2p_x^1 \approx \overset{*}{\pi} 2p_y^0$

= one unpaired e^- present.

whereas $N_2O_2^{2-}$ and F_2 have paired electrons and show diamagnetic nature.

$N_2 = \sigma 1s^2 \sigma^* 1s^2 \sigma 2s^2 \sigma 2p_z^2$
$\pi 2p_x^2 \approx \pi 2p_y^2$

O_2^{2-} and $F_2 = \sigma 1s^2 \sigma^* 1s^2$
$\sigma 2s^2 \sigma^* 2s^2 \sigma 2p_z^2\ \pi 2p_x^2$
$\approx \pi 2p_y^2 \pi^* 2p_x^2 \approx \pi^* 2p_y^2$

Thus, option (a) is correct.

4. (b) Set of quantum number (a), (c) and (d) are not possible but (b) is possible.

In (a), *n* cannot be zero.

In (c), and (d) the value of *l* cannot be equal to *n*.

So, option (b) is correct.

5. (a) Both (A) and (R) are true and (R) is the correct explanation of (A).

6. (b) $SnCl_2$ is a bent molecule. The structure is as follow

Sn with lone pair; Sn–Cl 242 pm; Cl–Sn–Cl 95°

7. (a) $PCl_5 \rightleftharpoons PCl_3 + Cl_2$

	PCl_5	PCl_3	Cl_2
Initial mol	0.1	0	0
At equil.	0.1–x	x	x

Total number of moles at equilibrium

$= 0.1 - x + x + x = 0.1 + x$

$\Rightarrow p_{\text{total}} = 1$ bar

$\Rightarrow p_{PCl_3} = p_{Cl_2} = \frac{x}{0.1+x} \times 1$ bar

$p_{PCl_5} = \frac{0.1-x}{0.1+x} \times 1$ bar

$\Rightarrow$ No. of moles $= \frac{pV}{RT}$

$\Rightarrow 0.1 + x$

$$= \frac{1\text{ bar} \times 8\text{ L}}{0.082\text{ L bar mol}^{-1}\text{ K}^{-1} \times 540\text{ K}}$$

$= 0.18$

$\Rightarrow x = 0.08$ mol

$$\Rightarrow K_p = \frac{p_{PCl_3} \times p_{Cl_2}}{p_{PCl_5}}$$

$$= \frac{\left(\frac{x}{0.1+x}\right)^2}{\left(\frac{0.1-x}{0.1+x}\right)} = \frac{x^2}{(0.1)^2 - x^2}$$

$$K_p = \frac{(0.08)^2}{(0.1)^2 - (0.08)^2} = 1.78\text{ bar}$$

8. (d) Number of possible isomeric ethers (structural only) of $C_5H_{12}O$ is 6.

I. $CH_3—CH_2—CH_2—CH_2—OCH_3$

II. $CH_3—CH_2—CH(OCH_3)—CH_3$

III. $CH_3—CH(CH_3)—CH_2—OCH_3$

IV. $CH_3—C(CH_3)(OCH_3)—CH_3$

V. $CH_3—CH_2—CH_2—OC_2H_5$

VI. $CH_3—CH(OC_2H_5)—CH_3$

9. (a) Both (A) and (R) are true and (R) is the correct explanation of (A).

$$\text{R–C}\equiv\text{CH} + NaNH_2 \longrightarrow \text{R–C}\equiv\text{C}^-Na^+ + NH_3$$

(C≡CH: Strong acid; $NaNH_2$: Strong base)

10. (d) R_f (retardation factor) is a measure used in thin layer chromatography. It is the ratio of distance moved by substance and that of solvent. R_f determines relative adsorption of each component of the mixture. It does not determine the refractive index.

Thus, option (d) is not correct.

11. (a) Isoelectronic species have same bond order.

$CN^- = 6 + 7 + 1 = 14$ electrons

$O_2^- = 8 + 8 + 1 = 17$ electrons

$NO^+ = 7 + 8 - 1 = 14$ electrons

$N_2^{2+} = 7+7-2 = 12$ electrons

$CO = 6+8 = 14$ electrons

12. (c) Species given in (i), (iv) and (v) are anti aromatic as they have $4n\pi e^-$ s.

13. (d) $\Delta S^{\ominus}_{vap} = \dfrac{\Delta_{vap}H^{\ominus}}{T_b}$

Here, $\Delta_{vap}\overset{\ominus}{H} = 26.0$ kJ/mol

$T_b = 35°C = 308$ K

$\Delta_{vap}S^{\ominus} = \dfrac{26.0\times10^3}{308\ (K)}$ (J/mol)

$= 84.415$ J/K

14. (c) The correct match is

A-III, B-IV, C-I, D-II.

A. At constant pressure the addition of an inert gas has no effect on the formation of N_2 and O_2 gases.
B. Increase in pressure, shifts the equilibrium towards less gaseous species.
C. In heterogeneous equilibrium, only gaseous species are considered as solids do not have pressure. Hence, $K_p = p_{Total}$
D. If the volume of the PCl_5 increases the formation of PCl_3 and Cl_2 increases so, a decrease in volume will favour the backward reaction.

15. (b) Among the species only IV and V are aromatic in nature.

IV. 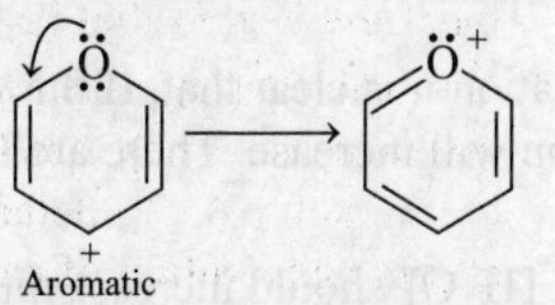 [structure] ⟶ [structure] Aromatic

Aromatic because of $(4n+2)$ π-electrons in a closed, cyclic loop as well as they are conjugated.

V. 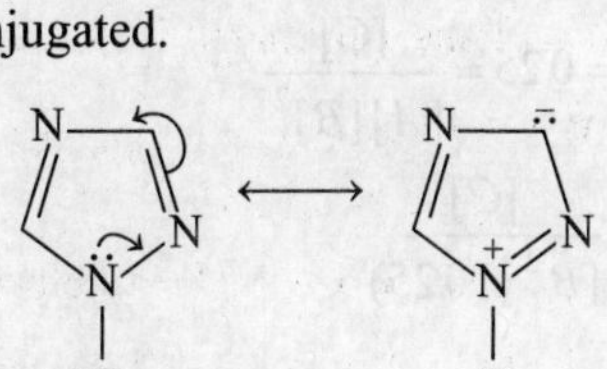 [structure] ⟷ [structure]

Aromatic

16. (c) Since the alkene (C_6H_{10}) on ozonolysis gives a single dialdehyde containing six C-atoms.

Therefore, the alkene must be cyclohexene.

17. (c) $CH_3-\underset{\underset{CH_3}{|}}{C}=CH_2 + HBr$

$\xrightarrow[\text{Anti-Markovnikov's addition}]{\text{Peroxide}} CH_3-\underset{\underset{CH_3}{|}}{CH}-CH_2Br$

Thus, the compound formed is given in option (c).

18. (b) Lassaigne's test is used to detect halogen, sulphur and nitrogen and phosphorus.

19. (a) The reaction will proceed according to Markovnikov's rule.

$CH_3CH_2-\underset{\underset{CH_3}{|}}{C}=CH-CH_3 + HO^-Cl^+ \longrightarrow$

$CH_3CH_2-\overset{\overset{OH}{|}}{\underset{\underset{H_3C}{|}}{C}}-\underset{\underset{Cl}{|}}{CHCH_3}$

20. (c) Less the heat of combustion, more stable is substance. Thus graphite is stable than diamond

21. (d)

(a) Electrons in 2s and 2p-orbitals have different screening effect. Hence, their Z_{eff} is different.

Z_{eff} of 2s-orbital > Z_{eff} of 2p-orbital

Therefore, it is not correct.

(b) Energy of 2s-orbital < energy of 2p-orbital.

Hence, it is not correct.

(c) Z_{eff} of 1s-orbital ≠ Z_{eff} of 2s-orbital.

Hence, it is incorrect.

(d) For the two electrons of 2s-orbital, the value of m_s is $+\frac{1}{2}$ and $-\frac{1}{2}$.

Hence, it is correct.

22. (a)

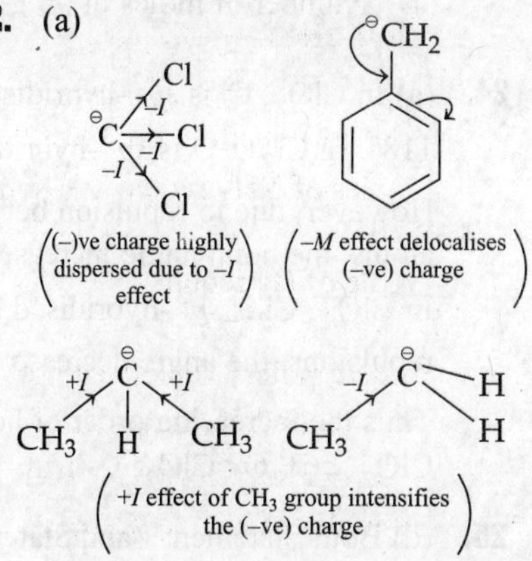

[structures: $\overset{\ominus}{C}Cl_3$ with –I arrows; benzyl carbanion $C_6H_5\overset{\ominus}{C}H_2$]

((–)ve charge highly dispersed due to –I effect) (–M effect delocalises (–ve) charge)

$CH_3 \xrightarrow{+I} \overset{\ominus}{C}(H) \xleftarrow{+I} CH_3$ $\quad CH_3 \xrightarrow{-I} \overset{\ominus}{C}H_2$

(+I effect of CH_3 group intensifies the (–ve) charge)

–I effect exerting group stabilises the carbanion by the dispersal of their (–ve) charge while +I effect exerting groups destabilises the carbanion by increasing electron density on them.

Resonance stabilised carbanion are stable due to the involvement of their lone pair of electron with the delocalisation of π-electrons of attached phenyl group.

Hence, the correct order of decreasing stability of the carbanions is

$\overset{\ominus}{C}Cl_3 > C_6H_5\overset{\ominus}{C}H_2$

$> CH_3\overset{\ominus}{C}H_2 > (CH_3)_2\overset{\ominus}{C}H$

23. (b) The correct match is

A-II, B-III, C-I, D-IV.

A. Number of moles of CO_2 molecules

$= \dfrac{\text{Mass in gram of } CO_2}{\text{Molecular mass of } CO_2}$

$= \dfrac{88}{44} = 2$ mol

B. 1 mol of a substance $= N_A$ molecules

$= 6.022\times10^{23}$ molecules

= Avogadro's number

$= 6.022 \times 10^{23}$ molecules of $H_2O = 1\,\text{mol}$

C. 22.4 L of O_2 at STP = 1 mol

5.6 L of O_2 at STP $= \frac{5.6}{22.4}$ mol = 0.25 mol

D. Number of moles of 96 g of $O_2 = \frac{96}{32}$ mol = 3 mol

24. (a) In ClO_2, Cl is sp^2-hybridised and the bond angle is 118°. In Cl_2O, O is sp^3-hybridised.

However, due to repulsion between two large sized Cl atoms, the bond angle increase from 109.5° to 111°.

In ClO_2^-, Cl is sp^3-hybridised but due to *lp-bp* repulsions, the angle decrease from 109.5° to 103°.

Thus the increasing order of bond angle is

$ClO_2^- < Cl_2O < ClO_2$.

25. (d) Both Statement I and Statement II are correct.

26. (b) For polyatomic molecules/ions, bond order is given as $\text{B.O} = 1 + \frac{\text{Number of double bond}}{\text{Number of delocalisation position}}$

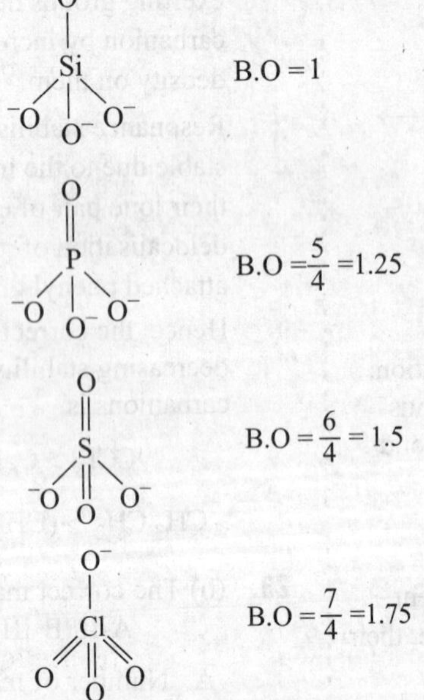

Bond length is inversely proportional to B.O.

27. (a) Oxidation number of Mn in all the given compounds are as follows

In $\overset{x}{\text{Mn}}\overset{-1}{\text{Cl}_2}$: $x + 2(-1) = 0$

$\Rightarrow \; = +2$

In $\overset{x}{\text{Mn}}\overset{-2}{\text{O}_2}$: $x + 2(-2) = 0$

$\Rightarrow x = +4$

In $\overset{x}{\text{Mn}}\overset{-1}{(\text{OH})_3}$: $x + 3(-1) = 0$

$\Rightarrow x = +3$

In $\overset{+1}{\text{K}}\overset{x}{\text{Mn}}\overset{-2}{\text{O}_4}$: $1(+1) + x + 4(-2) = 0 \Rightarrow x = +7$

Thus increasing order of oxidation number of Mn is

$MnCl_2 < Mn(OH)_3 < MnO_2 < KMnO_4$

28. (a)

Element	Atomic number	Percentage	Number of moles	Simple ratio
C	12	48	$\frac{48}{12} = 4$	1
H	1	8	$\frac{8}{1} = 8$	2
N	14	56	$\frac{56}{14} = 4$	1

Empirical formula is $= CH_2N$

Empirical formula mass = 28

Now, 200 mL of compound = 1 g

$\therefore$ 22400 mL of compound $= \frac{1}{200} \times 22400 = 112\,\text{g}$

= molecular mass

$$n = \frac{\text{molecular mass}}{\text{empirical formula mass}}$$

$$= \frac{112}{28} = 4$$

So, the molecular formula $= (CH_2N)_4 = C_4H_8N_4$

29. (d) The blue colour is due to formation of $Fe_4[Fe(CN)_6]_3$.

30. (c) The correct match is A-IV, B-III, C-II, D-I.

31. (c) $K = \frac{[CO(g)][H_2(g)]}{[H_2O(g)]}$

From the above equation it is clear that, If the volume is halved, concentration will increase. There are two terms in the numerator.

To keep K constant, $[H_2O]$ should increase much more.

32. (b) $A(g) + 2B(g) \longrightarrow C(g)$

	$A(g)$	$2B(g)$	$C(g)$
$(t = 0)$	n	4	0
At equil.	$n - 1$	$4 - 2$	1

$$K_C = 0.25 = \frac{[C]}{[A][B]^2}$$

$$\Rightarrow \quad [A] = \frac{[C]}{[B^2](0.25)}$$

$$\frac{n-1}{5} = \frac{1/5}{0.25 \times \frac{2^2}{5^2}} = 25$$

$\Rightarrow$ $n = 26$ moles

33. (a) Relative contributing resonance structures is inversely proportional to its energy but directly to its stability.

So, lesser the energy, the greater is its contribution. Thus, statement (a) is incorrect.

34. (b) N_2 and NO^+ both are diamagnetic as they don't have any unpaired electrons. Also, both have $14e^-$ so, they are isoelectronic.

Thus, both, (A) and (R) are true but (R) is not the correct explanation of (A).

35. (b) The correct match is A-III, B-IV, C-II, D-I.

36. (b) The complete reaction is as follows

$CH_3-HC=CH-C_6H_4-OH$ $\xrightarrow{H^+}$

$CH_3-CH_2-\overset{+}{C}H-C_6H_4-OH$ (More stable)

$CH_3-\overset{+}{C}H-CH_2-C_6H_4-OH$ (Less stable)

$\downarrow$

$CH_3-CH_2-CH(Br)-C_6H_4-OH$

37. (b) Number of electrons in $CH_3^+ = 6+3-1=8$

Number of electrons in $NH_2^- = 7+2+1=10$

Number of electrons in $NH_4^+ = 7+4-1=10$

Number of electrons in $NH_3 = 7+3=10$

Number of electrons in $CH_4 = 6+4=10$

So, 4 species are isoelectronic.

38. (c) (A) is true but (R) is false.

The correct form of (R) is,

The active electrophile in the nitration reaction is NO_2^+.

39. (b) Using the formula,

$$\bar{\nu} \text{ wave number} = \bar{R}_H Z^2 \left[\frac{1}{n_1^2} - \frac{1}{n_2^2}\right]$$

$\bar{\nu} \propto Z^2$ if n_1 and n_2 are same.

$$\frac{\bar{\nu}_1}{\bar{\nu}_2} = \frac{Z_1^2}{Z_2^2}$$

$$\Rightarrow \frac{x}{\bar{\nu}_2} = \frac{2^2}{4^2}$$

$$\frac{x}{\bar{\nu}_2} = \frac{4}{4\times 4}$$

$$\Rightarrow \bar{\nu}_2 = 4x\,\text{cm}^{-1}$$

40. (a) Among the given options. $H_2C=C=CH_2$ is a non a planar compound.

The presence of even number of double bonds in a molecule lead to a non-planar structure due to arrangement of the *p*-orbitals.

$\overset{1}{H_2C}=\overset{2}{C}=\overset{3}{CH_2}$

p_z p_z p_y p_y

p_z and p_y orbitals of C-1 and C-3 are perpendicular.

41. (b) K_{sp} (AgCl) > K_{sp} (AgI)

Hence, AgI is precipitated before AgCl.

$[Ag^+]$ to precipitated

$$Cl^- = \frac{1\times 10^{-10}}{0.05} = 2\times 10^{-9}\text{ M}$$

$$[I^-] \text{ at this stage} = \frac{K_{sp}(\text{AgI})}{[Ag^+]} = \frac{4\times 10^{-16}}{2\times 10^{-9}} = 2\times 10^{-7}\text{ M}$$

42. (c) The peroxide ion O_2^{2-} has 18 electrons arranged in the following manner:

$KK\sigma 2s^2, \sigma^* 2s^2, \sigma 2p_z^2, \pi 2p_x^2 \simeq \pi 2p_y^2, \pi^* 2p_x^2 \simeq \pi^* 2p_y^2$

All the electrons are paired.

Thus, O_2^{2-} ion is diamagnetic.

Bond order = (bonding electrons – anti-bonding electrons)/2 = (10 – 8)/2 = 1

43. (a) The correct match is

A-III, B-IV, C-I, D-II.

$\Delta H = \Delta E + \Delta n_g RT$

(A) $C(s) + O_2(g) \longrightarrow CO_2(g)$

$\Delta n_g = 1 - 1 = 0$

$\therefore \Delta H = \Delta E$

(B) $N_2(g) + 3H_2(g) \longrightarrow 2NH_3(g)$

$\Delta n_g = 2 - (1 + 3) = -2$

$\therefore \Delta H = \Delta E - 2RT$

(C) $PCl_5(g) \longrightarrow PCl_3(g) + Cl_2(g)$

$\Delta n_g = (1 + 1) - 1 = 1$

$\therefore \Delta H = \Delta E + RT$

(D) $2SO_2(g) + O_2(g) \longrightarrow 2SO_3(g)$

$\Delta n_g = 2 - (2 + 1) = -1$

$\therefore \Delta H = \Delta E - RT$

44. (d) Both Statement I and Statement II are correct.

45. (b) The change in enthalpy for the system is positive. It is because on heating.

$$N_2O_4 \overset{\Delta}{\rightleftharpoons} 2NO_2,$$

If NO_2 is formed more, it means $\Delta H = +$ ve because endothermic reactions are favoured with increase in temperature.

CHEMISTRY -XIth

MIND MAP

- Some Basic Concepts of Chemistry
- Structure of Atom
- Classification of Elements and Periodicity in Properties
- Chemical Bonding and Molecular Structure
- Thermodynamics
- Chemical Equilibrium
- Ionic Equilibrium
- Redox Reactions
- *p*-Block Elements-I
- Purification and Characterisation of Organic Compounds
- Some Basic Principles of Organic Chemistry
- Hydrocarbons

MEDACE

Test 1

Syllabus
- Matter and Its Nature, Dalton's Atomic Theory
- Concept of Atom, Molecule, Element and Compound
- Laws of Chemical Combinations

NCERT Page 4 to 16

For deeper insight **Scan the QR Code**

Chapter 01

Matter and Its Nature

- Anything which occupies space and has mass is called matter.
- There are five states of matter namely, solid, liquid, gas, Bose-Einstein condensate and plasma.
- These states of matter are interconvertible by changing the conditions of temperature and pressure. $\text{Solid} \underset{\text{Cool}}{\overset{\text{Heat}}{\rightleftharpoons}} \text{Liquid} \underset{\text{Cool}}{\overset{\text{Heat}}{\rightleftharpoons}} \text{Gas}$

States of Matter

- **Solids**
- Particles are held very close to each other.
- Have definite volume and shape.
- Not much freedom of movement of particles.
- **Liquids**
- Particles are close
- Have freedom to move
- Have definite volume
- Takes the shape of container
- **Gases**
- Particles are distanced
- Have freedom to move
- No definite volume or shape
- Completely fill the space they are in.
- **Bose-Einstein Condensate**
- This state is conceptualised by cooling a gas of extremely low density to supercooled condition.
- **Plasma** It is seen as a state containing gaseous ions and free electrons, e.g. neon lights, stars.

Classification of Matter

Matter
- Mixture
  - Homogeneous mixture
  - Heterogeneous mixture
- Pure substances
  - Elements
  - Compounds

Physical and Chemical Properties of Matter

- Physical properties are the characteristic that do not cause any change in the identity or the composition of the substance. e.g. Colour, hardness, density, boiling point.
- Chemical properties are the characteristics of matter that are measurable and observable only during a chemical change .e.g. Reactivity, oxidation state.

Mixtures and Pure Substance

Two or more substances mix together in any ratio to give mixture. These are of following two types.

- **Homogeneous mixtures** These are the mixtures in which components completely mix with each other. e.g. Air, tea, sugar solution etc.
- **Heterogeneous mixtures** These are the mixtures in which composition is not uniform throughout and components do not mix with each other. e.g. Salt and sugar, stone and pulses etc.
- Constituent particles of **pure substances** have fixed composition they can be classified into following two types
- **Elements** These are the species containing only one type of particles. These may exist as atoms or molecules. e.g. Na, K, H_2, O_2 etc.

Atoms of different elements

- **Compounds** These are the species which are obtained from combination of two or more atoms. e.g. H_2O, NH_3, CO_2 etc.

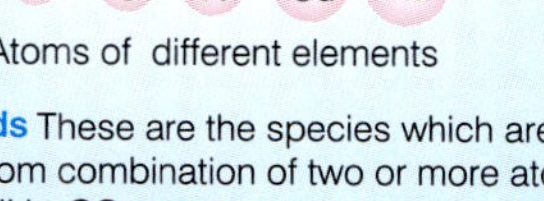

Water molecule (H_2O)

Carbon dioxide molecule (CO_2)

Concept of Atom and Molecule

- **Atom** It is the smallest particle of matter that takes part in a chemical reaction and is not capable of independent existence.
- **Molecule** It is the smallest particle of matter which is capable of independent existence but do not take part in a chemical reaction.

Measurement of Physical Properties

- **Mass and weight** Mass of a substance is the amount of matter present in it.
- Weight of a substance is the force exerted by gravity.
- **Volume** Amount of space occupied by a substance.
- It has unit of $(\text{length})^3$.
- Litre is used extensively where, $1L = 1000\ cm^3 = 1\ dm^3$.
- **Density** It is defined as amount of mass per unit volume. Mathematically, $\text{Density} = \frac{\text{Mass}}{\text{Volume}}$
- **Temperature**
- It is the measure of hotness or coldness of a body
- The three common scales to measure temperature is °C (degree Celcius), °F (degree Fahrenheit) and K (Kelvin).

Base Physical Quantity and Their Units

Base physical quantity	Symbol	Name of SI unit	Symbol for SI unit
Length	l	metre	m
Mass	m	kilogram	kg
Time	t	second	s
Electric current	I	ampere	A
Thermodynamic Temperature	T	Kelvin	K
Amount of substance	n	mole	mol
Luminous intensity	I_v	candela	cd

Above 7 quantities are **base units**. While other quantities that are derived from these base quantities are called as **derived units**.

Dimensional Analysis

- The method used to convert units from one system to the other is called factor label method or unit factor method.
- Required unit = Given value x conversion factor.

Prefixes

Multiple	Prefix	Symbol	Multiple	Prefix	Symbol
10^{-1}	deci	d	10^1	deca	da
10^{-2}	centi	c	10^2	hecto	h
10^{-3}	milli	m	10^3	kilo	k
10^{-6}	micro	μ	10^6	mega	M
10^{-9}	nano	n	10^9	giga	G
10^{-12}	pico	p	10^{12}	tera	T

Scientific Notation

- Representation of large numbers in the form of $N \times 10^n$, where, n can be negative or positive.
- If decimal moves towards right, n is positive. If decimal is moved towards left, n is negative.
- In multiplication, n is added.
- In division, n is subtracted.

Significant Figures

These are meaningful digits which are known with certainty plus one which is estimated or uncertain. Rules for determining number of significant figures are

- All non-zero digits are significant.
- Zeroes preceding to first non-zero digit are non-significant.
- Zeroes between two non-zeroes are significant.
- Zeroes on the right side of decimal are significant.

Dalton's Atomic Theory

- **Postulates**
- Matter consists of indivisible atoms.
- All the atoms of a given element have identical properties including identical mass. Atoms of different elements differ in mass.
- Compounds are formed when atoms of different elements combine in a fixed ratio.
- Chemical reactions involve rearrangement of atoms. These are neither created nor destroyed in a chemical reaction.
- **Limitations**
- Could not explain laws of gaseous volumes.
- Could not explain why atoms combines with each other.

Laws of Chemical Combination

Law of conservation of mass	Law of definite proportion	Law of multiple proportion	Law of gaseous volumes	Avogadro's law
Lavoisier	Joseph Proust	John Dalton	Gay Lussac	Amedeo Avogadro

Laws of Chemical Combination

- **Law of Conservation of Mass**
- Given by Antoine Lavoisier.
- Matter can neither be created nor be destroyed.
- There is no net change in mass during a chemical change or physical change.
- **Law of Definite Proportions**
- Given by Joseph Proust.
- A compound always contains exactly the same proportions of elements by weight e.g. H_2O (from tap)–H–22.22%, O –77.78%. H_2O (from lab)–H – 22.22%, O –77.78%
- **Law of Multiple Proportions**
- Given by Dalton.
- If two elements can combine to form more than one compound, the mass of one element that combine with a fixed mass of the other element, are in the ratio of small whole numbers.
- **Gay Lussac's Law of Gaseous Volumes**
- Given by Gay-Lussac.
- When gases combine or produced in a chemical reaction, they do so in a simple ratio by volume provided all gases are at same temperature and pressure.
- **Avogadro's Law**
- Given by Avogadro's.
- Equal volumes of gases at same temperature and pressure should contain equal number of molecules.

Test 2

Syllabus
- Atomic and Molecular Masses
- Percentage Composition
- Empirical and Molecular Formula

NCERT Page 16 to 20

For deeper insight **Scan the QR Code**

Chapter 01

Atomic Mass

- It is measured by comparing mass of an atom with the mass of a particular atom chosen as standard.
- Represents the mass of an atom.
- Denoted by amu (Atomic mass unit)

$$\text{Atomic mass} = \frac{\text{Mass of one atom of the element}}{1/12^{th} \text{ part of the mass of one atom of C-12}}$$

- $1 \text{ amu} = \frac{1}{12}$ (Mass of an atom of C-12) $= 1.660 \times 10^{-24}$ g

Relative Atomic Mass

Relative atomic mass of the atom of an element is defined as the average mass of the atom, as compared to 1/12th the mass of one carbon-12 atom.

Gram Atomic Mass

- Atomic mass of an element expressed in gram is called its gram atomic mass or gram atom. e.g. The atomic mass of hydrogen is 1.008 amu and thus, a gram atom of hydrogen is 1.008g.
  Gram atomic mass = atomic mass expressed in gram = gram atom
- Gram atom and mass of an atom of the element are different terms.
- For example mass of one atom of oxygen is

$$\frac{16 \text{g/mol}}{6.022 \times 10^{23} \text{ mol}^{-1}} = 2.66 \times 10^{-23} \text{g}$$

whereas its gram atomic mass is 16 amu.
- To convert gram atomic mass into amu divide by N_A (Avogadro number).

Average Atomic Mass

- Defined for elements existing in more than one isotopes.
- Each isotope has different mass.
- Average atomic mass is calculated by taking into account the masses and the % abundance of these isotopes.

Isotope	Atomic mass	Percentage
1	A_1	X_1
2	A_2	X_2

Then average atomic mass, $\overline{A} = \frac{A_1X_1 + A_2X_2}{X_1 + X_2}$

For more than two isotopes it is given by

$\frac{\Sigma x_i A_i}{\Sigma x_i}$ (x_i = % abundance, A_i = mass)

Dulong and Petit's Method to Calculate Average Atomic Mass

- According to this method, the approximate atomic mass of solid elements except Be, B, C and Si, is related to their specific heats as

$$\text{Average atomic mass} = \frac{6.4}{\text{specific heat}}$$

- Mass spectrometer is used to determine the atomic mass experimentally.

Molecular Mass

- Defined for a molecule.
- Is equal to sum of atomic masses of all the elements present.
- It is normally calculated for covalent compounds as they have a definite molecular structure.
- It is obtained by multiplying the atomic mass of each element by the number of its atoms and adding them together.
  For example molecular mass of CO_2
  = 1× atomic mass of C + 2× atomic mass of O
  = (1×12+2×16)u
  = (12+32)u=44u

Formula Mass

- It is defined as the sum of the atomic masses of all atoms in the formula unit of the compound.
- Normally calculated for ionic compounds.
- Defined for compounds like, NaCl which does not exist as a single entity.
- It is taken in terms of amu or u (Unified mass).

Packing of Na^+ and Cl^- ions in sodium chloride

Equivalent Mass

The number of parts by mass of a substance that combines with or displaces 1.008 parts by mass of hydrogen or 8.0 parts of oxygen or 35.5 parts of chlorine is called its equivalent mass (EM).

Gram Equivalent Mass

Quantity of a substance in grams numerically equal to its equivalent mass is called its gram equivalent mass (GEM) or gram equivalent.

$$\text{GEM of the substance} = \frac{\text{Mass of the substance in grams}}{\text{Number of GEM}}$$

Generalised Expression for Equivalent Mass (EM)

$$\text{EM} = \frac{\text{Atomic mass/formula mass /molecular mass}}{n\text{-factor}}$$

where,
- n-factor for an element = its valency
- n-factor for an acid=its basicity, i.e. number of H^+ ions released by it.
- n-factor for a base=its acidity, i.e. number of OH^- groups present in it.
- n-factor for salt=total positive or negative charge.
- n-factor for reducing agent=Number of electrons lost per molecule or total change in oxidation number.
- n-factor for oxidising agent=Number of electrons gained per molecules or total change in oxidation number.
- n-factor for radicals=Number of units of change.

Relation between molar mass (m) and equivalent weight of acids

Acid	Type	Number of H^+ cation present per unit	Equivalent weight
CH_3COOH	Monobasic	1	$= m$
HCl	Monobasic	1	$= m$
H_3PO_2	Monobasic	1	$= m$
H_2SO_4	Dibasic	2	$= m/2$
H_3PO_3	Dibasic	2	$= m/2$
H_3PO_4	Tribasic	3	$= m/3$

Relation between molar mass (m) and equivalent weight of bases

Base	Type	Number of OH^- ions per unit	Equivalent mass
KOH	Monoacidic	1	$= m$
NH_4OH	Monoacidic	1	$= m$
NaOH	Monoacidic	1	$= m$
$Ba(OH)_2$	Diacidic	2	$= \frac{m}{2}$
$Al(OH)_3$	Triacidic	3	$= \frac{m}{3}$

Steps to Calculate Molecular Formula

The molecular formula of a substance may be determined from the empirical formula multiply empirical formula by n to get the molecular formula.

Important Points Related to Different Types of Masses

- Atomic and molecular masses of elements and compounds respectively are always constant but equivalent mass may vary with change of valency.
- The valencies of elements forming isomorphous compounds, i.e. the compounds that have similar constitution and chemical formulae are same, e.g. valencies of Cr, Se and S in K_2CrO_4, K_2SeO_4 and K_2SO_4 are same.
- The molecular mass of a volatile compound can be determined by using the relation.
  Molecular mass = 2× Vapour density

Percentage Composition

The percentage of any element or constituent in a compound is the number of parts by mass of that element or constituent present in 100 parts by mass of the compound.

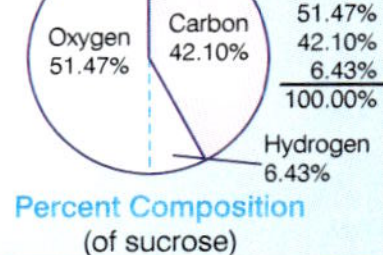

Percent Composition (of sucrose)

Steps to Calculate Percentage Composition

Step I Calculate the molecular mass of the compound from its formula by adding the atomic masses of all the elements present.

Step II Calculate the mass percent of the element by using the expression

Percentage or mass % of an element or constituent

$$= \frac{\text{mass of that element in the compound}}{\text{molar mass of the compound}} \times 100$$

Use of Percentage Composition

It helps in determining the molecular formula of a compound. Moreover, it is also helpful to check the purity of a given sample.

Empirical Formula

It shows simplest whole number ratio of different atoms present in a compound.
It is obtained by following steps.
- Divide mass of all elements by atomic weight.
- Divide all the obtained values with lowest obtained value
- Make the obtained number, a whole number if not.
- Write the obtained number below the symbol of the element in subscript.

Molecular Formula

It is the formula showing exact number of atoms present in a molecule.

$$n = \frac{\text{Molecular formula mass}}{\text{Empirical formula mass}}$$

Test 3

Syllabus
- Mole Concept
- Molar Mass
- Chemical Equations and Stoichiometry

NCERT Page 20 to 24

For deeper insight **Scan the QR Code**

Chapter 01

Mole Concept

Mole It is base quantity for amount of substance.
One mole of a substance always means 6.023×10^{23} entities of that substance. It is called Avogadro's number, represented by N_A.
It can be defined as
- The amount which weighs exactly same as its atomic mass in gram or molecular weight/formula weight in gram.
- The amount which has same number of entities, i.e. atoms, molecules or other particles as there are atoms in exactly 0.012 kg (or 12 g) of carbon-12 isotope. This number is equal to Avogadro's number, i.e. 6.023×10^{23} entities.

(i) 1 mole of particles $= 6.023 \times 10^{23}$ particles or 1 mol = 22.4 L, for gases [only in STP]
(ii) Number of moles
$$= \frac{\text{Mass}}{\text{Atomic or molar mass}}$$
(iii) Number of molecules
$$= N_A \times \text{Number of moles}$$
(iv) Number of atoms
$$= \text{Number of molecules} \times \text{Atomicity}$$

Mole
- 6.022×10^{23} particles
- Mass of 1 mole is molar mass
- Volume of 1 mole gas is molar volume
- Molar volume at STP is 22.4L or 22400mL

Formula Used to Convert into Moles

- Number of moles of molecule
$$= \frac{\text{weight in gram}}{\text{molecular/formula weight}}$$
- Number of moles of atoms $= \dfrac{\text{weight in gram}}{\text{atomic weight}}$
- Number of moles of particles $= \dfrac{\text{number of particles}}{\text{Avogadro's number}}$
- Number of moles of gases
$$= \frac{\text{volume of gas at STP (in L)}}{22.4}$$

Stoichiometry

- The word 'stoichiometry' is derived from two greek words-stoicheion (meaning element) and metron (meaning measurement).
- It refers to the calculations based on the quantitative relationship between the reactants and products.
- The purpose of these reactions is to predict the relationship between the amounts of the reactants and products of chemical reaction.

- $CH_4(g) + 2O_2(g) \longrightarrow CO_2(g) + 2H_2O(g)$
- One mole of $CH_4(g)$ reacts with two moles of $O_2(g)$ to give one mole of $CO_2(g)$ and two moles of $H_2O(g)$.
- One molecule of $CH_4(g)$ reacts with 2 molecules of $O_2(g)$ to give one molecule of $CO_2(g)$ and 2 molecules of $H_2O(g)$.
- 22.7 L of $CH_4(g)$ reacts with 45.4 L of $O_2(g)$ to give 22.7 L of $CO_2(g)$ and 45.4 L of $H_2O(g)$
- 16 g of $CH_4(g)$ reacts with 2×32 g of $O_2(g)$ to give 44 g of $CO_2(g)$ and 2×18 g of $H_2O(g)$.

From these relationship, the given data can be interconverted as follows
mass $\rightleftharpoons$ moles $\rightleftharpoons$ no. of molecules
$$\frac{\text{Mass}}{\text{Volume}} = \text{Density}$$

Stoichiometric Calculations

- Various steps involved in calculations are
- Write balanced chemical equation.
- Write the relative number of moles or relative masses of reactants and products involved below their formulae.
- In case of gases write 22.4 L at STP in place of 1 mole.
- Apply unitary method to make required calculations.

Stoichiometric Relationships and Steps to Solve Related Problems

- **Mole-Mole Relationship**
In this relationship, the mole of one of the reactants/products is to be calculated, if mole of the other one is given.
To solve the problems by this method follow the instructions given below
– **Step I** Write the balanced chemical equation to represent the chemical change.
– **Step II** Write down the number of moles below the formula of the reactants and products. The stoichiometric coefficients in the balanced chemical reactions represent the relative number of moles of different reactants and products.
– **Step III** Use unitary method and calculate the unknown amount of substance.
- **Mass-Mass Relationship**
In this relationship, the mass of one of the reactants/products is to be calculated.

If masses of the others are given.
To solve the given problem by this method follow the instructions given below
– **Step I** Write the balanced chemical equation.
– **Step II** Write the relative mass of each of the reactants and products by calculating it from their molecular formula.
– **Step III** Apply unitary method to calculate the unknown quantity.
- **Mass-Mole Relationship**
In this relationship, the mass or mole of one of the reactants/products is to be calculated if we have the mole or mass of other.
To solve problems by mass-mole relationship, follow the instructions given below
– **Step I** Write down the balanced chemical equation.
– **Step II** Calculate the molecular mass of each reactant and product and also write number of moles.
– **Step III** Apply unitary method to calculate unknown quantity.
- **Mass-Volume relationship**
In this relationship, mass or volume of one of the reactants or products is calculated from the mass or volume of other substances.
To solve problems by mass-volume relationship, follow the instructions given below
– **Step I** Write down the balanced chemical equation.
– **Step II** Write down the mass of various solid reactants and products.
– **Step III** Gases are usually expressed in terms of volumes. Volume of a gas at any temperature and pressure is converted into mass by using the relation
$pV = \frac{m}{M} \times RT$, where m is mass of gas in grams, M is its molar mass and R is gas constant.
– **Step IV** Unknown quantity is calculated by using unitary method.
- **Volume-Volume Relationship**
In this relationship, the volume of one of reactants/products is given and that of the other is to be calculated. To solve problems (specially related to a complete gaseous phase reaction) by this method, follow the steps given below.
– **Step I** Write down the balanced chemical equation.
– **Step II** Write down the volume of reactants and products below their formula with the help of the fact that 1g molecule of every gaseous substance occupies 22.4 L at NTP.

Limiting Reagent

- If a chemical reactions involves two or more reactants then the reactant which gets consumed completely and limits the amount of product formed is called limiting reagent.
- Limiting reagent, limits the amount of product formed.
- The other reagent present in the larger amounts is called excess reagent.
- Amount of H_2O is determined by amount of O_2 present. As O_2 is the limiting reagent.

Visualizing Limiting Reagent

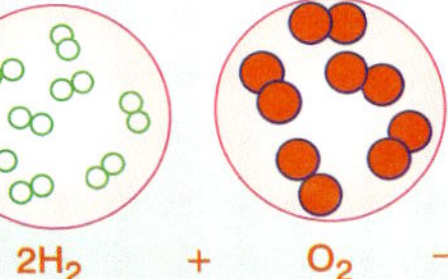
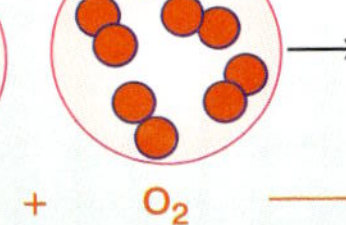
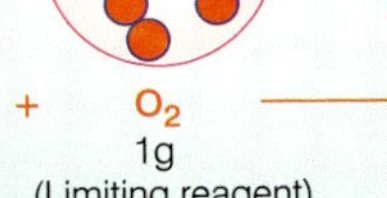

$2H_2$ + O_2 $\longrightarrow$ $2H_2O$
1g (Excess) + 1g (Limiting reagent) → 1.125 g

Concentration of Solutions

Amount of substance can be expressed in following ways
- **Mass Percent**
It is defined as the mass of substance per 100 g of solution.
$$\text{Mass (\%)} = \frac{w_{solute}}{W_{solution}} \times 100$$
- **Mole Fraction**
It is the ratio of moles of a substance to the total number of moles present in the solution.
$$\text{Mole fraction of } X_A = \frac{\text{Moles of } A}{\text{Total moles}}$$
Mole fraction of B $(X_B) = 1 - X_A$
Mole fraction can not exceed 1.
- **Molarity** (M)
It is defined as the number of moles of solute present per litre of solution.
$$\text{Molarity}(M) = \frac{\text{No. of moles of solute}}{\text{Volume of solution (in L)}}$$
- **Molality** (m)
It is defined as number of moles of solute present in 1 kg of solvent. It does not vary with temperature.
$$\text{Molality}(m) = \frac{\text{No. of moles of solute}}{\text{Mass of solvent (in kg)}}$$
- **Normality**
It is defined as the number of gram-equivalents of solute per litre of solution.
$$N = \frac{\text{Gram equivalents of solute}}{\text{Volume of solution (in L)}}$$

Test 1

Syllabus
- Preliminary Models and Nature of Electromagnetic Radiation, Photoelectric Effect

For deeper insight **Scan the QR Code**

Cathode Rays and Discovery of Electron

When a high voltage electric current is passed through a gas filled evacuated tube following results are observed.

- **At normal pressure 760 mm of Hg** The gas remain non-conducting even at very high voltage ≈ 10,000V.
- **At a pressure range of 10^{-2}-10^{-3}mm of Hg** The gas become conducting and some rays are visible which cause certain materials to glow.
- **At a pressure ≈10^{-4} mm of Hg** The gas remains conducting and the previous glow gets fainted. A new green glow behind anode at the walls of glass tube is observed.

Gas at low pressure
To vacuum pump
Cathode
Anode
High voltage
Porous anode

- **Properties of Cathode Rays** Cathode rays travel in straight line path from cathode towards anode and cast shadows of metallic objects placed in their path.
- These rays show deflection by electric and magnetic field both. The nature of the cathode rays is independent of
  (i) the nature of the cathode and
  (ii)the gas in the discharge tube.
- Thus, we can say that cathode rays contain negatively charged particles. These particles were called electrons by Stoney.

Positive Rays and Discovery of Protons

- Goldstein observed that while cathode rays were streaming away from the cathode, there were coloured rays produced simultaneously which passed through the perforated cathode and caused a glow on the wall opposite to the anode.

These rays are known as **canal rays** or **anode rays**.

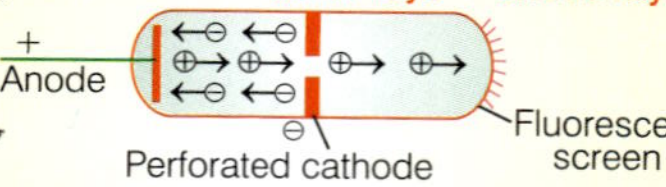

- **Properties of Canal Rays** Unlike cathode rays, mass of positively charged particles depends upon the nature of gas present in the cathode ray tube. These are simply the positively charged gaseous ions. The charge to mass ratio of the particles depends on the gas from which these originate.
- The behaviour of these particles in the magnetic or electrical field is opposite to that observed for electron or cathode rays.

Discovery of Neutrons

Chadwick (in 1932) bombarded beryllium (Be) sheet with high speed alpha (α) particles and noticed the emission of neutral particles, i.e. neutrons of mass nearly equal to protons and with no charge.

They are usually represented as,

$$_4Be^9 + {_2He^4} \longrightarrow {_6C^{12}} + \underset{\text{Neutron}}{_0n^1}$$

Subatomic Particles

Particle	Charge	Mass (kg)	Location	Discovery
Electron (e)	-1.6×10^{-19}	9.1×10^{-31}	Outside nucleus	J.J Thomson
Proton (p)	$+1.6\times10^{-19}$	1.6726×10^{-27}	Nucleus	E. Rutherford
Neutron (n)	0	1.6749×10^{-27}	Nucleus	J. Chadwick

Atomic Models

- Different atomic models were proposed to explain the distributions of the charged particles in an atom. Some of these atomic models are
- Thomson's atomic model
- Rutherford's atomic model

Thomson Atomic Model

- **J.J. Thomson** in 1898, proposed that an atom consists of a uniform sphere (radius approximately 10^{-10}m) of positive charge with electrons embedded into it in such a way to give most stable electrostatic arrangement.
- He visualised atom as a pudding or cake of positive charge with plum or seed (electrons) embedded into it. Thus, this model of atom is known as **plum pudding model or raisin pudding model or watermelon model**.

The main feature of this model is that almost all the mass of atom is assumed to be uniformly distributed over the atom.

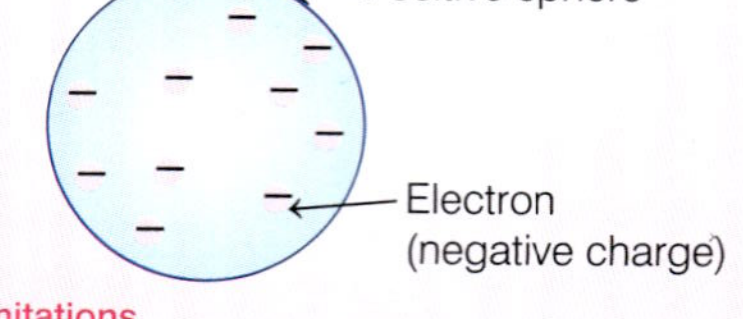

Limitations
- It could not satisfactorily explain the results of some later experiments, like gold foil scattering experiments of Rutherford.

Rutherford's Atomic Model

- Given in 1911, based on α-particle scattering experiment.
- Positive charge and most of the mass of atoms was densely concentrated in an extremely small region called **nucleus**.
- Nucleus is surrounded by electrons that move around the nucleus with high speed in circular path called **orbits**.
- Resembles solar system.
- **Drawback** This model fails to explain.
- Stability of atom.
- Electronic structure of atom.

Rutherford's α-Particles Scattering Experiment

- The gold foil has a circular fluorescent ZnS screen around it. Whenever an α-particle struck the screen, a tiny flash of light (scintillations) was produced at that point.

Gold foil
Source of alpha particles (Like radium, a radioactive substance)
Lead plate
Photographic plate

Scattering of α-particles by metal foil

Undeflected α-particles
Nucleus
α-particles deflected back
α-particles deflected by small angles

- Observations and conclusions of Rutherford experiment are given in following table.

Observations	Conclusions
Most of the α-particles passed through the gold foil undeflected.	It indicates that most of the space within the atom is empty.
A small fraction of the α-particles was deflected by small angles.	The positive charge is concentrated in a very small volume which repelled and deflected the positively charged α-particles.
A very few α-particles bounce back, i.e. deflected by nearly 180°.	It indicates that the volume occupied by nucleus is very small in comparison to the total volume of the atom.

- Alpha particles consist of two protons and two neutrons bound together to form $_2He^4$ nucleus. These particles have net spin of zero.

Dual Nature of EM radiation

- Possess both wave like and particle like character. Wave nature given by James Maxwell electrically charged particle under acceleration produces electromagnetic wave $c = \nu\lambda$ and $\nu = c/\lambda$.
- **Particle nature** Black body radiation emitted by a black body.

Wave Nature

- Clerk Maxwell showed that radiant energy has wave properties and called them electromagnetic waves or electromagnetic radiations. All these radiations travel with the speed of light and do not require any medium for their propagation or transmission.
- These radiations contain oscillating electric and magnetic fields perpendicular to each other.

Particle Nature

- **Black Body Radiation**
- The ideal body, which emits and absorbs all possible frequencies is called a black body and the radiations emitted by this body are called black body radiations. Such bodies when hot are known to emit radiations over a wide range of wavelengths and in doing so, they show colour change as shown below.

$$\text{Dull red} \xrightarrow{\Delta} \text{Red} \xrightarrow{\Delta} \text{White} \xrightarrow{\Delta} \text{Blue}$$

- At a given temperature, the relation of intensity of emitted radiation and its wavelength is shown below.

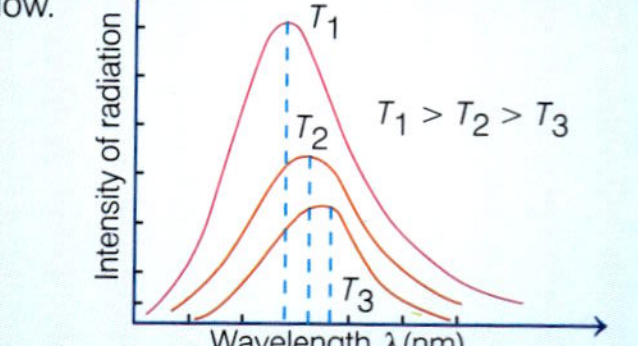

Intensity of radiation *vs* wavelength curve

- **Photoelectric Effect**
- When a light of certain frequency strikes the surface of a metal, electrons are ejected or given out from the metal surface. This phenomenon of ejection of the electrons from the metal surface under the influence of incident radiation is called photoelectric effect.
- The electrons ejected from a substance in this manner are called photoelectrons.

Test 2

Syllabus

- Spectrum of the Hydrogen Atom
- Bohr Model of a Hydrogen Atom- Its Postulates, Relation for the Energy of the Electron and Radii of the Different Orbits, Limitations of Bohr's Model

NCERT Page 37 to 49

For deeper insight **Scan the QR Code**

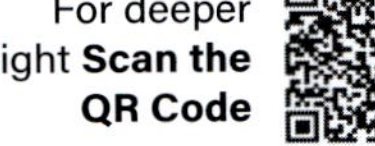

Development Leading to the Bohr's Model of atom

- In 1913 Neils Bohr introduced his atomic model which tried to explain the drawbacks of Rutherford atomic models.
- Two developments played a major role in the development of Bohr's model. These are as follows
  (i) **Dual nature of electromagnetic radiation** The electromagnetic radiation possess both wave like and particle like properties.
  (ii) **Quantisation of energy** Results of atomic spectra gave the evidence that energy is quantised.

Bohr's Atomic Model

Major postulates of Bohr's atomic model are

- The revolution of electrons around nucleus occur in circular paths of fixed radius and energy.
- These paths are called **orbits** or **stationary states** or **energy shells** or **stationary energy orbits** and are arranged concentrically around the nucleus.
- These are designated either as K, L, M, N etc., or 1, 2, 3 ....
- The integers (1, 2, 3...) were designated as n or principal quantum numbers by Bohr.
- Only those orbits are valid in which the angular momentum is quantised, i.e. have the value as an integral multiple of $h/2\pi$.
- Thus, angular momentum (M_eVr) of these orbitals can be $nh/2\pi$ where, $n=1, 2, 3, 4$ ......

- The energy of an electron within the orbit does not changes with time, i.e. during its course of revolution, the electron neither loses energy nor gains energy.
- An electron can move from one energy level to another through quantum or photon jumps only.
- When it resides in an orbit with lowest energy, it is said to be in **ground state**.
- It can jump from its lower energy level to higher energy level after absorbing energy. Here, at higher energy level, it is said to be in **excited state**.

Bohr's Calculations

- **Radii of various orbit**

$$r_n = r_0\frac{n^2}{Z} = 0.529 \times \frac{n^2}{Z}\text{ Å}$$

- **Energy of revolving electron**

$$E = -21.8\times10^{-12}\times\frac{Z^2}{n^2}\text{erg}$$

$$E = -21.8\times10^{-19}\times\frac{Z^2}{n^2}\text{J}$$

- The negative sign in all formulae of energy does not have any numerical implication. This sign only signifies that the energy of electron in an atom is lower than the energy of a free electron at infinity. The highest negative value is given for $n=1$ corresponding to most stable orbit.
- When $n=\infty$, $E=0$ which corresponds to an ionised atom, i.e. the electron and nucleus are infinitely separated.

$$H \longrightarrow H^+ + e^- \qquad \text{(ionisation)}$$

- **Bohr velocity**

$$v = 2.18\times10^8\frac{Z}{n}\text{cm/s}$$

Limitations of Bohr's Model

Bohr left the following facts unexplained

- Fine structure of atom.
- Spectrum of multi-electron systems.
- **Zeeman effect**, i.e. effect of magnetic field on an excited atom.
- **Stark effect**, i.e. effect of electric field on an excited atom.
- **Splitting**, i.e. resolution of spectral lines occur in both the effects.
- Three dimensional existence of atom.
- Dual nature of matter and especially electron.

Bohr Sommerfeld Model

Bohr along with Sommerfeld suggested the existence of elliptical orbits along with circular orbits. This had the situation of nuclei at one of the foci of ellipse and was used to explain the fine structure in hydrogen spectrum.

- So, an electron can move only from its ground state to its excited state after absorbing energy or from its excited state to ground state after releasing energy.
- During transition between two stationary states of different energies, the frequency of radiation absorbed or emitted is given by

$$v = \frac{E_2 - E_1}{h}$$

This expression is called **Bohr's frequency rule**.

Hydrogen Spectrum by Bohr's Model

- According to Bohr's model, although electrons revolve in stationary energy orbits, but these can undergo transitions as shown below.

An electron absorbs a photon of light while it jumps from a lower energy orbit and a photon is emitted while it returns to the original lower energy level.

- These transitions were proved responsible for the spectrum of an atom. In fact, Bohr explained the spectrum of hydrogen through these transitions.

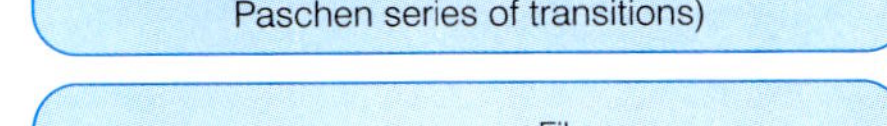

Transitions of the electron in the hydrogen atom (The diagram shows the Lyman, Balmer and Paschen series of transitions)

Spectrum

- The spectrum of hydrogen can be obtained by passing the light through spectrograph.
- This light being emitted from the discharge tube contain hydrogen at low temperature.
- It can be of following types
  (i) Emission and absorption spectra
  (ii) Line spectra or atomic spectra.
- Actually the electric discharge dissociates molecules and energetically excited hydrogen atoms are produced.
  These hydrogen atoms emit electromagnetic radiations of discrete frequencies.
- The spectrum obtained consists of large number of sharp lines each of which corresponds to a particular frequency.
  These lines are present in UV, visible and infra-red regions of electromagnetic spectrum.

Series	n_1	n_2	Spectral Region
Lyman	1	2, 3...	Ultraviolet
Balmer	2	3, 4...	Visible
Paschen	3	4, 5...	Infrared
Brackett	4	5, 6...	Infrared
Pfund	5	6, 7...	Infrared

The Spectral Lines for Atomic Hydrogen

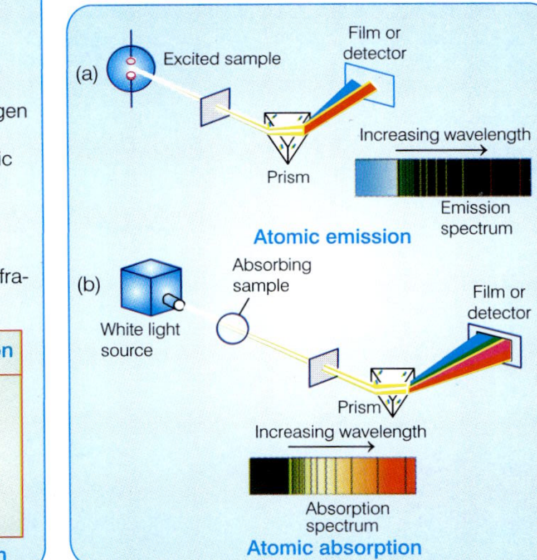

Test 3

Syllabus

Dual Nature of Matter: de-Broglie Relationship and Heisenberg Uncertainty Principle, Quantum Mechanical Model of Atom, Its Important Features, Quantum Numbers and their Significance, Rules For Filling Electrons in Orbitals, Aufbau Principle, Pauli's Exclusion Principle and Hund's Rule, Electronic Configuration of Elements

NCERT Page 49 to 67

For deeper insight **Scan the QR Code**

Chapter 02

Dual Nature of Matter : de-Broglie Equation

- The wave associated with matter waves is called de-Broglie matter wave. He also derived an expression for it, with the help of Planck's equation and Einstein's mass energy relationship. This expression is given below. $\lambda = \frac{h}{mv} = \frac{h}{p}$ where, $p = mv$ (momentum)
- In case kinetic energy, E of the particle is given, the de-Broglie wavelength can be calculated by the formula. $\lambda = \frac{h}{\sqrt{2mE}}$ (where, $p = \sqrt{2mE}$)
- For a charged particle of charge q following modification in de-Broglie equation is visible. $\lambda = \frac{h}{\sqrt{2eVm}}$

Heisenberg Uncertainty Principle

- It is impossible to predict accurately and simultaneously the position and momentum of microscopic particles like an electron.

$$\Delta x \times \Delta p_x \geq \frac{h}{4\pi}$$

- One of the important implications of the Heisenberg Uncertainty principle is that it rules out existence of definite paths or trajectories of electrons and other similar particles. The trajectory of an object is determined by its location and velocity at various moments.
- The effect of Heisenberg uncertainty principle is significant only for motion of microscopic objects and is negligible for that of macroscopic objects.

Shapes of Atomic Orbitals

- **s-orbital** Boundary surface diagram is centered on nucleus. The sphere has a region having probability of finding an e^- about 90%. With n, size increases. $4s > 3s > 2s > 1s$.
- **p-orbital** The shape of p-orbitals is dumbbell. It has lobes on either side of plane passing through nucleus.
- **d-orbital** There are total five types of d-orbitals. These orbitals are d_{xy}, d_{yz}, d_{zx}, $d_{x^2-y^2}$, d_{z^2}. Represented by the plane in which the orbital lies. Has shape of a double dumb-bell except d_{z^2}.

3-D Representation of Atomic Orbitals

s-orbital, p_x-orbital, p_y-orbital, p_z-orbital, $d_{x^2-y^2}$-orbital, d_{xy}-orbital, d_{yz}-orbital, d_{xz}-orbital, d_{z^2}-orbital

Quantum Mechanical Model

- Takes into account dual behaviour of matter.
- Schrodinger equation for any system (atom) whose energy does not change is as $\hat{H}\psi = E\psi$.
- **Schrodinger Equation**
- Energy of electrons is quantised. Follows Heisenberg principle and only talks about probability. Defines ψ as wave function for any electron in an atomic orbital as

$$\frac{\partial^2\Psi}{dx^2} + \frac{\partial^2\Psi}{dy^2} + \frac{\partial^2\Psi}{dz^2} + \frac{8\pi^2 m}{h^2}(E - V)\,\Psi = 0$$

Energy of Orbitals

- The orbitals having same energy are called **degenerate orbitals**.
- Existing state of any electron is ground state
- Any other state other than ground state is called excited state.
- For a shell number n, $s<p<d<f$ (Order of energy)
- Effective nuclear charge (Z_{eff}):

$$Z_{eff} = Z - \sigma \ (\sigma\text{-shielding})$$

- Electrons in the outer shells experience less nuclear charge due to shielding by electrons in inner shells.

$Z_{eff} \propto \frac{1}{l}$ value, hence $s < p$ (Energy)

Graphs of ψ and ψ^2 with Distance (r)

- Plots of orbital wave function ψ (r) as a function of distance r of 1s and 2s orbitals are

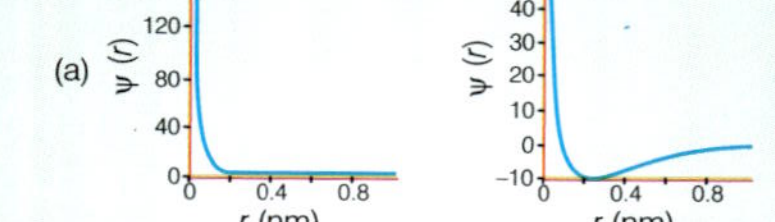

- Plots of the variation of probability density ψ^2 (r) as a function of distance r of electron in 1s and 2s orbitals.

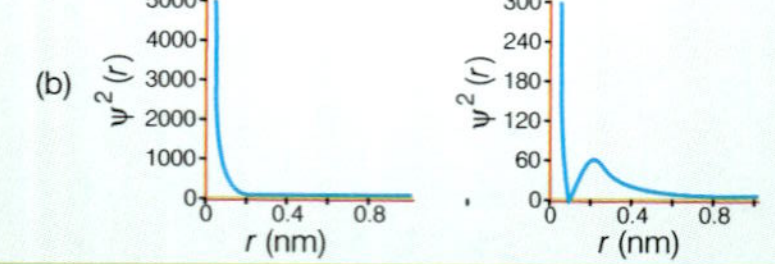

Nodes

- Regions where probability of finding an electron is zero.
- **Total nodes** in an orbital $= n - 1$
- **Radial nodes** Regions of zero probability across an axis. It is calculated by $(n - l - 1)$
- **Angular nodes** Regions of zero probability across a plane. It is given by value of 'l'.

Quantum Numbers

- **Principal Quantum Number (n)** tells about size and energy of an orbital.

$n = 1\ 2\ 3\ 4 \ldots$

Shell $= K\ L\ M\ N \ldots$

- **Azimuthal Quantum Number (l)**
- Tells about number of subshells and shapes of orbitals. $l = 0 \ldots n - 1$
  For s-orbital, $l = 0$, For p-orbitals $l = 1$
  For d-orbitals $l = 2$, For f-orbitals $l = 3$
- **Magnetic Orbital Quantum Number (m_l):**
- Tells about number of orbitals in any subshell.
- For any l, $(2l + 1)$ values of m_l are possible.
- **Electron Spin Quantum Number (m_s)**
- The value of s is $+1/2$ and $-1/2$, which signifies the spin or rotation or direction of electron on it's axis during movement.

Magnetic field; S, N; N, S

Filling of Orbitals

The filling of electrons into the orbitals of different atoms takes place according to Aufbau principle which is based on the Pauli's exclusion principle, the Hund's rule of maximum multiplicity and relative energies of the orbitals.

Aufbau Principle

- Atoms are filled in order of increasing energies.
- Orbitals are arranged on the basis of $(n + l)$ rule
  $1s < 2s < 2p < 3s$
  $< 3p < 4s < 3d$
  $< 4p < 5s < 4d < 5p$
  $< 6s < 4f < 5d < 6p$
  $< 7s$

1s; 2s 2p; 3s 3p 3d; 4s 4p 4d 4f; 5s 5p 5d 5f; 6s 6p 6d; 7s 7p

Pauli's Principle

- No two electrons in an atom can have same set of quantum numbers.
- Only two electrons can occupy the same orbitals with opposite spin.
  Maximum electrons in a shell $= 2n^2$.

Hund's Rule

Pairing of an electrons (e^-) in a subshell (s,p,d,f) does not take place until each orbital get one e^- in that subshell or singly occupied.

e.g. ⥮ | ↿ ↿ (Correct) ⥮ | | (Incorrect)

Symmetric Distribution

- Symmetry leads to stability
- Electrons in the same subshell do not shield one another effectively. Experience equal nuclear charge.

Exchange Energy

- Electrons having same spin tend to exchange positions. Energy released due to this exchange provides stability. More exchanges are possible when the subshell is fully or half-filled.and so on giving a total of 10 exchanges.

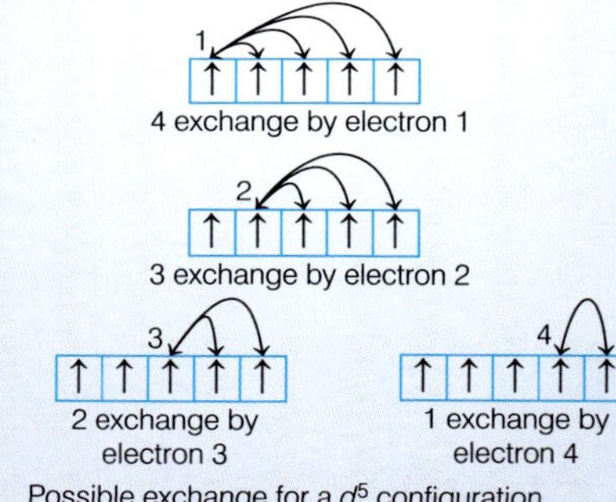

Possible exchange for a d^5 configuration.

Electronic Configuration

- Electron orbit the central nucleus in shells. Each shell can hold $2n^2$ electrons, where n is the principal quantum number.
- In electronic configuration $[nX^Y]$ n represents principal quantum number. X is the type of orbital and y is the number of electrons in the orbitals of the subshell e.g. potassium has 19 electrons and its electron configuration is written as

$$1s^2 2s^2 2p^6 3s^2 3p^6 4s^1$$

- Electronic configurations of ions can be determined by using the same building up principle $[nX^Y]$.e.g. K^+ is the same as potassium but one electron has been removed, therefore it is $1s^2 s^2 2p^6 3s^2 3p^6$.
- Take care with d-block ions, as 4s fills before 3d, but it also empties before 3d when forming ions. For two electrons in the same orbital, the spin must be opposite to minimize the repulsion.

Test 1

Syllabus

- Modern Periodic Law and Present Form of the Periodic Table
- *s*, *p*, *d* and *f*-Block Elements

NCERT Page 74 to 85

For deeper insight **Scan the QR Code**

Chapter 03

Genesis of Periodic Classification

- Dobereiner's Triads

Element	At. wt.	Element	At. wt.
Li	7	Ca	40
Na	23	Sr	88
K	39	Ba	137

- Put elements in several groups of triads.
- Atomic weight and properties of middle element was an average of the other two elements.
- Limitation
  Worked only for a few elements.

Newlands' Law of Octaves

- It is based on law of octaves.
- Arranged elements in increasing order of atomic weights.
- Made observation that every 8th element had properties similar to first element.

Musical scale	Sa	Re	Ga	Ma	Pa	Dha	Ni
Element	Li	Be	B	C	N	O	F
Atomic weight	7	9	11	12	14	16	19
Element	Na	Mg	Al	Si	P	S	Cl
Atomic weight	23	24	27	29	31	32	35.5
Element	K	Ca					
Atomic weight	39	40					

- Limitation
  Worked only for elements upto calcium.

Lothar Meyer's Atomic Volume Curve

- The German Chemist Lothar Meyer in 1870, independently introduced the idea of periodicity in properties of the elements from study of their atomic volumes [gram atomic mass/density].

Atomic volume (cm^3)

Atomic mass (u)

Position of alkali metals at maxima

Position of alkaline earth metals

Position of halogens

Position of transition elements at minima

Mendeleev's Periodic Table

- Periodic Law
- Properties, both physical and chemical are a periodic function of their atomic weights.
- Arranged elements in horizontal rows and vertical columns in order of increasing atomic weights.
- Elements with similar properties occupied the same group. Emphasis was put on similarities in properties rather than atomic weights.
- Characteristics
- The table consists of 9 vertical columns called groups and 7 horizontal rows called periods.
- The groups are marked from 0 to VIII of which group I to VII are subdivided into sub-groups A and B.
- The group VIII has three similar elements placed together at one place. These are called transition triads, e.g. Fe, Co and Ni; Ru, Rh and Pd; Os, Ir and Pt etc.
- Limitations
- I with lower atomic weight than that of Te was placed after Te with higher atomic weight.
- Irregularities in properties of lanthanides and actinides.
- Elements with similar properties were kept at different places while those with different properties were kept together. e.g. Cd and Hg placed with dissimilar elements like Ba, Mg and Ca. While Cu and Hg despite having similarity were kept at different positions.
- No separate place was allotted to allotropes.

Modern Periodic Law

- Irregularities in X-ray spectra of elements was observed by Henry moseley in 1913.
- For ν frequency, $\sqrt{\nu}$ *vs* atomic number gave a straight line plot.
- Periodic law Physical and chemical properties of the elements are periodic function of their atomic number.

Characteristics

- Starting from hydrogen to uranium, there are 92 elements which are arranged in different periods.
- In the 6th period, 14 elements after lanthanum (Z=57) to lutetium (Z=71) are given one position in III B group termed as lanthanides.
- In same period, 14 elements after actinium (Z=89) to lawrencium (Z=103) are also added to same place and called as actinides.

Long Form of Periodic Table

- *s* and *p*-block–representative elements
- *f*-block–inner transition elements
- *d*-block–transition elements

1 IA	2 IIA	3 IIIA	4 IVA	5 VA	6 VIA	7 VIIA	8 ←	9 VIII	10 →	11 IB	12 IIB	13 IIIB	14 IVB	15 VB	16 VIB	17 VIIB	18 0
1 H $1s^1$																	2 He $1s^2$
3 Li $2s^1$	4 Be $2s^2$											5 B $2s^22p^1$	6 C $2s^22p^2$	7 N $2s^22p^3$	8 O $2s^22p^4$	9 F $2s^22p^5$	10 Ne $2s^22p^6$
11 Na $3s^1$	12 Mg $3s^2$											13 Al $3s^23p^1$	14 Si $3s^23p^2$	15 P $3s^23p^3$	16 S $3s^23p^4$	17 Cl $3s^23p^5$	18 Ar $3s^23p^6$
19 K $4s^1$	20 Ca $4s^2$	21 Sc $3d^14s^2$	22 Ti $3d^24s^2$	23 V $3d^34s^2$	24 Cr $3d^54s^1$	25 Mn $3d^54s^2$	26 Fe $3d^64s^2$	27 Co $3d^74s^2$	28 Ni $3d^84s^2$	29 Cu $3d^{10}4s^1$	30 Zn $3d^{10}4s^2$	31 Ga $4s^24p^1$	32 Ge $4s^24p^2$	33 As $4s^24p^3$	34 Se $4s^24p^4$	35 Br $4s^24p^5$	36 Kr $4s^24p^6$
37 Rb $5s^1$	38 Sr $5s^2$	39 Y $4d^15s^2$	40 Zr $4d^25s^2$	41 Nb $4d^45s^1$	42 Mo $4d^55s^1$	43 Tc $4d^55s^2$	44 Ru $4d^75s^1$	45 Rh $4d^85s^1$	46 Pd $4d^{10}$	47 Ag $4d^{10}5s^1$	48 Cd $4d^{10}5s^2$	49 In $5s^25p^1$	50 Sn $5s^25p^2$	51 Sb $5s^25p^3$	52 Te $5s^25p^4$	53 I $5s^25p^5$	54 Xe $5s^25p^6$
55 Cs $6s^1$	56 Ba $6s^2$	57 La* $5d^16s^2$	72 Hf $4f^{14}5d^26s^2$	73 Ta $5d^36s^2$	74 W $5d^46s^2$	75 Re $5d^56s^2$	76 Os $5d^66s^2$	77 Ir $5d^76s^2$	78 Pt $5d^96s^1$	79 Au $5d^{10}6s^1$	80 Hg $5d^{10}6s^2$	81 Tl $6s^26p^1$	82 Pb $6s^26p^2$	83 Bi $6s^26p^3$	84 Po $6s^26p^4$	85 At $6s^26p^5$	86 Rn $6s^26p^6$
87 Fr $7s^1$	88 Ra $7s^2$	89 Ac** $6d^17s^2$	104 Rf	105 Db	106 Sg	107 Bh	108 Hs	109 Mt	110 Ds	111 Rg	112 Cn	113 Nh	114 Fl	115 Mc	116 Lv	117 Ts	118 Og

Inner-transition elements (*f*-block elements)

*Lanthanoids $4f^n5d^{0-1}6s^2$	58 Ce $4f^25d^06s^2$	59 Pr $4f^35d^06s^2$	60 Nd $4f^45d^06s^2$	61 Pm $4f^55d^06s^2$	62 Sm $4f^65d^06s^2$	63 Eu $4f^75d^06s^2$	64 Gd $4f^75d^16s^2$	65 Tb $4f^95d^06s^2$	66 Dy $4f^{10}5d^06s^2$	67 Ho $4f^{11}5d^06s^2$	68 Er $4f^{12}5d^06s^2$	69 Tm $4f^{13}5d^06s^2$	70 Yb $4f^{14}5d^06s^2$	71 Lu $4f^{14}5d^16s^2$
**Actinoids $5f^n6d^{0-2}7s^2$	90 Th $5f^06d^27s^2$	91 Pa $5f^26d^17s^2$	92 U $5f^36d^17s^2$	93 Np $5f^46d^17s^2$	94 Pu $5f^66d^07s^2$	95 Am $5f^76d^07s^2$	96 Cm $5f^76d^17s^2$	97 Bk $5f^96d^07s^2$	98 Cf $5f^{10}6d^07s^2$	99 Es $5f^{11}6d^07s^2$	100 Fm $5f^{12}6d^07s^2$	101 Md $5f^{13}6d^07s^2$	102 No $5f^{14}6d^07s^2$	103 Lr $5f^{14}6d^17s^2$

Demerits

- Position of hydrogen is inappropriate as it resembles both alkali metals and halogens.
- Lanthanides and actinides are not merged in the main body of the table.

Notation for IUPAC Nomenclature of Elements

Digit	Name	Abbreviation	Digit	Name	Abbreviation
0	nil	n	5	pent	p
1	un	u	6	hex	h
2	bi	b	7	sept	s
3	tri	t	8	oct	o
4	quad	q	9	enn	e

Nomenclature of Element with Atomic Number >100

At.No.	Name	At.No.	Name
101	Unnilunium (Unu)	108	Unniloctium (Uno)
102	Unnilbium (Unb)	109	Unnilennium (Une)
103	Unniltrium (Unt)	110	Ununnillium (Uun)
104	Unnilquadium (Unq)	111	Unununium (Uuu)
105	Unnilpentium (Unp)	112	Ununbium (Uub)
106	Unnilhexium(Unh)	113	Ununtrium (Uut)
107	Unnilseptium (Uns)	114	Ununquadium (Uuq)

Description of Periods

Period	*n*	Subshell	No. of elements	Element	Name of period
1	1	1*s*	2	$_1H$–$_2He$	Shortest
2	2	2*s*,2*p*	8	$_3Li$–$_{10}Ne$	Short
3	3	3*s*,3*p*	8	$_{11}Na$–$_{18}Ar$	Short
4	4	4*s*,3*d*,4*p*	18	$_{19}K$–$_{36}Kr$	Long
5	5	5*s*,4*d*,5*p*	18	$_{37}Rb$–$_{54}Xe$	Long
6	6	6*s*,4*f*,5*d*,6*p*	32	$_{55}Cs$–$_{86}Rn$	Longest
7	7	7*s*,5*f*,6*d*	32	$_{87}Fr$–$_{118}Og$	Longest

Electronic Configuration

- Group 1 Alkali metals → ns^1
- Group 2 Alkaline earth metals → ns^2
- Group 11 Coinage metals → $ns^1 (n-1)d^{10}$
- Group 12 Zinc family → $ns^2 (n-1)d^{10}$
- Group 13 Boron Family → $ns^2 np^1$
- Group 14 Carbon Family → $ns^2 np^2$
- Group 15 Pnictogens → $ns^2 np^3$
- Group 16 Chalcogens → $ns^2 np^4$
- Group 17 Halogens → $ns^2 np^5$
- Group 18 Noble gases → $ns^2 np^6$

Test 2

Syllabus

- Periodic Properties and their Trends-1 (Atomic Radius, Ionisation Enthalpy, Electron Gain Enthalpy, Electronegativity, Metallic Character)

NCERT Page 85 to 92

For deeper insight **Scan the QR Code**

Periodic Properties of Elements

- The reoccurrence of similar physical and chemical properties after regular intervals when elements are arranged in the order of increasing atomic number is called **periodicity**.
- The reason for periodicity is the repetition of similar valence shell electronic configuration at regular interval. The properties which show periodicity are called **periodic properties**.

Atomic Radius

- The distance from the centre of the nucleus to the outermost shell containing electrons is called **atomic radius**.
- It may be covalent, metallic or van der Waals' radii.
- It decreases along a period from left to right but increases on moving down the group.

Measurement of Atomic Radius

- Atomic radius can be measured by following approaches

Atomic radius → Covalent radius, Metallic radius, Ionic radius; Ionic radius → Cationic radius, Anionic radius

- **Covalent radius** It is one-half of the internuclear distance between the centres of nuclei of two identical or almost identical atoms bonded by a single covalent bond.
- **Metallic radius** It is one-half of the internuclear distance between two adjacent metal atoms in the closely packed metallic crystal lattice.
- **Ionic radius** The distance from the centre of nucleus to the most distant electron cloud bond to it within an ion.
- **Cationic radius** A cation is formed by the loss of one or more electrons from an atom. Radius of cation is always smaller than parent atom.
- **Anionic radius** An anion is formed by the gain of one or more electrons to an atom. The size of anion is always larger than that of corresponding neutral atom.

Isoelectronic Species

- These species are cations, anions or atoms which contain equal number of electrons but different size (ionic or atomic radii) due to different value of atomic number.
- Greater is the value of Z lesser is the radii of isoelectronic species.

Factors Affecting Atomic Radius

- As the number of shells in an atom increase, atomic radius increases.
  Atomic radius varies inversely with nuclear charge, i.e.
  $$\text{atomic radius} \propto \frac{1}{\text{nuclear charge}}$$
- Atomic radius vary directly with shielding effect, i.e. greater the shielding effect, larger will be the atomic radius.

Ionisation Enthalpy

- It is the energy required to remove an electron from an isolated gaseous atom.
- It decreases down the group and increases along a period from left to right.

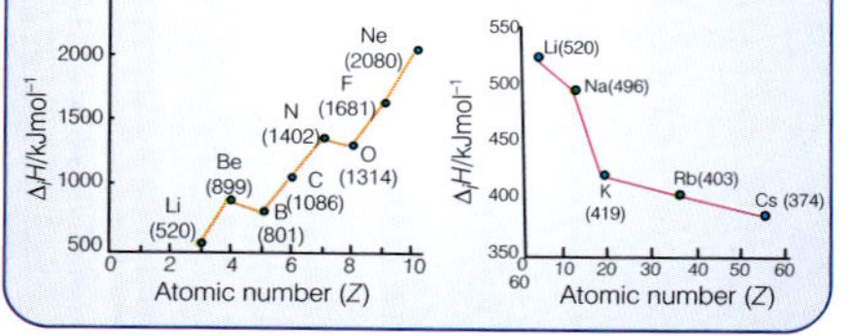

Factors Affecting Ionisation Enthalpy

- **Atomic size** Larger the atomic size, smaller is the I.E.
  $$\text{IE} \propto \frac{1}{\text{Atomic size}}$$
- **Effective nuclear charge** (Z_{eff}) IE increases with the increase in nuclear charge between outermost electrons and nucleus.
- **Screening effect** Higher screening effect on the outermost electrons causes less attraction from the nucleus and hence electron can be easily removed, which leads electron to the lower value of I.E.
  $$\text{IE} \propto \frac{1}{\text{Screening effect}}$$
- **Penetration power of sub-shells** The order of attraction of subshell towards nucleus. (Penetration power) is $s > p > d > f$.
- **Stability of half-filled and fully-filled orbitals electronic configuration** If an atom has fully-filled or half-filled orbitals, such an arrangement is highly stable
  Therefore, their first ionisation energy is higher than both of its neighbour in the periodic table.
- **Oxidation state** I.E. $\propto$ oxidation state of an atom e.g. $Fe^{3+} > Fe^{2+} > Fe$

Electron Gain Enthalpy

It is the energy change occurring during the conversion of an atom into an anion. It also follows the same trends as ionisation enthalpy.

Element	$\Delta_{eg}H$ (kJ mol^{-1})	Element	$\Delta_{eg}H$ (kJ mol^{-1})
H	−73	F	− 328
Li	−60	Cl	− 349
Na	−53	Br	− 325
O	−141	He	+ 48
S	−200	Ne	+116

Factors Affecting Electron Gain Enthalpy

- **Size of atom** Greater the atomic radius of the atom, lower is the magnitude of electron gain enthalpy.
  $$\Delta_{eg}H \propto \frac{1}{r_{\text{atom}}\text{ (Atomic radius)}}$$
- **Effective nuclear charge** Greater the effective nuclear charge, higher will be the magnitude of electron gain enthalpy.
- **Penetration power** More penetrating are subshells of the valence shells, easier is the addition of electron to that subshell.
  Hence, magnitude of electron gain enthalpy for addition of electron shows the following order
  $$s>p>d>f$$
- **Electronic configuration** If an atom has fully-filled or half-filled orbitals, it's stability is higher than expected from its position in the periodic table. For all such cases, the value of electron gain enthalpy will be positive, e.g. noble gases.
  $$\Delta_{eg}H \propto \frac{1}{\text{stability of electronic configuration}}$$

Electronegativity

It is the electron attracting power of an element in a compound. It also follows the same trend as IE. It is not a measurable quantity.

$A—B \rightarrow A^+ + B^-$ (E.N. of B > E.N. of A)

$A—B \rightarrow A^- + B^+$ (E.N. of A > E.N. of B)

Atom	EN Value	Atom	EN Value
Li	1.0	F	4.0
Na	0.9	Cl	3.0
N	3.0	Br	2.8

$$\text{EN} \propto \frac{1}{\text{Atomic size}}$$

$$\text{E.N} \propto Z_{eff} \propto \frac{\text{Positive charge}}{\text{Negative charge}}$$

Factors Affecting Electronegativity

- **Atomic size** As atomic size decreases electronegativity increases.
  $$\text{Electronegativity} \propto \frac{1}{\text{Atomic size}}$$
- **Effective nuclear charge** (Z_{eff}) As Z_{eff} increases. electronegativity increases. Electronegativity $\propto Z_{eff}$
  Electronegativity does not depend on filled or half-filled orbitals, because it is the tendency to attract bonded electron, not to gain electron from outside.
- **Hybridisation state of an atom** As s-character increases the electronegativity also increases.
  Electronegativity $\propto$ % of s-character in hybridised atom

	sp >	sp^2 >	sp^3
s-character	50%	33%	25%
Electronegativity	3.25	2.75	2.5

This is because s-orbital is nearer to nucleus so by increasing s-character in hybridisation state, electronegativity also increase.

Electropositive or Metallic Character

The tendency of an element to form the cation by the loss of electrons is called its electropositive character or metallic character. $M(g) \longrightarrow M^+(g) + e^-$

- **Metals** There are 91 metals out of 118 elements. These are electropositive elements.
  Their characteristic properties include high thermal and electrical conductivity, high tensile strength, high malleability and ductility, high elasticity, high density, high melting and boiling points.
- **Non-metals** There are 20 non-metals. These are electronegative elements and have the tendency to gain electrons to attain negative charge.
  Their distinguishing properties are almost opposite to those of metals. They have low thermal and electrical conductivity, low density, low melting and boiling points.
- **Metalloids** These are seven elements (Si, Ge, As, Sb, Te, Po and At) which have their properties intermediate to those of metal and non-metals.
  The tendency of an element to lose electron is closely connected to the IE of the element.
  The smaller the IE of an element, the greater will be its tendency to lose electrons and thus greater will be its metallic character. Further , the tendency to oxidise itself provides reducing property to the elements thus, smaller the IE, greater the metallic character hence greater the reducing nature.

Trend in Periodic Table

Metallic character decreases across the period while it increases on moving down the group.
This tendency varies inversely with ionisation energy and electronegativity of an element.

Test 3

Syllabus
- Periodic Properties and their Trends-2 (Lattice Enthalpy, Hydration Enthalpy, Oxidation State and Chemical Properties)

NCERT Page 92 to 95

For deeper insight **Scan the QR Code**

Chapter 03

Lattice Energy

It can be defined as the energy required to convert one mole of an ionic solid into gaseous ionic constituents.

Periodic Trends in Lattice Energy

- Lattice energy is affected by ionic size and ionic charge.
- As ionic size increases, lattice energy decreases. Therefore, lattice energy decreases on moving down the group.
- It increases on going from left to right in a period.

Hydration Energy

- Energy released when one mole of gaseous ions dissolves in water to form an infinitely dilute solution.
- The size of ion and its charge determines the extent of hydration.

Trends in Hydration Enthalpy

- Hydration enthalpy decreases down the group and increases on moving left to right in a period. It depends on charge density.
- Greater is the charge density, more easily it attracts the lone pair of oxygen atom from H_2O molecule and more easily it is hydrated and hence, more energy is released.
- If the hydration energy is greater than lattice energy, then the enthalpy of solution is negative (heat is released), otherwise it is positive (heat is absorbed).
- The hydration energy should not be confused with solvation energy, which is the change in Gibb's free energy (not enthalpy) as solute in the gaseous state is dissolved.

Valency

- It is the combining capacity of an element and can never be equal to zero.
- It is only a number and is not assigned a-positive or negative charge.

Trends in Valency

- On moving from left to right it increases from 1 to 7 with respect to hydrogen and then decreases to 1 with respect to oxygen.
- On moving down the group, it remains same.

Chemical Reactivity

- It is highest at the two extremes of a period and is lowest at the centre. This is because the elements present at left extreme of a period have the lowest ionisation enthalpy and that present at the right extreme have the highest electron affinity.
- Highly reactive elements are always found in combined state. In the groups, the reactivity of former elements (that present at left extreme) increases while that of latter (present at right extremes) decreases.

1	2	13	14	15	16	17	18
Na	Mg	Al	Si	P	S	Cl	Ar
Very reactive			Least reactive			Very reactive	Inert
Chemical reactivity Decreases			Chemical reactivity Increases				

Nature of Oxyacids

- When non-metal oxides are dissolved in water, they form oxyacids.
- Generally atoms having less electronegativity than oxygen form oxyacids.
- **Acidic strength** The acidic strength of oxyacids of an element increases with the increase of oxygen atom in it.
- **Exception** The strength of oxyacids of phosphorus increases in the order
$$H_3PO_4 < H_3PO_3 < H_3PO_2$$
- **Basicity** of an oxyacid is equal to the number of —OH groups present in the molecule.

Calculation of Valency

- The valency can be calculated from the concept based on the electronic configuration.
- According to this concept valency for IA, IIA, IIIB, IVB group elements it is equal to number of valence electron and from VB to zero group, it is [8– (number of valence electron)].

Valency = No. of valence e^-

	IA	IIA	IIIB	IVB
	ns^1	ns^2	ns^2np^1	ns^2np^2
Valence shell e^-	1	2	3	4
Valency	1	2	3	4

Valency = (8–No. of valence e^-)

	VB	VIB	VIIB	0
	ns^2np^3	ns^2np^4	ns^2np^5	ns^2np^6
Valence shell e^-	5	6	7	8
Valency	3	2	1	0
	(8–5) = 3			(8–8) = 0

Oxidation States

- It is the residual charge left on an atom of a molecule when other atoms of the molecule are removed as ions. Its value can be zero, positive, negative or fractional. An element can have different oxidation states in different compounds, e.g. Oxidation state of N in NO_2, NO, N_2O_3 and N_2O_5 are +4, +2, +3 and +5 respectively.
- In case of alkali and alkaline earth metals it is fixed, i.e. +1 and +2 respectively.
- It is generally variable for other elements. Higher *p*-block elements exhibit more stability for lower oxidation state due to inert pair effect, e.g. Pb^{4+} is less stable than Pb^{2+}.
- In case of *d*-block elements, maximum oxidation state $=(n-1)d\,e^-$(unpaired) $+ns\,e^-$.
- In general, the stability of the higher oxidation states is in the order $3d < < 4d < 5d$.

Reducing and Oxidising Properties

- Reducing agents provide electrons, thus metals act as good reducing agents. The reducing power of elements in the periodic table shows the following trend.

Decrease (across the period)
Reducing power of elements
Increase (down the group)

- Oxidising agents accept electrons, thus non-metals are good oxidising agents.
- The oxidising power of elements shows following trend in the periodic table.

Increase (across the period)
Oxidising power of elements
Decrease (down the group)

- Thus, alkali metals are most powerful reducing agents while halogens are most powerful oxidising agents in the periodic table.

Nature of Oxide

- Non-metals oxides are acidic in nature, semi-metal oxides are amphoteric in nature while metal oxides are basic in nature.
- Acidic nature of oxides increases along a period from left to right but decreases on moving down the group.
- Basic nature of oxides decreases across the period on moving from left to right while it increases on moving down the group.

Amphoteric oxides	Neutral oxides
Reacts with acids as well as bases	Does not react with an acid or a base
BeO_2, Al_2O_3, ZnO, Cr_2O_3	CO, N_2O, NO

Other Properties of Elements

- **Melting and boiling points** There is no regular trend in the variation of melting and boiling points in a group or period.
- In a period, noble gases have very low melting and boiling points due to the presence of very weak van der Waals' forces of attractions between the monoatomic molecules.
- **Density** There is no regular trend in the variation of density in a group or period.
- In general, stronger and compact binding leads to high density.
- **Atomic volume** Volume occupied by one gram atom of an element in solid state is called its atomic volume.
- Atomic volume is equal to atomic weight/density. It increases on moving down the group.
- On moving from left to right in a period atomic volume first decreases and becomes minimum in the middle and then again begins to increase.

Anomalous Behaviour of Second Period Elements

- The first element of each of the group 1 (Li), group 2 (Be) and group 13-17 (B to F) differs from the other members of their respective groups in many aspects.
- e.g. Lithium and beryllium unlike other members of their groups form compounds which possess covalent character while other members of their groups form ionic compounds.
- Lithium (group 1) resembles magnesium (group 2) and beryllium resembles aluminium [group 13]. This similarity in properties of elements placed diagonally to each other is called diagonal relationship.

Li	Be	B	C
Na	Mg	Al	Si

- The reasons attributed for such chemical behaviour are (a) small size (b) large charge/radius ratio (c) high electronegativity of the elements (d) absence of any vacant *d*-orbital.

Summary of Trends

Periodic property	Variation	
	Along a period	Along a group
Atomic radius	Decreases	Increases
Ionic radius	Decreases	Increases
Metallic nature	Decreases	Increases
Electron gain enthalpy	Increases	Decreases
Ionisation energy	increases	Decreases
Electronegativity	Increases	Decreases
Basic nature of oxides	Decreases	Increases
Acidic nature of oxides	Increases	Decreases
Reducing power	Decreases	Increases

Test 1

Syllabus

- Kossel-Lewis Approach to Chemical Bond Formation
- Concept of Ionic Bonds: Formation of Ionic Bond, Factors Affecting the Formation of Ionic Bonds, Lattice Enthalpy
- Covalent Bonding, Concept of Electronegativity, Fajans' Rule, Dipole Moment

NCERT Page 100 to 110

For deeper insight **Scan the QR Code**

Chapter 04

Electrovalent or Ionic Bond

- The electrostatic force of attractions between an anion and a cation formed by complete transfer of electrons.
- Difference in electronegativities of two atoms must be about two or more.
  e.g. NaCl, $MgCl_2$ etc.
- Electropositive atom forms a cation while electronegative forms an anion.

Factors Affecting the Formation of Ionic Bonds

The formation of an ionic bond is related to the ease of formation of cations and anions.

All those factors which help in the formation of ions are given below in a summarised way

- The ionisation enthalpies involved should be low so that the metal atom forms a positive ion easily.
- The quantitative values of electron gain enthalpies should be high, (in negative value) so that the non-metal atom forms a negative ion easily.
- Lattice enthalpies involved should be high.

Coordinate Bond

- Formed between atoms having excess and deficiency of electrons.
- One atom completely transfers its electrons into an empty orbital of another atom. e.g. NH_4^+, CO.

Lattice Enthalpy

- The energy required to completely separate one mole of a solid ionic compound into gaseous constituent ions. For example, the lattice enthalpy of NaCl is 788 kJ mol^{-1}. This means that 788 kJ of energy is required to separate one mole of solid NaCl into one mole of Na^+ (g) and one mole of Cl^- (g) to an infinite distance.
- This process involves both the attractive forces between ions of opposite charges and the repulsive forces between ions of like charges. This solid crystal being three dimensional; it is not possible to calculate lattice enthalpy directly from the interaction of forces of attraction and repulsion only. Factors associated with the crystal geometry have to be included.

Cl^- →
Na^+ →

Kossel-Lewis Approach

- **Atoms** can combine either by transfer of valence electrons from one atom to another or by sharing of valence electrons in order to have a complete octet in their valence shell.
  This is known as **octet rule**. Valence shell electrons are outer shell electrons that take part in reactions.
- **Limitations of Octet Rule**

Not applicable on atoms/molecules which

- have less than four outer electrons. e.g BF_3
- have an extra energy level to accept electrons e.g. PF_5
- have odd number of electrons e.g NO, ClO_2
- could not explain shape, relative stability of molecules.

Covalent Bond

Electrostatic force of attraction developed between the nucleus of one atom and electron cloud of another atom having shared equal number of electrons.

- **Polar covalent bond**
  shared electron are directed more towards the atom having greater electronegativity. e.g. NH_3, H_2O etc.
- **Non-polar covalent bond**
  shared electrons are equally attracted by the two atoms as they have same electronegativity e.g. H_2, Cl_2 etc.
- **Conditions**
  Favourable conditions for covalent bond formation are as follows
- Electronegativity difference between the combining atom should be small.
- Combining atoms should have incomplete valence shell electronic configurations.

Fajans' Rule

- Magnitude of covalent character in an ionic bond depends upon the extent of polarisation caused by cation.
- Polarising power (cation)
  $$\propto \frac{1}{\text{size of cation}}$$
- Smaller cations usually possess higher charge, thus causes more polarisation of anion.
- The polarising power of those cations which don't have inert gas configuration will be more in comparison to cations having inert gas configuration.
- Polarisability (anion) ∝ size of anion.
- Larger anions will be more easily polarised in comparison to smaller anions.

Lewis Representation of Simple Molecules (the Lewis Structures)

The Lewis dot structures provide a picture of bonding in molecules and ions in terms of the shared pairs of electrons and the octet. e.g.

Molecules/Ion	Lewis Representation
O_2	:Ö=Ö:
CO_3^{2-}	$[:\ddot{O}-C(=\ddot{O}:)-\ddot{O}:]^{2-}$

Formal Charge

The difference between the number of valence electrons of that atom in an isolated or free state and the number of electrons assigned to that atom in the Lewis structure. It is expressed as:

Formal charge on an atom in a Lewis structure = [Total number of valence electrons in the free atom] − [Total number of non-bonding (lone pair electrons)] −(1/2) [Total number of bonding (shared) electrons]

Dipole Moment

- Molecules having polar covalent bonds possess dipole moment.
- Dipole moment (μ) = electric charge (q) × separation (d)
- It is measured in 'Debye' unit. (D).
- 1D = 10^{-18} esu cm = 3.33×10^{-30} C-m
- Net dipole moment

$$(\mu) = \sqrt{\mu_1^2 + \mu_2^2 + 2\mu_1\mu_2\cos\theta}$$

$$\%\text{ ionic character} = \frac{\mu_{obs}}{\mu_{ionic}} \times 100$$

$\overset{\delta^+}{H}$—$\overset{\delta^-}{F}$

$\mu = 0.8 \times 10^{-30}$ C-m $\quad$ $\mu = 4.9 \times 10^{-30}$ C-m

Types of molecule	Example	Dipole moment (μ)
Molecule (AB)	HCl, H_2	1.07, 0
Molecule (AB_2)	H_2O	1.85
Molecule (AB_3)	NH_3	1.47
Molecule (AB_4)	CH_4	0

Bond Parameters

- **Bond Length**
  The average distance between the nuclei of two bonded atoms in a molecule.

r_A r_B A B

Factors affecting Bond Length

(i) **Size of the atoms**
Bond length depends upon the size of the atoms and nature of bonds. It increases with increase in the size of the atoms, e.g. bond length increases as the size of halogen increases in hydrogen halides.

$$H—F < H—Cl < H—Br < H—I$$

(ii) **Multiplicity of bonds** Bond length decreases as the bond multiplicity increases. This is because larger the number of electrons shared by the two atoms greater will be the attractive force between electrons and nuclei and consequently, lesser is the bond length. The carbon-carbon lengths follows the order

$$C \equiv C < C = C < C — C$$

(iii) **Type of hybridisations**
Greater is s-character, shorter is the hybridised orbital and hence, shorter is the bond length.

$$C \overset{sp}{\equiv} C < CH_2 \overset{sp^2}{=} CH_2 < CH_3 \overset{sp^3}{—} CH_3$$

- **Bond Angle** It is the angle between the orbitals containing bonding electron pairs around the central atom.

109°28 — Tetrahedral (no lone pair); 107° — One lone pair so less than tetrahedral; 104.5° — Two lone pairs; 120° — No lone pair (trigonal planar)

- **Bond enthalpy** The amount of energy required to break one mole of bond in gaseous state.
- **Bond order** Number of bonds between two atoms in a molecule e.g. H—C≡C—H, B.O = 3
  H—S—H, B.O = 1

Resonance

- The number of structures which describe a molecule accurately.
- All structures have similar energy and similar bonding and non-bonding pairs.
- A hybrid of all the resonating structures is known as **resonance hybrid**. e.g.

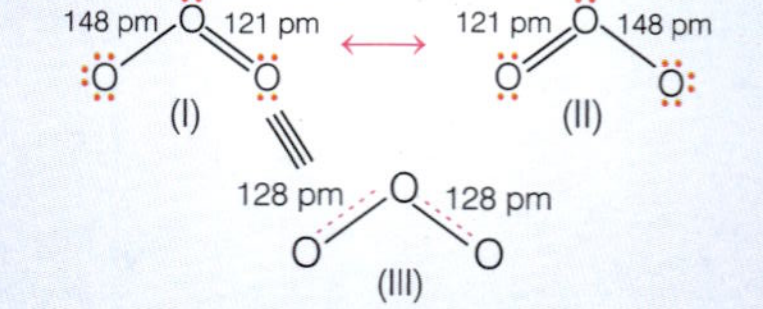

Resonance hybrid

Test 2

Syllabus
- The Concept of Hybridisation Involving s, p and d-Orbitals
- VSEPR Theory and Shapes of Simple Molecules
- Valence Bond Theory: Its Important Features

NCERT Page 110 to 125

For deeper insight **Scan the QR Code**

Hybridisation

Mixing of different shapes and approximate equal energy atomic orbitals, and redistribution of energy to form new orbitals, of same shape and same energy is known as hybrid orbitals and the phenomenon is called hybridisation.

$$H=\frac{1}{2}[V+M-C+A]$$

where, V = valence electrons
M = monovalent atoms
C or A = number of cations or anions.

e.g. NH_4^+, Hybridisation $=\frac{1}{2}[5+4-1]=\frac{8}{2}=4=sp^3$

H = 2 → sp
H = 3 → sp^2
H = 4 → sp^3
H = 5 → sp^3d
H = 6 → sp^3d^2

Types of hybridisation	No. of hybrid orbitals	Shape of molecule	Bond angle
sp	2	Linear	180°
sp^2	3	Trigonal planar	120°
sp^3	4	Tetrahedral	109.5°
dsp^2	4	Square planar	90°
dsp^3 or sp^3d	5	Trigonal bipyramidal	120° and 90°
d^2sp^3 or sp^3d^2	6	Octahedral	90°

Conditions for Hybridisation

- The orbitals present in the valence shell of the atom are hybridised.
- Orbitals undergoing hybridisation should have nearly same energies.
- Promotion of electron is not essential before hybridisation occurs.
- It is not necessary that only half-filled orbitals participate in hybridisation. In some cases, even filled orbitals of valence shell vacant orbitals take part in hybridisation.

Salient Features of Hybridisation

- The number of hybrid orbitals formed is exactly equal to the number of orbitals taking part in the process.
- The electronic charge in hybrid orbitals is concentrated more in one direction as shown below.

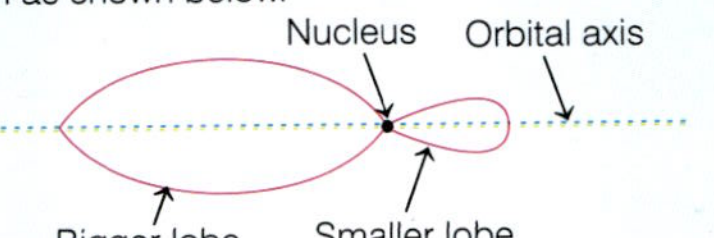

A hybrid orbitals

- This property make the hybrid orbitals to overlap with the atomic orbitals to a greater extent and hence, give stronger bonds.
- Atomic orbitals can mix together effectively to give hybrid orbitals only when they are of almost same energy and same symmetry.
- Same atom can assume different hybrid states under different situations.
- The distribution and shapes of hybrid orbitals differ from that of the atomic orbitals which are taking part in the process of hybridisation.

Bent's Rule

It explains the relationship between the orbital hybridisation of central atom and electronegativities of substituents in a molecule.

- % s-character ∝ bond strength
- % s-character ∝ bond angle
- % s-character ∝ 1/bond length
- In sp-hybridisation, s = 0.5 or 50%, p = 50%
- In sp^2 hybridisation, s = 33.33%, p = 66.66%

Drago's Rule

- Element of 3rd period or below do not allow hybridisation in molecule when they form compound with less electronegative elements. e.g PH_3, SiH_4, AsH_3 do not undergo hybridisation.
- Bond angle observed in drago molecules is nearly equal to 90°.

Valence Bond Theory

- Formation of a covalent bond between two atoms occurs by pairing of electrons present in valence shell having opposite spins.
- Directional orbitals (p,d and f) have stronger overlaps while non-directional(s) have weaker overlaps.
- Bond strength ∝ directional nature ∝ 1/size of orbital
- Sigma (σ) bonds are formed from head on overlap while π-bond are formed from side wise overlap.
- **Limitations**
- Could not explain paramagnetism of O_2.
- Could not explain formation of odd e^- bond.
- Failed to explain bonding in electron deficient molecules like B_2H_6.
- Failed to explain formation of coordinate bond in which both electrons are contributed by one of the bonded atoms.

Types of Overlapping

- **Sigma (σ) bond**
- A bond formed between two atoms by the overlap of single occupied orbitals along their axes (end to end overlap) is called sigma (σ) bond.
- Free rotation about σ bonds are possible.

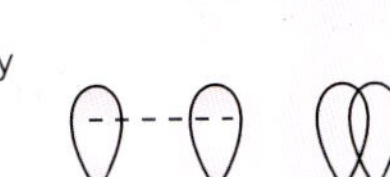

- **π-bond**
- π-bonds are those which are formed by the side wise or lateral overlapping of p and d-orbitals.
- Free rotations are not possible.
- π-bonds are weaker than σ bonds but multiple bonds are stronger than single bonds.

Triple bond > Double bond > Single bond.

p-p overlap

VSEPR Theory

- The shape of the molecules is determined by repulsions between all of the electron pairs present (lone pairs as well as bonded pairs)
- The order of strength of these repulsion is as

$lp-lp > lp-bp > bp-bp$

- Magnitude of repulsion is dependent on E.N difference between central atom and side atoms.
- Multiple bonds cause more repulsion than single bond.
- Geometries of simple molecules on the basis of VSEPR theory having one or more lone pairs of electrons.

Type of molecule	No. of bonding pair	No. of lone pair	Structure and geometry	Shape	Example
AB_2E	2	1	Trigonal planar	Bent	SO_2, O_3
AB_3E	3	1	Tetrahedral	Trigonal pyrami -dal	NH_3, PCl_3
AB_2E_2	2	2	Tetrahedral	Bent	H_2O,
AB_4E	4	1	Trigonal bipyramidal	See -saw	SF_4
AB_3E_2	3	2	Trigonal bipyramidal	T-shape	ClF_3
AB_5E	5	1	Octahedral	Square pyram -idal	BrF_2
AB_4E_2	4	2	Octahedral	Square planar	XeF_4
ABE_3	1	3	$\ddot{A}$ — B	Linear	HF, HCl

Test 3

Syllabus

- MOT's : Its Important Features, LCAO's, Types of Molecular Orbitals (Bonding, Antibonding) σ and π-Bonds, Molecular Orbital Electronic Configuration of Homonuclear Diatomic Molecules, Concept of Bond Order, Bond Length and Bond Energy, Elementary Idea of Metallic Bonding, Hydrogen Bonding and Its Applications

NCERT Page 125 to 132

For deeper insight **Scan the QR Code**

Chapter 04

Molecular Orbital Theory

S.No	With 2s-2p Mixing			Without 2s-2p Mixing		
Element	B_2	C_2	N_2	O_2	F_2	Ne_2
Bond order	1	2	3	2	1	0
Magnetic Properties	Paramagnetic	Diamagnetic	Diamagnetic	Paramagnetic	Diamagnetic	–
Valence electron Configuration	$(\sigma 2s)^2(\sigma^*2s)^2$ $\pi 2p_x^2$	$(\sigma 2s)^2(\sigma^*2s)^2$ $\pi 2p_x^2 \approx \pi 2p_y^2$	$(\sigma 2s)^2(\sigma^*2s)^2$ $\pi 2p_x^2 \approx \pi 2p_y^2$ $(\sigma 2p_z)^2$	$(\sigma 2s)^2(\sigma^*2s)^2$ $(\sigma 2p_z)^2(\pi 2p)^4$ $(\pi^*2p_x)^2$	$(\sigma 2s)^2(\sigma^*2s)^2$ $\sigma 2p_z^2$ $\pi 2p_x^2 \approx$ $\sigma 2p_y^2$ $\pi^*2p_x^2 \approx$ $\pi^*2p_y^2$	$(\sigma 2s)^2(\sigma^*2s)^2$ $\pi 2p_x^2 \approx \pi 2p_y^2$ $\sigma 2p_z^2$ $\pi^*2p_x^2 \approx$ $\pi^*2p_y^2$ $\sigma^*2p_z^2$
Interpretation	A	B	C	D	E	F

A Molecule exists stable with single bond. Two electron in π-bonding molecular orbital are unpaired, hence it is paramagnetic.
B Molecule exists stable with a double bond. It has 0 unpaired electrons hence, diamagnetic.
C Molecule exists, stable having a triple bond. It has 0 unpaired electrons hence, diamagnetic in nature.
D Molecule exists, stable with a double bond. It is paramagnetic in nature as it has two unpaired electrons in its π-electron antibonding molecular orbital.
E Molecule exists, stable with a single bond. It is diamagnetic in nature as no unpaired electrons are present.
F Molecule unstable and does not exist. As it's non-existent, it's magnetic character can't be determined.

LCAO

- Molecular orbitals are formed by the linear combination of atomic orbitals.The number of molecular orbitals formed is equal to the number of atomic orbitals combined.
- When two atomic orbitals combine they form one bonding molecular orbital of lower energy and one anti-bonding molecular orbital of higher energy.The molecular orbitals are filled in accordance with Aufbau principle obeying Pauli's exclusion principle and Hund's rule.
- **Condition for LCAO** The combining atoms orbitals must have the same or nearly the same energy. The combining atomic orbitals must have the same symmetry about the molecular axis. e.g having the same z-axis as molecular axis.
  The combining atomic orbitals must overlap to the maximum extent.

Formation of Bonding and Antibonding Orbitals

Molecular Orbitals by LCAO

Case I When two waves are in phase, the waves adds up and constructive interference occurs. The amplitude of new wave is, Ψ_{MO} or $\Psi_b = \Psi_A + \Psi_B$ (Bonding MO). Here, Ψ_{MO} is also called Ψ_g, i.e. GERADE MO corresponding to increased electron density between the two nuclei due to in phase overlap.

Case II When two waves are out of phase, the wave are subtracted from each others and destructive interference occurs. The amplitude of new wave is Ψ_{MO} or $\Psi_b = \Psi_A + \Psi_B$ (Antibonding MO).

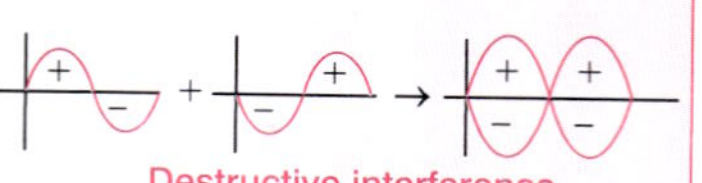

Application

- Bond order $= 1/2\,(N_b - N_a)$
  N_b = number of bonding electrons.
  N_a = number of antibonding electrons.
- **Nature of bond** Integral bond order values of 1, 2, 3 correspond to single, double and triple bonds.
- **Bond length** Bond order can be taken as an approximate of bond length. Bond order $\propto$ 1/bond length.
- Electrons present in a bonding MO tend to hold the nuclei together and stabilise a molecule whereas electrons present in an anti-bonding MO destabilise a molecule because of more mutual repulsions between the electrons.
- A bonding MO posses lower energy while an anti-bonding MO possess higher energy than the parent atomic orbital.

N_2 Molecule and O_2 Molecule

- $KK(\sigma 2s)^2\,(\sigma^*2s)^2\,(\pi 2p_x)^2 \approx (\pi 2p_y)^2\,(\sigma 2p_z)^2$

  Bond order $= \frac{1}{2}(8-2) = 3$

  Increasing energy; 2p; 2p; $\sigma^*(2p_z)$; $\pi^*(2p_x)\pi^*(2p_y)$; $\sigma(2p_z)$; $\pi(2p_x)\,\pi(2p_y)$; σ^*2s; 2s He; 2s He; $\sigma 2s$

- $[KK\,(\sigma 2s)^2\,(\sigma^*2s)^2\,(\sigma 2p_z)^2\,(\pi 2p_x)^2 \approx (\pi 2p_y)^2\,(\pi^*2p_x)^1 \approx \pi^*2p_y^1]$

  Bond order $= \frac{1}{2}(8-4) = 2$

  Increasing energy; $\sigma^*(2p_z)$; $\pi^*2p_x\,\pi^*2p_y$; $\pi 2p_x = \pi 2p_y$; $\sigma 2p_z$; σ^*2s; O (AO); O (AO); σ 2s; O_2 (MO)

Hydrogen Bond

Binds H-atom of one molecule with electronegative atoms (mainly F, O,N) of another molecule.

- **Intramolecular H-bonding** Formed between H-atom and an electronegative atom within the same molecule.
- **Intermolecular H-bonding** Formed between two different molecules of same or different compounds.

δ^- O H H δ^+ δ^+; Hydrogen bond; →O; →H

Types of H-Bonds

There are two types of H-bonds
- Intermolecular hydrogen bond
- Intramolecular hydrogen bond
- **Intermolecular hydrogen bond** is formed between two different molecules of the same or different compounds. For example, H-bonding in alcohol or H_2O molecule.
- **Intramolecular hydrogen bond** is formed when hydrogen atom is in between the two highly electronegative (F, O, N) atoms present with in the same molecule.
  For example, in o-nitrophenol the hydrogen is in between the two oxygen atoms.

Metallic Bonding

- It is the strong electrostatic attraction between positive metal ions and negative delocalised electrons in a metal lattice
- Metals have a fixed lattice structure of positive ions.
  The outer shell of electrons is delocalised, which can carry current.
- Metals have high melting and boiling points due to the large amounts of energy needed to overcome the metallic bonds.
- The greater the charge of a metal ion, the more electrons are delocalised. The smaller the size of the metal ions, the closer they are to the delocalised electrons. This results in stronger bonds and a higher melting point.
- Metals are malleable and ductile. The ions can slide and move past each other as there are no bonds holding specific ions together.

Metallic Bond Examples

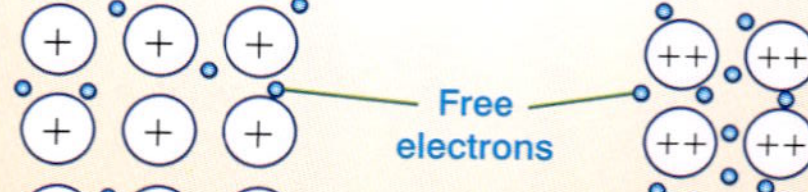
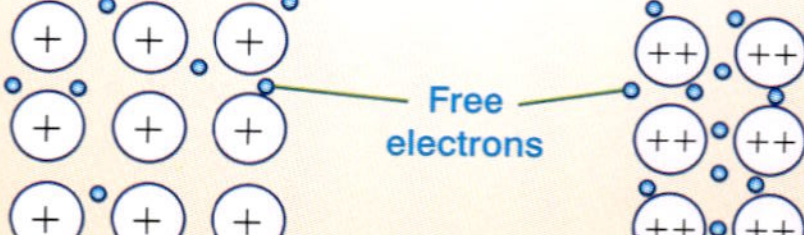

Test 1

Syllabus
- Fundamentals of Thermodynamics : System and Surrounding, Extensive and Intensive Properties, State Function, Types of Processes
- First Law of Thermodynamics : Concept of Work, Heat, Internal Energy, Enthalpy

NCERT Page 136 to 144

For deeper insight **Scan the QR Code**

Chapter 05

Thermodynamics

The branch of science which deals with study of different forms of energy and their interconversions due to physical or chemical transformations.

Thermodynamic Terms

- **System** Specified part of the universe which is under observation.
- **Surroundings** Remaining part of the universe which can interact with the system.
- **Boundary** The wall that separates the system from the surroundings.

Types of System
- **Open system** Can exchange both matter and energy.
- **Closed system** Can exchange energy but not matter.
- **Isolated system** Neither matter nor energy can be exchanged.

(a) Open system (b) Closed system

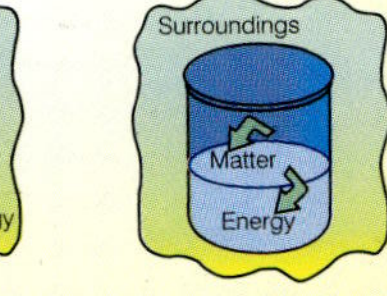

(c) Isolated system

Thermodynamic Processes

Isobaric process Thermodynamic process in which the pressure remains constant. $dp=0$

Isochoric process Thermodynamic process in which the volume remains constant. $dV=0$

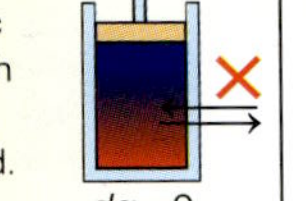

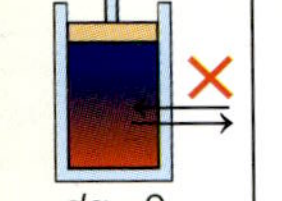

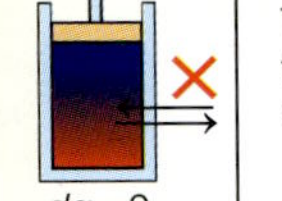

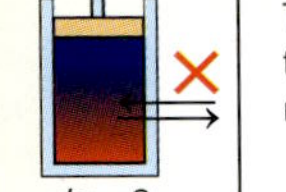

Adiabatic process Thermodynamic process in which there is no heat transfer involved. $dq=0$

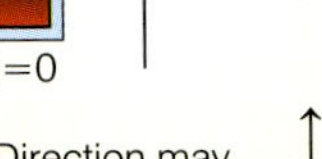

Isothermal process The process in which the temperature remains constant. $dT=0$

- **Reversible process** Direction may be reversed at any stage
- **Irreversible process** Proceeds only in one direction and cannot be reversed.
- **Cyclic process** It is a sequence of processes that leaves the system in same state in which it started.

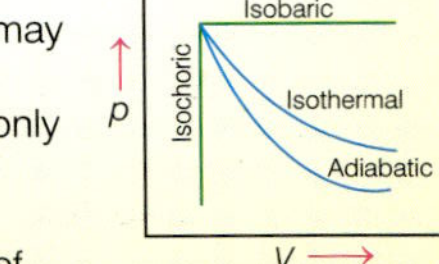

pV graph for various thermodynamic processes

Thermodynamic Properties

- **Intensive properties**
  Do not depend upon the quantity or size of matter present in the system, e.g. pressure, temperature, density, surface tension, viscosity, specific heat, melting and boiling points, etc.
- **Extensive properties**
  Depend upon the quantity or size of matter present in the system, e.g. mass, volume, internal energy, enthalpy, etc.

Note Extensive properties are additive but intensive properties are not.

State and Path Functions

- **State function** Properties which depend only on the initial and final state of a system. These are independent of the path or manner by which the state is reached are called the state function. Thus, most of the common variables are infact state functions. e.g. Pressure (p), volume (V), temperature (T), entropy (S), enthalpy (H).
- **Path function** Properties which depend upon the path followed. e.g. Work and heat.

Sign Convention

While studying thermodynamics, we should keep certain sign conventions in our mind.
- Whenever work is done on the system (compression), the work will be positive while if work is done by the system (expansion), then the work will be negative.
- The heat (q) will be positive, when heat is transferred from surroundings to the system and (q) is negative when heat is transferred from the system to the surroundings.

Work (W)

It is defined as the product of intensity factor and the capacity factor. Intensity factors are such factors that are responsible for the work, e.g. force, pressure, surface tension etc. While capacity factors are the measure of extent of work done, e.g. displacement, change in volume, change in length etc. The SI unit of work is Joule (J).

$W = -2.303\, nRT \log \frac{V_f}{V_i}$ (for isothermal reversible process).

$W = p_{ext}(V_f - V_i)$ (for isothermal irreversible process.)

- In vacuum, $p_{ext} = 0$, so $W = 0$
- Work done in adiabatic expansion,

$$W = C_V \Delta T = \frac{R}{\gamma - 1}(T_2 - T_1)$$

- Work done in irreversible adiabatic expansion.

$$\Delta U = W = 0$$

- The temperature of a gas decreases during adiabatic expansion, meaning cooling occurs. Conversely, the temperature increases during adiabatic compression meaning the system gets warmed.
- Work done will be maximum if the external pressure is infinitesimally smaller than the internal pressure of the gas.

First Law of Thermodynamics

Energy can neither be created nor be destroyed although it can be changed from one form to another.
Expression : $\Delta U = q + w$ where, $\Delta U = (U_2 - U_1)$

- **Internal energy change (ΔU)**
- Heat absorbed or evolved by the system at constant volume.
- It is the sum of all types of energies as a system.
- It changes with heat or work or matter changes in system.
- For all isothermal processes, $\Delta U = 0$.
- **Heat (q)** Mode of energy exchanged between the system and the surroundings as a result of temperature difference between them.
- **Enthalpy change (ΔH)** It is the total heat content of a system at constant pressure.

$$\Delta H = \Delta U + \Delta n_g RT \; [\Delta n_g = n_p - n_R]$$
$$\Delta H = \Delta U + p\Delta V$$

where,
n_p = number of moles of product and
n_R = number of moles of reactants.

- **Case I** When $\Delta n_g = 0$, then $\Delta H = \Delta U$
- **Case II** When $\Delta n_g < 0$, then $\Delta H < \Delta U$
- **Case III** When $\Delta n_g > 0$, then $\Delta H > \Delta U$

For reactions involving only solids or liquids,
$\Delta V = 0, \Delta H = \Delta U$

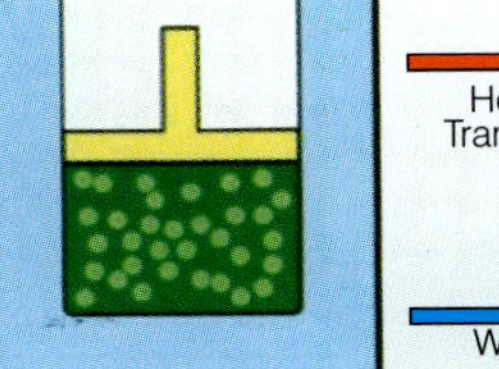

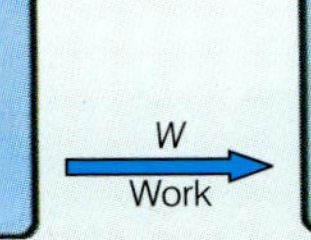

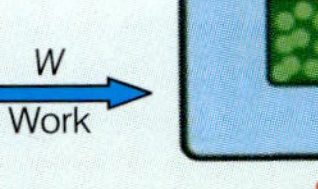

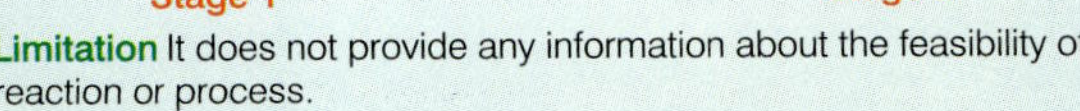

- **Limitation** It does not provide any information about the feasibility of a reaction or process.

Important Points Related to Work

- The magnitude of work in isothermal irreversible expansion increases as the number of steps involved increases.
- The magnitude of work will be more in isothermal irreversible compression than isothermal reversible compression, for the same change in volume.
- The magnitude of work decreases as the number of steps involved increases.
- The temperature of gas decreases in adiabatic expansion, i.e. cooling occurs while the temperature increases in adiabatic compression (i.e. the system gets warmed).
- In any adiabatic process (expansion or compression), the final temperature of the gas in reversible process is lower than that in irreversible process.

Test 2

Syllabus

- Hess's Law of Constant Heat Summation
- Enthalpies of Bond Dissociation, Combustion, Atomisation, Formation, Sublimation, Phase Transition, Hydration, Ionisation and Solution, Heat Capacity

NCERT Page 144 to 157

For deeper insight **Scan the QR Code**

Chapter 05

Thermochemical Equations

A balanced chemical equation together with the value of its $\Delta_r H$ is called a thermochemical equation.

e.g. $C_2H_5OH(l) + 3O_2(g) \longrightarrow 2CO_2(g) + 3H_2O(l)$

$$\Delta_r H^\circ = -1367 \text{ kJ/mol}$$

Sign Convention for Thermochemical Equation

- The coefficients in a balanced thermochemical equation refers to the number of moles of reactants and products involved in the reaction.
- The numerical value of $\Delta_r H^\circ$ refers to the number of moles of substance specified by an equation.
- Standard enthalphy change $\Delta_r H^\circ$ will have units as kJ mol^{-1}.

Reaction Enthalpy

- **Standard enthalpy of reaction ($\Delta_r H^\circ$)** Enthalpy change of a reaction when all the participating substances are in their standard states.
- **Standard enthalpy of formation ($\Delta_f H^\circ$)** Enthalpy change accompanying the formation of one mole of a substance from its constituents in their standard states.
- **Enthalpy change during phase transformation** Enthalpy change accompanying the conversion of 1 mole of a substance from one state to another.

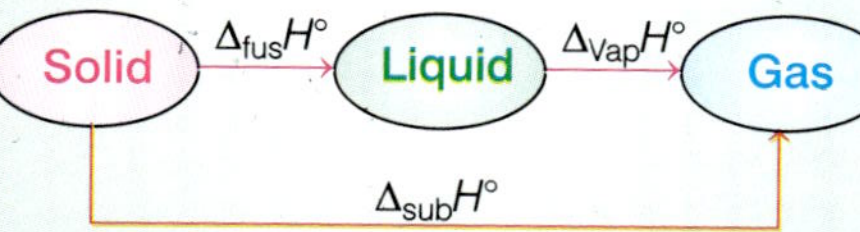

- Enthalpy of fusion $(\Delta_{fus}H^\circ) = T_m\Delta S^\circ$
- Enthalpy of vaporisation $(\Delta_{vap}H^\circ) = T_b\Delta S^\circ$
- Enthalpy of sublimation $(\Delta_{sub}H^\circ) = T_{sub}\Delta S^\circ$

Enthalpy of Different Types of Reactions

- **Enthalpy of combustion ($\Delta_c H$)** Change in enthalpy when one mole of a substance is completely burnt in oxygen.

$$C(s) + O_2(g) \longrightarrow CO_2(g)$$

- **Enthalpy of atomization ($\Delta_a H$)** Change in enthalpy on breaking one mole of bonds completely to obtain atoms in gas phase.

$$CH_4(g) \longrightarrow C(g) + 4H(g)$$

- **Bond enthalpy** Standard enthalpy of reaction is related to bond enthalpies of reactant and product in gas phase.

$$\Delta_r H^\circ = \Sigma B.E_{reactants} - \Sigma B.E_{products}$$

- **Enthalpy of neutralisation** Enthalpy change occurred. when one equivalent of an acid is neutralised by one equivalent of a base.
- **Enthalpy of solution** Enthalpy change when one mole of a substance dissolves in a fixed amount of solvent.

$$\Delta_{sol}H^\circ = \Delta_{lattice}H^\circ + \Delta_{hyd}H^\circ$$

Hess's Law

Total heat change (ΔH) accompanying a chemical reaction is the same whether the reaction takes place in one or more steps. $\Delta H = \Delta H_1 + \Delta H_2 + \Delta H_3$

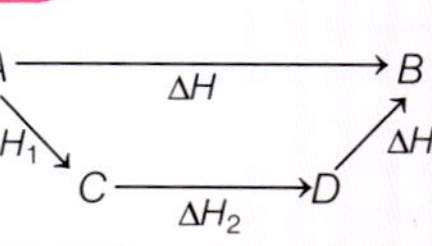

Application of Hess's Law

This law can be used to

- determine the enthalpies of formation.
- determine the enthalpies of extremely slow reactions.
- determine the enthalpies of transition.
- determine the bond enthalpy.
- determine the resonance energy.
- determine the lattice energy.

Born Haber's Cycle

- Born-Haber cycle, devleloped by Max Born and Fritz Haber is an approach to calculate energy involved during a process and is based on the Hess's law of constant heat summation.
- Born-Haber cycle can be utilised to calculate lattice energy of crystals like NaCl.

$Na(s) + \frac{1}{2}Cl_2(g) \xrightarrow{\Delta H^\circ} NaCl(s)$; $\Delta_{sub}H^\circ$; $\frac{1}{2}\Delta_{bond}H^\circ$; $Cl(g) \xrightarrow{\Delta_{eg}H^\circ} \overset{\ominus}{Cl}(g)$; $Na(s) \xrightarrow{\Delta_i H^\circ} Na^+(g)$; $\Delta_{lattice}H^\circ$

Born-Haber cycle for NaCl

Steps involved in formation of NaCl are

(i) $Na(s) \longrightarrow Na(g)$; $\Delta_{sub}H^\circ = 108.4$ kJ mol^{-1}

(ii) $Na(g) \longrightarrow Na^+(g) + e^-(g)$; $\Delta_i H^\circ = 496$ kJ mol^{-1}

(iii) $\frac{1}{2}Cl_2(g) \longrightarrow Cl(g)$; $\Delta_{bond}H^\circ = 121$ kJ mol^{-1}

(iv) $Cl(g) + e^-(g) \longrightarrow Cl^-(g)$; $\Delta_g H^\circ = -348.6$ kJ mol^{-1}

(v) $Na^+(g) + Cl^-(g) \longrightarrow Na^+Cl^-(s)$; $\Delta_{lattice}H^\circ = U$

- **Enthalpy of reaction ($\Delta_r H$)** The enthalpy change accompanying a reaction is called the reaction enthalpy.

$$\Delta_r H = \Delta H_{products} - \Delta H_{reactants}$$

- **Enthalpy of formation** Heat change in formation of 1 mole of substance at 298 K and 1 atm pressure (standard enthalpy of formation).

$$\frac{1}{2}N_2 + \frac{3}{2}H_2 \rightleftharpoons NH_3, \quad \underset{a}{A} + \underset{b}{B} \rightleftharpoons \underset{c}{C} + \underset{d}{D}$$

$\Delta H_{reaction}$ = Heat of formation of products–Heat of formation of reactants $= (c + d) - (a + b)$

- **Lattice energy** The enthalpy change which occurs when one mole of an ionic compound dissociates into its ions in gaseous state.

$$NaCl(s) \longrightarrow Na^+(g) + Cl^-(g) ; \Delta H^\circ = +788 \text{ kJmol}^{-1}$$

- **Enthalpy of dilution** Enthalpy change associated with the addition of a specific amount of solute to the specified amount of solvent.

Heat Capacity

- The quantity of heat required to raise the temperature of system by one degree is called **heat capacity** of that system.
- This is denoted by C and it is a path function.

Heat capacity $C = \frac{dq}{dT}$, $q = C \times m \times \Delta T$

- **Molar heat capacity** It is heat Capacity for one mole of the substance and is the quantity needed to raise the temperature of one mole by one degree.
- If C is the heat capacity of the system, then its molar heat capacity C_m is given by $C_m = C/n$.
- **Specific heat capacity** It is the quantity of heat required to raise the temperature of one unit mass of substance by one degree celsius.
- **Heat capacity at constant pressure (C_p)** It represents the rate of increase of enthalpy of system with temperature.

$$C_p = \left(\frac{dQ}{dT}\right)_p \text{ when } \Delta p = 0; \; C_p = \left(\frac{dH}{dT}\right)_p$$

- **Heat capacity at constant volume (C_V)** It represents the rate of increase of internal energy of system with temperature.

$$C_V = \left(\frac{dq}{dT}\right)_V, \Delta V = 0, C_V = \left(\frac{dU}{dT}\right)_V$$

- **Relation between C_p and C_V** $\quad C_p - C_V = R; \; \frac{C_p}{C_V} = \gamma$
- The value of γ gives the information about the atomicity of gases.
- C_p is always greater than C_V.

ΔH Measurement: Water Calorimetry

- Measurement of heat change at constant pressure can be done in a calorimeter called water calorimeter.
- When the pressure is constant, the heat change for the process is equal to ΔH. $q_p = \Delta H$
- In exothermic reaction, heat is evolved and system loses heat to the surrounding. So, q_p and $\Delta_r H$ are negative.
- In endothermic reaction, heat is absorbed. So, q_p and $\Delta_r H$ will be positive.

Thermometer
Foamed polystyrene cup
Reaction mixture

ΔU Measurement: Bomb Calorimetry

- Measurement of heat change at constant volume is done by using bomb calorimeter.
- Here, a steel vessel (the bomb) is filled with oxygen at about 30 atm of pressure is immersed in known amount of water to ensure that no heat is lost to the surrounding. A stirrer is suspended in the sealed water bath to dissipate the heat produced from the calorimeter.
- A thermometer is also suspended in it to monitor the change in the temperature.

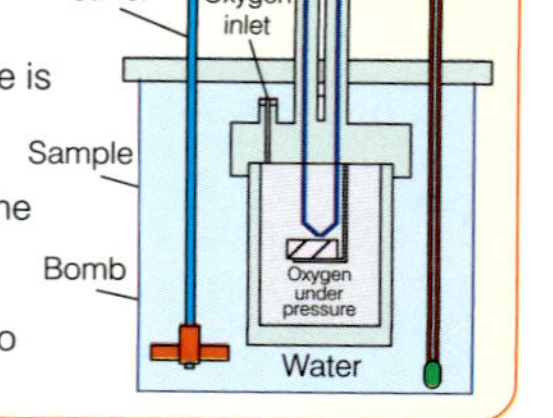

Test 3

Syllabus

- Second Law of Thermodynamics : Spontaneity of Processes, ΔS of Universe and ΔG of the System as Criteria for Spontaneity, ΔG° and Equilibrium Constant

NCERT Page 157 to 163

For deeper insight **Scan the QR Code**

Chapter 05

Second Law of Thermodynamics

- All spontaneous processes are accompanied by an increase in total entropy of the universe.
  $\Delta S_{uni} = \Delta S_{sys} + \Delta S_{surr}$
- No system is 100% efficient.
- It is impossible for a cyclic process to transfer heat from a body at lower temperature to one at higher temperature without conversion of some work to heat.

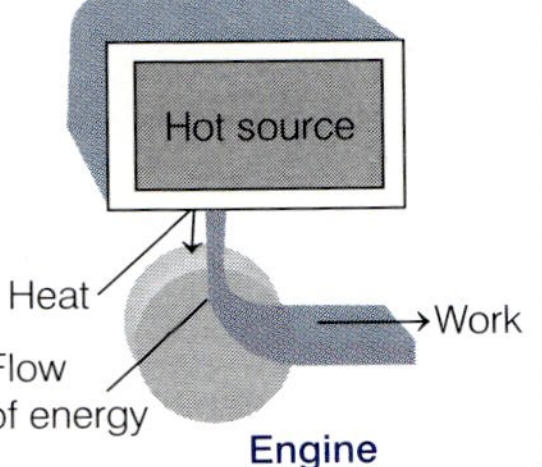

Spontaneity

- It refers to the ability of a process to occur on its own.
- A spontaneous process is an irreversible process and may only be reversed by some external agency.
- It does not tell about the rate of the reaction or process.
- The tendency to attain the minimum energy, i.e. decrease in enthalpy is responsible for the spontaneity or feasibility of a reaction but it is not true for all the cases.

Gibbs Energy and Spontaneity

- Gibbs free energy (G) is the net energy available to do useful work.
- $\Delta_r G = \Sigma \Delta_f G^\circ_{product} - \Sigma \Delta_f G^\circ_{reactants}$
- Gibbs-Helmholtz equation:
  $\Delta G = \Delta H - T\Delta S$
  $\Delta G^\circ = \Delta H^\circ - T\Delta S^\circ$ (standard)
  $\Delta G^\circ = -nFE^\circ$
  [where, ΔG = change in Gibbs' free energy, ΔH = enthalpy change, ΔS = change in entropy]
- If $\Delta G > 0$, process is non-spontaneous
- If $\Delta G < 0$, process is spontaneous.
- If $\Delta G = 0$, process is in equilibrium.

Effect of Temperature on Spontaneity of Reactions

$\Delta_r S^\circ$	$\Delta_r H^\circ$	$\Delta_r G^\circ$	Spontaneous/ Non-spontaneous process
+	−	–ve at all temperatures	Spontaneous at all temperature.
−	−	–ve at low temperature but +ve at high temperature	Spontaneous at low temperature but non-spontaneous at high temperature.
−	+	–ve at all temperature	Spontaneous at high temperature.
+	+	+ve at low temperature	Non-spontaneous at low temperature, spontaneous at high temperature.

Entropy

- It is a measure of the disorder or randomness of a system or energy unavailable to do work.
- It is denoted by S.
- It is a state function, i.e. depends only on the initial and final state of the systems.
- Unit is $JK^{-1}\ mol^{-1}$.

Factors Affecting Entropy

- **Phase of matter** Gas > Liquid > Solid,
- **Temperature** Higher temperature, higher entropy.
- **Volume** Higher volume, higher entropy.
- **Number of particles** Higher number of particles, higher entropy.

Types of Entropy

- **Entropy of vaporisation** Amount of entropy increased when a liquid goes into vapour state, is called entropy of vaporisation.
  Liquid $\rightleftharpoons$ Vapour
- **Entropy of fusion** The amount of entropy increased when a solid melts into liquid state is called as entropy of fusion.
  Solid $\rightleftharpoons$ Liquid

Entropy Change in Various Processes

Change in entropy for ideal gas under different conditions is calculated by using following formulaes.

1. Isothermal process

$$\Delta S = nR \ln \frac{V_2}{V_1} = nR \ln \frac{p_1}{p_2}$$ [As p and V are inversely related]

2. Isochoric process

$$\Delta S = nC_V \ln \frac{T_2}{T_1} = nC_V \ln \frac{p_2}{p_1}$$ [As p and T are directly related]

3. Isobaric process

$$\Delta S = nC_p \ln \frac{T_2}{T_1} = nC_V \ln \frac{V_2}{V_1}$$ [As V and T are directly related]

- Entropy change in reversible process
  $\Delta S_{total} = \Delta S_{system} + \Delta S_{surrounding} = 0$
- Entropy change in irreversible process
  $\Delta S_{total} = \Delta S_{system} + \Delta S_{surrounding}$
  $= q\left[\frac{T_1 - T_2}{T_1 T_2}\right]$

Entropy changes during phase transformations are

$$\Delta_{fus} S = \frac{\Delta_{fus} H}{T_m}, \Delta_{vap} S = \frac{\Delta_{vap} H}{T_b}, \Delta_{sub} S = \frac{\Delta_{sub} H}{T_{sub}}$$

Spontaneity and Entropy

- Positive and negative values of ΔS shows the spontaneous and non-spontaneous processes respectively.
- When an isolated system is in equilibrium, the entropy is maximum.
- At equilibrium, $\Delta S = 0$
- For spontaneous change, $\Delta S > 0$.
- For non-spontaneous reactions, $\Delta S < 0$.
- A thermodynamically irreversible process is always accompanied by increase in entropy of the universe while in case of reversible process, entropy remains constant.
- Most of the natural phenomenon are irreversible in nature.

Entropy Effects Associated with Melting and Freezing Points

Change	Temperature	Sign of (a) ΔS_{sys}	Sign of (b) ΔS_{surr}	Comparison of (a) and (b)	ΔS_{surr}	Spontaneity
Melting (Solid → Liquid)	(i) > melting point	+	−	>	>0	Spontaneous
	(ii) = melting point	+	−	=	=0	Equilibrium
	(iii) < melting point	+	−	<	<0	Non -spontaneous
Freezing (Liquid → Soild)	(i) > melting point	−	+	>	<0	Non -spontaneous
	(ii) = melting point	−	+	=	=0	Equilibrium
	(iii) < melting point	−	+	<	>0	Spontaneous

Gibbs Energy Change and Equilibrium

Gibbs energy change, $\Delta_r G$ is related to the equilibrium constant of the reaction as,

$$\Delta_r G^\circ = -2.303\ RT \log K$$

ΔG°	log K	K	Conclusion
$\Delta G^\circ = 0$	$\log K = 0$	1	The equilibrium mixture contains comparable amounts of reactants and products (for 1 M concentration and 1 atm partial pressures).
$\Delta G^\circ < 0$	$\log K > 0$	$K > 1$	The equilibrium mixture contains mainly products, exothermic reactions.
$\Delta G^\circ > 0$	$\log K < 0$	$K < 1$	The equilibrium mixture contains mainly reactants, endothermic reactions.

Test 1

Syllabus

- Meaning of Equilibrium, Concept of Dynamic Equilibrium, Equilibrium Involving Physical Processes : Solid-Solid, Liquid-Gas and Solid-Gas, Their Characteristics, Law of Chemical Equilibrium, Equilibrium Constant (K_p and K_C) and their Significance, Significance of ΔG and $\Delta G°$ in Chemical Equilibrium

NCERT Page 168 to 184

For deeper insight **Scan the QR Code**

Chapter 06

Physical Equilibrium

- The equilibrium established between different physical states (or phases) of a substance at a particular temperature is called physical equilibrium.
- As there are three physical states of matter, solid, liquid and gas so there are three types of physical equilibrium.
- Generally observed in phase transformation processes.
- Solid-Liquid Equilibrium:
  Ice (s) $\rightleftharpoons$ Water (l) (in an insulated flask)
  $r_{\text{melting of ice}} = r_{\text{freezing of water}}$
  At fixed temperature and pressure, the change is at equilibrium.
- Liquid-Gas Equilibrium:
  Water (l) $\rightleftharpoons$ Vapour (g); $r_{\text{boiling of water}} = r_{\text{condensation}}$
- Solid-Gas Equilibrium:
  I_2 (solid) $\rightleftharpoons$ I_2 (vapour); $r_{\text{sublimation}} = r_{\text{condensation}}$

Chemical Equilibrium

- Analogous to physical equilibrium.
- Involves chemical changes.
- When rates of forward and backward reactions become equal, concentration of reactants and products remain constant.

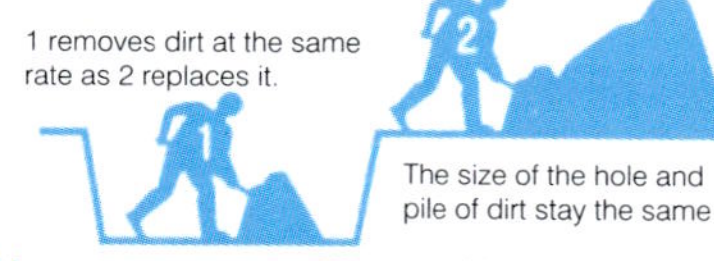

- **Homogeneous equilibrium** All the reactants and products are in the same phase.
  $N_2(g) + 3H_2(g) \rightleftharpoons 2NH_3(g)$

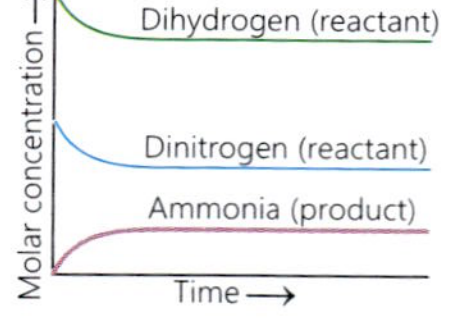

- **Heterogeneous equilibrium** Reactants and products are in two or more different phases.
  $C(s) + H_2O(g) \rightleftharpoons CO(g) + H_2(g)$

For heterogeneous equilibrium processes, concentration of solid species and pure solvents are not considered, as they do not change in considerable amount.

Law of Mass Action

- The law of mass action states that, the rate of a chemical reaction is directly proportional to the product of the reactant concentration values.
- For the general reaction:
  $$aA + bB \rightleftharpoons cC + dD$$
  The law gives a formula for the equilibrium constant:
  $$K_C = \frac{[C]^c\,[D]^d}{[A]^a\,[B]^b}$$

Calculating the Equilibrium Concentration

It can be determine by the steps:

- Write balance chemical equation.
- 'x' as the amount of the reactant or product.
- Calculate the equilibrium concentration of each reactant and product from the stoichiometry.
- Write expression for K_C or K_p.
- Substitute the values of equilibrium concentration and equilibrium constant.
- From the values of x, calculate the equilibrium concentrations of different substances.

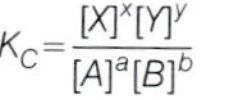

Equilibrium Constant

- For reactions in solutions,
  For the reaction,
  $$aA(aq) + bB(aq) \rightleftharpoons xX(aq) + yY(aq);$$
  $$K_C = \frac{[X]^x[Y]^y}{[A]^a[B]^b}$$
  K_C = equilibrium constant in terms of molar concentration and this equilibrium equation is also known as law of mass action.
- For reactions involving gases
  For the reaction,
  $$aA(g) + bB(g) \rightleftharpoons yY(g);$$
  $$K_p = \frac{[p_Y]^y}{[p_A]^a[p_B]^b}$$
  K_p = equilibrium constant in terms of partial pressure.
  where, p_A and p_B are the partial pressure of A and B respectively.
- Units of Equilibrium constant
- If $\Delta n_g = 0$, both K_C and K_p have no units
- If $\Delta n_g > 0$, unit of $K_C = (\text{mol L}^{-1})^{\Delta n_g}$, unit of $K_p = (\text{atm})^{\Delta n_g}$
- If $\Delta n_g < 0$, unit of $K_C = (\text{L mol}^{-1})^{\Delta n_g}$, unit of $K_p = (\text{atm}^{-1})^{\Delta n_g}$

Relation between K_p and K_C

- $K_p = K_C\,(RT)^{\Delta n}$; If $\Delta n = 0, K_p = K_C$;
  If $\Delta n = +$ ve, $K_p > K_C$; If $\Delta n = -$ ve, $K_p < K_C$
- Equilibrium constant for the reverse reaction $K'_C = \frac{1}{K_C}$
- Equilibrium constant for the reaction which is divided by $n\,K'_C = \sqrt[n]{K_C}$
- Equilibrium constant for the reaction which is multiplied by n, $K'_C = (K_C)^n$
- Equilibrium constant for the reaction taking place in n steps $K'_C = K_1 \times K_2 \times K_3 \dots K_n$
- The value of equilibrium constant for a particular reaction is always constant and it only depends upon the temperature of reaction.
- It is independent of the initial concentration of reactant.
- The value of equilibrium constant is not effected by the addition of a catalyst to the reaction. e.g.

Relation Between K_p and K_C for Some Chemical Reactions

	Equilibrium	Δn_g	$K_p = K_C\,(RT)^{\Delta n_g}$
1.	$H_2(g) + I_2(g) \rightleftharpoons 2HI$	0	$K_p = K_C$
2.	$N_2O_4(g) \rightleftharpoons 2NO_2(g)$	1	$K_p = K_C(RT)$
3.	$2SO_2(g) + O_2(g) \rightleftharpoons 2SO_3(g)$	−1	$K_C = K_p(RT)$
4.	$N_2(g) + 3H_2(g) \rightleftharpoons 2NH_3(g)$	−2	$K_C = K_p(RT)^2$
5.	$C(s) + O_2(g) \rightleftharpoons CO_2(g)$	0	$K_p = K_C$
6.	$NH_4HS(s) \rightleftharpoons NH_3(g) + H_2S(g)$	2	$K_p = K_C(RT)^2$
7.	$NH_3(g) + H_2O(l) \rightleftharpoons NH_4OH(l)$	− 1	$K_C = K_p(RT)$

Relationship between Equilibrium Constant (K_C), Reaction Quotient (Q_C) and Gibbs Energy (G)

The value of K_C is independent of the rate of reaction. Instead it is directly related to the thermodynamics of the reaction.

ΔG for a reaction under any set of conditions is related to its value under standard conditions, i.e. $\Delta G°$ by the equation

$$\Delta G = \Delta G° + 2.303\,RT \log Q_C$$

Under equilibrium condition,

$$\Delta G = 0 \Rightarrow Q_C = K_C$$
$$\Delta G° = -\,2.303\,RT \log K_C$$

Significance of ($\Delta G°$)

Significance of $\Delta G°$ can be explained from the following points.

- If $\Delta G° < 0$, $\log K_C > 0 \Rightarrow K_C > 1$
  Hence, reaction is spontaneous in forward direction.
- If $\Delta G° > 0$, $\log K_C < 0 \Rightarrow K_C < 1$
  Hence, reaction is non-spontaneous or a reaction proceeds in the forward direction to such a small extent that a very small amount of the product is formed.
- If $\Delta G° = 0$, $\log K_C = 0 \Rightarrow K_C = 1$
  Hence, it represents equilibrium.
- If $\Delta G°$ is large negative number, $K_C >> 1$, the forward reaction is nearly complete.
- If $\Delta G°$ is a very small positive number, $K_C << 1$, then reverse reaction is nearly complete.

Applications of Chemical Equilibrium

- **Predicting the extent of reaction:**
  $K_C > 10^3$ [Forward reaction is favoured.]
  $K_C < 10^{-3}$ [Reverse reaction is favoured.]
  $10^{-3} < K_C < 10^3$ [Both reactants and products are present in equilibrium]

A $\xrightleftharpoons{K>>1}$ B   A $\xrightleftharpoons{K<<1}$ B   A $\xrightleftharpoons{K\approx 1}$ B

- **Predicting the direction of reaction:**
  For this, reaction quotient Q is defined.
  Q is same as K however in Q, concentrations are not necessarily equilibrium concentration.

– **Step 1** Write the balanced equation for the reaction.
– **Step 2** Under the balanced equation make a table that lists for each substance involved in reaction. Initial concentration, change in concentration, equilibrium concentration.
– **Step 3** Substitute the equilibrium concentrations into the equilibrium equation for the reaction and solve.
– **Step 4** Calculate equilibrium concentrations from the calculated value of concentration of substance.
– **Step 5** Check results by substituting them into the equilibrium equation.

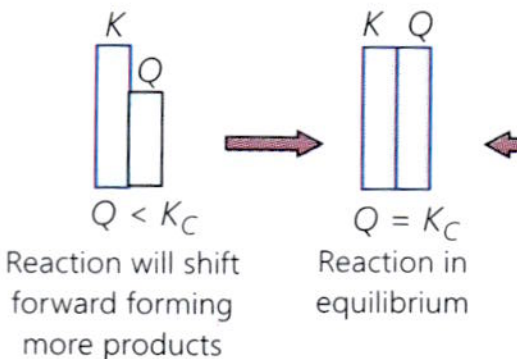
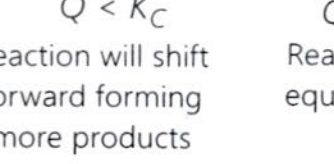

Test 2

Syllabus
- Significance of ΔG and ΔG° in Chemical Equilibrium
- Factors Affecting Equilibrium : Concentration, Temperature and Pressure
- The Effect of Catalyst : Le-Chatelier's Principle

NCERT Page 184 to 188

For deeper insight **Scan the QR Code**

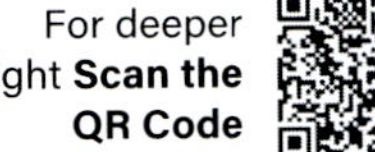

Le-Chatelier's Principle

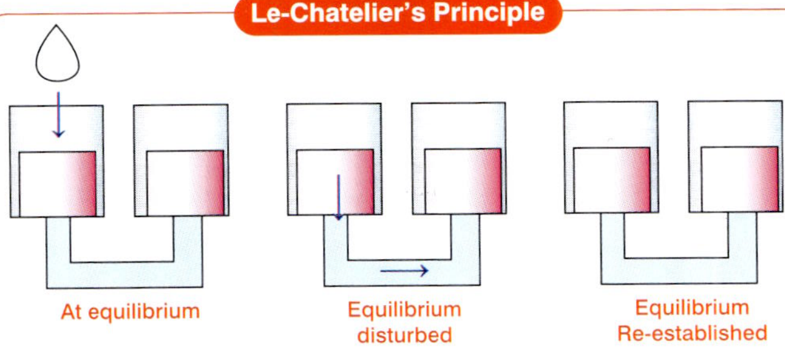

- It states that when a change is made to the conditions of a dynamic equilibrium, the system moves to counteract the change, causing changes in quantities of reactants and products.
- This is applicable to all physical and chemical equilibrium.

Factors Affecting Equilibrium

Concentration

Reactant concentration increased → The equilibrium position shifts to reduce the reactant concentration. → **Reaction forming Products favoured** In the example below the new equilibrium mixture will contain a higher concentration C and D.

Reduces Reactant Concentration

$A + 2B \rightleftharpoons C + D$

Reduces Production concentration

Increasing concentration of one side favours the other

Product concentration increased → The equilibrium position shifts to reduce the product concentration → **Reaction forming Reactants favoured** In the example above the new equilibrium mixture contain a higher concentration A and B.

Temperature

Temperature increased ↑°C → The equilibrium position shifts to reduce the temperature. ↓°C → **The endothermic reaction will be favoured** In the example below the new equilibrium mixture will contain more A and B and less C and D. (ENDO)

Exothermic (Increases temperature)

$A + 2B \rightleftharpoons C + D$

(decreases temperature) Endothermic

If the forward reaction is exothermic the backward reaction will be endothermic and *vice-versa*.

Temperature decreased ↓°C → The equilibrium position shifts to increase the temperature. ↑°C → **The exothermic reaction will be favoured** In the example above the new equilibrium mixture less contain more C and B and less A and B. (EXO)

Pressure

Pressure increased ↑Pa → The equilibrium position shifts to reduce the pressure. ↓Pa → **Side of reaction with fewer gas molecules favoured** In the example below the new equilibrium mixture will contain more C and D, and lesser A and B.

Decreases Pressure (fewer gas molecules on right)

$A + 2B \rightleftharpoons C + D$

(more gas molecules on left) Increases Pressure

If the number of gas molecules is the same on either side then changing pressure will have no effect.

Pressure decreased ↓Pa → The equilibrium position shifts to increase the pressure. ↓Pa → **Side of reaction with more gas molecules favoured** In the example above the new equilibrium mixture will contain more A and B, and less C and D.

Catalyst

- Adding a catalyst does not change the position of equilibrium but increases the rate at which the equilibrium is established.
- If catalyst will form an extra path through which the reaction rate go fast by lowering the activation energy.

R_f = Rate of forward reaction

$R_f = R_b$

System at equilibrium

$R_f = R_b$ (in presence of catalyst)

R_b = Rate of backward reaction

Rate of reaction ⟶ ; Time ⟶ ; O

Addition of Inert Gas

- **At constant volume** There will be no change in equilibrium at constant volume when inert gas is added.
- **At constant pressure** When an inert gas is added at constant pressure the equilibrium will shift towards greater number of moles.

Effect of Concentration Change

Effect of addition of H_2 on change of concentration for the reactants and products in the reaction,

$$H_2(g) + I_2(g) \rightleftharpoons 2HI(g)$$

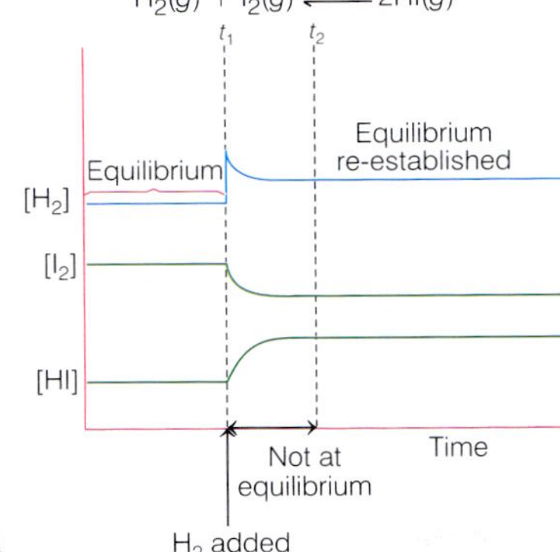

Application of Le-Chatelier's Principle

Haber Process

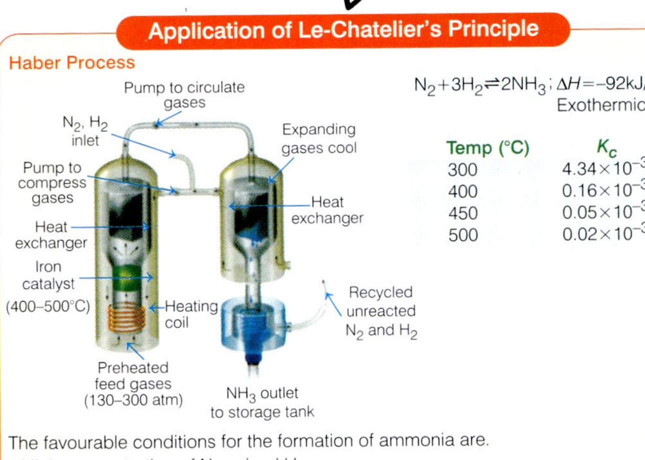

$N_2 + 3H_2 \rightleftharpoons 2NH_3$; $\Delta H = -92$ kJ/mol Exothermic

Temp (°C)	K_c
300	4.34×10^{-3}
400	0.16×10^{-3}
450	0.05×10^{-3}
500	0.02×10^{-3}

The favourable conditions for the formation of ammonia are.
- High concentration of N_2 or/and H_2
- High pressure
- Low temperature (as the reaction is exothermic).
- To enhance rate of reaction, catalyst, finely divided iron containing molybdenum (act as promoter) is used.

Study of favourable conditions for the specific direction of the given equilibrium.

Equilibrium reaction	Direction of changing p		Direction of changing T	
	$p\uparrow$	$p\downarrow$	$T\uparrow$	$T\downarrow$
$N_2(g) + 3H_2(g) \rightleftharpoons NH_3(g) - Q$	Forward	Backward	Backward	Forward
$PCl_5(g) \rightleftharpoons PCl_3(g) + Cl_2(g)$	Backward	Forward	Forward	Backward
$2HI(g) \rightleftharpoons H_2(g) + I_2(g)$	No effect	No effect	Forward	Backward
$H_2O(l) \rightleftharpoons H_2O(g)$	Backward	Forward	Forward	Backward
$NH_3(g) + H_2O(l) - Q \rightleftharpoons NH_4OH(l)$	Forward	Backward	Backward	Forward

Test 1

Syllabus
- Various Concepts of Acids and Bases (Arrhenius, Bronsted-Lowry and Lewis)
- Weak and Strong Electrolytes
- Acid-Base
- Ionisation of Electrolytes
- Ionisation Constants
- Ionisation of Water

NCERT Page 188 to 193 Page 195 to 200

For deeper insight **Scan the QR Code**

Chapter 07

Ionic equilibrium

It is a type of equilibrium that involves ions in aqueous solution.

Ostwald's Dilution Law

- It relates the dissociation constant of the weak electrolyte with the degree of dissociation and the concentration of the weak electrolyte.

$$K_a = \frac{C\alpha^2}{1-\alpha}$$

where, K_a = dissociation constant of weak acid
α = degree of dissociation

- Ostwald's dilution law states that the weak electrolyte undergoes complete ionisation at infinite dilution only.
- Applicable only for weak electrolytes.

Arrhenius Theory of Acids and Bases

- **Acids** Acids dissociate in water to give H^+ ions.
  $HA(aq) \rightleftharpoons A^-(aq) + H^+(aq)$
- Common acids include, hydrochloric acid (HCl), sulphuric acid (H_2SO_4) and nitric acid (HNO_3)
- This process of *HA* separating into A^- and H^+ ions is called dissociation.
- **Bases** Bases dissociate in water to give OH^- ions. $XOH\ (aq) \longrightarrow X^+(aq) + OH^-(aq)$
- Common bases include sodium hydroxide (NaOH), potassium hydroxide (KOH) and ammonia (NH_3).

Bronsted-Lowry Acid and Base

- Bronsted-Lowry Acid is a species that can donate protons.
  $HA\ (aq) + H_2O\ (l) \longrightarrow H_3O^+\ (aq) + A^-\ (aq)$
- Bronsted-Lowry Base is a species that can accept protons.
  $B\ (aq) + H_2O(l) \longrightarrow BH^+\ (aq) + OH^-\ (aq)$
- Conjugate acid-base pairs are a pair of species that are interconverted by the gain or loss of a proton.

$$\underset{\text{Acid}}{HCl(aq)} + \underset{\text{Base}}{H_2O(l)} \rightleftharpoons \underset{\text{Conjugate acid}}{H_3O^+(aq)} + \underset{\text{Conjugate base}}{Cl^-(aq)}$$

(Adds proton; Loses proton)

- **Monobasic acids** each molecule can release one proton, e.g. HCl.
  $HCl(aq) \longrightarrow H^+\ (aq) + Cl^-\ (aq)$
- **Dibasic acids** each molecule can release two protons per molecule, e.g. H_2SO_4.
  $H_2SO_4\ (aq) \longrightarrow 2H^+\ (aq) + SO_4^{2-}\ (aq)$

Lewis Acid and Base

Lewis Base	Lewis Acid
Electron pair donor	Electron pair acceptor
• lone-pair donor	• lone-pair acceptors
• nucleophiles	• electrophiles
• Bronsted bases	• metal cations
• ligands	• metal atom
• electron-rich π-systems	• electron-poor π-systems

$$\underset{\text{Lewis base}}{A:} + \underset{\text{Lewis acid}}{B} \longrightarrow \underset{\text{Adduct}}{A - B}$$

Electrolytes

- Substance which allow the flow of electricity through their aqueous solutions or their molten form.
- These are of two types strong electrolytes and weak electrolytes.
- **Strong electrolytes** dissociate completely into ions.
- **Weak electrolytes** dissociate partially into ions.

Polybasic Acids and Polyacidic Bases

- Acids having more than one ionisable proton are called polybasic or polyprotic acids. e.g. H_2SO_4, H_3PO_4, $H_2C_2O_4$ etc.
- Bases having more than one hydroxide ions are called polyacidic base. e.g. H_3BO_3, $Mg(OH)_2$, $Al(OH)_3$ etc.
- Their dissociation is a multi-step process due to presence of protons in conjugate bases.
- **Ionisation constant of some common polyprotic acids** Polybasic acids like ortho-phosphoric acid ionises in three steps and each step has its own ionisation constant. e.g.

Step I $H_3PO_4 \overset{k_1}{\rightleftharpoons} H^+ + H_2PO_4^-$

Step II $H_2PO_4^- \overset{k_2}{\rightleftharpoons} H^+ + HPO_4^{2-}$

Step III $HPO_4^{2-} \overset{k_3}{\rightleftharpoons} H^+ + PO_4^{3-}$

- The overall dissociation constant (*k*) of ortho-phosphoric acid is given by the relation $k = k_1 \times k_2 \times k_3$
- Dissociation constants like k_2, k_3 are smaller than k_1 and follows the order $k_1 < k_2 < k_3$.
- As a proton is removed, it becomes difficult to remove another proton due to presence of negative charge and increased electrostatic forces.

Factors Affecting Acid Strength

- In a group of periodic table, H — *A* bond strength is a more important factor in determining acidity than its polar nature.
  e.g.

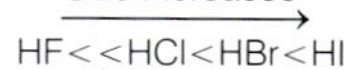

Size increases →
HF << HCl < HBr < HI
Acid strength increases →

- In the same period of the periodic table, H — *A* bond polarity becomes the deciding factor for determining the acidic strength. As the electronegativity of *A* increases, the strength of the acid increases.
  e.g.

Electronegativity of *A* increases →
$CH_4 < NH_3 < H_2O < HF$
Acid strength increases →

Ionisation of Acids and Bases

- A strong acid is an acid which completely dissociates in water or aqueous solution.
- A weak acid is an acid which partially dissociates in water or aqueous solution.
- The dissociation constant for a weak acid, K_a is used to measure the strength of a weak acid.

$$HA\ (aq) \rightleftharpoons A^-\ (aq) + H^+\ (aq)$$

$$K_a = \frac{[A^-]\ [H^+]}{[HA]}$$

- $[A^-]$ = conjugate base concentration
- $[H^+]$ = H^+ ion concentration
- $[HA]$ = acid concentration
- The greater the strength of an acid, the greater its K_a value.
- The pH of a weak acid can be calculated by using the concentration of the acids and K_a
- It is assumed $[H^+] = [A^-]$

$$K_a = \frac{[A^-][H^+]}{[HA]} = \frac{[H^+][H^+]}{[HA]}$$

- The concentration of *HA* present is given by the concentration of *HA* before any dissociation minus the concentration of H^+ ions:

$$K_a = \frac{[H^+]^2}{[HA] - [H^+]}$$

- As the degree of dissociation of the weak acid is very small:

$$[HA] - [H^+] \approx [HA];\ K_a = \frac{[H^+]^2}{[HA]}$$

- $[H^+] = \sqrt{K_a \times [HA]}$ the ion concentration can be used to find the pH. Similarly, for a weak base *BOH*.

$$BOH\ (aq) \rightleftharpoons B^+ + OH^-$$

$$K_b = \frac{[B^+]\ [OH^-]}{[BOH]} \text{ or } K_b = \frac{[OH^-]^2}{[BOH]}$$

Ionic Product of Water

- Species that can act as both an acid and a base are called amphoteric, e.g. water.
- Water slightly dissociates into hydroxide and hydroxonium ions.
  $2H_2O(l) \rightleftharpoons OH^-\ (aq) + H_3O^+\ (aq)$
  $2H_2O(l) \rightleftharpoons OH^-\ (aq) + H^+\ (aq))$
- The equilibrium constant for the dissociation of water is

$$K_C = \frac{[OH^-]\ [H^+]}{[H_2O]}$$

- The concentration of H_2O is constant for a given temperature
  $K_C \times [H_2O] = [OH^-]\ [H^+]$
- Ionic product of water,
  $K_w = [OH^-]\ [H^+]$
- K_w like other equilibrium constants, only changes with temperature.
- K_w can be used to calculate the pH of a strong base from its concentration
- $K_w = [H_3O^+][OH^-] = 10^{-14}$
- Acidic : $[H_3O^+] > [OH^-]$
- Neutral : $[H_3O^+] = [OH^-]$
- Basic : $[H_3O^+] < [OH^-]$
- The released H^+ ion from an acid is not free floating proton. They are not stable on their own, thus, it exist in combined form with water molecules giving hydronium ion (H_3O^+).
- These ions formed during the dissociation of acids in water is the basis of the properties of various acids.

Characteristics of Water

- Number of H_2O moles in 1litre water $= \frac{1000}{18} = 55.5$ mole
- Molar concentration of $H_2O = 55.5\text{mol L}^{-1}$
- Number of H_2O molecules in 1 litre water $= 55.5N_A$ (N_A = Avogadro's number)
- In water (No. of H_2O molecules :No. of H^+ ions) $= 55.5N_A : 10^{-7}N_A = 55.5 \times 10^7 : 1$ i.e. one H^+ ion is obtained from 55.5×10^7 H_2O molecules.
- The equilibrium constant for the self ionisation of water is called **ionic product of water**.
- Water is a very weak electrolyte so, a poor conductor of electricity.

Test 2

Syllabus

- Solubility of Sparingly Soluble Salts and Solubility Products
- Common Ion Effect

NCERT Page 200 to 201, Page 204 to 206

For deeper insight **Scan the QR Code**

Salt

- **Soluble salt**
  - Solubility is more than 0.1 M.
  - Such salts are in the form of ions in solution. 100% ionisation. e.g. NaCl, $CaCl_2$, CaF_2
- **Less soluble salt**
  - Solubility is more than 0.01M and less than 0.1M.
  - Possess ionic equilibrium. e.g. $Ca(OH)_2$, $MgSO_4$
- **Sparingly soluble salt**
  - Solubility less than 0.01M.
  - Sparingly soluble. e.g. AgCl, $Mg(OH)_2$, $BaSO_4$

Example of Different Types of Salt

- 1 : 1 type salt–AgCl, $BaSO_4$
- 1 : 2 or 2 : 1 type salt–PbI_2, $CaCl_2$
- 1 : 3 type salt–$FeCl_3$, $AlCl_3$

Solubility and Solubility Product

Solubility (*S*) Concentration of a substance in a saturated solution.

Solubility product (K_{sp}) It is defined as the product of concentration of ions in a saturated solution.

$$A_xB_y(s) \longrightarrow xA^{y+} + yB^{x-}$$

$$K_{sp} = [A^{y+}]^x . [B^{x-}]^y$$

- Total solubility of an ion is the product of solubility of salt and the stoichiometry of the ion.

e.g. $Ag_2CO_3 \longrightarrow 2Ag^+ + CO_3^{2-}$

Solubility $\quad S \qquad 2S \qquad S$

- Presence of a common ion decreases the solubility.

K_{sp} and Solubility of Salts

Types of salt	General formula	Solubility (S) and Solubility product (K_{sp})
1 : 1	*AB*	$S^2 = K_{sp}$ or $K_{sp} = S^2$
1 : 2 or 2 : 1	AB_2 or A_2B	$S = \sqrt[3]{\frac{K_{sp}}{4}}$ or $K_{sp} = 4S^3$
1 : 3	AB_3	$S = \sqrt[4]{\frac{K_{sp}}{27}}$ or $K_{sp} = 27S^4$

Factors Affecting the Solubility

Solubility is mainly affected by following four factors, i.e. temperature, pressure, polarity and molecular size.

- **Effect of temperature** Solubility increases with temperature for most solids dissolved in liquid water.
- **Effect of pressure** Solubility of a gas in a solvent increases with increase in pressure and decreases with decrease in pressure of gas.
- **Effect of polarity** In most of the cases, polar solute dissolve in a polar solvent while a non polar solute dissolves in a non polar solvent.
- **Effect of molecular size** Solubility decreases as the molecular size increases.

The more the carbon atoms added, the less soluble it will be.

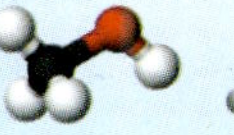

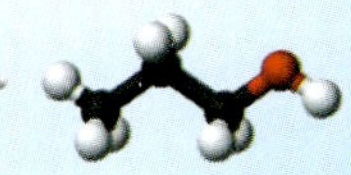

Most soluble — Least soluble

Uses of Solubility product

- Cation analysis is based on the principles of K_{sp} and common ion effect.
- The decrease in the ionisation (solubility) of a weak electrolyte in the presence of a common ion from a strong electrolyte. e.g. Ionisation of H_2S (weak acid) decreases in presence of HCl (H^+ is the common ion).
- **Group I**
  Cations (Ag^+, Hg_2^+, Pb^{2+}) are precipitated as chlorides since their values are low.
- **Group II**
  Cations (Pb^{2+}, Cu^{2+}, Cd^{2+}, Hg^{2+}, Bi^{3+}, Sb^{3+}) are precipitated as their sulphides since their K_{sp} values are decreased because of low value due of common ion effect.
- **Group III**
  Cations (Al^{3+}, Fe^{3+}, Cr^{3+}) are precipitated as their hydroxides, Since their K_{sp} values are decreased by the addition NH_4Cl and NH_4OH
- **Group IV**
  Cations (Zn^{2+}, Mn^{2+}, Ni^{2+}) are precipitated as their sulphides since their K_{sp} value are decreased due to increased [S^{2-}] concentration.

Solubility Product *vs* Ionic Product

Solubility product	Ionic product
• Solubility product is the concentration of ions of electrolyte, each raised to the power of their coefficients in the balanced chemical equation in a saturated solution. • Applicable only to saturated solutions. • At constant temperature, its value is constant for a given electrolyte.	• It is the product of concentration of ions of the electrolyte, each raised to the power of their coefficients in the balanced chemical equation in solution at any concentration. • Applicable to all types of solutions of any concentration. • The value keeps changing with concentration.

Prediction of Precipitate Formation

- Q_{sp} is the ion product or reaction quotient and is based on initial conditions of the reaction.
- Q_{sp} can then be compared to K_{sp}.
- To predict if a precipitation occurs:
- Precipitation should occur if $Q_{sp} > K_{sp}$.
- Precipitation cannot occur if $Q_{sp} < K_{sp}$.
- A solution is just saturated if $Q_{sp} = K_{sp}$.

A supersaturated solution will precipitate if a seed crystal is added

Importance of Common Ion Effect

Salt analysis, food processing, and other important chemical tasks are done through this effect. Moreover, it regulates buffers in the gravimetry technique.

Common Ion Effect

If an ionic equilibrium, $AB \rightleftharpoons A^+ + B^-$, a salt containing a common ion (e.g. *AC* or *BD*) is added, the equilibrium shifts in the backward direction. This is called common ion effect.

The results can be easily explained on the basis of Le-Chatelier's principle.

To the solution of the weak base, NH_4OH if NH_4Cl is added which provides the common NH_4^+ ions, dissociation of NH_4OH is suppressed:

$$NH_4OH \rightleftharpoons NH_4^+ + OH^-$$

$$NH_4Cl \longrightarrow NH_4^+ + Cl^-$$

- **Effect of common ion on solubility of sparingly soluble salt.**
- Adding a common cation or anion shifts a solubility equilibrium in the direction predicted by Le-Chatelier's principle.
- This results in decrease in solubility of any sparingly soluble salt due to presence of a soluble salt that contains a common ion.

Effect of Common Ion on Solubility

- Addition of a soluble salt that contains one of the ions of the "insoluble" salt, decreases the solubility of the "insoluble" salt.
- For example, addition of NaCl to the solubility equilibrium of solid $PbCl_2$ decreases the solubility of $PbCl_2$.

$$PbCl_2(s) \rightleftharpoons Pb^{2+}(aq) + 2Cl^-(aq)$$

Addition of Cl^- shifts the equilibrium to the left.

The effect of a common ion on solubility

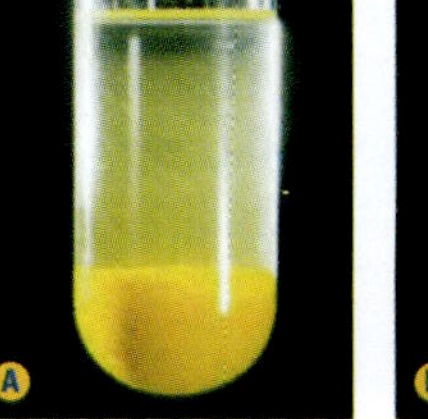

- The added chloride ions shifts the equilibrium reaction towards reactant side creating more solid lead (II) chloride.

Test 3

Syllabus
- pH Scale
- Hydrolysis of Salts
- Buffer Solutions
- pH of Solutions

NCERT
Page 193 to 194
Page 201 to 204

For deeper insight **Scan the QR Code**

pH

- The concentration of H^+ ions, often written as $[H^+]$, present in a solution determines how acidic it is.
- The pH scale Is logarithmic to cover the wide range of hydrogen ion concentrations in aqueous solution.
- $pH = -\log_{10}[H^+]$

0 1 2 3 4 5 6 7 8 9 10 11 12 13 14

Low pH, High (H^+), Acidic — High pH, Low (H^+), Basic

- The greater the concentration of H^+ ions, the lower the pH value, and the more acidic the solution is $-[H^+] = 10^{-pH}$.

pH and pOH Values

- For a weak monobasic acid:
  $pH = -\log[H_3O^+], = -\log\sqrt{K_a \cdot C}$
  $pH = \frac{1}{2}(pK_a - \log C)$
- For a monoacidic base:
  $pOH = -\log[OH^-] = -\log\sqrt{K_b \cdot C}$
  $pH = 14 - pOH = 14 - \frac{1}{2}[pK_b - \log C]$
- For mixture of acids and bases
  $[H^+] = \sqrt{C_1 K_{a_1} + C_2 K_{a_2}}$
- where, C_1 = concentration of acid 1,
  C_2 = concentration of acid 2.
  K_{a_1} and K_{a_2} are dissociation constants of acid 1 and 2 respectively.
  $[OH^-] = \sqrt{C_1 K_{b_1} + C_2 K_{b_2}}$

Effect of pH on Solubility

- The solubility of an ionic solute may be greatly affected by pH if an acid-base reaction also occurs as the solute dissolves.
- In other words, some salts will not dissolve well in pure water, but will dissolve in an acid or base.
- If the anion (A^-) of the salt/precipitate is that of a weak acid, the salt/precipitate will dissolve more when in a strong acid (H^+ ions will form HA with A^-).
- However, if the anion of the precipitate is that of a strong acid, adding a strong acid will have no effect on the precipitate dissolving more.

Relation Between K_a and K_b

K_a, K_b, pK_a and pK_b describe the acidity or alkalinity of a solution. They predict acid and base strength.

$$K_w = K_a \times K_b$$
$$pK_w = pK_a + pK_b$$
$$pK_a + pK_b = 14 \text{ (at 25°C)}$$

$$pK_a = -\log K_a$$
$$pK_b = -\log K_b$$

Buffer Solutions

- **Acidic buffer** They have pH value < 7.
- **Basic buffer** They have pH value > 7.
  Buffer system present in blood is $H_2CO_3 + NaHCO_3$.
- **Henderson-Hesselbalch Equation**
  This equation is used to calculate the pH of a buffer solution.
  (i) For acidic buffer,
  $$pH = pK_a + \log\frac{[salt]}{[acid]}$$
  (ii) For basic buffer,
  $$pOH = pK_a + \log\frac{[salt]}{[base]}$$
  and $pH = 14 - pOH$
  Here, $pK_a = -\log K_a$, $pK_b = -\log K_b$ and K_a and K_b are dissociation constants of acid and base.
  If addition of a strong acid or base changes the pH of a buffer by a unit, the buffer solution is assumed to be destroyed, i.e.
  New $pH = pK_a \pm 1$
  This means the ratio,
  $$\frac{[salt]}{[acid]} \text{ or } \frac{[salt]}{[base]} = 10 \text{ or } \frac{1}{10}$$

Application of Buffer Solutions

- Normal blood have a pH of 7.4 due to buffer nature. This pH is maintained by
  (a) buffer of carbonic acid
  ($H_2CO_3 + NaHCO_3$)
  (b) buffer of phosphoric acid
  ($H_2PO_4^-$, HPO_4^{2-})
- Acetate buffer ($CH_3COOH + CH_3COONa$) is used for precipitation of lead chromate quantitatively.
- Buffers are used as preservatives of foods and fruits.
- Buffers are used in paper manufacture, drugs, dyes, inks, electroplating etc.

Buffer Capacity

It is defined as the number of moles of acid or base added in 1 L of solution to change the pH by unity.

$$\text{Buffer capacity } (\phi) = \frac{\text{number of moles of acids or base added to 1L of buffer}}{\text{change in pH of buffer solution}}$$

Salt Hydrolysis

- Salt + Water $\rightleftharpoons$ Acid + Base
  Hydrolysis constant: $K_h = \frac{[Acid][Base]}{[Salt]}$
- Degree of hydrolysis (h) is the fraction of total salt that has undergone hydrolysis.

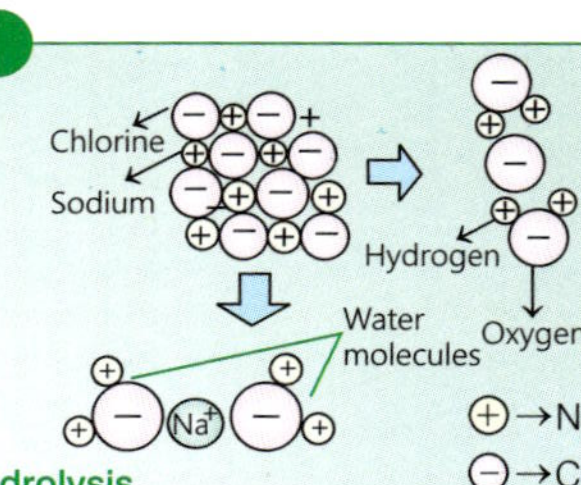

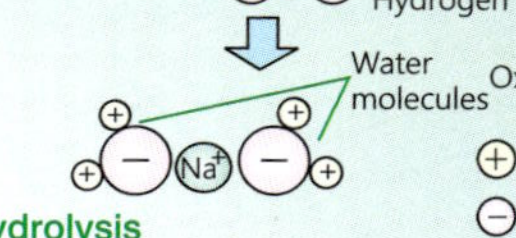

Various Formulae for Salt Hydrolysis

Salt	Nature	Degree of Hydrolysis	pH	K_h
NaCl (strong acid + strong base)	Neutral	No hydrolysis	——	——
CH_3COONa (weak acid + strong base)	Basic	$h = \sqrt{\frac{K_w}{CK_a}}$	$pH = \frac{1}{2}[pK_w + pK_a + \log C]$	$\frac{K_w}{K_a}$
NH_4Cl (strong acid + weak base)	Acidic	$h = \sqrt{\frac{K_w}{CK_b}}$	$pH = \frac{1}{2}[pK_w - pK_b - \log C]$	$\frac{K_w}{K_b}$
CH_3COONH_4 (weak acid + weak base)	*	$h = \sqrt{\frac{K_w}{K_a \times K_b}}$	$pH = \frac{1}{2}[pK_w + pK_a - pK_b]$	$\frac{K_w}{K_a \times K_b}$

* can be neutral, acidic or basic.

Applications of Hydrolysis

The applications of hydrolysis are as follows
- Hydrolysis of sugar is known as inversion. Sucrose is hydrolysed to release glucose and fructose.
- Hydrolysis is used for dissolution of salt of a mild acid and a base in water.
- Using hydrolysis, strong acids can be hydrolysed as well. When suphuric acid is dissolved in water, bisulphate and hydronium is produced.
- Acid-base catalysed hydrolysis is a very good application of hydrolysis.
- In biological systems, hydrolysis is catalysed by using enzymes, ATP is a good example for this chemical reaction.
- Hydrolysis is used for digestion of proteins, fats and carbohydrates.

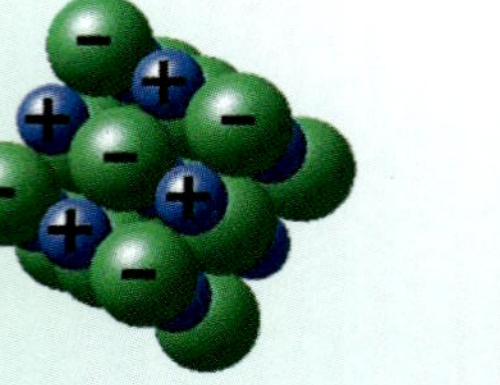

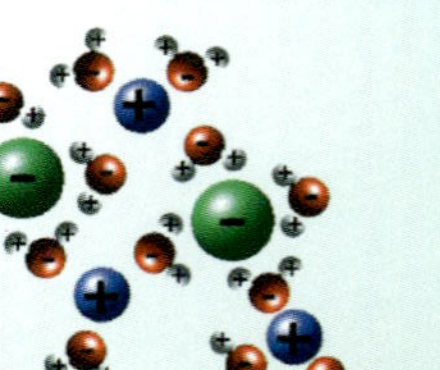

Test 1

Syllabus
- Electronic Concept of Oxidation and Reduction
- Oxidation Number
- Rules for Assigning Oxidation Number

NCERT
Page 235 to 237
Page 239 to 241
Page 245

For deeper insight **Scan the QR Code**

Oxidation

It is defined as loss of electrons during a reaction or an increase in oxidation number.

- **Addition of oxygen or other electronegative element**
  $2Mg + O_2 \longrightarrow 2MgO$
  $SnCl_2 + Cl_2 \longrightarrow SnCl_4$
- **Removal of Hydrogen or other electropositive element**
  $H_2S + Cl_2 \longrightarrow 2HCl + S$
- **Loss of electron**
- The half reaction that involve loss of electrons are called oxidation reactions. $K \longrightarrow K^+ + e^-$

Oxidation
Atom Loses Electron

- So, oxidation can be summarised as addition of oxygen/electronegative element to a substance or removal of hydrogen/electropositive element from a substance.
- **Oxidising agent or oxidant**
- It is the species, which itself undergoes reduction and oxidises other substance.
- It acts as electron acceptor.

Reduction

It is defined as gain of electrons during a reaction or a decrease in oxidation number.

- **Addition of hydrogen or other electropositive element**
  $Cl_2 + H_2 \longrightarrow 2HCl$
  $HgCl_2 + Hg \longrightarrow Hg_2Cl_2$
- **Removal of oxygen or other electronegative element**
  $2FeCl_3 + H_2 \longrightarrow 2FeCl_2 + 2HCl$
- **Gain of electron**
- The half reactions that involve gain of electrons are called reduction reactions. $Br_2 + 2e^- \longrightarrow 2Br^-$

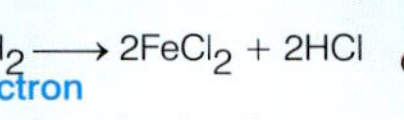

  So, reduction can be summarised as removal of oxygen / electronegative element from a substance or addition of hydrogen / electropositive element to a substance.
- **Reducing agent or Reductant** Substance which supplies hydrogen or removes oxygen. This substance itself gets oxidised while reducing the other substance.
- They acts as electron donor.
- Oxidation and reduction never takes place. independently, i.e. there is no chemical process that involves only reduction or oxidation.
- Whenever there is oxidation, that will be always associated with reduction.

Oxidation Numbers

- This is a number representing the number of electrons lost or gained by an atom in a compound.

Rules to Assign Oxidation Number

1. Oxidation number of an element in free elemental state or uncombined state zero.
2. In polyatomic ion, the algebraic sum of all the oxidation numbers of atom of the ion must be equal to the charge on the ion.
3. The oxidation number of oxygen in most of the compounds is –2.
   In peroxides the oxidation number is –1 while in superoxides it is –1/2.
   In OF_2 and O_2F_2 the assigned oxidation number of oxygen is +2 and +1 respectively.
4. Oxidation number of hydrogen is + 1 in most of its compounds (in metal hydrides it is – 1).
5. Oxidation number of fluorine is always –1 in its compounds.
6. Alkali metals have oxidation number +1 and alkaline earth metals have oxidation number +2 always in the compounds.
7. The algebraic sum of the oxidation number of all the atoms in a compound must be zero.
   $\overset{-1\ \ x\ \ -2}{KMnO_4}$ $1 + x \times 4(-2) = 0 \Rightarrow x = +7$

Application of Oxidation Number

Following are the applications of oxidation number.

- **Acidic character** Greater the oxidation number of the element forming oxyacids, greater is the acid strength except for oxyacids of phosphorous.
  Order : $H_2S_2O_3 < H_2SO_3 < H_2SO_4$
  $HCl < HClO < HClO_2 < HClO_3 < HClO_4$
- **Basic strength** Greater the oxidation number of the element in conjugate bases, smaller is the basic strength.
  Basic strength of conjugate bases of oxyacids of Cl will be in the order
  $ClO_4^- < ClO_3^- < ClO_2^- < ClO^-$.
- **Prediction of oxidising and reducing agent**
- Oxidising agent in the substance whose oxidation number decreases in the chemical reaction.
- Reducing agent is the substance whose oxidation number increases in the chemical reaction.
- **Prediction of redox reactions**
  It is used to define oxidation, reduction or redox reactions as.

$$\overset{+7}{MnO_4^-} + 5Fe^{2+} + 8H^+ \longrightarrow 5Fe^{3+} + Mn^{2+} + 4H_2O$$

Oxidation ($Fe^{2+} \to Fe^{3+}$); Reduction ($MnO_4^- \to Mn^{2+}$)

Exceptions in Oxidation Number

These are exceptional behaviour of some elements on assigning the oxidation number.

Carbon suboxide
$O = \overset{+2}{C} = \overset{0}{C} = \overset{+2}{C} = O$

Fe_3O_4
$\overset{+2}{FeO}.\overset{+3}{Fe_2O_3}$

Tribromooctaoxide
$O = \overset{+6}{Br} - \overset{+4}{Br} - \overset{+6}{Br} = O$ (each Br with double-bonded O above and below)

$CaOCl_2$
$Ca(\overset{+1}{O}\overset{-1}{Cl})Cl$

CrO_5
Cr (+6) bonded to one O (–2) by double bond and to two peroxide O–O groups (each O –1)

Tetrathionate ion
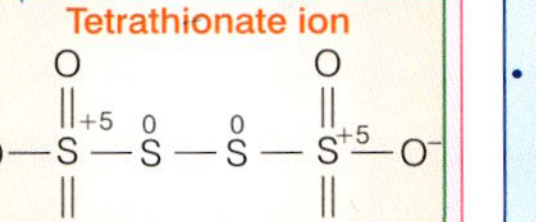
$^-O - \overset{+5}{S} - \overset{0}{S} - \overset{0}{S} - \overset{+5}{S} - O^-$ (each terminal S with double-bonded O above and below)

Assigning Oxidation Number

Rules	Oxidation Number	Example
Elements	Zero (0)	N_2, Cl_2, O_2, P_4, S_8
Monoatomic ions	Same as charge	$Na^+(+1)$, $Mg^{2+}(+2)$
Hydrogen		
Generally	+ 1	H_2O, H_2S, HCl
with binary compound	– 1	LiH, CaH_2, KH
Oxygen	– 2 (mostly)	H_2O, CaO, NaOH
In peroxides	– 1	H_2O_2, BaO_2
In superoxides	–1/2	KO_2, CsO_2
In fluorides	+ 1, + 2	O_2F_2, OF_2 (respectively)
Alkali metals	+ 1	Li, Na, K, etc.
Alkaline earth metals	+ 2	Be, Mg, Ca, etc.
Fluorine (most electronegative)	– 1 (always)	HF, OF_2, LiF
Sulphides	– 2	H_2S, ZnS

Example for Assigning Oxidation Number

- Same atom in a compound can have different oxidation state. e.g. $Na_2S_2O_3$.

Na — O — S_1 — O — Na (with S_2 attached to S_1 by arrow, and O double-bonded to S_1)

- Here, S_1 and S_2 both are sulphur atoms but they have different oxidation states (O.S.)
- Oxidation state of $S_1 = 6$
- Oxidation state of $S_2 = -2$ (it is accepting two electrons from S_1)
- Average oxidation state of $S = \frac{6-2}{2} = 2$

Paradox of Fractional O.N.

- Fractional oxidation state is the average oxidation number of the element under consideration and the structural parameters reveal that the element for which fractional oxidation number is realised, is present in different oxidation state.
- In $S_4O_6^{2-}$, oxidation number of two S atoms is five and other two S is zero.

202 pm, 102°, 212 pm, 104°

- In Fe_3O_4, oxidation number of two Fe atoms is +3 and one Fe is +2.
- In Br_3O_8, oxidation number of two Br atoms are +6 while other one has +4.Average oxidation number of Br in $Br_3O_8 = \frac{16}{3}$

Stock Notation

- Oxidation states are written in Roman numeral after the symbol of metal in molecular formula.
- Cation + (Oxidation number in Roman Numeral) + anion. e.g. Au(I) Cl.

Naming the Acid and its Ions

Oxoanions	Formula	Acids	Formula
Bromate (I)	BrO^-	Bromic (I)	HBrO
Bromate (III)	BrO_2^-	Bromic (III)	$HBrO_2$
Bromate (V)	BrO_3^-	Bromic (V)	$HBrO_3$
Bromate (VII)	BrO_4^-	Bromic (VII)	$HBrO_4$
Chromate(VI)	CrO_4^{2-}	Chromic (VI)	H_2CrO_4

Important Points Related to Oxidation Number

- I group elements always shows +1 oxidation number.
- II group elements always shows +2 oxidation number.
- III group elements shows +3 oxidation number but +1 becomes more stable on going down the group (due to inert pair effect).
- IV group shows –4 to +4 oxidation number.
- V group shows –3 to +5 oxidation number.
- VI group shows –2 to +6 oxidation number.
- VII group shows –1 to +7 oxidation number.
- Inert gases show zero oxidation number.

Test 2

Syllabus
- Redox Reactions
- Balancing of Redox Reactions

NCERT
Page 238
Page 242 to 244
Page 246 to 251

For deeper insight **Scan the QR Code**

Chapter 08

Types of Redox Reactions

These reactions can be classified as
- Combination reaction
- Decomposition reaction
- Displacement reaction
  – Metal displacement reaction
  – Non-metal displacement reaction
- Disproportionation reaction

Combination Reaction

- These reaction involves combination of two or more atoms to give a single product.
- Its general expression is $A+B \longrightarrow C$

$CH_4(g) + 2O_2(g) \longrightarrow CO_2(g)+2H_2O(l)$

- For such a reaction either A and B or both A and B must be in the elemental form for such a reaction to be redox reaction.

Decomposition Reaction

- These reaction involves splitting of a compound into two or more simpler products. In which one of the obtained component should be in elemental state.
- It is the opposite of combination reaction.

$2H_2O(l) \xrightarrow{\Delta} 2H_2(g)+O_2(g)$

Displacement Reaction

- These reaction involve displacement of one atom (or ion) by other atom of same nature.
- These reactions help in estimating the reactivity of metals and non-metals.

e.g. $X+YZ \longrightarrow XZ + Y$

Metal Displacement Reaction

In this reaction, one metal displaces the other metal.

$CuSO_4(aq) + Zn(s) \longrightarrow Cu(s) + ZnSO_4(aq)$

Non-metal Displacement Reaction

In this reaction, non-metal is displaced by metal or non-metal.

$Mg(s) + 2H_2O(l) \longrightarrow Mg(OH)_2(s) + H_2(g)$

Disproportionation Reaction

In this reaction, the same element is oxidised as well as reduced.

$Cl_2(g)+2OH^-(aq) \longrightarrow ClO^-(aq)+Cl^-(aq) + H_2O(l)$

$S_8(s)+12OH^-(aq) \longrightarrow 4S^{2-}(aq) +2S_2O_3^{2-}(aq) + 6H_2O(l)$

Redox Reactions

- The reactions which involve both oxidation and reduction.
- Oxidising agents cause oxidation of other species, and so are themselves reduced.
- Reducing agents cause reduction of other species, and so are themselves oxidised.
- In the reaction below. H is reduced, Na is oxidised.

$$2\overset{+1}{H}Cl + 2\overset{0}{Na} \longrightarrow 2\overset{+1}{Na}Cl + \overset{0}{H_2}$$

- These reaction may be divided in two parts

(i) Oxidation half-reaction
(ii) Reduction half-reaction

Applications of Redox Reactions

- Redox reactions are used in redox titration, e.g. titration of MnO_4^- with Fe^{2+} or $C_2O_4^{2-}$ iodometric titrations etc.

(i) In one situation, the reagent itself is intensely coloured, e.g. permanganate ion MnO_4^- Here MnO_4^- ; acts as the self Indicator. The visible end point in this case is achieved after the last of the reductant (Fe^{2+} or $C_2O_4^{2-}$) is oxidised and the first lasting tinge of pink colour appears at MnO_4^- concentration as low as 10^{-6} mol dm^{-3} (10^{-6} mol L^{-1}).
This ensures a minimal 'overshoot' in colour beyond the equivalence point, the point where the reductant and the oxidant are equal in terms of their mole stoichiometry.

(ii) If there is no dramatic auto-colour change (as with MnO_4^- titration), there are indicators which are oxidised immediately after the last bit of the reactant is consumed, producing a dramatic colour change. The best example is afforded by $Cr_2O_7^{2-}$ which is not a self-indicator, but oxidises the indicator substance diphenylamine just after the equivalence point to produce an intense blue colour thus signalling the end point.

(iii) There is yet another method which is interesting and quite common. Its use is restricted to those reagents which are able to oxidise I^- ions, say, e.g. Cu(II).

$2Cu^{2+} (aq) + 4\,I^- (aq) \longrightarrow Cu_2I_2 (s) + I_2 (aq)$

- This method relies on the facts that iodine itself gives an intense blue colour with starch and has a very specific reaction with thiosulphate ions ($S_2O_3^{2-}$) , which too is a redox reaction.

$I_2 (aq) + 2\,S_2O_3^{2-} (aq) \longrightarrow 2I^- (aq) + S_4O_6^{2-} (aq)$

I_2 though insoluble in water, remains in solution containting KI as KI_3.

Balancing of Redox Reactions

1. Identify oxidation and reduction half equations.
2. Make total increase and total decrease in oxidation number equal two both half equation.
3. Balance all atoms except O and H.
4.

Acidic	Basic
• Oxygen with H_2O • Hydrogen with H^+	• Charge with OH^- • Oxyen with H_2O

Oxidation Number Method

Steps involved in it are

(i) Write ionic equation.
(ii) Assign oxidation number and balance all other atoms except H and O.
(iii) Predict change in oxidation number.
(iv) Balance charge.
(v) Balance H and O.

e.g. $Zn+HNO_3 \longrightarrow Zn(NO_3)_2+NH_4NO_2+ H_2O$

- **Skeleton equation with oxidation number**

$$\overset{0}{Zn} + \overset{+1+5-2}{HNO_3} \longrightarrow \overset{+2+5-2}{Zn(NO_3)_2} + \overset{-3+1+5-2}{NH_4NO_3} + \overset{+1-2}{H_2O}$$

- **Change in oxidation number**

$$\overset{0}{Zn} \longrightarrow \overset{+2}{Zn}(NO_3)_2,\; H\overset{+5}{N}O_3 \longrightarrow \overset{-3}{N}H_4NO_3$$

- Increase in oxidation number of Zn = 2
Decrease in oxidation number of N = 8, then

$4Zn+NHO_3 \longrightarrow 4Zn(NO_3)_2+NH_4NO_3$

- Addition of HNO_3 on LHS, addition of H_2O on RHS will balance the equation:

$4Zn + 10HNO_3 \longrightarrow 4Zn(NO_3)_2 + NH_4NO_3 + 3H_2O$

Electrochemical Series

- The arrangement of standard electrode potential of various electrode in their decreasing order is called **electromotive** or **electrochemical** or **activity series.**
- In this series, the oxidising agents are arranged in the decreasing order of their strength, i.e. the tendency of oxidation half reaction goes on decreasing on moving from top to bottom.
- **Application of electrochemical series**

(i) Predicting the strength of oxidant or reductant
- a negative $E°$ means that the redox couple is a stronger reducing agent than H^+/H_2 couple.
- a positive $E°$ means that the redox couple is a weaker reducing agent than H^+/H_2 couple.

(ii) Comparing the reactivity of metals.
(iii) Predicting feasibility of a cell reaction.

Ion Electron Method

Steps involved in it are

(i) Write ionic equation and indicate the oxidation number of all elements.
(ii) Split it into two halves. One is oxidation half and other is reduction half.
(iii) Balance all other atoms which undergoes oxidation, reduction except H and O.
(iv) Balance charge with addition of electrons.
(v) Add half equation and cancel any term common to both sides.
(vi) Verify balanced equation.
(vii) Convert ionic equation into molecular form.

e.g. $MnO_2 + HCl \longrightarrow MnCl_2 + H_2O + Cl_2$

- **Ionic form**

$MnO_2 + H^+ + Cl^- \longrightarrow Mn^{2+} + H_2O + Cl_2$

- **Half reactions**

$Cl^- \longrightarrow Cl_2$, $MnO_2 + H^+ \longrightarrow Mn^{2+} + H_2O$

- **Balance half reaction**

$2Cl^- \longrightarrow Cl_2$, $MnO_2 + 4H^+ \longrightarrow Mn^{2+} + 2H_2O$

- **Addition of electrons and balanced reaction**

$2Cl^- \longrightarrow Cl_2 + 2e^-$

$MnO_2 + 4H^+ + 2e^- \longrightarrow Mn^{2+} + 2H_2O$

- **Addition of both half-reactions**

$2Cl^- + MnO_2 + 4H^+ \longrightarrow Cl_2 + Mn^{2+} + 2H_2O$

$MnO_2 + 4Cl^- + 4H^+ \longrightarrow Cl_2 + Mn^{2+} + 2Cl^- + 2H_2O$

- **Molecular form**

$MnO_2 + 4HCl \longrightarrow MnCl_2 + Cl_2 + 2H_2O$

Useful Terms in Electrode Process

- **Electrode** It is a metal rod dipped in its salt solution.
- **Anode** The electrode at which oxidation occurs.
- **Cathode** The electrode at which reduction occurs.
- **Redox couple** It is the combination of oxidised and reduced forms, e.g. Zn^{2+}/Zn.
- **Electrode potential** It is the potential associated with an electrode.
- **Standard electrode potential** It is the electrode potential measured in standard conditions.
- **Electrolytic cell** It converts electrical energy into chemical energy.
- **Electrochemical cell** It converts chemical energy into electrical energy e.g. Daniell cell, lead storage battery etc.
- **Salt-bridge** It completes the circuit and maintain electrical neutrality.
- **Electrochemical series** A series of decreasing $E°$, e.g. $F^- > Au > Br^- > Cu > Ag > H_2 >$ Pb > Sn > Fe > Cr > Zn > Al > Mg > Na > Ca > K > Li.

Anode (Oxidation) – Zn, $ZnSO_{4(aq)}$; Salt-bridge KCl; Cathode (Reduction) + Cu, $CuSO_4$; e^-

Test 1

Syllabus
- Electronic Configuration and General Trends in Physical and Chemical Properties of Elements
- Unique Behaviour of Boron

NCERT Page 307 to 314

For deeper insight **Scan the QR Code**

Introduction

- *p*-block elements are the elements in which the last electron enters in the outermost *p*-orbital.
- The number of *p*-orbitals are three so, the maximum number of electrons that can be accomodated in a set of *p*-orbital is six.

Abundance and Electronic Configuration

Al is the most abundant metal and third most abundant element by mass in the Earth's Crust.

Electronic Configuration of Elements of Group 13

- The general electronic configuration of *p*-block elements is [N.G.]$ns^2 np^{1-6}$ where, N.G.=noble gas for 13 group element.
- The electronic configuration of group 13 elements is [N.G.]$ns^2 np^1$.

Element	Atomic number	Electronic configuration
Boron (B)	5	[He] $2s^2 2p^1$
Aluminium (Al)	13	[Ne] $3s^2 3p^1$
Gallium (Ga)	31	[Ar] $3d^{10} 4s^2 4p^1$
Indium (In)	49	[Kr] $4d^{10} 5s^2 5p^1$
Thallium (Tl)	81	[Xe] $4f^{14} 5d^{10} 6s^2 6p^1$
Nihonium (Nh)	113	[Rn] $5f^{14} 6d^{10} 7s^2 7p^1$

Physical Properties

- **Atomic radii** On moving down the group for each successive member one extra shell of electron is added. So, atomic radius increases (Except for Ga and Al).
  $$B < Ga < Al < In < Tl$$
- **Ionisation enthalpy** There is a discontinuity in I.E. between Al and Ga and between In and Tl due to inability of *d* and *f*-electron to compensate increase in nuclear charge.
  $$B > Tl > Ga > Al > In$$
- **Electronegativity** It decreases from B to Al then increases marginally. B>Tl>In>Ga> Al
- **Melting point** Boron has unusually high M.P. while others have low M.P.
  $$B > Al > Tl > In > Ga$$

Chemical Properties

- Shows +1 and +3 oxidation states.
- Stability of +1 and +3 states respectively are
  $$Al^+ < Ga^+ < In^+ < Tl^+$$
  $$Al^{3+} > Ga^{3+} > In^{3+} > Tl^{3+}$$
- **BF_3** and **BCl_3** are electron deficient and behave as **Lewis acid**.
- **Reactions with air** Amorphous boron and aluminium metal on heating in air form B_2O_3 and Al_2O_3 respectively.
  $$2M(s) + 3O_2(g) \xrightarrow{\Delta} 2M_2O_3(s)$$
- With dinitrogen at high temperature they form nitrides.
  $$2M(s) + N_2(g) \xrightarrow{\Delta} 2MN(s) \quad (M=\text{element})$$
- **Reactions with acids and alkalies**
  $$2M(s) + 6HCl(aq) \rightarrow 2M^{3+}(aq) + 6Cl^- + 3H_2(g)\uparrow$$
  $$2M(s) + 2NaOH + 6H_2O(l) \longrightarrow 2Na^+[M(OH)_4]^-(aq) + 3H_2(g)$$
  [Boron does not react with acids and alkalies.]
- Aluminium dissolves in dil.HCl and liberates dihydrogen.
- **Reaction with halogens** These elements react with halogens to form trihalides (except TlI_3).
- $2M(s) + 3X_2(g) \longrightarrow 2MX_3(s) \quad (X=F, Cl, Br, I)$
- The relative strength of Lewis acids of boron trihalides increases in the order
  $$BF_3 < BCl_3 < BBr_3 < BI_3$$
- This order can be explained on the basis of the tendency of the halogen atom to back donate its electrons to boron atom and makes it less electron deficient.
- Amongst the trihalides of group 13, BF_3 and $AlCl_3$ are widely used as Lewis acid catalysts.

Metallic and Reducing Character

- **Metallic character** Boron is the only non-metal in the group, aluminium is a metal but shows many properties similar to boron gallium, indium and thallium are almost exclusively metallic in character. The overall order of electropositive character is B<Tl<In<Ga<Al. In Ga to Tl, d^{10} and (in case of Tl) do not shield the nuclear charge effectively and thus these metals are less electropositive.
- **Reducing character** The reducing power of group 13 elements decreases down the group from aluminium to thallium as the electrode potential values increase. Thus, the reducing power follows the trend. Al>Ga>In>Tl

Anomalous Behaviour of Boron

- Cannot extend covalency beyond four.
- Exhibits allotropy and exists in crystalline and amorphous form.
- Has higher melting and boiling points comparatively.

Among group 13 elements, only boron forms several oxyacids, all of which are obtained by adding one or more molecules to one or more B_2O_3 molecules as

$$B_2O_3 + 3H_2O \longrightarrow 2H_3BO_3 \text{ or } 3B(OH)_3 \text{ (Orthoboric acid)}$$
$$B_2O_3 + H_2O \longrightarrow 2H_3BO_2 \text{ (Metaboric acid)}$$
$$2B_2O_3 + 3H_2O \longrightarrow H_6B_4O_9 \text{ (Pyroboric acid)}$$
$$3B_2O_3 + 2H_2O \longrightarrow H_4B_6O_{11} \text{ (Hexaboric acid)}$$
$$4B_2O_3 + 3H_2O \longrightarrow H_4B_8O_{15} \text{ (Octaboric acid)}$$

B forms only covalent compounds on account of its high ionisation enthalpy while Al forms covalent compounds in anhydrous state and ionic compounds in aqueous solutions.

Diborane

- Simplest known hydride of boron.
- $4BCl_3 + 3LiAlH_4 \xrightarrow{\text{Ether}} 2B_2H_6 + 3LiCl + 3AlCl_3$
- Structure contains two 3 centre-2 electron bonds known as "Banana bonds".

(Structure labels: 122°, 97°, 1.19Å, 1.77Å, 2C — 2e bond, 3c — 2e bond)

- The given structure shows bonding in diborane. Each B atom uses sp^3 hybrids for bonding. Out of the four sp^3 hybrids on each B atom, one is without an electron shown with broken lines.
- The terminal B — H bonds are normal 2-centre-2-electron bonds.
- Diborane undergoes cleavage reactions with Lewis bases to give borane adducts.
- It is used as a precursor to synthesise other boron compounds borazine.
  $$3B_2H_6 + 6NH_3 \xrightarrow{\Delta} 2B_3N_3H_6 + 12H_2$$
- $B_3N_3H_6$ is known as "inorganic benzene" in view of its ring structure with alternate BH and NH groups.

Boric Acid

- Weak monobasic acid (Lewis acid)
  $$H_3BO_3 + 2H_2O \longrightarrow [B(OH)_4]^- + H_3O^+$$
- Heating effect
  $$\underset{\text{Metaboric acid}}{H_3BO_3} \xrightarrow[\Delta]{273K} HBO_2 \xrightarrow[\Delta]{433K} \underset{\text{Tetraboric acid}}{H_2B_4O_7} \xrightarrow[\text{hot}]{\text{Red}} \underset{\text{Boron trioxide (boric anhydride)}}{B_2O_3}$$
- Forms 6 H-bonds in aqueous solution.

Borax

- Its general formula is $Na_2B_4O_7 \cdot 10H_2O$ / $Na_2[B_4O_5(OH)_4] \cdot 8H_2O$.
- Aqueous solution of borax is alkaline in nature.
  $$Na_2B_4O_7 + 7H_2O \longrightarrow 2NaOH + 4H_3BO_3$$
- Borax bead test (Detection of transition metal)
  $$Na_2B_4O_7 \cdot 10H_2O \xrightarrow{\Delta} Na_2B_4O_7 \xrightarrow{\text{Heat}} \underset{\text{Sodium Metaborate}}{2NaBO_2} + \underset{\text{Boric anhydride Glassy mass (Borax bead)}}{B_2O_3}$$
- There are 5 B — O — B bridge bonds.

Transition metal	Colour
Cu/Co	Blue

Uses • As flux
- Water softening agent
- As antiseptic
- In making enamel
- Manufacture of glass

Compounds of Al

- **$AlCl_3$**
- $Al_2O_3 + 3C + 3Cl_2 \xrightarrow{\text{Heat}} 2AlCl_3 + 3CO$
- Aqueous solution is acidic due to the formation of HCl.
- $Al_2O_3 + 3H_2O \longrightarrow Al(OH)_3 + 3HCl$
- Anhy. $AlCl_3$ is covalent and dimeric.

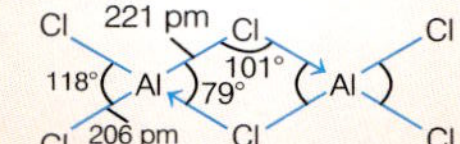

Uses of Boron and Aluminium and their Compounds

- Boron fibres are used in making bullet proof vests.
- Light composite material of boron is used in aircraft
- Boron-10 (^{10}B) isotope has high ability to absorb neutron, so, it is used in nuclear industry as protective shields and control rods.
- Borax and boric acid is used in the manufacture of heat resistant glasses.
- Aluminium is used in packing utensil making, transportation industry etc.

Test 2

Syllabus
- Electronic Configuration and General Trends in Physical and Chemical Properties of Elements
- Unique Behaviour of Carbon

NCERT Page 314 to 322

For deeper insight **Scan the QR Code**

Chapter 09

Introduction

Carbon, silicon, germanium, tin, lead and flerovium are the members of group 14.

Abundance and Electronic Configuration

C is the seventeenth and Si is the second most abundant element by mass in the Earth's crust.

Electronic Configuration of Elements of Group 14

Element	Atomic number	Electronic configuration
Carbon (C)	6	[He] $2s^2 2p^2$
Silicon (Si)	14	[Ne] $3s^2 3p^2$
Germanium (Ge)	32	[Ar] $3d^{10} 4s^2 4p^2$
Tin (Sn)	50	[Kr] $4d^{10} 5s^2 5p^2$
Lead (Pb)	82	[Xe] $4f^{14} 5d^{10} 6s^2 6p^2$

Physical Properties

- **Covalent radii** Increases down the group,
  $C < Si < Ge < Sn < Pb$
- **Ionisation enthalpy** Decreases down the group but Pb is an exception.
  $C > Si > Ge > Sn < Pb$
- **Electronegativity** Does not show much variation and is almost same for all except C.
  $C > Si \approx Ge \approx Sn < Pb$
- **Melting points and boiling point** Have higher MP and BP than group 13 elements and decreases down the group.
  M.P. $C > Si > Ge > Pb > Sn$
  B.P. $C > Si > Ge > Sn > Pb$
- **Metallic character**
  Increases down the group.

Uses of Carbon

- Graphite is used for electrodes in batteries and industrial electrolysis.
- Being highly porous, activated charcoal is used in adsorbing poisonous gases.
- Used in water filters to remove organic contamination and in air conditioning.
- Carbon black is used as black pigment in black ink and as filler in automobile tyres.

Chemical Properties

- Common oxidation states are +4 and +2
- Compounds are generally covalent.
- +4 is more stable for earlier elements (C,Si, Ge).
- +2 is more stable on going down the group due to inert pair effect. (Pb^{2+})
- Pb does not show catenation.
- Catenation power of carbon family is higher than boron family and nitrogen family as well.

Element	General formula of hydrides	Common name	Known number of hydride (n)
Carbon (C)	C_nH_{2n+2}	Alkane	$n = 1$ to 100
Silicon (Si)	Si_nH_{2n+2}	Silane	$n = 1$ to 8
Germanium (Ge)	Ge_nH_{2n+2}	Germane	$n = 1$ to 9
Tin (Sn)	$Sn_n H_{2n+2}$	Stannane	$n = 1$ or 2

- The tetrahalide of carbon, i.e. CCl_4 cannot be hydrolysed by water since it cannot expand its covalency beyond 4 due to the absence of d-orbitals.
- The tetrachloride of other element, $SiCl_4$, $GeCl_4$, $SnCl_4$ and $PbCl_4$ are easily hydrolysed due to presence of vacant d-orbital which accept OH^- from water molecules. The ease of hydrolysis follows the sequence
  $(SiCl_4 < GeCl_4 < SnCl_4 < PbCl_4)$
- Order of thermal stability of tetrahalides
  $CX_4 > SiX_4 > GeX_4 > SnX_4 > PbX_4$.
- Most of the MX_4 are covalent in nature except SnF_4 and PbF_4. These elements can form halides of formula MX_2 and MX_4.
- Except carbon, all other members react directly with halogen under suitable condition to make halides.

Reactions

With oxygen

$M(s) + O_2 \xrightarrow{\text{Limited supply}} MO(g)$

$M(s) + O_2 \xrightarrow{\text{Excess}} MO_2(g)$

Nature of oxides : GeO-acidic, SnO and PbO (Amphoteric)]

CO_2, SiO_2, GeO_2 (Acidic)
SnO_2 and PbO_2 (Amphoteric)

With water

- C, Si and Ge are not affected by water.
- Pb is unaffected by water due to protective oxide film formation.
- $\underset{\text{(Steam)}}{Sn + 2H_2O} \xrightarrow{\Delta} SnO_2 + 2H_2$

With halogen

- $M + 2X_2 \longrightarrow MX_4$

Anomalous Behaviour of Carbon

- Carbon shows –4 to +4 oxidation states.
- Melting point and boiling point of C are very high.
- It can form multiple $p\pi$-$p\pi$ bonds with itself.
- Shows a property called catenation.
- Exists in allotropic forms.
- Its covalency is limited to four while other members can expand it to six.
- The reason for this anomaly is smaller size, higher electronegativity, higher I.E. and unavailability of d-orbitals.

Allotropes of Carbon

(i) Crystalline allotropes

- **Diamond**
  - Rigid 3-D lattice network.
  - All carbons are sp^3 hybridised.
  - Insulator of electricity but a conductor of heat.
  - It is the hardest known substance on the earth.
  - Used for making dyes, abrasive for sharpening.
- **Graphite**
  - A layered structure
  - Each carbon is sp^2-hybridised.
  - Good conductor of electricity.
  - The cleaves easily between the layers and therefore, it very soft and slippery.
  - It is used as dry lubricant in machines at high temperature

141.5 pm
340 pm

- **Buckminster fullerene**
  - It is C_{60} molecule.
  - Shape like soccer ball.
  - It has 20,6-membered and 12, 5-membered rings.
  - Each C is sp^2-hybridised.

(ii) Amorphous allotropes

- Carbon black
- Charcoal
- Coke

Compounds of Carbon

- **CO**
  - $HCOOH \xrightarrow[373K]{\text{Conc. } H_2SO_4} CO + H_2O$
  - Coal gasification
    $\underset{\text{(Steam)}}{C + H_2O} \longrightarrow \underset{\text{Syn gas / Water gas}}{CO + H_2}$
  - Producer gas $(CO + N_2)$
  - With Hb it forms 300 times stable carboxy haemoglobin as compared to oxyhaemoglobin
- **CO_2**
  - Solid CO_2-Dry ice (Refrigerant)
  - CO_2 in water gives carbonic acid (maintain pH 7.26-7.42)

Carbon Dioxide

Relative contribution of various greenhouse gases to total global warming.

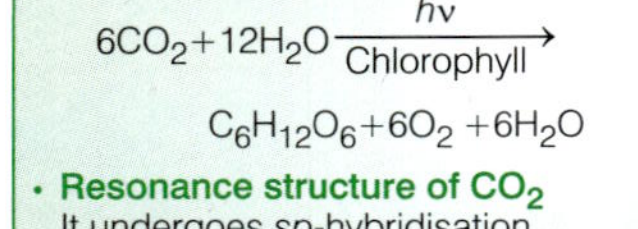

- **Photosynthesis** The process of removal of CO_2 from atmosphere.
  $6CO_2 + 12H_2O \xrightarrow[\text{Chlorophyll}]{h\nu} C_6H_{12}O_6 + 6O_2 + 6H_2O$
- **Resonance structure of CO_2**
  It undergoes sp-hybridisation.
  The resonance structure are shown as
  $:\ddot{O}^- - C \equiv \overset{+}{O}: \leftrightarrow :\ddot{O} = C = \ddot{O}: \leftrightarrow :\overset{+}{O} \equiv C - \ddot{O}:^-$

Compounds of Silicon

- **Silicones**
  - General formula $(R_2SiO)n$
  - $R_2SiCl_2 + 2H_2O \xrightarrow{\text{Hydrolysis}} \underset{\text{(Linear chain silicones)}}{R_2Si(OH)_2} + 2HCl$
  - $RSiCl_3 + 3H_2O \longrightarrow \underset{\text{(Cross linked silicones)}}{RSi(OH)_3} + 3HCl$
  - $R_3SiCl \longrightarrow$ Stopping agent /Dimer

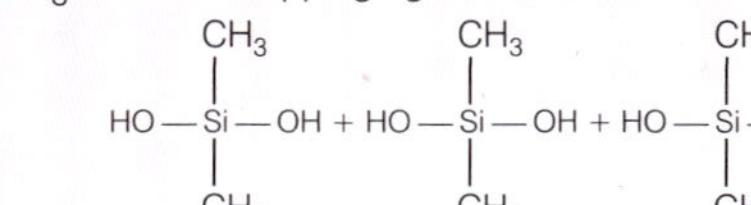

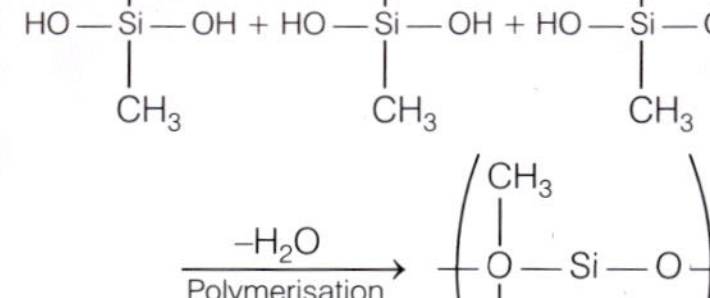

- **Silicates**
  - Basic unit is SiO_4^{4-} (tetrahedral).
  - In SiO_4^{4-} silicon atom is bonded to four oxygen atoms in tetrahedron fashion.
  - When silicate units are linked together, they form chain, ring, sheet of 3-D structures.
- **Silica**
  - SiO_2-sand, quartz (piezoelectric).
  - Insoluble in H_2O and inert at room temperature.
  - Reacts with HF (etching of glass)
    $4HF + SiO_2 \longrightarrow SiF_4 + 2H_2O$
    $SiF_4 + 2HF \longrightarrow H_2SiF_6$
  - 3D network covalent solid.
- **Zeolites**
  - Sodium aluminium silicates $(Na_2Al_2Si_2O_8 \cdot xH_2O)$
  - Used for purification of H_2O to remove hardness of water.
  - ZSM-5 is a shape selective catalyst used to convert alcohol to gasoline.

Test 1

Syllabus
- Crystallisation
- Sublimation
- Distillation
- Differential Extraction
- Chromatography-Principles and their Applications

NCERT Page 278 to 284

For deeper insight **Scan the QR Code**

Methods of Purification of Organic Compounds

Based on the nature of the compound and the impurity present in it, there are various methods that are used for the purification of organic compound.

Solids: Sublimation, Crystallisation

Liquid or gas: Distillation, Differential extraction, Chromatography

Crystallisation

- **Principle** It is based on the difference in the solubilities of the compound and the impurities in a suitable solvent.
- **Process** The impure compound is dissolved in a solvent in which it is sparingly soluble at room temperature but appreciably soluble at higher temperature. The solution is concentrated to get a nearly saturated solution.
  On cooling the solution, pure compound crystallises out and removed by filtration. The filtrate contains impurities and small quantity of the compound. The solvents commonly used for dissolving organic solids are water, alcohol, ether, chloroform, benzene, petroleum ether, etc.

Sublimation

- **Principle**
  This process is employed for those solids which convert directly into vapours on heating without converting into liquid phase and the vapours upon cooling give back solid.

$$\text{Solid} \underset{\text{Cool}}{\overset{\text{Heat}}{\rightleftharpoons}} \text{Vapour}$$

- **Process**
- In this process, the impure solid is taken into China dish and is covered with a perforated filter paper.
- An inverted funnel is placed over the dish and its stem is plugged with cotton.
  The diagram is shown below.
- The dish is heated gently and the substance volatilises as a result. The substance now called **sublimate** is collected over the inner cold surface of the funnel.
- The non-volatile impurities are left behind in the China dish.
- The perforated filter paper allows only the vapours to go upwards and prevent the sublimate from falling back down into the dish.

Cotton plug
Sublimate
Perforated filter paper
Crude solid

Sublimation

- **Application**
  Impure samples of naphthalene, anthracene, camphor, dry ice, salicylic acid can be purified by the method provided, the impurities are non-volatile.

Distillation

This method is used to separate
(i) volatile liquids from non-volatile impurities.
(ii) the liquids having sufficient difference in their boiling points.

Types of Distillation

Simple distillation:
To separate liquids which have sufficient difference in b.p. For e.g Chloroform (334K) and aniline (457K)

Fractional distillation:
To separate liquids which have small difference in b.p. For e.g To separate different fractions of crude oil in petroleum industry.

Vacuum distillation (distillation under reduced pressure):
This method is used to purify liquids having very high boiling points but they decompose at or below their boiling points.
e.g. Glycerol is separated from spent-lye in soap industry.

Steam distillation:
To separate substances which are steam volatile and are immiscible with water.
e.g. Aniline, nitrobenzene,

Differential Extraction

This method is used when the organic compound is less soluble in the organic solvent, a very large quantity of solvent would be required to extract even a very small quantity of the compound.

Differential Extraction Principle

Based on difference in solubility of organic compounds in different solvents.

When an organic compound is present in an aqueous medium, it is separated by shaking it with an organic solvent in which it is more soluble than in water.

The organic solvent and *aq.* solvent should be immiscible with each other so that they form two distinct layers which can be separated by separating funnel.

The organic solvent is later removed by distillation or evaporation to get back organic compound.

Solvent layer
Organic compound in aqueous layer
Before extraction

Organic compound in solvent layer
Aqueous layer
After extraction

Chromatography

- **Adsorption chromatography** It is based on fact that different compounds are adsorbed on an adsorbent to different degrees.e.g. Silica gel or alumina are commonly used adsorbents.
- **Column chromatography** It involves the separation of a mixture over a column of adsorbent packed in glass tube. e.g. Mixture of naphthalene and benzophenone

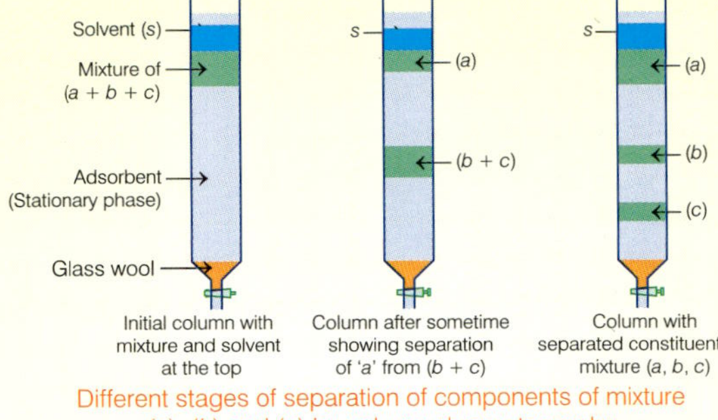

Different stages of separation of components of mixture (a), (b) and (c) by column chromatography

Thin layer chromatography
It involves separation of substances of a mixture over a thin layer of an adsorbent coated on glass plate.
e.g. Detection of amino acids using ninhydrin solution.

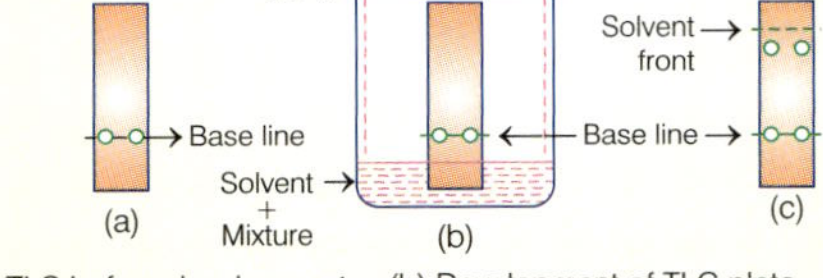

(a) TLC before development (b) Development of TLC plate
(c) TLC after development

- **Partition chromatography** It is based on continous differential partitioning of components of a mixture between stationary and mobile phase.
- **Paper chromatography** It is a type of partition chromatography. In it a special quality paper known as chromatography paper is used. It contains water trapped in it, which acts as the stationary phase. e.g. Separation of sugars from amino acids.

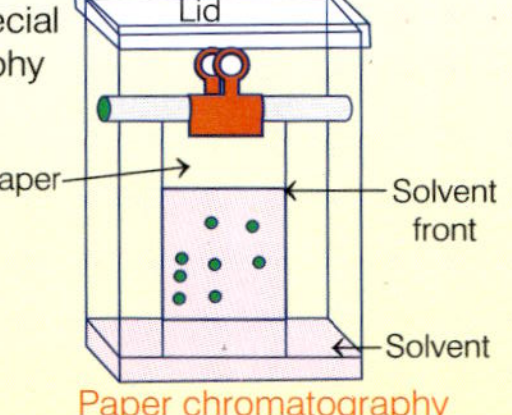

Paper chromatography (liquid-liquid chromatography)

- **Retardation factor (R_f)** It is a fraction which, express degree of adsorption of each component.

$$R_f = \frac{\text{Distance moved by component of mixture from base line}}{\text{Distance moved by mobile phase}}$$

Test 2

Syllabus
- Detection of Nitrogen, Sulphur, Phosphorus and Halogens

NCERT Page 284 to 285

For deeper insight **Scan the QR Code**

Chapter 10

Qualitative Analysis of Organic Compounds

This analysis of organic compound is a non-quantitative method of analysing organic compounds to determine the composition, structure and purification.

Detection of Carbon and Hydrogen

- **Method/detection reagent**
- Heat the compound with copper (II) oxide
- $C + 2CuO \xrightarrow{\Delta} 2Cu + CO_2$
- $2H + CuO \xrightarrow{\Delta} Cu + H_2O$
- **Procedure**
- CO_2 reacts with lime water which develops turbidity and confirms carbon.
- H_2O reacts with anhyd. $CuSO_4$ and develops blue colour confirms hydrogen.
- **Chemical reactions**
- $\underset{\text{(Lime water)}}{CO_2 + Ca(OH_2)} \longrightarrow \underset{\text{(Milkiness)}}{CaCO_3} \downarrow + H_2O$
- $5H_2O + \underset{\text{(White)}}{CuSO_4} \xrightarrow{\Delta} \underset{\text{(Blue)}}{CuSO_4 \cdot 5H_2O}$
- The mixture is heated in a hard glass test tube which is fitted with a bulb containing delivery tube as shown.
- The other end of delivery tube is dipped in a tube containing lime water.
- The bulb of delivery tube contains anhydrous $CuSO_4$ in it.

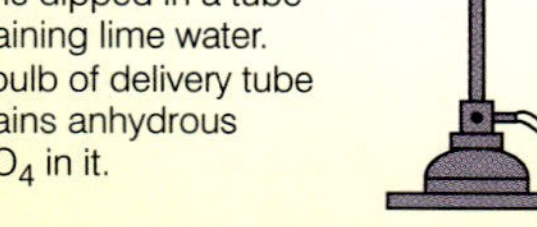

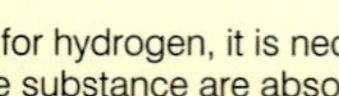

- **Note**

While testing for hydrogen, it is necessary that the apparatus, copper oxide and the substance are absolutely dry. Cupric oxide being hygroscopic in nature and strongly heated just before use.

Test for Sulphur

- **Method/detection reagent**
- Lassaigne's extract (Na_2S) • $2Na + S \xrightarrow{\Delta} Na_2S$ (LE)
- **Procedure**
- Add acetic acid and lead acetate to Lassaigne's extract to get a black precipitate.
- Add sodium nitroprusside to Lassaigne's extract to get **violet** colour confirms sulphur.
- **Chemical reactions**

$S^{2-} + Pb^{2+} \longrightarrow \underset{\text{(Black)}}{PbS\downarrow}$ • $S^{2-} + [Fe(CN)_5NO]^{2-} \longrightarrow \underset{\text{(Violet)}}{[Fe(CN)_5NOS]^{4-}}$

Detection of Other Elements

- Elements like nitrogen, phosphorus, halogens and sulphur. Present in an organic compounds are detected by 'Lassaigne's test'.
  It involves two steps which are as follows
  (i) Preparation of Lassaigne's extract.
  (ii) Detection of elements using Lassaigne's extract.
- To prepare Lassaigne's extract, the organic substance is fused with small quantity of Na pieces in a fusion tube. The red hot tube is plunged into distilled water contained in a China dish. The contents of dish are boiled for couple of minutes, then cooled and filtered.
- The filtered liquid is called sodium extract or Lassaigne's extract. The Lassaigne's extract is usually alkaline. If not, it is made alkaline by adding a few drops of NaOH.
- During fusion, the elements like N, S, F, Cl, Br, I, etc., are present in the organic compound, get fused with Na and convert into their ionic form.

Test for Halogen

- **Method/detection reagent**

Lassaigne's extract (NaX)

$Na + X \xrightarrow{\Delta} NaX$ (X=Cl, Br, I)

- **Procedure**
- Acidify Lassaigne's extract with HNO_3 and then add $AgNO_3$ a white ppt. soluble in NH_4OH shows presence of chlorine.
- Yellow ppt. sparingly soluble in NH_4OH shows presence of bromine.
- A yellow ppt. insoluble in NH_4OH shows presence of iodine.
- **Chemical reactions**

$X^- + Ag^+ \longrightarrow \underset{\text{(ppt.)}}{AgX}$

(X represents a halogen Cl, Br or I)

Note

- In the detection of halogens if cyanide and sulphide are not removed before adding silver nitrate solution, these radicals will combine with silver nitrate and produce white and black precipitate of AgCN and Ag_2S respectively.
- H_2SO_4 cannot be used instead of HNO_3 as it gives white ppt. of Ag_2SO_4 with $AgNO_3$ which interfere with the test of chlorine.

Test for Nitrogen and Sulphur Together

- **Method/detection reagent**
- Lassaigne's extract (NaSCN)

$Na + C + N + S \xrightarrow{\Delta} NaSCN$

- **Procedure**
- Boil Lassaigne's extract with acetic acid and lead acetate.
- Formation of blood red colour and no prussian blue colour.
- **Chemical reactions**

$FeCl_3 + NaSCN^- \longrightarrow \underset{\text{(Blood red)}}{[Fe(SCN)]Cl_2} + NaCl$

Test for Phosphorus

- **Method/detection reagent**
- Heat the compound with (oxidising agent) sodium peroxide. $P \xrightarrow{Na_2O_2 \cdot \text{Boil}} Na_3PO_4$
- **Procedure**
- Solution is boiled with nitric acid and then treated with ammonium molybdate.
- Formation of yellow colouration or ppt. indicate the presence of phosphorus.
- **Chemical reactions**

$Na_3PO_4 + 3HNO_3 \longrightarrow H_3PO_4 + 3NaNO_3$

$H_3PO_4 + \underset{\text{Ammonium molybdate}}{12(NH_4)_2MoO_4} + 21HNO_3 \longrightarrow$

$\underset{\text{Ammonium phosphomolybdate (yellow ppt.)}}{(NH_4)_3PO_4 \cdot 12MoO_3} + 21NH_4NO_3 + 12H_2O$

Layer Test For Bromine and Iodine

- The presence of nitrogen and sulphur does not interfere in this test. In this test, add a little sodium extract and acidify with dil. HNO_3 or dil.H_2SO_4 . Then add $CHCl_3$ or CCl_4 and excess of chlorine water. If organic layer becomes yellow or brown, bromine is present and if violet, iodine is present.

$2NaBr + Cl_2 \longrightarrow 2NaCl + Br_2$

$CHCl_3 + Br_2 \longrightarrow$ Yellow brown layer

$2NaI + Cl_2 \longrightarrow 2NaCl + I_2$

$CHCl_3 + I_2 \longrightarrow$ Violet layer

Beilstein Test for Halogens

If organic compound gives blue or green colour at the tip of red hot copper wire, it indicates the presence of halogens in the organic compound. Several halogen free compounds such as pyridine, purines, urea, thiourea, etc., also give green colour to the flame, thus this test is not very reliable.

Note Since, CuF_2 is non-volatile, fluorine does not give this test.

Test for Nitrogen

- **Method/detection reagent**
- Lassaigne's extract (NaCN)

$Na + C + N \xrightarrow{\Delta} NaCN$

- **Procedure**
- Boil Lassaigne's extract (LE) with $FeSO_4$ and then acidify with conc. H_2SO_4.
- Formation of prussian blue colour confirms nitrogen.
- **Chemical reactions**

$6NaCN + Fe^{2+} \longrightarrow [Fe(CN)_6]^{4-}$

$3[Fe(CN)_6]^{4-} + 4Fe^{3+} \xrightarrow{xH_2O} \underset{\text{(Prussian blue)}}{Fe_4[Fe(CN)_6]_3 \cdot xH_2O}$

Test 3

Syllabus

- Quantitative Analysis (Basic Principles Only)
- Estimation of Carbon, Hydrogen, Nitrogen, Halogens, Sulphur, Phosphorus and Numerical Problems in Organic Quantitative Analysis

NCERT Page 285 to 290

For deeper insight **Scan the QR Code**

Quantitative Analysis

- After qualitative analysis of elements, the next step in the determination of molecular formula of an organic compound is the estimation of various elements by mass, i.e. finding the percentage composition of the substance by mass.
- Quantitative analysis refers to the analysis in which the amount or concentration of an analyte may be expressed and determined (estimated as the numerical value in the given appropriate units).

CHN Elemental Analyser

- The estimation of elements in an organic compound is carried out with automatic experimental techniques using microquantities of the compound.
- The elements C,H and N present in an organic compound are determined by this instrument called CHN elemental analyser.

Carbon and Hydrogen

Liebig's combustion method In this method, a known mass of organic compound is heated with pure and dry cupric oxide in a excess of stream of pure and dry oxygen.
Where, carbon is oxidised to carbon dioxide while hydrogen is oxidised to water.

$$C_xH_y + \left(x+\frac{y}{4}\right)O_2 \xrightarrow{\Delta} xCO_2 + \frac{y}{2}H_2O$$

$$C + 2CuO \longrightarrow CO_2 + 2Cu$$

$$2H + 2CuO \longrightarrow H_2O + 2Cu$$

Sample in platinum boat, CuO pallets, Excess oxygen, Pure dry oxygen, Furnace, Combustion tube, Anhyd. $CaCl_2$, KOH tube

Apparatus used for the estimation of carbon and hydrogen

From the mass of CO_2 and H_2O, the percentage of C and H can be calculated by using,

$$\%\text{ of carbon} = \frac{12}{44}\times\frac{M_{CO_2}}{M_{OC}}\times 100$$

$$\%\text{ of hydrogen} = \frac{2}{18}\times\frac{M_{H_2O}}{M_{OC}}\times 100$$

where, M_{OC} = mass of organic compound
M_{H_2O} = mass of water
M_{CO_2} = mass of carbon dioxide

Nitrogen

- **Kjeldahl's method** Nitrogen in organic compound is converted into ammonium sulphate.

$$O.C + H_2SO_4 \xrightarrow{\Delta} (NH_4)_2SO_4 \xrightarrow{2NaOH,\ \Delta} 2NH_3 + 2H_2O + Na_2SO_4$$

$$2NH_3 + H_2SO_4 \longrightarrow (NH_4)_2SO_4\ ;\ \%\text{ of N} = \frac{1.4\,M\times 2\times(V-V/2)}{m}$$

- In this method, nitrogen containing compound is treated with concentrated H_2SO_4 to get ammonium sulphate which liberates ammonia on treating with NaOH, ammonia is absorbed in known volume of standard acid.
- **Duma's method**

$$C_xH_yN_z + \left(2x+\frac{y}{2}\right)CuO \longrightarrow xCO_2 + \frac{y}{2}H_2O + \frac{z}{2}N_2 + \left(2x+\frac{y}{2}\right)Cu$$

$$\frac{p_1V_1}{T_1} = \frac{760\times V_{STP}}{273}$$

$$\%(N) = \frac{V_{STP}}{22400}\times\frac{28}{m}\times 100$$

Volume of nitrogen collected = V_1mL, Temperature = T, K
p_1 = Atmospheric pressure – Aqueous tension

- Kjeldahl's method is not applicable to compounds containing nitrogen in the ring. e.g. Pyridine, pyrrole etc., and compounds containing nitro and azo (—N═N—) groups. It is because nitrogen in these compounds is not completely converted into $(NH_4)_2SO_4$.

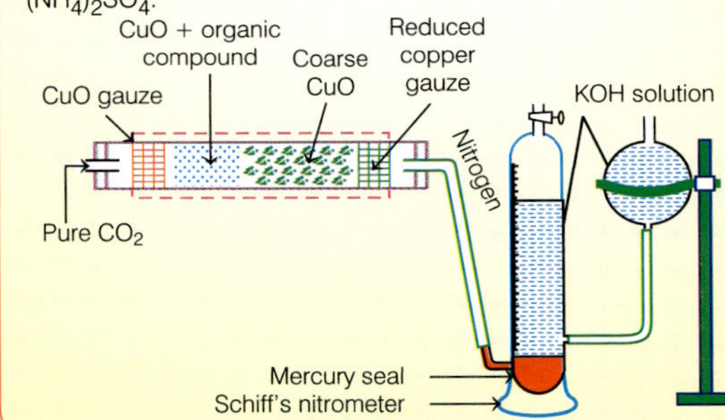

Summary

1. Define the problem → 2. Select a method → 3. Sampling → 4. Sample preparation → 5. Eliminate interferences → 6. Perform the Measurement → 7. Calculate the results and report writing

Halogens

Carius method This method is based on the fact that when an organic compound containing halogen (Cl, Br or I) is heated in a sealed tube with fuming nitric acid in presence of silver nitrate, silver halide is formed. From the mass of silver halide formed, the percentage of the halogen can be calculated.

$$\%\text{ of Cl} = \frac{35.5}{143.5}\times\frac{\text{Mass of AgCl formed}}{\text{Mass of organic compound taken}}\times 100$$

$$\%\text{ of Br} = \frac{80}{188}\times\frac{\text{Mass of AgBr formed}}{\text{Mass of organic compound taken}}\times 100$$

$$\%\text{ of I} = \frac{127}{235}\times\frac{\text{Mass of AgI formed}}{\text{Mass of organic compound taken}}\times 100$$

Sulphur

When an organic compound containing sulphur is heated with fuming nitric acid, sulphur is oxidised to sulphuric acid. This is precipitated as barium sulphate by adding barium chloride solution. From the amount of barium sulphate, percentage of sulphur can be calculated.

$$S + HNO_3\ (\text{fuming}) \xrightarrow{\Delta} H_2SO_4$$

$$H_2SO_4 + BaCl_2 \longrightarrow BaSO_4 + 2HCl$$

$$\%\text{ of S} = \frac{32}{233}\times\frac{\text{Mass of }BaSO_4\text{ formed }(W_1)}{\text{Mass of organic compound taken }(W)}\times 100$$

Phosphorus

The organic compound containing phosphorus is heated with fuming nitric acid. Phosphorus is oxidised to phosphoric acid. It is precipitated as magnesium ammonium phosphate, $MgNH_4PO_4$, by the addition of magnesia mixture ($MgSO_4 + NH_4OH + NH_4Cl$).The magnesium ammonium phosphate is washed, dried and ignited when it is converted to magnesium pyrophosphate ($Mg_2P_2O_7$).

$$2MgNH_4PO_4 \longrightarrow Mg_2P_2O_7 + 2NH_3 + H_2O$$

From the mass of magnesium pyrophosphate, the percentage of phosphorus in the compound can be calculated

$$\%\text{ of P} = \frac{62}{222}\times\frac{\text{Mass of }Mg_2P_2O_7\text{ formed }(W_1)}{\text{Mass of substance taken }(W)}\times 100$$

$$\%\text{ P} = \frac{31\times W_{APM}\times 100}{1877\times W}$$ (where, W=mass of substance taken)

Oxygen

- The usual method of determining the percentage of oxygen in organic compounds is by the method of difference.
- All the elements except oxygen present in the organic compound are estimated and the total of their percentages is subtracted from 100 to get the percentage of oxygen.
- Percentage of oxygen can also be calculated by using the formula,

$$\text{Percentage of oxygen} = \frac{32\times m_1\times 100}{88\times m}$$

Test 1

Syllabus

- Tetravalency of Carbon, Shapes of Simple Molecules, Hybridisation (s and p), Classification of Organic Compounds Based on Functional Groups and Those Containing Halogens, Oxygen, Nitrogen and Sulphur

NCERT Page 256 to 270

For deeper insight **Scan the QR Code**

Chapter 11

Vital Force Theory of Organic Compounds

- Berzelius proposed that the organic compound synthesized due to some super natural force, this was called vital force theory.
- In 1828, Friedrich Wohler discovered that it was possible to convert the inorganic salt ammonium cyanate into the organic compound urea.

$$\underset{\text{Ammonium cyanate}}{NH_4CNO} \xrightarrow{\text{Heat}} \underset{\text{Urea}}{NH_2CONH_2}$$

- In modern practice, organic chemistry is defined as the study of compounds of carbon.
- However, there are certain compounds of carbon that are inorganic compounds. These are as follows

$CO \rightarrow$ Carbon monoxide
$KCN \rightarrow$ Potassium cyanide
$CaCO_3 \rightarrow$ Calcium carbonate

Hence, more precise definition of organic chemistry would be "the study of hydrocarbons and the compounds which could be their derivatives.

Sigma (σ) and Pi (π) Bonding in Organic Compounds

Carbon has a unique property that it can form two types of covalent bonds, i.e. the σ-bond by head on or axial overlapping and the π-bond by sidewise overlapping of orbitals.

(i) Sigma bond is formed by linear overlapping of orbitals.

- s and s-orbitals
- s and p_x, p_y or p_z-orbitals
- Hybrid orbitals

(ii) Since, σ-bonds are formed by axial or linear overlapping so, it is strong in nature.

(iii) π-bonds are formed by axial or linear overlapping of

- p_y – and p_y – orbitals
- p_z – and p_z – orbitals

(iv) π-bonds are weaker than σ-bonds. Bond dissociation energy of π-bond is lower than that of σ-bond.

All single bonds are sigma bonds (σ).
Double bond contains one σ and one π-bond.
Triple bond contains one σ and two π-bonds.

All σ | 5σ and 1π | 3σ and 2π

Tetravalency of Carbon

- August Kekule and Archibald Scott Couper independently proposed that in all organic compounds carbon is tetravalent.
- It always forms four bonds when it combines with other elements to form stable compounds.
- It has sp^3-hybridisation and four valencies are directed towards four corners of tetrahedral structure.

Structural Representation of Organic Compounds

Structures of organic compounds are represented in following ways.

- **Two Dimensional Representation**

(i) **Complete structural formula or Dash structure** Here, all the bonds (either single, double or triple) present are shown by dash (–).

e.g. Ethane, Ethene, Ethyne ($H-C\equiv C-H$)

(ii) **Condensed structural formula** Here, all the bonds except double or triple bonds are omitted.

e.g. $\underset{\text{Ethane}}{CH_3CH_3}$, $\underset{\text{Ethene}}{H_2C=CH_2}$, $\underset{\text{Ethyne}}{HC\equiv CH}$

(iii) **Bond line structural formula** In this structure, bonds are represented by *zig-zag* lines and the terminal denote methyl groups.

Butane | But-1-ene | But-1-yne

- **Three Dimensional Representation**
- The Following conventions are used to represent an organic molecule three-dimensionally (3-D).
- Groups lying in the plane of paper is shown by normal line.
- Bonds projecting out of the plane of paper and towards the observer is shown by solid-wedge.
- The bond projecting out of the plane of paper but away from observer is shown by dashed-wedge thus, the 3-D structure of methane molecule on paper can be represented as

Bonds in the plane of paper | Dashed-wedge (bond away from observer) | Solid-wedge (bond towards observer)

Classification of Organic Compounds

On the Basis of Structure

A. Acyclic or open chain compound
These are the compounds with a linear structure, rather than a cyclic one. It consists of straight chain and branched chain compounds. They are also called as aliphatic compounds.

$\underset{\text{Ethane}}{CH_3-CH_3}$, $CH_3-CH(CH_3)-CH_3$ *Iso*-butane

B. Cyclic or closed chain or ring compound
These compounds are divided in two parts as

1. Homocyclic or carbocyclic compounds
These compounds are the ring structures made up of only carbon in the ring and hydrogen atoms. These are of two types.

(i) **Alicyclic compounds** These compounds contain carbon atoms joined in the form of a ring but don't follow Huckel's rule.

(ii) **Aromatic compounds** These are the compounds that consist of conjugated planar ring systems accompanied by delocalized pi-electrons in place of individual alternate double and single bonds. They follow the Huckel's rule of aromaticity.

(a) Benzenoid compounds (have benzene ring) (b) Non-benzenoid compounds (don't have benzene ring)

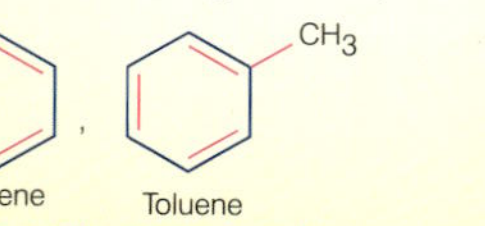

Benzene, Toluene, Tropone

2. Heterocyclic compounds
These compounds are the cyclic compounds that have atoms of atleast two different elements as members of its ring.

On the Basis of Functional Group and Homology

(i) **Single bond containing compounds**
The compounds containing only single bonds are referred to as alkanes. These compounds have the names with the suffix -ane.

e.g. Alkane $\left(-\overset{|}{\underset{|}{C}}-\overset{|}{\underset{|}{C}}-\right)$

(ii) **Double/Triple bond containing compounds**
The compounds which contain double or triple bonds in their structures are referred to as alkenes or alkynes. They have names with suffix -ene or -yne respectively.

e.g. Alkenes $>C=C<$
Alkynes $-C\equiv C-$

(iii) **Halogen derivatives**
The compounds made from hydrocarbons by replacing one or more H-atoms with the same number of halogen atoms.
e.g. $R-X$

(iv) **Oxygen containing compounds**
The compounds which have oxygen as a functional group in their structure are referred to as oxygen containing compounds.
e.g. Alcohols, aldehydes, carboxylic acids, etc.

(v) **Nitrogen containing compounds**
The compounds which are formed as the addition of nitrogen atoms in their structure are referred to as nitrogen containing compounds.

Nomenclature

- Complete IUPAC name of an organic compound consists of five parts.
Secondary prefix + Primary prefix + Word root + Primary suffix + Secondary suffix
- For naming of benzene compounds, substituents is placed as prefix to word benzene.
- In case of disubstituted benzene, 1, 2, 1, 3 and 1, 4 are used to indicate the position.
- Decreasing priority order for selection of a principal functional group is
$COOH > -COOR > -COCl > -CONH_2 - CN > -CHO > -C=O > -OH > -NH_2$ > Alkene > Alkyne

Rules for IUPAC Naming

Rule 1 Select the longest possible carbon chain.
Rule 2 Numbering of parent chain is done from that side where functional group, multiple bond and substituents get the lowest number.
Rule 3 Lowest sum rule If first substituent sets same number from all side then chain selected should have lowest sum of all substituents numbering.
Rule 4 Alphabet rule Naming should be done in alphabetical order if the numbering of all substituents is same.
Rule 5 If the molecule has more than one functional group, the functional group with highest priority assigned the lowest number.

Test 2

Syllabus

- **Homologous Series :** Isomerism-Structural and Stereoisomerism

NCERT Page 270 to 271

For deeper insight **Scan the QR Code**

Chapter 11

Isomerism

- Isomers are compounds with the same molecular formula but a different arrangement of atoms.
- The phenomenon of existence of two or more compounds possessing the same molecular formula but different properties is called a isomerism.

Types of Isomerism

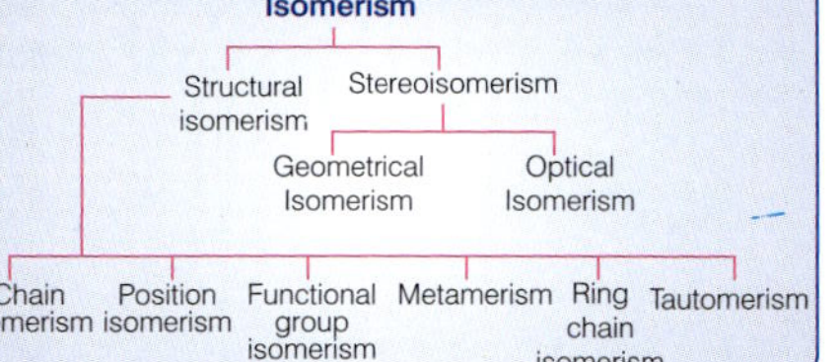

Structural Isomerism

Structural isomers are the compounds with the same molecular formula but a different structural formula.

- **Chain isomerism** When two or more compounds have similar molecular formula but different carbon skeletons, they are called as chain isomerism.

  Pentane, 2-methyl butane, 2-2 dimethyl propane

  This phenomenon is called chain isomerism.
- **Position isomerism** When two or more compounds having different positions of functional group on the carbon chain they are called as position isomers. e.g

  Propan -1-ol, Propan -2-ol
- **Functional isomerism** Two or more compounds having different functional groups but same formula. e.g.

  Propanone, Propanal
- **Metamerism** Two or more compounds having different alkyl group on either side of the functional group. e.g.

  Methoxy propane, Ethoxyethane
- **Ring chain isomerism** When two or more compounds have same molecular formula but have open form (chain) isomer as well as in ring isomer. e.g. C_4H_8.

  But-1-ene, Cyclobutane

Stereoisomerism

Compounds that have same chemical formula and sequence of covalent bonds but differ in spatial arrangement are called stereoisomers. This phenomenon is called stereoisomerism.

- **Geometrical Isomerism**
- They are of two types, i.e. *cis* and *trans*.
- *cis*-isomers have same groups on same side of double bond.
- *trans*-isomers have same groups on *anti* to each other.
- For compounds not having same groups, the priority of each groups is considered according to CIP rule.
- *E/Z* notation is followed in case of different substituents.

e.g. *cis*, *trans*; (*Z*) - zusammen, (*E*)-entgegen

- **Optical Isomers**
- **Enantiomers** Non-superimposable mirror image of a compound are called enantiomers. e.g

  (*S*), (*R*) Enantiomers

  Diastereomers In compounds having at least two chiral carbon atoms. Isomers having different configuration about one carbon atom. e.g

  Diastereomers

  ***Meso*-compounds** These are compounds which have at least two centres which are having same substituents but different configuration around carbon centre.

Important Point Related to Structural Isomerism

- **Chain isomers** will always differ in their physical properties. They may or may not show dissimilar chemical property.
- **Position isomerism** is true only for those compounds having monovalent groups, i.e. functional groups with one free valency, like —OH, —X, —CHO etc.
- Compounds with polyvalent functional groups like —C(=O)—, —O—, —N(H)— does not show this isomerism. e.g. $CH_3CH_2COCH_2CH_3$ and $CH_3COCH_2CH_2CH_3$ must not be considered as position isomers.
- Due to difference in position of groups or atoms these isomers shows difference in physical and chemical properties.
- If two compounds with same molecular formula contain different functional groups, then it can never be chain or position isomerism, there will always be **functional isomerism**.
- If two molecules contain same functional group, then it can never be position isomerism. It will always be **metamerism**.

Tautomerism

It arises due to migration of H-atom from one atom to the other within the same molecule.

e.g. Keto ⇌ Enol

Conditions for Exhibiting Geometrical Isomerism

Following two elaborations are the required conditions for exhibiting geometrical isomerism.

There should be frozen rotation about two atoms in the molecules, e.g.

(i) >C=C<, i.e. alkenes there is frozen rotation about C—C double bond.

(ii) i.e. cycloalkanes there is frozen rotation about carbon-carbon single bond.

(iii) >C=N, i.e. there is oximes and imines frozen rotation about carbon-nitrogen double bond.

(iv) —N=N—, i.e. azo compounds there is frozen rotation about nitrogen-nitrogen double bond.

Both the atoms of above written bonds should contain different substituents.

E - form and *Z* - form

- When two same priority group is attached on the opposite side of double bonded carbon, then it is called as *E*-form.
- When two same priority groups are attached on the same side of double bonded carbon, then it is called as *Z*-form.

Calculation of Number of Geometrical Isomers

S.No.	Nature of compound	No. of G.I. (n=No. of stereocentres)
I.	Compound with dissimilar ends	2^n
II.	Compounds with similar ends and even stereocentres	$2^{n-1}+2^{\frac{n}{2}-1}$
III.	Compound with similar ends and odd stereocentre	$2^{n-1}+2^{\left(\frac{n+1}{2}-1\right)}$

Calculation of Number of Optical Isomerism

- For molecules which are not divisible into two equal halves and have n number of assymmetric C-atoms.
- Number of optically active forms $= 2^n = a$
- Number of enantiomeric pairs $= a/2$
- Number of racemic mixtures $= a/2$
- Number of *meso* forms $= 0$
- In molecules which are divisible into two equal halves,

Case I When n=even number,

- Number of optically active forms $= (a) = 2^{n-1}$
- Number of enantiomeric forms $= a/2$
- Number of racemic mixtures $= a/2$

Case II When n=odd number,

- Number of optically active forms $= (a) = 2^{n-1} - 2^{\left(\frac{n-1}{2}\right)}$
- Number of enantiomeric pairs $= a/2$
- Number of racemic mixtures $= a/2$

Syllabus

- Covalent Bond Fission - Homolytic and Heterolytic: Free Radicals, Carbocations and Carbanions, Stability of Carbocation and Free Radicals, Electrophiles and Nucleophiles, Electronic Displacement of Organic Molecules, Inductive Effect, Electromeric Effect, Resonance and Hyperconjugation.
- Common Types of Organic Reactions : Substitution, Addition, Elimination and Rearrangement.

NCERT Page 271 to 278

For deeper insight **Scan the QR Code**

Inductive Effect

Inductive effect Displacement of σ-electrons along a saturated C-chain towards electronegative atom.

– I effect Order of decreasing strength of – I effect due to EWG is

$—NO_2 > —CN > —COOH > —F > —Cl > —Br.$

+I effect Order of decreasing strength of + I effect due to EDG is

$(CH_3)_3C— > (CH_3)_2CH— > CH_3CH_2— > CH_3 > H—$

Electromeric Effect

A temporary effect that involves transfer of electrons of a multiple bond towards one of the bonded atoms in the presence of an attacking reagent.

+E effect $CH_3—CH{=}CH_2 + H^{\oplus} \longrightarrow CH_3—\overset{\oplus}{C}H—CH_3$

–E effect $>C{=}C< + CN^- \longrightarrow >C(CN)—\overset{-}{C}<$

Resonance or Mesomeric Effect

Defined as polarity developed in a molecule by interaction of two π-bonds or between a π bond and a lone pair.

+ R or + M effect groups

— OH, — OR, — OCOR, — SH, — SR, — NH_2, —NHR, — NR_2 etc.

–R or –M effect groups

— COOH, — CO, —CHO, —COOR, —CN, — NO_2 etc.

Hyperconjugation

Involves delocalisation of σ electrons of C—H bond of an alkyl group attached to an atom or system with unshared p-electrons.

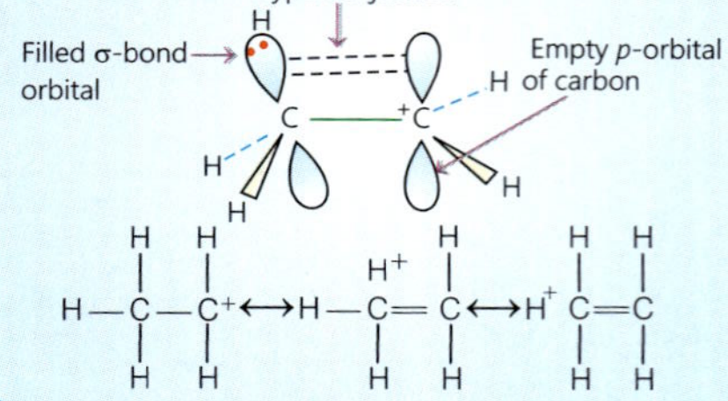

Fission of a Covalent Bond

- A covalent bond can get cleaved either by (i) heterolytic cleavage, or by (ii) homolytic cleavage.
- In heterolytic cleavage, the bond breaks in such a fashion that the shared pair of electrons remains with one of the fragments.
- In homolytic cleavage, the bond breaks in such a fashion that the each fragement contains one electron.

The general reaction is depicted as follows

Organic molecule (substrate) $\xrightarrow{\text{Attacking reagent}}$ [Intermediate] ⟶ Product(s) ↳ By products

Attacking Reagents

Electrophiles These are positively charged or neutral molecules having electron deficient atom, seeking a site of high electron density.

Positively charged

H_3O^+, X^+ (where X = Cl, Br, I) $\overset{+}{N}O_2$, $\overset{+}{N}O$, NH_4^+, SO_3H^+, $C_6H_5N_2^+$, R^+, RCO^+

Neutral BF_3, $AlCl_3$, $FeCl_3$, $BeCl_2$ $ZnCl_2$, SO_3, CO_2, CS_2, CX_4, $RCOCl$, $:CCl_2$

Nucleophiles They are negatively charged or neutral molecules having electron-rich atom with unshared electron pair, seeking electron deficient site to attack. They are also called **Lewis bases** (Electron-pair donors).

Negatively charged

H^-, OH^- X^-, CN^-, N_3^-, RO^-, R^-, RS^-, SH^-, HSO_3, NO_2^-, NH_2^-, $RCOO^-$, $HC\equiv C^-$

Neutral NH_3, $H_2\ddot{O}$, $R\ddot{O}H$, $R\ddot{O}R$, $R\ddot{S}H$, $RMgX$, $Ph_3\ddot{P}$ RLi, $LiAlH_4$ etc.

Reaction Intermediates

Free radical	Carbocation	Carbanion	Carbene
Electrically neutral, highly unstable, e^- deficient	- + ve charge on C, - Electrophilic, Lewis acid	- –ve charge on C, - Nucleophilic, Lewis base	- Neutral, divalent with 2-unshared electrons -Both nucleophilic and electrophilic
sp^2, planar	sp^2, planar	sp^3 (Non-conjugated), pyramidal sp^3 (Conjugated), planar	(i) sp^2 (singlet):  (ii) sp (triplet) : $R—\ddot{C}—R$
Paramagnetic	Diamagnetic	Diamagnetic	(i) Diamagnetic (ii) Paramagnetic
Order $Ph_3C > Ph_2CH > PhCH_2 > 3° > 2° > 1° > CH_3 > CH_2{=}CH_2$ e.g. Wurtz reaction • Anti-Markov-nikov's addition • Kolbe's electrolysis	**Order** 3°>2°>1° e.g. Pinacol-pinacolone rearrangement • Electrophilic addition reaction of alkenes, alkynes and alkadienes.	**Order** 1°>2°>3° e.g. Aldol condensation • Cannizzaro's reaction • Perkin reaction • Knovenagel reaction	e.g. Carbylamine reaction • Reimer-Tiemann reaction • Wittig reaction • Wolff rearrangement

Favourable Factors for Homolysis

- The major factor which favours homolysis is zero or a small difference in electronegativity between the two atoms of a bond.
- Homolytic bond fission takes place in gaseous phase or in the presence of non-polar solvents (CCl_2, CS_2) .
- Presence of peroxide, UV light, heat (≥ 500°C), electricity also favour homolysis.

Favourable Factors for Heterolysis

- Heterolysis is seen in polar covalent bonds and is favoured by polar solvents.
- The energy required for the heterolytic bond fission is always greater than that for homolytic bond fission due to electrostatic force of attraction between ions.

Types of Organic Reactions

Substitution Reactions

(Replacement of an atom by different atoms.)

Reaction is done by

- Free radical (e.g. Wurtz reaction)
- Ionic: Electrophilic (by electrophiles), S_E; Nucleophilic (by nucleophiles), S_N

S_N1	S_N2
• Unimolecular	• Bimolecular
• First order	• Second order
• Two steps reaction	• One step reaction
(i) $R:X \xrightleftharpoons{\text{Slow}} R^+ + X^-$	$R:X + Nu \longrightarrow R:Nu + :X^-$
(ii) $R^+ + Nu^- \xrightarrow{\text{Fast } R:Nu}$	**(Through transition state)**
• Low and milds concentration of nucleophile.	• High and strong concentration of nucleophile.
• Solvent of high polarity.	• Solvents of low polarity.
• Catalysed by Lewis and Bronsted acids.	• Catalyst not involved.
• e.g. Hydrolysis of *tert*-butyl halide.	• e.g. Hydrolysis of methyl halide.

Addition Reactions

(Compounds containing = or ≡ bonds.)

$>C\overset{\sigma}{\underset{\pi}{=}}C< + X_2 \longrightarrow >C(X)\overset{\sigma}{—}C(X)<$

Reaction is done by

- Free radical—(e.g. Peroxide effect)
- Ionic: Nucleophilic (A_N); Electrophilic (A_E) (e.g.Markovnikov's rule)

Elimination Reactions

(Reverse of addition reaction.)

- **α-elimination** Two atoms or groups are lost from the same carbon atom to form carbene.

$OH^- + H—CCl_2(Cl) \longrightarrow :CCl_2 + H_2O + Cl^-$

- **β-elimination** Two atoms or groups are lost from adjacent carbon atoms to form an unsaturated compound.

$>C(H)—C(X)< \longrightarrow >C{=}C< + HX$

Rearrangement Reactions

(Migration of an atom/group within the molecule).

$NH_4CNO \xrightarrow{\Delta} NH_2CONH_2$

Test 1

Syllabus

- **Alkanes** : Classification, Isomerism, IUPAC Nomenclature, General Method of Preparation, Properties and Reactions, Conformations, Sawhorse and Newman Projections (of Ethane), Mechanism of Halogenation.

NCERT Page 296 to 306

For deeper insight **Scan the QR Code**

Chapter 12

Alkanes

- These are the homologous series made up of saturated hydrocarbons, containing only carbon and hydrogen atoms joined by sigma bonds.
- They are also called as **paraffins**.
- **Structure** They have tetrahedral geometry with sp^3 hybridisation and 109.5° bond angle.
- **General formula** C_nH_{2n+2}
- **Nomenclature**
  Root word + ane = alkane name
- **Isomerism** They exhibit mainly structural isomerism, i.e. chain and conformational.

Structures

Methane Ethane Propane

Physical Properties

- Amongst alkanes, C_1 to C_4 are gases; C_5 to C_{17} are liquids, C_{18} and above are solids.
- Boiling point increases with molecular mass, as branching increases, the boiling point decreases in the isomers.
  e.g. *n*-pentane > *iso*-pentane > *neo*-pentane
- Intermolecular van der Waals' forces increases with increase of the molecular size or surface area of the molecule.
- Alkanes with even number of C-atoms are symmetrical and pack more compactly. Hence, they possess higher melting point than the alkanes with odd number of carbon atoms.
- They are colourless and odourless.
- They are non-polar and hydrophobic.

Preparation

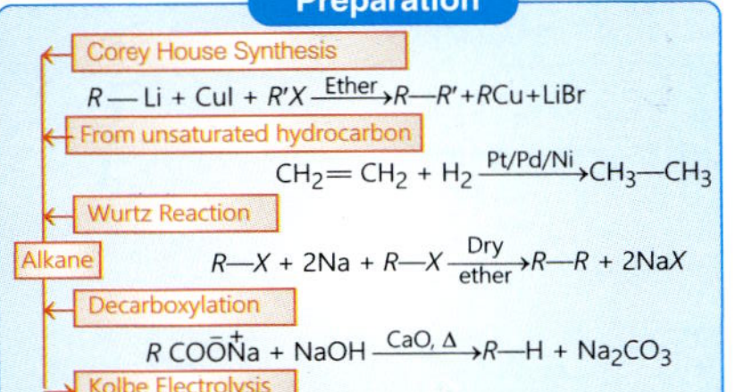

Conformations

- **Staggered** The most stable form in which groups are as far apart as possible.
- **Eclipsed** The least stable form in which groups are as close as possible.
- ***Skew or Gauche*** All the possible conformation between the above conformations are called *skew* or *Gauche* conformations.
- **Order of Stability**
  Staggered > *Skew* > Eclipsed > Fully eclipsed

Representation of Conformers

Conformers can be represented with the help of following two models.

- **Sawhorse projection** In this projection, the molecule is seen along the molecular axis. It is projected on paper by drawing the central C — C and as a some what longer straight line. Upper end of the line is tilted towards right or left hand side.

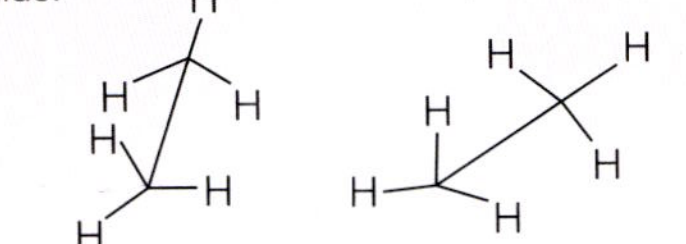

Eclipsed Staggered

- **Newman projection** In this projection, bond connecting two carbon atoms such that C — C bond appears to be head observer. The carbon atom nearer to eye is represented by a point.

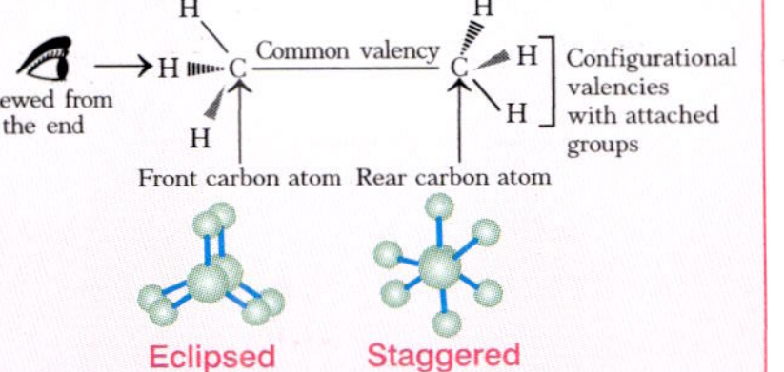

Important Points Related to Preparation

- **Hydrogenation** It is the process of addition of dihydrogen gas to alkenes and alkynes in the presence of finely divided catalyst like platinum, palladium or nickel to form alkanes.
- Alkyl halide on treatment with sodium metal in dry ethereal solution gives higher alkanes. This reaction is called **Wurtz reaction**.
- The process of elimination of carbon dioxide from a carboxylic acid is called **decarboxylation**.

Stability of the Conformation of Cyclohexane

Potential energy in kJ/mol; I Chair; II Half chair; III Twist boat; IV Half chair; VI Boat; VII Twist boat; V Chair; 46.0 kJ/mol; 23.0 kJ/mol; 29.7 kJ/mol; 67 kJ/mol

Relative potential energies of the various conformations of cyclohexane.

- **Nitration**
  Higher alkanes, i.e. those having more than five carbon atoms can be nitrated when heated with fuming HNO_3 This reaction is called **liquid phase nitration**. e.g.

  $$C_6H_{14}+HNO_3 \longrightarrow C_6H_{13}NO_2+H_2O$$

  For nitration of lower alkanes, a technique called **vapour phase nitration** is used. In this a mixture of the lower hydrocarbons and nitric acid vapours is passed through the silica tube at highly elevated temperature of 400-500°C. The reaction also involves cleavage of C—C linkage alongwith C—H linkage, resulting to a mixture of nitroalkanes as

  $$C_2H_6+HONO_2 \longrightarrow C_2H_5NO_2+CH_3NO_2+H_2O$$

  Nitration just like halogenation also follows free radical mechanism.
- **Sulphonation**
  Sulphonation is normally given by alkanes with minimum 6C-atoms onwards, i.e. hexane onwards. Lower alkanes except those having tertiary hydrogen atom can't get sulphonated. It is done by fuming H_2SO_4 as,

  $$(CH_3)_3CH + H_2S_2O_7 \longrightarrow (CH_3)_3CSO_3H + H_2O$$

  iso-butane (contains one 3°C); Oleum; *t*-butylsulphonic acid
- **Isomerisation**

  $$CH_3CH_2CH_2CH_3 \xrightarrow[\text{270°C, 35atm}]{AlCl_3/HCl} CH_3—\underset{H}{\overset{CH_3}{C}}—CH_3$$

  n-butane; *Iso*-butane
- **Pyrolysis** Decomposition of higher alkane into lower alkane by the application of heat is called pyrolysis or cracking. It is a free radical reaction.
- **Reaction with steam** Methane reacts with steam at 1273 K in the presence of nickel catalyst to form carbon monoxide and dihydrogen.

Chemical Properties

- The reaction in which hydrogen atom of alkanes are substituted by different atom or group are called as **substitution reaction**.
- **Halogenation** Substitution of 3° > 2° > 1° H-atom by halogens in the order $F_2 > Cl_2 > Br_2 > I_2$. They proceed *via* free radicals chain mechanism.

  $$R—H + X_2 \xrightarrow{UV} R—X + HX$$

  $$CH_4 + Cl_2 \longrightarrow CH_2—Cl + CH_2—Cl_2 + CH—Cl_3 + CCl_4$$

  Abstraction of H atoms → 3° > 2° > 1°
  Stability of free radicals → 3° > 2° > 1°

Mechanism This reaction follows free radical mechanism and involves the following steps

Step I Initiation step – single

$$X-X \xrightarrow{h\nu \text{ or Homolysis}} X^\bullet + X^\bullet$$ Free radicals

Step II Propagation steps – multiple

$$R-H + X^\bullet \longrightarrow R^\bullet + HX$$
$$R^\bullet + X-X \longrightarrow RX + X^\bullet$$

Step III Termination steps – multiple

$$X^\bullet + X^\bullet \rightarrow X_2;\ R^\bullet + X^\bullet \rightarrow RX;\ R^\bullet + R^\bullet \rightarrow R-R$$

- **Reactivity and selectivity of alkane** These are inversely related with each other.
  Reactivity $Cl_2 > Br_2$; Selectivity $Cl_2 < Br_2$
- **Combustion** Alkanes on heating in the presence of air or dioxygen are completely oxidised to carbon dioxide and water with the evolution of large amount of heat. The general combustion equation for any alkane is $C_nH_{2n+2} + \left(\frac{3n+1}{2}\right)O_2 \longrightarrow nCO_2 + (n+1)H_2O$

  $$CH_4(g) + 2O_2(g) \longrightarrow CO_2(g) + 2H_2O(l) + \text{Heat}$$
  $$2C_2H_6(g) + 7O_2(g) \longrightarrow 4CO_2(g) + 6H_2O(l) + \text{Heat}$$
- **Controlled oxidation** Alkanes on heating with a regulated supply of dioxygen or air at high pressure and in the presence of suitable catalyst gives different oxidation product.

  $$2CH_4 + O_2 \xrightarrow[\text{100atm}]{\text{Cu/523K}} 2CH_3OH$$
  $$CH_4 + O_2 \xrightarrow[\Delta]{Mo_2O_3} HCHO + H_2O$$
  $$2R-CH_3 + 3O_2 \xrightarrow[\Delta]{(CH_3COO)_2Mn} 2R—COOH + 2H_2O$$
- **Aromatisation** *n*-alkanes having six or more carbon atoms on heating to 773K at 10-20 atmospheric pressure in the presence of oxides of vanadium, molybdenum or chromium supported over alumina gets dehydrogenated and cyclised to benzene and its homologous.

  $$CH_3CH_2CH_2CH_2CH_2CH_3 \xrightarrow[\text{773K, 10–20atm}]{Cr_2O_3/V_2O_5 \text{ or } Mo_2O_3} \text{Benzene}$$ *n*-hexane

  It involves cyclisation and dehydrogenation.

Test 2

Syllabus

- **Alkenes** : IUPAC Nomenclature, General Method of Preparations Geometrical Isomerism, Mechanism of Electrophilic Addition, Addition of Hydrogen, Halogens, Water, Hydrogen Halide (Markownikoff's and Peroxide Effect), Ozonolysis and Polymerisation

NCERT Page 306 to 314

For deeper insight **Scan the QR Code**

Chapter 12

Alkenes

- These are the homologous series made up of unsaturated hydrocarbons containing at least one C$=$C double bond.
- Their general formula is C_nH_{2n}.
- **Nomenclature** Root word + ene = alkene
- **Structure** Due to electron pair repulsion, alkenes have a trigonal planar shape with a bond angle of 120°.
  C$=$C — contains both a σ-bond and a π-bond. π-bonds are formed due to the overlap of adjacent *p*-orbitals above and below the carbon atoms.
- π-bond restricts the rotation around the planar C$=$C double bond, leading to stereoisomerism in some alkenes.

Physical Properties

- The first three members are gases, the next fourteen are liquid and the higher ones are solids.
- All alkenes are colourless and odourless except ethene and they are insoluble in water.
- Their boiling point increases with increase in molar mass. Boiling point of *cis* form is higher as compared to their *trans*-isomers. However, melting point is higher in case of *trans*-isomers.
- Generally *trans*-isomers has almost zero dipole moment and thus exhibits weaker intermolecular attractions.
- They are insoluble in water but soluble in non-polar solvents.
- Alkenes are lighter than water. However, their density increases with increase in molecular mass.

Diels-Alder Reaction

- This reaction is also called as cycloaddition as a new cycle is generated in this reaction.
- Basically in this reaction a conjugated diene is attacked by an olefin which is called as dienophile.
- The equation of reaction is as follows

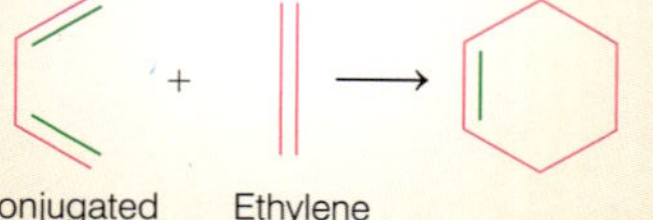

Conjugated diene + Ethylene (dienophile) ⟶

Preparation of Alkenes

Alkene

- **By Dehydrohalogenation**
  $$CH_3CH_2Br \xrightarrow[\Delta]{Alc.KOH} CH_2{=}CH_2 + KBr + H_2O$$
- **Birch Reduction**
  $$R{-}C{\equiv}C{-}R \xrightarrow{Na/Liq.NH_3} \underset{H}{\overset{R}{>}}C{=}C\underset{R}{\overset{H}{<}}$$
- **Hydroboration**
  $$3H{-}C{\equiv}C{-}H \xrightarrow{BH_3 in THF} CH_2{=}CH_2 + CH_2{=}CH{-}CH{=}CH_2$$
- **From Alkynes**
  $$RC{\equiv}C{-}R' + H_2 \xrightarrow[H_2]{Pd/C} \underset{H}{\overset{R}{>}}C{=}C\underset{H}{\overset{R'}{<}}$$
  cis-alkene
  $$RC{\equiv}CR' + H_2 \xrightarrow[H_2]{Na/Liq.\ NH_3} \underset{H}{\overset{R}{>}}C{=}C\underset{R'}{\overset{H}{<}}$$
  trans-alkene
- **By Dehalogenation**
  $$CH_2Br{-}CH_2Br + Zn \longrightarrow CH_2{=}CH_2 + ZnBr_2$$
  $$CH_3CHBr{-}CH_2Br + Zn \longrightarrow CH_3CH{=}CH_2 + ZnBr_2$$
- **By Acidic Dehydration**
  $$H{-}\underset{H}{\overset{H}{C_\beta}}{-}\underset{OH}{\overset{H}{C_\alpha}}{-}H \xrightarrow[\Delta]{Conc.\ H_2SO_4} CH_2{=}CH_2 + H_2O$$

Chemical Properties

- Alkenes are highly reactive compounds due to the presence of exposed π-electrons cloud in them as these π-electrons are less tightly held between the two carbon atoms.
- These compounds show electrophilic reactions in which electrophiles [or electron deficient species] attack the loosely held π-electrons of alkenes.
- They largely show, electrophilic addition and substitution reactions.

Important Points of Preparation

- **Dehydrohalogenation** For dehydrohalogenation is 3°>2°>1° for alkyl halide. In elimination reaction, when alternatives are available then, more substituted alkene will be preferred.
- **Saytzeff rule** In elimination reaction, when alternatives are available then, the H-atom will be removed from that C-atom that contains less number of hydrogen.
- **Dehalogenation** Dihalides in which two halogen atoms are attached to two adjacent carbon atoms are called ***vicinal* dihalides**.
  Dihalides in which two halogen atoms are attached on same carbon atom is called ***geminal* dihalide**.
- **Lindlar's catalyst** Pd poisoned with $BaSO_4$ or $CaCO_3$ in quinoline or xylene.
- **Birch catalyst** Na or Li in Liquid NH_3.
- **Hydroboration-Oxidation** An alcohol is formed.
  $$\underset{\text{Alkene}}{RCH{=}CH_2} \xrightarrow{BH_3\ in\ THF} (RCH_2CH_2)_3B \xrightarrow[NaOH]{H_2O_2} \underset{1^\circ\ \text{alcohol}}{3RCH_2CH_2OH} + H_3BO_3$$
- C — B bond is oxidised to C — OH bond.
- No rearrangement, *syn* addition.
- Similar to anti-Markovnikov addition of H, OH to an alkene.

Chemical Reactions

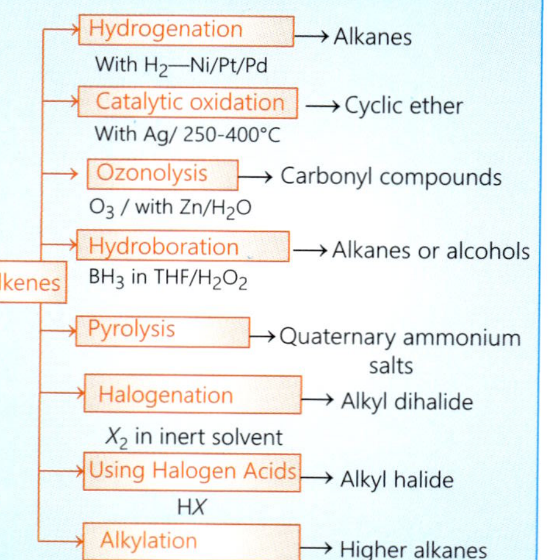

Polymerisation

Alkenes can undergo addition reactions with themselves to form a long chain polymer molecules. This reaction is addition polymerisation.

$$n\ \underset{R_2}{\overset{R_1}{>}}C{=}C\underset{R_4}{\overset{R_3}{<}} \longrightarrow \left[-\underset{R_2}{\overset{R_1}{C}}-\underset{R_4}{\overset{R_3}{C}}- \right]$$

Markownikoff's Rule

The rule states that negative part of the addendum (adding molecule) gets attached to that carbon atom which possesses lesser number of hydrogen atom.

e.g. $H_3C{-}CH{=}CH_2 + HBr \longrightarrow H_3C{-}CH(Br){-}CH_3$
2- bromopropane

Anti-Markownikoff's Addition

- In the presence of peroxide, addition of HBr to unsymmetrical alkenes takes place contrary to Markownikoff's rule.
- It is also called as peroxide or Kharasch effect.

$$CH_3{-}CH{=}CH_2 + HBr \xrightarrow{(C_6H_5CO)_2O_2} CH_3CH_2CH_2Br$$
1- bromopropane

Chemical Tests Used to Distinguish Ethane and Ethene

- **Br_2 solution (in CCl_4)** When ethane is treated with Br_2 solution (in CCl_4) then no effect or no change is visible.
  However, when ethene is treated with Br_2 solution (in CCl_4) then Br_2 solution is decolourised due to addition reaction.
- **Aqueous/alkaline $KMnO_4$ (Baeyer's reagent)** When ethane is treated with Baeyer's reagent then no effect or no change is visible.
  However, when ethene is treated with Baeyer's reagent then $KMnO_4$ is decolourised and a brown/black precipitate of MnO_2 is formed.

Uses of Ethene

- It is used in making polythene and synthetic chemicals.
- It is also used for producing oxy-ethylene flame, which is used for cutting and welding of metals.
- It is used for artificially ripening the fruits
- It is used in making epoxyethene, which is used in the manufacturing of detergent.

Test 3

Syllabus

- **Alkynes** : Acidic Character, Addition of Hydrogen, Halogen, Water, Hydrogen Halides and Polymerisation, Directive Influence of Functional Group, Friedal-Craft Alkylation, Acylation.
- Aromatic Hydrocarbon-Nomenclature, Benzene-Structure and Aromaticity, Mechanism of Electrophilic Substitution, Halogenation, Nitration,

NCERT Page 314 to 325

For deeper insight **Scan the QR Code**

Alkynes

- **General formula** C_nH_{2n-2}
- **Nomenclature**
  Root word + yne = alkyne
- **Structure** Triple bonded carbon are *sp*-hybridised with linear shape and 180° bond angle. They have atleast one C≡C bond.

Physical Properties

- First three members are gases, the next eight are liquids and the higher ones are solid.
- All alkynes are colourless.
- They are weakly polar in nature.
- Their melting point, boiling point and density increase with increase in molar mass.
- Boiling points are greater than that of alkenes and alkanes of nearly equal molecular weight.

Preparation

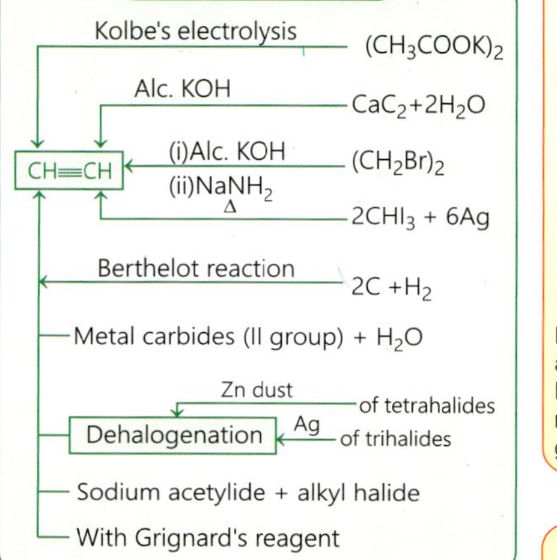

Important Points of Preparation

- On industrial scale, ethyne is prepared by treating calcium carbide with water.
- Alkynes can also be prepared by treatment of *vicinal* dihalides with alcoholic potassium hydroxide that undergo dehydrohalogenation.
- In Kolbe's electrolysis method, electrolysis of potassium fumarate produces acetylene with the liberation of CO_2 and H_2 at anode respectively.

Chemical Properties

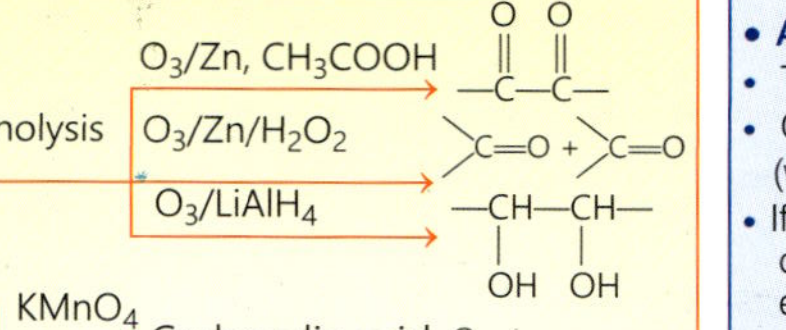

Like alkanes and alkenes, alkynes do not react with water. However, one molecule of H_2O can be reacted with mercuric sulphate and dil. H_2SO_4 to give carbonyl compound.

Important Point Related to Chemical Properties

Acidic strength Acetylene and terminal alkynes are acidic in nature. Acidic nature is due to *sp*-hybridisation present. Internal alkynes are non acidic in nature as they lack replaceable H.

The order of pK_a of alkynes, alkene and alkane is in the order. alkyne > alkene > alkane

- In **addition reactions**, the product formed depends upon the stability of vinylic cation.
- **Polymerisation** In polymerisation reaction alkynes, aromatic compounds are produced.
- **Addition of Halogens** Addition of alkynes with halogens (Br_2) can be used as a test for unsaturation.

Aromaticity

- **Aromatic molecule**
- These are planar, cyclic and completely conjugated.
- Contains $(4n+2)\pi$-electrons, (where, n=an integer).
- If on ring closure, the *p*-electron energy of an open chain polyene decreases. e.g. [6] annulene (benzene)
- **Anti-aromatic molecule**
- These are planar, cyclic and completely conjugated.
- Contains $4n$ π-electrons, (where, n-an integer).
- Upon ring closure, the π-electrons energy increases. e.g.[4] annulene (cyclobutadiene).
- **Non-aromatic molecule**
- These are non-planar, non-cyclic and not completely conjugated
- If on ring closure, the π-electron energy remains the same. e.g. Alkanes, alkenes and 1, 3, 5-cyclobutadiene.

Physical Properties of Aromatic Hydrocarbon

- These are non-polar molecules.
- These are colourless liquid or solids with a characteristic aroma.
- These are immiscible with water but miscible with organic solvents and burn with sooty flame.
- **Boiling point** of arenes increases with increase in the molecular size due to increase in van der Waals' forces of attraction.
- **Melting point** depends on molecular size and symmetry. Among *o-*,*m-* and *p*-xylenes, the *p*-isomer has the highest melting point.

Chemical Properties of Aromatic Hydrocarbon

- These are less reactive than alkenes and alkynes because their π-electrons are involved in delocalisation and not available for addition reactions.
- Under special conditions, they can also undergo addition and oxidation reactions.

Carcinogenicity and Toxicity

- Benzene and polynuclear hydrocarbon containing more than two benzene rings fused together are toxic and called carcinogenic.
- These polynuclear hydrocarbons are formed by incomplete combustion of organic materials.

Preparations of Benzene

Reaction	Reagent	Starting material
Dehydroxylation	Zn/dust, Δ	Phenol
Polymerisation	Red hot Cu/Fe	Acetylene
Reduction	H_3PO_2/H_2O	Benzene diazonium chloride
Hydrogenation		Halobenzenes
Hydrolysis		Phenyl magnesium chloride
Decarboxylation	NaOH/CaO	Sodium salt of carboxylic acids

Chemical Reactions of Benzene

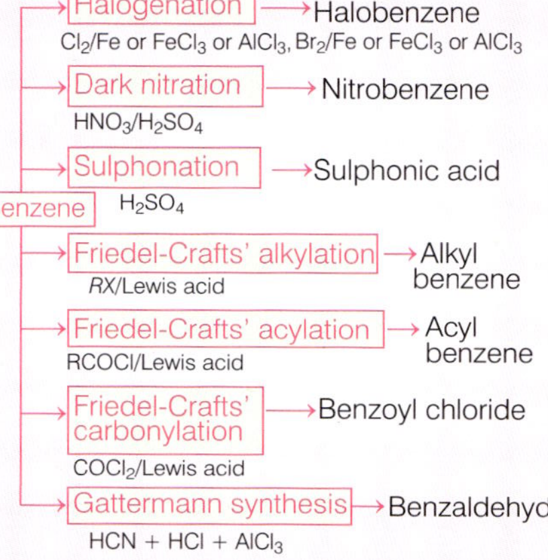

Directive Influence of Functional Group

Towards electrophilic substitution

(i) —NH_2,— NHR,— $NHCOCH_3$, —OH, — CH_3 — C_2H_5 etc., are *o*/*p* - directing activating groups.

(ii) Halogens are *o*/*p*-directing but deactivating.

(iii) — NO_2, — CN,— CHO,— CO_2, — COOH, —SO_3H etc., are *meta*-directing and deactivating groups.

OMR SHEET

ROLL No.

1	1	1	1	1	1	1	1	1	1
2	2	2	2	2	2	2	2	2	2
3	3	3	3	3	3	3	3	3	3
4	4	4	4	4	4	4	4	4	4
5	5	5	5	5	5	5	5	5	5
6	6	6	6	6	6	6	6	6	6
7	7	7	7	7	7	7	7	7	7
8	8	8	8	8	8	8	8	8	8
9	9	9	9	9	9	9	9	9	9
0	0	0	0	0	0	0	0	0	0

TEST BOOKLET No.

1	1	1	1	1	1	1
2	2	2	2	2	2	2
3	3	3	3	3	3	3
4	4	4	4	4	4	4
5	5	5	5	5	5	5
6	6	6	6	6	6	6
7	7	7	7	7	7	7
8	8	8	8	8	8	8
9	9	9	9	9	9	9
0	0	0	0	0	0	0

TEST BOOKLET Code

Q No.	Response				Q No.	Response			
001	a	b	c	d	051	a	b	c	d
002	a	b	c	d	052	a	b	c	d
003	a	b	c	d	053	a	b	c	d
004	a	b	c	d	054	a	b	c	d
005	a	b	c	d	055	a	b	c	d
006	a	b	c	d	056	a	b	c	d
007	a	b	c	d	057	a	b	c	d
008	a	b	c	d	058	a	b	c	d
009	a	b	c	d	059	a	b	c	d
010	a	b	c	d	060	a	b	c	d
011	a	b	c	d	061	a	b	c	d
012	a	b	c	d	062	a	b	c	d
013	a	b	c	d	063	a	b	c	d
014	a	b	c	d	064	a	b	c	d
015	a	b	c	d	065	a	b	c	d
016	a	b	c	d	066	a	b	c	d
017	a	b	c	d	067	a	b	c	d
018	a	b	c	d	068	a	b	c	d
019	a	b	c	d	069	a	b	c	d
020	a	b	c	d	070	a	b	c	d
021	a	b	c	d	071	a	b	c	d
022	a	b	c	d	072	a	b	c	d
023	a	b	c	d	073	a	b	c	d
024	a	b	c	d	074	a	b	c	d
025	a	b	c	d	075	a	b	c	d
026	a	b	c	d	076	a	b	c	d
027	a	b	c	d	077	a	b	c	d
028	a	b	c	d	078	a	b	c	d
029	a	b	c	d	079	a	b	c	d
030	a	b	c	d	080	a	b	c	d
031	a	b	c	d	081	a	b	c	d
032	a	b	c	d	082	a	b	c	d
033	a	b	c	d	083	a	b	c	d
034	a	b	c	d	084	a	b	c	d
035	a	b	c	d	085	a	b	c	d
036	a	b	c	d	086	a	b	c	d
037	a	b	c	d	087	a	b	c	d
038	a	b	c	d	088	a	b	c	d
039	a	b	c	d	089	a	b	c	d
040	a	b	c	d	090	a	b	c	d
041	a	b	c	d	091	a	b	c	d
042	a	b	c	d	092	a	b	c	d
043	a	b	c	d	093	a	b	c	d
044	a	b	c	d	094	a	b	c	d
045	a	b	c	d	095	a	b	c	d
046	a	b	c	d	096	a	b	c	d
047	a	b	c	d	097	a	b	c	d
048	a	b	c	d	098	a	b	c	d
049	a	b	c	d	099	a	b	c	d
050	a	b	c	d	100	a	b	c	d

DECLARATION BY THE CANDIDATE

I declare that particulars and signature on this OMR Answer sheet are mine and are Name as in Attendance Sheet. I fruther declare that particulars filled in and Signature as well as the circles darkened on this ORIGINALCOPY is same as in OFFICE COPY.

Signature with time (in running handwriting)

CANDIDATE's NAME (in running handwriting)

MOTHER's NAME (in running handwriting)

FATHER's NAME (in running handwriting)

CANDIDATE LEFT HAND IMPRESSION

SIGNATURE OF INVIGILATOR'S WITH TIME

1

2

MEDACE

OMR SHEET

ROLL No.

1	1	1	1	1	1	1	1	1	1
2	2	2	2	2	2	2	2	2	2
3	3	3	3	3	3	3	3	3	3
4	4	4	4	4	4	4	4	4	4
5	5	5	5	5	5	5	5	5	5
6	6	6	6	6	6	6	6	6	6
7	7	7	7	7	7	7	7	7	7
8	8	8	8	8	8	8	8	8	8
9	9	9	9	9	9	9	9	9	9
0	0	0	0	0	0	0	0	0	0

TEST BOOKLET No.

1	1	1	1	1	1	1
2	2	2	2	2	2	2
3	3	3	3	3	3	3
4	4	4	4	4	4	4
5	5	5	5	5	5	5
6	6	6	6	6	6	6
7	7	7	7	7	7	7
8	8	8	8	8	8	8
9	9	9	9	9	9	9
0	0	0	0	0	0	0

TEST BOOKLET Code

Q No.	Response				Q No.	Response			
001	a	b	c	d	051	a	b	c	d
002	a	b	c	d	052	a	b	c	d
003	a	b	c	d	053	a	b	c	d
004	a	b	c	d	054	a	b	c	d
005	a	b	c	d	055	a	b	c	d
006	a	b	c	d	056	a	b	c	d
007	a	b	c	d	057	a	b	c	d
008	a	b	c	d	058	a	b	c	d
009	a	b	c	d	059	a	b	c	d
010	a	b	c	d	060	a	b	c	d
011	a	b	c	d	061	a	b	c	d
012	a	b	c	d	062	a	b	c	d
013	a	b	c	d	063	a	b	c	d
014	a	b	c	d	064	a	b	c	d
015	a	b	c	d	065	a	b	c	d
016	a	b	c	d	066	a	b	c	d
017	a	b	c	d	067	a	b	c	d
018	a	b	c	d	068	a	b	c	d
019	a	b	c	d	069	a	b	c	d
020	a	b	c	d	070	a	b	c	d
021	a	b	c	d	071	a	b	c	d
022	a	b	c	d	072	a	b	c	d
023	a	b	c	d	073	a	b	c	d
024	a	b	c	d	074	a	b	c	d
025	a	b	c	d	075	a	b	c	d
026	a	b	c	d	076	a	b	c	d
027	a	b	c	d	077	a	b	c	d
028	a	b	c	d	078	a	b	c	d
029	a	b	c	d	079	a	b	c	d
030	a	b	c	d	080	a	b	c	d
031	a	b	c	d	081	a	b	c	d
032	a	b	c	d	082	a	b	c	d
033	a	b	c	d	083	a	b	c	d
034	a	b	c	d	084	a	b	c	d
035	a	b	c	d	085	a	b	c	d
036	a	b	c	d	086	a	b	c	d
037	a	b	c	d	087	a	b	c	d
038	a	b	c	d	088	a	b	c	d
039	a	b	c	d	089	a	b	c	d
040	a	b	c	d	090	a	b	c	d
041	a	b	c	d	091	a	b	c	d
042	a	b	c	d	092	a	b	c	d
043	a	b	c	d	093	a	b	c	d
044	a	b	c	d	094	a	b	c	d
045	a	b	c	d	095	a	b	c	d
046	a	b	c	d	096	a	b	c	d
047	a	b	c	d	097	a	b	c	d
048	a	b	c	d	098	a	b	c	d
049	a	b	c	d	099	a	b	c	d
050	a	b	c	d	100	a	b	c	d

DECLARATION BY THE CANDIDATE

I declare that particulars and signature on this OMR Answer sheet are mine and are Name as in Attendance Sheet. I fruther declare that particulars filled in and Signature as well as the circles darkened on this ORIGINALCOPY is same as in OFFICE COPY.

Signature with time (in running handwriting)

CANDIDATE's NAME (in running handwriting)

MOTHER's NAME (in running handwriting)

FATHER's NAME (in running handwriting)

CANDIDATE LEFT HAND IMPRESSION

SIGNATURE OF INVIGILATOR'S WITH TIME

1

2

MEDACE

OMR SHEET

ROLL No.

1	1	1	1	1	1	1	1	1	1
2	2	2	2	2	2	2	2	2	2
3	3	3	3	3	3	3	3	3	3
4	4	4	4	4	4	4	4	4	4
5	5	5	5	5	5	5	5	5	5
6	6	6	6	6	6	6	6	6	6
7	7	7	7	7	7	7	7	7	7
8	8	8	8	8	8	8	8	8	8
9	9	9	9	9	9	9	9	9	9
0	0	0	0	0	0	0	0	0	0

TEST BOOKLET No.

1	1	1	1	1	1	1
2	2	2	2	2	2	2
3	3	3	3	3	3	3
4	4	4	4	4	4	4
5	5	5	5	5	5	5
6	6	6	6	6	6	6
7	7	7	7	7	7	7
8	8	8	8	8	8	8
9	9	9	9	9	9	9
0	0	0	0	0	0	0

TEST BOOKLET Code

Q No.	Response			
001	a	b	c	d
002	a	b	c	d
003	a	b	c	d
004	a	b	c	d
005	a	b	c	d
006	a	b	c	d
007	a	b	c	d
008	a	b	c	d
009	a	b	c	d
010	a	b	c	d
011	a	b	c	d
012	a	b	c	d
013	a	b	c	d
014	a	b	c	d
015	a	b	c	d
016	a	b	c	d
017	a	b	c	d
018	a	b	c	d
019	a	b	c	d
020	a	b	c	d
021	a	b	c	d
022	a	b	c	d
023	a	b	c	d
024	a	b	c	d
025	a	b	c	d
026	a	b	c	d
027	a	b	c	d
028	a	b	c	d
029	a	b	c	d
030	a	b	c	d
031	a	b	c	d
032	a	b	c	d
033	a	b	c	d
034	a	b	c	d
035	a	b	c	d
036	a	b	c	d
037	a	b	c	d
038	a	b	c	d
039	a	b	c	d
040	a	b	c	d
041	a	b	c	d
042	a	b	c	d
043	a	b	c	d
044	a	b	c	d
045	a	b	c	d
046	a	b	c	d
047	a	b	c	d
048	a	b	c	d
049	a	b	c	d
050	a	b	c	d

Q No.	Response			
051	a	b	c	d
052	a	b	c	d
053	a	b	c	d
054	a	b	c	d
055	a	b	c	d
056	a	b	c	d
057	a	b	c	d
058	a	b	c	d
059	a	b	c	d
060	a	b	c	d
061	a	b	c	d
062	a	b	c	d
063	a	b	c	d
064	a	b	c	d
065	a	b	c	d
066	a	b	c	d
067	a	b	c	d
068	a	b	c	d
069	a	b	c	d
070	a	b	c	d
071	a	b	c	d
072	a	b	c	d
073	a	b	c	d
074	a	b	c	d
075	a	b	c	d
076	a	b	c	d
077	a	b	c	d
078	a	b	c	d
079	a	b	c	d
080	a	b	c	d
081	a	b	c	d
082	a	b	c	d
083	a	b	c	d
084	a	b	c	d
085	a	b	c	d
086	a	b	c	d
087	a	b	c	d
088	a	b	c	d
089	a	b	c	d
090	a	b	c	d
091	a	b	c	d
092	a	b	c	d
093	a	b	c	d
094	a	b	c	d
095	a	b	c	d
096	a	b	c	d
097	a	b	c	d
098	a	b	c	d
099	a	b	c	d
100	a	b	c	d

DECLARATION BY THE CANDIDATE

I declare that particulars and signature on this OMR Answer sheet are mine and are Name as in Attendance Sheet. I fruther declare that particulars filled in and Signature as well as the circles darkened on this ORIGINALCOPY is same as in OFFICE COPY.

Signature with time (in running handwriting)

CANDIDATE's NAME (in running handwriting)

MOTHER's NAME (in running handwriting)

FATHER's NAME (in running handwriting)

CANDIDATE LEFT HAND IMPRESSION

SIGNATURE OF INVIGILATOR'S WITH TIME

1

2

MEDACE

OMR SHEET

ROLL No.

1	1	1	1	1	1	1	1	1	1
2	2	2	2	2	2	2	2	2	2
3	3	3	3	3	3	3	3	3	3
4	4	4	4	4	4	4	4	4	4
5	5	5	5	5	5	5	5	5	5
6	6	6	6	6	6	6	6	6	6
7	7	7	7	7	7	7	7	7	7
8	8	8	8	8	8	8	8	8	8
9	9	9	9	9	9	9	9	9	9
0	0	0	0	0	0	0	0	0	0

TEST BOOKLET No.

1	1	1	1	1	1	1
2	2	2	2	2	2	2
3	3	3	3	3	3	3
4	4	4	4	4	4	4
5	5	5	5	5	5	5
6	6	6	6	6	6	6
7	7	7	7	7	7	7
8	8	8	8	8	8	8
9	9	9	9	9	9	9
0	0	0	0	0	0	0

TEST BOOKLET Code

Q No.	Response				Q No.	Response			
001	a	b	c	d	051	a	b	c	d
002	a	b	c	d	052	a	b	c	d
003	a	b	c	d	053	a	b	c	d
004	a	b	c	d	054	a	b	c	d
005	a	b	c	d	055	a	b	c	d
006	a	b	c	d	056	a	b	c	d
007	a	b	c	d	057	a	b	c	d
008	a	b	c	d	058	a	b	c	d
009	a	b	c	d	059	a	b	c	d
010	a	b	c	d	060	a	b	c	d
011	a	b	c	d	061	a	b	c	d
012	a	b	c	d	062	a	b	c	d
013	a	b	c	d	063	a	b	c	d
014	a	b	c	d	064	a	b	c	d
015	a	b	c	d	065	a	b	c	d
016	a	b	c	d	066	a	b	c	d
017	a	b	c	d	067	a	b	c	d
018	a	b	c	d	068	a	b	c	d
019	a	b	c	d	069	a	b	c	d
020	a	b	c	d	070	a	b	c	d
021	a	b	c	d	071	a	b	c	d
022	a	b	c	d	072	a	b	c	d
023	a	b	c	d	073	a	b	c	d
024	a	b	c	d	074	a	b	c	d
025	a	b	c	d	075	a	b	c	d
026	a	b	c	d	076	a	b	c	d
027	a	b	c	d	077	a	b	c	d
028	a	b	c	d	078	a	b	c	d
029	a	b	c	d	079	a	b	c	d
030	a	b	c	d	080	a	b	c	d
031	a	b	c	d	081	a	b	c	d
032	a	b	c	d	082	a	b	c	d
033	a	b	c	d	083	a	b	c	d
034	a	b	c	d	084	a	b	c	d
035	a	b	c	d	085	a	b	c	d
036	a	b	c	d	086	a	b	c	d
037	a	b	c	d	087	a	b	c	d
038	a	b	c	d	088	a	b	c	d
039	a	b	c	d	089	a	b	c	d
040	a	b	c	d	090	a	b	c	d
041	a	b	c	d	091	a	b	c	d
042	a	b	c	d	092	a	b	c	d
043	a	b	c	d	093	a	b	c	d
044	a	b	c	d	094	a	b	c	d
045	a	b	c	d	095	a	b	c	d
046	a	b	c	d	096	a	b	c	d
047	a	b	c	d	097	a	b	c	d
048	a	b	c	d	098	a	b	c	d
049	a	b	c	d	099	a	b	c	d
050	a	b	c	d	100	a	b	c	d

DECLARATION BY THE CANDIDATE

I declare that particulars and signature on this OMR Answer sheet are mine and are Name as in Attendance Sheet. I fruther declare that particulars filled in and Signature as well as the circles darkened on this ORIGINALCOPY is same as in OFFICE COPY.

Signature with time (in running handwriting)

CANDIDATE's NAME (in running handwriting)

MOTHER's NAME (in running handwriting)

FATHER's NAME (in running handwriting)

CANDIDATE LEFT HAND IMPRESSION

SIGNATURE OF INVIGILATOR'S WITH TIME

1

2

MEDACE

OMR SHEET

ROLL No.

1	1	1	1	1	1	1	1	1	1
2	2	2	2	2	2	2	2	2	2
3	3	3	3	3	3	3	3	3	3
4	4	4	4	4	4	4	4	4	4
5	5	5	5	5	5	5	5	5	5
6	6	6	6	6	6	6	6	6	6
7	7	7	7	7	7	7	7	7	7
8	8	8	8	8	8	8	8	8	8
9	9	9	9	9	9	9	9	9	9
0	0	0	0	0	0	0	0	0	0

TEST BOOKLET No.

1	1	1	1	1	1	1
2	2	2	2	2	2	2
3	3	3	3	3	3	3
4	4	4	4	4	4	4
5	5	5	5	5	5	5
6	6	6	6	6	6	6
7	7	7	7	7	7	7
8	8	8	8	8	8	8
9	9	9	9	9	9	9
0	0	0	0	0	0	0

TEST BOOKLET Code

Q No.	Response				Q No.	Response			
001	a	b	c	d	051	a	b	c	d
002	a	b	c	d	052	a	b	c	d
003	a	b	c	d	053	a	b	c	d
004	a	b	c	d	054	a	b	c	d
005	a	b	c	d	055	a	b	c	d
006	a	b	c	d	056	a	b	c	d
007	a	b	c	d	057	a	b	c	d
008	a	b	c	d	058	a	b	c	d
009	a	b	c	d	059	a	b	c	d
010	a	b	c	d	060	a	b	c	d
011	a	b	c	d	061	a	b	c	d
012	a	b	c	d	062	a	b	c	d
013	a	b	c	d	063	a	b	c	d
014	a	b	c	d	064	a	b	c	d
015	a	b	c	d	065	a	b	c	d
016	a	b	c	d	066	a	b	c	d
017	a	b	c	d	067	a	b	c	d
018	a	b	c	d	068	a	b	c	d
019	a	b	c	d	069	a	b	c	d
020	a	b	c	d	070	a	b	c	d
021	a	b	c	d	071	a	b	c	d
022	a	b	c	d	072	a	b	c	d
023	a	b	c	d	073	a	b	c	d
024	a	b	c	d	074	a	b	c	d
025	a	b	c	d	075	a	b	c	d
026	a	b	c	d	076	a	b	c	d
027	a	b	c	d	077	a	b	c	d
028	a	b	c	d	078	a	b	c	d
029	a	b	c	d	079	a	b	c	d
030	a	b	c	d	080	a	b	c	d
031	a	b	c	d	081	a	b	c	d
032	a	b	c	d	082	a	b	c	d
033	a	b	c	d	083	a	b	c	d
034	a	b	c	d	084	a	b	c	d
035	a	b	c	d	085	a	b	c	d
036	a	b	c	d	086	a	b	c	d
037	a	b	c	d	087	a	b	c	d
038	a	b	c	d	088	a	b	c	d
039	a	b	c	d	089	a	b	c	d
040	a	b	c	d	090	a	b	c	d
041	a	b	c	d	091	a	b	c	d
042	a	b	c	d	092	a	b	c	d
043	a	b	c	d	093	a	b	c	d
044	a	b	c	d	094	a	b	c	d
045	a	b	c	d	095	a	b	c	d
046	a	b	c	d	096	a	b	c	d
047	a	b	c	d	097	a	b	c	d
048	a	b	c	d	098	a	b	c	d
049	a	b	c	d	099	a	b	c	d
050	a	b	c	d	100	a	b	c	d

DECLARATION BY THE CANDIDATE

I declare that particulars and signature on this OMR Answer sheet are mine and are Name as in Attendance Sheet. I fruther declare that particulars filled in and Signature as well as the circles darkened on this ORIGINALCOPY is same as in OFFICE COPY.

Signature with time (in running handwriting)

CANDIDATE's NAME (in running handwriting)

MOTHER's NAME (in running handwriting)

FATHER's NAME (in running handwriting)

CANDIDATE LEFT HAND IMPRESSION

SIGNATURE OF INVIGILATOR'S WITH TIME

1

2

MEDACE

OMR SHEET

ROLL No.

1	1	1	1	1	1	1	1	1	1
2	2	2	2	2	2	2	2	2	2
3	3	3	3	3	3	3	3	3	3
4	4	4	4	4	4	4	4	4	4
5	5	5	5	5	5	5	5	5	5
6	6	6	6	6	6	6	6	6	6
7	7	7	7	7	7	7	7	7	7
8	8	8	8	8	8	8	8	8	8
9	9	9	9	9	9	9	9	9	9
0	0	0	0	0	0	0	0	0	0

TEST BOOKLET No.

1	1	1	1	1	1	1
2	2	2	2	2	2	2
3	3	3	3	3	3	3
4	4	4	4	4	4	4
5	5	5	5	5	5	5
6	6	6	6	6	6	6
7	7	7	7	7	7	7
8	8	8	8	8	8	8
9	9	9	9	9	9	9
0	0	0	0	0	0	0

TEST BOOKLET Code

Q No.	Response				Q No.	Response			
001	a	b	c	d	051	a	b	c	d
002	a	b	c	d	052	a	b	c	d
003	a	b	c	d	053	a	b	c	d
004	a	b	c	d	054	a	b	c	d
005	a	b	c	d	055	a	b	c	d
006	a	b	c	d	056	a	b	c	d
007	a	b	c	d	057	a	b	c	d
008	a	b	c	d	058	a	b	c	d
009	a	b	c	d	059	a	b	c	d
010	a	b	c	d	060	a	b	c	d
011	a	b	c	d	061	a	b	c	d
012	a	b	c	d	062	a	b	c	d
013	a	b	c	d	063	a	b	c	d
014	a	b	c	d	064	a	b	c	d
015	a	b	c	d	065	a	b	c	d
016	a	b	c	d	066	a	b	c	d
017	a	b	c	d	067	a	b	c	d
018	a	b	c	d	068	a	b	c	d
019	a	b	c	d	069	a	b	c	d
020	a	b	c	d	070	a	b	c	d
021	a	b	c	d	071	a	b	c	d
022	a	b	c	d	072	a	b	c	d
023	a	b	c	d	073	a	b	c	d
024	a	b	c	d	074	a	b	c	d
025	a	b	c	d	075	a	b	c	d
026	a	b	c	d	076	a	b	c	d
027	a	b	c	d	077	a	b	c	d
028	a	b	c	d	078	a	b	c	d
029	a	b	c	d	079	a	b	c	d
030	a	b	c	d	080	a	b	c	d
031	a	b	c	d	081	a	b	c	d
032	a	b	c	d	082	a	b	c	d
033	a	b	c	d	083	a	b	c	d
034	a	b	c	d	084	a	b	c	d
035	a	b	c	d	085	a	b	c	d
036	a	b	c	d	086	a	b	c	d
037	a	b	c	d	087	a	b	c	d
038	a	b	c	d	088	a	b	c	d
039	a	b	c	d	089	a	b	c	d
040	a	b	c	d	090	a	b	c	d
041	a	b	c	d	091	a	b	c	d
042	a	b	c	d	092	a	b	c	d
043	a	b	c	d	093	a	b	c	d
044	a	b	c	d	094	a	b	c	d
045	a	b	c	d	095	a	b	c	d
046	a	b	c	d	096	a	b	c	d
047	a	b	c	d	097	a	b	c	d
048	a	b	c	d	098	a	b	c	d
049	a	b	c	d	099	a	b	c	d
050	a	b	c	d	100	a	b	c	d

DECLARATION BY THE CANDIDATE

I declare that particulars and signature on this OMR Answer sheet are mine and are Name as in Attendance Sheet. I fruther declare that particulars filled in and Signature as well as the circles darkened on this ORIGINALCOPY is same as in OFFICE COPY.

Signature with time (in running handwriting)

CANDIDATE's NAME (in running handwriting)

MOTHER's NAME (in running handwriting)

FATHER's NAME (in running handwriting)

CANDIDATE LEFT HAND IMPRESSION

SIGNATURE OF INVIGILATOR'S WITH TIME

1

2

MEDACE

OMR SHEET

ROLL No.

1 2 3 4 5 6 7 8 9 0

TEST BOOKLET No.

1 2 3 4 5 6 7 8 9 0

TEST BOOKLET Code

Q No.	Response
001–100	ⓐ ⓑ ⓒ ⓓ

DECLARATION BY THE CANDIDATE

I declare that particulars and signature on this OMR Answer sheet are mine and are Name as in Attendance Sheet. I fruther declare that particulars filled in and Signature as well as the circles darkened on this ORIGINALCOPY is same as in OFFICE COPY.

Signature with time (in running handwriting)

CANDIDATE's NAME (in running handwriting)

MOTHER's NAME (in running handwriting)

FATHER's NAME (in running handwriting)

CANDIDATE LEFT HAND IMPRESSION

SIGNATURE OF INVIGILATOR'S WITH TIME

1

2

MEDACE

OMR SHEET

ROLL No.

1	1	1	1	1	1	1	1	1	1
2	2	2	2	2	2	2	2	2	2
3	3	3	3	3	3	3	3	3	3
4	4	4	4	4	4	4	4	4	4
5	5	5	5	5	5	5	5	5	5
6	6	6	6	6	6	6	6	6	6
7	7	7	7	7	7	7	7	7	7
8	8	8	8	8	8	8	8	8	8
9	9	9	9	9	9	9	9	9	9
0	0	0	0	0	0	0	0	0	0

TEST BOOKLET No.

1	1	1	1	1	1	1
2	2	2	2	2	2	2
3	3	3	3	3	3	3
4	4	4	4	4	4	4
5	5	5	5	5	5	5
6	6	6	6	6	6	6
7	7	7	7	7	7	7
8	8	8	8	8	8	8
9	9	9	9	9	9	9
0	0	0	0	0	0	0

TEST BOOKLET Code

Q No.	Response				Q No.	Response			
001	a	b	c	d	051	a	b	c	d
002	a	b	c	d	052	a	b	c	d
003	a	b	c	d	053	a	b	c	d
004	a	b	c	d	054	a	b	c	d
005	a	b	c	d	055	a	b	c	d
006	a	b	c	d	056	a	b	c	d
007	a	b	c	d	057	a	b	c	d
008	a	b	c	d	058	a	b	c	d
009	a	b	c	d	059	a	b	c	d
010	a	b	c	d	060	a	b	c	d
011	a	b	c	d	061	a	b	c	d
012	a	b	c	d	062	a	b	c	d
013	a	b	c	d	063	a	b	c	d
014	a	b	c	d	064	a	b	c	d
015	a	b	c	d	065	a	b	c	d
016	a	b	c	d	066	a	b	c	d
017	a	b	c	d	067	a	b	c	d
018	a	b	c	d	068	a	b	c	d
019	a	b	c	d	069	a	b	c	d
020	a	b	c	d	070	a	b	c	d
021	a	b	c	d	071	a	b	c	d
022	a	b	c	d	072	a	b	c	d
023	a	b	c	d	073	a	b	c	d
024	a	b	c	d	074	a	b	c	d
025	a	b	c	d	075	a	b	c	d
026	a	b	c	d	076	a	b	c	d
027	a	b	c	d	077	a	b	c	d
028	a	b	c	d	078	a	b	c	d
029	a	b	c	d	079	a	b	c	d
030	a	b	c	d	080	a	b	c	d
031	a	b	c	d	081	a	b	c	d
032	a	b	c	d	082	a	b	c	d
033	a	b	c	d	083	a	b	c	d
034	a	b	c	d	084	a	b	c	d
035	a	b	c	d	085	a	b	c	d
036	a	b	c	d	086	a	b	c	d
037	a	b	c	d	087	a	b	c	d
038	a	b	c	d	088	a	b	c	d
039	a	b	c	d	089	a	b	c	d
040	a	b	c	d	090	a	b	c	d
041	a	b	c	d	091	a	b	c	d
042	a	b	c	d	092	a	b	c	d
043	a	b	c	d	093	a	b	c	d
044	a	b	c	d	094	a	b	c	d
045	a	b	c	d	095	a	b	c	d
046	a	b	c	d	096	a	b	c	d
047	a	b	c	d	097	a	b	c	d
048	a	b	c	d	098	a	b	c	d
049	a	b	c	d	099	a	b	c	d
050	a	b	c	d	100	a	b	c	d

DECLARATION BY THE CANDIDATE

I declare that particulars and signature on this OMR Answer sheet are mine and are Name as in Attendance Sheet. I fruther declare that particulars filled in and Signature as well as the circles darkened on this ORIGINALCOPY is same as in OFFICE COPY.

Signature with time (in running handwriting)

CANDIDATE's NAME (in running handwriting)

MOTHER's NAME (in running handwriting)

FATHER's NAME (in running handwriting)

CANDIDATE LEFT HAND IMPRESSION

SIGNATURE OF INVIGILATOR'S WITH TIME

1

2

MEDACE

OMR SHEET

ROLL No.

1	1	1	1	1	1	1	1	1	1
2	2	2	2	2	2	2	2	2	2
3	3	3	3	3	3	3	3	3	3
4	4	4	4	4	4	4	4	4	4
5	5	5	5	5	5	5	5	5	5
6	6	6	6	6	6	6	6	6	6
7	7	7	7	7	7	7	7	7	7
8	8	8	8	8	8	8	8	8	8
9	9	9	9	9	9	9	9	9	9
0	0	0	0	0	0	0	0	0	0

TEST BOOKLET No.

1	1	1	1	1	1	1
2	2	2	2	2	2	2
3	3	3	3	3	3	3
4	4	4	4	4	4	4
5	5	5	5	5	5	5
6	6	6	6	6	6	6
7	7	7	7	7	7	7
8	8	8	8	8	8	8
9	9	9	9	9	9	9
0	0	0	0	0	0	0

TEST BOOKLET Code

Q No.	Response				Q No.	Response			
001	a	b	c	d	051	a	b	c	d
002	a	b	c	d	052	a	b	c	d
003	a	b	c	d	053	a	b	c	d
004	a	b	c	d	054	a	b	c	d
005	a	b	c	d	055	a	b	c	d
006	a	b	c	d	056	a	b	c	d
007	a	b	c	d	057	a	b	c	d
008	a	b	c	d	058	a	b	c	d
009	a	b	c	d	059	a	b	c	d
010	a	b	c	d	060	a	b	c	d
011	a	b	c	d	061	a	b	c	d
012	a	b	c	d	062	a	b	c	d
013	a	b	c	d	063	a	b	c	d
014	a	b	c	d	064	a	b	c	d
015	a	b	c	d	065	a	b	c	d
016	a	b	c	d	066	a	b	c	d
017	a	b	c	d	067	a	b	c	d
018	a	b	c	d	068	a	b	c	d
019	a	b	c	d	069	a	b	c	d
020	a	b	c	d	070	a	b	c	d
021	a	b	c	d	071	a	b	c	d
022	a	b	c	d	072	a	b	c	d
023	a	b	c	d	073	a	b	c	d
024	a	b	c	d	074	a	b	c	d
025	a	b	c	d	075	a	b	c	d
026	a	b	c	d	076	a	b	c	d
027	a	b	c	d	077	a	b	c	d
028	a	b	c	d	078	a	b	c	d
029	a	b	c	d	079	a	b	c	d
030	a	b	c	d	080	a	b	c	d
031	a	b	c	d	081	a	b	c	d
032	a	b	c	d	082	a	b	c	d
033	a	b	c	d	083	a	b	c	d
034	a	b	c	d	084	a	b	c	d
035	a	b	c	d	085	a	b	c	d
036	a	b	c	d	086	a	b	c	d
037	a	b	c	d	087	a	b	c	d
038	a	b	c	d	088	a	b	c	d
039	a	b	c	d	089	a	b	c	d
040	a	b	c	d	090	a	b	c	d
041	a	b	c	d	091	a	b	c	d
042	a	b	c	d	092	a	b	c	d
043	a	b	c	d	093	a	b	c	d
044	a	b	c	d	094	a	b	c	d
045	a	b	c	d	095	a	b	c	d
046	a	b	c	d	096	a	b	c	d
047	a	b	c	d	097	a	b	c	d
048	a	b	c	d	098	a	b	c	d
049	a	b	c	d	099	a	b	c	d
050	a	b	c	d	100	a	b	c	d

DECLARATION BY THE CANDIDATE

I declare that particulars and signature on this OMR Answer sheet are mine and are Name as in Attendance Sheet. I fruther declare that particulars filled in and Signature as well as the circles darkened on this ORIGINALCOPY is same as in OFFICE COPY.

Signature with time (in running handwriting)

CANDIDATE's NAME (in running handwriting)

MOTHER's NAME (in running handwriting)

FATHER's NAME (in running handwriting)

CANDIDATE LEFT HAND IMPRESSION

SIGNATURE OF INVIGILATOR'S WITH TIME

1

2

MEDACE

OMR SHEET

ROLL No.

1	1	1	1	1	1	1	1	1	1
2	2	2	2	2	2	2	2	2	2
3	3	3	3	3	3	3	3	3	3
4	4	4	4	4	4	4	4	4	4
5	5	5	5	5	5	5	5	5	5
6	6	6	6	6	6	6	6	6	6
7	7	7	7	7	7	7	7	7	7
8	8	8	8	8	8	8	8	8	8
9	9	9	9	9	9	9	9	9	9
0	0	0	0	0	0	0	0	0	0

TEST BOOKLET No.

1	1	1	1	1	1	1
2	2	2	2	2	2	2
3	3	3	3	3	3	3
4	4	4	4	4	4	4
5	5	5	5	5	5	5
6	6	6	6	6	6	6
7	7	7	7	7	7	7
8	8	8	8	8	8	8
9	9	9	9	9	9	9
0	0	0	0	0	0	0

TEST BOOKLET Code

Q No.	Response			
001	a	b	c	d
002	a	b	c	d
003	a	b	c	d
004	a	b	c	d
005	a	b	c	d
006	a	b	c	d
007	a	b	c	d
008	a	b	c	d
009	a	b	c	d
010	a	b	c	d
011	a	b	c	d
012	a	b	c	d
013	a	b	c	d
014	a	b	c	d
015	a	b	c	d
016	a	b	c	d
017	a	b	c	d
018	a	b	c	d
019	a	b	c	d
020	a	b	c	d
021	a	b	c	d
022	a	b	c	d
023	a	b	c	d
024	a	b	c	d
025	a	b	c	d
026	a	b	c	d
027	a	b	c	d
028	a	b	c	d
029	a	b	c	d
030	a	b	c	d
031	a	b	c	d
032	a	b	c	d
033	a	b	c	d
034	a	b	c	d
035	a	b	c	d
036	a	b	c	d
037	a	b	c	d
038	a	b	c	d
039	a	b	c	d
040	a	b	c	d
041	a	b	c	d
042	a	b	c	d
043	a	b	c	d
044	a	b	c	d
045	a	b	c	d
046	a	b	c	d
047	a	b	c	d
048	a	b	c	d
049	a	b	c	d
050	a	b	c	d

Q No.	Response			
051	a	b	c	d
052	a	b	c	d
053	a	b	c	d
054	a	b	c	d
055	a	b	c	d
056	a	b	c	d
057	a	b	c	d
058	a	b	c	d
059	a	b	c	d
060	a	b	c	d
061	a	b	c	d
062	a	b	c	d
063	a	b	c	d
064	a	b	c	d
065	a	b	c	d
066	a	b	c	d
067	a	b	c	d
068	a	b	c	d
069	a	b	c	d
070	a	b	c	d
071	a	b	c	d
072	a	b	c	d
073	a	b	c	d
074	a	b	c	d
075	a	b	c	d
076	a	b	c	d
077	a	b	c	d
078	a	b	c	d
079	a	b	c	d
080	a	b	c	d
081	a	b	c	d
082	a	b	c	d
083	a	b	c	d
084	a	b	c	d
085	a	b	c	d
086	a	b	c	d
087	a	b	c	d
088	a	b	c	d
089	a	b	c	d
090	a	b	c	d
091	a	b	c	d
092	a	b	c	d
093	a	b	c	d
094	a	b	c	d
095	a	b	c	d
096	a	b	c	d
097	a	b	c	d
098	a	b	c	d
099	a	b	c	d
100	a	b	c	d

DECLARATION BY THE CANDIDATE

I declare that particulars and signature on this OMR Answer sheet are mine and are Name as in Attendance Sheet. I fruther declare that particulars filled in and Signature as well as the circles darkened on this ORIGINALCOPY is same as in OFFICE COPY.

Signature with time (in running handwriting)

CANDIDATE's NAME (in running handwriting)

MOTHER's NAME (in running handwriting)

FATHER's NAME (in running handwriting)

CANDIDATE LEFT HAND IMPRESSION

SIGNATURE OF INVIGILATOR'S WITH TIME

1

2

MEDACE

OMR SHEET

ROLL No.

1	1	1	1	1	1	1	1	1	1
2	2	2	2	2	2	2	2	2	2
3	3	3	3	3	3	3	3	3	3
4	4	4	4	4	4	4	4	4	4
5	5	5	5	5	5	5	5	5	5
6	6	6	6	6	6	6	6	6	6
7	7	7	7	7	7	7	7	7	7
8	8	8	8	8	8	8	8	8	8
9	9	9	9	9	9	9	9	9	9
0	0	0	0	0	0	0	0	0	0

TEST BOOKLET No.

1	1	1	1	1	1	1
2	2	2	2	2	2	2
3	3	3	3	3	3	3
4	4	4	4	4	4	4
5	5	5	5	5	5	5
6	6	6	6	6	6	6
7	7	7	7	7	7	7
8	8	8	8	8	8	8
9	9	9	9	9	9	9
0	0	0	0	0	0	0

TEST BOOKLET Code

DECLARATION BY THE CANDIDATE

I declare that particulars and signature on this OMR Answer sheet are mine and are Name as in Attendance Sheet. I fruther declare that particulars filled in and Signature as well as the circles darkened on this ORIGINALCOPY is same as in OFFICE COPY.

Signature with time (in running handwriting)

CANDIDATE's NAME (in running handwriting)

Q No.	Response				Q No.	Response			
001	a	b	c	d	051	a	b	c	d
002	a	b	c	d	052	a	b	c	d
003	a	b	c	d	053	a	b	c	d
004	a	b	c	d	054	a	b	c	d
005	a	b	c	d	055	a	b	c	d
006	a	b	c	d	056	a	b	c	d
007	a	b	c	d	057	a	b	c	d
008	a	b	c	d	058	a	b	c	d
009	a	b	c	d	059	a	b	c	d
010	a	b	c	d	060	a	b	c	d
011	a	b	c	d	061	a	b	c	d
012	a	b	c	d	062	a	b	c	d
013	a	b	c	d	063	a	b	c	d
014	a	b	c	d	064	a	b	c	d
015	a	b	c	d	065	a	b	c	d
016	a	b	c	d	066	a	b	c	d
017	a	b	c	d	067	a	b	c	d
018	a	b	c	d	068	a	b	c	d
019	a	b	c	d	069	a	b	c	d
020	a	b	c	d	070	a	b	c	d
021	a	b	c	d	071	a	b	c	d
022	a	b	c	d	072	a	b	c	d
023	a	b	c	d	073	a	b	c	d
024	a	b	c	d	074	a	b	c	d
025	a	b	c	d	075	a	b	c	d
026	a	b	c	d	076	a	b	c	d
027	a	b	c	d	077	a	b	c	d
028	a	b	c	d	078	a	b	c	d
029	a	b	c	d	079	a	b	c	d
030	a	b	c	d	080	a	b	c	d
031	a	b	c	d	081	a	b	c	d
032	a	b	c	d	082	a	b	c	d
033	a	b	c	d	083	a	b	c	d
034	a	b	c	d	084	a	b	c	d
035	a	b	c	d	085	a	b	c	d
036	a	b	c	d	086	a	b	c	d
037	a	b	c	d	087	a	b	c	d
038	a	b	c	d	088	a	b	c	d
039	a	b	c	d	089	a	b	c	d
040	a	b	c	d	090	a	b	c	d
041	a	b	c	d	091	a	b	c	d
042	a	b	c	d	092	a	b	c	d
043	a	b	c	d	093	a	b	c	d
044	a	b	c	d	094	a	b	c	d
045	a	b	c	d	095	a	b	c	d
046	a	b	c	d	096	a	b	c	d
047	a	b	c	d	097	a	b	c	d
048	a	b	c	d	098	a	b	c	d
049	a	b	c	d	099	a	b	c	d
050	a	b	c	d	100	a	b	c	d

MOTHER's NAME (in running handwriting)	FATHER's NAME (in running handwriting)

CANDIDATE LEFT HAND IMPRESSION	SIGNATURE OF INVIGILATOR'S WITH TIME
	1
	2

MEDACE

OMR SHEET

ROLL No.

1	1	1	1	1	1	1	1	1	1
2	2	2	2	2	2	2	2	2	2
3	3	3	3	3	3	3	3	3	3
4	4	4	4	4	4	4	4	4	4
5	5	5	5	5	5	5	5	5	5
6	6	6	6	6	6	6	6	6	6
7	7	7	7	7	7	7	7	7	7
8	8	8	8	8	8	8	8	8	8
9	9	9	9	9	9	9	9	9	9
0	0	0	0	0	0	0	0	0	0

TEST BOOKLET No.

1	1	1	1	1	1	1
2	2	2	2	2	2	2
3	3	3	3	3	3	3
4	4	4	4	4	4	4
5	5	5	5	5	5	5
6	6	6	6	6	6	6
7	7	7	7	7	7	7
8	8	8	8	8	8	8
9	9	9	9	9	9	9
0	0	0	0	0	0	0

TEST BOOKLET Code

Q No.	Response				Q No.	Response			
001	a	b	c	d	051	a	b	c	d
002	a	b	c	d	052	a	b	c	d
003	a	b	c	d	053	a	b	c	d
004	a	b	c	d	054	a	b	c	d
005	a	b	c	d	055	a	b	c	d
006	a	b	c	d	056	a	b	c	d
007	a	b	c	d	057	a	b	c	d
008	a	b	c	d	058	a	b	c	d
009	a	b	c	d	059	a	b	c	d
010	a	b	c	d	060	a	b	c	d
011	a	b	c	d	061	a	b	c	d
012	a	b	c	d	062	a	b	c	d
013	a	b	c	d	063	a	b	c	d
014	a	b	c	d	064	a	b	c	d
015	a	b	c	d	065	a	b	c	d
016	a	b	c	d	066	a	b	c	d
017	a	b	c	d	067	a	b	c	d
018	a	b	c	d	068	a	b	c	d
019	a	b	c	d	069	a	b	c	d
020	a	b	c	d	070	a	b	c	d
021	a	b	c	d	071	a	b	c	d
022	a	b	c	d	072	a	b	c	d
023	a	b	c	d	073	a	b	c	d
024	a	b	c	d	074	a	b	c	d
025	a	b	c	d	075	a	b	c	d
026	a	b	c	d	076	a	b	c	d
027	a	b	c	d	077	a	b	c	d
028	a	b	c	d	078	a	b	c	d
029	a	b	c	d	079	a	b	c	d
030	a	b	c	d	080	a	b	c	d
031	a	b	c	d	081	a	b	c	d
032	a	b	c	d	082	a	b	c	d
033	a	b	c	d	083	a	b	c	d
034	a	b	c	d	084	a	b	c	d
035	a	b	c	d	085	a	b	c	d
036	a	b	c	d	086	a	b	c	d
037	a	b	c	d	087	a	b	c	d
038	a	b	c	d	088	a	b	c	d
039	a	b	c	d	089	a	b	c	d
040	a	b	c	d	090	a	b	c	d
041	a	b	c	d	091	a	b	c	d
042	a	b	c	d	092	a	b	c	d
043	a	b	c	d	093	a	b	c	d
044	a	b	c	d	094	a	b	c	d
045	a	b	c	d	095	a	b	c	d
046	a	b	c	d	096	a	b	c	d
047	a	b	c	d	097	a	b	c	d
048	a	b	c	d	098	a	b	c	d
049	a	b	c	d	099	a	b	c	d
050	a	b	c	d	100	a	b	c	d

DECLARATION BY THE CANDIDATE

I declare that particulars and signature on this OMR Answer sheet are mine and are Name as in Attendance Sheet. I fruther declare that particulars filled in and Signature as well as the circles darkened on this ORIGINALCOPY is same as in OFFICE COPY.

Signature with time (in running handwriting)

CANDIDATE's NAME (in running handwriting)

MOTHER's NAME (in running handwriting)

FATHER's NAME (in running handwriting)

CANDIDATE LEFT HAND IMPRESSION

SIGNATURE OF INVIGILATOR'S WITH TIME

1

2

OMR SHEET

ROLL No.

1	1	1	1	1	1	1	1	1	1
2	2	2	2	2	2	2	2	2	2
3	3	3	3	3	3	3	3	3	3
4	4	4	4	4	4	4	4	4	4
5	5	5	5	5	5	5	5	5	5
6	6	6	6	6	6	6	6	6	6
7	7	7	7	7	7	7	7	7	7
8	8	8	8	8	8	8	8	8	8
9	9	9	9	9	9	9	9	9	9
0	0	0	0	0	0	0	0	0	0

TEST BOOKLET No.

1	1	1	1	1	1	1
2	2	2	2	2	2	2
3	3	3	3	3	3	3
4	4	4	4	4	4	4
5	5	5	5	5	5	5
6	6	6	6	6	6	6
7	7	7	7	7	7	7
8	8	8	8	8	8	8
9	9	9	9	9	9	9
0	0	0	0	0	0	0

TEST BOOKLET Code

Q No.	Response				Q No.	Response			
001	a	b	c	d	051	a	b	c	d
002	a	b	c	d	052	a	b	c	d
003	a	b	c	d	053	a	b	c	d
004	a	b	c	d	054	a	b	c	d
005	a	b	c	d	055	a	b	c	d
006	a	b	c	d	056	a	b	c	d
007	a	b	c	d	057	a	b	c	d
008	a	b	c	d	058	a	b	c	d
009	a	b	c	d	059	a	b	c	d
010	a	b	c	d	060	a	b	c	d
011	a	b	c	d	061	a	b	c	d
012	a	b	c	d	062	a	b	c	d
013	a	b	c	d	063	a	b	c	d
014	a	b	c	d	064	a	b	c	d
015	a	b	c	d	065	a	b	c	d
016	a	b	c	d	066	a	b	c	d
017	a	b	c	d	067	a	b	c	d
018	a	b	c	d	068	a	b	c	d
019	a	b	c	d	069	a	b	c	d
020	a	b	c	d	070	a	b	c	d
021	a	b	c	d	071	a	b	c	d
022	a	b	c	d	072	a	b	c	d
023	a	b	c	d	073	a	b	c	d
024	a	b	c	d	074	a	b	c	d
025	a	b	c	d	075	a	b	c	d
026	a	b	c	d	076	a	b	c	d
027	a	b	c	d	077	a	b	c	d
028	a	b	c	d	078	a	b	c	d
029	a	b	c	d	079	a	b	c	d
030	a	b	c	d	080	a	b	c	d
031	a	b	c	d	081	a	b	c	d
032	a	b	c	d	082	a	b	c	d
033	a	b	c	d	083	a	b	c	d
034	a	b	c	d	084	a	b	c	d
035	a	b	c	d	085	a	b	c	d
036	a	b	c	d	086	a	b	c	d
037	a	b	c	d	087	a	b	c	d
038	a	b	c	d	088	a	b	c	d
039	a	b	c	d	089	a	b	c	d
040	a	b	c	d	090	a	b	c	d
041	a	b	c	d	091	a	b	c	d
042	a	b	c	d	092	a	b	c	d
043	a	b	c	d	093	a	b	c	d
044	a	b	c	d	094	a	b	c	d
045	a	b	c	d	095	a	b	c	d
046	a	b	c	d	096	a	b	c	d
047	a	b	c	d	097	a	b	c	d
048	a	b	c	d	098	a	b	c	d
049	a	b	c	d	099	a	b	c	d
050	a	b	c	d	100	a	b	c	d

DECLARATION BY THE CANDIDATE

I declare that particulars and signature on this OMR Answer sheet are mine and are Name as in Attendance Sheet. I fruther declare that particulars filled in and Signature as well as the circles darkened on this ORIGINALCOPY is same as in OFFICE COPY.

Signature with time (in running handwriting)

CANDIDATE's NAME (in running handwriting)

MOTHER's NAME (in running handwriting)

FATHER's NAME (in running handwriting)

CANDIDATE LEFT HAND IMPRESSION

SIGNATURE OF INVIGILATOR'S WITH TIME

1

2

MEDACE

OMR SHEET

ROLL No.

1	1	1	1	1	1	1	1	1	1
2	2	2	2	2	2	2	2	2	2
3	3	3	3	3	3	3	3	3	3
4	4	4	4	4	4	4	4	4	4
5	5	5	5	5	5	5	5	5	5
6	6	6	6	6	6	6	6	6	6
7	7	7	7	7	7	7	7	7	7
8	8	8	8	8	8	8	8	8	8
9	9	9	9	9	9	9	9	9	9
0	0	0	0	0	0	0	0	0	0

TEST BOOKLET No.

1	1	1	1	1	1	1
2	2	2	2	2	2	2
3	3	3	3	3	3	3
4	4	4	4	4	4	4
5	5	5	5	5	5	5
6	6	6	6	6	6	6
7	7	7	7	7	7	7
8	8	8	8	8	8	8
9	9	9	9	9	9	9
0	0	0	0	0	0	0

TEST BOOKLET Code

Q No.	Response				Q No.	Response			
001	a	b	c	d	051	a	b	c	d
002	a	b	c	d	052	a	b	c	d
003	a	b	c	d	053	a	b	c	d
004	a	b	c	d	054	a	b	c	d
005	a	b	c	d	055	a	b	c	d
006	a	b	c	d	056	a	b	c	d
007	a	b	c	d	057	a	b	c	d
008	a	b	c	d	058	a	b	c	d
009	a	b	c	d	059	a	b	c	d
010	a	b	c	d	060	a	b	c	d
011	a	b	c	d	061	a	b	c	d
012	a	b	c	d	062	a	b	c	d
013	a	b	c	d	063	a	b	c	d
014	a	b	c	d	064	a	b	c	d
015	a	b	c	d	065	a	b	c	d
016	a	b	c	d	066	a	b	c	d
017	a	b	c	d	067	a	b	c	d
018	a	b	c	d	068	a	b	c	d
019	a	b	c	d	069	a	b	c	d
020	a	b	c	d	070	a	b	c	d
021	a	b	c	d	071	a	b	c	d
022	a	b	c	d	072	a	b	c	d
023	a	b	c	d	073	a	b	c	d
024	a	b	c	d	074	a	b	c	d
025	a	b	c	d	075	a	b	c	d
026	a	b	c	d	076	a	b	c	d
027	a	b	c	d	077	a	b	c	d
028	a	b	c	d	078	a	b	c	d
029	a	b	c	d	079	a	b	c	d
030	a	b	c	d	080	a	b	c	d
031	a	b	c	d	081	a	b	c	d
032	a	b	c	d	082	a	b	c	d
033	a	b	c	d	083	a	b	c	d
034	a	b	c	d	084	a	b	c	d
035	a	b	c	d	085	a	b	c	d
036	a	b	c	d	086	a	b	c	d
037	a	b	c	d	087	a	b	c	d
038	a	b	c	d	088	a	b	c	d
039	a	b	c	d	089	a	b	c	d
040	a	b	c	d	090	a	b	c	d
041	a	b	c	d	091	a	b	c	d
042	a	b	c	d	092	a	b	c	d
043	a	b	c	d	093	a	b	c	d
044	a	b	c	d	094	a	b	c	d
045	a	b	c	d	095	a	b	c	d
046	a	b	c	d	096	a	b	c	d
047	a	b	c	d	097	a	b	c	d
048	a	b	c	d	098	a	b	c	d
049	a	b	c	d	099	a	b	c	d
050	a	b	c	d	100	a	b	c	d

DECLARATION BY THE CANDIDATE

I declare that particulars and signature on this OMR Answer sheet are mine and are Name as in Attendance Sheet. I fruther declare that particulars filled in and Signature as well as the circles darkened on this ORIGINALCOPY is same as in OFFICE COPY.

Signature with time (in running handwriting)

CANDIDATE's NAME (in running handwriting)

MOTHER's NAME (in running handwriting)

FATHER's NAME (in running handwriting)

CANDIDATE LEFT HAND IMPRESSION

SIGNATURE OF INVIGILATOR'S WITH TIME

1

2

MEDACE

OMR SHEET

ROLL No.

1	1	1	1	1	1	1	1	1	1
2	2	2	2	2	2	2	2	2	2
3	3	3	3	3	3	3	3	3	3
4	4	4	4	4	4	4	4	4	4
5	5	5	5	5	5	5	5	5	5
6	6	6	6	6	6	6	6	6	6
7	7	7	7	7	7	7	7	7	7
8	8	8	8	8	8	8	8	8	8
9	9	9	9	9	9	9	9	9	9
0	0	0	0	0	0	0	0	0	0

TEST BOOKLET No.

1	1	1	1	1	1	1
2	2	2	2	2	2	2
3	3	3	3	3	3	3
4	4	4	4	4	4	4
5	5	5	5	5	5	5
6	6	6	6	6	6	6
7	7	7	7	7	7	7
8	8	8	8	8	8	8
9	9	9	9	9	9	9
0	0	0	0	0	0	0

TEST BOOKLET Code

DECLARATION BY THE CANDIDATE

I declare that particulars and signature on this OMR Answer sheet are mine and are Name as in Attendance Sheet. I fruther declare that particulars filled in and Signature as well as the circles darkened on this ORIGINALCOPY is same as in OFFICE COPY.

Signature with time (in running handwriting)

CANDIDATE's NAME (in running handwriting)

Q No.	Response			
001	a	b	c	d
002	a	b	c	d
003	a	b	c	d
004	a	b	c	d
005	a	b	c	d
006	a	b	c	d
007	a	b	c	d
008	a	b	c	d
009	a	b	c	d
010	a	b	c	d
011	a	b	c	d
012	a	b	c	d
013	a	b	c	d
014	a	b	c	d
015	a	b	c	d
016	a	b	c	d
017	a	b	c	d
018	a	b	c	d
019	a	b	c	d
020	a	b	c	d
021	a	b	c	d
022	a	b	c	d
023	a	b	c	d
024	a	b	c	d
025	a	b	c	d
026	a	b	c	d
027	a	b	c	d
028	a	b	c	d
029	a	b	c	d
030	a	b	c	d
031	a	b	c	d
032	a	b	c	d
033	a	b	c	d
034	a	b	c	d
035	a	b	c	d
036	a	b	c	d
037	a	b	c	d
038	a	b	c	d
039	a	b	c	d
040	a	b	c	d
041	a	b	c	d
042	a	b	c	d
043	a	b	c	d
044	a	b	c	d
045	a	b	c	d
046	a	b	c	d
047	a	b	c	d
048	a	b	c	d
049	a	b	c	d
050	a	b	c	d

Q No.	Response			
051	a	b	c	d
052	a	b	c	d
053	a	b	c	d
054	a	b	c	d
055	a	b	c	d
056	a	b	c	d
057	a	b	c	d
058	a	b	c	d
059	a	b	c	d
060	a	b	c	d
061	a	b	c	d
062	a	b	c	d
063	a	b	c	d
064	a	b	c	d
065	a	b	c	d
066	a	b	c	d
067	a	b	c	d
068	a	b	c	d
069	a	b	c	d
070	a	b	c	d
071	a	b	c	d
072	a	b	c	d
073	a	b	c	d
074	a	b	c	d
075	a	b	c	d
076	a	b	c	d
077	a	b	c	d
078	a	b	c	d
079	a	b	c	d
080	a	b	c	d
081	a	b	c	d
082	a	b	c	d
083	a	b	c	d
084	a	b	c	d
085	a	b	c	d
086	a	b	c	d
087	a	b	c	d
088	a	b	c	d
089	a	b	c	d
090	a	b	c	d
091	a	b	c	d
092	a	b	c	d
093	a	b	c	d
094	a	b	c	d
095	a	b	c	d
096	a	b	c	d
097	a	b	c	d
098	a	b	c	d
099	a	b	c	d
100	a	b	c	d

MOTHER's NAME (in running handwriting)	FATHER's NAME (in running handwriting)

CANDIDATE LEFT HAND IMPRESSION	SIGNATURE OF INVIGILATOR'S WITH TIME
	1
	2

MEDACE

OMR SHEET

ROLL No.

1	1	1	1	1	1	1	1	1	1
2	2	2	2	2	2	2	2	2	2
3	3	3	3	3	3	3	3	3	3
4	4	4	4	4	4	4	4	4	4
5	5	5	5	5	5	5	5	5	5
6	6	6	6	6	6	6	6	6	6
7	7	7	7	7	7	7	7	7	7
8	8	8	8	8	8	8	8	8	8
9	9	9	9	9	9	9	9	9	9
0	0	0	0	0	0	0	0	0	0

TEST BOOKLET No.

1	1	1	1	1	1	1
2	2	2	2	2	2	2
3	3	3	3	3	3	3
4	4	4	4	4	4	4
5	5	5	5	5	5	5
6	6	6	6	6	6	6
7	7	7	7	7	7	7
8	8	8	8	8	8	8
9	9	9	9	9	9	9
0	0	0	0	0	0	0

TEST BOOKLET Code

Q No.	Response				Q No.	Response			
001	a	b	c	d	051	a	b	c	d
002	a	b	c	d	052	a	b	c	d
003	a	b	c	d	053	a	b	c	d
004	a	b	c	d	054	a	b	c	d
005	a	b	c	d	055	a	b	c	d
006	a	b	c	d	056	a	b	c	d
007	a	b	c	d	057	a	b	c	d
008	a	b	c	d	058	a	b	c	d
009	a	b	c	d	059	a	b	c	d
010	a	b	c	d	060	a	b	c	d
011	a	b	c	d	061	a	b	c	d
012	a	b	c	d	062	a	b	c	d
013	a	b	c	d	063	a	b	c	d
014	a	b	c	d	064	a	b	c	d
015	a	b	c	d	065	a	b	c	d
016	a	b	c	d	066	a	b	c	d
017	a	b	c	d	067	a	b	c	d
018	a	b	c	d	068	a	b	c	d
019	a	b	c	d	069	a	b	c	d
020	a	b	c	d	070	a	b	c	d
021	a	b	c	d	071	a	b	c	d
022	a	b	c	d	072	a	b	c	d
023	a	b	c	d	073	a	b	c	d
024	a	b	c	d	074	a	b	c	d
025	a	b	c	d	075	a	b	c	d
026	a	b	c	d	076	a	b	c	d
027	a	b	c	d	077	a	b	c	d
028	a	b	c	d	078	a	b	c	d
029	a	b	c	d	079	a	b	c	d
030	a	b	c	d	080	a	b	c	d
031	a	b	c	d	081	a	b	c	d
032	a	b	c	d	082	a	b	c	d
033	a	b	c	d	083	a	b	c	d
034	a	b	c	d	084	a	b	c	d
035	a	b	c	d	085	a	b	c	d
036	a	b	c	d	086	a	b	c	d
037	a	b	c	d	087	a	b	c	d
038	a	b	c	d	088	a	b	c	d
039	a	b	c	d	089	a	b	c	d
040	a	b	c	d	090	a	b	c	d
041	a	b	c	d	091	a	b	c	d
042	a	b	c	d	092	a	b	c	d
043	a	b	c	d	093	a	b	c	d
044	a	b	c	d	094	a	b	c	d
045	a	b	c	d	095	a	b	c	d
046	a	b	c	d	096	a	b	c	d
047	a	b	c	d	097	a	b	c	d
048	a	b	c	d	098	a	b	c	d
049	a	b	c	d	099	a	b	c	d
050	a	b	c	d	100	a	b	c	d

DECLARATION BY THE CANDIDATE

I declare that particulars and signature on this OMR Answer sheet are mine and are Name as in Attendance Sheet. I fruther declare that particulars filled in and Signature as well as the circles darkened on this ORIGINALCOPY is same as in OFFICE COPY.

Signature with time (in running handwriting)

CANDIDATE's NAME (in running handwriting)

MOTHER's NAME (in running handwriting)

FATHER's NAME (in running handwriting)

CANDIDATE LEFT HAND IMPRESSION

SIGNATURE OF INVIGILATOR'S WITH TIME

1

2

MEDACE

OMR SHEET

ROLL No.

1	1	1	1	1	1	1	1	1	1
2	2	2	2	2	2	2	2	2	2
3	3	3	3	3	3	3	3	3	3
4	4	4	4	4	4	4	4	4	4
5	5	5	5	5	5	5	5	5	5
6	6	6	6	6	6	6	6	6	6
7	7	7	7	7	7	7	7	7	7
8	8	8	8	8	8	8	8	8	8
9	9	9	9	9	9	9	9	9	9
0	0	0	0	0	0	0	0	0	0

TEST BOOKLET No.

1	1	1	1	1	1	1
2	2	2	2	2	2	2
3	3	3	3	3	3	3
4	4	4	4	4	4	4
5	5	5	5	5	5	5
6	6	6	6	6	6	6
7	7	7	7	7	7	7
8	8	8	8	8	8	8
9	9	9	9	9	9	9
0	0	0	0	0	0	0

TEST BOOKLET Code

Q No.	Response				Q No.	Response			
001	a	b	c	d	051	a	b	c	d
002	a	b	c	d	052	a	b	c	d
003	a	b	c	d	053	a	b	c	d
004	a	b	c	d	054	a	b	c	d
005	a	b	c	d	055	a	b	c	d
006	a	b	c	d	056	a	b	c	d
007	a	b	c	d	057	a	b	c	d
008	a	b	c	d	058	a	b	c	d
009	a	b	c	d	059	a	b	c	d
010	a	b	c	d	060	a	b	c	d
011	a	b	c	d	061	a	b	c	d
012	a	b	c	d	062	a	b	c	d
013	a	b	c	d	063	a	b	c	d
014	a	b	c	d	064	a	b	c	d
015	a	b	c	d	065	a	b	c	d
016	a	b	c	d	066	a	b	c	d
017	a	b	c	d	067	a	b	c	d
018	a	b	c	d	068	a	b	c	d
019	a	b	c	d	069	a	b	c	d
020	a	b	c	d	070	a	b	c	d
021	a	b	c	d	071	a	b	c	d
022	a	b	c	d	072	a	b	c	d
023	a	b	c	d	073	a	b	c	d
024	a	b	c	d	074	a	b	c	d
025	a	b	c	d	075	a	b	c	d
026	a	b	c	d	076	a	b	c	d
027	a	b	c	d	077	a	b	c	d
028	a	b	c	d	078	a	b	c	d
029	a	b	c	d	079	a	b	c	d
030	a	b	c	d	080	a	b	c	d
031	a	b	c	d	081	a	b	c	d
032	a	b	c	d	082	a	b	c	d
033	a	b	c	d	083	a	b	c	d
034	a	b	c	d	084	a	b	c	d
035	a	b	c	d	085	a	b	c	d
036	a	b	c	d	086	a	b	c	d
037	a	b	c	d	087	a	b	c	d
038	a	b	c	d	088	a	b	c	d
039	a	b	c	d	089	a	b	c	d
040	a	b	c	d	090	a	b	c	d
041	a	b	c	d	091	a	b	c	d
042	a	b	c	d	092	a	b	c	d
043	a	b	c	d	093	a	b	c	d
044	a	b	c	d	094	a	b	c	d
045	a	b	c	d	095	a	b	c	d
046	a	b	c	d	096	a	b	c	d
047	a	b	c	d	097	a	b	c	d
048	a	b	c	d	098	a	b	c	d
049	a	b	c	d	099	a	b	c	d
050	a	b	c	d	100	a	b	c	d

DECLARATION BY THE CANDIDATE

I declare that particulars and signature on this OMR Answer sheet are mine and are Name as in Attendance Sheet. I fruther declare that particulars filled in and Signature as well as the circles darkened on this ORIGINALCOPY is same as in OFFICE COPY.

Signature with time (in running handwriting)

CANDIDATE's NAME (in running handwriting)

MOTHER's NAME (in running handwriting)

FATHER's NAME (in running handwriting)

CANDIDATE LEFT HAND IMPRESSION

SIGNATURE OF INVIGILATOR'S WITH TIME

1

2

MEDACE

OMR SHEET

ROLL No.

1	1	1	1	1	1	1	1	1	1
2	2	2	2	2	2	2	2	2	2
3	3	3	3	3	3	3	3	3	3
4	4	4	4	4	4	4	4	4	4
5	5	5	5	5	5	5	5	5	5
6	6	6	6	6	6	6	6	6	6
7	7	7	7	7	7	7	7	7	7
8	8	8	8	8	8	8	8	8	8
9	9	9	9	9	9	9	9	9	9
0	0	0	0	0	0	0	0	0	0

TEST BOOKLET No.

1	1	1	1	1	1	1
2	2	2	2	2	2	2
3	3	3	3	3	3	3
4	4	4	4	4	4	4
5	5	5	5	5	5	5
6	6	6	6	6	6	6
7	7	7	7	7	7	7
8	8	8	8	8	8	8
9	9	9	9	9	9	9
0	0	0	0	0	0	0

TEST BOOKLET Code

Q No.	Response				Q No.	Response			
001	a	b	c	d	051	a	b	c	d
002	a	b	c	d	052	a	b	c	d
003	a	b	c	d	053	a	b	c	d
004	a	b	c	d	054	a	b	c	d
005	a	b	c	d	055	a	b	c	d
006	a	b	c	d	056	a	b	c	d
007	a	b	c	d	057	a	b	c	d
008	a	b	c	d	058	a	b	c	d
009	a	b	c	d	059	a	b	c	d
010	a	b	c	d	060	a	b	c	d
011	a	b	c	d	061	a	b	c	d
012	a	b	c	d	062	a	b	c	d
013	a	b	c	d	063	a	b	c	d
014	a	b	c	d	064	a	b	c	d
015	a	b	c	d	065	a	b	c	d
016	a	b	c	d	066	a	b	c	d
017	a	b	c	d	067	a	b	c	d
018	a	b	c	d	068	a	b	c	d
019	a	b	c	d	069	a	b	c	d
020	a	b	c	d	070	a	b	c	d
021	a	b	c	d	071	a	b	c	d
022	a	b	c	d	072	a	b	c	d
023	a	b	c	d	073	a	b	c	d
024	a	b	c	d	074	a	b	c	d
025	a	b	c	d	075	a	b	c	d
026	a	b	c	d	076	a	b	c	d
027	a	b	c	d	077	a	b	c	d
028	a	b	c	d	078	a	b	c	d
029	a	b	c	d	079	a	b	c	d
030	a	b	c	d	080	a	b	c	d
031	a	b	c	d	081	a	b	c	d
032	a	b	c	d	082	a	b	c	d
033	a	b	c	d	083	a	b	c	d
034	a	b	c	d	084	a	b	c	d
035	a	b	c	d	085	a	b	c	d
036	a	b	c	d	086	a	b	c	d
037	a	b	c	d	087	a	b	c	d
038	a	b	c	d	088	a	b	c	d
039	a	b	c	d	089	a	b	c	d
040	a	b	c	d	090	a	b	c	d
041	a	b	c	d	091	a	b	c	d
042	a	b	c	d	092	a	b	c	d
043	a	b	c	d	093	a	b	c	d
044	a	b	c	d	094	a	b	c	d
045	a	b	c	d	095	a	b	c	d
046	a	b	c	d	096	a	b	c	d
047	a	b	c	d	097	a	b	c	d
048	a	b	c	d	098	a	b	c	d
049	a	b	c	d	099	a	b	c	d
050	a	b	c	d	100	a	b	c	d

DECLARATION BY THE CANDIDATE

I declare that particulars and signature on this OMR Answer sheet are mine and are Name as in Attendance Sheet. I fruther declare that particulars filled in and Signature as well as the circles darkened on this ORIGINALCOPY is same as in OFFICE COPY.

Signature with time (in running handwriting)

CANDIDATE's NAME (in running handwriting)

MOTHER's NAME (in running handwriting)

FATHER's NAME (in running handwriting)

CANDIDATE LEFT HAND IMPRESSION

SIGNATURE OF INVIGILATOR'S WITH TIME

1

2

MED+ACE

OMR SHEET

ROLL No.

1	1	1	1	1	1	1	1	1	1
2	2	2	2	2	2	2	2	2	2
3	3	3	3	3	3	3	3	3	3
4	4	4	4	4	4	4	4	4	4
5	5	5	5	5	5	5	5	5	5
6	6	6	6	6	6	6	6	6	6
7	7	7	7	7	7	7	7	7	7
8	8	8	8	8	8	8	8	8	8
9	9	9	9	9	9	9	9	9	9
0	0	0	0	0	0	0	0	0	0

TEST BOOKLET No.

1	1	1	1	1	1	1
2	2	2	2	2	2	2
3	3	3	3	3	3	3
4	4	4	4	4	4	4
5	5	5	5	5	5	5
6	6	6	6	6	6	6
7	7	7	7	7	7	7
8	8	8	8	8	8	8
9	9	9	9	9	9	9
0	0	0	0	0	0	0

TEST BOOKLET Code

Q No.	Response			
001	a	b	c	d
002	a	b	c	d
003	a	b	c	d
004	a	b	c	d
005	a	b	c	d
006	a	b	c	d
007	a	b	c	d
008	a	b	c	d
009	a	b	c	d
010	a	b	c	d
011	a	b	c	d
012	a	b	c	d
013	a	b	c	d
014	a	b	c	d
015	a	b	c	d
016	a	b	c	d
017	a	b	c	d
018	a	b	c	d
019	a	b	c	d
020	a	b	c	d
021	a	b	c	d
022	a	b	c	d
023	a	b	c	d
024	a	b	c	d
025	a	b	c	d
026	a	b	c	d
027	a	b	c	d
028	a	b	c	d
029	a	b	c	d
030	a	b	c	d
031	a	b	c	d
032	a	b	c	d
033	a	b	c	d
034	a	b	c	d
035	a	b	c	d
036	a	b	c	d
037	a	b	c	d
038	a	b	c	d
039	a	b	c	d
040	a	b	c	d
041	a	b	c	d
042	a	b	c	d
043	a	b	c	d
044	a	b	c	d
045	a	b	c	d
046	a	b	c	d
047	a	b	c	d
048	a	b	c	d
049	a	b	c	d
050	a	b	c	d

Q No.	Response			
051	a	b	c	d
052	a	b	c	d
053	a	b	c	d
054	a	b	c	d
055	a	b	c	d
056	a	b	c	d
057	a	b	c	d
058	a	b	c	d
059	a	b	c	d
060	a	b	c	d
061	a	b	c	d
062	a	b	c	d
063	a	b	c	d
064	a	b	c	d
065	a	b	c	d
066	a	b	c	d
067	a	b	c	d
068	a	b	c	d
069	a	b	c	d
070	a	b	c	d
071	a	b	c	d
072	a	b	c	d
073	a	b	c	d
074	a	b	c	d
075	a	b	c	d
076	a	b	c	d
077	a	b	c	d
078	a	b	c	d
079	a	b	c	d
080	a	b	c	d
081	a	b	c	d
082	a	b	c	d
083	a	b	c	d
084	a	b	c	d
085	a	b	c	d
086	a	b	c	d
087	a	b	c	d
088	a	b	c	d
089	a	b	c	d
090	a	b	c	d
091	a	b	c	d
092	a	b	c	d
093	a	b	c	d
094	a	b	c	d
095	a	b	c	d
096	a	b	c	d
097	a	b	c	d
098	a	b	c	d
099	a	b	c	d
100	a	b	c	d

DECLARATION BY THE CANDIDATE

I declare that particulars and signature on this OMR Answer sheet are mine and are Name as in Attendance Sheet. I fruther declare that particulars filled in and Signature as well as the circles darkened on this ORIGINALCOPY is same as in OFFICE COPY.

Signature with time (in running handwriting)

CANDIDATE's NAME (in running handwriting)

MOTHER's NAME (in running handwriting)

FATHER's NAME (in running handwriting)

CANDIDATE LEFT HAND IMPRESSION

SIGNATURE OF INVIGILATOR'S WITH TIME

1

2

MEDACE

OMR SHEET

ROLL No.

1	1	1	1	1	1	1	1	1	1
2	2	2	2	2	2	2	2	2	2
3	3	3	3	3	3	3	3	3	3
4	4	4	4	4	4	4	4	4	4
5	5	5	5	5	5	5	5	5	5
6	6	6	6	6	6	6	6	6	6
7	7	7	7	7	7	7	7	7	7
8	8	8	8	8	8	8	8	8	8
9	9	9	9	9	9	9	9	9	9
0	0	0	0	0	0	0	0	0	0

TEST BOOKLET No.

1	1	1	1	1	1	1
2	2	2	2	2	2	2
3	3	3	3	3	3	3
4	4	4	4	4	4	4
5	5	5	5	5	5	5
6	6	6	6	6	6	6
7	7	7	7	7	7	7
8	8	8	8	8	8	8
9	9	9	9	9	9	9
0	0	0	0	0	0	0

TEST BOOKLET Code

Q No.	Response	Q No.	Response
001	a b c d	051	a b c d
002	a b c d	052	a b c d
003	a b c d	053	a b c d
004	a b c d	054	a b c d
005	a b c d	055	a b c d
006	a b c d	056	a b c d
007	a b c d	057	a b c d
008	a b c d	058	a b c d
009	a b c d	059	a b c d
010	a b c d	060	a b c d
011	a b c d	061	a b c d
012	a b c d	062	a b c d
013	a b c d	063	a b c d
014	a b c d	064	a b c d
015	a b c d	065	a b c d
016	a b c d	066	a b c d
017	a b c d	067	a b c d
018	a b c d	068	a b c d
019	a b c d	069	a b c d
020	a b c d	070	a b c d
021	a b c d	071	a b c d
022	a b c d	072	a b c d
023	a b c d	073	a b c d
024	a b c d	074	a b c d
025	a b c d	075	a b c d
026	a b c d	076	a b c d
027	a b c d	077	a b c d
028	a b c d	078	a b c d
029	a b c d	079	a b c d
030	a b c d	080	a b c d
031	a b c d	081	a b c d
032	a b c d	082	a b c d
033	a b c d	083	a b c d
034	a b c d	084	a b c d
035	a b c d	085	a b c d
036	a b c d	086	a b c d
037	a b c d	087	a b c d
038	a b c d	088	a b c d
039	a b c d	089	a b c d
040	a b c d	090	a b c d
041	a b c d	091	a b c d
042	a b c d	092	a b c d
043	a b c d	093	a b c d
044	a b c d	094	a b c d
045	a b c d	095	a b c d
046	a b c d	096	a b c d
047	a b c d	097	a b c d
048	a b c d	098	a b c d
049	a b c d	099	a b c d
050	a b c d	100	a b c d

DECLARATION BY THE CANDIDATE

I declare that particulars and signature on this OMR Answer sheet are mine and are Name as in Attendance Sheet. I fruther declare that particulars filled in and Signature as well as the circles darkened on this ORIGINALCOPY is same as in OFFICE COPY.

Signature with time (in running handwriting)

CANDIDATE's NAME (in running handwriting)

MOTHER's NAME (in running handwriting)

FATHER's NAME (in running handwriting)

CANDIDATE LEFT HAND IMPRESSION

SIGNATURE OF INVIGILATOR'S WITH TIME

1

2